GREAT BRITAIN:
FOREIGN POLICY
AND
THE SPAN OF EMPIRE

VOLUME IV

GREAT BRITAIN: FOREIGN POLICY AND THE SPAN OF EMPIRE

1689-1971
A Documentary History

Edited with Commentaries by
Joel H. Wiener
City College of New York

Introduction
J. H. Plumb
Christ's College, Cambridge

CHELSEA HOUSE PUBLISHERS
in association with
McGRAW HILL BOOK CO.
New York   Toronto   London   Sydney

Executive Editor: *LEON FRIEDMAN*

Project Editor: *JEANETTE MORRISON*

Editorial Staff: *ALICE SHERMAN, JOAN TAPPER*

Some of the selections in this book are used by permission of the holders of copyright and publication rights, listed among Acknowledgments following the Bibliography in Volume IV, and may not be reproduced without their consent.

Library of Congress Cataloging in Publication Data

Wiener, Joel H. comp.
Great Britain: foreign policy and the span of empire, 1689-1971.
Bibliography
1. Gt. Brit.—Foreign relations—Sources.
2. Gt. Brit.—Colonies—History—Sources.
3. Commonwealth of Nations—History—Sources.   I. Title.
DA45.W53   327.42   78-179375
ISBN 0-07-079730-7

Printed and bound in the United States of America

2 3 4 5 6 7 8 9 0 HDBP 7 5 4 3

CONTENTS

Volume IV

INVOLVEMENT IN ASIA AND THE NEAR EAST

GOVERNOR EYRE CONTROVERSY

DEVELOPING SELF-GOVERNMENT AND THE DEFINITION OF IMPERIAL TIES

EXPANSION INTO AFRICA

DISSOLUTION OF THE EMPIRE
1914–Present

DISSOLUTION OF THE OTTOMAN EMPIRE

FORMATION OF THE BRITISH COMMONWEALTH OF NATIONS

THE CONCEPT OF TRUSTEESHIP IN AFRICA

MOVEMENT TOWARD INDIAN INDEPENDENCE

CONFLICT IN THE MIDDLE EAST

THE END OF EMPIRE

INVOLVEMENT IN ASIA AND THE NEAR EAST

*Speech by William E. Gladstone in the House of Commons Attacking
the Second China War, 3 March 1857**

*   *   *

Having, Sir, adverted to the arguments founded on the municipal and international law, I now ask, how does this question stand on the higher ground of natural justice? I say higher ground, because it is the highest ground of all. My right hon. Friend was forbidden to appeal to the principles of Christianity. I grant that it is painful to have them brought into discussions of this kind: but at the same time any man, feeling the application of Christian principles to the position in which he is placed, might find it difficult under the circumstances altogether to refrain from giving expression to his deepest convictions. However, as it seems to give offence, I will make no appeal to those principles; but I will appeal to that which is older than Christianity, because it was in the world before Christianity—to that which is broader than Christianity, because it extends in the world beyond Christianity,—and to that which underlays Christianity, for Christianity itself appeals to it,—I appeal to that justice which binds man to man. I ask the House to take with me a short survey of the position in which we stand in China. We have spoken of the treaty obligations of China towards ourselves; but let not our treaty obligations to China be forgotten. For what purpose did we acquire Hong Kong? Have you looked to the terms of the treaty on that point? The purpose for which you acquired it is stated in the following passage: —

> His Majesty the Emperor of China cedes to the Queen of Great Britain the island of Hong Kong, it being obviously necessary and desirable that British subjects should have some port whereat they might careen and refit their ships when required.

That was the purpose of the cession of Hong Kong, and to that purpose, if we were to act in conformity with the spirit of the treaty, it should be applied. I confess I heard with astonishment the statement of my right hon. Friend the Vice President of the Board of Trade the other evening upon this subject. He rose from his seat and said that he would introduce to the House something not mentioned before. It certainly had not been mentioned before, and it has not been mentioned since, and I very much doubt whether it will ever be mentioned again. He told us that Hong Kong had been handed over to Her Majesty by the Emperor of China, and that at the period of the cession the Emperor

*Hansard, 3.s., CXLIV, 1798–1809.

himself had virtually clothed and invested the population of the island with British rights. I certainly never heard what I should consider a more ingenious argument, if it had only the slightest foundation in fact. But of the 60,000 Chinese at the present moment in Hong Kong, how many were there at the time when it first became a British possession? My right hon. Friend stated the number the other night at 1,000, but if I am rightly informed it did not in reality amount to more than 500; and that is the largest number of Chinese who could have been included in the cession of the island made by the Emperor of China. But there is no ground whatever for the claim put forward by the right hon. Gentleman in this case. The purpose for which Hong Kong was ceded is clearly indicated in the treaty itself; it was that it might afford a port for careening and refitting our ships. But that is not your only treaty obligation towards China. There is another. It is the 12th Article of the Supplementary Treaty: —

> A fair and regular tariff of duties and other dues having now been established, it is to be hoped that the system of smuggling which has heretofore been carried on between English and Chinese merchants—in many cases with the open connivance and collusion of the Chinese Custom House officers—will entirely cease; and the most peremptory proclamation to all English merchants has been already issued on this subject by the British Plenipotentiary, who will also instruct the different Consuls to strictly watch over and carefully scrutinize the conduct of all persons being British subjects trading under his superintendence.

By that article you have contracted, under the most solemn obligations to put down smuggling to the very best of your power. Is there anything peculiar in your smuggling trade on the coast of China? It is the worst, the most pernicious, demoralizing, and destructive of all the contraband trades that are carried on upon the surface of the globe. It is partly a trade in salt. That, of course, can be open to no objection beyond the fact that it is contraband. But it is also partly a trade in opium. Have you struggled to put down that trade? I ask the Prime Minister who will, no doubt, address the House to-night, have the British Government struggled to put down that trade? They may say that they did struggle to put it down, but they found that it was too strong for them. Then, I will ask another question—whether they have done anything to encourage that trade? Yes, Sir, they have done the very thing that is now in issue. They have created this fleet of lorchas. What has been its purpose? What has been its effect? I refer you to the very words of your own authority, page 7 of the correspondence, where it is said that the granting of the registers to these colonial vessels has been eminently beneficial to Hong Kong. That passage was quoted by the Lord Advocate. He is a gentleman of so much intelligence that, as he appeared not to have gathered the sense of it, I infer that he cannot have read these papers. It was beneficial to the colony? And why was it beneficial? Because it increased this coasting trade. It has already added to and still tends to increase the coasting trade in goods the manufacture of Great Britain or in the produce of India, such as cotton, opium, &c. It is quite plain that this coasting trade mainly has reference to smuggling purposes. There can be no doubt about it. Unfortunately, the quantity of British goods which you send to China is still extremely small. Your greatest and most valuable trade with China is this trade in opium. It is a smuggling trade. You promised to put it down; you bound yourselves by the terms of the treaty as far as possible to suppress it. You received Hong Kong for the purpose of careening and refitting your vessels; and instead of that you have located those 60,000 Chinese within it, and from them you find the means of sustaining and organizing a fleet of coasters whose business it is to enlarge, who have enlarged, and who are enlarging, that smuggling traffic that you are bound by treaty to put down. So stands the case so far as the treaty is concerned. And, now, having taken Hong Kong for purposes that you have not fulfilled, having applied it to different purposes, having failed entirely, or rather not having *bonâ fide* endeavoured to put down this smuggling trade, which on the contrary has grown largely since the treaty, having organized this coasting trade for purposes which included an enlargement of that smuggling trade, you accumulate all these acts of injustice by trumping up a claim built upon technicalities to cover this coasting fleet with the British flag; and when we are told that such proceedings ought not to be endured, then you reproach us with indifference to the honour of the ensign of our country. Was there ever such a series of mockeries? But you have confessed that the case of the *Arrow* is satisfied. I will not weary the House by quoting the words of Consul Parkes on that subject. There is no doubt about their meaning. They have been cited over and over again in this debate. He undoubtedly confesses in these documents that the case of the *Arrow* is satisfied; and you are now, in point of fact, engaged, as I will show, in bombarding and burning a city in order that your envoy may enter within it. My right hon. Friend the Secretary of State for the Colonies made a complaint on the part of Her Majesty's Government that gentlemen were irreverently in the habit of speaking of the war with China. He said there is no war with China. I agree with him; there is not war with China. [MR. LABOUCHERE: *With* China.] I thank my right hon. Friend for that correction. There is not war *with* China. No, Sir, there is not war with China, but what is there? There is hostility. There is bloodshed. There is a trampling down of the weak by the strong. There is the terrible and abominable retaliation of the weak upon the strong. You are now occupied in this House by revolting and harrowing details about a Chinese baker who has poisoned bread, by proclamations for the capture of British heads, and the waylaying of a postal steamer. And these things you think strengthen your case. Why, they deepen your guilt. They place you more completely in the wrong. War taken at the best is a frightful scourge to the human race; but because it is so the wisdom of ages has surrounded it with strict laws and usages, and has required formalities to be observed which shall act as a curb upon the wild passions of man, to prevent that scourge from being let loose unless under circumstances of full deliberation and from absolute necessity. You have dispensed with all these precautions. You have turned a consul into a diplomatist, and that metamorphosed consul is forsooth to be at liberty to direct the whole might of England against the lives of a defenceless people. While war is a scourge and curse to man it is yet attended with certain compensations. It is attended with acts of heroic self-sacrifice and of unbounded daring. It is ennobled by a consciousness that you are meeting equals in the field, and that while you challenge the issue of life or death you at least enter into a fair encounter. But you go to China and make war upon those who stand before you as women or children. They try to resist you; they call together their troops; they load their guns; they kill one man and wound another in action, but while they are doing so you perhaps slay thousands. They are unable to meet you in the field. You have no equality of ground on which to meet them. You can earn no glory in such warfare. And it is those who put the British flag to such uses that stain it. It is not from them that we are to hear rhetorical exaggerations on the subject of the allegiance that we owe to the national standard. Such is the case of the war in China. And what of the people—who have no means of offering you open resistance—who are women and children before you—what do they do when you make war with them? They resort to those miserable and detestable contrivances for the destruction of their enemies which their weakness teaches them. It is not the first time in the history of the world. Have you never read of those rebellions of the slaves which have risen to the dignity of being called wars, and which stand recorded in history as the servile wars? Is it not notorious that among all the wars upon record those have been the most terrible, ferocious, and destructive? And why? Because those who have been trampled upon have observed no limit in the gratification of their feeling of revenge against their oppressors; and however wrong may have been their excesses in the abstract, those excesses could not become a just subject of complaint on the part of those who had provoked them. Every account that reaches us of the cruelties and the atrocities to which this war gives rise only deepens the pain and the shame with which I look back, and with which I trust the majority of this House will look back, on the origin of this deplorable contest. Something has been said by the hon. and learned Member for Hertford (Mr. T. Chambers) on the subject of what he considered the limited nature of the destruction and the havoc that have taken place in this case, and the hon. and learned Gentleman read a document dated the 10th of November, for the purpose of sustaining his views upon that point. But documents of the 10th of November have by this time become obsolete and superannuated. We have much later intelligence; and I remember that the hon. Member for Cornwall (Mr. Kendall) eulogised for its humanity a later account which has reached us to the effect that our fleet had been firing cannon balls into Canton at "moderate intervals." But your agents do not appear now to confine themselves to those "moderate intervals." I have received a letter, dated the 14th of January, which has not been published in the journals, and, therefore, I trust the House will attend to it, as it is written by one of our officers and shows the real character of our operations against China. He says—

> On Monday morning, at daylight, fire parties were told off from the *Encounter, Barracouta, Niger,* the 59th, and, last not least, the Dutch Folly. The orders were to advance as near as possible to the city wall, and all the

suburbs from Shamen Fort down to the Dutch Folly were to be burnt. This was well accomplished, and by nine o'clock there was a tremendous conflagration, having been fired in so many places. The naval, I am glad to say, had no casualties. Not so the 59th; they had what I consider a severe loss—two killed, eleven seriously and two slightly wounded;—had a narrow escape, as also one of our fire party. They were surprised and nearly cut off by a hundred and more men, but the revolvers and cutlasses told well, and they rushed clear. We then commenced 'carcasses' and fireballs from the Folly into the city, and got up a tremendous fire, which was much aided by a very strong breeze, which blew all day, and they only got the fire under in the city about noon on Tuesday. It must have done great damage. The entire suburbs from Shamen Fort to 400 yards beyond this fort in the French Folly direction is now a mass of ruins.

Sir, that is the state of things that existed on the 14th of January. That is the state of things to which, as early as circumstances permit, but, unhappily, I fear, too late, the wisdom and firmness of Parliament have been called upon to apply a remedy. And, now, when this matter has been discussed, when the cause has been sustained by learning, eloquence, zeal, and feeling, worthy as relates to the other House of Parliament, and worthy as relates to some portion of the debate in this House, of the best days of Parliamentary history, that which calls itself wordly wisdom steps in and warns us against the exercise of the authority of Parliament, which seeks to put an effectual check upon these deplorable proceedings. We are told to take care what we are about. We are told to support our representatives. But we have swept away the rubbish which has been talked with respect to Sir. John Bowring. We have got so far in the consideration of this question that we are not dealing judicially with Sir John Bowring. As far as we are dealing with persons at all, it is with the Government by whom these proceedings have been approved that we are now dealing; but we are dealing much more with the vast interests of humanity which are at stake, and with respect to which we are told that they, and they alone, ought to guide us. But we are told to beware of an adverse vote of the House of Commons. We are told to consider the effect of such a vote upon the Chinese. We are told to consider the ruinous consequences to our trade. We are asked if we wish to extend the ruinous conflagration which has broken out, and to injure those interests of humanity which it is our duty to assert. That is the argument, and I will make this concession to those who use it. Our last accounts from China are up to the middle of January, and we are now debating this question on the 3rd of March. No human wisdom can tell, and I, for one, am not bold enough to conjecture what has happened since, or what may happen within the three months that have elapsed from the date of the last advices, and before the decision of Parliament can reach China. But, Sir, I must say, that if I look to the continuation of the influences that have been at work there can be nothing darker than the prospect before us, and I, for one, should have not the smallest hope. You amused us with the story that the population of Canton were rising against the authorities. On the contrary, we are now assured by contrary accounts that the populace are arming to a man to do their best—I will not say to fight, for they are unequal to that great operation—but to expose themselves, and to die in the quarrel which you have forced upon them. But of all the cases in which warlike operations were ever begun I do not know of any in which the political problem to be solved was so simple. What do we want from the Chinese? They are not making war on us. If the vote of Parliament had induced the Chinese to make war upon us that would be a different matter. With a good heart and a clear conscience, we could then apply the full strength of the British Empire. But there is nothing so improbable as that they should make war on us. They have never shown that skill or daring necessary for undertaking aggressive operations. Sir, it is we who are making war upon them; and for what are we making war? What are we asking from the Chinese? Sir John Bowring has proposed our entrance into Canton. But the Government have never told us that this is an adequate cause for the war. They have never told us even that they consider our entrance into Canton desirable. It is impossible for me to say whether it is desirable; but I own I lean to the opinion of Yeh, the Chinese Commissioner, and that I am inclined to believe that our entrance into Canton, if it were conceded, would be more mischievous than beneficial. I, for one, therefore, see no reason why we should make war for the purpose of obtaining a thing which, so far from being desirable, is likely to be mischievous. Sir, I repeat, there never was a case in which the solution of the political problem was so simple; for the actual state of war has never been constituted. This is a happy thing. I might almost say it is a providential circumstance, if we consider it in regard to the solution of the difficulty. The state of war has not been regularly and legally constituted, and that freedom which we now possess for correcting the proposals of our agents would have been lost if war had been regularly and formally declared. But, Sir, I am not content with that mode of dealing with such an argument. I find an appeal has been made to this House which appears to me to be a false and illegitimate appeal. It appears to me the basest that could be made under existing circumstances. It is an appeal to fear, which is seldom a rightful and noble sentiment, and it is to that fear which is the basis of the worst kind of fear—the fear of being thought afraid. The Government are afraid of the mischievous impression that will be produced upon the Chinese if the acts of our officials are disavowed. Sir, let us consider fairly, impartially, and at large the moral impressions that must now be produced, and that cannot be avoided. Let us weigh the evil and the good upon one side and the other, and I have no fear of the result. Hereafter we shall be told by the noble Lord of the wise caution that we ought to display, of the solemn predicament in which we are placed, of the political mischief which may ensue. The noble Lord will, no doubt, draw some shadowy pictures of the dangers, the confusion, the weakness, and the paralysis of British power in the East. But what is the foundation of British power in the East— what is the foundation of the promise to be permanent and useful of that British power? It is not now a question as if the Chinese are alone concerned, for the debate has been prolonged night after night, and your words have gone throughout the whole earth. The confessions and avowals of the supporters of the Government have been, it appears to me, perfectly fatal either to the continuance of that policy or else to the character and fame of England. When you talk of the consequences, and talk of injustice, and then say that we must go on with that injustice; when you speak of the necessity of appealing to the law of force in respect of the Chinese; when you say that it is by force only that your influence can be supported, I am bound to remind you that that has not been the general tone of the language used in this debate. The opponents of the Resolution of my hon. Friend have not generally ascended to that height of boldness, although a few amongst them have attempted to justify the proceedings that have taken place. I heard the speech of the hon. and learned Member for Hertford in support of the Government, but I did not understand that he approved them. I heard the able and vigorous speech of my hon. and learned Friend the Attorney General, but I thought he eschewed that portion of the case. I doubt whether my right hon. Friend the Secretary of State for the Home Department justified the proceedings. Many of those who intend to support the Government have openly condemned the proceedings that have taken place. The hon. Gentleman the Member for Cornwall condemns them. The hon. Member for Norfolk condemns them. Members more than I could name have condemned the proceedings. I will ask what the effect will be throughout the world if it goes forth that in the debates held in the two Houses of Parliament the majority of speakers condemned the proceedings, and that even among those who sustained the Government with their vote there was a large number who condemned these proceedings? Why, Sir, the opinion will be that England is a Power which, while it is higher and more daring in its pretensions to Christianity than any other Power on the face of the globe, yet that in a case where her own worldly interests were concerned, and where she was acting in the remote and distant East, when fairly put to it and asked whether she would do right or wrong, she was ready to adopt for fear of political inconvenience the principle,—"I will make the law of wrong the law of my Eastern policy, and will lay the foundation of that empire which is my proudest boast in nothing more nor less than huge injustice." Sir, this is not my opinion. I will not believe that England will lay the foundations of its Eastern empire on such unstable ground as this. I believe, on the contrary, that if you have the courage to assert your prerogative as the British House of Commons, you will pursue a course more consistent with sound policy as well as the eternal principles of justice.

Sir, how stands the case at present? I have just now supposed that the House are going to negative the Resolution. That will go forth as the seal of our disgrace. But let me reverse the picture and suppose that the House will adopt the Resolution, and then what will the House do, and what will be the history of this case? Its history will read well for England and for the nineteenth century. Its history will, then, be this,—The subordinate officers of England, in a remote quarter of the globe, misconstrued the intentions of their country; they acted in violation of the principles of right; the Executive Government failed to check them. The appeal was next made to the House of Lords, and made as such an appeal ought to be made, for the cause was worthy of the eloquence, and the eloquence was worthy of the cause. It was made to nobles and it was made to bishops, and it failed. But it does not rest with subordinate functionaries abroad, it does not rest with the Executive Government, it does not rest with the House of Lords, finally, and in the last resort, to say what shall be the policy of England and to what purpose shall her power be directed. Sir, that function lies within these walls. Every Member of the House of Commons is proudly conscious that he belongs to an assembly which in its collective capacity is the paramount power of the State. But if it is the paramount power of the State it can never separate from that paramount power a similar and paramount responsibility. The vote of the House of Lords will not acquit us; the sentence of the Government will not acquit us. It is with us that it lies to determine whether this wrong shall remain unchecked and uncorrected. And at a time when sentiments are so much divided, every man I trust, will give his vote with the recollection and the consciousness that it may depend upon his single vote whether the miseries, the crimes, the atrocities that I fear are now proceeding in China are to be discountenanced or not. We have now come to the crisis of the case. England is not yet committed. But if an adverse vote be given—if an adverse division reject the Motion of my hon. Friend, to-morrow morning, England will have been committed. With you then, with us, with every one of us, it rests to show that this House, which is the first, the most ancient, and the noblest temple of freedom in the world, is also the temple of that everlasting justice without which freedom itself would be only a name or only a curse to mankind. And I cherish the trust and belief that when you, Sir, rise in your place to-night to declare the numbers of the division from the chair which you adorn, the words which you speak will go forth from the walls of the House of Commons, not only as a message of mercy and peace, but also as a message of British justice and British wisdom, to the farthest corners of the world.

Speech by the Prime Minister, Viscount Palmerston, in the
House of Commons Defending the Second China War, 3 March 1857*
[Palmerston's Cabinet resigned after its defeat on this issue but he
triumphed in the subsequent General Election and was returned to power.]

*   *   *

Let us, Sir, inquire what was the event which has given rise to these unfortunate occurrences. I will not go into the legal question. I think that much of the legal argument as to whether the lorcha was or was not a British vessel would have been very proper if this case had been before the Court of Admiralty or the Judicial Committee of the Privy Council upon a question whether this ship, having been captured by an enemy of England or of China, was or was not a legal prize and liable to be condemned; but I hold that that dissertation, however interesting it may have been, and however valuable and

*Hansard, 3.s., CXLIV, 1813–24.

important may be the legal knowledge which has been brought to bear upon this question in both Houses of Parliament, does not touch the bottom of this matter. We have a treaty with China, and that treaty says that British vessels shall not be boarded, and men taken out of them without a previous application to the British Consul. The whole question is, what did the Chinese know and believe this vessel to be? Did they or did they not consider her to be a British vessel? I say that they did. The whole question turns upon that; and when it is said that it was a falsehood on the part of Sir John Bowring when he said that the Chinese Government did not know that the licence had expired, I say, on the contrary, that that is a correct statement of the real principle at issue between the British and the Chinese authorities, and, in fact, contains the gist of the whole transaction; and I say that, instead of this being a flagitious attempt at imposition, it was a statement of the principle upon which the question between the British and Chinese authorities was to be adjusted. If the Chinese, knowing and believing—whether rightly or wrongly believing—that this was a British vessel, nevertheless in violation of the treaty boarded her, carried off her crew, and hauled down her colours. I say that it is immaterial to the question whether by the technicalities of the law you can or cannot show that at that moment she had not a right to be protected. The *animus* of an insult, the *animus* of violation of the treaty was in the Chinese, and you had a right to demand not only an apology for the wrong that was done, but an assurance that it should not be repeated. But, I think, it has been shown that, in point of fact, this vessel was, to all intents and purposes, entitled to protection as a British vessel. Although the licence had expired five days, yet the register was good until the return of the lorcha to her port. Why, Sir, I never before heard such a quibble as that by which it is maintained that the lorcha was not at sea because she was in the river at Canton. Sir, I was ashamed, in a serious argument in this House, to see a distinction of that kind taken. The provision that the register should continue good while the vessel was at sea means of course that it should be in force as long as the voyage in which she was engaged kept her out of her port, and the miserable distinction between her being at sea and being in a river I certainly did not expect to hear taken in this House. What, then, is the history of the *Arrow*? Why, that she had obtained a register; that she went to Macao, where she took in a cargo; and that she conveyed part of that cargo to Canton. What does she there, and what must she have done according to established regulation? She must have deposited, and did deposit, her register with the British Consul, who thereupon communicated with the Hoppo, to obtain permission for the landing of her cargo. That permission was given, and the cargo was landed. It consisted of rice. There was no pretence that it was contraband; and it must have been landed with the cognizance of the customhouse officers of Canton. The vessel lay five or six days opposite that town; and I say that the Chinese authorities must have known that she was a British vessel engaged in a legal trade—that she had not violated any Chinese law, and was therefore entitled to the protection which the 9th Article of the treaty afforded her. Nevertheless, they choose, in contravention of that treaty, at the moment when she was about to sail, to board her and carry off her crew. The question has been raised whether the British ensign was flying. What evidence have we, may I ask, upon that point? We have the evidence of Kennedy, the master of the *Arrow*, and also of Leach, the master of the *Dart*, who being both within fifty yards of the lorcha at the time, state that they saw the flag hauled down from the mizen peak by a mandarin soldier, and likewise— an important point that has not been sufficiently dwelt upon—that they saw the 'blue-peter' hauled down. I say this is important, because it is an answer to one of the main arguments of Yeh, who states that the lorcha could not have had the British ensign flying, inasmuch as no vessel is allowed to hoist British colours from the moment she casts anchor until the moment she is about to get under way. Why, she was about to get under way. Everybody knows that the 'blue-peter' is a sign of immediate departure. It is perfectly clear, therefore, that the vessel was about to get underweigh, and the argument of Commissioner Yeh is thus at once disposed of. The master was preparing to go on board, and the *Arrow* would probably have been underweigh within a few minutes after-wards had not the Chinese officers come and boarded her. Then another excuse is that there was no foreigner on board, and therefore they did not believe she was a British vessel, but concluded that she must be Chinese. True, there was no foreigner on board at the time when the Chinese officials entered her, but then the master went on board with two other British subjects before they left the ship, and he was actually on board while they were still alongside. Could there have been any doubt in their minds that he was on board? Why, Kennedy, knowing enough Chinese to communicate with them in their own language, represented to them the injury they would do him if they took away the whole crew; and he asked them to leave him two of the men, and they did leave him two, in consequence of his own special application. I say, then, away with the excuse—the falsehood—the "flagitious falsehood" of the Chinese authorities—that there was no British ensign flying and no foreigner on board the lorcha at the time when the men were taken away. Well, what was the allegation urged by them in defence of the course they were pursuing? It was quite different from the allegation subsequently put forward by Yeh when he had got evidence better suited for his purpose. The allegation made by the officer commanding the party was, that there was on board the *Arrow* an old man who was supposed to be the father of a pirate. On that ground they seized him, on the Chinese principle that relatives are made to answer for relatives; and no doubt if they could not have found the pirate himself they would have cut off this old man's head. But why did they take the rest of the crew? They wanted them, they said, as witnesses, to give information on the matter in question. Well, was that statement made only to the master of the lorcha? It was repeated afterwards to Consul Parkes when he applied to the proper authorities for the release of the men. They said that it was done on account of the old man whose son was supposed, somewhere or other, to have been engaged in piracy. Subsequently, however, Yeh—with that ability, which I do not deny that he possesses—Commissioner Yeh, I repeat, whose forbearance we have heard so much praised—though the chief forbearance which I think he exhibits is a forbearance to tell the truth—Yeh, however, with that conciliatory spirit which is said to animate him, shifts his ground, sends in a new and a different story. And what is that story? Why, that a certain man, a sailor, having been some months before attacked in his own vessel by a band of pirates, and plundered, was able to recognize one of the pirates by two circumstances—the one was that he wore a red turban, the other that he had lost a front tooth. As for the red turban, I do not know whether that is a distinguishing mark sufficient to enable one to say whenever he meets a person wearing it that he is a pirate, and ought to be seized. The tale, however, is that while sailing up the Canton river the accuser passed the lorcha, the *Arrow*, and identified on board of her the very pirate by whom his ship had been plundered—a men, be it observed, whom he could only recognise by observing that he had lost a front tooth. They say that eyesight is keener and quicker in warm climates than in these colder regions; but this, I think, cannot be denied, that a man who could distinguish in rapidly passing another vessel in a river whether one man of the crew had or had not lost a front tooth would be a valuable addition to one of our sharp-shooting regiments, where I am sure he would make an admirable and most successful rifleman. If a gross outrage could only be justified by such an absurd story as that, it only shows how hardly put to it Commissioner Yeh must have been to invent a ground for its commission. But it having been committed, what was our demand? An apology and an assurance that such a violation of the treaty should not be repeated. And it was not until forbearance had been shown by our commander for some days, and a refusal on the part of the Chinese authorities to grant any satisfaction, that measured hostilities were resorted to, first in the shape of reprisals by the seizure of a junk, and afterwards by an attack on some of their forts. The hon. Member for the West Riding is very fond of referring us to the United States, as a model to be imitated in all respects, both in our institutions and our conduct. What, then was the conduct of the American Commodore when an outrage was offered about the same time to his flag? An American boat rowing along the river, after the dispute with us had begun, was fired into by one of the Chinese forts. She hoisted the American flag, and that was fired upon. That was an insult which undoubtedly required reparation. But, at the same time, it was not an outrage of the same kind as the deliberate violation of a treaty. It might have been caused by an accidental mistake of a single gunner stationed in the fort, or the use of the American flag might have been deemed the stratagem of an English boat wishing to pass by in security by pretending to belong to the United States. The United States' commander, however, very properly thought that it required atonement; and what was the course he pursued. Some people are fond of a word and a blow. The United States' commander preferred a blow and a word. He judged that it was better to punish first and ask for explanations afterwards—that it was better in the first place to knock down the offending fort, and after that to demand from Yeh an apology and a guarantee for the future. He inverted our course of proceeding. His demand, when made, was precisely the same as ours, only his attack went first, and the demand followed after it. But was that all? He destroyed the fort—he demanded reparation from the Chinese; and twenty-four hours were given them to make their apology. Before that interval had elapsed the American captain, with a shrewd eye, saw that something was going on in the fort near which he lay that indicated that at the end of the twenty-four hours, if the answer was unfavourable, his position might not be so good as it was at the beginning of that time, and he accordingly renewed his hostile operations without waiting for the expiration of the period allowed to the Chinese to deliberate whether they would give an explanation and make an apology. The hon. Member for the West Riding, who is so fond of making the conduct of the Americans a model for our imitation, must admit, then, that our proceedings evinced extreme forbearance compared with the proceedings of those whom he would have us to copy. Well, Sir, we demanded reparation. And for what? Was it a matter of little consequence? You may say, what did it signify if a few men were taken out of a small vessel?—you might have overlooked it and have said, if it happens again we will make it a serious matter. But, Sir, this was only one out of many acts of deliberate violation of our treaty rights. We had by the treaty of Nankin a right for all British subjects to enter and reside in, without molestation, certain five cities of China, of which Canton is one. In the case of Canton that right has been pertinaciously refused. We had a right by the treaty to a certain quantity of land to be given, either in the city or immediately adjoining the city, for the purposes of commercial business; and it was distinctly stated that, as the wants of the British community could not be defined beforehand, so no particular limit should be placed as to the quantity of land to be devoted to their uses. Well, Sir, the fulfilment of that stipulation has been determinately refused to us at Canton. We have had a small area of ground allotted in which all foreign merchants are confined; and, as I know from official information, direct communications have been made to the Chinese authorities on this subject; we have stated that we wished land to be assigned to us, we care not in what particular direction, for the purpose of warehousing British property; but our applications have been in vain. In vain are cited our treaty rights to have this land: the demand has never been complied with. And the consequence has been that a great quantity of British merchandise has been stored in Chinese warehouses instead of where it ought to have been, in British warehouses under the custody of the British merchants themselves. There was a systematic determination on the part of the Canton author-ities to refuse to us all our treaty rights as far as it was possible to deny them. Well, what were the grounds of that refusal? It was that the people of Canton were so barbarous, so unruly, so savage, so hostile to foreigners, that it would not be safe for British or any foreign subjects to attempt to enter the city. Now, Sir, the hon. Member for the West Riding himself gave us a complete refutation of that excuse of Yeh and his predecessors. He read us a statement showing that British officers and subjects had walked through the suburbs of Canton and had been treated with the utmost civility and kindness—that there was curiosity to ascertain the quality of the clothes worn by the foreign visitors—some inclination to examine their dress—but there was not the slightest indication of insult or molestation during the course of a long promenade. Well, Sir, does the wall of Canton mark such a division between barbarism and civilization, between brutality and good humour, that those living in the suburbs will receive strangers in this way, while those who happen to reside within the walls will act in the way Yeh suggests? I think we may very fairly assume that the people within the walls would be as courteous as the people outside the walls; and that if foreigners were permitted to enter the city, the people there would take the same interest in them as those outside have practically shown they do. And, Sir, what is the character of the Chinese people in general? What happens in the other towns? If Canton were the only Chinese town with which we had intercourse, we might, from want of knowing better, give credit to Yeh, and suppose that he knew his countrymen better than we did. But there is Shanghai—fully as important a city as Canton, and proving more and more important every day—a populous city itself, and adjoining a populous district. No difficulty is there made; British subjects are admitted within the town; social intercourse exists between the Chinese and British subjects; and everything proceeds in the most ample harmony and good nature. So far from any difficulty arising, even now, from the accounts that have of course been received from Canton, no interruption of good feeling has occurred between the Chinese and foreigners in Shanghai, or, indeed, in any of the other Chinese ports. I say then, Sir, this is a falsehood—another of those Chinese falsehoods—"flagitious falsehoods"—by which Yeh and his predecessors have endeavoured to find excuses for violating the treaty which the Emperor entered into with this country. I say, Sir, this violation of our treaty in regard to the lorcha is not the first or only one that occurred, but a part of a deliberate system to strip us step by step of our treaty rights, to set the population of the city against us for purposes of their own, and to give an undue advantage to others against British subjects. The most important right was violated—a right of the utmost importance to us. How could any commerce between Canton and Hong Kong be carried on in British vessels under British license if those vessels are to be liable to all the caprices of Chinese police or Chinese authorities, and to have their whole crews carried off at the moment of sailing. It so happened that at the time of the occurrence the subject of this discussion, this lorcha did not happen to have any cargo on board; but it might have happened that she had a valuable cargo, and thus she would have been stripped of all hands and left exposed to all the risks of damage from want of a proper crew, to say nothing of the loss which all merchants know to arise from the detention of a vessel which is ready to sail. Then I say the right which was violated was a most important right—a right most important to the whole British commerce between Hong Kong and Canton, a commerce which is continually growing, and which is carried on almost entirely by vessels of this description. It was said this vessel had been a pirate. That has been disproved, and at the particular time she was certainly engaged in lawful commerce. Had there been any doubt about her character, application ought to have been made to the Consul. There was not even a pretence on which an application could have been made to the

Consul, for the old man who was seized was not accused of being concerned in any crime, but was a relation of a man who was suspected.

Well, Sir, was the Chinese Governor of Canton a man of that mildness of character, of that justice and forbearance, that our authorities might have been satisfied with a mere remonstrance and an assurance that no such thing would occur again? Why, all the equivocations of Yeh in replying to our communications, and in escaping from that assurance, show that in his mind there was a reservation, and that he would commit the same offence when the opportunity again occurred. His answer was, no Chinese vessel in future shall take men out of any British lorcha "without reason." Well, who is to judge of that reason? Why, the Chinese themselves. The very object of the treaty was to prevent the Chinese from setting up their own reason as a sufficient ground for interfering with the just rights and privileges of British vessels. Again, he says that it belongs to Chinese officials to arrest Chinese criminals on board British vessels. But that is entirely setting aside the right which we by treaty have acquired for our Consul to intervene, and is an arrogation to the Chinese authorities of privileges which by the treaty do not belong to them—that is, a right to judge of the criminality of persons aboard these vessels. I do not think, throughout the course of this debate, however extreme may have been the opinions of hon. Gentlemen, that any one has ventured to defend this inhuman monster. I do not think any one has asserted that these men were legally seized because they were Chinese subjects. The hon. Member for the West Riding has asked what would happen if a British vessel went into a Spanish port and Spanish criminals were taken out of that ship? He also says, "You refuse to permit the authorities of another country to board your vessels to take criminals; yet do you not yourselves, in your own ports, subject foreigners coming in foreign vessels to your own municipal regulations and laws?" Undoubtedly, Sir, we do. But those who thus argue have omitted the circumstance of the treaty, which overrides all international obligations, and which was specially constructed for the very purpose of overriding those obligations. It is well known that in all our treaties with nations less civilized than those in Europe, engagements of this sort are necessarily entered into. In Turkey, for instance, British subjects are not to be taken without the presence of the British Consul; in Persia the same; and in China the stipulation is still more necessary. Why, if the Canton authorities had really been the mild, the gentle, the humane, the forbearing people which they have been so assiduously represented to be, one might have trusted to them, and have said, "We believe in future you will have recourse to the British Consul or other British authorities." But look at the ferocious system of administration which has prevailed in China, and especially in Canton—though I confess that what we have been told in the course of this debate exceeded any notion I had on the subject. We have been told that in the course of a few months 70,000 heads—Chinese heads—have been struck off by the axe of the executioner of the barbarous Yeh. We have further been told that the remains of 5,000 or 6,000 people were left reeking in the place of public execution; that the authorities had not even taken the trouble of removing those mutilated remains from the view of the new victims coming to execution. Sir, I am almost afraid to believe that 70,000 executions took place within less than a year; but I am afraid it is too true. And what must we say of the barbarity of the Government under which those executions had taken place? There is another circumstance, Sir, which I have been several times assured of, though when I first heard it I thought it must be a joke. But I have heard from more than one person locally connected with China, that persons condemned to death may for about 200 dollars get a substitute to represent them at the place of execution. I believe it is too true. The argument used to these substitutes is, "Your life is very precarious; you have no certainty that you may not be beheaded in a few months by the caprice of some official without getting anything for it. How much better, therefore, is it that you should take what will enable you to maintain yourself in luxury for a fortnight, and to leave something behind for your family." What a picture does that give of the state of society among these much be-praised and be-lauded people! These barbarities are committed by the ruling authorities. Undoubtedly it is by them that all those cruelties to Europeans of which we have recently read have been instigated. The first act of Yeh upon the breaking out of the dispute was to issue a reward for the heads of Englishmen, and he next put out a proclamation declaring that he had taken secret means of extirpating that hated race. We have seen by the latest accounts from Hong Kong how these secret methods are carried into effect—by the atrocious murder of eleven Europeans in the *Thistle*, and by the poisoning of the food of the European community of Hong Kong. Yet, to my utter astonishment, the right hon. Gentleman, the Member for the University of Oxford, instead of displaying that generous zeal and those honourable sentiments which he has so much at command on subjects much less deserving of them, repeated, though not in the same words yet in the same spirit, the justification which he put forth in the discussion on Chinese affairs some fifteen years ago. It was alleged then that the Chinese had poisoned their wells—"Of course they poisoned their wells," said the right hon. Gentleman. Now, the right hon. Gentleman has undertaken to defend ("No! no!")—yes, Sir, I say he has undertaken to defend these atrocities. ("No! no!"). He says it is the natural and necessary recourse of the weak against the strong; and if, therefore, a nation should be too weak to resist its enemies in open fight, that, according to the right hon. Gentleman's view, is a sufficient justification for the perpetration of the basest and most atrocious acts which disgrace mankind. ("No! no!") I was the more sorry to hear that formal, elaborate, and studied defence—("No! no!")—because I had framed an excuse which I believed in my own mind to be the true one for the words which escaped the right hon. Gentleman in the former debate. I did not believe that he meant to justify the poisoning of the wells. What I believe he meant was, that the Chinese were such a barbarous nation, that they were capable of such enormities; that they combined such cruelty with treachery, that it was only natural they should have resorted to this flagrant atrocity. But I grieve to say that upon the present occasion the language of the right hon. Gentleman, and the manner in which he dealt with the subject, indicate to my mind that he was framing a sort of excuse for these terrible crimes—("No! no!")—that he was arguing that the weakness of the Chinese justified their recourse to means of defence which even savage nations— which even nations far less civilized than they—which even the Caffres and the Indians would shrink from with horror. ("No! no!").

* * *

Account of Lord Elgin's Mission to China and of the Events Leading to the Treaty of Tien-tsin by His Private Secretary, Laurence Oliphant, July 1858*

* * *

Although, in the ordinary course of diplomatic routine, it is considered unnecessary to procure, before ratification, the assent of the sovereign to a treaty negotiated between specially appointed plenipotentiaries, Lord Elgin decided upon adopting the course followed by Sir Henry Pottinger in the Treaty of Nankin, and obtaining the imperial assent to the treaty, the ratifications of which, it had been arranged, should be exchanged at Pekin within the period of a year from the date of its signature. His intention to this effect was expressed to the commissioners, who, accordingly, four days after it was signed, forwarded to his lordship a communication in which they stated that they had received an imperial autograph rescript to the following effect: "We have perused your memorial and know all. Respect this." As the fact of the emperor's cognizance of "all" did not by any means imply his assent to it; the embassador replied that he "was still awaiting his majesty's approval to the conditions of the treaty." In answer to which, the commissioners stated that, "as soon as we shall have in person presented the originals of the different nations' treaties, with the seals and signatures, to his majesty at the capital, and received the ratification of them in the imperial autograph, it shall be transmitted, with all speed, to Shanghai for the information of your excellency."

Lord Elgin, in reply to the above communication, states "that he can not consider peace to be re-established until he shall have been satisfied of the emperor's entire acceptance of the conditions agreed to by the commissioners as his majesty's plenipotentiaries. That the undersigned is neither acting nor insisting upon more than is justified by the usage of the empire, is shown by the decree of the late emperor, a copy of which he has the honor to inclose. Within a few days of its arrival at Nankin, Sir H. Pottinger began to move his fleet down the Yang-tse-Kiang. The undersigned is bound to require an assurance, similarly complete, of the purpose of his present majesty to abide by the engagement entered into on his behalf. Without such an assurance the undersigned can not quit Tientsin, and delay in procuring it will leave him no other

**Oliphant, *Narrative of the Earl of Elgin's Mission to China and Japan*, 289–300.

alternative but to order up to that city the large body of troops which has arrived from Hong Kong, and is now lying in the Gulf of Pechelee."

This letter was followed up by a prompt requisition for barrack accommodation for the 59th regiment, which had recently arrived in the Gulf in the troop-ship Adventure. It produced an immediate effect, the commissioners replying the same day, and promising to procure the required assent, all difficulty on the subject being removed from their minds by the fact which had been brought to their notice of the existence of a precedent.

Accordingly, on the 4th of July, or only two days afterward, a letter was received from the commissioners with the following inclosure: "On the 23d day of the 5th moon of the 8th year of Hien Fung (3d of July), the great council had the honor to receive the following imperial decree:

"Kweiliang and his colleagues have submitted for our perusal copies of the treaties of the different nations. These have been negotiated and sealed by Kweiliang and his colleague. As Kweiliang and his colleague now represent that the different nations are desirous of having our autograph acknowledgment as evidence of their validity, we (hereby signify) our assent to all the propositions in the English and French, and in the Russian and American treaties, as submitted to us in their previous memorial by these ministers, and we command that the course pursued be in accordance therewith. Respect this."

With reference to this imperial decree, Mr. Wade states in his note on the above document that "these Shang-yu imperial decrees are never in autograph. They are prepared by the council, and go forth as the will of the emperor. It will be remembered with what ceremony Kweiliang produced that declaring the powers with which he and Hwashana were invested at their first conference with Lord Elgin." It will be observed that this decree, which was only forced out of the emperor by Lord Elgin's pertinacity, was in general terms, and applied to the treaties made by the other powers as well as ourselves.

The 59th were actually on their way up the river in gun-boats when this letter arrived. Their advance was at once countermanded, and they returned to Hong Kong without ever having reached Tientsin, but not without having done good service.

It was, indeed, with feelings of the deepest regret and disappointment that, in consequence of the news which now arrived from Canton, Lord Elgin found himself compelled to give this order, and to abandon his original intention of visiting Pekin in order to present to the emperor the letter with which he had been accredited by her majesty. The very success which had attended our operations hitherto, and the facility with which they had been carried out, only furnished a more unmistakable proof of the ease with which we might have reached Pekin, had we been at Tientsin two months earlier, when Canton and its neighborhood were still tranquil, when the Chinese were unprepared, and the climate was that of an English spring. The political importance of such an achievement it is impossible to overestimate. The much-vexed question of the reception of a British minister at the capital would have been set at rest forever, and under peculiarly favorable conditions.

Now, unfortunately, every thing combined to induce his excellency to abandon the idea. A Tartar force had collected in the neighborhood of the capital during the last two months, and, although a visit to Pekin after the signature of the treaty of peace would not have had a hostile character, yet it would have been distasteful to the emperor, and it must, in common prudence, have preceded the evacuation of Tientsin by the allied force. A state of affairs had, however, arisen in the south that made it imperative that neither the naval nor military force should be detained in the north any longer than was absolutely necessary. Moreover, the sun was in its most fatal month, and a march of fifty miles would be attended with serious consequences, while the *eclat* and prestige by any such movement would have been very much neutralized by the dilatory nature of the negotiations, and the apparent vacillation at the outset.

Thus every one of those evil results, as arising out of the delay, which had been anticipated by Lord Elgin at Shanghai more than three months before, and to avoid which he felt justified in proceeding to the north without waiting for the admiral, had been realized.

On the 26th of May Lord Elgin had received a communication from General Straubenzee assuring him of the perfect tranquillity of Canton, and of his ability to spare a large share of his troops for operations in the north, should they become necessary. In consequence of this assurance, Lord Elgin did not hesitate, immediately on his arrival at Tientsin, to write to him requesting him to send up the force available for the purpose, and on the 30th of June these reached the Gulf. They brought with them, however, intelligence of a totally altered condition of affairs from that which had existed only a few weeks previously. Sufficient time had elapsed since our first appearance in the Gulf to enable the Chinese government to instigate the Braves to attack Canton. Their assaults on the city, the expedition of our troops to the White Cloud Mountains, and the increased audacity of the Braves in consequence of the unsuccessful issue of this operation, was news which imparted to the state of matters at Canton a more serious aspect than they had yet worn. Although, from our previous acquaintance with both the foreign and Chinese community, we were aware that the panic which existed in the south was probably to a great extent groundless, still the representations generally made of the nature of the crisis were too urgent to be disregarded. From the effect they produced in England some idea may be formed of the sensation they were calculated to create at Tientsin.

To keep troops in the north after the treaty had received the emperor's assent, and when it was reported that the British community at Hong Kong were to be ruthlessly massacred, and the British garrison in Canton ignominiously expelled, for want of a sufficient military force to protect the one place and retain the other, would be clearly unjustifiable; and Lord Elgin at once returned the whole force to General Straubenzee, in the earnest hope that they might arrive in time to enable him to restore confidence by administering to the Braves that lesson, without which, according to the opinion generally entertained, they would never be imbued with a proper respect for British authority. With this view he reminded his excellency "that the power of resorting to such hostile operations as they might deem necessary for the security of their military position at Canton was reserved to the commanders-in-chief, in the most ample terms, in the communication addressed by the plenipotentiaries to the government of China, which formed the subject of my letter to yourself and Sir Michael Seymour, dated the 6th of February last."

Before leaving Tientsin Lord Elgin intimated his desire to meet the commissioners in a semi-official manner; and accordingly, on the morning of the 6th of July, we proceeded to the "Temple of the Winds, which was not so distant as that at which the former interviews were held, and there paid a friendly visit to the commissioners, in the course of which Lord Elgin alluded to the state of affairs in the south, and the conduct of the imperial commissioner Hwang. Had he insisted upon it, there is no doubt he might have procured this worthy's disgrace, instead of leaving this to be done on a future day. Lord Elgin was, however, unwilling to use language which might seem to imply that we were unable to cope with the Canton Braves, and he therefore contented himself with warning the commissioners that the conduct Hwang was pursuing in the south would lead to a recurrence of those scenes which they must deplore equally with himself. Kweiliang replied in the same spirit, and expressed his earnest hope that the troubles at Canton were now at an end, and that the treaty just concluded would inaugurate a more peaceful era in the relations of the Celestial Empire with foreigners. He promised to use his influence to put a stop to the proceedings of the Governor General Hwang.

Since our last interview with this venerable old man, news have been received of the death of Yu, the first minister of the Council of State. This gave Kweiliang the highest rank in the empire.

The ambassador adverted to the expediency of a Chinese officer of rank being sent to England as embassador, and asked the portly Hwashana whether he would like to go in that capacity to which that sedate and imperturbable old aristocrat replied, "That if the emperor ordered him to go, he would go; but if the emperor did not order him to go, he would not go." Lord Elgin then complimented him on his eminence as a scholar and a poet, and referred to the distinction which was conferred upon him by his having taken the degree of Han, an allusion which caused him somewhat to relax as he acknowledged the compliment with an air of grim gratification. The allusion to his poetical compositions was met by an offer on his part to present Lord Elgin with a copy of some of them, and a goodly supply of volumes accordingly followed us on our return to the yamun, containing the metrical effusions of this accomplished "imperial expositor of the classics." As I am not aware that the poem of a Chinese cabinet minister has ever yet appeared in print, I take this opportunity of giving publicity to the following stanzas, as a specimen of those which have, during the intervals of his political labors, flowed from the pen of his excellency Hwashana. It is just possible that their merit is due rather to Mr. Wade's elegant translation than to the poetic talent of the composer.

Hwashana's Complaint when, on his second mission to Moukhden, the Capital of Manchouria, he finds himself once more at the Inn at Chalau.

I.

On toward the sister capital once more,
By duty called, I track my distant way;
The watch-dog notes my wheel, as droops the night
O'er the thatched cot, and slowly tramp my steeds
Up the wild pass, in autumn's mourning sad,
Joyless the moon. And now in chamber lone,
Beneath his single lamp, the traveler dreams
Of house and home, an hundred leagues behind.
Where are his rhymes these panels bore of old?
Vain search! o'er Lu-ho let him listless pore.

II.

Where herds and swine once lay, a hostel now.
Chalau is won at last. My car is staid,
As sunset, slanting, strikes its roof, and chill
The widespread bars admit the evening's breath.
Forlorn the scene—a very "Walk in Dew."
Envoy of majesty! so known to whom?
Peace where the state hath need—no word of care;
Turn to thy muse—let verse these walls adorn.

I leave to competent critics the task of discussing the merits of this production; but in justice to a humbler poet, who became well known to us during our trip to the north, and whose gentle and amiable character impressed us all in his favor, I venture to insert a composition which I think bears off the palm from his exalted competitor. Old Chang was one of those not very old men who have probably been known as "old Chang" all their lives. He was a not unfavorable specimen of the literary class of China—a good scholar, an efficient spy in behalf of his own government, a gentleman in his manners, a great humbug, and a confirmed opium-smoker. He did not speak a word of English, though he had lived with Mr. Wade as teacher for many years, and in that capacity accompanied us to Tientsin. The poem, also translated and versified by Mr. Wade, which was written on a fan in memory of the occasion, was thus headed:

Two stanzas of verses, in five words each, presented by Chang-Tung-Yau to Wade his pupil, and literary acquaintance of nine years' standing, with whom he had been a shipmate to Taku, and at Tientsin, on finding himself several months on board the same vessel with him. Composed on the 5th moon of the year Wu Wu (June, 1854).

I.

So best, in lettered toil thine aim
To aid the world—by one fair deed
To earn a thousand autumns' fame.
The day's capricious will why heed?
Fitful as down upon the air
A bubble that the waters bear,
Is all our glory's fleeting pride.
Thy pastime in the leisure hour
The nicely-studied rhyme to pair;
Nor titles win thy praise, nor power—
And well, for all is change. Though fair
The moon, yet dark the evening's doom:
Changeful our lot, as light and gloom
Play o'er the blue stream's tide.

II.

Nine years since first we met are sped,
Thenceforth in friendly union bound;
Now six long moons one deck we tread.
Our night-lamp trimm'd, we chat the round
Of earth's affairs; the burning day
On weighty labors pours its ray;
We part inditing matters grave
For me, my part fled vainly by,
And with what haste! No longer proud,
But free I stray, as floats on high,
Now clustering, now dispersed, the cloud.
Home to my books—I ask no more—
With age my limbs and travel sore;
Give me my hillside cave.

Hwashana's volume was not the only present Lord Elgin received from the commissioners; nine enormous earthen jars of wine, of dimensions sufficient for Morgiana to smother thieves in, made their appearance just as we were leaving the yamun.

The same afternoon we bade a final adieu to the "Temple of Supreme Felicity," and embarked on board the Firm gun-boat. A flowing tide swept us down to the Gulf in eight hours, and that night we had the satisfaction of once more finding ourselves on board the good ship Furious. As as she had now remained without moving from her dismal anchorage for three months, our appearance was hailed with some pleasure, as the signal for a change to new and more lively scenes.

As we found that we should just have time, on our way back to Shanghai, to visit the Great Wall, we steered a northeasterly course after we had weighed anchor the following day. Before dark we saw the Sha-liu-tien, or "Sand-hill Fields," extensive sand-banks rising but a few feet above the water, remarkable only for being a favorite and profitable fishing-ground, and for a square joss-house painted white to serve as a beacon, and which, situated at one corner, is the only building visible.

The following morning found us off the high land of the department of Shuntien, in the province of Chih-li. Unfortunately, the weather was thick and lowering; the mountains were capped with clouds; and we could only judge of their height when we caught an occasional glimpse of a peak rising from two to three thousand feet above the sea-level. In fine weather there is no difficulty in finding the Great Wall, which is seen for miles scoring with an irregular line the sides of the steepest hills, and crossing their highest ridges. To-day, however, we looked in vain for any such indication of its existence; dense masses of cloud rolled along the base of the range; while misty drizzling rain rendered our search neither hopeful nor agreeable. About 9 A.M. we passed a large walled city, near which a mass of solid masonry abutted on the sea, with a tower or two in rear. This answered in some degree to Lord Jocelyn's description of the locality, but, according to the chart, the position was placed some miles farther on. We therefore followed the coast for two more hours, until we shoaled the water to five fathoms, without observing any sign of the Wall.

It was now evident that we had passed the object of our search, and that the walled town we had observed was Shan-hai, described as being situated at the point where the Great Walls abuts on the sea. The north shore of the Gulf of Leatung, along which we had since been steaming, was the most beautiful piece of coast scenery we had seen in China. Rich plains, covered with the brightest verdure, rose in swelling undulations from the sea to the magnificent range of peaked mountains in rear. Villages were scattered plentifully over them. Snug farm-houses nestled in clumps of wood, and innumerable cattle dotted the landscape, as though they had been sown upon it broadcast. Every thing indicated a prosperous rural population, occupying a champaign of much fertility and picturesque beauty.

We were sorry to turn our backs upon it without either prosecuting our voyage to the new port of Neu-chwang, from which we were scarce fifty miles distant, or returning to inspect more closely the far-famed Wall; but the heavy fogs would have decided the question against farther exploration, even had not our anxiety to reach Shanghai in time for the departure of the mail influenced Lord Elgin in avoiding any farther delay. A rapid and prosperous passage of four days to Shanghai from this point enabled us to secure this latter object.

Prior to leaving Tientsin Lord Elgin had acquainted the admiral with his intention of proceeding at an early date to Japan, at the same time adverting to the state of affairs at Canton, and informing his excellency that the conclusion of the treaty would release the naval forces from any farther service in the north of the empire. As the complexion of the news received from Canton on our arrival at Shanghai, however, was not in any degree improved, Lord Elgin determined to postpone his departure for Japan, in order to consult with the admiral upon the course to be pursued in that quarter.

The following fortnight we passed at Shanhai in a state of some anxiety, as the admiral did not appear, and the condition of Canton seemed to be getting worse by each successive mail: not until the 26th were we cheered by the arrival of the Coromande in the river, the admiral having made a slow passage from the north in his flag-ship, which was then lying at the Rugged Island. He had been more fortunate than ourselves in his trip to the Great Wall, which was visited both by his excellency and Baron Grots.

On the day previous to the arrival of the Admiral Lord Elgin received the intelligence from Pekin that five commissioners had been appointed to proceed to Shanghai for the settlement of the tariff, and the framing of those general trade-regulations which must necessarily be drawn up as a supplemental part of the treaty. Of these commissioners, two were our old friends Kweiliang and Hwashana, to whom was added the governor general of the Two Kiangs, Ho-Kwei-tsick, one of the most highly esteemed men in the empire for learning and administrative ability. Two other mandarins of less note completed the commission.

As no commissioners of the eminence of these mandarins had been demanded for the revision of the tariff, etc., their appointment to this function was a spontaneous act, on the part of the government, of some significance; and their position and character were such that, whatever idea Lord Elgin might at one time have entertained of proceeding to Canton instead of Japan was now abandoned, as he considered it above all things essential that he should not lose the opportunity which the visit of the commissioners would afford him of exerting that influence which personal intercourse would, he doubted not, enable him to acquire over them.

Though the Treaty of Tientsin effected the great object of revolutionizing the system under which our political and commercial relations with the empire were to be for the future conducted, there were many most important details to be considered in the altered conditions under which these latter were to be worked out, and the embassador perceived with no little satisfaction that these might now be arranged by himself in accordance with the spirit of the treaty, and with that deliberation and solemnity which they deserved; nor, indeed, however deeply interested he might feel in the state of affairs then existing at Canton, did he consider that their settlement fell within the province of a civilian. The city was under a purely military government. It is true, the Governor Pih-kwei was exercising certain functions as a Chinese authority, but he did so only with the sufferance of General Straubenzee, and as an assistance to that officer in preserving peace and order: should the general have found his presence an obstruction rather than an aid to his administration, it was in his power at any time to suspend him from his functions, and turn him out of the city or keep him in confinement, as, indeed, for some part of the time he did.

Lord Elgin was strongly impressed with the notion that the most thorough and satisfactory way of restoring quiet to Canton was to inflict a summary chastisement upon those who disturbed the peace there; and accordingly, in a letter to General Straubenzee, informing his excellency of the expected arrival of the commissioners above named, and of his intention to meet them at Shanghai, the embassador goes on to say: "It is not impossible that I may be able to induce these high officers to take some active steps to check the proceedings of the Braves at Canton; but, looking at the present state of affairs in that quarter as portrayed in your excellency's dispatch of the 22d instant, and in the reports I have received from Mr. Parkes, I can not help thinking that it would be very desirable that any such intimation by the Chinese authorities should be preceded by some vigorous decisive action on our part, showing our power to control and punish the Braves.

> It is for your excellency to determine how such a blow can be most effectually struck; but I trust you will excuse me for making a suggestion which is prompted by the expected arrival of the imperial commissioners, and the anomalous state of affairs at Canton.

Lord Elgin also wrote a letter to the admiral immediately on his arrival at Shanghai, calling his excellency's attention "to the continued existence in that quarter of a state of affairs to which it is most important an arrest should be put at the earliest period," and proceeding in terms almost identical with those I have quoted as already addressed to General Straubenzee. In reply to the communication, the admiral stated that it was his intention, prior to going south, to proceed to Nagasaki for the purpose of delivering over the yacht Emperor to the government of Japan, and watering the Calcutta.

During this period of our stay at Shanghai the climate was more oppressively hot than I ever remember to have felt it in any part of the world. The thermometer did not show a higher temperature than at Tientsin, but there was a stifling heaviness in the atmosphere which acted in a most depressing manner both on health and spirits. Cases of death by sun-stroke were of daily occurrence, chiefly among the sailors in the shipping which crowded the river. Upward of a hundred merchantmen, waiting hopelessly for cargoes, were lying at anchor under the broiling sun, their lists of sick daily increasing under the deleterious influence of the climate.

As two or three weeks must elapse before the arrival of the commissioners, Lord Elgin determined to escape for the interval to Japan, and return in time to meet their excellencies at Shanghai. In the mean time certain changes had taken place in the "personnel" of the mission. Mr. Bruce had proceeded to England with the treaty of Tientsin immediately on our return to Shanghai; Mr. Jocelyn had arrived to relieve Mr. Cameron, who went home on his promotion; and Mr. Morrison returned to England. With our party thus reduced, we embarked on board the Furious on the last day of July, 1858, delighted under any circumstances to escape from the summer heats of Shanghai, were it only for a few weeks, but our gratification increased by the anticipation of visiting scenes which have ever been veiled in the mystery of a jealous and rigid seclusion.

*   *   *

---

*Agreement between Great Britain and Egypt for the
Purchase of Suez Canal Shares (Initiated by Benjamin Disraeli),
25 November 1875**

Agreement entered into this 25th day of November, in the year of Our Lord 1875, between Major-General Edward Stanton, C.B., Her Britannic Majesty's Agent and Consul-General in Egypt, acting on behalf of Her Britannic Majesty's Government, on the one part, and his Excellency Ismail Sadek Pasha, Egyptian Minister of Finance, acting on behalf of His Highness the Khedive of Egypt, on the other part.

Whereas His Highness the Khedive has proposed to sell to Her Britannic Majesty's Government the whole of his shares in the Suez Canal Company, and whereas Her Britannic Majesty's Government has proposed to purchase from His Highness the Khedive 177,642 shares in the said Suez Canal Company for the sum of 4,000,000*l.* sterling:

**British and Foreign State Papers*, LXVI, 670–71.

Now it is hereby witnessed that His Highness the Khedive agrees to sell to Her Britannic Majesty's Government the whole of his shares in the Suez Canal Company, being to the number of 176,602 shares, not, as supposed by Her Britannic Majesty's Government, 177,642 shares; and Her Britannic Majesty's Government agrees to purchase the same for the sum of 4,000,000*l.* sterling, less the proportionate value of the 1,040 shares, the difference between 177,-642 and 176,602, and Her Britannic Majesty's Government agrees to recommend to Parliament to sanction the contract.

Her Britannic Majesty's Government undertakes that on the 1st of December next, on the deposit of the shares in the hands of Her Majesty's Agent and Consul-General in Egypt, the sum of 1,000,000*l.* sterling shall be held at the disposal of the Egyptian Government in the hands of Messrs. N. de Rothschild and Sons, of London; and that the remaining 3,000,000*l.* sterling, less the amount to be deducted for the value of the 1,040 shares above-mentioned, shall be provided in the months of December and January next, as may be arranged between the Egyptian Government and Messrs. Rothschild and Sons.

The Egyptian Government undertakes to pay to Her Britannic Majesty's Government interest at the rate of 5 per cent. per annum on the whole amount of the purchase money of the said 176,602 shares, in equal half-yearly payments, the said payments to be made in London on the 1st of June and the 1st of December in each year, until such times as the coupons of the said shares shall be liberated from the engagement now existing with the Suez Canal Company; and the Egyptian Government further engages that the amount of the said interest shall be charged on the revenues of Egypt.

Debate in the House of Commons on the Purchase of Suez Canal Shares Including Disraeli's Defense of His Actions, 8 August 1876*

* * *

MR. RYLANDS said, he could not regard the possession of the Suez Canal shares as necessary or advantageous. The holding of the shares would not alone keep open our route to our Indian Empire. The share certificates would not prevent a hostile fleet from closing the passage of the Canal in the event of an European complication; in one way only could that route be kept open, and that was by having a more powerful fleet than any that could be brought against us. Our fleet being swept away, what power was there in these £4,000,000 of worthless paper? Surely his hon. Friend the Member for Pembroke (Mr. E. J. Reed) did not suppose that the destinies of European nations could be determined by

*Hansard, 3.s., CCXXXI, 835–45, 848–54.

means of scraps of paper? No justification for the action which Government had taken could be based upon ground such as that. Then what security did the shares offer for the route to India, seeing that with or without the possession of the shares still the only safeguard was a powerful fleet? Looking at the transaction from a business point of view he would like to ask the Government whether they had conducted the purchase in a businesslike manner. In the first place, why was the transaction entered into at all? That was a question the importance of which demanded a fuller discussion than it had received, and the opportunity for that discussion should have been provided at an earlier part of the Session. The Bill before the House was first mentioned some months ago, and it was brought in by the right hon. Gentleman the Chancellor of the Exchequer some time back, and now when the House was weary, when there was but a thin attendance of Members, and those anxious to get away, they were called upon to discuss this Bill. The right hon. Gentleman the Member for the University of London (Mr. Lowe) had challenged the Government to lay before the House the reasons which induced such a large expenditure of public money; he (Mr. Rylands) would not venture to attempt to add force to that appeal, for he felt sure that it would receive the attention of the right hon. Gentleman the Chancellor of the Exchequer. He would content himself with taking lower ground, and looking at it merely as a business transaction he asked why did the Government purchase an article for £4,000,000 with a guarantee of 5 per cent when that same article could have been bought in Paris for £3,800,000, with a guarantee of 10 or 12 per cent? Unless in the reports which had reached him the truth was grossly misrepresented, £1,500,000 had been considered the full market value of the shares. Such was the statement which appeared in *The Times* newspaper, and he had seen no contradiction. But it was asked what guarantee was there that the Khedive would pay the 10 or 12 per cent when it was known that he was actually borrowing money for which he was paying 20 and 25 per cent, and people were not disposed to lend the Khedive money at any price. But that consideration applied equally to the guarantee of 5 per cent, and there was no reason why Government should buy the shares upon higher terms than they were offered at. Her Majesty's Government, however, met the Khedive with most unusual generosity; they thought they ought to deal with him handsomely, that it was a great international undertaking, and that the Khedive could not be treated in an ordinary business manner. There was an elevation of sentiment about this; but, still, he (Mr. Rylands) failed to see in it a justification for giving for the shares a price beyond what any other capitalist would have offered. The Government were led to suppose that other parties were negotiating for the purchase of the shares; but he was inclined to believe that the English Government were imposed upon in these operations. Then after paying £4,000,000 we were absolutely unable to qualify our directors upon the company, and to get out of this absurd position when three directors were appointed we were obliged to purchase shares for £8,000 more. And so it came to this—that our commercial interest upon the Board was represented by £8,000 worth of shares, and upon the power of that sum our representatives depended! Whether we were right in the question of the qualification or whether we were wrong he was not prepared to say. One question he would like to put, and that was, whether steps had been taken to secure compensation to Sir Daniel Lange, who lost the position he held with the Company owing to the action of the Government in publishing a private letter sent by him. That gentleman was closely connected with the progress of that great work, and he endeavoured to serve his country. Some satisfaction was due to him from the Government of this country, whose inconsiderate conduct had led to his dismissal. Turning to another matter he expressed his strong disapprobation of the way in which the salary of Mr. Rivers Wilson had been increased in consequence of his having been made a director. If the duties of his office were not sufficient to occupy his attention then let other work be provided for him; but he objected to his holding two positions with two salaries. The action taken by Her Majesty's Government in effecting the purchase of the Suez Canal shares had led to serious pecuniary losses being suffered by many persons owing to the state into which the market for Egyptian securities was thrown by the transaction, and much distress and privation had followed. A week before the Suez Canal purchase, Egyptian Stock stood at 54, and it gradually went up to 60, then a large purchase was made at 61—the price next day was 64, and the day after the announcement appeared in *The Times* of the Suez purchase, and the Stock went up to 74. Some parties, who were in the secret, had made large amounts by their transactions. After a time a reaction occurred, and the Stock fell. What did the Government do then? They commissioned a most important member of their own body to proceed to Egypt under circumstances which led people to believe that the fact foreshadowed a great policy—namely, the taking of Egypt by the hand by the Government of England. Then, again, Egyptian Stocks went up, and people held the bonds with some confidence. What happened then? The right hon. Gentleman the Member for Shoreham (Mr. Stephen Cave) sent in a Report, and Egyptian Stock was very firm and rising; but the right hon. Gentleman at the head of the Government stated that the Report must not be published; and then what happened? Down went Egyptian Stock; and so it remained for some time. But on a certain Friday morning there were large orders for the purchase of the Stock from France. No one understood what it meant. The day passed. All the Stock that could be procured was purchased, and the Stock Exchange closed; but in the House of Commons, about half-past 1 o'clock on Saturday morning, the Chancellor of the Exchequer got up in his place and said that they had received intelligence by telegraph that the Khedive assented to the Report of the right hon. Gentleman. What happened then? Why, the following morning up went the Stock. So that there were people who on Friday knew about the telegram, and that the announcement would be made, and the result was that those people in France or Egypt operated in the Stock, and they again made a large plunder; but when the Report came out and was found not to justify the expectations it had given rise to, down went the Stock again. In the same way, Mr. Rivers Wilson was allowed to proceed to Egypt, and that fact enabled the

Stock-jobbers to operate, and the Stock again went up and down. The right hon. Gentleman the Member for the University of London said that the Egyptian policy of the Government was a drama in four acts; but it differed from all other dramas in this—that the grand letting off of fireworks and the transformation scene came first, and now it was ending in a good deal of gloom and disappointment. He did not know how the Government could justify what had been done in the matter. Their policy was, he believed, in any case an unfortunate policy, and might lead to an involvment of this country in Egyptian affairs in a very serious manner. He believed that finally the purchase would not be of importance to this country, while the way in which the negotiations were carried on was a source of great loss to our countrymen. He felt sure that it would come to be looked upon as one of the greatest mistakes the Government had made.

THE CHANCELLOR OF THE EXCHEQUER said, he should gladly have waited until any other hon. Members who desired to address the House had done so, but the statement just made by the hon. Member for Burnley (Mr. Rylands) was of so very serious a character, if he understood it rightly, that he was bound at once to ask an explanation of it, and at the same time to complain, as he did most seriously, that the hon. Member, if he had anything of the sort to say, had not mentioned it long ago, or given him notice of his intention to say what he had said. What he understood the hon. Gentleman to say was this—that upon the morning of a certain day, on the evening of which he (the Chancellor of the Exchequer) read a telegram to the House stating that the Khedive had authorized the publication of the Report of his right hon. Friend the Member for Shoreham (Mr. Cave), orders were sent for the purchase of Egyptian Stock from parties abroad with the knowledge that he was in receipt of that telegram, and was going to communicate it to the House.

MR. RYLANDS: Oh, I beg your pardon.

THE CHANCELLOR OF THE EXCHEQUER: I certainly so understood the hon. Member.

MR. RYLANDS: I am quite sure the right hon. Gentleman will believe me when I say I meant to cast no personal imputation whatever upon him. It was the last thing that would come into my mind. I believe fully in the high honour of the right hon. Gentleman. What I stated was that some people knew that the telegram was going to be sent, and allowed it to be known, and on their own knowledge took means of operating on the market. They must have known in Cairo, or France, or elsewhere in the morning that it was to be sent in the evening.

THE CHANCELLOR OF THE EXCHEQUER was anxious that the matter should be made perfectly clear, because in the way the words of the hon. Member were used they involved a serious charge against himself. [Mr. RYLANDS: "Oh, no, no!" Several hon. MEMBERS: "Hear, hear!"] He accepted, of course, the disclaimer of the hon. Gentleman, and he felt sure that every one would feel that it was impossible that such a thing could have occurred. He at once and frankly acknowledged that it was to him and his Colleagues matter of most serious anxiety, and had occasioned them the greatest regret, that, in consequence of the transactions that had been going on, there had been from time to time speculations on the Stock Exchange, and that, as they were informed, considerable sums of money had been won and lost on this matter. He hardly knew what one could say on such a matter. This, however, he confidently said, on the part of the Government—that no private information had ever been given or made use of, to the best of their belief, on the subject; and he earnestly entreated that, if there was any suspicion of that kind in any quarter, full inquiry might be made, so that, even at this late period of the Session, steps might be taken to ascertain that there was no foundation whatever for any imputation of that kind. He could believe that among all those different transactions some persons might have obtained some information, and there might have been reason to suppose this, that, or the other, and that some speculations that were very good and some that were very bad might have been made; but he wished to state the facts exactly as they occurred with respect to the publication or non-publication of his right hon. Friend's Report. When that Report was handed to them by his right hon. Friend, they communicated with the Khedive and informed him that they proposed to publish it. Well, the Khedive objected, in the telegram which would be found among the Papers. His right hon. Friend at the head of the Government, in answer to a Question put soon after the receipt of the telegram, gave the answer that had been commented upon, and that answer, unfortunately, was misunderstood. His right hon. Friend intended to have said that the Khedive objected to the publication of the Report, not permanently, but in consequence of the then unsettled question of the financial relations of Egypt. His right hon. Friend adverted to what was in his mind at the time the communications were going on between this Government and the Khedive as to the appointment of a Commissioner from England, but it was understood by the public in another sense, and, unfortunately, that misunderstanding gave a blow to Egyptian credit which they very much regretted for the sake of the Khedive. The consequence was that his noble Friend (the Earl of Derby) sent a telegram to the Khedive informing him that the non-publication of the Report was injurious to his credit. The Khedive thereupon sent a telegram to say that he was ready to agree to the Report being published. That telegram was received at the Foreign Office late at night, not earlier than between 11 or 12 o'clock. His right hon. Friend at the head of the Government was absent, the business was going on, and he thought he could not do better than, at the earliest moment he could, read the telegram to the House. What was done was done in the regular course of official business, and it had been a matter of extreme pain and regret to the Government that any person should have been injuriously affected. As to what communication might have been going on between the Khedive and persons at Cairo or elsewhere he knew nothing; but of this he could entirely assure the House—that if the

shadow of a doubt existed in the mind of any hon. Member, or if any hon.
Member was aware that among any class in the country any impression or
suspicion existed that there was anything in the matter, so far as Her Majesty's
Government was concerned, that ought to be inquired into, he implored them,
he adjured them in the name of the honour of the Government and of the
House, not to allow the matter to rest, but to bring it at once into a condition in
which it could be fully inquired into. He would now endeavour to answer the
different points which had been mooted in the course of the debate. The right
hon. Gentleman the Member for the University of London (Mr. Lowe) asked
what was their precise position with regard to this undertaking? Well, they had
waited until the general meeting of the Company, which was to have been held
in June, but was not held till July, in order to ascertain the arrangements the
Company were prepared to recommend. The managing body recommended—
M. de Lesseps especially—the increase of the number of directors to 24, and
agreed that the new directors should be nominated by the British Government.
The understanding was that they must be duly qualified and elected in the
manner described by the statutes of the Company. M. de Lesseps gave the
Government to understand that it was presumed they would not nominate
persons who would be offensive on any grounds to the shareholders, but that if
any such person was nominated it should, on the fact becoming known, be in
the power of the English Government to name his successor. It was the
impression of Her Majesty's Government that their duty was to nominate
persons who should represent the interest, amounting to the value of 176,000
shares, which the Government had in the Canal; but M. de Lesseps pointed out
that there still was a question, which had never been decided, as to the precise
amount of right which these shares during the time their coupons were detached
from them gave to the shareholders. It was competent for the British Government to have brought that question before a French Law Court for decision;
but they thought that, looking to the whole spirit of the arrangement, and their
desire to enter into this matter on the fullest terms of confidence and goodwill
with the Company, it was not desirable to raise contentious questions, and that
it would be better that they should see that the directors were qualified in
accordance with the statutes of the Company. They did not abandon their claim
to vote on account of their own shares, but they thought that the simplest way
would be to purchase a certain number of qualifying shares, and place them in
the hands of the gentlemen who might be the representatives of Her Majesty's
Government on the Council. This view was communicated to M. de Lesseps,
and was considered by the legal advisers engaged on both sides of the question,
the result being, as far as Her Majesty's Government was concerned, a conviction that the course taken opened no legal difficulties as far as the final
settlement of the question was concerned. If, however, it should appear hereafter that legal difficulties really existed, the step taken was one that could be
retraced when occasion arose. These gentlemen did not go there to represent
their own interests, they went there to represent the interests of the country
which nominated them; and the Government were convinced, from their knowl-

edge of the character and ability of these gentlemen, that they would represent effectively the interests of this country. It had been suggested that the mode in which they were appointed, or nominated, was one which implied humiliation as far as they were personally concerned; and the hon. Member for Burnley (Mr. Rylands) had gone the length of saying that one of them (Mr. Rivers Wilson) ought not, if appointed at all, to receive any payment for the duty additional to that which he at present received as a servant of the Government. The duties which Mr. Wilson at present discharged were highly important, but they did not occupy the whole of his time, nor was his salary by any means extravagant, and it was believed that he might very well give one day in a month to the Suez Canal business, with a small additional payment to recompense him for the work, and pay the expenses which he would have to incur. The question of the right of voting in meetings of the Company by the directors appointed by the English Government had been raised, and upon that question he could pronounce no authoritative decision; but in any case he thought the question was one of infinitesimal importance. The advantage which they had gained in respect of this matter was really that which was stated by the hon. Member for Pembroke (Mr. E. J. Reed)—namely, the moral position which they had acquired in dealing with these questions. The surtax arrangement was just one of the questions in point. Though the question was settled at Constantinople, yet it was settled subject to certain protests, and in a manner that always left you with the apprehension that the question might be re-opened, and re-opened in a very awkward manner. The Government should have insisted upon the matters that had been agreed to; but their object was to avoid the necessity of having to invoke the armed interference of the Khedive, or of the Turkish Government, or of our own Power. When hon. Gentlemen talked about keeping open the Canal by the power of our Fleet, of course we might; but the object was to avoid using force, and to put ourselves in a position where we would be able to deal with all these questions in a much more satisfactory manner. These were the general considerations which induced the Government to make the purchase, and nothing had occurred since to cause them to doubt their soundness. Colonel Stokes and Mr. Rivers Wilson had been in Paris, and had attended one of the meetings of the Council, and in their Report to him they stated that they had been received in the most amicable manner; that they had been treated with the fullest confidence and in a spirit which promised that the best possible relations would exist between us and the managers of this great Company; and that they had been very much struck with what they saw of the administration and the general management of the undertaking. Every person who had read the Company's last Report would have seen that, as far as prosperity was concerned, the undertaking was in a very flourishing condition, for at the present time, when commercial affairs were not particularly bright, it showed that the receipts of the Canal were going on in a most satisfactory manner, inasmuch as last year the excess of receipts over expenditure had increased by about 17 per cent over that of the previous year, while at the same time the expenses had scarcely been increased at all. The question of surtax was still in this position—that it was impossible for Her Majesty's Government to adopt M. de Lesseps' proposals merely as for this country, as it was necessary to obtain the concurrence of other countries which were interested in the matter. Communications had been going on with the different Governments which would shortly be laid before Parliament, and they were, so far as they had gone, generally in favour of the arrangement which had been come to, which showed to the shipping interest with certainty what the duties would be that they would have to pay year by year. The right hon. Gentleman had asked questions with reference to the probability of the Khedive continuing to pay the £ 200,000 per annum; but he thought that those were questions which the right hon. Gentleman, to a certain extent at least, was as qualified to answer as he was himself. It was a very hard matter to say whether or not at some time or another a difficulty might occur in the payment of the money, but his own belief was that the money would be paid. It was paid on the last occasion, and he saw no reason why it should not be paid in future. In conclusion, he could only acknowledge and regret the lateness of the period when this matter had been brought forward—it certainly ought to have been discussed at a much earlier period of the Session. Her Majesty's Government, however, were waiting for the action of the Company and for the meeting to which he had referred and which had explained to the House the manner in which the undertaking was being carried on. In consequence of the mode in which the Business of the House had been transacted it was impossible to get time earlier in the Session for the discussion of the subject. All he could say was that so far as the Government were concerned, the reasons which induced them to make this purchase stood good, that his faith had not been shaken by anything that had taken place, and though there might have been some exaggeration in the minds of the people at the time when the purchase was announced, his own belief was that in making that purchase they had arrived at a good and sound conclusion.

Mr. RYLANDS disclaimed all intention of throwing imputations upon Her Majesty's Government in reference to this subject.

THE CHANCELLOR OF THE EXCHEQUER thought that there was some ambiguity in the expressions which had been used by the hon. Member that rendered it imperative upon him to offer the explanations he had done of the conduct of the Government in the matter.

* * *

LORD ELCHO said, it was natural the Opposition should criticize a transaction of this kind, but it was refreshing to see the hon. Member for Pembroke (Mr. E. J. Reed) cast aside the trammels of Party and treat this as a great national question. As such he believed it would be viewed by the constituencies, who, if appealed to, would throw the carping criticism of the Opposition to the winds, and give their verdict that politically the purchase was a bold and a wise act. Had the Government not availed themselves of their opportunity, and not purchased those shares, he had no doubt the Opposition would then have criticized their omission to secure for England the interest she was entitled to possess in so great an undertaking. England possessed the largest number of shares in the Canal, and her interests, politically and commercially, in it would no doubt be well represented by the three directors whom she had appointed to watch over and represent them. Government had, in fact, recovered the position for England which Lord Palmerston had lost.

THE MARQUESS OF HARTINGTON: Until my noble Friend addressed the House I was under the impression that Members of the Opposition had criticized the measure submitted to the House by the Government. The noble Lord appears to be of opinion that the discussion which has occurred is not criticism, but carping. I do not think it much matters whether he calls it criticism or carping. We criticize the measures of the Government in the best way we are able, and I can assure him we shall not be deterred from that duty by the epithet he chooses to apply to that humble criticism. Although it is to be regretted in one sense that this debate should have been brought on so late in the Session, it is not altogether unfortunate, because of the instructive comparison that might be drawn with respect to the treatment of this subject between the opening of the Session and its close. At the opening of the Session the transaction was almost in the first blush of its prosperity and popularity. And the minimizing explanation, although it had, I believe, to a certain extent set in already, had not attained the full vigour and strength that it has now at the close of the Session arrived at. It would be extremely instructive, if we had time to make a comparison between some of the speeches delivered at the commencement of the Session and the speech of the right hon. Gentleman the Chancellor of the Exchequer to-night. All traces of high policy have now vanished from the speeches of the Government; their high policy remains, in a feeble and diluted form, in the speeches of the noble Lord the Member for Haddingtonshire and my hon. Friend the Member for Pembroke (Mr. E. J. Reed). Nothing is now said about the high road to India and the chain of fortresses in which the Suez Canal was to form a link. This line has altogether vanished from the speeches of the Government, and we are told to look for the advantage of this transaction to the improved tone of M. de Lesseps. We are told that nothing can be more friendly than the communications between Colonel Stokes and M. de Lesseps. That is easy to be understood; but it may be doubted whether the improved tone of our correspondence is worth £4,000,000 of public money. The right hon. Gentleman can no doubt point to two results. He can point to the appointment of three directors on the Board, and he can point to the satisfactory and amicable arrangements come to between Colonel Stokes and M. de Lesseps on the surtax. He says M. de Lesseps made a great concession in the matter of the appointment of directors. But that is the very thing M. de Lesseps wanted us to do five years ago. In the negotiations in 1871 it was stated that M. de Lesseps "recoiled with horror" from the idea of the management of the Canal passing into the hands of a foreign Power. He declared he never would be a party for the placing of the management of the Canal in other than French hands, but he trusted to see the introduction of English directors on a French Board. At the same time, this was only to "give an appearance of importance without its actual possession." These being M. de Lesseps' views in 1871, no doubt M. de Lesseps did not see any reason to change them; but these being M. de Lesseps' views, I do not think it was necessary to spend £4,000,000 to get M. de Lesseps to agree to what he desired in 1871. The negotiatons on the surtax are said to have gone on smoothly; and they may have ended in a satisfactory result; but that result has been brought about not by concessions on the part of M. de Lesseps, but on the part of Colonel Stokes and the English Government. The surtax was to have terminated at an earlier date than that now fixed upon, and it is not wonderful that M. de Lesseps and the French Direction should show a conciliatory spirit, when all the concessions were made, not on the other side, but on ours. It is quite unnecessary to say what will be the effect in time of war. I doubt whether it will have any effect in time of war. I cannot agree with the hon. Member for Pembroke that by the influence we have acquired through these shares in the Canal we should have acquired the right in time of war to seize upon the whole, and to disregard not only our own rights, but those of our co-partners. It may be my own fault, but I am unable to follow that argument of my hon. Friend. It would be the same as if we should acquire an interest in the railways of a neighbouring State, with which we at some time might be at war, in order that we might have a moral right to take possession of those railways in case of an invasion of the country. I do not believe that this purchase will have any effect upon the possession of the Canal in time of war. What must happen in time of war must be decided by contingencies. It is impossible to foresee what can only be decided upon at the moment. What the House wants to know is what will be the effect on certain ordinary creditors in the Canal in time of peace. Many Members of this House who are competent to give an opinion think our position is not improved by anything that has taken place, and that our interests are not so simple and well-defined as before. Up to the present year the Government was the representative of a nation which made use of the Canal to a vastly greater extent than any other European nation. It had certain rights secured to it under the concessions, and at all events occupied a definite and well-defined position as the representative of the greatest trading nation of the world. Now the Government is not merely the representative of the customers of the Canal—it has become a co-partner in managing the Canal, and a co-partner under very different circumstances from the other shareholders. In that way it seems to me that the position of the Government is particularly complicated, and I fail to see that it is in any way strengthened. It appears to me, on the contrary, that the Government will be somewhat shy in future in embarking in these commercial enterprizes, or in interfering in the pecuniary affairs of other nations. It was impossible for hon. Members not to sympathize with the Chancellor of the Exchequer when he spoke of the deep regret with which he had learnt of the Stock Exchange gambling transactions which had resulted from the action of the Government. The House was not surprised that the right hon. Gentleman should have so warmly as he did repudiated the suspicion that the Government was in any way a party to transactions of this character; but it showed how extremely inconvenient, and how much to be deprecated, it is that the Government should have taken any part whatever in transactions such as those to which I have referred, and that they should have to trust to the right hon. Gentleman to rise and repudiate any idea of such a thing. There is no doubt that clever and unscrupulous persons, apparently acting in Egypt or in other parts of the world, have made use of the knowledge they acquired of the intention of the Government in this country to act on the Stock Exchange in London, Paris, and other places in a manner not creditable to the British Government. I do not think we can be proud of the part which the Government of England played on the Stock Exchange in Europe; but I do think it will be a lesson to the Government to avoid for the future being mixed up in such transactions.

MR. DISRAELI: Sir, there seems to be one fallacy that pervades all the remarks of hon. Members on the opposite side of the House on this subject, and that is the assumption on their part that our interest in an institution cannot be at the same time political and commercial. Take, for example, the National Debt. That is a political institution. It is so in a special degree, and never could have existed had it not been founded upon the most delicate of all political considerations—national credit. It depends upon political considerations. Its prosperity and its influence in the world depend upon political considerations. Yet I suppose hon. Gentlemen will hardly agree that it must not be considered a commercial institution, or the declaration of our dividends would not be met in due time with the same regularity and promptness as they are at present. For my own part, I never deviated—nor am I aware that my Colleagues ever deviated—from the declarations we made when we announced the purchase of these shares. We purchased them from high political considerations; and had it not been for those considerations we should never have entered into those negotiations. But having bought those shares, it became our duty to make every arrangement and take every precaution that the country should not be financially and commercially a loser. While, therefore, we thought we had accomplished a great political object, we were at the same time anxious to prevent the country from experiencing any loss. It seems to me the position is so clear that there cannot be any misapprehension that political and commercial principles can exist in the same institution, notwithstanding the unauthorized remarks of the noble Lord and others who preceded him. Nor do I think the noble Lord was particularly fortunate in his argument that M. de Lesseps, when he offered to consent to the appointment of three English directors some time ago, said that they would exercise no influence except as directors, if they were introduced into the Board on the part of the English proprietors. It is very true that in 1871 M. de Lesseps did make that remark, and insisted upon it. He said that the three English directors would be nothing more than three individuals who would exercise that influence which by their qualifications under the charter of the Company they might possess. But in 1871, when M. de Lesseps made that observation, England had not purchased half the shares in the Company.

Therefore, all the arguments of the noble Lord based upon the remarks made by M. de Lesseps at that time go for nothing at all, and do not apply to the circumstances with which we have to deal at present. Nor is there anyone who can doubt the contrast between the two cases. Suppose that in 1871 English directors had been appointed in the manner referred to, and suppose that in the present case the English directors were appointed after the purchase of the Canal, is there any body of men either in this country or on any of those Stock Exchanges of Europe with which the noble Lord seems so familiar, who would hesitate to say which three individuals would exercise the greatest influence? Every man of sense must know that the three English directors now to be appointed would occupy a totally different position from the three individuals whose appointment in 1871 was suggested by M. de Lesseps. Then the noble Lord says my right hon. Friend the Chancellor of the Exchequer entirely disregarded all political considerations, and founded his observations on commercial considerations. My right hon. Friend very properly, on a Bill of this kind, made observations which he argued out completely, so far as financial and commercial considerations can go. To-night my right hon. Friend, as I listened to his arguments, never for a moment deviated from the political position which the Government assumed with regard to this queston. He argued in this way. He said one of the great advantages of this is that we obtain our object in an amicable manner, which otherwise might be obtained only by painful controversy, and probably by force. What is that but a political consideration, and of the highest kind. What does that prove? That we obtain this object, not for financial and commercial considerations, though it is our duty not to neglect these financial and commercial considerations, but for our political considerations. Now, with regard to what the noble Lord says about the influence of the conduct of Her Majesty's Government on the Stock Exchanges of Europe, all I can say is I am innocent in the matter. I have never allowed considerations of what would happen on the Stock Exchanges of Europe to prevent me from doing that in public which I think would be for the advancement of the welfare of this country. If we were to be arrested in our conduct of the high matters which are involved in the government of a great country like England merely, by considerations of what the effect of our words would be upon the Stock Exchanges of Europe, I think we should be in a position which, as a public man, I should feel to be utterly disgraceful. Sir, I hope this Bill will pass without any opposition. I feel sure myself that the feeling of the country is not changed as to this great enterprize. I cannot doubt that the hon. Member for Birkenhead (Mr. Mac Iver) spoke with justice when he expressed the opinion of the powerful community in which he lives. I believe that the people of the country have not changed one iota the sentiments which influenced them at the commencement of the Session; that they look upon this act on the part of Her Majesty's Government as a political and patriotic act; and as such, if ever the matter is made a subject of controversy, and I am before my countrymen, I shall be ready to appeal to them with the utmost confidence.

*   *   *

Debate in the House of Lords on the Second Afghan War, 4 August 1879*

VISCOUNT CRANBROOK: My Lords, it now becomes my duty, the war with Afghanistan having been happily concluded, and a Treaty of Peace having been signed with the Ameer, to call your Lordships' attention to the services which have been rendered by those who had charge of the conduct of the war in that country. The sole object of the Resolution which I will propose will be not a discussion of the policy of the war, upon which your Lordships have already given an opinion, but simply to look at the military operations which have taken place, and which are of a character, as your Lordships will agree, creditable to this country, and have justified the confidence that was felt in the Officers by whom those operations have been carried on. It is my intention to look now at the Treaty which has been concluded, not in its political aspect, but simply as bringing the war to an end—at the peace which has been established and at the work done by our soldiers in the field. I will not trespass upon your Lordships now by discussing the Articles of the Treaty—we may have an opportunity of doing that hereafter—at present, as I have said, I regard it merely as the conclusion of the war and the beginning of the peace. Although, in the Resolution I shall propose, there are some whose names have not been mentioned among those who have been conspicuous in the field, still I think your Lordships would not feel justified in passing them over. Among them is the name of that distinguished officer who negotiated the Treaty with the Ameer and brought the war to a conclusion, Major Cavagnari. Before the affairs in Afghanistan his name was not much known in England; but now it is deservedly well known for the intelligence and sagacity which enabled him to bring about the Treaty of Peace which, in less skilful hands, might have failed. His power of understanding the Afghan Ruler, and his insight into the Native character, enabled him in a shorter time than, perhaps, any person with less skill and penetration into character could have done, to bring to a conclusion a Treaty of Peace which is likely to have the best results. I am sure that Major Cavagnari will bring to the conduct of the business with which he is intrusted at Cabul the same skill, tact, and prudence which have raised him to his present position, and which in the future, I believe, will obtain for him still greater recognition. Perhaps your Lordships will also allow me to say one word about another officer, Major Sandeman, who had charge of the negotiations at Khelat. He was placed in a position of great responsibility—it was necessary that all his proceedings should be in perfect harmony with all that was doing elsewhere, and the satisfactory relations into which we have been brought with the Khan and the useful results as regarded the conduct of the war in Afghanistan are in no small degree due to the admirable qualities which Major

*Hansard, 3.s., CCXLIX, 2–20.

Sandeman brought to bear upon the mission which he had in charge. There-fore, I have thought it right to mention Major Sandeman before I pass on to consider the services which were rendered by the officers who actually conduct-ed the campaign. But, my Lords, before referring to these special services, there are some special circumstances connected with the campaign to which I should like to allude. I will mention, first, that which has been spoken of in the newspapers during the last three or four days in terms which gave me great pain, because I thought there was great exaggeration. No doubt, there was at one time some anxiety as to cholera; but, according to the official information, this has, in the main, passed away. The statement that the 10th Hussars and the 17th Regiment had suffered very severely from disease was very much exagger-ated. It is true that the 10th Hussars did suffer very much in coming back from Afghanistan to their quarters beyond Peshawur. It was also said that the officers were very much to blame for having led their men back by long marches through such a country at a period of the year when there is so much greater danger of cholera than at other seasons. Now, I have been allowed to see a private letter from one of the most distinguished officers serving in the Khyber Pass; I believe I may mention his name—it is Colonel Jenkins, who commands the Guides. He says—

> The march down was very trying. The heat was very great, and at every 100 yards of the route there was a dead camel or bullock. Besides this, there was cholera, and some of the regiments suffered very severely. In spite of all this, I am convinced the Government did right to get the army back from Afghanistan. If the troops had refrained on the road between Peshawur and Gandamack all the hot weather, they would have lost far more than they did in marching down, and they would still have had the march to do in the autumn, which is the most unhealthy part of the year.

It is not true, then, that the officers who marched the men back have acted with rashness and imprudence. On the contrary, they acted with the greatest caution in getting the troops into a position in which they might suffer less. I come now to another point. Your Lordships will have observed in the history of this campaign that until the period at which the troops were marched back very little disease has been mentioned. I am, therefore, fully justified in calling attention to the services of the Medical Staff, and to the great skill and judgment which, looking to the healthy condition of the men, they must have exercised. Then, as to the Transport and Commissariat, no one can suppose that any great expedition, such as this, conducted on three lines, could be effected in a smooth and easy way. Much has been said of the difficulties with which the Transport and Commissariat Departments had to contend. Those difficulties were of a very serious kind; and the more praise, therefore, should be given to those who overcame them, though, no doubt, with considerable loss of camels and beasts of burden, and some delay in consequence. There is no period at which a march of some 500 miles from the Indus towards the North-West would not be considered an operation of a gigantic character in connection with the difficulties of route and of transport and commissariat; and great credit is due to these branches of the Service by which these difficulties were overcome, so that the men kept their health and received their rations without fail throughout the whole of that long march. And here, again, I must bring in one name which has not been mentioned in the active operations of the war. I allude to the aid rendered to the Transport Service by Sir Richard Temple. When Sir Richard Temple found that there were these difficulties he went up himself, and by his personal exertions got together 20,000 camels, and assisted in the most material way to overcome those obstacles which threatened to impede the march of the columns. I am bound, therefore, not to forget the name of Sir Richard Temple, though he is not among those whose names will be found in the Resolution.

And now, my Lords, for the campaign itself. There may be those who would have been more interested had this war been one of great battles and even of great disasters; but I have no such circumstances to mention to your Lordships. I may say that every operation has been conducted with success, and with less bloodshed than has ever accompanied a war of equal proportion. I rejoice to think that it has been so. Comparatively, it has been a bloodless campaign; and had it not been for the melancholy disaster which befel the 10th Hussars, upon which we cannot help looking with great regret, and thinking that blame must attach somewhere, we should have had to lament no great loss. That disaster— the facts concerning which do not appear to have clearly come to light— resulted in a loss of one officer and 46 men to that splendid regiment. That was a severe blow, and the regiment has also since that period sustained losses by cholera. Such things, my Lords, I am afraid will happen in all wars. That, however, has been the only serious disaster in this war, and otherwise the loss of life has been small compared with the great results which have been attained.

Your Lordships will remember that the time allowed by the Ultimatum expired on the 20th of November last; and upon the 21st of November, such was the diligence and care which had been displayed in the preparations, though no steps had been taken before to move the troops, and no threats had been used to the Ameer until the Ultimatum was sent, the troops immediately crossed the Frontier. I think, my Lords, you will agree with me that that reflects the highest credit on the Governor General, the Commander-in-Chief, the Generals, as well as upon the Adjutant and Quartermaster General, that 40,000 men were put on the march, that the Frontier was crossed at all points, on the 21st of the month, the day when the march began. If your Lordships will take into consideration the amount of work and labour necessary to bring about so great a result without disturbance to the Military Forces of India except at one or two points, you will see that it reflects the greatest credit on all concerned. The Frontier was crossed in three columns. General Sir Samuel Browne, a name well known in Indian affairs, crossed it on the morning of the 21st. In the course of that afternoon, he attacked Ali Musjid, his Forces turned the fortress, and in the course of the night the garrison fled up the Khyber Pass, leaving the guns behind, and were intercepted partly by the Khyberees and partly by our own troops, who, by a difficult march, cut off their retreat. Practically, on the very day and the night which succeeded the passage, Sir Samuel Browne was in possession of the fortress. This success, achieved at the very outset of the campaign, had the effect of breaking up and demoralizing the Forces of the Ameer on that side of Afghanistan, and, so far as those Forces were concerned, there was no longer any opposition in that quarter. Shere Ali had gone on a different system from his predecessor. Dost Mahomed relied on the Tribal Forces; but Shere Ali raised a body of 60,000 to 70,000 troops, which he armed and trained in the European fashion. This was a course which alienated the Tribes, and broke the bond between him and them, and when the regular regiments were broken up there was no longer opposition. In a few days, therefore, Sir Samuel Browne entered into Dakka, the great military camp of the Ameer, and subsequently ascertaining that Jellalabad was undefended, and that no resistance would be offered to its occupation, advanced to that place. In consequence of these successful operations, his further advance on Gandamak was made chiefly for sanitary reasons, and that he might secure a healthy situation for his troops; but it had a very important political effect in expediting negotiations, because that movement produced the impression of a probable advance of our Army on Cabul. Negotiations were accordingly entered into with Yakoob Khan, who sent in his submission on the 8th of May. I must not allow your Lordships to suppose that Sir Samuel Browne's column had no fighting at all other than that that had taken place at Ali Musjid. On the contrary, there was a good deal of fighting with the predatory Tribes, who made attacks on our communications. Some of those Tribes thought they were beyond the reach of European troops; but General Maude soon proved to them that this was by no means the case.

I must now take your Lordships to the other two lines. Coming to the Candahar Column, General Biddulph was continually pressing on from the period I have mentioned in December, and I think that he reached his destination at the mouth of the Khojak Pass on the 9th of December. There he was joined by General Stewart, and the columns then marched together on Candahar. This march was through a comparatively friendly country, though the difficulties of the ground and of the Khojak Pass were very great. The columns reached Candahar on the 9th of January, where they were received with great courtesy by the Deputy Governor and the principal inhabitants of the place. There have been, it is true, some isolated acts of fanaticism perpetrated by individuals. These columns still remain in possession of Candahar, until the time shall arrive for its being handed over, as agreed upon, to the Ameer. It was found necessary to feel in different directions for the enemy, and, accordingly, General Biddulph went 75 miles further to Girischk, while General Stewart made his way to Khilabi Ghilzie. With the exception of an attack made on General Biddulph as he retired towards Candahar, there was no great occasion for fighting; but that attack afforded an opportunity of showing that our Cavalry, under that gallant and able officer, Colonel Malcolmson, were far superior to the Afghan Cavalry, who were put to flight. And here I may remark that on his way back to India General Biddulph rendered a great service in exploring and making known to us a tract of country and a route available for troops and artillery with which previously we were unacquainted.

General Roberts, with some 5,500 men, crossed the Kurrum River. He found that the Army of the Ameer had retired 40 miles on that side, and that the Ameer was preparing to make his great defence on the Peiwar Kotal. There were rocks of great steepness, the position was in front impregnable, and the place was defended by some 4,000 men. General Roberts took three days to make reconnoissances, and on the 1st of December, by a circuitous and most difficult march, he turned the position, and with a force of Highlanders, Goorkhas, and Sikhs, and at the height of 8,000 feet, attacked it in the rear and captured it. General Roberts commenced his attack early in the morning, was admirably supported by Kelso with his guns, and it was not till dusk that the enemy gave way, and, upon his executing another flank movement which would have intercepted their retreat, fled in the direction of the Shutur-Gardan Pass, followed closely up by General Roberts. From that height he looked down upon the plains of Cabul, but withdrew, and contented himself with watching the Pass until it was effectually closed by the snows, and has since been in quiet possession of the Kurrum Valley to Ali Keyl.

I must here mention one officer—Wigram Battye, of the Guides—who greatly distinguished himself, and whose death India and England must deplore. In truth, however, India is rich in officers of that description, and others have been found in his family—men of great military capacity, who are always ready to sacrifice their lives gallantly in the service of their country.

My Lords, I have not attempted, in making these remarks, to show that this was a great campaign in the way of battles; nor have we, I am glad to say, to bewail any grave disaster. These men have served their country with courage and devotion, their leaders have received honours from Her Majesty, and it now remains for the Houses of Parliament to do honour not only to the officers in command, but also to every soldier who has fought under the flag, and they are embodied in the Resolution I am about to move. I am sure there is not one of your Lordships who does not recognize in this campaign the bravery of the soldiers who have been employed in it. I ask you to give due honour to their patience under hardship, to the gallantry which they have displayed in every encounter, and to that great combination of military qualities which has enabled them, in an incredibly short time, to achieve a great success—bloodless in its character, but one which, I hope, will secure the permanent peace of India. In thanking all those who have been engaged in this campaign, you will encourage others to take a like course to that which has been followed by those who have won such honours for the name of England. The noble Viscount concluded by moving the Resolution.

Moved to resolve,
1. That the Thanks of this House be given to the Right Honourable Lord Lytton, Viceroy and Governor-General of India, for the ability and judgment with which the resources of the British Empire in India have been applied to the support of the Military operations in Afghanistan:

2. That the Thanks of this House be given to
    General Sir Frederic P. Haines, G.C.B., G.C.S.I.;
    Lieutenant-General Sir Donald Martin Stewart, K.C.B.;
    Lieutenant-General Sir Samuel James Browne, K.C.B., K.C.S.I.,
    V.C.;
    Lieutenant-General Sir Frederick Francis Maude, K.C.B., V.C.;
    Major-General Sir Michael Anthony Shrapnell Biddulph, R.A.,
    K.C.B.;
    Major-General Sir Frederick Sleigh Roberts, R.A., K.C.B., V.C.;
    and the other Officers of the Army, both European and Native, for the
    intrepidity, skill, and perseverance displayed by them in the Military
    operations in Afghanistan, and for their indefatigable zeal and
    exertions throughout the late Campaign:
3. That this House doth highly approve and acknowledge the valour and
    perseverance displayed by the Non-Commissioned Officers and Pri-
    vate Soldiers, both European and Native, employed in Afghanistan,
    and that the same be signified to them by the Commanders of the
    several Corps, who are desired to thank them for their gallant
    behaviour:
4. That the said Resolutions be transmitted by the Lord Chancellor to the
    Viceroy and Governor-General of India, and that his Lordship be
    requested to communicate the same to the several Officers referred
    to therein.

EARL GRANVILLE: My Lords, I rise with great pleasure to express my warm concurrence in the Vote of Thanks to the Army which has been proposed by the noble Viscount. In proposing this Motion, the noble Viscount has properly adhered, on several points, to the precedents which bear most closely upon the present case. The Resolutions, *mutatis mutandis,* are the same as those proposed at the close of the last Afghan War, and nearly the same as those proposed at the final suppression of the Indian Mutiny. He has also adhered to those precedents in abstaining from making any observations on the policy or results of the war. But there is a point, and an important one, on which he seems to have entirely departed from previous precedents. Charges have been constantly brought against Her Majesty's Government of the extraordinary economy with which they furnish information to a Parliament which is always ready, by a large majority, to register facts accomplished without their knowledge. Her Majesty's Government always repudiate and deny this accusation—it is unlucky that, on this occasion, their proceedings tend to support this accusation. On looking back to the case of the close of the last Afghan War, I find that the Duke of Wellington and Sir Robert Peel gave a fortnight's Notice of the Vote of Thanks—explaining that they postponed it for so long in order to comply with former precedents; that Papers containing full information with regard to the military operations should be in the hands of Peers and Members for a considerable time before they were asked to vote Thanks. I find that four more days were given to both Houses, in order to give more time for consideration of these Papers. We are now asked to vote, without, as far as I am aware, a single scrap of Paper having been laid before Parliament on the subject. The technical objection to this proceeding seems so strong that I hardly know how Her Majesty's Government could, with propriety, resist if we were to press strongly for a delay until the Papers were laid before us. On the 10th of March

I asked when a statement would be made, and when Papers would be presented regarding this war? The noble Viscount replied that it would not be convenient at that moment to do so; but he promised that, on the earliest opportunity, he would do both. Five months have now elapsed, peace has been made, a Treaty signed, and we have had no statement and no Papers bearing on this particular question. The noble Viscount has given us a clear and interesting account of the military operations; but he has not supported that account by a single despatch. We have been up to this time left to gather our information as we best can. I am, however, bound to say that I cordially accept what the noble Viscount has told us about the services of the Army. All the accounts which we have received concur as to the judgment, energy, and ability of our officers, and the discipline, courage, and endurance of their men. They have fully and nobly fulfilled the prognostications made with regard to them, and their only regret was that of a soldier—but is one in which we cannot agree—that the foe did not prove to be more worthy of their steel. Have we, however, the same assurance as to the Governor General, whose name—I admit, according to precedent—has been introduced? On the occasion of the Thanks to Lord Canning, Lord Derby in this House, the noble Earl opposite (the Earl of Beaconsfield) in the House of Commons, while they stated that they reserved their final opinion, made strong attacks upon Lord Canning. The noble Earl opposite spoke of Lord Canning's inconsistency, and of his incoherence—of his want of vigilance and energy; and he blamed him, curiously enough, for having during the Mutiny gagged the Indian Press. I imagine, at this time, the noble Earl would not be the last to acknowledge that never was a man suddenly placed in a more responsible position than Lord Canning, and that in that position he showed the wisdom of a great statesman, the energy of a great administrator, and the justice and calm courage of an English Christian. The moral I draw from this is, that in Opposition we may be too prone to blame, and I do not wish to form any rash judgment as to the manner in which Lord Lytton has shown ability and judgment in applying the resources of India to this war. But we are asked to affirm a certain proposition, without any Papers, and with nothing but a statement of a most general character from the Secretary of State for India. And as to other sources of information nothing can be more absolutely contradictory. On the one hand, correspondents—evidently in possession of information, sometimes of a semi-official character—have been loud in their praise of the ability, decision, and energy of Lord Lytton. On the other, exactly opposite language has been held; and not only censure applied, but particular facts alleged. Thus, it has been stated that Lord Lytton, without authority from Her Majesty's Government, gave positive orders for an attack upon the Khyber Pass without an adequate Force, which must have ended in a great disaster, and which was only stopped by the obstinate determination of the Commander-in-Chief, Sir Frederick Haines; and that since that time the relations between the Governor General and the Commander-in-Chief have not been of a cordial character. It will be satisfactory if Her Majesty's Government can deny these allegations. It would be still more satisfactory if they could, like

Lord Palmerston, refer to a letter from the Commander-in-Chief referring in enthusiastic terms to the great services rendered by the Governor General to the military authorities. It has been stated in the same way that the march of General Stewart on Candahar, as it turned out, was successful; but it was due to an accident on which the Governor General had no right to rely; that snow generally falls in Bolan and round Quetta in November—it did not fall on this occasion till the end of February; that, if the season had been an ordinary one, at the time we had 12 regiments and batteries struggling through the Bolan Pass, that Pass would have been swept by hurricanes of wind and snow, rendering all progress impossible. As there is neither food nor forage in the Pass, any compulsory halt would have caused the death of both horses and baggage animals, besides great mortality among the men. It is said that General Stewart was opposed to an advance into Afghanistan until seven months' supplies had been collected for his column at Quetta; but that he was ordered on; and in order to do so he had to take on 20,000 camels which the Commissariat had collected there for the conveying of supplies at Quetta; that not one of these camels ever got back to Sukkur, and that the consequence was that when Biddulph and Stewart's united columns got to Candahar the transport train which was to have supplied them with food from their base on the Indus was no longer in existence, and to preserve them from starvation 8,000 men were immediately withdrawn to India; that about 4,000 men remained in Candahar; but carriage was so deficient that even this small Force could not have moved collectively for 50 miles in any direction—that it was in fact isolated, and, if the resistance of the Afghans had not collapsed, would have been in great danger. Whether these allegations affecting the question of the judgment of the Governor General which we are called upon to praise are true or not I have no means of knowing. The facts must be known to the Government, and it will be satisfactory if they give some explanations. In our state of doubt, it would be better not to be called upon to give a vote. My only excuses for agreeing to do so are these—that the noble Earl himself gave me an example, when he withdrew his Motion of the Previous Question in the case of Lord Canning, on the ground that the Government had avoided calling upon the House for any expression of opinion on the policy of the war. A still better excuse is my strong desire that nothing should occur which can diminish the appearance of cordial and complete unanimity with which a brave and successful Army receives the great compliment of the Thanks of this House. The late Lord Lawrence and my noble Friend the late Governor General (the Earl of Northbrook), although strongly opposed to the war, always maintained that the invasion of Afghanistan by our Army would be almost certain of success. The Army has nobly fulfilled these prognostications, and is entitled to the best Thanks of this House.

THE DUKE OF CAMBRIDGE: My Lords, I desire to say a few words on this Motion, which I most cordially support—entirely, of course, upon military grounds. As Head of the Army, it is my duty to be fully cognizant of all circumstances connected with the operations of war in any part of Her Majesty's Dominions; and it has, therefore, fallen to my lot to follow with great care the advance of the separate columns forming the Army which executed the recent campaign in Afghanistan. The noble Viscount the Secretary of State for India has so well given the details connected with those three columns that it is unnecessary for me to go over them again. But I entirely endorse every word he has said on military grounds as to the ability with which those columns were conducted, and as to the energy displayed both by those in command and by the troops under their orders. There can be no doubt that the great difficulty of this campaign has been that of transport. I will only say that this campaign has not been singular in that respect. The real difficulty of all our campaigns, particularly in recent years, has been that of transport. People are disposed to think that transport can be easily found when great operations are to be undertaken; but it is the very thing which you cannot find under such circumstances. My noble Friend who has been in India (Lord Napier of Magdala) and also my noble and gallant Friend on the Cross Benches (Lord Strathnairn) must be aware of the immense difficulty of finding transport and of the enormous amount that is required there. I think it ought to be clearly understood that it is impossible to improvise the transport which is necessary, and that if we are to have it available when it is indispensable, we must keep up permanently a very considerable nucleus of transport, whether in India or elsewhere. As regards the conduct of these operations, whether by General Stewart and General Biddulph, who acted in concert, or by General Roberts, General Browne, or General Maude, I cannot think that there is anything to choose between these various officers. They have all had very grave and difficult duties to perform, and they have performed them in a manner not only thoroughly worthy of the high reputation they had already won before this war commenced, but also so as to add largely to that reputation. The late campaign in Afghanistan has been short, and comparatively bloodless; but it has been attended with great difficulties. One of those difficulties has been connected with the keeping open our communications. Communication through the Khyber Pass, especially, has been a very great difficulty. Sir Samuel Browne was in command of the troops at Ali Musjid, and then went to the front; and another division followed under General Maude, who, in conjunction with some of Sir Samuel Browne's troops, kept up the communications—a task requiring great tact and judgment. There was one misfortune, which we must all deplore— namely, that which befell the 10th Hussars; but I believe it was simply one of those accidents which must sometimes occur in war. I do not believe there was anyone to blame in the matter. It is always a difficult matter for mounted troops to cross a difficult ford in the night; and, at the same time, it is often essential that it should be done at night, because if not conducted at night the object of the operation would be frustrated. The risk, therefore, had to be run, and, unfortunately, a good many men and one officer were drowned; but after reading the evidence given at the inquiry I really believe that no special blame can be attached to anyone. Besides, it is not certain that there was not a freshet of water that would carry the horses off their legs, and which would subside as suddenly as it had arisen. I do not know that I need say more, except that, while I feel satisfied from all I hear that the European troops of Her Majesty's Army have behaved in a manner highly to their credit, and in a way deserving of your Lordships' commendation, they were cordially and fully supported by the Native troops. This is the largest campaign we have had in India for some time, and we have had no recent opportunity of seeing of what kind of troops our Native Army was composed. I think the result is highly satisfactory, and shows the Native Army to be in a very serviceable condition both for the field as well as for garrison work. The officers have always been conspicuous for their gallant conduct, and the recent war has shown that they are now as brave and efficient as they ever have been. Another point is the question of the Cavalry. We have heard it said that the days of Cavalry are gone by, and that they are an expensive arm of the Service, and that they can now be dispensed with, and that such a step would greatly tend to economize the expenditure for the Army. My Lords, I believe that no greater mistake was ever made. I believe that Cavalry is as essential as ever, or even more so, because movements in the field are now much more rapid than they used to be; so that unless you have a good body of Cavalry, to be the eyes and ears of your Army, you would be in a most dangerous position. The Cavalry in India, whether Native or European, have displayed the utmost gallantry. They have performed acts of great valour now, as on all former occasions; they have showed themselves in every respect good soldiers, and highly qualified for the duties which they are called upon to perform. The highest tribute is also due to the Commander-in-Chief in India and to the Quartermaster General. They have acted in the most cordial manner with the various authorities in regard to the different operations of the war. I must also say one word in regard to Sir Neville Chamberlain, who was acting Military Member of the Council during a part of the war, and whose experience and assistance were most beneficial to the Governor General during the period that he acted. He took the place of another gallant and distinguished Officer—Sir Allen Johnson—who was absent from ill-health, but who was able to return to his duties before the war was over. I think it right just to state their names. My Lords, I cordially and entirely support the Vote of Thanks which has been proposed.

THE EARL OF NORTHBROOK, as he had the honour of being personally acquainted with nearly all the officers who had filled high commands in the war, and as he had upon a former occasion expressed his confidence, both in the Army and in the measures taken to make the campaign successful, wished only to say that he most heartily and cordially joined in the Vote of Thanks. The remarks of the noble Viscount the Secretary of State for India, and of the illustrious Duke, rendered it wholly unnecessary for him (the Earl of Northbrook) to enter into any details. He felt sure that the Native Army would be gratified, not only with the honour conferred on them by the Thanks of the House, but also by the expression of opinion of the illustrious Duke. If there had been no very great military operations, yet there had been long marches, considerable privations, and exposure to heat and cold to be endured such as were calculated to try the discipline of any troops. It was most satisfactory to all who had been connected with the administration of the Army in India that nothing whatever had been said against the discipline or behaviour of the troops employed.

LORD NAPIER OF MAGDALA, who was indistinctly heard, said, he could scarcely venture to make any observations after the addresses made to their Lordships by the noble Viscount and by His Royal Highness; but he rose to address to their Lordships a few words which he thought were due in justice to Lord Lytton. First, he considered that Lord Lytton deserved the greatest credit for his just appreciation of the powers of resistance of Shere Ali and his Army. Secondly, he thought he deserved the highest credit for his treatment of the Native Princes, and his just estimate of their loyalty and that of the people of India, which enabled him to conduct the war to a successful conclusion with a very slight addition to the British troops in India. There were a few remarks which were also due to the Generals commanding and their troops. He thought it had been little appreciated that war in these mountains was a warfare against the forces of Nature; and the success of our troops, with little loss, had, perhaps, led people unacquainted with the character of the mountains in which the several operations had been conducted to make light of the difficulties they had had to encounter. Those mountains abounded at every step with natural fortifications—natural citadels of the most difficult and inaccessible character. Every hill and ravine and every defile was thoroughly well known to their Native occupants, while our policy had made them a sealed book to our officers. Of course, reconnoissances were most difficult where each ravine might contain an enemy who never left a prisoner alive. Too much credit could not be given to the Generals and their troops for the skill and bravery with which they overcame those difficulties. He had known and watched the rise of nearly all the principal officers engaged. They had most fully justified the expectations that he had formed of them, and he had noticed their progress with the greatest joy. The conduct of the British troops was, as it ever had been, most brilliant, and deserved every credit. With regard to the Native troops, the House was aware that there had been much discussion regarding them. No one could give too high praise to the British Army; but there were facts connected with the Native Army which he thought would cause all to admit that the policy of placing Natives in the position of officers, and not treating them merely as nonentities, as they were before that policy was adopted, had proved a just and wise policy. Therefore, he desired to bring to their notice the conduct of the Native officers of the Indian Army. Yussen Khan, an Afridi Jemadar of the 24th Punjab Native Infantry, had conducted negotiations with the Afridis of the Bazaar Valley, during Generals Tyler's and Maude's expeditions, and was mainly instrumental in procuring satisfactory terms of peace. This man was a young Afridi Mullick, brought into a direct commission in 1873. Subadar-Major Azeez Khan, of the 5th Punjab Infantry, died of wounds received at the Peiwar

Pass. His commanding officer reported of him as his right-hand man, and that he could better have spared any other officer, British or Native. Reisaldar Mahomed Kahn, corps of Guides, would not desert the body of his commanding officer, Wygram Battye, in the action with the Khugiani, but remained and fell with him. Subadar Faiz Tallab, a Khuttuck of the 1st Punjab Infantry, was on detached command with 30 men in the Atchakzai country, in the vicinity of the Khojak Pass, and was warned that he would be attacked by a large body of the enemy. There was no time for him to send in for reinforcements, so he struck his tents, threw up a sunga, and awaited the attack, which was carried on by about 400 Atchakzais, whom Faiz Tallab's party drove off with very heavy loss. This man was admitted to the Order of Merit for his conspicuous gallantry and ready resource on this occasion. Lastly, his dear friend and comrade, Gholam Hussein Khan, after fighting our battles for 30 years, and rendering us great diplomatic services, was now the Governor of Candahar, where, by his wisdom and justice, he had become most popular with the Afghans, and had won the respect and regard of everyone in our own Army. With such examples as these, he thought there could never again be a question of not placing the Native officers in positions of command.

Viscount Cranbrook: I am extremely gratified that my noble and gallant Friend has spoken, as he informed me that he would do, in the terms which he has done of the Native Army. I feel, myself, that I made an omission in not more specially referring to the services of that Army, and, perhaps, your Lordships will now forgive my adding this one word on the subject. Besides our own Native troops there was a contingent of 4,000 furnished by some of the Native Princes, and one of those Princes has been awarded the Grand Cross of the Star of India. With regard to the absence of despatches, I felt the difficulty to which the noble Earl (Earl Granville) referred. The despatches narrating all that has happened have not yet come home. I expected that they would have been here by this time, and I understand that they are coming. The precedents of the Duke of Wellington and Sir Robert Peel scarcely apply to this case. We knew, day by day, through the public journals from their Correspondents on the spot, every incident that has taken place, and I have furnished every telegram which gave any information with regard to operations in the field. Such was not the case in the time to which the noble Earl referred. I think that it may be said that, generally, your Lordships are in full possession of the facts of the war. With regard to Lord Lytton, this is the first time that I have heard he gave any directions with regard to the force to be used against Ali Musjid. Sir Samuel Browne crossed the Frontier, and the same day he attacked Ali Musjid; and it was abandoned in the night, and occupied next day. I do not see how there could have been such orders. In regard to the commissariat of the Candahar column, Lord Lytton gave all the orders that were necessary. The difficulties were immense; there was great difficulty in obtaining beasts of burthen, and a long line had to be maintained; and it would be rather a strong measure to hold Lord Lytton, who was at Calcutta or Simla, responsible for the conduct of the details of the commissariat on that line. General Biddulph has informed me that the difficulties with regard to the commissariat of this column have been greatly exaggerated.

Motion *agreed to, nemine dissentiente.*

> Ordered, That the Lord Chancellor do communicate the said Resolutions to the Viceroy and Governor-General of India, and that his Lordship be requested to communicate the same to the several Officers referred to therein.

Letter from General Sir Frederick Roberts Defending His Conduct during the Battle of Char-Asiab and at Kabul during the Second Afghan War, 13 February 1880*
[This letter was read by Viscount Cranbrook in the House of Lords.]

I am extremely grateful to you for so kindly writing to me with regard to attacks being made on me in certain quarters respecting ill-treatment of prisoners and wounded at the battle of Char-Asiab, and also for forwarding to me a copy of the article in *The Fortnightly Review* for December, headed "Martial Law in Cabul." I think that a short explanation of what has really occurred since we entered Afganistan last September will enable you to satisfy all those who may refer to the subject in Parliament that wounded Afghans have not been ill-treated, and that there is no foundation for the remarks made by Mr. Harrison in *The Fortnightly Review*. With regard to the burning of Afghan bodies at the battle of Char-Asiab, I would beg to say that I first heard of the circumstances from the newspapers, and that I at once directed a Court of Inquiry to investigate the matter, the proceedings of which have some time since been forwarded for the information of the Commander-in-Chief and Government of India. It would appear that the act was committed in the rear of the troops engaged by two or three Goorkhas who were by themselves, and by the evidence given life must have been as good as extinct at the time the clothes were set on fire. I need not assure you that no blame for the act in question can be attached to any officer of the force under my command, and that with this exception every consideration has been shown to the wounded and the dead, inasmuch as they have been treated as if they were our own soldiers, and after Char-Asiab some of the wounded Afghans were taken into hospital and placed alongside of our own wounded men. This fact, I think, speaks for itself as regards the general

*Hansard, 3.s., CCL, 580–82.

treatment of the Afghans who fought against us. With reference to martial law having been proclaimed within a radius of 10 miles round Cabul, I can safely affirm that for many reasons it was absolutely necessary to do so, the chief one being to prevent the inhabitants carrying firearms and other weapons which might render it possible for them to make sudden attacks on soldiers and other individuals belonging to this force. Had this precaution not been taken, I venture to say that, living as we are among a nation of fanatics, murders would have been of frequent occurrence. I am not at all in favour of martial law, and shall be glad to see it discontinued, as soon as some other form of government can be decided upon. As to the Proclamation published relative to the treatment of soldiers and others concerned in the attack on the Embassy and of those who had apparently shown themselves to be rebels against the Ameer by fighting against us, I would mention that at the time the Proclamation was issued Yakoob Khan was outwardly our friend, and repeatedly spoke to me of the people who fought against us at Char-Asiab as rebels to his rule; and on that account they were referred to in the terms of the Proclamation. As to men being hanged for the simple fact of their having fought against us, such was not the case. Rewards were certainly offered for their capture; but this was done with a view of arresting those who, directly or indirectly, has taken part in the massacre of the several members of the British Embassy. All convicted of such a crime would, I believe, have been sentenced to death in any country, whether civil or martial law had been in force. The Kotwal (chief magistrate of the city) was found guilty of having excited the troops to the massacre, of having taken an active part in dishonouring the dead bodies, and of having subsequently instigated the troops and people of Cabul to resist our advance. On these accounts he was hanged. As to prisoners taken in fight being shot, such is totally devoid of truth, further than in one or two instances summary punishment has been inflicted on individuals who have been found mutilating our wounded soldiers; indeed, all the wounded that have fallen into the enemy's hands at different times have been treated in the most cruel manner and horribly mutilated. With regard to the men who were not implicated in the attack on the Embassy, some short time after Yakoob Khan had been made a prisoner an amnesty was proclaimed, and the people of every district visited by our troops have invariably been informed that those soldiers have nothing to fear from us; but, on the other hand, if they came in and gave up their rifles or guns they would receive the amount authorized for the same. This was fully understood, and a considerable number of arms have from time to time been brought in. Recently, quite irrespective of any action taken by us, the Mollahs have been preaching a 'jehad,' or religious war, and have by these means got together by coertion, practical as well as religious, a gigantic collection of people. On reaching Cabul this mass was joined by all the riff-raff of the city and neighbouring villages; but the Kazilbashis, merchants, and respectable inhabitants, so far from throwing in their lot with our opponents, held aloof, and from time to time gave us valuable information. The greater portion also of the Sidars of Cabul remained during the disturbances in our camp. As soon as I was aware that the enemy had been completely dispersed I published a general amnesty, feeling that the people generally were not be blame for what had occurred, and the quickest way of restoring order was to invite the people to Cabul and to let them see that they could trust implicitly to our forbearance and generosity. At the same time the Civil Dispensary was re-established, and notice was sent through the city and to all the neighbouring villages inviting the wounded to hospital and assuring them that they had nothing to fear. Many wounded have been brought in and are being taken every care of. Afghans are naturally very suspicious and require time to be re-assured; but so many Maliks and other headmen had responded to the Amnesty Proclamation that yesterday I was enabled to hold a Durbar at which nearly 200 of the principal men who had fought against us were present. Others will doubtless follow their example, and I hope in time the country will quiet down. Referring to the administration of affairs in the city and surroundings of Cabul, I can conscientiously say that our rule from the first has been extraordinarily mild and lenient. No harsh measure of any kind have been adopted. On the contrary, I have since had reason to regret that, from a desire not to do anything that could possibly set the people against us, I abstained, on our first occupation of Sherpur, from levelling the forts and enclosures by which it is surrounded on all sides, and which during the late siege, by affording shelter to the enemy, were the causes of much annoyance and some loss to us. Two proofs which to my mind are fairly conclusive as to the feelings of security and trust which the people of Cabul city and adjoining villages reposed in us are the rapid manner in which the city filled immediately the enemy dispersed, and the fact that since our arrival there had not been a single complaint against a European soldier, and only a few of a trivial nature against one or two men belonging to the Native regiments. The strictest discipline has been maintained, and there has not been an instance of violence against the people, notwithstanding that our soldiers have witnessed the cruel treatment of their comrades on every occasion of their falling into the enemy's hands. There is one point mentioned by Mr. Harrison in *The Fortnightly Review*—namely, that civilian special correspondents have been prevented from accompanying the force under my command—

in answer to which I would like to say a few words. I certainly never received any orders prohibiting civilian correspondents accompanying the force, and from the first one has been in my camp. He had considerable difficulty in reaching Ali-khel before the force marched, as our movements were very rapid after the order for an advance on Cabul was received. This may have prevented other correspondents joining me at the time. Had any come they would have received every assistance. Some correspondents have arrived since we reached this. No restrictions whatever are placed on them, and they are allowed to send any telegrams they please, even when the information contained in them is incorrect, always excepting such information as by nature of its inaccuracy is calculated to produce an evil effect.

out treats as unlawful. But after these nine inquiries, throughout which the conduct of certain individuals is assumed to be illegal, there is a tenth inquiry which comes to this—whether Her Majesty's Government, after inquiry, are of opinion that such conduct and proceedings were illegal? Now, I think that we are all agreed that the Law Advisers of the Crown, from whatever party the Government of this country may be formed, generally speaking, are men most eminent in their profession, and if the hon. Gentleman is of opinion that it is possible that the Law Advisers of the Crown may be of opinion that these acts are not illegal, I think the hon. Gentleman is hardly justified in assuming throughout his inquiries that they are illegal, and he might have made these inquiries without proceeding on that assumption. But it is not merely that the questions are put in a form which, if not noticed, might, perhaps, lead to great inconvenience, that I think the course pursued by the hon. Gentleman objectionable, but so far as I can judge, though brought forward with great apparent precision, they do not appear in their allegations to be as accurate as could be desired. In the first place, throughout these questions the hon. Gentleman seems entirely oblivious of the fact that the proceedings complained of took place during the existence of martial law. That is the first feature which strikes one amid these numerous interrogatories, and there seems throughout a very great confusion in the mind of the hon. Gentleman on the nature of martial law, because we have this remarkable expression—certain persons being spoken of as if their cases were decided without trial or alleged trial by court martial; we have such expressions as "on charges not cognizable by a military court." Then there is another charge that the case was decided "without observance of the rules prescribed by the Articles of War." Then, in a third case, we are told that persons have been "tried in time of peace by military courts irregularly composed," and other allegations of the same kind have been made. But in a state of martial law there can be no irregularity in the constitution of the courts. Martial law supersedes ordinary law, and the hon. Gentleman seems throughout these questions to assume that in a state of martial law courts martial are to be held according to the terms and conditions under which they would be held when the Mutiny Act was in existence. But in a state of martial law the Mutiny Act, like other Acts, would be suspended, so that here, throughout, there is a source of extreme irregularity and inaccuracy in these questions. There are also, so far as I am acquainted with the subject—of course, I am not versed in the complications of it like the hon. Gentleman—inquiries which ought not to have been made in such cases, and which are founded on the assumption of absolutely illegal conduct. In the case of Ensign Cullen and Dr. Morris, for instance, the hon. Gentleman asks "whether any steps have been or will be taken to bring to trial Ensign Cullen and Dr. Morris for putting three men to death without trial; and Dr. Morris for shooting one William Gray?" Now, in the evidence taken before the Commissioners it is particularly stated that this was a charge not proved, and that the evidence for and against was equally conflicting; the Commissioners themselves recommend further inquiry, and I believe that that further inquiry is now taking place. Assuredly, under these circumstances, the hon. Gentleman is not justified in asking whether the Government are going to interfere and to try persons for putting to death men without trial when we have authentic records on the table of the House which seem to point to a different conclusion. Now, there is a very strong charge here with regard to Colonel Nelson, at the time Brigadier General in Jamaica. We are asked "whether any steps have been taken or will be taken to bring to trial Colonel Nelson for, among other things, unlawfully putting to death certain men and women, one of whom was in a state of pregnancy, who had been previously flogged." Now it is patent that in the evidence taken before the Commissioners it has been shown that no one was flogged without trial by Colonel Nelson, and no woman known to be in a state of pregnancy was tried; and therefore I think the hon. Gentleman was not justified in so decidedly pronouncing that a person serving Her Majesty was guilty of crimes which have not been proved. I feel it my duty, as these are questions of a remarkable character, to make these explanations. In the first place, I cannot countenance the hon. Gentleman assuming throughout that these proceedings were illegal. That is at least a question of controversy, upon which there may be a difference of opinion. But throughout these questions the hon. Gentleman takes for granted that these have been illegal acts, and that these proceedings have taken place without authority. Secondly, I think the hon. Gentleman ought to have taken care, in putting these questions, that they should be simply and severely accurate in their allegations. Having made these observations, which I think I am justified in doing, although I do not myself approve long questions being addressed to Ministers, or long answers being given by Ministers—for, generally speaking, when they are requisite, it is more convenient to have a debate upon the matter—yet I hope the House will not think it intrusive on my part if I tell them now what really has been done in these affairs. When these unhappy events took place in Jamaica the late Government thought it their duty to advise Her Majesty to appoint a Commission to proceed to the island, and there, with all the advantage of local inquiry and observation, to investigate what had occurred. I think the late Government took a prudent and proper course. That Commission was formed of eminent men, who possessed the public confidence; and whatever controversy there may be on other parts of this question, I think it will be generally admitted that by their acuteness and assiduity these eminent persons have quite justified the confidence placed in them by the Sovereign and the country. Well, Sir, the late Government, acting upon the Report of their own Commission, considered the case of the Governor, and dismissed him from his post. That appears to me to be conclusive as regards the case of Governor Eyre. He was dismissed. Those who ask that further steps should be taken seem to me to confuse errors of conduct and errors of judgment with *malice prepense*. But I wholly mistake the House of Commons if they would ever sanction such an opinion. Now, with regard to the subordinate officers, either naval or military, the late Government, after deliberating upon the Report of their own Commissioners, gave instructions to the Admiralty and the Horse Guards to investigate and report upon the conduct of the officers connected respectively with those Departments. The Admiralty, after investigating the subject, decided that no fresh inquiry was requisite, and they approved the conduct of the Admiral on the station. The Horse Guards, as I am informed, have not made up their minds upon the instructions with which they were furnished, and no one grudges them sufficient time to arrive at a decision of so momentous a character. Under these circumstances, I am at a loss to understand why the hon. Gentleman is thus pressing us for information, and why he is so impatient to ask us what steps are or have been taken. If, upon consideration, Her Majesty's Government should feel it their duty to address fresh instructions to the Horse Guards or the Admiralty, we shall do our duty. But our fresh instructions would be of course founded upon fresh information, and we should only act after having taken the opinion of the Law Officers of the Crown. The present state of affairs is that the late Government considered the conduct of Governor Eyre and dismissed him. They referred it to the Admiralty and the Horse Guards, under the instructions of the Government, to consider the conduct of the officers employed. The Admiralty did not disapprove the conduct of the Admiral, and the Horse Guards have not yet come to any decision. This being the state of the case, I am not prepared to offer any further information to the hon. Gentleman.

Testimony against Governor Eyre, 15 May 1868*

*   *   *

WALTER REA, on his oath, saith: I was in Jamaica in October, 1865, a seaman on board the Wolverine; we went to Morant Bay on the 12th October. The day after that the Governor came to Morant Bay. He came into the tent at night and read martial law to us from a paper. About 100 seamen and marines were in the tent. After reading martial law, the Governor said he hoped we should do our duty. The next morning I went with a party of seamen and marines to Easington, which is twenty-eight miles, I should think, from Morant Bay; there were thirty seamen and twenty marines. Lieutenant Oxley commanded us. We had our rifles and cutlasses and forty rounds of ammunition, and our orders were to shoot at any one we saw running away that we could not capture. These orders were obeyed in three cases on the way to Easington; the first was, we saw a man running behind some bushes on the coast, I should say twelve men fired at him, and wounded him; he ran into the sea, and Lieutenant O'Connor, of the marines, ran to the beach with his revolver and shot him. That man was not armed. I think he offered no resistance, he only tried to escape. The next case was a man playing a flute outside a cottage; he tried to run into the bush, and one man shot at and wounded him, another one

*Report of the Case of the Queen v. Edward John Eyre, 6–12.

afterwards shot him dead, and two of them then threw him up into the bush. This man offered no resistance, only when he saw us he ran away. I didn't hear him call out or say anything. After that the advanced-guard caught a man and passed him aft to the body of seamen; he tried to escape into the sugar-cane, and one marine shot him in the thigh and brought him down, and afterwards a sergeant shot him. He made no resistance and had no arms, he only said when the sergeant pointed at him, "Don't shoot, massa." We had about fifty prisoners in the rear, and some of them said this man had been seen in a market-place with a sugar-cane knife, the length of a cutlass, brandishing it about and trying to get the people to rebel. We got to Easington about four that afternoon; we took about fifty prisoners on the road. We met with no resistance at all on the road. At Easington we found no disturbance at all. We loopholed every window and shutter in the Court-house, and stationed men at each window and door. The police brought in prisoners at Easington and I twice mounted guard. Lieutenant Errington and Mr. Ramsay came there whilst I was at Easington. I was told to full-cock my rifle and fix my cutlass by Lieutenant Errington, and told if one man, who was condemned to die, should move or make the least resistance, I was to shoot him. He was afterwards shot by two men. There were three other men in the same room; one man had forty-eight lashes, and the other two were let off. We flogged a man who worked for Mr. Brown, and gave him three dozen because he would not bring the provisions up. We stayed at Easington four or five days, and brought a good many prisoners back to Morant Bay. They were all put in a tent and a black sentry put over them. After that our party was sent to Stoney Gut, about eleven miles from Morant Bay. I can't remember the day. We were sent off to Stoney Gut immediately. We went into the village; a female fired a pistol off and hit nobody, she was afterwards captured; there was no other resistance, there was nobody there; it was day-break when we got there. We pulled down about twenty houses there that day. The next day a party of the 6th Foot were burning the houses, so we burnt houses. We cut down the bread-fruit and cocoa-nut trees. I think we remained three days at Stoney Gut; when we left all the houses were destroyed. I should say fifty or sixty houses altogether were destroyed. All the fruit-trees were cut down. We lived on the live stock, pigs and other animals, where we could catch them; some ran into the bush. After being three days at Stoney Gut we returned to Morant Bay; we went to Easington again for a day or two, and came back to Morant Bay. I saw twelve (I think) executions the day before we came off to the ship. I saw them hanged; they allowed us a quarter of an hour to see the men hanged. The men stood on a plank, and the piece that went across was a bamboo, and a man stood atop to make the rope fast. I saw Gordon in custody, but did not see him hanged.

Cross-examined: If a person got into the bush, you would never catch them, or in the sugar-cane. Our whole number, when we got to Stoney Gut, was 100 about. We had been increased. There were about 100 black soldiers, a battery of artillery, and the blue jackets and marines at Morant Bay. Stoney Gut would be a formidable position for an enemy to hold. It commanded the road to Kingston, and the bush surrounded it. It was not a plain country through which we marched, there was so much bush and wood. It was very rainy at this time, and the rivers much swollen, and that makes keeping communication open much more difficult. We had one or two of our horses and carts washed away, going to Easington. Stoney Gut is a somewhat inaccessible place to reach; we couldn't get artillery there. I should think we had great difficulty in getting a bag of biscuit there. We had to march there in single file. I don't think when we got there that Paul Bogle had been taken. We found females' dresses, and glass and china, they told us had come from Morant Bay. I should think the dresses were above the condition of the persons who lived at Stoney Gut. There is a place called White Horses, on the road to Easington; there was no marks of a disturbance there that I saw. I don't remember if there's a house there. It's a cliff, with a narrow road, and a deep valley. A sugar-knife is about three feet long, and very heavy; there were several found at Stoney Gut. Jamaica is very mountainous; they rise steeply from the shore; in some places there's a level country inland, and then the mountains begin again. The roads are generally in the track of the rivers; we had to cross about twelve going to Easington. In the summer the rivers are dry, and in the rainy season flooded. Hayti is about one day's sail from Jamaica.

By the Court: I have sailed to Hayti myself. None of the prisoners we took going to Easington had arms. We saw no one with arms going to Stoney Gut. It was dark. From the time that I landed at Morant Bay till I quitted that part of the country, I saw no disturbance.

FREDERICK AUGUSTUS BURT, being on his oath, saith: I was at Kingston, Jamaica, in October, 1865. I remember the time of the proclamation of martial law. There was then no outbreak or breach of the peace; nothing more than a little excitement from what had taken place at Morant Bay. The Courts of Justice were open, and so continued during the time martial law was pro-claimed. On the 21st October I was arrested by an ordinary policeman; he produced no warrant. He took me to the barracks on no charge whatever. I think two policemen joined him afterwards. I was locked up at the barracks. I requested to know what I was locked up for, and to see the custos and the superintendent of police. I saw neither, nor informed why, nor was I informed of any charge. When first taken to the barracks, I was put into an ordinary cell, and then removed by one of the officers to the guard-room, and had a mattress given me for the night. On Sunday 22nd, I was removed from the barracks, and taken to the Up Park Camp by a detachment of soldiers. At the camp I was put in a cell with two others; Signor Beneyiyne was one. I was there made to take off my boots; I received them again after a day or two. I know Dr. Bruce; he was brought into the same cell two or three days later. There was no bed or furniture in the cell. I was kept there a few days, and afterwards removed to . . . . I saw men flogged, and I was ordered to witness it. Whilst in the cell, I was visited by Mr. Bicknell, the police magistrate of Kingston; he asked me a number of questions, and took down the answers. I requested to know what I was arrested for, and how long I should be detained. He told me he saw no reason for detaining me, and had he the power he'd release me at once. I was not so released. I afterwards saw General O'Connor. We were ordered out of our cells on the occasion of his visiting the camp. I asked him on what grounds I had been arrested, and told him that as an Englishman I thought I had a right to know. He did not appear to give any definite answer, but said he didn't know the grounds, and said I should not go back to the cells, but be taken to the officers' quarters. I was detained altogether twenty days. No charge was ever made against me. I had nothing in the least to do with the disturbance at Morant Bay. I know the handwriting of George William Gordon. The document shown to me is in his handwriting.

Cross-examined: I was about nine years in Jamaica. I think the population was 450,000. The country is thinly populated and scattered. I think there are nearly 400,000 black and coloured persons, and the rest white. I should think there were more than 13,000 whites, as stated in the census. I won't swear the census wasn't right.

Re-examined by the Court: The black population includes the Maroons. I think it was three or four days after my arrest that I saw Mr. Bicknell, and two days after that that I saw General O'Connor.

ALEXANDER PHILLIPS, on his oath, saith: I am a native of Jamaica, and lived there in 1865, in the Parish of Vere and County of Middlesex. My residence was about forty-three miles from the nearest point of the district where martial law was proclaimed. I was not engaged in any business at the time. I had some freehold property. Directly or indirectly I had nothing whatever to do with the outbreak. I was arrested 24th October, 1865, by Lieutenant Sinclair, and a body of men, volunteers. No charge whatever was made against me. Lieutenant Sinclair informed me he was authorised by his Excellency the Governor to arrest me, search my house, and seize all my papers. I was put on horseback and conveyed to the Court-house at Alley, and placed in the custody of the military. I know Dr. Bruce, and had known him a long time. He lived in Vere, and I saw him in custody at Alley. He was under guard in a room apart from me. The next day he was put into a gig; he was handcuffed, and his left arm lashed to the gig with a rope. I was handcuffed, lashed with a rope, and put into a cart, and taken to Spanish Town. We stopped at Old Harbour, and had refreshment. It's thirty miles from Alley to Spanish Town. From Old Harbour Dr. Bruce was put into the same van as me. At Spanish Town is what is called the King's House, where Mr. Eyre lived. I was taken in front of that house. Lieutenant Sinclair was there, and he asked for his Excellency the Governor, and said he had brought the prisoners, Dr. Bruce, Phillips, and another. His Excellency said he was sorry we had met with such bad weather, and he ordered him to convey us to the Volunteer Station at Spanish Town, where we were accordingly taken. We remained there about three hours. Dr. Bruce's handcuffs were taken off; my rope was taken off, but I wore the handcuffs still, and so did the other prisoner, Morris. We were put into a carriage and conveyed to Up Park Camp, which was in the proclaimed district. We remained there that night and the following day, and about six in the evening we were taken to Kingston, put into a boat, and rowed to Port Royal, and put on board the Wolverine, and next morning we were taken to Morant Bay. Dr. Bruce was then delivered into the custody of Mr. Ramsay, who acted for the military as Provost-marshal. I saw Dr. Bruce again on 20th November; he was then in custody. He was released about the last week in December. I was not in court when his case came on. After 20th December I saw him at Vere. I was sent to the cell in the prison amongst the prisoners who were called rebels. My hand-cuffs were taken off, but both hands were tied with rope, and I was kept in that state all the time. No charge whatever was ever made against me. I never inquired why I was detained, and I was never told; I never had the opportunity to inquire. I saw Gordon Ramsay during the time I was confined. I was released on 4th November; I was flogged and released. Four sailors were ordered to flog me; the orders were given by Lieutenant Adcock. I had a hundred lashes from a navy cat. I was not told at all why I was flogged. I did not ask why. I was only told to take off my clothes and receive a hundred lashes. I said to Lieutenant Adcock before the flogging commenced that it was impossible I could receive the flogging in my state of health. He requested to see my back. I showed it to him, and he said I had a good back to receive it. I was in bad health at this time, and my health suffered most severely from the flogging. Lieutenant Adcock requested me to kneel after the flogging before him, and I did so. He requested me to bless the Queen and damn every black man. I did that. He told me to go and receive a pass, and go away. No doctor was present when I was flogged, and after it was over I went on the public road, and had to shift for myself. I had severe fever, and sat on the road side, unable to move, and a boy assisted me to put on my clothes. I went to far end of the bay, and sat under a bamboo tree in a fainting state with fever. My brother found me there, and he got me to a house, and it was some time before I was well enough to be removed to his house. I was confined in bed in this house two weeks with the severe wounds in my back, and then I returned home. I was never tried, nor told what I was arrested for. I didn't see persons flogged, but I heard a great number before I was flogged. I was afterwards tried by a special commission in February, 1866. The result was an acquittal. I was tried for conspiracy. Dr. Bruce was tried with myself and other prisoners. I was first subpoenaed in behalf of the Crown, and whilst waiting I was told I was indicted, and a true bill found against me. Dr. Bruce was acquitted also. Morris was not tried; he was flogged at Morant Bay. I saw some executions at Morant Bay; I was taken out, with other prisoners, to see them four times; I saw forty-nine executions; I saw Samuel Clark executed. Ten more were indicted with me for conspiracy; all were acquitted. The case was broken down for six of the prisoners. Four were sent for trial, Dr. Bruce, Levine, Kelly, Smith, and myself. The Attorney-General made a speech, and told the jury the men were indicted for conspiracy, but hoped they wouldn't link their names with Paul Bogle. The indictment charged us with conspiracy, with Bogle and others, to set aside the Queen's authority. Witnesses were called against me. Mr. Phillips was my counsel, and he spoke to the jury, who acquitted me.

Question put—Objected to by prosecuting Counsel: I have brought an action against Mr. Eyre. There is a fund formed to enable me to bring the action. I have not received any direct authority from Mr. Mill and Mr. Taylor to mention their names in getting subscriptions. I have seen the document now shown me before. I know Mr. Biggs and Mr. Camerovzow. They are not appointed by me or by my authority to collect subscriptions. Messrs. Shaen and Roscoe are my attorneys. Mr. Shaen never told me that permission had been obtained for me to use Messrs. Taylor and Mill's names in recommending me for subscriptions. Mr. Camerovzow told me so, and that he was treasurer to the fund and also Mr. Pringle, my agent, told me so. I think it was in March last that I knew of this fund being commenced. I have been ten months in this country. I have received some assistance from the fund that is raised for me, not from any other source. I draw on Mr. Shaen for what money I require. I began to draw upon him last year, I think in August. Mr. Shaen paid my expenses from Jamaica here. I was examined twice before the Royal Commissioners. I mentioned Ensign Taylor, but I never mentioned Lieutenant Adcock before the Commissioners, because I did not know his name.

Re-examined: I have nothing whatever to do with this present prosecution. I have been subpoenaed, and I am come in consequence of that. I did not volunteer to come at all. I was subpoenaed three different times. I have had nothing to do with the criminal proceedings; it's only my action I am concerned. I used Ensign Taylor's name as the person of whom I received the pass, his being the only name I knew of the officers. I produce the pass.

*   *   *

DEVELOPING SELF-GOVERNMENT AND
THE DEFINITION OF IMPERIAL TIES

Dispatch from the Home Secretary, Sir G. Cornewall Lewis, to the
Governor of New Zealand, T. Gore Browne, Justifying the
British Government's Refusal to Meet
Demands for Military Assistance to Suppress the
Maori Disturbances, 26 July 1860*

I have received, and Her Majesty's Government has very carefully considered, your recent despatches respecting the disturbances in New Zealand.

The present posture of affairs I collect to be this: That Wiremu Kingi and the Taranaki tribes have receded from the immediate neighbourhood of New Plymouth, discouraged apparently by Captain Cracroft's successful attack on their pah; that no other tribes have as yet declared themselves on the side of the insurgents; and that there is reason to hope that none will so declare themselves. But you point out as a matter of much importance that the position taken by the Waikatos is one which if persevered in will be inconsistent with the due maintenance of the Queen's authority in the islands.

The reinforcements sent from other points of Australia have raised the number of troops in New Zealand to about 1,800 men, besides volunteers and a naval brigade of about 500 men furnished from the ships of war which are now on the coast of New Zealand. There are now four and will shortly be five such ships.

I do not, however, collect from your despatches that any volunteers have offered to come forward in aid of Her Majesty's Government except those persons who have armed in defence of their own homes, or have been compelled to leave them.

Under these circumstances, you and your advisers request that three regiments of infantry and one of artillery may be sent out, partly in order to provide against the possibility of a general rising of the natives, and partly in order to enable you to take, under any circumstances which may occur, a commanding tone respecting the various questions at issue between the settlers and the Maories.

The Native Secretary, I observe, has remarked that with less than 5,000 troops (involving an expense of about 150,000*l.* per annum) it would not be possible to defend all the outlying settlements in the colony; and Mr. Richmond closes his able and interesting memorandum with the following words:

Parliamentary Papers, 1861, XLI, Cmd. 2798, 261–63.

Justice, therefore, and humanity require that England should freely recognise the onerous duties cast upon her by the colonization of New Zealand. To avert such calamities as seem to impend, it is indispensable to place at the disposal of the Governor a military and naval force adequate to support him in a policy of equal justice to the two races which have been placed by Providence in a relation to each other, so singular and difficult.

I must at once say that in the present posture of affairs, and with the demands for troops which exist, or may be expected in other quarters, it is impossible for Her Majesty's Government to comply with your desire to receive 3,000 or 4,000 soldiers, in addition to your present force. Measures, however, have been taken to dispatch the 14th Regiment at once for the relief of the 65th, which will be allowed to remain in the colony for the present, in case on the arrival of the 14th the immediate danger should not have passed over. I trust that it will have passed. And if this should prove the case I cannot but believe that wise government and prudent conduct on the part of the settlers will do far more than an increased military force to maintain the relations between the Europeans and natives on a satisfactory footing.

Meantime I must observe, that, although it is the desire of Her Majesty's Government to provide fully for the performance of those duties which the mother country owes to her colonies, I cannot silently accept what appears to be the colonial estimate of those responsibilities.

England cannot undertake the defence, against a nation of warlike savages, of a number of scattered farms or villages, selected, not with any view to such defence, but to the profitable pursuit of peaceful industry, and subject to the risks which necessarily attend the occupation of land in the midst of an uncivilized population.

Nor can Her Majesty's Government undertake to provide such a force as will secure the colonists against prospective difficuties. Immediate and imminent dangers must be met as they arise. But a policy which requires the continual presence of a large force carries, in most cases, its condemnation on its face.

What is the degree of protection which the inhabitants of a British colony are entitled to expect from the Home Government is a matter on which it is impossible to speak in the abstract. It is no doubt necessary to punish aggression, to defend the centres of population, to maintain a hold upon the keys of the country. But beyond this the amount of assistance given must depend on the demands to which the military and naval forces of the country are subjected elsewhere, and on the urgency of the case as shown, not merely by demands for assistance, but by the disposition of the colonists to adopt their share of the necessary expenses, to incur for the defence of their neighbours the dangers and inconveniences of personal service, and to place in the hands of the Home Government the power of controlling the treatment of those whom they are called upon to subdue.

And I cannot refrain from observing, that neither your despatches nor Mr. Richmond's memorandum indicate any definite intention on the part of the colonists to contribute to the expense of the troops whom they demand; that the volunteering appears to be confined to the particular localities threatened; and that Mr. Richmond, while calling upon the Home Government to adopt the expenses of the war, does not even hint at the propriety of investing it with any larger powers than they at present possess for dealing with the native question out of which these expenses arise. I may add that a Bill introduced into Parliament to provide an effectual machinery for the exercise by the Crown of the powers reserved to it by the Constitutional Act is threatened with a determined opposition by gentlemen professing to represent the feelings of the colonists.

This you will perceive on perusing a pamphlet which I enclose in another despatch.

I allude to these circumstances, not of course as relieving the Home Government from the duty of supporting the colony against a pressing danger, but because they must materially affect the disposition of the British Government and people to undertake that indefinite expenditure of blood and treasure to which Mr. Richmond invites them.

*Speech by John Bright in the House of Commons
Criticizing the British North America Bill,
28 February 1867**

Although this measure has not excited much interest in the House or in the country, yet it appears to me to be of such very great importance that it should be treated rather differently, or that the House should be treated rather differently in respect to it. I have never before known of any great measure affecting any large portion of the empire or its population which has been brought in and attempted to be hurried through Parliament in the manner in which this bill is being dealt with. But the importance of it is much greater to the inhabitants of those provinces than it is to us. It is on that account alone that it might be expected we should examine it closely, and see that we commit no error in passing it.

The right hon. Gentleman has not offered us, on one point, an explanation which I think he will be bound to make. This bill does not include the whole of the British North American Provinces. I presume the two left out have been left out because it is quite clear they did not wish to come in. [Mr. Adderley: 'I am glad I can inform the hon. Gentleman that they are, one of them at least, on the point of coming in.'] Yes; the reason of their being left out is because they were not willing to come in. They may hereafter become willing, and if so the bill will admit them by a provision which appears reasonable. But the province of Nova Scotia is also unwilling to come in, and it is assumed that

*Bright, *Speeches on Questions of Public Policy*, I, 157–63.

because some time ago the Legislature of that province voted a resolution partly in favour of some such course, therefore the population is in favour of it.

For my part I do not believe in the propriety or wisdom of the Legislature voting on a great question of this nature with reference to the Legislature of Nova Scotia, if the people of Nova Scotia have never had the question directly put to them. I have heard there is at present in London a petition complaining of the hasty proceeding of Parliament, and asking for delay, signed by 31,000 adult males of the province of Nova Scotia, and that that petition is in reality signed by at least half of all the male inhabitants of that province. So far as I know, the petition does not protest absolutely against union, but against the manner in which it is being carried out by this scheme and bill, and the hasty measures of the Colonial Office. Now, whether the scheme be a good or bad one, scarcely anything can be more foolish, looking to the future, than that any of the provinces should be dragged into it, either perforce, by the pressure of the Colonial Office, or by any hasty action on the part of Parliament, in the hope of producing a result which probably the populations of those provinces may not wish to see brought about.

I understand that the general election for the Legislature of Nova Scotia, according to the constitution of that colony, will take place in the month of May or June next; that this question has never been fairly placed before the people of that province at an election, and that it has never been discussed and decided by the people; and seeing that only three months or not so much will elapse before there will be an opportunity of ascertaining the opinions of the population of Nova Scotia, I think it is at least a hazardous proceeding to pass this bill through Parliament, binding Nova Scotia, until the clear opinion of that province has been ascertained. If, at a time like this, when you are proposing a union which we all hope is to last for ever, you create a little sore, it will in all probability become a great sore in a short time, and it may be that the intentions of Parliament will be almost entirely frustrated by the haste with which this measure is being pushed forward.

The right hon. Gentleman the Chancellor of the Exchequer, I think, in the early part of the evening, in answer to a question from this side, spoke of this matter as one of extreme urgency. Well, I cannot discover any urgency in the matter at all. What is urgent is this, that when done it ought to be done wisely, and with the full and free consent of all those populations who are to be bound by this Act and interested in its results. Unless the good-will of those populations is secured, in all probability the act itself will be a misfortune rather than a blessing to the provinces to which it refers.

The right hon. Gentleman amused me in one part of his speech. He spoke of the filial piety—rather a curious term—of these provinces, and their great anxiety to make everything suit the ideas of this country; and this was said particularly with reference to the proposition for a Senate selected, not elected, for life, by the Governor-General of Canada. He said they were extremely anxious to follow as far as possible the institutions of the mother country. I have not the smallest objection to any people on the face of the earth following our institutions if they like them. Institutions which suit one country, as we all know, are not very likely to suit every other country. With regard to this particular case, the right hon. Gentleman said it is to be observed that Canada has had a nominated council, and has changed it for an elected one, and that surely they had a right if they pleased to go back from an elected council to a nominated council. Well, nobody denies that, but nobody pretends that the people of Canada prefer a nominated council to an elected council. And all the wisdom of the wise men to whom the right hon. gentleman the member for Oxford has referred in such glowing terms, unless the experience of present and past times goes for nothing, is but folly if they have come to the conclusion that a nominated council on that continent must be better than an elected council. Still, if they wish it, I should not interfere and try to prevent it. But I venture to say that the clause enabling the Governor-General and his Cabinet to put seventy men in that council for life inserts into the whole scheme the germ of a malady which will spread, and which before very long will require an alteration of this Act and of the constitution of this new Confederation.

But the right hon. Gentleman went on to say that with regard to the representative assembly—which, I suppose, is to be called according to his phrase the House of Commons—they have adopted a very different plan. There they have not followed the course of this country. They have established their House of Representatives directly upon the basis of population. They have adopted the system which prevails in the United States, which upon every ten years' summing up of the census in that country the number of members may be changed, and is by law changed in the different States and districts as the rate of population may have changed. Therefore, in that respect his friends in Canada have not adopted the principle which prevails in this country, but that which prevails in the United States. I believe they have done that which is right, and which they have a right to do, and which is inevitable there. I regret very much that they have not adopted another system with regard to their council or senate, because I am satisfied—I have not a particle of doubt with regard to it—that we run a great danger of making this Act work ill almost from the beginning.

They have the example of thirty-six States in the United States, in which the Senate is elected, and no man, however sanguine, can hope that seventy-two stereotyped provincial peers in Canada will work harmoniously with a body elected upon a system so wide and so general as that which prevails in the States of the American Union. There is one point about which the right hon. Gentleman said nothing, and which I think is so very important that the Member for Oxford, his predecessor in office, might have told us something about it. We know that Canada is a great country, and we know that the population is, or very soon will be, something like 4,000,000, and we may hope that, united under one government, the province may be more capable of defence. But what is intended with regard to the question of defence? Is everything to be done for the province? Is it intended to garrison its fortresses by English troops? At the present moment there are, I believe, in the province 12,000 or 15,000 men.

There are persons in this country, and there are some also in the North American provinces, who are ill-natured enough to say that not a little of the loyalty that is said to prevail in Canada has its price. I think it is natural and reasonable to hope that there is in that country a very strong attachment to this country. But if they are to be constantly applying to us for guarantees for railways, and for grants for fortresses, and for works of defence, then I think it would be far better for them and for us—cheaper for us and less demoralising for them—that they should become an independent State, and maintain their own fortresses, fight their own cause, and build up their own future without relying upon us. And when we know, as everybody knows, that the population of Canada is in a much better position as regards the comforts of home, than is the great bulk of the population of this country, I say the time has come when it ought to be clearly understood that the taxes of England are no longer to go across the ocean to defray expenses of any kind within the Confederation which is about to be formed.

The right hon. Gentleman has never been an advocate for great expenditure in the colonies by the mother country. On the contrary, he has been one of the members of this House who have distinguished themselves by what I will call an honest system for the mother country, and what I believe is a wise system for the colonies. But I think that when a measure of this kind is being passed, having such stupendous results upon the condition and the future population of these great colonies, we have a right to ask that there should be some consideration for the revenue and for the taxpayers of this country. In discussing this Bill with the delegates from the provinces, I think it was the duty of the Colonial Secretary to have gone fairly into this question, and, if possible, to have arranged it to the advantage of the colony and the mother country.

I believe there is no delusion greater than this—that there is any party in the United States that wishes to commit any aggression upon Canada, or to annex Canada by force to the United States. There is not a part of the world, in my opinion, that runs less risk of aggression than Canada, except with regard to that foolish and impotent attempt of certain discontented not-long-ago subjects of the Queen, who have left this country. America has no idea of anything of the kind. No American statesman, no American political party, dreams for a moment of an aggression upon Canada, or of annexing Canada by force. And therefore, every farthing that you spend on your fortresses, and all that you do with the idea of shutting out American aggression, is money squandered through an hallucination which we ought to get rid of. I have not risen for the purpose of objecting to the second reading of this Bill. Under the circumstances I presume it is well that we should do no other than read it a second time. But I think the Government ought to have given a little more time. I think they have not treated the province of Nova Scotia with that tenderness, that generosity, and that consideration which is desirable when you are about to make so great a change in its affairs and in its future. For my share, I want the population of these provinces to do that which they believe to be best for their own interests— to remain with this country if they like it, in the most friendly manner, or to become independent States if they wish it. If they should prefer to unite themselves with the United States, I should not complain even of that. But whatever be their course, there is no man in this House or in those provinces who has a more sincere wish for their greatness and their welfare than I have who have taken the liberty thus to criticise this Bill.

British North America Act, an Act for the Union of Canada, Nova Scotia, and New Brunswick, and the Government Thereof (30 Vict., c. 3), 29 March 1867*

Whereas the Provinces of *Canada, Nova Scotia,* and *New Brunswick* have expressed their Desire to be federally united into One Dominion under the Crown of the United Kingdom of *Great Britain* and *Ireland*, with a Constitution similar in Principle to that of the United Kingdom:

And whereas such a Union would conduce to the Welfare of the Provinces and promote the Interests of the *British* Empire:

And whereas on the Establishment of the Union by Authority of Parliament it is expedient, not only that the Constitution of the Legislative Authority in the Dominion be provided for, but also that the Nature of the Executive Government therein be declared:

And whereas it is expedient that Provision be made for the eventual Admission into the Union of other Parts of *British North America:*

Be it therefore enacted and declared by the Queen's most Excellent Majesty, by and with the Advice and Consent of the Lords Spiritual and Temporal, and Commons, in this present Parliament assembled, and by the Authority of the same, as follows:

I.—Preliminary

1. This Act may be cited as The *British North America* Act, 1867.

2. The Provisions of this Act referring to Her Majesty the Queen extend also to the Heirs and Successors of Her Majesty, Kings and Queens of the United Kingdom of *Great Britain* and *Ireland*.

II.—Union

3. It shall be lawful for the Queen, by and with the Advice of Her Majesty's Most Honourable Privy Council, to declare by Proclamation that, on and after

Public General Statutes, II, 5–9, 11, 13–18, 21–24.

a Day therein appointed, not being more than Six Months after the passing of this Act, the Provinces of *Canada, Nova Scotia,* and *New Brunswick* shall form and be One Dominion under the Name of *Canada;* and on and after that Day those Three Provinces shall form and be One Dominion under that Name accordingly.

4. The subsequent Provisions of this Act shall, unless it is otherwise expressed or implied, commence and have effect on and after the Union, that is to say, on and after the Day appointed for the Union taking effect in the Queen's Proclamation; and in the same Provisions, unless it is otherwise expressed or implied, the Name *Canada* shall be taken to mean *Canada* as constituted under this Act.

5. *Canada* shall be divided into Four Provinces, named *Ontario, Quebec, Nova Scotia,* and *New Brunswick.*

6. The Parts of the Province of *Canada* (as it exists at the passing of this Act) which formerly constituted respectively the Provinces of *Upper Canada* and *Lower Canada* shall be deemed to be severed, and shall form Two separate Provinces. The Part which formerly constituted the Province of *Upper Canada* shall constitute the Province of *Ontario;* and the Part which formerly constituted the Province of *Lower Canada* shall constitute the Province of *Quebec.*

7. The Provinces of *Nova Scotia* and *New Brunswick* shall have the same Limits as at the passing of this Act.

8. In the general Census of the Population of *Canada* which is hereby required to be taken in the Year One thousand eight hundred and seventy-one, and in every Tenth Year thereafter, the respective Populations of the Four Provinces shall be distinguished.

III.—Executive Power

9. The Executive Government and Authority of and over *Canada* is hereby declared to continue and be vested in the Queen.

10. The Provisions of this Act referring to the Governor General extend and apply to the Governor General for the Time being of *Canada*, or other the Chief Executive Officer or Administrator for the Time being carrying on the Government of *Canada* on behalf and in the Name of the Queen, by whatever Title he is designated.

11. There shall be a Council to aid and advise in the Government of *Canada*, to be styled the Queen's Privy Council for *Canada;* and the Persons who are to be Members of that Council shall be from Time to Time chosen and summoned by the Governor General and sworn in as Privy Councillors, and Members thereof may be from Time to Time removed by the Governor General.

12. All Powers, Authorities, and Functions which under any Act of the Parliament of *Great Britain,* or of the Parliament of the United Kingdom of *Great Britain* and *Ireland*, or of the Legislature of *Upper Canada, Lower Canada, Canada, Nova Scotia,* or *New Brunswick*, are at the Union vested in or exerciseable by the respective Governors or Lieutenant Governors of those

Provinces, with the Advice, or with the Advice and Consent, of the respective Executive Councils thereof, or in conjunction with those Councils, or with any Number of Members thereof, or by those Governors or Lieutenant Governors individually, shall, as far as the same continue in existence and capable of being exercised after the Union in relation to the Government of *Canada,* be vested in and exerciseable by the Governor General, with the Advice or with the Advice and Consent of or in conjunction with the Queen's Privy Council for *Canada,* or any Members thereof, or by the Governor General individually, as the Case requires, subject nevertheless (except with respect to such as exist under Acts of the Parliament of *Great Britain* or of the Parliament of the United Kingdom of *Great Britain* and *Ireland*) to be abolished or altered by the Parliament of *Canada.*

13. The Provisions of this Act referring to the Governor General in Council shall be construed as referring to the Governor General acting by and with the Advice of the Queen's Privy Council for *Canada.*

14. It shall be lawful for the Queen, if Her Majesty thinks fit, to authorize the Governor General from Time to Time to appoint any Person or any Persons jointly or severally to be his Deputy or Deputies within any Part or Parts of *Canada,* and in that Capacity to exercise during the Pleasure of the Governor General such of the Powers, Authorities, and Functions of the Governor General as the Governor General deems it necessary or expedient to assign to him or them, subject to any Limitations or Directions expressed or given by the Queen; but the Appointment of such a Deputy or Deputies shall not affect the Exercise by the Governor General himself of any Power, Authority, or Function.

15. The Command-in-Chief of the Land and Naval Militia, and of all Naval and Military Forces, of and in *Canada,* is hereby declared to continue and be vested in the Queen.

16. Until the Queen otherwise directs, the Seat of Government of *Canada* shall be *Ottawa.*

IV.—Legislative Power

17. There shall be One Parliament for *Canada,* consisting of the Queen, an Upper House styled the Senate, and the House of Commons.

18. The Privileges, Immunities, and Powers to be held, enjoyed, and exercised by the Senate and by the House of Commons and by the Members thereof respectively shall be such as are from Time to Time defined by Act of the Parliament of *Canada,* but so that the same shall never exceed those at the passing of this Act held, enjoyed, and exercised by the Commons House of Parliament of the United Kingdom of *Great Britain* and *Ireland* and by the Members thereof.

19. The Parliament of *Canada* shall be called together not later than Six Months after the Union.

20. There shall be a Session of the Parliament of *Canada* once at least in every Year, so that Twelve Months shall not intervene between the last Sitting of the Parliament in one Session and its first Sitting in the next Session.

The Senate

21. The Senate shall, subject to the Provisions of this Act, consist of Seventy-two Members, who shall be styled Senators.

22. In relation to the Constitution of the Senate *Canada* shall be deemed to consist of Three Divisions:

1. *Ontario;*
2. *Quebec;*
3. The Maritime Provinces, *Nova Scotia* and *New Brunswick;* which Three Divisions shall (subject to the Provisions of this Act) be equally represented in the Senate as follows: *Ontario* by Twenty-four Senators; *Quebec* by Twenty-four Senators; and the Maritime Provinces by Twenty-four Senators, Twelve thereof representing *Nova Scotia,* and Twelve thereof representing *New Brunswick.*

In the Case of *Quebec* each of the Twenty-four Senators representing that Province shall be appointed for One of the Twenty-four Electoral Divisions of *Lower Canada* specified in Schedule A. to Chapter One of the Consolidated Statutes of *Canada.*

23. The Qualifications of a Senator shall be as follows:

(1.) He shall be of the full Age of Thirty Years:

(2.) He shall be either a natural-born Subject of the Queen, or a Subject of the Queen naturalized by an Act of the Parliament of *Great Britain,* or of the Parliament of the United Kingdom of *Great Britain* and *Ireland,* or of the Legislature of One of the Provinces of *Upper Canada, Lower Canada, Canada, Nova Scotia,* or *New Brunswick,* before the Union, or of the Parliament of *Canada* after the Union:

(3.) He shall be legally or equitably seised as of Freehold for his own Use and Benefit of Lands or Tenements held in Free and Common Socage, or seised or possessed for his own Use and Benefit of Lands or Tenements held in Franc-alleu or in Roture, within the Province for which he is appointed, of the Value of Four thousand Dollars, over and above all Rents, Dues, Debts, Charges, Mortgages, and Incumbrances due or payable out of or charged on or affecting the same:

(4.) His Real and Personal Property shall be together worth Four thousand Dollars over and above his Debts and Liabilities:

(5.) He shall be resident in the Province for which he is appointed:

(6.) In the Case of *Quebec* he shall have his Real Property Qualification in the Electoral Division for which he is appointed, or shall be resident in that Division.

24. The Governor General shall from Time to Time, in the Queen's Name, by Instrument under the Great Seal of *Canada,* summon qualified Persons to the Senate; and, subject to the Provisions of this Act, every Person so summoned shall become and be a Member of the Senate and a Senator.

*   *   *

The House of Commons

37. The House of Commons shall, subject to the Provisions of this Act, consist of One hundred and eighty-one Members, of whom Eighty-two shall be elected for *Ontario,* Sixty-five for *Quebec,* Nineteen for *Nova Scotia,* and Fifteen for *New Brunswick.*

38. The Governor General shall from Time to Time, in the Queen's Name, by Instrument under the Great Seal of *Canada,* summon and call together the House of Commons.

39. A Senator shall not be capable of being elected or of sitting or voting as a Member of the House of Commons.

40. Until the Parliament of *Canada* otherwise provides, *Ontario, Quebec, Nova Scotia,* and *New Brunswick* shall, for the Purposes of the Election of Members to serve in the House of Commons, be divided into Electoral Districts as follows: . . .

41. Until the Parliament of *Canada* otherwise provides, all Laws in force in the several Provinces at the Union relative to the following Matters or any of them, namely, the Qualifications and Disqualifications of Persons to be elected or to sit or vote as Members of the House of Assembly or Legislative Assembly in the several Provinces, the Voters at Elections of such Members, the Oaths to be taken by Voters, the Returning Officers, their Powers and Duties, the Proceedings at Elections, the Periods during which Elections may be continued, the Trial of controverted Elections, and Proceedings incident thereto, the vacating of Seats of Members, and the Execution of new Writs in case of Seats vacated otherwise than by Dissolution,—shall respectively apply to Elections of Members to serve in the House of Commons for the same several Provinces.

Provided that, until the Parliament of *Canada* otherwise provides, at any Election for a Member of the House of Commons for the District of *Algoma,* in addition to Persons qualified by the Law of the Province of *Canada* to vote, every Male *British* Subject, aged Twenty-one Years or upwards, being a Householder, shall have a Vote.

*   *   *

49. Questions arising in the House of Commons shall be decided by a Majority of Voices other than that of the Speaker, and when the Voices are equal, but not otherwise, the Speaker shall have a Vote.

50. Every House of Commons shall continue for Five Years from the Day of the Return of the Writs for choosing the House (subject to be sooner dissolved by the Governor General), and no longer.

51. On the Completion of the Census in the Year One thousand eight hundred and seventy-one, and of each subsequent decennial Census, the Representation of the Four Provinces shall be readjusted by such Authority, in such Manner, and from such Time, as the Parliament of *Canada* from Time to Time provides, subject and according to the following Rules:

(1.) *Quebec* shall have the fixed Number of Sixty-five Members:

(2.) There shall be assigned to each of the other Provinces such a Number of Members as will bear the same Proportion to the Number of its Population (ascertained at such Census) as the Number Sixty-five bears to the Number of the Population of *Quebec* (so ascertained):

(3.) In the Computation of the Number of Members for a Province a fractional Part not exceeding One Half of the whole Number requisite for entitling the Province to a Member shall be disregarded; but a fractional Part exceeding One Half of that Number shall be equivalent to the whole Number:

(4.) On any such Re-adjustment the Number of Members for a Province shall not be reduced unless the Proportion which the Number of the Population of the Province bore to the Number of the aggregate Population of *Canada* at the then last preceding Re-adjustment of the Number of Members for the Province is ascertained at the then latest Census to be diminished by One Twentieth Part or upwards:

(5.) Such Re-adjustment shall not take effect until the Termination of the then existing Parliament.

52. The Number of Members of the House of Commons may be from Time to Time increased by the Parliament of *Canada,* provided the proportionate Representation of the Provinces prescribed by this Act is not thereby disturbed.

Money Votes; Royal Assent

53. Bills for appropriating any Part of the Public Revenue, or for imposing any Tax or Impost, shall originate in the House of Commons.

54. It shall not be lawful for the House of Commons to adopt or pass any Vote, Resolution, Address, or Bill for the Appropriation of any Part of the Public Revenue, or of any Tax or Impost, to any Purpose that has not been first recommended to that House by Message of the Governor General in the Session in which such Vote, Resolution, Address, or Bill is proposed.

55. Where a Bill passed by the Houses of the Parliament is presented to the Governor General for the Queen's Assent, he shall declare, according to his Discretion, but subject to the Provisions of this Act and to Her Majesty's Instructions, either that he assents thereto in the Queen's Name, or that he withholds the Queen's Assent, or that he reserves the Bill for the Signification of the Queen's Pleasure.

56. Where the Governor General assents to a Bill in the Queen's Name, he shall by the first convenient Opportunity send an authentic Copy of the Act to One of Her Majesty's Principal Secretaries of State, and if the Queen in Council within Two Years after Receipt thereof by the Secretary of State thinks fit to disallow the Act, such Disallowance (with a Certificate of the Secretary of State of the Day on which the Act was received by him) being signified by the Governor General, by Speech or Message to each of the Houses of the Parliament or by Proclamation, shall annul the Act from and after the Day of such Signification.

57. A Bill reserved for the Signification of the Queen's Pleasure shall not have any Force unless and until, within Two Years from the Day on which it was presented to the Governor General for the Queen's Assent, the Governor General signifies, by Speech or Message to each of the Houses of the Parliament or by Proclamation, that it has received the Assent of the Queen in Council.

An Entry of every such Speech, Message, or Proclamation shall be made in the Journal of each House, and a Duplicate thereof duly attested shall be delivered to the proper Officer to be kept among the Records of *Canada*.

V.—Provincial Constitutions

Executive Power

58. For each Province there shall be an Officer, styled the Lieutenant Governor, appointed by the Governor General in Council by Instrument under the Great Seal of *Canada*.

59. A Lieutenant Governor shall hold Office during the Pleasure of the Governor General; but any Lieutenant Governor appointed after the Commencement of the First Session of the Parliament of *Canada* shall not be removeable within Five Years from his Appointment, except for Cause assigned, which shall be communicated to him in Writing within One Month after the Order for his Removal is made, and shall be communicated by Message to the Senate and to the House of Commons within One Week thereafter if the Parliament is then sitting, and if not then within One Week after the Commencement of the next Session of the Parliament.

*   *   *

61. Every Lieutenant Governor shall, before assuming the Duties of his Office, make and subscribe before the Governor General or some Person authorized by him Oaths of Allegiance and Office similar to those taken by the Governor General.

62. The Provisions of this Act referring to the Lieutenant Governor extend and apply to the Lieutenant Governor for the Time being of each Province, or other the Chief Executive Officer or Administrator for the Time being carrying on the Government of the Province, by whatever Title he is designated.

63. The Executive Council of *Ontario* and of *Quebec* shall be composed of such Persons as the Lieutenant Governor from Time to Time thinks fit, and in the first instance of the following Officers, namely,—the Attorney General, the Secretary and Registrar of the Province, the Treasurer of the Province, the Commissioner of Crown Lands, and the Commissioner of Agriculture and Public Works, with in *Quebec* the Speaker of the Legislative Council and the Solicitor General.

64. The Constitution of the Executive Authority in each of the Provinces of *Nova Scotia* and *New Brunswick* shall, subject to the Provisions of this Act, continue as it exists at the Union until altered under the Authority of this Act.

65. All Powers, Authorities, and Functions which under any Act of the Parliament of *Great Britain,* or of the Parliament of the United Kingdom of

Great Britain and *Ireland,* or of the Legislature of *Upper Canada, Lower Canada,* or *Canada,* were or are before or at the Union vested in or exerciseable by the respective Governors or Lieutenant Governors of those Provinces, with the Advice or with the Advice and Consent of the respective Executive Councils thereof, or in conjunction with those Councils, or with any Number of Members thereof, or by those Governors or Lieutenant Governors individually, shall, as far as the same are capable of being exercised after the Union in relation to the Government of *Ontario* and *Quebec* respectively, be vested in and shall or may be exercised by the Lieutenant Governor of *Ontario* and *Quebec* respectively, with the Advice or with the Advice and Consent of or in conjunction with the respective Executive Councils, or any Members thereof, or by the Lieutenant Governor individually, as the Case requires, subject nevertheless (except with respect to such as exist under Acts of the Parliament of *Great Britain,* or of the Parliament of the United Kingdom of *Great Britain* and *Ireland,*) to be abolished or altered by the respective Legislatures of *Ontario* and *Quebec.*

*   *   *

Legislative Power

1.—Ontario. 69. There shall be a Legislature for *Ontario* consisting of the Lieutenant Governor and of One House, styled the Legislative Assembly of *Ontario.*

70. The Legislative Assembly of *Ontario* shall be composed of Eighty-two members, to be elected to represent the Eighty-two Electoral Districts set forth in the First Schedule to this Act.

2.—Quebec. 71. There shall be a Legislature for *Quebec* consisting of the Lieutenant Governor and of Two Houses, styled the Legislative Council of *Quebec* and the Legislative Assembly of *Quebec.*

72. The Legislative Council of *Quebec* shall be composed of Twenty-four Members, to be appointed by the Lieutenant Governor, in the Queen's Name, by Instrument under the Great Seal of *Quebec,* One being appointed to represent each of the Twenty-four Electoral Divisions of *Lower Canada* in this Act referred to, and each holding Office for the Term of his Life, unless the Legislature of *Quebec* otherwise provides under the Provisions of this Act.

73. The Qualifications of the Legislative Councillors of *Quebec* shall be the same as those of the Senators for *Quebec.*

*   *   *

VI.—Distribution of Legislative Powers

Powers of the Parliament

91. It shall be lawful for the Queen, by and with the Advice and Consent of the Senate and House of Commons, to make Laws for the Peace, Order, and good Government of *Canada,* in relation to all Matters not coming within the Classes of Subjects by this Act assigned exclusively to the Legislatures of the Provinces; and for greater Certainty, but not so as to restrict the Generality of the foregoing Terms of this Section, it is hereby declared that (notwithstanding

anything in this Act) the exclusive Legislative Authority of the Parliament of *Canada* extends to all Matters coming within the Classes of Subjects next herein-after enumerated; that is to say,—

1. The Public Debt and Property.
2. The Regulation of Trade and Commerce.
3. The raising of Money by any Mode or System of Taxation.
4. The borrowing of Money on the Public Credit.
5. Postal Service.
6. The Census and Statistics.
7. Militia, Military and Naval Service, and Defence.
8. The fixing of and providing for the Salaries and Allowances of Civil and other Officers of the Government of *Canada*.
9. Beacons, Buoys, Lighthouses, and *Sable Island*.
10. Navigation and Shipping.
11. Quarantine and the Establishment and Maintenance of Marine Hospitals.
12. Sea Coast and Inland Fisheries.
13. Ferries between a Province and any *British* or Foreign Country or between Two Provinces.
14. Currency and Coinage.
15. Banking, Incorporation of Banks, and the Issue of Paper Money.
16. Savings Banks.
17. Weights and Measures.
18. Bills of Exchange and Promissory Notes.
19. Interest.
20. Legal Tender.
21. Bankruptcy and Insolvency.
22. Patents of Invention and Discovery.
23. Copyrights.
24. *Indians*, and Lands reserved for the *Indians*.
25. Naturalization and Aliens.
26. Marriage and Divorce.
27. The Criminal Law, except the Constitution of Courts of Criminal Jurisdiction, but including the Procedure in Criminal Matters.
28. The Establishment, Maintenance, and Management of Penitentiaries.
29. Such Classes of Subjects as are expressly excepted in the Enumeration of the Classes of Subjects by this Act assigned exclusively to the Legislatures of the Provinces.

And any Matter coming within any of the Classes of Subjects enumerated in this Section shall not be deemed to come within the Class of Matters of a local or private Nature comprised in the Enumeration of the Classes of Subjects by this Act assigned exclusively to the Legislatures of the Provinces.

*   *   *

*Second Report of the Royal Commission on the Defense of
British Possessions and Commerce Abroad Recommending
Australia and New Zealand Take a Greater Share
in Their Own Defenses, 23 March 1882**

*   *   *

Having thus summarized the evidence which has been brought before us in respect of each of the Australian Colonies and New Zealand, we will proceed to state the general conclusions at which we have arrived.

It is, in our opinion, plainly necessary to maintain at each fortified place a small body of fully trained artillerymen, permanently enrolled. This was the unanimous opinion of the Commission and Military Committee, and of the witnesses, not only from New South Wales, but from Victoria and South Australia. There were and probably will be, differences of opinion as to the organization of such a force; the period for which the men should be engaged, the numbers required, and so forth; but these points must be locally decided, and we need to no more than refer to them.

We consider it further desirable to create a reserve of men who have passed through the permanent forces as an economical means of increasing, in times of emergency, the number of efficient gunners. Upon this point there was also an unanimity of opinion in New South Wales; and it appears that the same view was entertained in Victoria and South Australia, though in New South Wales it was considered that the reserve might be partly composed of volunteer militia.

It is clear from the evidence that, however good the volunteer forces may be, they cannot become efficient without daylight drill and periods of continuous training. Where the value of labour is high, as it is in Australia, the time required for these military exercises cannot be given gratuitously, and it follows that, without payment for their time, it is impossible to raise forces upon which dependence could be placed in time of war. Any military expedition directed against Australia would be composed of regular and disciplined troops, which the colonial forces could not hope to meet on anything like equal terms, unless their first line of defence be organized with as near an approximation to the efficiency of regular troops as they are able to attain. For these reasons, it is desirable that each Colony should maintain a limited volunteer militia force, comprising, if possible, artillery, engineers, and infantry, sufficiently trained, and paid for the time devoted to training.

From a purely militant point of view we apprehend that it would be best to have a small permanent infantry force, which would not only be well officered and well drilled, but would serve as a model and school for the volunteers. But, as we have before observed, the great object is to secure permanence in the defence forces, and it may be doubted whether that would be obtained by establishing a force, the maintenance of which would be exposed to attacks on

**Parliamentary Papers*, 1887, LVI, Cmd. 6091, I, 326–28.

the ground of economy. We believe, upon the whole, that the organization of a volunteer militia, enrolled and paid, as in South Australia, for actual work done, and supplemented by an unpaid volunteer force, infantry and mounted, would be most likely to meet the requirements of all the Australian Colonies, and to acquire a permanent character. This latter force would cost the Colony nothing except, perhaps, a small capitation fee, and a sum for instruction, arms, and ammunition.

All the witnesses agree in describing the existing volunteer forces as composed of men of good physique, with zeal and every disposition to perfect themselves in drill. Existing defects would be best remedied by the establishment of a school of instruction for officers, on the principle of the Military College in Canada. But in the present circumstances of the Australian Continent an efficient school could hardly be created and maintained except by the joint action of the several Colonies. This is a question which will need much consideration; but if approached with judgment, it ought not to present any insuperable difficulty. It is satisfactory to find that the Sydney Commission were unanimous in recommending not only a school for instruction for the Colony of New South Wales, but also a central school, on a plan somewhat similar to that in Canada. If such a school were established it would, we think, be desirable, as in the case of Canada, to offer commissions in your Majesty's service to a limited number of cadets.

We believe that the colonial forces would derive the highest advantage from the presence and superintendence of an experienced officer of rank and distinction, either stationed for a certain number of years, not exceeding five, in Australia, or sent out from England from time to time. Upon the whole, Colonial opinion seems in favour of the former plan, and we concur in thinking it the best. The charge should, of course, be divided amongst the several Colonies, and the officer should be chosen by the military authorities in this country, with special reference to his personal qualifications for the post. All the witnesses agree in believing that such an appointment would be welcomed in the Colonies, and would more than anything else tend to raise the tone of discipline and bring about uniformity in organization and equipment.

To avoid misunderstanding, it would be desirable that the scope of the duties of such an officer should be distinctly defined and agreed to by all the Colonies interested. Speaking generally, his duties should be to conduct periodical inspections of the local forces, and of the military establishments in each Colony; and to advise and act as referee of the several Governments in military questions and questions of discipline. In time of peace he should not perform any act of executive command, nor in any way interfere with the Commandants. In time of war he should assume supreme direction of the military affairs of the Colonies.

We have already alluded to the services of Sir W. D. Jervois, and we desire now to draw attention to those of Colonel Scratchley, who has been actively engaged during the last four years in superintending the construction of the works, inspecting the local forces, and generally advising the Governments of the several Colonies on matters connected with their defences. The success which has attended the mission of these two distinguished officers—marked, as it has been, by conspicuous zeal and ability in carrying out a difficult and delicate task—affords strong presumptive evidence of the feasibility of such a measure as we propose, and points to the advantage which the Colonies derive from the presence of well selected Imperial officers.

Although it may not be expedient to press upon the Colonial Governments to take steps at once to secure joint action of the different colonial forces, the advantages gained by troops, whether permanent or volunteer, occasionally meeting and training in concert, are so manifest that such an officer would doubtless feel it his duty to advise an experiment in this direction. Such advice, given with tact and judgment, and shown to be practicable, would have weight with the Colonial authorities.

The advantage derived from competent officers and instructors from the Imperial service being attached to colonial corps having been brought to our notice, we think that applications to the Imperial Government for the services of such officers or instructors, whether military or naval, should receive prompt compliance; their services to be in all cases for a limited period, during which they should be paid by the Colony where they may be serving.

We think it most desirable that an efficient torpedo corps should be maintained in each Colony. A torpedo corps and artillery stand in the same category, and are of first importance in any system of defence. We agree with Colonel Scratchley in thinking that, whilst maintaining the character of the corps as a military body, efficiency in purely military drill is not necessary, but that, the nature of the work being exceptional, more training is required than for the ordinary military exercises.

There are other points in connection with the land forces which have been brought to our notice: but those above referred to seem to us the most important, and, indeed, essential to their efficiency.

We will conclude our observations by stating that there are some ports, the cost of defending which it is hardly reasonable to expect a single Colony to bear, and with regard to which we think the Australian Governments might well consider the expediency of providing the defence in common. King George's Sound in Western Australia is a strong case in point. The harbour is an admirable one, and the evidence we have received shows that, though of considerable importance from a commercial point of view, it is not of much use to your Majesty's ships. But, we do not anticipate that the Colony of Western Australia would be able to provide and maintain defences at her sole expense, although Colonel Scratchley is disposed to think that she could do so with some assistance.

With regard to the larger question of the naval defence of Australia generally as an integral portion of the British Empire and of Australian commerce on the high seas, the time, in our opinion, has arrived when the Colonies may reasonably be expected to take upon themselves some share of that defence—a burden hitherto exclusively borne by the mother-country.

Looking to the fact that only one Colony has availed itself of the powers given by the Colonial Naval Defence Act, and that the vessel acquired by Victoria as a sea-going ship has practically been converted into a vessel for harbour defence, we do not suggest that these Colonies should maintain sea-going ships of their own for action beyond their territorial waters. To such a plan there are many objections; and even if the Colonies were willing to undertake the heavy expenditure of purchasing such ships, it is doubtful whether considering the rapid changes in the construction and armament of sea-going vessels of war, they would long continue to be efficient.

But we see no reason why the Australian Colonies should not make a moderate contribution in money towards the cost of that squadron which is maintained by the mother-country for the protection of interests common to the Colonies and herself.

How the amount of contribution should be calculated is a matter of detail and would require further discussion: but speaking generally, it would seem that each Colony should pay a sum proportioned to its commerce and population, and it would be desirable that the amount should be periodically revised.

We are aware that at the Intercolonial Conference held at Sidney in January, 1881, a Resolution was adopted in the following terms: —

> That, in the opinion of this Conference, considering the large Imperial interests involved, the naval defence of these Colonies should continue to be the exclusive charge of the Imperial Government, and that the strength of the Australian squadron should be increased. That the members of this Conference pledge themselves to use all legitimate endeavours to procure the efficient fortifications and land defence of the several ports of the Australian Colonies at the cost of the several Colonies interested.

In the face of that Resolution we hesitate to recommend that a formal proposal should at this moment be made to the several Colonies on the subject; but we think that no fair opportunity should be lost of bringing and keeping the matter before the Australian people, and if this is done with tact and judgment we cannot doubt that, with a continuance of the good feeling which now happily exists, public opinion in Australia will soon be ripe for a satisfactory settlement of the question.

Experience has shown that war evokes a hearty spirit of loyalty in your Majesty's Australian Dependencies, and there is reason to hope that considering their fast-increasing prosperity, the larger Colonies will, before long, be prepared, even in times of peace, to accept the principle of a contribution towards the cost of the Australian squadron, and that the other Colonies will follow their example.

The Colonies will recognize that in the protection of commerce in the Australian seas their interest is not less than that of the mother-country, and whilst Great Britain will willingly bear the greater share in the defence of her dependencies, a glance at the subjoined Table will show how wide is the disproportion in taxation for defence purposes borne by the populations of the United Kingdom and Australia respectively.

* * *

Correspondence in Preparation for the First Colonial
Conference together with a Report of the Conference,
November 1886 – July 1887*

25TH NOVEMBER, 1886

You will no doubt have remarked that in the Queen's Speech on the prorogation of Parliament, Her Majesty was pleased to refer to Her Colonial and Indian Possessions in the following terms:

> I have observed with much satisfaction the interest which, in an increasing degree, is evinced by the people of this country in the welfare of their Colonial and Indian fellow subjects; and I am led to the conviction that there is on all sides a growing desire to draw closer in every practicable way the bonds which unite the various portions of the Empire. I have authorised communications to be entered into with the principal Colonial Governments with a view to the fuller consideration of matters of common interest.

2. The communications thus promised with the Colonies have engaged the careful consideration of Her Majesty's Government, and they have come to the conclusion that the Queen should be advised to summon a Conference, to meet in London in the early part of next year, at which representatives of the principal Colonial Governments will be invited to attend for the discussion of those questions which appear more particularly to demand attention at the present time. I request you to inform your Ministers of this proposal, which I am confident will be very satisfactory to them, and to express the hope which I entertain of their cordial co-operation.

3. In the opinion of Her Majesty's Government, the question which is at once urgent and capable of useful consideration at the present time is that of organisation for military defence. The patriotic action of the Colonies in offering contingents of troops to take part in the Egyptian campaign made a deep and lasting impression on the public mind, and was the first practical result of much careful work during recent years. It is a necessity of the case that the measures which have been taken in each Colony, as well for the organisation of the local forces as for the construction of local defensive works, are, to a great extent, not yet fully understood and appreciated in other parts of the Empire. The close and thorough examination of the whole subject of Imperial Defence, which was completed by the Royal Commission presided over by the Earl of Carnarvon, has led

Parliamentary Papers, 1887, LVI, Cmd. 5091, vii–xiii.

to the execution of extensive and important defensive works in various parts of the Empire; and the cordial co-operation offered to Her Majesty's Government by the Colonies in carrying out this policy indicates their desire to arrive, so far as may at present be practicable, at a common basis of action. This work is still being actively pressed on with the assistance of a Standing Committee, which is continuously occupied with matters relating to Colonial Defence.

4. Much yet remains to be done; and it is of course unavoidable that secrecy should continue to be observed with regard to many of the defensive measures in progress or in contemplation. The time has, however, now arrived when an attempt may fairly be made to attain to a better understanding as to the system of defence which may be established throughout the Empire. For this purpose an interchange of knowledge as to the state of preparation or as to the capabilities of organisation in each Colony, would lead to a more thorough understanding of their wants and wishes; but whilst Her Majesty's Government would thus be prepared to recommend for the consideration of the Conference certain principles calculated to promote the general defence of the Empire, it is not our intention in calling the Conference to commit either the Imperial Government or any Colony to new projects entailing heavy expenditure, but rather to secure that the sums which may be devoted to this purpose may be utilized to the fullest extent, with complete knowledge of all the conditions of the problem.

5. Second only in importance to this great question is one concerning in a special degree the interests of the Empire in time of peace. The promotion of commercial and social relations by the development of our postal and telegraphic communications could be considered with much advantage by the proposed Conference. It is a subject the conditions of which are constantly changing. New requirements come into existence, and new projects are formulated, every year. It is obviously desirable that the question of Imperial intercommunication should be considered as a whole, in order that the needs of every part of the Empire may, as far as practicable, be provided for, and that suggestions may be obtained from all quarters as to the best means of establishing a complete system of communications without that increased expenditure which necessarily results from isolated action.

6. Two leading subjects for consideration have been referred to, but it is not impossible that there may be some other important question which in the general opinion of the Colonial Governments might properly and usefully be brought under consideration. But I should deprecate the discussion at the present time of any of the subjects falling within the range of what is known as Political Feder-

ation. There has been no expression of Colonial opinion in favour of any steps in that direction; and Her Majesty's Government are of opinion that there would be no advantage in the informal discussion of a very difficult problem before any basis has been accepted by the Governments concerned. It might, indeed, be detrimental to the ultimate attainment of a more developed system of united action if a question not yet ripe for practical decision were now to be brought to the test of a formal examination.

7. The Conference will necessarily be purely consultative, and it will therefore not be material that the Colonies should have equal or proportional representation upon it. The desire of Her Majesty's Government would rather be that its constitution should be sufficiently comprehensive to include, in addition to the Agent-General or other specially deputed representative of each Government, any leading public man who may be at liberty to come to England next year, and may be specially qualified to take a useful part in the deliberations. It will, I think, be convenient that I should preside at the Conference, and I need not say that I anticipate much advantage to myself and to Her Majesty's Government from the opportunities of acquiring information which will thus be afforded to me.

8. I will only add, in conclusion, that I am confident that your Government will, as I do, feel deep interest in this first attempt to bring all parts of Her Majesty's Empire into joint deliberation. However modest the commencement may be, results may grow out of it affecting, in a degree which it is at present difficult to appreciate, the interests of the Empire and of the Civilized world.

I have, &c.,

Edward Stanhope

To The Governors of Colonies
Under Responsible Government

P.S.—My own opinion is that the best time for meeting would be the month of April or May, but I should be glad in this matter to be guided by the general opinion of the Colonial Governments.

25th NOVEMBER, 1886

I have the honour to enclose a copy of a despatch which I have addressed to the Governors of the Colonies under Responsible Government, inviting the Governments of those Colonies to nominate a representative, or representatives, to take part in a Conference which it is proposed to hold next year for the purpose of discussing certain questions of common interest to all parts of the Empire.

It is the wish of Her Majesty's Government that, in the consideration of these questions, the interests of all the Colonies should be duly considered at the Conference; and in the case of any Crown

Colony which may not send a special representative, I shall take care that proper provision is made for securing such consideration.

If, however, you are in a position to furnish me with the name of any high officer or leading public man connected with your Colony who is likely to be in London during the spring of next year, I shall be able, should circumstances render it desirable, to arrange for his presence at the Conference on any occasion on which matters specially affecting your Colony are likely to come under discussion.

I have, &c.,

Edward Stanhope

To The Governors Of The
Crown Colonies

23RD JULY, 1887

I have the honour to transmit to you the Report of the proceedings of the recent Colonial Conference, together with copies of papers which were laid before it.

The invitation to the Conference contained in Mr. Stanhope's despatch of the 25th of November last met with a prompt and gratifying acceptance in all quarters. The self-governing Colonies sent as their delegates Ministers, ex-Ministers, or other distinguished Colonists; while, at Meetings in which the Crown Colonies were interested, representative gentlemen, deputed by the local Governments or invited by myself, were present and took part in the proceedings.

The opening meeting was held on April the 4th, and the Conference closed on the 9th of May.

The first meeting was attended by the Prime Minister and many of my colleagues, as well as by members of the late Ministry, former Secretaries and under Secretaries of State for the Colonies, members of both Houses of Parliament, and other eminent men well known for their interest in matters relating to the Colonies. The meeting was addressed by the Marquis of Salisbury, Earl Granville, Mr. Stanhope, myself, and the representatives of the Colonies, whose speeches will be found in the Report of the Proceedings.

Subsequently, when questions specially concerning particular departments have been under consideration, the Conference has had the advantage of the presence and assistance in its deliberations of the members of Her Majesty's Government presiding over such departments together with other departmental officers and experts.

These arrangements, I have every reason to believe, met with the approval of the Conference; and I am deeply sensible of the loyal support which I received from all its members, and of the courteous and considerate spirit which animated the meetings throughout, and maintained the harmony of their proceedings unbroken.

The Report is a verbatim account of all that passed, except that the discussion of the questions relating to the Pacific Islands is not included, and that in one or two other cases I have thought it desirable, in the exercise of my discretion, to omit short portions of the discussion which were of a conversational character, or had no practical bearing on the business under consideration.

I will now refer briefly to the main results arrived at on the various questions submitted to the Conference; though it must be remembered that as the Conference was assembled for consultation and discussion only, its members were not empowered to bind their Governments to any final decisions upon the questions submitted.

The subject of the organization of Colonial Defence comes first in order of importance, and that position was assigned to it by my predecessor, Mr. Stanhope, who now fills the office of Secretary of State for War.

There can be no doubt that the time had arrived for mutual discussion of this important subject. The great efforts which have been made by many of the Colonies in the direction of local defence, have not, perhaps, been sufficiently realized in this country, and on all accounts it was desirable that this vitally important question should be fully considered. I believe that the Conference has been productive of the greatest good in the opportunity for the interchange of information which it has afforded; and I trust that it will lead to a consolidation of the great military resources of the Empire for purposes of mutual defence.

Summary statements forming a valuable and interesting record of the progress of all the self-governing colonies in matters relating to defence, were laid before the Conference, and will be confidentially communicated to the Colonial Governments; but it is not desirable to include them among the published papers. These statements are extremely gratifying to Her Majesty's Government as shewing the energy, ability, and self-sacrifice with which the Colonies have contributed their share towards the general defence of the Empire. Thus, dealing with *personnel* only, it appears that in the Dominion of Canada the available force of active militia, together with the permanent corps, amounts to nearly 37,000 men; in the Australasian Colonies the total armed strength is no less than 34,000; and in the Cape and Natal there are trained forces of 5,500 and 1,500 men respectively. There is, moreover, in each case a large reserve which can be drawn upon in case of need.

Valuable information was also given in the concise account supplied by Mr. Stanhope of the measures taken with regard to the first-class coaling stations which are being fortified for the purpose of maintaining communication with the distant dependencies of the Empire, and protecting the floating trade in the event of war.

I have been able, after consulting the Earl of Carnarvon, who was President of the Royal Commission on the Defence of British Possessions and Commerce abroad, to include among the papers important extracts from the Reports of that Commission. At my request Lord Carnarvon has been good enough to undertake the necessary revision of those Reports, and the Secretary of State for War, as well as the First Lord of the Admiralty, have concurred in their publication.

The special subject of the defences of the Cape of Good Hope (Table Bay and Simon's Bay) was discussed by Mr. Stanhope and myself with the representatives from South Africa. The Imperial Government has undertaken, in the case of Table Bay, to provide an armament, estimated at £75,000, the superintendence of the works, and all special technical fittings, the Cape Government agreeing to find the sites (where necessary), the materials and the labour for the erection of the necessary works. With regard to the fortification of Simon's Bay, it has been agreed that the Imperial Government shall defray the entire cost.

Proposals for the defence of King George's Sound (Princess Royal Harbour) and Torres Straits (Thursday Island) formed the subject of another special discussion. Her Majesty's Government proposed that the cost of erecting, maintaining, and defending such works as are considered necessary should be borne by the United Australasian Colonies. Having, however, at a period of great emergency offered to provide such armament as could then be sent out immediately, Her Majesty's Government did not desire to recede from that offer, and accordingly proposed to provide a muzzle-loading armament, considered by the War Office to be sufficiently effective, which could be gradually replaced by new type guns, as soon as the Colonies were in a position to provide them.

The Australasian representatives were, however, of opinion that a new type armament should be provided at once as the Imperial contribution; but in view of the heavy expenditure on armament which is being incurred in accordance with the recommendations of the Royal Commission for more important stations elsewhere, Mr. Stanhope and myself were unable to do more than promise full consideration of the views put forward.

The most valuable decision arrived at by means of the Conference was that relating to the increase of the Australasian squadron, for the protection of the floating trade. Proposals had been made on the subject by the Admiralty through Admiral Tryon, by whom preliminary negotiations had been entered into with the Premiers of New South Wales, Victoria, and Queensland at a meeting held in Sydney on board H.M.S. "Nelson," in April 1886. The Australasian representatives have now unanimously agreed that the terms of the approved agreement, which will be found in the proceedings of the 6th of May, should be submitted by the respective Colonial Governments to their Parliaments for ratification. The agreement is for ten years, in the first instance, and under its terms five fast cruisers and two torpedo gunboats will be added to the squadron under the command of the Admiral, such vessels to be retained for service within the limits of the Australasian station,—the Colonies agreeing to pay for maintenance a sum not exceeding £91,000 per annum, and for depreciation a percentage of 5 per cent. on the initial cost, which, with other incidental charges, is estimated to amount to a further sum not exceeding £35,000 per annum.

Other matters of a general character in connection with the subject of Colonial Defence were brought forward, as, for example, the engagement under improved and favourable conditions of active and retired Imperial officers for service in Colonial forces, and the question of the employment of Colonial forces beyond the limits of the Colony to which they belong. Mr. Stanhope also willingly agreed to meet the wishes expressed at the Conference for the appointment of an Imperial Officer as Inspecting Officer of the Australian local forces, and as Military Adviser to the several Governments, for the purpose of conducting periodical inspections of the local forces and military defences.

Several subjects relating to the improvement of Postal and Telegraphic communication between the Colonies and the Mother country also engaged the careful consideration of the Conference.

The three Postal questions to which I invited attention were (1) the scheme for an Imperial Penny postage; (2) the question of the Australasian and South African Colonies joining the Postal Union; (3) the renewal of the arrangements for carrying the mails to Australia.

With regard to (1), I gathered that in the general opinion of the Conference the reduction of postage to a penny would be impracticable for financial reasons.

With respect to (2), the representatives clearly expressed the unwillingness of the Colonies to enter the Postal Union without adequate representation, to which they considered that a comparison with other countries possessing votes entitled them. They also felt debarred from doing so on account of the anticipated diminution of Postal Revenue.

The third question, which more immediately concerned the three Colonial Governments who have undertaken to provide the subsidy, was only partially discussed, as the negotiations were already far advanced. Several representatives, however, expressed a decided opinion in favour of the resumption of a cheaper supplementary service by sea only; and it was further urged that negotiations should be entered into with the French and Italian Governments for the reduction of the present transit rates.

The important proposals of the Canadian Pacific Railway Company for a service of powerful steamers between Vancouver and Hong Kong, by way of Japan, was not discussed at length in the Conference, being already under the consideration of Her Majesty's Government. Attention was, however, called by the Canadian representatives to this scheme, as well as to that for establishing a line of steamers from Vancouver to Australia, and it was stated that the mails could be carried to Australian and Asiatic ports in considerably less time, and at less cost, by these Pacific routes than at present.

In connection with the subject of telegraphic communication, the proposal of an alternative line to Australia was prominently brought forward. The Colonial representatives were of opinion that their Governments would not, unless the Imperial Government also contributed, be willing to subsidize another company in addition to the Eastern Extension Telegraph Company; and on behalf of the Imperial Post Office, it was stated that the question of such a subsidy could not be entertained by that department. While, therefore, I expressed my willingness to bring before Her Majesty's Government the wishes of the members of the Conference that a line might be constructed for military purposes, to be exclusively controlled by the Government, I could not hold out any hope that such a scheme would be favourably received.

Two alternative routes were suggested, one by way of the Cape of Good Hope, and the other from Vancouver. The latter was warmly advocated by the representatives of the Dominion of Canada, as being a route deserving to be placed in competition with the existing line in point of speed, convenience, and economy, and as possessing the additional advantage of passing entirely over British territory by means of the Canadian Pacific Railway which has recently been brought to a successful completion. The Conference expressed their admiration at the energy and enterprise shown in carrying out that great undertaking, and marked their sense of the Imperial importance of the connecting link thus established by their ready assent to the two propositions submitted by Sir Alexander Campbell on this subject on the 6th of May. On the other hand, proposals were submitted on behalf of the Eastern Extension Telegraph Company for a reduction of the telegraph rates upon the condition of a guarantee from the Colonial Governments.

The questions connected with the Pacific Islands to which I made reference in my opening speech were fully discussed.

Her Majesty's Government having desired to receive a frank expression of the opinion of the Australasian representatives on the position of affairs in the New Hebrides and elsewhere in the Pacific, and to give full and unreserved explanations, it was thought desirable to place no restrictions upon the discussion, which consequently ranged over a wide field, comprising suggestions as to British policy, and comments upon the policy and action of foreign powers, which it would not be advantageous to publish. It has therefore been decided that the detailed account of the proceedings in relation to this subject should not be included in the Report. I may, however, state that while the Australasian representatives generally concurred in expressing dissatisfaction at the present position of British interests in the Pacific, there was a divergence of opinion as to the course which might be most beneficial to their interests in the future; and it was ultimately agreed unanimously that the proposal of Her Majesty's Government to preserve the neutrality of the New Hebrides under a joint Anglo-French Naval Commission was a satisfactory one, and should be pressed on as speedily as possible, being the best that could, in the present circumstances, be adopted.

A strong protest, however, was placed on record against any further deportation of French Recidivists to New Caledonia, or any extension of that system to other islands in the Pacific.

With regard to Samoa, the Conference approved the proposal now being considered at Washington by representatives of Germany, the United States, and this country, that one of the three Great Powers having interests in the group should for a term control native affairs there.

The settlement of the administration of British New Guinea upon a proper footing with a view to the assumption of the Queen's sovereignty over the southern portion of the island has also been accomplished, and the draft bill approved by the Conference and included among the Papers given in the Appendix sets forth the conditions of the arrangement. The Colony of Queensland, concurrently with the Colonies of New South Wales and Victoria, has engaged to defray the cost of administration to the extent of £15,-000 a year for ten years, whilst Her Majesty's Imperial Government will provide a suitable steam vessel, with the cost of its maintenance for three years, at an estimated total cost of £ 29,000.

Various questions in connection with trade were debated, such as the adoption by the Colonies of similar legislation to that proposed in the Mother country with regard to merchandize marks and patents, and the effect of foreign bounties upon the sugar trade of the Colonies. In regard to this last question, the representatives generally urged that in justice to Colonial industries and trade which are injuriously affected by the sugar bounties, Her Majesty's Government should spare no effort to bring about the abolition of that unsound system.

Among the suggestions put forward was a proposal that commerce within the Empire should be encouraged by imposing a duty of an equal rate on all imports entering the Empire from foreign countries, and that the revenue thereby acquired should be applied to the defence of the Empire.

It was also urged that permission should be given to the self-governing Colonies to enter into direct negotiations with foreign Powers in regard to Trade matters, as had been allowed in the case of Canada.

Another important series of questions discussed related to the Enforcement of Colonial Judgments and Orders in Bankruptcy, and Winding-up of Companies. The desirability of establishing a common procedure was fully recognised, and a general agreement arrived at as to the principles of two draft bills on the subject, which will be found among the printed papers. Consideration was also given to the best method of giving effect to Colonial Wills, whether by resealing the Probate, or some other procedure, and complaint was made of the cost of proving such wills in England, when the only property involved might be shares upon the Colonial Register of an English Company.

Three questions of interest to the Colonial Governments in connection with their loans were also brought forward, viz., the Investment of Trust Funds in Colonial Stock, the Stamp Duties on the Transfer of Colonial Inscribed Stock, and the position of Unclaimed Dividends on Colonial Stock.

Advantage was taken of the Conference to elicit the views of its members with regard to the best means to be adopted for the preservation of life at sea, a subject which has recently been investigated by a Royal Commission; and the question of conducting the next census of the Empire in 1891 under identical conditions in all parts of Her Majesty's Possessions was considered.

The only other subject to which I need allude is the suggestion which has been made that it would be desirable to extend the Queen's style and title so as to include a reference to the Colonies. The members of the Conference were invited to express an opinion upon it, and were generally favourable to the proposal. It was, however, thought desirable to ascertain the views of the Colonial Governments, and their replies, as far as they have yet been received, do not indicate any general wish for the change, though there would be a ready acquiescence if Her Majesty should think it desirable.

I have further to add that on the 4th of May the Colonial representatives proceeded to Windsor and personally presented to the Queen addresses on behalf of the Colonies they represented, as well as a joint address of loyal congratulation, to which her Majesty returned a most gracious reply. The terms of the joint address and of Her Majesty's reply are appended to this despatch.

Many other addresses of a similar character from all parts of Her Majesty's Colonial dominions have been received at this time, and have been duly laid by me before the Queen; and Her Majesty has commanded me to take this occasion of expressing her appreciation of the great loyalty and affection of Her Colonies, as well as the sincere pleasure with which Her Majesty has learnt the success of the Conference.

I have, &c.,

H. T. Holland

The Officer
Administering The Government

---

*Official Text Summarizing the Proceedings
of the Colonial Conference, June – July 1897**

On Thursday, the 24th of June, the Prime Ministers of Canada, New South Wales, Victoria, New Zealand, Queensland, Cape Colony, South Australia, Newfoundland, Tasmania, Western Australia, and Natal, assembled at the Colonial Office, Downing Street, for the discussion of certain Imperial questions with the Secretary of State for the Colonies. It was decided that the proceedings should be informal and that the general results only should be published. With the view of giving a definite direction to the discussion, the Secretary of State [JOSEPH CHAMBERLAIN] in opening the proceedings, set forth the subjects which he considered might usefully be discussed, so as to secure an interchange of views upon them, and where they were ripe for a statement of opinion, a definite resolution in regard to them, in the following speech:

"I have made arrangements for a full shorthand report of all our proceedings, which will be confidential, unless we otherwise desire, but copies, of course, will be furnished to every gentleman for reference, and possibly later on, if we come to any conclusions, we may consider further whether it is desirable or not that any public statement should be made. In the meantime, until we come to a united conclusion upon the subject, the proceedings will be treated as absolutely confidential.

I desire at the outset of these proceedings to offer to you, on behalf of Her Majesty's Government, a hearty and cordial welcome. You will have seen in your short visit to this country that all parties,

Parliamentary Papers, 1897, LIX, Cmd. 8596, 4–15.

and all classes, are animated by the most affectionate feelings of regard towards our Colonial fellow subjects. I think that you may also feel that the main object of your visit has already been to a great extent accomplished. The great pageant to which you contributed so interesting a feature has shown to this country, to the Colonies, and to all the world, the strength, the power, the resources, and the loyalty of the British Empire. It was, I think we shall all agree, a most remarkable and absolutely unparalleled demonstration of personal loyalty to a Sovereign and of the essential unity of the Empire.

Her Majesty's Government, while very anxious to take this opportunity of an interchange of views with you on many matters of common interest, have carefully avoided suggesting anything in the nature of a formal Conference. We do so, in the first place because we do not wish to detract in any way from the personal character of this visit, and also because we do not desire to take advantage of your presence to force upon you discussions on which you might be unwilling at this moment to enter. On the other hand we are open to consider in the most friendly and the most favourable way any representations which may be made to us by the representatives of the self-governing Colonies, having regard to the present or the future relations between the different parts of the Empire, and in this respect we are in the position of those who desire rather to learn your views than to press ours upon you. I might, I think, upon this sit down and invite your opinions, but it has been suggested to me, and it seems reasonable to suppose, that it might be convenient to you at this, our preliminary meeting, if I were to state as briefly as I can the subjects which appear to us to be most worthy of our joint consideration, and then it will be for you to say whether these subjects, or any of them, are such as you would like to consider more formally and in detail, in which case I hope we may arrange for subsequent interviews with that object; but to-day I will state for your consideration a list of subjects, and I will ask you to give me your views as to the way in which they should subsequently be dealt with.

Political Relations

Now, gentlemen, undoubtedly the greatest, the most important, and at the same time the most difficult of all the subjects which we could consider is the question of the future relations, political and commercial, between the self-governing Colonies and the United Kingdom. I do not think that it is necessary for me to argue at all upon the advantages of such closer union. Strong as is the bond of sentiment, and impossible as it would be to establish any kind of

relations unless that bond of sentiment existed, I believe we all feel
that it would be desirable to take advantage of it, and to still further
tighten the ties which bind us together. In this country, at all events,
I may truly say that the idea of federation is in the air. Whether with
you it has gone as far, it is for you to say, and it is also for you to
consider whether we can give any practical application to the principle. It may well be that the time is hardly ripe for anything definite
in this regard. It is quite true that our own constitution and your
constitutions have all been the subject of very slow growth and that
they are all the stronger because they have been gradually consolidated, and so perhaps with Imperial Federation: if it is ever to be
accomplished it will be only after the lapse of a considerable time
and only by gradual steps.

And undoubtedly one of those steps to which we must all attach
very great importance is the grouping of the Colonies. We rejoice in
this country that Canada has already shown the way, with results
which everyone has seen have conduced greatly to her strength and
to her prosperity. We observe, with the most lively interest, the
proceedings which are taking place in Australia with the same view.
We know that in South African politics the same idea has bulked
very largely in the past, and probably will come to the front again.
In regard to all these matters it is not for us to offer advice; it is not
for us to press upon you in any shape our interference or our
assistance. If it be possible for us in any way to help you to give
effect to your own desires, I need not say that we are entirely at
your service; but, in the meanwhile, I can assure you, on behalf, I
am sure, of the people of this country that we most heartily wish
success to your efforts, believing, as I have said, that it will in your
case, as it has already done in the case of Canada, conduce to your
prosperity and to your power. But as regards the larger question,
and anything in the nature of a federation of the Empire, the subject
seems to me to depend entirely upon the feeling which exists in the
Colonies themselves. Here you will be met half way. The question is
whether up to the present time there is such a genuine popular
demand for closer union as would justify us in considering practical
proposals to give it shape.

I feel that there is a real necessity for some better machinery of
consultation between the self-governing Colonies and the mother
country, and it has sometimes struck me—I offer it now merely as a
personal suggestion—that it might be feasible to create a great
council of the Empire to which the Colonies would send representative plenipotentiaries,—not mere delegates who were unable to
speak in their name, without further reference to their respective
Governments, but persons who by their position in the Colonies, by
their representative character, and by their close touch with Colonial

feeling, would be able, upon all subjects submitted to them, to give really effective and valuable advice. If such a council were to be created it would at once assume an immense importance, and it is perfectly evident that it might develop into something still greater. It might slowly grow to that Federal Council to which we must always look forward as our ultimate ideal.

And to a council of this kind would be committed, in the first instance, the discussion of all minor subjects of common interest, and their opinion would be taken and would weigh most materially in the balance before any decision were come to either by this country or by the legislatures of the several Colonies in regard to such matters.

There is only one point in reference to this which it is absolutely necessary that we all should bear in mind. It may be that the time has come, and if not I believe it will come, when the Colonies will desire to substitute for the slight relationship which at present exists a true partnership, and in that case they will want their share in the management of the Empire which we like to think is as much theirs as it is ours. But, of course, with the privilege of management and of control will also come the obligation and the responsibility. There will come some form of contribution towards the expense for objects which we shall have in common. That, I say, is self evident, but it is to be borne in mind, even in these early stages of the consideration of the subject.

Now, gentlemen, in connection with this subject we have already made a small advance, upon which I congratulate myself, since it was accomplished during my term of office, though it was prepared by my predecessors; and it may have in the future important results. The Judicial Committee of the Privy Council is the great Judicial Court of Appeal of the Empire. It is the nearest approach, the closest analogy, to the Supreme Court of the United States. It is a body of almost universal and world wide reputation and authority, and it is our desire naturally, in pursuit of the ideas which I am venturing to put before you, to increase its authority, if that be possible, and to give it a more representative character, and with that view we have most gladly secured the appointment as Privy Councillors of distinguished Judges from the courts of Canada, of Australia, and of South Africa, and they now will take their seats on equal terms with the other members of the Judicial Committee. Well, gentlemen, that is a good beginning, but I do not think that you can feel that at present the arrangement is on a permanent footing. There are objections to the present system which will present themselves to every mind. The Judges who have been chosen have hitherto been Judges who are still in active practice. That at the outset raises a considerable difficulty. It will be difficult for these Judges, even if it were consistent with our general idea of what is right, to take part in appeals in regard to cases upon which they have already decided. And another difficulty is that by the necessity of their position the greater part of their time will be spent in the colonies from which they come. They will only be here for indefinite periods, and, as it were on casual occasions. It is impossible to arrange the business of the Privy Council or to delay the suitors to meet their convenience, and the result of that is that though they would sit as Judges of the Privy Council, it may very often happen that they would not be present or be able to serve precisely on the occasions on which they might be most useful. Now all that could be altered by the Colonies themselves, and this is one of the subjects which I recommend to your attention. If these gentlemen were appointed solely and entirely for the purpose of representing the groups of Colonies on the Privy Council, they could reside permanently in this country, and not being themselves actively engaged in judicial work at home, they could sit and assist the Privy Council in all cases in which their respective Colonies were engaged; and I think this would go very far to strengthen the position of the Privy Council, and at the same time to give to all the Colonies a security that justice would be done when they appeal to this great institution. May I note in passing a matter of some importance in regard to the proposed Australian Federation Bill; it appears in that Bill to be suggested that if it is passed appeals should only go to the Privy Council upon constitutional questions. I venture most respectfully to urge the reconsideration of that suggestion. Nothing is more desirable in the interests of the Colonies, in the interests of the United Kingdom and of the British Empire, than an uniformity of law, and that uniformity can only be obtained by occasional appeals to the highest tribunal, settling once for all the law for all parts of the Empire; and I confess I think it would be a great loss to the Colonists if they surrendered the opportunity of getting this judicial decision upon difficult and complicated points of law which from time to time may arise in the local courts.

Defence

I have said that the question to which I first directed your attention—that of closer relations—is greater than all the rest. I may say that it covers all the rest, because, of course, if Federation were established, or anything approaching to it, all these other questions to which I am now about to call your attention would be settled by whatever was the representative body of the Federation, and among them, and in the very first rank, must of necessity come the question of Imperial defence. Gentlemen, you have seen something of the military strength of the Empire; you will see on Saturday an astounding representation of its naval strength, by which alone a Colonial Empire can be bound together. You are aware that that representation—great, magnificent, unparalleled as it will be—is nevertheless only a part of the naval forces of the Empire spread in every part of the globe. The great Mediterranean fleet is still at its full force; the fleets on the various stations are all up to their normal strength, and the fleet which you will see on Saturday next is merely the Reserve and the Home fleet, ready to go anywhere, at any time, in the interests of the Colonies and of the United Kingdom.

This gigantic navy, and the military forces of the United Kingdom, are maintained, as you know, at heavy cost. I think the charge upon the Exchequer is at the present time something like 35 millions sterling per annum, and it constitutes more than one-third of the total income of the country. Now, these fleets, and this military armament, are not maintained exclusively, or even mainly, for the benefit of the United Kingdom, or for the defence of home interests. They are still more maintained as a necessity of empire, for the maintenance and protection of Imperial trade and of Imperial interests all over the world, and if you will for a moment consider the history of this country during, say, the present century, or, I would say, during the present reign, you will find that every war, great or small, in which we have been engaged, has had at the bottom a colonial interest, the interest, that is to say, either of a colony, or of a great dependency like India. That is absolutely true, and is likely to be true to the end of the chapter. If we had no Empire, there is no doubt whatever that our military and our naval resources would not require to be maintained at anything like their present level.

Now I venture to say that that must necessarily be the case in the future. Look at the condition of the Colonies. Assume,—although I am almost ashamed to assume it, even for the purpose of argument,—assume that these Colonies were separated from the mother country. What would be the position of the great Dominion of Canada? The Dominion of Canada is bordered for 3,000 miles by a most powerful neighbour, whose potentialities are infinitely greater than her actual resources. She comes into conflict in regard to the most important interests with the rising power of Japan, and even in regard to some of her interests with the great empire of Russia. Now, let it not be supposed for a moment that I suggest as probable—I hardly like to think that it is even possible—that there should be a war between Canada, or on behalf of Canada, either with the United States of America, or with any of the other Powers with which she may come into contact, but what I do say is this, that if Canada had not behind her to-day, and does not continue to have behind her this great military and naval power of Great Britain, she would have to make concessions to her neighbours, and to accept views which might be extremely distasteful to her in order to remain permanently on good terms with them. She would not be able to, it would be impossible that she should, herself control all the details of her own destiny; she would be, to a greater or less extent, in spite of the bravery of her population and the patriotism of her people, she would still be, to a great extent, a dependent country.

Look at Australia again. I need not dwell on the point at any length, but we find the same thing. The interests of Australia have already, on more than one occasion, threatened to come into conflict with those of two of the greatest military nations of the Continent, and military nations, let me add, who also possess each of them a very large, one of them an enormous, fleet. There may be also questions of difficulty arising with Eastern nations, with Japan or even with China, and under those circumstances the Australasian Colonies are in precisely the same position as the Dominion of Canada. In South Africa, in addition to the ambitions of foreign countries, to which I need not further allude, our Colonies there have domestic rivals who are heavily armed, prepared both for offence and for defence; and again I say, nothing could be more suicidal or more fatal than for any of those great groups of Colonies either to separate themselves in the present stage from the protecting forces of the mother country, or to neglect themselves to take their fair share in those protective resources.

What, then, I want to urge upon you is, and in doing so, I think I am speaking to those who are already converted, that we have a common interest in this matter, and certainly it has been a great pleasure to us, a great pride to us, that Australia, in the first instance, offered voluntarily a contribution in aid of the British Navy besides taking her full share of her own military defences. Now we have to recognize that the Cape Colony has followed in that patriotic course. I do not know upon what conditions these gifts may be offered or continued, but, at all events, the spirit in which they have been made is most heartily reciprocated in this country. The amount, of course, is at the present time absolutely trifling, but that is not the point. We are looking to the Colonies as still children, but rapidly approaching manhood. In the lifetime, perhaps, of some of us, we shall see the population doubled, and certainly in the lifetime of our descendants there will be great nations where now there are comparatively sparse populations; and to establish in the early days this principle of mutual support and of a truly Imperial patriotism, is a great thing of which our Colonial statesmen may well be proud.

I shall be very glad to hear the views of the Premiers in regard to this question of any contribution which they think the Colonies would be willing to make in order to establish this principle in regard to the naval defence of the Empire. As regards the military defence of the Empire, I am bound to say that we are still behindhand, although a great deal has been done in recent years. As you know, the Colonial Defence Committee of experts has been sitting, and has accomplished already, with the assistance of the Colonies, a very great improvement in the state of things which existed before; but I cannot say from the information at my disposal that with all the magnificent resources of the Colonies their organisation at present is satisfactory. This is more a matter of detail, and I do not propose to dwell upon it now, but I would remind the Premiers assembled that if war breaks out war will be sudden, and there will be no time for preparation then. Therefore it is of the first importance that we, all having a common interest, should have beforehand a scheme of common defence against any possible or at all events any probable enemy, and we ought to have these schemes of defence before us. In the case of some of the Colonies schemes have already been prepared; in others no scheme has been prepared or concerted up to the present time, and I believe it is most desirable that that omission should be repaired. It is also most desirable in Australia especially, and to a lesser extent, although still to an important extent in South Africa, that there should be an uniformity in regard to the military preparations. An uniformity of arms is, I need scarcely say, of immense importance, as it gives us interchangeability of weapon, and there are also uniformity of equipment, some central provision for stores, and for the military instruction of the local forces, all of which can be arranged with the assistance of the Colonies, and, I believe, very much to their advantage.

Exchange of Military Forces

But I am looking forward to something more than that. The interchangeability in the several groups is a matter of great importance, but how much greater it would be if there were interchangeability between the whole forces of the Empire, between the forces which you have in the several Colonies and the forces of which you have seen some examples at home since you came to these shores. That is a matter which also can be arranged, and to which we shall bring at all events the utmost good will. If you have, as Canada has at Kingston, an important military college, it may be possible for us to offer occasionally to the cadets of that college commissions in the British Army. But a still more important matter which has suggested itself to my mind, and which now I desire to commend to your earnest attention, is a proposal which may be described as the interchangeability of military duties. To put it into plain English it means this: that, for instance, a Canadian regiment should come to this country, take up its quarters for a period of time, at least 12 months, with the British army, and form, during the whole time that it is in this country, a part of the British army, and that in return a similar regiment of British troops, or a brigade of artillery or cavalry, should go to Canada and should reside and exercise with the Canadian army, and form a part of that army. The idea is that this should be chiefly for the purpose of drill and instruction, and I cannot doubt that it will be of enormous advantage to the Canadian troops, and to the troops of the Colonies, to measure themselves against the regular army, and to learn the discipline and the manoeuvres which are practised on a large scale in this country.

But my imagination goes even further. It seems to me possible that although in the first instance the idea is that such a regiment coming to this country would come solely for that purpose and would not be engaged in military operations, yet if it were their wish to share in the dangers and the glories of the British army and take their part in expeditions in which the British army may be engaged, I see no reason why these colonial troops should not, from time to time, fight side by side with their British colleagues. That, however, is a matter which, like everything else which I am putting before you, is not a recommendation which has any pressure behind it; it is merely a suggestion to be taken up by you voluntarily if it commends itself to your minds. What I have suggested might take place with regard to Canada, I believe might equally take place with regard to such fine forces as those of which we have seen representatives from some of the Colonies of Australia, and might take place also with regard to the Sough African Colonies.

Commercial Relations

I pass on, then, to another question, and that is as to the future commercial relations between this country and her Colonies. How far is it possible to make those relations closer and more intimate? I have said that I believe in sentiment as the greatest of all the forces in the general government of the world, but at the same time, I should like to bring to the reinforcement of sentiment the motives which are derived from material and personal interest. But undoubtedly the fiscal arrangements of the different Colonies differ so much among themselves, and all differ so much from those of the mother country, that it would be a matter of the greatest complication and difficulty to arrive at any conclusion which would unite us commercially in the same sense in which the Zollverein united the empire of Germany. It may be borne in mind that the history of that Zollverein is most interesting and most instructive. It commenced entirely as a commercial convention, dealing in the first instance only partially with the trade of the empire, it was rapidly extended to include the whole trade of the empire, and it finally made possible and encouraged the ultimate union of the empire. But this is a matter upon which at the present time, rather than suggest any proposals of my own, I desire to hear the views of the gentlemen present.

In the meanwhile, however, I may say that I note a resolution which appears to have been passed unanimously at the meeting of the Premiers in Hobart, in which the desire was expressed for closer commercial arrangements with the Empire, and I think it was suggested that a Commission of Inquiry should be created in order to see in what way practical effect might be given to the aspiration. If that be the case, and if it were thought that at the present time you were not prepared to go beyond inquiry, if it were the wish of the other Colonies, of Canada and of the South African Colonies, to join in such an inquiry, Her Majesty's Government would be delighted to make arrangements for the purpose, and to accept any suggestions as to the form of the reference and the character and constitution of the Commission, and would very gladly take part in it.

But that brings me to another question connected with commercial relations, and of great importance. I refer to the treaties at present existing between the mother country, acting on behalf of the Colonies as well as of herself, and foreign countries. The question has been raised at various times in the shape of resolutions or suggestions from the Colonies that certain treaties, notably a treaty with Germany and a treaty with Belgium, should be denounced. It should be borne in mind that that is for us a most important question. Our trade with Germany and Belgium is larger than our trade with all the Colonies combined. It is possible that if we denounced those treaties Germany and Belgium would endeavour, I do not say whether they would succeed, but they might endeavour to retaliate, and for some time, at any rate, our commercial relations with these two countries might be disturbed. Therefore a step of that kind is one which can only be taken after the fullest consideration, and in deference to very strong opinion both in this country and in the Colonies. Now the question is brought to a practical issue, or may be brought to a practical issue, by the recent action of Canada. As all are aware, Canada has offered preferential terms to the mother country, and Germany and Belgium have immediately protested and claimed similar terms under these treaties. Her Majesty's Government desire to know from the Colonies whether, so far as they are concerned, if it be found that the arrangements proposed by Canada are inconsistent with the conditions of those treaties, they desire that those treaties shall be denounced. If that be the unanimous wish of the Colonies, after considering the effect of that denunciation upon them as well as upon us, because they also are concerned in the arrangements which are made by these treaties, then all I can say at the present time is that Her Majesty's Government will most earnestly consider such a recommendation from the Colonies, and will give to it the favourable regard which such a memorial deserves.

But I should add that there is another question which is still more difficult, but about which I only wish to offer a word of warning to the representatives present. Besides those two treaties which are very special in their terms, and which prevent the preferential arrangement, or which appear to prevent the preferential arrangement contemplated by Canada, we have a most favoured nation clause in all our treaties to which most of the Colonies are parties. I may explain that, under the terms of the Canadian resolution, if any foreign nation were to offer to Canada beneficial terms as defined in the resolution, Canada would then be bound to give to that country the same preference as is offered to Great Britain. Let me suppose, for instance, that it was a minor country like Holland, and assume for the sake of argument that Holland offered these advantages, thereupon Canada would be compelled to give the same terms to Holland that she now offers to the mother country. She would then be bound by most favoured nation treaties to give the same terms to practically every important commercial country in the world. It would be, I think, a matter of impossibility to denounce those treaties, because that involves the whole trade of the empire, and in some cases there is no term of denunciation in the treaties.

But of course the whole difficulty can be avoided—I only point it out in passing—the whole difficulty can be avoided by any colony which desires to make the preferential arrangement with the mother country, if that colony will confine its offer *nominatim* to the mother country and not make it to a foreign country, but if it is offered to a foreign country then, as I say, it will be controlled by the most favoured nation treaties throughout the world.

*   *   *

Consider what has been brought to your notice during your visit to this country. The United Kingdom owns as its brightest and greatest dependency that enormous Empire of India, with 300,000,000 of subjects, who are as loyal to the Crown as you are yourselves, and among them there are hundreds and thousands of men who are every whit as civilized as we are ourselves, who are, if that is anything, better born in the sense that they have older traditions and older families, who are men of wealth, men of cultivation, men of distinguished valour, men who have brought whole armies and placed them at the service of the Queen, and have in times of great difficulty and trouble, such for instance as on the occasion of the Indian Mutiny, saved the empire by their loyalty. I say, you, who have seen all this, cannot be willing to put upon those men a slight which I think is absolutely unnecessary for your purpose, and which would be calculated to provoke ill-feeling, discontent, irritation, and would be most unpalatable to the feelings not only of Her Majesty the Queen, but of all her people.

What I venture to think you have to deal with is the character of the immigration. It is not because a man is of a different colour from ourselves that he is necessarily an undesirable immigrant, but it is because he is dirty, or he is immoral, or he is a pauper, or he has some other objection which can be defined in an Act of Parliament, and by which the exclusion can be managed with regard to all those whom you really desire to exclude. Well, gentlemen, this is a matter I am sure for friendly consultation between us. As I have said, the Colony of Natal has arrived at an arrangement which is absolutely satisfactory to them, I believe, and remember they have, if possible, an even greater interest than you, because they are closer to the immigration which has already begun there on a very large scale, and they have adopted legislation which they believe will give them all that they want, and to which the objection I have taken does not apply, which does not come in conflict with this sentiment which I am sure you share with us; and I hope, therefore, that during your visit it may be possible for us to arrange a form of words which will avoid hurting the feelings of any of Her Majesty's subjects, while at the same time it would amply protect the Australian Colonies against any invasion of the class to which they would justly object. Now, gentlemen, I really owe you a humble apology for having detained you so long, but I thought that it might be to your convenience that this recapitulation should be made of some things which might be treated in our discussions, and I have only now to thank you very much for your kindness in listening to me so patiently, and to express a hope that you will be good enough to give me generally and at this stage in our proceedings your ideas as to the course which we should take in regard to our future meetings."

The commercial relations of the United Kingdom and the self-governing Colonies were first considered, and the following resolutions were unanimously adopted: —

1. That the Premiers of the self-governing Colonies unanimously and earnestly recommend the denunciation, at the earliest convenient time, of any treaties which now hamper the commercial relations between Great Britain and her Colonies.

2. That in the hope of improving the trade relations between the mother country and the Colonies, the Premiers present undertake to confer with their colleagues with the view to seeing whether such a result can be properly secured by a preference given by the Colonies to the products of the United Kingdom.

Her Majesty's Government have already given effect to the first of these resolutions by formally notifying to the Governments concerned their wish to terminate the commercial treaties with Germany and Belgium, which alone of the existing commercial treaties of the United Kingdom are in a bar to the establishment of preferential tariff relations between the mother country and the Colonies. From and after the 30th July 1898, therefore, there will be nothing in any of Her Majesty's treaty obligations to preclude any action which any of the Colonies may see fit to take in pursuance of the second resolution.

It is, however, right to point out that if any Colony were to go farther and to grant preferential terms to any Foreign Country, the provisions of the most favoured nation clauses in many treaties between Her Majesty and other powers, in which the Colonies are included, would necessitate the concession of similar terms to those countries.

On the question of the political relations between the mother country and the self-governing Colonies, the resolutions adopted were as follows: —

1. The Prime Ministers here assembled are of opinion that the present political relations between the United Kingdom and the self-governing Colonies are generally satisfactory under the existing condition of things.
    Mr. Seddon and Sir E. N. C. Braddon dissented.
2. They are also of opinion that it is desirable, whenever and wherever practicable, to group together under a federal union those colonies which are geographically united.
    Carried unanimously.
3. Meanwhile, the Premiers are of opinion that it would be desirable to hold periodical conferences of representatives of the Colonies and Great Britain for the discussion of matters of common interest.
    Carried unanimously.

Mr. Seddon and Sir E. N. C. Braddon dissented from the first resolution because they were of opinion that the time had already come when an effort should be made to render more formal the political ties between the United Kingdom and the Colonies. The majority of the Premiers were not yet prepared to adopt this position, but there was a strong feeling amongst some of them that with the rapid growth of population in the Colonies, the present relations could not continue indefinitely, and that some means would have to be devised for giving the Colonies a voice in the control and direction of those questions of Imperial interest in which they are concerned equally with the mother country.

It was recognised at the same time that such a share in the direction of Imperial policy would involve a proportionate contribution in aid of Imperial expenditure, for which at present, at any rate, the Colonies generally are not prepared.

Commonwealth of Australia Constitution Act
(63 & 64 Vict., c. 12), 9 July 1900*

Whereas the people of New South Wales, Victoria, South Australia, Queensland, and Tasmania, humbly relying on the blessing of Almighty God, have agreed to unite in one indissoluble Federal Commonwealth under the Crown of the United Kingdom of Great Britain and Ireland, and under the Constitution hereby established:

And whereas it is expedient to provide for the admission into the Commonwealth of other Australasian Colonies and possessions of the Queen:

Be it therefore enacted by the Queen's most Excellent Majesty, by and with the advice and consent of the Lords Spiritual and Temporal, and Commons, in this present Parliament assembled and by the authority of the same, as follows: —

1. This Act may be cited as the Commonwealth of Australia Constitution Act.

2. The provisions of this Act referring to the Queen shall extend to Her Majesty's heirs and successors in the sovereignty of the United Kingdom.

3. It shall be lawful for the Queen, with the advice of the Privy Council, to declare by proclamation that, on and after a day therein appointed, not being later than one year after the passing of this Act, the people of New South Wales, Victoria, South Australia, Queensland, and Tasmania, and also, if Her Majesty is satisfied that the people of Western Australia have agreed thereto, of Western Australia, shall be united in a Federal Commonwealth under the name of the Commonwealth of Australia. But the Queen may, at any time after the proclamation, appoint a Governor-General for the Commonwealth.

4. The Commonwealth shall be established, and the Constitution of the Commonwealth shall take effect, on and after the day so appointed. But the Parliaments of the several colonies may at any time after the passing of this Act make any such laws, to come into operation on the day so appointed, as they might have made if the Constitution had taken effect at the passing of this Act.

5. This Act, and all laws made by the Parliament of the Commonwealth under the Constitution, shall be binding on the courts, judges, and people of every State and of every part of the Commonwealth, notwithstanding anything in the laws of any State; and the laws of the Commonwealth shall be in force on all British ships, the Queen's ships of war excepted, whose first port of clearance and whose port of destination are in the Commonwealth.

6. "The Commonwealth" shall mean the Commonwealth of Australia as established under this Act.

*Public General Statutes, XXXVIII, 24–30, 32-35, 42.

"The States" shall mean such of the colonies of New South Wales, New Zealand, Queensland, Tasmania, Victoria, Western Australia, and South Australia, including the northern territory of South Australia, as for the time being are parts of the Commonwealth, and such colonies or territories as may be admitted into or established by the Commonwealth as States; and each of such parts of the Commonwealth shall be called "a State."

"Original States" shall mean such States as are parts of the Commonwealth at its establishment.

7. The Federal Council of Australasia Act, 1885, is hereby repealed, but so as not to affect any laws passed by the Federal Council of Australasia and in force at the establishment of the Commonwealth.

Any such law may be repealed as to any State by the Parliament of the Commonwealth, or as to any colony not being a State by the Parliament thereof.

8. After the passing of this Act the Colonial Boundaries Act, 1895, shall not apply to any colony which becomes a State of the Commonwealth; but the Commonwealth shall be taken to be a self-governing colony for the purposes of that Act.

9. The Constitution of the Commonwealth shall be as follows:

*   *   *

Chapter I. The Parliament

Part I.—General

1. The legislative power of the Commonwealth shall be vested in a Federal Parliament, which shall consist of the Queen, a Senate, and a House of Representatives, and which is herein-after called "The Parliament," or "The Parliament of the Commonwealth."

2. A Governor-General appointed by the Queen shall be Her Majesty's representative in the Commonwealth, and shall have and may exercise in the Commonwealth during the Queen's pleasure, but subject to this Constitution, such powers and functions of the Queen as Her Majesty may be pleased to assign to him.

*   *

Part II.—The Senate

7. The Senate shall be composed of senators for each State, directly chosen by the people of the State, voting, until the Parliament otherwise provides, as one electorate.

But until the Parliament of the Commonwealth otherwise provides, the Parliament of the State of Queensland, if that State be an Original State, may make laws dividing the State into divisions and determining the number of senators to be chosen for each division, and in the absence of such provision the State shall be one electorate.

Until the Parliament otherwise provides there shall be six senators for each Original State. The Parliament may make laws increasing or diminishing the number of senators for each State, but so that equal representation of the several Original States shall be maintained and that no Original State shall have less than six senators.

The senators shall be chosen for a term of six years, and the names of the senators chosen for each State shall be certified by the Governor to the Governor-General.

8. The qualification of electors of senators shall be in each State that which is prescribed by this Constitution, or by the Parliament, as the qualification for electors of members of the House of Representatives; but in the choosing of senators each elector shall vote only once.

9. The Parliament of the Commonwealth may make laws prescribing the method of choosing senators, but so that the method shall be uniform for all the States. Subject to any such law, the Parliament of each State may make laws prescribing the method of choosing the senators for that State.

The Parliament of a State may make laws for determining the times and places of elections of senators for the State.

*   *   *

Part III.— The House of Representatives

24. The House of Representatives shall be composed of members directly chosen by the people of the Commonwealth, and the number of such members shall be, as nearly as practicable, twice the number of the senators.

The number of members chosen in the several States shall be in proportion to the respective numbers of their people, and shall, until the Parliament otherwise provides, be determined, whenever necessary, in the following manner: —

(i.) A quota shall be ascertained by dividing the number of the people of the Commonwealth, as shown by the latest statistics of the Commonwealth, by twice the number of the senators:

(ii.) The number of members to be chosen in each State shall be determined by dividing the number of the people of the State, as shown by the latest statistics of the Commonwealth, by the quota; and if on such division there is a remainder greater than one-half of the quota, one more member shall be chosen in the State.

But notwithstanding anything in this section, five members at least shall be chosen in each Original State.

25. For the purposes of the last section, if by the law of any State all persons of any race are disqualified from voting at elections for the more numerous House of the Parliament of the State, then, in reckoning the number of the people of the State or of the Commonwealth, persons of that race resident in that State shall not be counted.

26. Notwithstanding anything in section twenty-four, the number of members to be chosen in each State at the first election shall be as follows: —

New South Wales	twenty-three;
Victoria	twenty;

Queensland	eight;
South Australia	six;
Tasmania	five;

Provided that if Western Australia is an Original State, the numbers shall be as follows: —

New South Wales	twenty-six;
Victoria	twenty-three;
Queensland	nine;
South Australia	seven;
Western Australia	five;
Tasmania	five.

27. Subject to this Constitution, the Parliament may make laws for increasing or diminishing the number of the members of the House of Representatives.

28. Every House of Representatives shall continue for three years from the first meeting of the House, and no longer, but may be sooner dissolved by the Governor-General.

29. Until the Parliament of the Commonwealth otherwise provides, the Parliament of any State may make laws for determining the divisions in each State for which members of the House of Representatives may be chosen, and the number of members to be chosen for each division. A division shall not be formed out of parts of different States.

In the absence of other provision, each State shall be one electorate.

* * *

34. Until the Parliament otherwise provides, the qualifications of a member of the House of Representatives shall be as follows: —

(i.) He must be of the full age of twenty-one years, and must be an elector entitled to vote at the election of members of the House of Representatives, or a person qualified to become such elector, and must have been for three years at the least a resident within the limits of the Commonwealth as existing at the time when he is chosen:

(ii.) He must be a subject of the Queen, either natural-born or for at least five years naturalized under a law of the United Kingdom, or of a Colony which has become or becomes a State, or of the Commonwealth, or of a State.

* * *

Part V.—Powers of the Parliament

51. The Parliament shall, subject to this Constitution, have power to make laws for the peace, order, and good government of the Commonwealth with respect to: —

(i.) Trade and commerce with other countries, and among the States:

(ii.) Taxation; but so as not to discriminate between States or parts of States:

(iii.) Bounties on the production or export of goods, but so that such bounties shall be uniform throughout the Commonwealth:

(iv.) Borrowing money on the public credit of the Commonwealth:

(v.) Postal, telegraphic, telephonic, and other like services:

(vi.) The naval and military defence of the Commonwealth and of the several States, and the control of the forces to execute and maintain the laws of the Commonwealth:

(vii.) Lighthouses, lightships, beacons and buoys:

(viii.) Astronomical and meteorological observations:

(ix.) Quarantine:

(x.) Fisheries in Australian waters beyond territorial limits:

(xi.) Census and statistics:

(xii.) Currency, coinage, and legal tender:

(xiii.) Banking, other than State banking; also State banking extending beyond the limits of the State concerned, the incorporation of banks, and the issue of paper money:

(xiv.) Insurance, other than State insurance; also State insurance extending beyond the limits of the State concerned:

(xv.) Weights and measures:

(xvi.) Bills of exchange and promissory notes:

(xvii.) Bankruptcy and insolvency:

(xviii.) Copyrights, patents of inventions and designs, and trade marks:

(xix.) Naturalization and aliens:

(xx.) Foreign corporations, and trading or financial corporations formed within the limits of the Commonwealth:

(xxi.) Marriage:

(xxii.) Divorce and matrimonial causes; and in relation thereto, parental rights, and the custody and guardianship of infants:

(xxiii.) Invalid and old-age pensions:

(xxiv.) The service and execution throughout the Commonwealth of the civil and criminal process and the judgments of the courts of the States:

(xxv.) The recognition throughout the Commonwealth of the laws, the public Acts and records, and the judicial proceedings of the States:

(xxvi.) The people of any race, other than the aboriginal race in any State, for whom it is deemed necessary to make special laws:

(xxvii.) Immigration and emigration:

(xxviii.) The influx of criminals:

(xxix.) External affairs:

(xxx.) The relations of the Commonwealth with the islands of the Pacific:

(xxxi.) The acquisition of property on just terms from any State or person for any purpose in respect of which the Parliament has power to make laws:

(xxxii.) The control of railways with respect to transport for the naval and military purposes of the Commonwealth:

(xxxiii.) The acquisition, with the consent of a State, of any railways of the State on terms arranged between the Commonwealth and the State:

(xxxiv.) Railway construction and extension in any State with the consent of that State:

(xxxv.) Conciliation and arbitration for the prevention and settlement of industrial disputes extending beyond the limits of any one State:

(xxxvi.) Matters in respect of which this Constitution makes provision until the Parliament otherwise provides:

(xxxvii.) Matters referred to the Parliament of the Commonwealth by the Parliament or Parliaments of any State or States, but so that the law shall extend only to States by whose Parliaments the matter is referred, or which afterwards adopt the law:

(xxxviii.) The exercise within the Commonwealth, at the request or with the concurrence of the Parliaments of all the States directly concerned, of any power which can at the establishment of this Constitution be exercised only by the Parliament of the United Kingdom or by the Federal Council of Australasia:

(xxxix.) Matters incidental to the execution of any power vested by this Constitution in the Parliament or in either House thereof, or in the Government of the Commonwealth, or in the Federal Judicature, or in any department or officer of the Commonwealth.

52. The Parliament shall, subject to this Constitution, have exclusive power to make laws for the peace, order, and good government of the Commonwealth with respect to—

(i.) The seat of government of the Commonwealth, and all places acquired by the Commonwealth for public purposes:

(ii.) Matters relating to any department of the public service the control of which is by this Constitution transferred to the Executive Government of the Commonwealth:

(iii.) Other matters declared by this Constitution to be within the exclusive power of the Parliament.

53. Proposed laws appropriating revenue or moneys, or imposing taxation, shall not originate in the Senate. But a proposed law shall not be taken to

appropriate revenue or moneys, or to impose taxation, by reason only of its containing provisions for the imposition or appropriation of fines or other pecuniary penalties, or for the demand or payment or appropriation of fees for licences, or fees for services under the proposed law.

The Senate may not amend proposed laws imposing taxation, or proposed laws appropriating revenue or moneys for the ordinary annual services of the Government.

The Senate may not amend any proposed law so as to increase any proposed charge or burden on the people.

The Senate may at any stage return to the House of Representatives any proposed law which the Senate may not amend, requesting, by message, the omission or amendment of any items or provisions therein. And the House of Representatives may, if it thinks fit, make any of such omissions or amendments, with or without modifications.

Except as provided in this section, the Senate shall have equal power with the House of Representatives in respect of all proposed laws.

54. The proposed law which appropriates revenue or moneys for the ordinary annual services of the Government shall deal only with such appropriation.

55. Laws imposing taxation shall deal only with the imposition of taxation, and any provision therein dealing with any other matter shall be of no effect.

Laws imposing taxation, except laws imposing duties of customs or of excise, shall deal with one subject of taxation only; but laws imposing duties of customs shall deal with duties of customs only, and laws imposing duties of excise shall deal with duties of excise only.

56. A vote, resolution, or proposed law for the appropriation of revenue or moneys shall not be passed unless the purpose of the appropriation has in the same session been recommended by message of the Governor-General to the House in which the proposal originated.

*   *   *

58. When a proposed law passed by both Houses of the Parliament is presented to the Governor-General for the Queen's assent, he shall declare, according to his discretion, but subject to this Constitution, that he assents in the Queen's name, or that he withholds assent, or that he reserves the law for the Queen's pleasure.

The Governor-General may return to the House in which it originated any proposed law so presented to him, and may transmit therewith any amendments which he may recommend, and the Houses may deal with the recommendation.

59. The Queen may disallow any law within one year from the Governor-General's assent, and such disallowance on being made known by the Governor-General by speech or message to each of the Houses of the Parliament, or by Proclamation, shall annul the law from the day when the disallowance is so made known.

60. A proposed law reserved for the Queen's pleasure shall not have any force unless and until within two years from the day on which it was presented

to the Governor-General for the Queen's assent the Governor-General makes known, by speech or message to each of the Houses of the Parliament, or by Proclamation, that it has received the Queen's assent.

Chapter II. The Executive Government

61. The executive power of the Commonwealth is vested in the Queen and is exerciseable by the Governor-General as the Queen's representative, and extends to the execution and maintenance of this Constitution, and of the laws of the Commonwealth.

62. There shall be a Federal Executive Council to advise the Governor-General in the government of the Commonwealth, and the members of the Council shall be chosen and summoned by the Governor-General and sworn as Executive Councillors, and shall hold office during his pleasure.

63. The provisions of this Constitution referring to the Governor-General in Council shall be construed as referring to the Governor-General acting with the advice of the Federal Executive Council.

64. The Governor-General may appoint officers to administer such departments of State of the Commonwealth as the Governor-General in Council may establish.

Such officers shall hold office during the pleasure of the Governor-General. They shall be members of the Federal Executive Council, and shall be the Queen's Ministers of State for the Commonwealth.

After the first general election no Minister of State shall hold office for a longer period than three months unless he is or becomes a senator or a member of the House of Representatives.

* * *

Chapter V. The States

106. The Constitution of each State of the Commonwealth shall, subject to this Constitution, continue as at the establishment of the Commonwealth, or as at the admission or establishment of the State, as the case may be, until altered in accordance with the Constitution of the State.

107. Every power of the Parliament of a Colony which has become or becomes a State, shall, unless it is by this Constitution exclusively vested in the Parliament of the Commonwealth or withdrawn from the Parliament of the State, continue as at the establishment of the Commonwealth, or as at the admission or establishment of the State, as the case may be.

108. Every law in force in a Colony which has become or becomes a State, and relating to any matter within the powers of the Parliament of the Commonwealth, shall, subject to this Constitution, continue in force in the State; and, until provision is made in that behalf by the Parliament of the Commonwealth, the Parliament of the State shall have such powers of alteration and of repeal in respect of any such law as the Parliament of the Colony had until the Colony became a State.

109. When a law of a State is inconsistent with a law of the Commonwealth, the latter shall prevail, and the former shall, to the extent of the inconsistency, be invalid.

* * *

Speech by Joseph Chamberlain at St. Andrew's Hall, Glasgow, Advocating Tariff Reform and a System of Imperial Preferences, 6 October 1903*

I am in a great city, the second of the Empire; the city which by the enterprise and intelligence which it has always shown is entitled to claim something of a representative character in respect of British industry. I am in that city in which Free Trade took its birth, in that city in which Adam Smith taught so long, and where he was one of my most distinguished predecessors in the great office of Lord Rector of your University, which it will always be to me a great honour to have filled. Adam Smith was a great man. It was not given to him, it never has been given to mortals, to foresee all the changes that may occur in something like a century and a half; but with a broad and far-seeing intelligence which is not common among men, Adam Smith did at any rate anticipate many of our modern conditions; and when I read his books I see how even then he was aware of the importance of home markets as compared with foreign; how he advocated retaliation under certain conditions; how he supported the Navigation Laws; how he was the author of a sentence which we ought never to forget, that 'Defence is greater than opulence.' When I remember, also, how he, entirely before his time, pressed for reciprocal trade between our colonies and the mother country, I say he had a broader mind, a more Imperial conception of the duties of the citizens of a great Empire, than some of those who have taught also as professors and who claim to be his successors. Ladies and gentlemen, I am not afraid to come here to the home of Adam Smith and to combat free imports, and still less am I afraid to preach to you preference with our colonies—to you in this great city whose whole prosperity has been founded upon its colonial relations. But I must not think only of the city, I must think of the country. It is known to every man that Scotland has contributed out of all proportion to its population to build up the great Empire of which we are all so proud—an Empire which took genius and capacity and courage to create, and which requires now genius and capacity and courage to maintain.

I do not regard this as a party meeting. I am no longer a party leader. I am an outsider, and it is not my intention—I do not think it would be right—to raise any exclusively party issues. But after what has occurred in the last few days, after the meeting at Sheffield, a word or two may be forgiven to me, who,

*Chamberlain, *Speeches*, II, 140–64.

although no longer a leader, am still a loyal servant of the party to which I belong.

I say to you, ladies and gentlemen, that that party whose continued existence, whose union, whose strength I still believe to be essential to the welfare of the country and to the welfare of the Empire, has found a leader whom every member may be proud to follow. Mr. Balfour in his position has responsibilities which he cannot share with us, but no one will contest his right—a right to which his high office, his ability, and his character alike entitle him—to declare the official policy of the party which he leads, to fix its limits, to settle the time at which application shall be given to the principles which he has put forward. For myself, I agree with the principles that he has stated. I approve of the policy to which he proposes to give effect, and I admire the courage and the resource with which he faces difficulties which, even in our varied political history, have hardly ever been surpassed. It ought not to be necessary to say any more. But it seems as though in this country there have always been men who do not know what loyalty and friendship mean, and to them I say that nothing that they can do will have the slightest influence or will affect in the slightest degree the friendship and confidence which exist and have existed for so many years between the Prime Minister and myself. Let them do their worst. Understand that in no conceivable circumstances will I allow myself to be put in any sort of competition, direct or indirect, with my friend and leader, whom I mean to follow. What is my position? I have invited a discussion upon a question which comes peculiarly within my province, owing to the office which I have so recently held. I have invited discussion upon it. I have not pretended that a matter of this importance is to be settled off-hand. I have been well aware that the country has to be educated, as I myself have had to be educated before I saw, or could see, all the bearings of this great matter; and therefore I take up the position of a pioneer. I go in front of the army, and if the army is attacked, I go back to it.

Meanwhile, putting aside all these personal and party questions, I ask my countrymen, without regard to any political opinions which they may have hitherto held, to consider the greatest of all great questions that can be put before the country, to consider it impartially if possible, and to come to a decision; and it is possible—I am always an optimist—it is possible that the nation may be prepared to go a little further than the official programme. I have known them to do it before, and no harm has come to the party; no harm that I know has come to those who as scouts, or pioneers, or investigators, or discoverers have gone a little before it. Well, one of my objects in coming here is to find an answer to this question. Is the country prepared to go a little further?

What are our objects? They are two. In the first place, we all desire the maintenance and increase of the national strength and the prosperity of the United Kingdom. That may be a selfish desire; but in my mind it carries with it something more than mere selfishness. You cannot expect foreigners to take the same views as we of our position and duty. To my mind Britain has played a great part in the past in the history of the world, and for that reason I wish Britain to continue. Then, in the second place, our object is, or should be, the realisation of the greatest ideal which has ever inspired statesmen in any country or in any age—the creation of an Empire such as the world has never seen. We have to cement the union of the states beyond the seas; we have to consolidate the British race; we have to meet the clash of competition, commercial now—sometimes in the past it has been otherwise—it may be again in the future. Whatever it be, whatever danger threatens, we have to meet it no longer as an isolated country; we have to meet it fortified and strengthened, and buttressed by all those of our kinsmen, all those powerful and continually rising states which speak our common tongue and glory in our common flag.

Those are two great objects, and, as I have said, we all should have them in view. How are we to attain them? In the first place, let me say one word as to the method in which this discussion is to be carried on. Surely it should be treated in a manner worthy of its magnitude, worthy of the dignity of the theme. For my part I disclaim any imputation of evil motive and unworthy motive on the part of those who may happen to disagree with me; and I claim equal consideration from them. I claim that this matter should be treated on its merits—without personal feeling, personal bitterness, and, if possible, without entering upon questions of purely party controversy, and I do that for the reason I have given; but also because, if you are to make a change in a system which has existed for nearly sixty years, which affects more or less every man, woman, and child in the kingdom, you can only make that change successfully if you have behind you not merely a party support—if you do not attempt to force it by a small majority on a large and unwilling minority, but if it becomes, as I believe it will become, a national policy in consonance with the feelings, the aspirations, and the interests of the overwhelming proportion of the country.

I was speaking just now of the characteristics of Glasgow as a great city; I am not certain whether I mentioned that I believe it is one of the most prosperous of cities, that it has had a great and continuous prosperity; and if that be so, here, more than anywhere else, I have to answer the question, Why cannot you let well alone? Well, I have been in Venice—the beautiful city of the Adriatic—which had at one time a commercial supremacy quite as great in proportion as anything we have ever enjoyed. Its glories have departed; but what I was going to say was that when I was there last I saw the great tower of the Campanile rising above the city which it had overshadowed for centuries, and looking as though it was as permanent as the city itself. And yet the other day, in a few minutes, the whole structure fell to the ground. Nothing was left of it but a mass of ruin and rubbish. I do not say to you, gentlemen, that I anticipate any catastrophe so great or so sudden for British trade; but I do say to you that I see signs of decay; that I see cracks and crevices in the walls of the great structure; that I know that the foundations upon which it has been raised are not broad enough or deep enough to sustain it. Now, do I do wrong, if I know this—if I even think I know it—do I do wrong to warn you? Is it not a most strange and inconsistent thing that while certain people are indicting the

Government in language which, to say the least of it, is extravagant, for not having been prepared for the great war from which we have recently emerged with success—is it not strange that these same people should be denouncing me in language equally extravagant because I want to prepare you now, while there is time, for a struggle greater in its consequences than that to which I have referred—a struggle from which, if we emerge defeated, this country will lose its place, will no longer count among the great nations of the world—a struggle which we are asked to meet with antiquated weapons and with old-fashioned tactics?

I tell you that it is not well to-day with British industry. We have been going through a period of great expansion. The whole world has been prosperous. I see signs of a change, but let that pass. When the change comes, I think even the Free Fooders will be converted. But meanwhile, what are the facts? The year 1900 was the record year of British trade. The exports were the largest we had ever known. The year 1902—last year—was nearly as good, and yet, if you will compare your trade in 1872, thirty years ago, with the trade of 1902—the export trade—you will find that there has been a moderate increase of £22,000,000. That, I think, is something like 7½ per cent. Meanwhile, the population has increased 30 per cent. Can you go on supporting your population at that rate of increase, when even in the best of years you can only show so much smaller an increase in your foreign trade? The actual increase was £22,000,000 under our Free Trade. In the same time the increase in the United States of America was £110,000,000, and the increase in Germany was £56,000,000. In the United Kingdom our export trade has been practically stagnant for thirty years. It went down in the interval. It has now gone up in the most prosperous times. In the most prosperous times it is hardly better than it was thirty years ago.

Meanwhile the protected countries which you have been told, and which I myself at one time believed, were going rapidly to wreck and ruin, have progressed in a much greater proportion than ours. That is not all; not merely the amount of your trade remained stagnant, but the character of your trade has changed. When Mr. Cobden preached his doctrine, he believed, as he had at that time considerable reason to suppose, that while foreign countries would supply us with our food-stuffs and raw materials, we should remain the mart of the world, and should send them in exchange our manufactures. But that is exactly what we have not done. On the contrary, in the period to which I have referred, we are sending less and less of our manufactures to them, and they are sending more and more of their manufactures to us.

I know how difficult it is for a great meeting like this to follow figures. I shall give you as few as I can, but I must give you some to lay the basis of my argument. I have had a table constructed, and upon that table I would be willing to base the whole of my contention. I will take some figures from it. You have to analyse your trade. It is not merely a question of amount; you have to consider of what it is composed. Now what has been the case with regard to our manufactures? Our existence as a nation depends upon our manufacturing capacity and production. We are not essentially or mainly an agricultural country. That can never be the main source of our prosperity. We are a great manufacturing country. In 1872, we sent to the protected countries of Europe and to the United States of America, £116,000,000 of exported manufactures. In 1882, ten years later, it fell to £88,000,000. In 1892, ten years later, it fell to £75,000,000. In 1902, last year, although the general exports had increased, the exports of manufactures to these countries had decreased again to £73,500,000, and the total result of this is that, after thirty years, you are sending £42,500,000 of manufactures less to the great protected countries than you did thirty years ago. Then there are the neutral countries, that is, the countries which, although they may have tariffs, have no manufactures, and therefore the tariffs are not protective—such countries as Egypt and China, and South America, and similar places. Our exports of manufactures have not fallen in these markets to any considerable extent. They have practically remained the same, but on the whole they have fallen £3,500,000. Adding that to the loss in the protected countries, and you have lost altogether in your exports of manufactures £46,000,000.

How is it that that has not impressed the people before now? Because the change has been concealed by our statistics. I do not say they have not shown it, because you could have picked it out, but they are not put in a form which is understanded of the people. You have failed to observe that the maintenance of your trade is dependent entirely on British possessions. While to these foreign countries your export of manufactures has declined by £46,000,000, to your British possessions it has increased £40,000,000, and at the present time your trade with the colonies and British possessions is larger in amount, very much larger in amount, and very much more valuable in the categories I have named, than our trade with the whole of Europe and the United States of America. It is much larger than our trade to those neutral countries of which I have spoken, and it remains at the present day the most rapidly increasing, the most important, the most valuable of the whole of our trade. One more comparison. During this period of thirty years in which our exports of manufactures have fallen £46,000,000 to foreign countries, what has happened as regards their exports of manufactures to us? They have risen from £63,000,000 in 1872 to £149,000,000 in 1902. They have increased £86,000,000. That may be all right. I am not for the moment saying whether that is right or wrong, but when people say that we ought to hold exactly the same opinion about things that our ancestors did, my reply is that I dare say we should do so if circumstances had remained the same.

But now, if I have been able to make these figures clear, there is one thing which follows—that is, that our Imperial trade is absolutely essential to our prosperity at the present time. If that trade declines, or if it does not increase in proportion to our population and to the loss of trade with foreign countries, then we sink at once into a fifth-rate nation. Our fate will be the fate of the empires and kingdoms of the past. We shall have reached our highest point, and indeed I am not certain that there are not some of my opponents who regard that with absolute complacency. I do not. As I have said, I have the misfortune to be an optimist. I do not believe in the setting of the British star, but then, I do not believe in the folly of the British people. I trust them. I trust the working classes of this country, and I have confidence that they who are our masters, electorally speaking, will have the intelligence to see that they must wake up. They must modify their policy to suit new conditions. They must meet those conditions with altogether a new policy.

I have said that if our Imperial trade declines we decline. My second point is this. It will decline inevitably unless while there is still time we take the necessary steps to preserve it. Have you ever considered why it is that Canada takes so much more of the products of British manufacturers than the United States of America does per head? Why does Australia take about three times as much per head as Canada? And why does South Africa—the white population of South Africa—take more per head than Australasia? When you have got to the bottom of that—and it is not difficult—you will see the whole argument. These countries are all protective countries. I see that the Labour leaders, or some of them, in this country are saying that the interest of the working class is to maintain our present system of free imports. The moment those men go to the colonies they change. I will undertake to say that no one of them has ever been there for six months without singing a different tune. The vast majority of the working men in all the colonies are Protectionists, and I am not inclined to accept the easy explanation that they are all fools. I do not understand why an intelligent man—a man who is intelligent in this country—becomes an idiot when he goes to Australasia. But I will tell you what he does do. He gets rid of a good number of old-world prejudices and superstitions. I say they are Protectionist, all these countries. Now, what is the history of Protection? In the first place, a tariff is imposed. There are no industries, or practically none, but only a tariff; then gradually industries grow up behind the tariff wall. In the first place, they are primary industries, the industries for which the country has natural aptitude or for which it has some special advantage—mineral or other resources. Then when those are established the secondary industries spring up, first the necessaries, then the luxuries, until at last all the ground is covered. These countries of which I have been speaking to you are in different stages of the protective process. In America the process has been completed. She produces everything; she excludes everything. There is no trade to be done with her beyond a paltry 6s. per head. Canada has been protective for a long time. The protective policy has produced its natural result. The principal industries are there, and you can never get rid of them. They will be there for ever, but up to the present time the secondary industries have not been created, and there is an immense deal of trade that is still open to you, that you may still retain, that you may increase. In Australasia the industrial position is still less advanced. The agricultural products of the country have been first of all developed.

Accordingly, Australasia takes more from you per head than Canada. In South Africa there are, practically speaking, no industries at all. Now, I ask you to suppose that we intervene in any stage of the process. We can do it now. We might have done it with greater effect ten years ago. Whether we can do it with any effect or at all twenty years hence I am very doubtful. We can intervene now. We can say to our great colonies: 'We understand your views and conditions. We do not attempt to dictate to you. We do not think ourselves superior to you. We have taken the trouble to learn your objections, to appreciate and sympathise with your policy. We know that you are right in saying you will not always be content to be what the Americans call a one-horse country, with a single industry and no diversity of employment. We can see that you are right not to neglect what Providence has given you in the shape of mineral or other resources. We understand and we appreciate the wisdom of your statesmen when they say they will not allow their country to be solely dependent on foreign supplies for the necessities of life. We understand all that, and therefore we will not propose to you anything that is unreasonable or contrary to this policy, which we know is deep in your hearts; but we will say to you, "After all, there are many things which you do not now make, many things for which we have a great capacity of production—leave them to us as you have left them hitherto. Do not increase your tariff walls against us. Pull them down where they are unnecessary to the success of this policy to which you are committed. Do that because we are kinsmen—without injury to any important interest— because it is good for the Empire as a whole, and because we have taken the first step and have set you the example. We offer you a preference; we rely on your patriotism, your affection, that we shall not be losers thereby." '

Now, suppose that we had made an offer of that kind—I won't say to the colonies, but to Germany, to the United States of America—ten or twenty years ago. Do you suppose that we should not have been able to retain a great deal of what we have now lost and cannot recover?

I will give you an illustration. America is the strictest of protective nations. It is so immoderate, so unreasonable, so unnecessary, that, though America has profited enormously under it, yet I think it has been carried to excessive lengths, and I believe now that a great number of intelligent Americans would gladly negotiate with us for its reduction. But until very recent times even this immoderate tariff left to us a great trade. It left to us the tin-plate trade, and the American tin-plate trade amounted to millions per annum, and gave employment to thousands of British work-people. If we had gone to America ten or twenty years ago and had said, 'If you will leave the tin-plate trade as it is, put no duty on tin-plate—you have never had to complain either of our quality or our price—we in return will give you some advantage on some articles which you produce,' we might have kept the tin-plate trade. It would not have been worth America's while to put a duty on an article for which it had no particular or special aptitude or capacity. If we had gone to Germany in the same sense, there are hundreds of articles which are now made in Germany which are sent to this country, which are taking the place of goods employing British labour, which they might have left to us in return for our concessions to them.

We did not take that course. We were not prepared for it as a people. We allowed matters to drift. Are we going to let them drift now? Are we going to lose the colonial trade? This is the parting of the ways. You have to remember that if you do not take this opportunity it will not recur. If you do not take it I predict, and I predict with certainty, that Canada will fall to the level of the United States, that Australia will fall to the level of Canada, that South Africa will fall to the level of Australia, and that will only be the beginning of the general decline which will deprive you of your most important customers, of your most rapidly increasing trade. I think that I have some reason to speak with authority on this subject. The colonies are prepared to meet us. In return for a very moderate preference they will give us a substantial advantage. They will give us in the first place, I believe they will reserve to us, much at any rate of the trade which we already enjoy. They will not—and I would not urge them for a moment to do so—they will not injure those of their industries which have already been created. They will maintain them, they will not allow them to be destroyed or injured even by our competition, but outside that there is still a great margin, a margin which has given us this enormous increase of trade to which I have referred. That margin I believe we can permanently retain, and I ask you to think, if that is of so much importance to us now, when we have only eleven millions of white fellow-citizens in these distant colonies, what will it be when, in the course of a period which is a mere moment of time in the history of states, that population is forty millions or more? Is it not worth while to consider whether the actual trade which you may retain, whether the enormous potential trade which you and your descendants may enjoy, be not worth a sacrifice, if sacrifice be required? But they will do a great deal more for you. This is certain. Not only will they enable you to retain the trade which you have, but they are ready to give you preference on all the trade which is now done with them by foreign competitors. I never see any appreciation by the free importers of the magnitude of this trade. It will increase. It has increased greatly in thirty years, and if it goes on with equally rapid strides we shall be ousted by foreign competition, if not by protective tariffs, from our colonies. It amounts at the present time to £47,000,000. But it is said that a great part of that £47,000,000 is in goods which we cannot supply. That is true, and with regard to that portion of the trade we have no interest in any preferential tariff, but it has been calculated, and I believe it to be accurate, that £26,000,000 a year of that trade might come to this country which now goes to Germany and France and other foreign countries, if reasonable preference were given to British manufactures. What does that mean? The Board of Trade assumes that of manufactured goods one-half the value is expended in labour—I think it is a great deal more, but take the Board of Trade figures— £13,000,000 a year of new employment. What does that mean to the United Kingdom? It means the employment of 166,000 men at 30s. a week. It means the subsistence if you include their families, of 830,000 persons; and now, if you will only add to that our present export to the British possessions of £96,000,000, you will find that that gives, on the same calculation, £48,000,000 for wages, or employment at 30s. a week to 615,000 work-people, and it finds subsistence for 3,075,000 persons. In other words, your colonial trade as it stands at present with the prospective advantage of a preference against the foreigner means employment and fair wages for three-quarters of a million of workmen, and subsistence for nearly four millions of our population.

Ladies and gentlemen, I feel deeply sensible that the argument I have addressed to you is one of those which will be described by the leader of the Opposition as a squalid argument. A squalid argument! I have appealed to your interests, I have come here as a man of business, I have appealed to the employers and the employed alike in this great city. I have endeavoured to point out to them that their trade, their wages, all depend on the maintenance of this colonial trade, of which some of my opponents speak with such contempt, and, above all, with such egregious ignorance. But now I abandon that line of argument for the moment, and appeal to something higher, which I believe is in your hearts as it is in mine. I appeal to you as fellow-citizens of the greatest Empire that the world has ever known; I appeal to you to recognise that the privileges of Empire bring with them great responsibilities. I want to ask you to think what this Empire means, what it is to you and your descendants. I will not speak, or, at least, I will not dwell, on its area, greater than that which has been under one dominion in the history of the world. I will not speak of its population, of the hundreds of millions of men for whom we have made ourselves responsible. But I will speak of its variety, and of the fact that here we have an Empire which with decent organisation and consolidation might be absolutely self-sustaining. Nothing of the kind has ever been known before. There is no article of your food, there is no raw material of your trade, there is no necessity of your lives, no luxury of your existence which cannot be produced somewhere or other in the British Empire, if the British Empire holds together, and if we who have inherited it are worthy of our opportunities.

There is another product of the British Empire, that is, men. You have not forgotten the advantage, the encouragement, which can be given by the existence of loyal men, inhabitants, indeed, of distant states, but still loyal to the common flag. It is not so long since these men, when the old country was in straits, rushed to her assistance. No persuasion was necessary; it was a voluntary movement. That was not a squalid assistance. They had no special interest. They were interested, indeed, as sons of the Empire. If they had been separate states they would have had no interest at all. They came to our assistance and proved themselves indeed men of the old stock; they proved themselves worthy of the best traditions of the British army, and gave us an assistance, a material assistance, which was invaluable. They gave us moral support which was even more grateful. That is the result of Empire. I should be wrong if, in referring to our white fellow-subjects, I did not also say, that in addition to them, if any straits befell us, there are millions and hundreds of millions of men born in tropical climes, and of races very different from ours, who, although they were prevented by political considerations from taking part in our recent struggle, would be in any death-throe of the Empire equally eager to show their loyalty and their devotion. Now, is such a dominion, are such traditions, is such a glorious inheritance, is such a splendid sentiment—are they worth preserving? They have cost us much. They have cost much in blood and treasure; and in past times, as in recent, many of our best and noblest have given their lives, or risked their lives, for this great ideal. But it has also done much for us. It has ennobled our national life, it has discouraged that petty parochialism which is the defect of all small communities. I say to you that all that is best in our present life, best in this Britain of ours, all of which we have the right to be most proud, is due to the fact that we are not only sons of Britain, but we are sons of Empire. I do not think, I am not likely to do you the injustice to believe, that you would make this sacrifice fruitless, that you would make all this endeavour vain. But if you want to complete it, remember that each generation in turn has to do its part, and you are called to take your share in this great work. Others have founded the Empire; it is yours to build firmly and permanently the great edifice of which others have laid the foundation. And I believe we have got to change somewhat our rather insular habits. When I have been in the colonies I have told them that they are too provincial, but I think we are too provincial also. We think too much of ourselves, and we forget—and it is necessary we should remember—that we are only part of a larger whole. And when I speak of our colonies it is an expression; they are not ours—in the sense that we possess them. They are sister states, able to treat with us from an equal position, able to hold to us, willing to hold to us, but also able to break with us. I have had eight years' experience. I have been in communication with many of the men, statesmen, orators, writers, distinguished in our colonies. I have had intimate conversation with them. I have tried to understand them and I think I do understand them, and I say that none of them desire separation. There are none of them who are not loyal to this idea of Empire which they say they wish us to accept more fully in the future, but I have found none who do not believe that our present colonial relations cannot be permanent. We must either draw closer together or we shall drift apart.

When I made that statement with all responsibility some time ago there were people, political opponents, who said: 'See, here is the result of having a Colonial Secretary. Eight years ago the colonies were devoted to the mother country. Everything was for the best. Preferences were not thought of. There were no squalid bonds. The colonies were ready to do everything for us. They were not such fools as to think we should do anything for them, but while things were in this happy state the Colonial Secretary came into office. Now it has all disappeared. We are told if we do not alter our policy we may lose our Empire.' It is a fancy picture, but I will not rest my case upon my own opinion. It is not I who have said this alone; others have said it before me. We have a statesman here in Scotland whose instincts are always right. What did he say many years before I came into office, in 1888? Lord Rosebery was speaking at

Leeds, and he said this: 'The people in this country will in a not too distant time have to make up their minds what position they wish their colonies to occupy with respect to them, or whether they desire their colonies to leave them altogether. It is, as I believe, absolutely impossible for you to maintain in the long run your present loose and indefinable relations and preserve these colonies as parts of the Empire. . . . I do not see that you can obtain the great boon of a peaceful Empire encircling the globe with a bond of commercial unity and peace without some sacrifice on your part.' Well, we have to consider, of course, what is the sacrifice we are called upon to make. I do not believe—no, let me first say if there be a sacrifice, if that can be shown, I will go confidently to my countrymen, I will tell them what it is, and I will ask them to make it. Nowadays a great deal too much attention is paid to what is called the sacrifice; no attention is given to what is the gain. But, although I would not hesitate to ask you for a sacrifice if a sacrifice were needed to keep together the Empire to which I attach so much importance, I do not believe that there would be any sacrifice at all. This is an arrangement between friends. This is a negotiation between kinsmen. Can you not conceive the possibility that both sides may gain and neither lose? Twelve years ago another great man—Mr. Cecil Rhodes— with one of those flashes of insight and genius which made him greater than ordinary men, took advantage of his position as Prime Minister of the Cape Colony to write letters, which have recently been published, to the Prime Minister of Canada and the Prime Minister of New South Wales, of that day. He said in one of these letters: 'The whole thing lies in the question—Can we invent some tie with our mother country that will prevent separation? It must be a practical one. The curse is that English politicians cannot see the future.'

Well, I ask the same question. Can we invent a tie which must be a practical one, which will prevent separation, and I make the same answer as Mr. Rhodes, who suggested reciprocal preference, and I say that it is only by commercial union, reciprocal preference, that you can lay the foundations of the confederation of the Empire to which we all look forward as a brilliant possibility. Now I have told you what you are to gain by preference. You will gain the retention and the increase of your customers. You will gain work for the enormous number of those who are now unemployed; you will pave the way for a firmer and more enduring union of the Empire. What will it cost you? What do the colonies ask? They ask a preference on their particular products. You cannot give them, at least it would be futile to offer them, a preference on manufactured goods, because at the present time the exported manufacture of the colonies is entirely insignificant. You cannot, in my opinion, give them a preference on raw material. It has been said that I should propose such a tax; but I repeat now, in the most explicit terms, that I do not propose a tax on raw materials, which are a necessity of our manufacturing trade. What remains? Food.

Therefore, if you wish to have preference, if you desire to gain this increase, if you wish to prevent separation, you must put a tax on food. The murder is out. I said that in the House of Commons, but I said a good deal more, but that is the only thing of all that I said that my opponents have thought it particularly interesting to quote, and you see that on every wall, in the headlines of the leaflets of the Cobden Club, in the speeches of the devotees of free imports, in the arguments of those who dread the responsibilities of Empire, but do not seem to care much about the possibility of its dissolution—all these, then, put in the forefront that Mr. Chamberlain says, 'You must tax food.' I was going to say that this statement which they quote is true. But it is only half the truth, and they never give you the other half. You never see attached to this statement that you must tax food the other words that I have used in reference to this subject, that nothing that I propose would add one farthing to the cost of living to the working man, or to any family in this country. How is that to be achieved? I have been asked for a plan. I have hesitated, because, as you will readily see, no final plan can be proposed until a Government is authorised by the people to enter into negotiations upon these principles. Until that Government has had the opportunity of negotiating with the colonies, with foreign countries, and with the heads and experts in all our great industries, any plan must be at the present time more or less of a sketch plan.

But at the same time I recognise that you have a right to call upon me for the broad outlines of my plan, and those I will give you if you will bear with me. You have heard it said that I propose to put a duty of 5s. or 10s. a quarter on wheat. That is untrue. I propose to put a low duty on foreign corn, no duty at all on the corn coming from our British possessions. But I propose to put a low duty on foreign corn not exceeding 2s. a quarter. I propose to put no tax whatever on maize, partly because maize is a food of some of the very poorest of the population, and partly also because it is a raw material for the farmers, who feed their stock with it. I propose that the corresponding tax which will have to be put on flour should give a substantial preference to the miller, and I do that in order to re-establish one of our most ancient industries in this country, believing that if that is done not only will more work be found in agricultural districts, with some tendency, perhaps, operating against the constant migration from the country into the towns, but also because by re-establishing the milling industry in this country, the offals, as they are called—the refuse of the wheat—will remain in the country and will give to the farmers or the agricultural population a food for their stock and their pigs at very much lower rates. That will benefit not merely the great farmer, but it will benefit the little man, the small owner of a plot or even the allotment owner who keeps a single pig. I am told by a high agricultural authority that if this were done so great an effect would be produced upon the price of the food of the animal that where an agricultural labourer keeps one pig now he might keep two in the future. I propose to put a small tax of about 5 per cent. on foreign meat and dairy produce. I propose to exclude bacon, because once more bacon is a popular food with some of the poorest of the population. And, lastly, I propose to give a substantial preference to our colonies upon colonial wines and perhaps upon colonial fruits. Well, those are the taxes, new taxes, or alterations of taxation which I propose as additions to your present burden.

But I propose also some great remissions. I propose to take off three-fourths of the duty on tea and half of the whole duty on sugar, with a corresponding reduction on cocoa and coffee. Now, what will be the result of these changes: in the first place upon the cost of living; in the second place upon the Treasury? As regards the cost of living, I have accepted, for the purpose of argument, the figures of the Board of Trade as to the consumption of an ordinary workman's family, both in the country districts and in the towns, and I find that if he pays the whole of the new duties that I propose to impose it would cost an agricultural labourer 16½ farthings per week more than at present, and the artisan in the town 19½ farthings per week. In other words, it would add about 4d. per week to the expenditure of the agricultural labourer and 5d. per week on the expenditure of the artisan. But, then, the reduction which I propose, again taking the consumption as it is declared by the Board of Trade, the reduction would be—in the case of the agricultural labourer 17 farthings a week; in the case of the artisan 19½ farthings a week.

Now, gentlemen, you will see, if you have followed me, that upon the assumption that you pay the whole of the new taxes yourselves, the agricultural labourer would be half a farthing per week to the better, and the artisan would be exactly in the same position as at present. I have made this assumption, but I do not believe in it. I do not believe that these small taxes upon food would be paid to any large extent by the consumers in this country. I believe, on the contrary, they would be paid by the foreigner.

Now, that doctrine can be supported by authoritative evidence. In the first place, look at the economists—I am not speaking of the fourteen professors— but take John Stuart Mill, take the late Professor Sidgwick, and I could quote others now living. They all agree that of any tax upon imports, especially if the tax be moderate, a portion, at any rate, is paid by the foreigner, and that is confirmed by experience. I have gone carefully during the last few weeks into the statistical tables not only of the United Kingdom, but of other countries, and I find that neither in Germany, nor in France, nor in Italy, nor in Sweden, nor in the United Kingdom, when there has been the imposition of a new duty or an increase of an old duty, has the whole cost over a fair average of years ever fallen upon the consumer. It has always been partly paid by the foreigner. Well, how much is paid by the foreigner? That, of course, must be a matter of speculation, and, there again, I have gone to one of the highest authorities of this country—one of the highest of the official experts whom the Government consult—and I have asked him for his opinion, and in his opinion the incidence of a tax depends upon the proportion between the free production and the taxed production. In this case the free production is the home production and the production of the British colonies. The taxed production is the production of the foreigner, and this gentleman is of opinion that if, for instance, the foreigner supplies, as he does in the case of meat, two-ninths of the consumption, the consumer only pays two-ninths of the tax. If he supplies, as he does in the case of corn, something like three-fourths of the consumption, then the consumer pays three-fourths of the tax. If, as in dairy produce, he supplies half of the consumption, then the consumer pays half of the tax. Well, as I say, that is a theory that will be contested, but I believe it to be accurate, and at all events, as a matter of curiosity, I have worked out this question of the cost of living upon that assumption, and I find that, if you take that proportion, then the cost of the new duties would be 9½ farthings to the agricultural labourer and 10 farthings to the artisan, while the reduction would still be 17 farthings to the labourer and 19½ farthings to the artisan. There, gentlemen, you see my point. If I give my opponents the utmost advantage, if I say to them what I do not believe, if I grant that the whole tax is paid by the consumer, even in that case my proposal would give as large a remission of taxation on the necessary articles of his life as it imposes. As a result of the advantage upon other necessary articles, the budget at the end of the week or the result at the end of the year will be practically the same even if he pays the whole duty. But if he does not pay the whole duty, then he will get all the advantages to which I have already referred. In the case of the agricultural labourer he will gain about 2d. a week, and in the case of the town artisan he will gain 2½d. a week.

I feel how difficult it is to make either interesting or intelligible to a great audience like this the complicated subject with which I have to deal. But this is my opening declaration, and I feel that I ought to leave nothing untold; at all events, to lay the whole of the outlines of my scheme before the country.

Now, the next point, the last point I have to bring before you, is that these advantages to the consumer will involve a loss to the Exchequer. And you will see why. The Exchequer when it reduces tea or sugar loses the amount of the tax on the whole consumption, but when it imposes a tax on corn or upon meat it only gains the duty on a part of the consumption, since it does not collect it either upon the colonial or upon the home production. Well, I have had that worked out for me, also by an expert, and I find, even making allowance for growth in the colonial and home production which would be likely to be the result of the stimulus which we give to them—and after making allowances for those articles which I do not propose to tax—the loss to the Exchequer will be £2,800,000 per annum. How is it to be made up? I propose to find it, and to find more, in the other branch of this policy of fiscal reform, in that part of it which is sometimes called 'retaliation' and sometimes 'reciprocity.' Now I cannot deal fully with that subject to-night. I shall have other opportunities, but this I will point out to you, that in attempting to secure reciprocity we cannot hope to be wholly successful. Nobody, I imagine, is sanguine enough to believe that America or Germany and France and Italy and all those countries are going to drop the whole of their protective scheme because we ask them to do so, or even because we threaten. What I do hope is that they will reduce their duties so that worse things may not happen to them. But I think we shall also have to raise ours. Now a moderate duty on all manufactured goods, not exceeding 10 per cent. on the average, but varying according to the amount of labour in these goods—that is to say, putting the higher rate on the finished manufactures upon which most labour would be employed—a duty, I say, averaging 10 per cent. would give the Exchequer, at the very least, £9,000,-

000 a year, while it might be nearer £15,000,000 if we accept the Board of Trade estimates of £148,000,000 as the value of our imports of manufactured and partly manufactured goods. Nine millions a year—well, I have an idea that the present Chancellor of the Exchequer would know what to do with a full purse. For myself, if I were in that onerous position—which may Heaven forfend—I should use it in the first place to make up this deficit of £2,800,000 of which I have spoken; and, in the second place, I should use it for the further reduction both of taxes on food and also of some other taxes which press most hardly on different classes of the community. Remember this, a new tax cannot be lost if it comes to the Chancellor of the Exchequer. He cannot bury it in a stocking. He must do something with it, and the best thing he can do with it is to remit our taxation. The principle of all this policy is that whereas your present taxation, whether it be on food or anything else, brings you revenue and nothing but revenue, the taxation which I propose, which will not increase your burdens, will gain for you in trade, in employment, in all that we most want to maintain, the prosperity of our industries. The one is profitless taxation, the other scientific taxation.

I have stated, then, the broad outline of the plan which I propose. As I have said, this can only be filled up when a mandate has been given to the Government, when they have the opportunity which they desire to negotiate and discuss. It may be that when we have these taxes on manufactured goods, we might be willing to remit or reduce them if we could get corresponding advantages from the country whose products would thus be taxed. It cannot, therefore, be precisely stated now what they would bring in or what we should do, but this is clear that, whatever happened, we should get something. We should either get something in the shape of a reduction of other taxation or something in the shape of a reduction of those prohibitive tariffs which now hamper so immensely our native industries. There will be, according to this plan, as I have said, no addition to the cost of living, but only a transfer from one item to another.

It remains to ask, what will the colonies say? I hear it said sometimes by people who have never, I think, visited the colonies and do not know much about them, that they will receive this offer with contempt, that they will spurn it, or that if they accept it they will give nothing in return. Well, I differ from these critics. I do not do this injustice to the patriotism or the good sense of the colonies. When the prime ministers, representing all the several States of the Empire, were here, this was the matter of most interesting discussion. Then it was that they pressed upon the Government the consideration of this question. They did not press—it is wrong, it is wicked, to say that they pressed it in any spirit of selfishness, with any idea of exclusive benefit to themselves. No, they had Mr. Rhodes's ideal in their minds. They asked for it as a tie, a practical tie, which should prevent separation, and I do not believe that they will treat ungenerously any offer that we may now be able to make them. They had not waited for an offer. Already Canada has given you a preference of 33 1/3 per cent., South Africa has given you a preference of 25 per cent., New Zealand has offered a preference of 10 per cent. The premier of Australia has promised to bring before Parliament a similar proposal. They have done all this in confidence, in faith which I am certain will not be disappointed—in faith that you will not be ungrateful, that you will not be unmindful of the influences which have weighed with them, that you will share their loyalty and devotion to an Empire which is theirs as well as ours, and which they also have done something to maintain.

It is because I sympathise with their object, it is because I appreciate the wisdom, ay, the generosity of their offer, it is because I see that things are moving and that an opportunity now in your hands once lost will never recur; it is because I believe that this policy will consolidate the Empire—the Empire which I believe to be the security for peace and for the maintenance of our great British traditions—it is for all these things, and, believe me, for no personal ambition that I have given up the office which I was so proud to hold, and that now, when I might, I think, fairly claim a period of rest, I have taken up new burdens, and come before you as a missionary of Empire, to urge upon you again, as I did in the old times, when I protested against the disruption of the United Kingdom, once again to warn you, to urge you, to implore you to do nothing that will tend towards the disintegration of the Empire, and not to refuse to sacrifice a futile superstition, an inept prejudice, and thereby to lose the results of centuries of noble effort and patriotic endeavour.

EXPANSION INTO AFRICA

Report from Commander Sholto Douglas to Commodore W. Edmonstone Describing a Commercial Expedition to the Niger Valley, 2 October 1861*

I arrived and anchored off the Nun bar on the evening of the 9th July. At about 9 P.M. a vessel arrived and anchored not far from me, this proved to be the "Sunbeam" from Bonny; the tide being favourable, I followed her over the bar the next morning, taking fourteen feet across. I remained a few days at the anchorage inside Palm Point, waiting for the "Sunbeam" discharging and receiving cargo; this time I employed in getting out and leaving on board the hulk all the heavy stores so as to lighten the ship as much as possible. Started for the ascent on the morning of July 13, at 9 P.M.; had not got very far before the ship took the ground in Louis Creek; came off the next day at high water, and after some detention from the shoals about Sunday Island, arrived at Angiana on the 17th, and had an interview with the Chiefs and head men; settled one or two little disputes that had arisen between the agent in charge of the factory and the native traders, and left again on the 19th leaving them apparently well satisfied. This factory is the one that was founded in November 1860 by the "Bloodhound;" since this date there has been a brisk trade in palm oil carried on, and latterly it has increased very much.

After leaving Angiana no difficulty was encountered on the bar marked in Glover's Chart at the south point of Wilberforce island, but just after passing the village Asasi again grounded at the mouth of the Brass Creek; after some trouble got off. In sounding for a channel sufficient water could not be found for the "Espoir," though the "Sunbeam" from her light draft of water was able to cross with facility; as the water was now expected to rise very rapidly warped close up to the bank in readiness to get over.

On the 27th July finding the water rising very slowly took advantage of the offer of Captain Walker of the services of the "Rainbow" (see Inclosure No. 2), and proceeded to lighten the ship by getting all stores, coals, &c., into this vessel and lashing her alongside; by this means I was able to bring the ship up from twelve feet to ten feet ten inches.

On the 30th July, as a boat was despatched down the river I took the opportunity of writing in hopes of it reaching and informing the senior officer of my being detained at this point.

*Parliamentary Papers, 1862, LXI, Cmd. 2958, 107–09.

August 6th, at 11 A.M., hauled and steamed the ship over the bank, and, after picking up anchors and cables, steamed up to Ekebre, where I anchored for the night.

My time at this point was not entirely wasted, as I frequently visited the villages near to me, explaining to them the objects of the ship's visit, and pointed out the advantages to be gained by trade and intercourse with foreigners. To this they appeared fully alive, and were most anxious a factory should be placed at their village. The Chiefs visited the ships, of which they saw more than they could ever have done before, as on previous occasions no vessels have ever remained more than a few hours.

After having again been on shore for a day, arrived off Kpetema on the 8th August. These villages are two on the right and two on the left bank. Without the slightest provocation they fired on the "Sunbeam" and "Rainbow," coming down the river in November 1859. The four of them might contain about 2,000 inhabitants. Having anchored off the largest on the left bank, I sent on shore to call the Chiefs on board. After some hesitation they came, and on my questioning them about the attack they flatly denied it. When confronted with Captain Walker they began to prevaricate, then wished to go on shore and talk it over, and at length, when I insisted on an answer as to their reason for such an unprovoked attack, they all, with one consent, made a rush to the ports and jumped overboard, not waiting for their canoes, which were lying alongside.

One chief I detained as he was in the act of jumping out of a port. The people who covered the banks not fifty yards distant immediately rushed to arms, and I expected them to open fire every minute. The interpreter hailed them repeatedly to come off and talk the matter over. This having no effect, I sent for the Chief I had detained, told him the fact of their not stopping to talk the matter over proved their guilt. I would let him go, and if his brother Chiefs did not return and make their people lay down their arms, I must open fire in a quarter of an hour. The time having fully expired, the people only increasing in numbers and filling the bush on both sides of the town, I at 1:30 P.M. opened fire. After clearing the town, I landed with the boats of the ship, and fired the town. I then weighed and dropped down to the lower villages, and destroyed them in the same manner; during which time the natives were keeping up a smart fire from the bush and high grass which surrounded the town closely on all sides, unfortunately killing John Clanny, Stoker, and severely wounding Geo. Williams, A.B., who died a few days afterwards. In this service I was ably assisted by Mr. Teppett, Gunner, and Mr. Southwick, Master's Assistant; also by Mr. Bunn, Assistant Paymaster, and Mr. Slaughter, Assistant Surgeon, who volunteered their services in the boats.

After waiting till dark, not far from the upper village, in hopes of being able to open communication, but no one being seen, I shifted up a few miles for the night. The next morning (August 9th) arrived off the village of Sabogrega; on nearing this line of villages, which are about a mile and a-half long, a white flag was displayed from various points; these villages also fired on the ships in October and November 1859, killing a mate and a seaman of the "Rainbow."

On my sending on shore, the boat, at first, was not allowed to land: after sending several times, a message was sent off "that the ships might pass, they would not stop or molest them." Nothing would induce the Chiefs to come off to the ship.

As I found I was wasting valuable time in the attempt to open communications with these people, after waiting two days I proceeded up the river, deeming the punishment inflicted on the Kpetema villages would be sufficient warning to these; moreover, if I should now attack Sabogrega, I did not know if I might not drive the other doubtful villages into hostility, as well as giving them time to band together to attack the ships on their way down, which, in the event of the ship having to return with many sick, or getting aground, would not be pleasant, as the deep-water passage is close under the bank on which most of the villages are built, and from which they look down on the deck of a ship passing. I remained a day off the villages of Oloben and Imblamah. The Chiefs came off to the "Sunbeam," and exchanged presents with Captain Walker. Though these villages did not fire in 1859 their character is doubtful. Owing to this, I took care to inform them, through the Interpreter, that they had nothing to fear if they did not molest the ships. The next village called at was Agheir, which fired on the "Sunbeam" and "Rainbow" on the passage up in July 1859, wounding Captain Wild, and again on the "Sunbeam" coming down in November. These people are a different tribe to those about them, and are reported to have emigrated from the Ware branch, and settled in their present position, from which they exact tribute from all canoes passing. The Chief made a statement that it was the people of an adjacent village who fired on the ships, without his knowledge or consent, for which he had punished them. He promises none of his people should offend again, and before I left a law was proclaimed in the village to punish any one who should do so.

I arrived at Aboh on the 15th August; and in anchoring found that the factory had totally disappeared; this agreed with the report that had reached Captain Walker at Angiana in January. I sent on shore to call the King on board. Ajie is the present King. The power seems to be divided between him and his brothers Akia and Tschukuma, all sons of the late Obi. Ajie came the first day, and in answer to questions about the factory, he stated that it was washed away in October 1860 by the uncommon rise of the river; that Mr. Cole, the agent who had been left in charge, was gone to the factory at Onitsha. He declined to answer any further questions until Mr. Cole arrived. A boat was accordingly sent from the "Sunbeam" for him. The Chiefs still frequented the ships daily, and received presents from Captain Walker, and all stated their intention of coming to talk the matter over on Mr. Cole's arrival. On the 19th I sent to tell the Chiefs that I was ready to see them, and that Mr. Cole had arrived. The messenger returned with an answer that I must come to the beach to them. On their arrival on the bank I sent to remind them of their promise, as well as of the facts that all palavers before had been held on board. They refused to come, and after several messages Ajie sent to say that as I had sent for him and would not see him, if I sent again he would not come. On sending this message he immediately returned to the town, accompanied by the Chiefs and their followers, of whom there were several hundred, mostly armed.

I inclose a statement of Mr. Cole's (Inclosure No. 3) regarding the plunder of the factory, and the treatment to which he was subjected. The Chiefs did not give me an opportunity of hearing their side of the question. I cannot but think there must have been some provocation given on the part of Mr. Cole, the more so as during the residence of another agent (Mr. Lyall) at the Aboh factory, affairs went on much more smoothly. They may, perhaps, have been partly induced to go so far as they did from no notice having been taken of the attack on the ships in 1859; the natives fancied they had driven us from the river entirely. The accounts of the factory were lost by Mr. Cole, who brought forward claims against the Chiefs for various goods; they again (as stated by Mr. Cole) brought counter-claims that the ground had never been paid for, and there were also large debts owing to Tschukuma, many of them of long standing.

Having waited till 3 P.M. on the 20th of August, in hopes of the King coming off, I weighed and proceeded up the river, intending again to try and communicate with them on my way down. I did not communicate with any towns between Aboh and Onitsha, though most of them are under the influence of Aboh, except Midoni Osomari, the town to which Tschukuma's mother belongs, has been at war with Aboh, but is now at peace. The Oko villages are, I believe, the highest point to which the influence of Aboh extends.

On the 23rd August, arrived and anchored off the Onitsha factory. The agent in charge reported all well, though various reports of an intended attack had reached him. The Aboh people had been trying to induce the Onitshas to join them in plundering the factory, telling them that no notice had been taken of the doings last year, or of the previous at Sabogrega.

The town of Onitsha is situated in the middle of a thick wood. These people are not a canoe people, seldom going on the water. One of their superstitions is that the King shall never see the river; he is consequently not allowed to leave his house except on very rare occasions. Another custom or superstition, the King never provides any mat or seat for any one native or foreigner visiting him. Since our first intercourse with these people in 1857 this has caused a number of disputes; latterly the King has allowed the Europeans visiting him to bring their own chairs. Further, shortly before my visit, the King sent to the factory saying there should be no more palaver about seats. On my arrival, I sent to say I intended to visit the King the next day, and trusted he would carry out his promise in this matter. The messenger returned with an answer that the King would do so.

The next day, on arriving at his house, I was much surprised to find the King sitting in state, with not a mat even prepared for us.

A few words ensued between the King and myself; so finding my position not very dignified, I turned my back on him, and returned on board.

The next day all the chief men of the town sent to say they would be glad to see me. I accordingly met them at the factory. They appeared sorry for what had taken place, but while they acknowledged it was a most foolish custom, regretted their inability to induce the King to give in. After this I made no attempt to visit the King, nor did I hear from him. The Chiefs were most friendly and civil to myself and officers whenever we visited the town.

From the King's confinement to his house he is perfectly ignorant of all affairs outside, and has accordingly taken advantage of it when appealed to in any dispute by the agent in charge of the factory, who has consequently received no redress.

Understanding that the state of the country was settled above this point, I did not deem it advisable to risk Her Majesty's ship by taking her to the Confluence. I accordingly informed Captain Walker, of the "Sunbeam," that I would wait his return from that point. I also took advantage of the opportunity to communicate with Dr. Baikie, and inform him of my proceedings in the Delta.

On the 14th September the "Sunbeam" returned, and after breaking up the factory I started, in company with her, on the 21st for the descent. Before leaving Onitsha I called the Chiefs, and explained to them that the factory was broken up on account of Mr. Laird's death, but the idea seemed to obtain with them that it was owing to the King's conduct. I have no doubt that if another factory is to be formed here, sooner than lose the benefits of our trade, they will concede the question of seats, if pressed.

Arriving at Aboh on the afternoon of the 21st, I sent to call on Tschukuma and his brothers. The boat returned late in the evening, stating that Ajie and Akia were at Oko, but he (Tschukuma) would come off the next day. Because he should have no excuse for not coming, I sent a boat, but now he was sick, and would come the next day. I sent again the third time on the 23rd. Mr. Southwick, Master's Assistant, was in the boat—the cutter manned by kroomen; no arms; the colours flying. After pulling some distance up the creek, he landed, and walked to Tschukuma's house, some 400 yards from the boat. According to my instructions, he informed Tschukuma I had sent a boat for him if he wished to come off, but he refused to do so.

On Mr. Southwick's leaving the house, a large number of people had collected outside, who attempted to seize him and two of the kroomen who had strayed from the boat. They all, however, reached the bank in safety, and shoved off, the natives following him down the bank, but not attempting to fire, though many had arms with them. It seemed to have been their object to detain him, if possible.

I now gave up all hopes of coming to any peaceable arrangement, or recovering any of the British property from these people. Even if my instructions had allowed me to do so, I did not feel justified in attacking a large town of this sort, of which the lowest estimated population is 8,000.

I could not approach closer than half-a-mile to the nearest point, while the more distant part is fully two miles. Shelling a town of such magnitude, &c., from one gun would have been absurd. I cannot but add that this attack on the boat was most unprovoked, and tends to show how little trust should be placed in these people.

Having well considered the subject, and determined not to act myself in the matter, I left the town as soon as possible, and proceeded down the river, and the towns I had formerly visited appeared friendly: the natives crowded the banks to see the ship, so I did not deem it necessary to again stop.

The Kpetema villages were rebuilt; the natives were not to be seen till passing the last village, when a few were visible; but, after the ship had left them a quarter of a mile astern, well out of range, they commenced firing, and kept it up for some time. This, I believe, was meant for a defiance or challenge for me to return and fight them; but as they had refrained from actually firing on the ship, I did not molest them. All the so-called hostile towns, as well as Imblamah and Oloheir, are, I believe, governed by independent Chiefs, yet at times they act together and assist one another.

I arrived at Angiana on the 24th, and, finding all well, proceeded to the anchorage at the Nun mouth, which I reached on the morning of the 25th. The "Sunbeam" arriving next day, after having broken up the Angiana factory, I remained at the mouth of the river preparing for sea till the 28th, when the bar being good I crossed at high-water. Outside I met the "Bloodhound," just arrived with provisions. These I received, and weighed the same evening to proceed to Lagos.

I am happy to state that no deaths from fever occurred during the eighty-one days the "Espoir" was in the river. The weather was very dry; no rain during July and August. The general health of the ship's company was very good for the first thirty days, after which cases of fever appeared, gradually increasing in number till the fifty-second day, when a third of the ship's company were sick. From this time the amount of fever gradually diminished, and ague appeared, from which, and the debilitating effects of the fever, many are, and will suffer for some time.

Speech by Lord Elcho in the House of Commons Attacking the Occupation of Egypt, 10 August 1882*

LORD ELCHO rose to ask the First Lord of the Treasury, Whether, before engaging in military operations, other than such as may be necessary for the defence of Alexandria, the protection of the Khedive, and the security of the Suez Canal, they will endeavour to ascertain the true state of feeling of the Egyptian Nation? The noble Lord said, he proposed slightly to amplify his Question, and with that view he should conclude with a Motion. He felt constrained to apologize for the course which he was about to take; but he was so deeply impressed with the gravity of the situation in Egypt that he could not forego making a few observations on the subject. Look where they would, the situation was grave—there was darkness all around. He had no wish to open up

*Hansard, 3.s., CCLXXIII, 1384–87.

the question of the general policy of Her Majesty's Government, or to enter into the general Egyptian Question. All he wished to do was to get a distinct and clear expression from the Government as to whom they were at war with. The first part of the present military operations consisted of the bombardment of Alexandria. Two reasons were given for that bombardment—namely, the protection of the Fleet, and the necessity of asserting their prestige after the murders that had taken place. The bombardment was followed by the despatch of troops to Egypt—not by any declaration of war, because there was no Power against whom they could declare war; but the reasons given for the despatch of troops were, as he understood, the necessity of putting a stop to, or crushing, military lawlessness, of restoring order where anarchy prevailed, and of restoring the authority of the Khedive. The Prime Minister had said at the Mansion House on Wednesday evening—

> It is true that we have gone to Egypt with the Forces of this country in the prosecution of the great interests of the Empire which it is our duty to cherish and defend.

Nothing could give him greater pleasure than to see his right hon. Friend coming forward as the defender of their Imperial interests. He admitted that, in the absence of the action of the Sovereign of that country, the Sultan, whose proper duty it was to maintain order, it might be right and just, considering the interests which England had in Egypt, and considering the necessity of making the Suez Canal secure, that they should endeavour to put a stop to military lawlessness, and restore order in that country. But what he wanted to know was this—was this question in Egypt simply one of military lawlessness and anarchy, or had they to deal, as was much more likely, with the Egyptian people? Now, how was the evidence? Was there any evidence one way or the other? He asked his hon. Friend the Under Secretary of State for Foreign Affairs the other day whether he could contradict or confirm the statement that a public meeting had taken place in Egypt to demand administrative reforms. His answer was that they had no information. On the 29th of last month another great meeting was held. Those present determined to support Arabi Pasha. Were they men of straw? A list containing the signatures of those who approved of the meeting included the names of the Minister of the Interior, 10 Princes, many Pashas, the Armenian Vicar, the Vicar of the Maronites, the Vicar of the Orthodox Greeks, the Grand Rabbi of Cairo, and Notables of all parts of Egypt. It might be said that in giving their signatures they acted under the duress of bayonets. There was no proof of that. As far as they knew, there was no evidence that it was not an absolutely free assembly of Egyptians. He was not aware that they had made any "Rules of Procedure" in Egypt, and he had not yet heard that in Egypt they had established the Caucus; and, therefore, everything tended rather to show that it was an absolutely free expression of free men managing their own affairs in that country. They had the testimony of an English gentleman who had arrived at Alexandria from Cairo that the meeting was held with open doors; and, in the absence of anything more distinct and definite, he thought they were justified in assuming that they were dealing with the Egyp-

tian people as a whole. But there was one other authority he knew of to support
the opinion that they were dealing with more than a mere army of rebels, and
that was the authority of the right hon. Gentleman the Prime Minister himself,
who, in his speech at the Mansion House, said—

> I do not deny that there is in Egypt something besides a military
> tyranny;

and:

> There are a section or class of men in Egypt who now wish to help the
> military tyranny which prevails.

Who was this section? Unless it could be shown that all the important
personages who signed the determination to which he referred—all the local
magnates, all the Ministers at Cairo, and all the heads of the Native religion—
were not acting freely, he was justified in saying that the section and class to
which the right hon. Gentleman referred was practically the whole of the
Egyptian people. His right hon. Friend would doubtless ask him—"What do
you wish us to do? Do you wish us to stop in our military action altogether? Do
you wish 30,000 men to be kept idle in Egypt, and that no further step should
be taken?" That was not what he wished at all. What he wished was this—that
the Government should proceed with their despatch of troops and the Military
Convention with the Sultan, occupy all the strategic points on the map at once,
and, having done that, they would be in such a strong position that they would
be able to find out what was the true state of affairs, and what course it was
necessary to take in regard to them. If, after having done that, they found that
it was simply a matter with regard to a rebel colonel and a mutinous Army,
they would find that the affair would suddenly come to naught; but if, on the
other hand, they discovered it to be the national will of the people, then they
had no right to interfere in order to prevent that national will being carried out.
If the people of Egypt had good ground for their objection to the Khedive—and
it was plainly shown that they had—then Her Majesty's Government had no
right to support the Khedive, and should allow the people of Egypt to manage
their own affairs. For his part, he should be glad if it could be shown that Her
Majesty's Government were justified in taking action for the restoration of order
in Egypt; but he hoped they would not act unadvisedly or hastily. In taking the
course he had he was aware that he was likely to render himself unpopular,
because, at the present moment, the nation was bent more or less on war; but
he hoped the Government would not listen to the irresponsible advice that they
obtained by the yard through the columns of the British Press, because, if they
did, they would be prepared to put all Europe up in arms against them, to risk
bringing the whole Mussulman population of the world against them, and to
treat the Turkish Government of Egypt as if it had no existence. The simple
object he had in putting his Question was to give them an opportunity of stating
with whom they were at war; whether it was a rebel colonel and a mutinous
soldiery or the Egyptian people? The noble Lord concluded by moving the
adjournment of the House.

Speech by Sir H. Drummond Wolff in the House of Commons
Criticizing the Occupation of Egypt, 10 August 1882*

SIR H. DRUMMOND WOLFF, in seconding the Motion, disclaimed any intention
to embarrass the Government in the military operations which they had undertaken. But, while desirous of assisting the Government to carry the war to a
successful issue, he would like to hear a statement from them as to its exact
objects. They were at that moment employed, he supposed, in conjunction with
Turkey, in suppressing an insurrection on the part of Arabi, who thought to
depose the Khedive. He could conceive that they might be very much bound to
support the Khedive, because he undertook the government of Egypt at their
request, and had shown himself all along to be a loyal ally. At the same time,
he could not conceive, if the people of Egypt really objected to him as their
Sovereign, that they had any right to retain him there against the consent of the
Egyptian people. When they recommended the King of Greece in 1864 they did
not undertake to maintain him in Greece, but made stipulations by which, in
case Greece wished at any time to get rid of him, he should have ample
provision for a living. If, in the same way, it were found that the present
Khedive was repugnant to the Egyptian people, this country was bound to
secure, not merely the safety of his life, but an ample provision befitting his
dignity. What he wanted to know was, what the Government intended to do in
Egypt? They would probably not find it difficult to suppress Arabi; but, after
that, were they going to maintain the occupation of Egypt indefinitely, or to
establish some form of popular government which would enable it to remain
independent of foreign occupation? He could conceive nothing more dangerous
than a British occupation of Egypt for the purpose of establishing Prince
Tewfik, unless, at the same time, Europe was given to understand that the
occupation would last no longer than was necessary to establish such a form of
government as would be acceptable to the people of Egypt, and enable them to
maintain order without any foreign intervention whatever. A great part of the
recent complications had arisen from the action of the Government on every
occasion being influenced by France. It was the object of France to suppress the
popular movement in Egypt. The Chamber of Notables professed no desire to
interfere with the international obligations of the country, and asked no more
than was the right of every Representative Body; yet, when Cherif Pasha asked
the Government of this country to suggest some compromise, no notice was
taken of the request. He would not go into the question of the Debts, because
that had been settled by the Control; but he could not help expressing his
anxious wish that the Control would not be established in the form in which it

*Hansard, 3.s., CCLXXIII, 1387–89.

had hitherto been conducted. These were matters on which everyone must feel anxious. They were anxious to know what was the policy of the Government in this intervention—whether they had any policy as to the future? They were anxious to know whether they were going to attempt to do what was impossible— namely, to re-establish the *status quo ante;* or whether they really and truly intended to establish such a state of things in Egypt as would, while maintaining the internal obligations Egypt had entered into, establish the liberties of the Egyptian people on a firm basis?

Motion made, and Question proposed, "That this House do now adjourn."

---

*Speech by the Prime Minister, William E. Gladstone, in the House
of Commons in Defense of the Decision to Intervene
in Egypt, 10 August 1882**

There is some difficulty on raising a great question of this kind in narrowing the issue, and the tendency is that the discussion, when once opened, should extend itself to a much wider field; and my noble Friend the Mover of this Motion will be able to see how this proposition is illustrated by the far greater scope of the speech of his Seconder, who entirely, in seconding the Motion, passed away from everything that was contained in the Question that gave rise to it, and really supplied a text upon which, if the House were so inclined, we might renew the debate of four nights which we had, I think, during the week before last. Well, now, Sir, I sincerely hope that the House will not accept the invitation which has thus been given; and I say that, not because I object to the spirit of most of the remarks of the hon. Gentleman who seconded the Motion. On the contrary, I commend his sympathies with the Egyptian people. It is a fair and proper question, indeed, to raise, whether, in conjunction with any Proclamation from the Sultan, or in connection with the commencement of the full operations contemplated, it may be right for Her Majesty's Government to convey a distinct and formal assurance in a shape likely to become known to the Egyptian people as to the nature and extent of the objects which we contemplate. I may, perhaps, draw the attention of the hon. Gentleman and of the House to a circumstance which is worth remembering. The subject has not escaped our attention, and, under the instructions of Her Majesty's Government, the Commander of the Fleet has already conveyed to the Khedive of Egypt distinct assurances upon those questions. Undoubtedly, at a later stage those assurances might be repeated and enlarged by someone with larger authority than that of the Admiral of the Squadron; but an assurance from him seemed the best adapted to the earlier stages of the proceedings. Sir, I must decline to enter at the present moment upon a definition of the objects of the

Hansard, 3.s., CCLXXIII, 1389–97.

military operations now proceeding; but I can go so far as to answer the hon. Gentleman when he asks me whether we contemplate an indefinite occupation of Egypt. Undoubtedly, of all things in the world, that is a thing which we are not going to do. It would be absolutely at variance with all the principles and views of Her Majesty's Government, and the pledges they have given to Europe, and with the views, I may say, of Europe itself. With respect to the Chamber of Notables, I must, in passing, say one word. That question is a question in respect to which our conduct and our exact proceedings have never been laid before the House. It may be necessary to lay them before the House; but as the proceedings were in some respects joint proceedings, I cannot at present give a definite answer as to producing the Papers. I only wish to point out that the House is not at the present time in possession of the evidence that would be necessary in order to enable it to form a conclusion upon the conduct of Her Majesty's Government with respect to the Chamber of Notables. There is one part of the remarks of the hon. Gentleman which I heard with unfeigned regret, and which I cannot help thinking, on reflection, will inspire him with some misgiving. He stated, and stated very fairly, that we were under very great and strong obligations to maintain in Egypt the position and authority of the Khedive, who has been placed in his present position with the very highest sanction and authority, and who has been completely faithful, under very difficult circumstances, to the obligations under which he came when he assumed them. Therefore, the hon. Gentleman most fairly and justly says that we are greatly bound to maintain the authority and position of the Khedive; but he goes on to say that if we should find that the Egyptian people were not in favour of his remaining in his present position, then it is a matter with which we have to do to see that a respectable and ample provision is made for him during his life. Now, Sir, why raise that question? If we wish to maintain the authority of a Ruler, one of the most unfortunate and left-handed methods of setting about it is to refer to contingencies before us not founded on the reasons of the case. Undoubtedly, if such language were adopted by the Government, instead of being, as I must say it is, repudiated by the Government, if the tendency was to give the impression that we were not, after all, more than half in earnest, if we were to give the impression that we had some secondary purpose—some latent idea—on which we intended to fall back, in case of need, with the view of bringing about a totally different state of things—

SIR H. DRUMMOND WOLFF: What I meant to say was that we were certainly not bound to maintain the Khedive by an indefinite occupation.

MR. GLADSTONE: I am very glad to accept any explanation which the hon. Gentleman makes for the purpose of obviating the inferences which may be too hastily drawn from his speech with regard to the position of the Khedive. The reason I do not speak fully on the question of the final arrangements with regard to Egypt is not because I differ from the hon. Gentleman, when he says that he thinks, after all that has now taken place, the re-establishment of the *status quo ante* can no longer be regarded as the definite and adequate purpose with which we are to move and to conduct our military operations—in that I agree with him, and I admit that the larger field of consideration is of necessity open to us—but it is because it would not be expedient at this stage of affairs that we should attempt to anticipate by declarations—necessarily delivered in a crude and in an immature condition of the evidence—that we should endeavour to anticipate by such declarations the results, which, according to our own positive engagements, must be arrived at with the intervention and under the authority of Europe, and which never could be adequately founded on the simple conclusions of any single Power in Europe. I pass now to the Question put by my noble Friend, and to the argument by which he supported it. It would, perhaps, be wrong in me to complain of my noble Friend giving the sanction of an old Member to this practice of moving the adjournment after he has so frankly admitted that it is a course requiring apology. I am thankful to believe that the time is near at hand when apology will no longer be necessary, and when the House, by positive and resolute methods, may take security against its occurrence. I fully admit to my noble Friend that he is justified in demanding from me an explanation of any words used by me at the Mansion House, and I will give him that explanation. He says I admitted that in Egypt we have something to deal with besides the Military Party. I am willing to give him that admission, and it is an admission which I think will be readily perceived to be really inherent in any attempt to describe thoroughly the facts as they are in Egypt with reference to its recent history and its present condition. There is no doubt that if we go back to the period antecedent to the establishment of the Foreign Control, we come upon a state of things when the cultivators of the soil in Egypt, who, like the cultivators of the soil in Ireland, may be said almost to form the bulk of the nation, were subject to a system of abominable oppression. But wherever there is oppression there are oppressors; there are instruments of that oppression; there are people who profit by it, people who live by it; and it is the oppressors of the people who most resent interference, and who most readily avail themselves of any opportunity that may offer for complaining of the means by which the interference is effected, and who are most ready to enter into any measures, whatever they may be, for the purpose of bringing back a state of things which was to them a paradise, but which to their fellow-countrymen was more like a hell. Those are the gentlemen whom I fully admit to be the allies of Arabi Pasha and of the Military Party. I need not go back upon the discussion of the question of the Foreign Control, which I have endeavoured myself to treat in what I may call an historical sense—that is to say, to recognize its advantages and its disadvantages. Its disadvantages have been that it might be represented, and not only so, but it might in some respects be said to be an interference with the fair rights of the Egyptian people, and a limitation of the development of their future institutions; but we must not forget the fact that it had considerable apology and justification from the state of things to which it applied, and that it is beyond all question that great practical benefits resulted from it, and from the substitution of European for Oriental methods in the administration of finances and the levying of taxes in Egypt. That is one thing which accounts for the nature of the very limited scope of the admission which I made when I said that something besides the Military Party might be found in support of Arabi Pasha. Then I come to the evidence which my noble Friend has given and to the question of the evidence which he has demanded of me. He desires that we should endeavour to ascertain the true state of feeling of the Egyptian people, but he does not desire that without limitation; because he says that he considers it right that we should take all the measures necessary for the defence of Alexandria, for the protection of the Khedive, and for the security of the Suez Canal, and I think he explained that to mean that we might take into our own possession the principal strategical points of the country. Well, I think if we take into our own possession the principal strategical points of the country we shall have very little occasion to quarrel with my noble Friend as to the limitation which he imposes upon us in respect to ascertaining the feeling of the people of Egypt; for after we have obtained the principal strategical points of the country we shall be in a condition, without prejudice to any of the objects that were in view, to make any inquiry we please into either the feeling of the Egyptian people or any other subject. But the matter is a serious one; and I wish to challenge the mode which my noble Friend takes of presenting what he appears to think is adequate evidence of a feeling of the people of Egypt favourable to Arabi Pasha and his confederates, for he is not the only one, after all, with whom we have to deal. He has a knot of other persons around him who find a considerable portion of the brains that are engaged in these mutinous and mischievous operations. I am very sorry that my noble Friend has found it his duty to raise a discussion at the present time; because, undoubtedly, although I do not anticipate very serious public mischief from it, I think the mind of this country is pretty well made up on the subject of the rights or wrongs of the quarrel in which we are engaged. [MR. O'DONNELL: No, no! *and cries of* "Hear, hear!"] I am very glad, therefore, to think that my noble Friend does stand, to a great degree, in that respect in an isolated position. I do not mean to say that there are no differences of opinion with regard to the question of intervention in the affairs of Egypt—that is quite a different matter—but I mean I believe the mind of the country is well made up in general as to the necessity, and as to the justice, of the cause which we have in hand, and is yet more clearly made up on the question whether it is or is not with the concurrence of the Egyptian people that we are now going in conflict. My noble Friend thinks he has evidence to produce, and he produces the evidence, and quoted from journals published under the permission of what I may call the rebellious and military Government in Cairo, which gives accounts of certain meetings and treats them as representing the sense of the people. I believe my noble Friend would find that these very same journals are the journals which have seriously reported for the information of the Egyptian people the sinking of the British iron-clads before Alexandria; and which, when Moubarek Pasha came down to Alexandria and saw for himself the British iron-clads afloat, propagated the story likewise for the information of the Egyptian people that the original iron-clads had been

sunk, and that they were a new set which had come to take their places! That is
the evidence drawn from such a source. The fact is that a system of falsification
is employed wholesale in Egypt with reference to the Khedive, with reference,
of course, to the English, and with reference to whatever obstructs or impedes
the plans of military violence. I think it is not difficult to understand that such a
system of falsification may prevail, when it is borne in mind that falsification
has been carried, avowedly and unquestionably carried in the case of this
Military Party in Egypt, beyond, I believe, any point it has ever been known to
reach in the history of the world. For that Party did not scruple to falsify the
most sacred of all obligations in war—namely, those attaching to the use of a
flag of truce, and while pretending to have pacification in view, not only had no
such purpose, but used the hours gained by the employment of that flag of truce
for the base and abominable purpose of conflagration and looting. [MR. O'DON-
NELL: No, no!] I believe I am speaking of a matter subject to no dispute, but
which is absolutely as certain as is the bombardment of Alexandria. My noble
Friend asks what evidence we have that we are not at variance with the
sentiments of the people of Egypt. Well, Sir, those who know that those who
decline the authority of Arabi Pasha are dismissed from their offices and
imprisoned; those who know that Arabi Pasha has set aside the authority of the
Notables; those who know that we have a large body of European and British
residents in Egypt—and if I except the unfortunate case of Mr. Blunt, which it
is not for me to explain, who, I believe, still remains under the delusions which
have been formed—I believe there is not one among these, even including
gentlemen who were formerly inclined to take a more favourable view, who has
the smallest idea, or who does not emphatically repudiate the idea, that Arabi
Pasha and his confederates are the representatives of the National movement. I
think I am bound to say that, besides those residents, we have the testimony of
official men—those connected with the Consulate and those connected with the
Control, gentlemen of high position, of high character. [MR. O'DONNELL: No!
and cries of "Order!"] I affirm that Sir Auckland Colvin, Sir Edward Malet,
Mr. Cartwright, Mr. Cookson, and the various other gentlemen who have been
connected with the official representation of this country in Egypt, are gentlemen of high character. The gentlemen I have named are all competent and fair
witnesses, and we may fall back with confidence upon their testimony were it
necessary. But the matter does not rest with them; there are public men of high
character in Egypt—Egyptians, Mahomedans, men known to the world—who
have borne high office in Egypt. Is there one of these men who has given the
smallest countenance, direct or indirect, to the cause of Arabi Pasha? Some of
them are men of well known character and reputation. There are Riaz Pasha,
who was at the head of the Egyptian Government; Cherif Pasha, who was at
the head of the Government only dismissed a few months ago; Sultan Pasha,
the head of the Chamber of Notables, and a Mahomedan of the highest
influence and best character. There is not one of these men who has not been
found on the side of the Khedive in support of his lawful authority. It is really
too late to raise a question of this kind, because the conclusion we have arrived

at, and on which we are acting, is not a British conclusion alone; it is the conclusion of all Europe. Europe has met together at Constantinople, and Europe has by its united voice and by its united appeal to the Sultan declared that the Power which has paralyzed the authority of the Khedive is an unlawful, a rebellious, and a mischievous Power, and has appealed to the Sultan to put it down by force of arms. Surely, under these circumstances, it is late for any Member of the British Parliament, not only when his country has definitely acted, but when Europe has acted and has delivered its own deliberate conclusion, it is too late to ask the question whether Arabi Pasha is or is not the representative of the Egyptian nation. I hold that the authority of the united Powers of Europe and the evidence afforded by their conclusion are the highest and the most conclusive of which the case admits, and it absolves us from the necessity of a minute discussion of this or that—evidence I need hardly call it—gossip or tittle-tattle, and those figments which newspapers, under the domain of military violence, would seek to palm off upon the world, representations which were thoroughly and entirely false. That is my answer to my noble Friend. We have not the results of formal inquiry, of which the case does not admit; but we have a mass of moral evidence, supported by intelligent testimony of every character and from every quarter unvaried and unbroken, and supported by the responsibility of every Government; it is a known, patent, and notorious fact that we have the judgment of the whole civilized world. That is my answer with regard to the Egyptian people. I trust the ulterior development of this question and the conduct and policy of this country will be such as to verify the assurance with which we have entered into the struggle we are about to commence—namely, that we are not making war against the Egyptian people; but that we are determined to put down those who are oppressing the people of Egypt, those who are, in our opinion, not only contemning the lawful authority of the country, but are likewise engaged in machinations contrary to liberty, having for their certain result, were they to succeed, the revival of all the abominable abuses and oppressions which formerly debased the condition of that country.

Account by Major-General Charles Gordon of the Final Days of the Siege of Khartoum, the Sudan, by the Forces of the Mahdi, 3–14 December 1884*
[The fortress fell on 25 January 1885 with no British troops surviving.]

December 3.—This morning Arabs fired eight rounds at us, and we replied; one of our shells struck their casemate. Numbers of Arabs left Mahdi's camp for the north. Arabs fired nine rounds into the town at night from the south lines. One shell fell into the garden of the Palace; this from the south lines. A

*Gordon, *Journals*, 378–95.

shell from Arabs at Goba fell in the garden, so it will be seen the attention which is being paid to the Palace.

Twenty shells fell in town yesterday, but none did any harm.

I think this is the programme, and though it is of doubtful morality, perhaps it is the shortest route out of a mess. "British Expedition comes up to relieve British subjects in distress, *nothing else;* it finds one of its subjects acting as ruler; it takes him away, and he, on going away, appoints Zubair ruler, subject to approval of Towfik, Zubair having been allowed to come up to Kartoum, as a private individual, to look after his family."

Now who can say anything to the British Government? It has had nothing to do with the appointment of Zubair, or with the Government of Towfik; it came up to relieve its subjects, and "Gordon is entirely responsible for the appointment of Zubair;" "even Towfik is not responsible, for Gordon did it on his own responsibility." This will be a splendid dodge; it first clears Her Majesty's Government of any blame, it puts the blame on me, and in the storm that is caused, I shall have been so effectually blackened that every one will forget the—well! we will not say it in direct words (count the months), we will call the DELAY; in fact, I expect the public will rather blame the Government for having sent any Expedition at all for such a style of British subject; the Government will chuckle over it all, and will preserve the *fiction* that they have nought to do with the Soudan or Egypt.

The Opposition will be perfectly wild at seeing the Ministry get out of the mess, with what one may call really credit, while the Anti-Slavery Society and Europe at large will empty their vials of wrath on me. Towfik and his pashas will wring their hands *openly* over such an act. . . . will get such kudos! For my part I shall get out of any of those wretched honours, for the Ministry will be only too glad to say, "We could not, you know, confer any honours on him after such very disreputable conduct," knowing well enough I would not take them if offered; and as I am not going to England again, and shall not see the papers, I shall not much mind the abuse. I think it is a splendid programme. Zubair must be given either £200,000 or £300,000 a year for two years, replenished magazines, and stores of all sorts, all the Expedition's boats and steamers, &c., &c., and must be aided for two months in small expeditions; besides the £200,000 or £300,000 for two years, he must have down on the nail £150,000 to £200,000.

I must clear, in disgrace, out of the country, to prevent any appearance of any connivance on the part of . . . in this arrangement, which he will or ought officially to deplore. I do not think Zubair will care for the Equator Province; he will agree to give that up; he will agree to uphold the Treaty of 1877 Slave Convention, and laugh as he does so. As for the Bahr Gazelle, I expect the Mahdi has it, and if so, his people will move up there, when Zubair by his politics recaptures Obeyed.

What a fearful row there will be. I know one man who will write: "Better, my dear Gordon, FAR better! to have died, than have so very far departed from the right path; nothing, no nothing can explain it away. A happy Christmas to you." . . . "This news from the Soudan is very satisfactory; I call it a great triumph, for it not only delivers us out of a dilemma, but it effectually settles our friends, and vitiates anything he may say as to the Delay." Any military operations undertaken after the proclamation of Zubair will be put down "as measures necessary to be undertaken to secure the return, unmolested, of the expeditionary force." 5 P.M. Artillery duel going on between our two guns and the Arab gun; our practice is very bad. The shells the Arabs fire from their Krupp gun reach the Palace Garden, but the report of their gun is not to be heard. The Arab shells from Goba fall just about 200 yards short of the Palace; but in its line there is just the second of suspense (after seeing them fire), while one hears the soft sighing of their shells coming nearer and nearer, till they strike. 7 P.M. *Another battle!* (the third to-day). The Arabs came down to the river and fired on the Palace; we could not stand *that*. 7.10 P.M. Battle over; we are as we were, minus some cartridges. 7.20 P.M. Battle begun again, because the buglers played "Salaam Effendina," the Arabs wasting ammunition. 8 P.M. The Arabs are firing from the south at the Krupps on the Palace; they (*i.e.* the Arabs) are at least 4000 yards distant; one hears the shells burst, but not the report of their gun; they reached the river close to the Palace.

December 4.—Omdurman Fort all right. They had a man wounded yesterday. There was a small battle at Bourré this morning. The Arabs at Goba are quiet after the exertions of yesterday. Firing was heard (on north) towards Shoboloha last night. Report in town says the steamers are near there.

Should the Zubair arrangement be accepted, then comes the question of the military action during two months, at end of which time the expeditionary force should be wending its way back. The driving away of the Arabs from the Dem at the north of the Palace will be immediate on the arrival of the troops; the Arabs will then hold on to El foun and to Giraffe. They will vacate the vicinity of Omdurman Fort; 1000 men will deal with El foun and Giraffe, supported by our tag-rag. First Giraffe, then El foun; but at the same time as this takes place, the retreat of Arabs ought to be cut off at Gitana from Kordofan by the steamers and another 1000 men; the Mahdi will return to Schatt, and the town will be free, and all the troops defending the lines will be available. Then comes the question of going inland and attacking the family of the Sheikh el Obeyed's son, two and a half hours inland, or else going on and attacking Mesalamieh. I think Sheikh el Obeyed's family will give in as soon as the Arabs are driven from El foun (an affair of an hour, *D.V.*). I tried to entice the Arabs at Goba into a fight this evening, but they would not be drawn, and only replied by two shells, which fell in the river. We played on them with the mitrailleuse, and made them move their gun, and then they fired two more shells, one which fell near the Palace in the river. With a good mitrailleuse, and a sharp operator, *with telescope sight*, no gun could be served with impunity at 2000 yards range, though it could be served *against artillery fire,* for at that range there is plenty of time to dodge under cover after seeing the flash ere the shell arrives. The band, principally of small boys, the men being on the lines, went on to the roof of the Palace to play (they always come on the eve of their Sabbath, the Friday). The Arabs heard them, and fired a volley at them; they, furious, threw down their instruments, and flew to arms, and a regular fusillade went on for some moments, the other places supporting the fire. The buglers are bugling now "Come to us, come to us," to the Arabs. (The Egyptian Government have the French calls, and can converse by bugle; I do not think we have.) Last night a *renegade* Dervish bugler in the Arab ranks replied, "Come to us, come to us."

December 5.—Small church parades. Three caravans of some size came in from the north to Mahomet Achmet's camp this morning. Two deserters came in from the Arabs. Fort at Omdurman all right. In store 737 ardebs of dhoora, 121,300 okes of biscuit.

We are going to make an attempt to relieve Omdurman Fort (really things are looking very black). The men who came in say the Mahdi is short of ammunition. The Arabs fired three shells at the palace this afternoon, which fell in the river. A soldier deserted to-day to the Arabs. 5 P.M. The Arabs fired two shells at the palace, which fell into the water (if *they only* knew! that if they sank the trail they would touch us up! their line is quite correct). 6.30 P.M. Since 3 P.M. we have been firing on them, and they on us, only wasting ammunition, for though our bullets reach them, few of theirs reach us. According to the men who came in from the Arabs, it is the pet detachment of the Mahdi who are opposite the Palace; they do not number more than one hundred, and are principally our Soudan soldiers. I have almost given up all idea of saving the town; it is a last resource, this attempt we make to open the route to the Omdurman Fort.

December 6.—(Certainly every fortified place ought to be provided with a hundred good telescopes.) The steamers went down and fired on the Arabs at Omdurman. We have £150 in cash in the treasury. In the affair to-day we had three killed and thirty-six wounded in the steamers, and Ferratch Ullah Bey reports he had five wounded at Omdurman Fort. The Arabs came down in good force, and must have lost.

I have given up all idea of landing at Omdurman: we have not the force to do it. The Arabs fired forty-five rounds from their guns at Mogrim and the steamers. We had two men wounded at Mogrim, and one killed. This is most distressing to have these poor fellows wounded and killed. To-morrow it will be 270 days 9 months that we have endured one continuous misery and anxiety. The Greeks who were at Mogrim say at least 300 or 400 Arabs were killed and wounded in to-day's engagement. The *Ismailia* was struck by four, and the *Bordeen* by two shells, but not in vital parts. I visited the steamers, and had weariness of heart at hearing the complaint of the men as to the robbery of their rations by the officers.

December 7.—The 270th day of our imprisonment. The Arabs fired from their guns at Goba 8 shells, one of which fell in the town near Palace, but did no harm. Omdurman reports the fort all right, one more man wounded there. A great force of Arabs strayed down near Omdurman last night, and left at dawn. The cock turkey has killed one of his companions, reason not known. (Supposed to be correspondence with Mahdi, or some harem infidelity.) Report in town that Berber surrendered, "*sans coup férir.*" I hope so. We are going to send the steamers down again to attack the Arabs at Omdurman at noon to-morrow. The Arabs fired nine shells at Bourré, and begun again their practice on the Palace, firing five shells, one of which came close to the roof of Palace.

A soldier escaped from the Arabs and came in; he says the Expeditionary Force has captured Berber. Two soldiers deserted to the Arabs to-day! The Arabs at Goba fired three shells this evening at the Palace; two fell close to it, one fell in the water. One shell from the Arabs at Bourré fell in the hospital. One of the shells of the Arabs this evening struck the building next the Palace, and stuck in the wall, about 9 feet from the ground. A man came in from the Arabs, who says the Expeditionary Force is approaching. I saw a body of horsemen going north to-day, very fast, from El foun. In the *Ismailia* were eighty bullet holes on the water line of her hull; in the *Bordeen* there were seventy-five bullet holes, ditto *in the last engagement!!!* These holes were stopped by screws made for the purpose. As for the bullet marks elsewhere they are not to be counted.

My belief is that the Mahdi business will be the end of slavery in the Soudan. The Arabs have invariably put their slaves in the front and armed them; and the slaves have seen that they were plucky, while their masters shirked: is it likely that those slaves will ever yield obedience to those masters as heretofore?

December 8.—The Arabs this morning fired twelve rounds from guns at Bourré, and five rounds at the North Fort and Palace. Two men came in from the Arabs; they say no Arabs have gone down towards Berber; that the report in the Arab camp was that Berber was captured; this report was four days old. 10 A.M. The steamers are going down to attack. Omdurman Fort reports "*All right.*" 10.30 A.M. The steamers are engaged; the Arabs have two nasty wasp batteries with regular embrasures, quite *á l'Europe.* (Query Slatin Bey's design.) Though we have protected the steam-chests of the steamers, one cannot help being very anxious. The Arabs at Goba are *silent.* Another soldier from the Arabs came in and states report of advance of the Expeditionary Force, who are coming by land. Every time I hear the guns fire I have a twitch of the heart of gnawing anxiety for my penny steamers. 11.30 A.M. The battle is over, and my penny boats are safe, thank God! (not in words only, but from my heart). We had two wounded on board the *Bordeen*, none on board the *Ismailia.* We are meditating an attack with 500 men on the 50 Arabs, who with their gun, are at Goba. The *Bordeen* was struck by four shells, the *Ismailia* by two shells, one of which destroyed a cabin: they had not much musketry fire, but the Arabs fired a great number of rounds; they had six guns playing on the steamers. At noon Arabs fired five shells at Bourré. In the evening they fired three shells against the Palace from Goba which fell in the town. Had we not cased the steam-chest of the *Ismailia* with wood she would have had her boiler blown up by one of the shells. The Arab rifle force of Goba is completely innocuous; we do not even hear their bullets, yet our bullets reach them, for they cannot stay in the open, and we can see the dust the bullets throw up that we fire. Wadji Barra, an Ameer of the Mahdi, on the north side, sent me a letter (in Appendix AB) asking me to surrender, and saying it is all lies about the Expedition, the Mahdi is evidently (like H.M.G.) offended with my curt answer to his last, and so his holiness will not write direct. Whenever we have what we call a victory we fire some fireworks at the main posts of our lines, which infuriates the Arabs, and puzzle them as to the reason. They were very angry to-night, and came down in a good number, and fired on the Palace several volleys. I ordered up the three buglers, who put them to flight. The letter Wadji Barra sent me was sent by a woman who came to the North Fort. I telegraphed the officer "Open the letter and tell me contents." He did so, and I answered, "Send the woman back to the Ameer and tell him to go, &c." I expect this irritated the Ameer, who ordered the advance of his men, and consequent expenditure of his ammunition.

December 9.—A party of sixty men, with ammunition, camels, and some horsemen, left the Dem of the Mahdi, and went north this morning. The Arabs on the right bank of the White Nile came over to the left bank of the Blue Nile, and went through some antics, so we suppose something is up. A man was wounded yesterday at Omdurman, which fort reports all right. Letter sent by Wadji Barra in Appendix AB. The Arabs fired yesterday not rifled shell, but round shell, which they must have got at Obeyed, which shows they are out of ammunition of the regulation sort. What called forth the letter from Wadji Barra (Appendix AB) was a paper I issued (Appendix CD) to the town, when I received Towfik's telegram saying he would hold the Soudan, and which I gave to a man to send to the Arabs. If Lord Palmerston was alive (or Forster was Premier) he would never leave the Soudan, without proclaiming the emancipation of the slaves. On 18th December, 1862, Lincoln proclaimed abolition of slavery in the United States; this would be a good day to issue such a proclamation in the Soudan. Wadji Barra's letter calls me Pasha of Kartoum, and says I have been deaf to all their entreaties. Stewart left this place *three months ago!* to-day. A man was wounded by the Arab fire at Bourré: they fired twelve rounds from these guns at the fort. I feel sure that the cause of the Mahdi's coming here is, that he got hold of Herbin's 'French Consul's' journal, written in a hostile critical spirit, and thinking it true, he advanced from Schatt. I expect Hansall, the Austrian Consul, also wrote in the style of Lamentations, for he also sent down a journal by the *Abbas*. It is remarkable that the very effort which I made to obtain the ear of Europe should have thus recoiled on us. I have for the present abandoned the attack on the Arabs at Goba, as Omdurman is more important, and as I expect the Arabs there have taken away their gun; it has not (up to 2 P.M.) fired to-day. I would like to ask the Mahdi—allowing *pro forma* that he is the Mahdi—what will be his ultimate work? Certainly his present work is not exhilarating, firing on his fellow-creatures night and day. The siege of Sevastopol lasted 326 days. We are at our 271st day. In their case they had always their communication open, and they dealt with an enemy who would recognise the rights of war; whereas we are not so placed. They, the Russians, were united, and had no civil population to deal with; yet I cannot say I think we are over great heroes (the fact is, that, if one analyses human glory, it is composed of nine-tenths twaddle, perhaps ninety-nine hundredths twaddle). We are only short of the duration of siege of Sevastopol 57 days, and we have had *no respite*, like the Russians had, during the winter of 1854-55; and neither Nicholas nor Alexander speculated on (well, we will not say what, but we will put it) "counting the months." Of course it will be looked on as very absurd to compare the two blockades, that of Sevastopol and Kartoum; but if properly weighed, one was just as good as the other. The Russians had money, we had none; they had skilled officers, we had none; they had no civil population, we had forty thousand; they had their route open and had news, we had neither.

December 10.—A slave came in to-day, he had been with Slatin. He says Slatin is still in chains, that there are two insurrections in Kordofan, and rumour is rife that the Expeditionary Force is near. Fort Omdurman is all right. The slave says the Arabs have not much ammunition. The Arabs fired thirty-one rounds at Bourré to-day, and wounded four men (one an officer, a Major Souleiman Effi, fatally). The Arabs have been firing stones to-day. Goba is quiet, they did not fire their gun to-day, or yesterday. I expect it has gone down to the riverbank. The slave who came in says the Mahdi's return to Kordofan is cut off by the insurrection in his rear; so we and he are like two rats in a box. (I wish *he* was *out* of the *box!*) I have ordered the two steamers to stay up at Bourré, towards which place the Arabs seem to be directing an unpleasant degree of attention. (Truly I am worn to a shadow with the food question; it is one continual demand.) Five men deserted to-day. The Arabs shape the stones they fire, like to the shells of their guns; they will soon spoil the rifling of their guns if they continue this.

December 11.—The Arabs fired their gun from Goba three times; one shell fell into the water before the Palace—two passed over it. I put down more mines at Bourré. I have given the whole garrison an extra month's pay in addition to the three months' they had before received—I will not (D.V.) hesitate to give them £100,000, if I think it will keep the town.

Three soldiers came in from the Arabs who report advance of the Expedition towards Berber. The Arabs fired fourteen rounds from their guns at Bourré. The officers say that there is a European directing the Arab guns there. (I wonder if it is that Frenchman who came from Dongola, and who, I thought, might have been Renan.) Sennaar is holding out and in great force (so say the three soldiers), so is Kassala. The Dem of the Mahdi is altered in appearance. They say he has sent off the families of his adherents into the interior.

3.30 P.M.—The Arabs fired three shells at the Palace from Goba; two went into the water, one passed over the Palace. This always irritates me, for it is so personal, and from one's own soldiers too! It is not very pleasant also to feel at any moment you may have a shell in your room, for the creatures fire at all hours. The steamers fired on the Arabs at Bourré this morning, and one of the Arab shells struck one steamer, and another struck a santal which we have there to defend the flank; but neither did any harm. Two soldiers deserted to the Arabs to-day—these men are generally those who have before been with the Arabs, and had deserted to us. The Arabs fired another shell at the Palace this evening, which burst in the air.

December 12.—Small Church Parade. I sincerely hope this will be the last we shall have to witness. We have in hand 1,796,000 rounds Remingtons ammunition; 540 rounds Krupp; 6000 rounds mountain gun ammunition; £ 140 in specie; £18,000 in paper in treasury!! £60,000 in town in paper. 110,000 okes of biscuits; 700 ardebs of dhoora. This morning I was told a long story of report concerning the expeditionary force being at El Damer, near the Atbara river; of how Berber had surrendered, &c. On tracing it, I found it was a fib put in circulation by one of the chief Ulemas, to encourage the people.

3.30 P.M. The Arabs fired two shells at the Palace; one burst in the air, the other fell in the water in a direct line with the window I was sitting at, distant about a hundred yards.

3.40 P.M. They fired another shell, which fell only fifty yards short of the Palace; another burst in the air. I have sent the buglers up to stop this target practice. All these shells are in good line for the west wing, in which the Arabs know I stop. They fired seven shells in all in this affair; though the Arabs have fired over two thousand shells at us, I do not think we have lost by artillery fire more than three men.

December 13.—The steamers went up and attacked the Arabs at Bourré (certainly this day-after-day delay has a most disheartening effect on every one. To-day is the 276th day of our anxiety). The Arabs appear, by all accounts, to have suffered to-day heavily at Bourré. We had none wounded by the Arabs; but one man, by the discharge of a bad cartridge, got a cut in neck: this was owing to the same cause as nearly blew out my eyes the other day. We are going to send down the *Bordeen* the day after to-morrow, and with her I shall send this journal. *If some effort is not made before ten days' time the town will fall.* It is inexplicable, this delay. If the Expeditionary Forces have reached the river and met my steamers, one hundred men are all that we require, just to show themselves.

I send this journal, for I have little hopes of saving it if the town falls. I put in (Appendix EF), the sort of arrangement I would make with Zubair Pasha for the future government of the Soudan. Ferratch Pasha is really showing an amount of vigour I did not give him credit for. Even if the town falls under the

nose of the Expeditionary Force, it will not, in my opinion, justify the abandonment of Senaar and Kassala, or of the Equatorial Province, by Her Majesty's
Government. All that is absolutely necessary is, for fifty of the Expeditionary
Force to get on board a steamer and come up to Halfeyeh, and thus let their
presence be felt; this is not asking much, but it must happen *at once;* or it will
(as usual) be too late. A soldier deserted to the Arabs to-day from the North
Fort. The buglers on the roof, being short of stature, are put on boxes to enable
them to fire over the parapet; one with the recoil of rifle was knocked right
over, and caused considerable excitement. We thought he was killed, by the
noise he made in his fall. The Arabs fired their Krupps continually into town
from the south front, but no one takes any notice of it. The Arabs at Goba only
fired one shell at the Palace to-day, which burst in the air.

December 14th. — Arabs fired two shells at the Palace this morning; 546
ardebs dhoora! in store; also 83,525 okes of biscuit! 10.30 A.M. The steamers
are down at Omdurman, engaging the Arabs, consequently I am on *tenter-
hooks!* 11.30 A.M. Steamers returned; the *Bordeen* was struck by a shell in her
battery; we had only one man wounded. We are going to send down the
Bordeen to-morrow with this journal. If I was in command of the two hundred
men of the Expeditionary Force, which are all that are necessary for the
movement, I should stop just below Halfeyeh, and attack the Arabs at that
place before I came on here to Kartoum. I should then communicate with the
North Fort, and act according to circumstances. NOW MARK THIS, if the
Expeditionary Force, and I ask for no more than two hundred men, does not
come in ten days, *the town may fall;* and I have done my best for the honour of
our country. Good bye.

C. G. Gordon

You send me no information, though you have lots of money.

C. G. G.

---

*Agreement between Great Britain and Germany Signed at
Berlin and Defining Their Respective Spheres of Influence
in Africa, 1 July 1890**
[*This Treaty includes the cession of Zanzibar
to Britain and Heligoland to Germany.*]

The Undersigned,

Sir Edward Baldwin Malet, Her Britannic Majesty's Ambassador Extraordinary and Plenipotentiary;

Sir Henry Percy Anderson, Chief of the African Department of Her Majesty's Foreign Office;

*British and Foreign State Papers, LXXXII, 35–47.

The Chancellor of the German Empire, General von Caprivi;

The Privy Councillor in the Foreign Office, Dr. Krauel;

Have, after discussion of various questions affecting the Colonial interests of Germany and Great Britain, come to the following agreement on behalf of their respective Governments.

Art. I

In East Africa the sphere in which the exercise of influence is reserved to Germany is bounded—

1. To the north by a line, which, commencing on the coast at the north bank of the mouth of the River Umba, runs direct to Lake Jipé; passes thence along the eastern side and round the northern side of the lake, and crosses the River Lumé; after which it passes midway between the territories of Taveita and Chagga, skirts the northern base of the Kilimanjaro range, and thence is drawn direct to the point on the eastern side of Lake Victoria Nyanza which is intersected by the 1st parallel of south latitude; thence, crossing the lake on that parallel, it follows the parallel to the frontier of the Congo Free State, where it terminates.

It is, however, understood that, on the west side of the lake, the sphere does not comprise Mount Mfumbiro; if that mountain shall prove to lie to the south of the selected parallel, the line shall be deflected so as to exclude it, but shall nevertheless return so as to terminate at the above-named point.

2. To the south by a line which, starting on the coast at the northern limit of the Province of Mozambique, follows the course of the River Rovuma to the point of confluence of the Msinje; thence it runs westward along the parallel of that point till it reaches Lake Nyasa; thence striking northward, it follows the eastern, northern, and western shores of the lake to the northern bank of the mouth of the River Songwe; it ascends that river to the point of its intersection by the 33rd degree of east longitude; thence it follows the river to the point where it approaches most nearly the boundary of the geographical Congo Basin defined in Article I of the Act of Berlin, as marked in the Map attached to the 9th Protocol of the Conference.

From that point it strikes direct to the above-named boundary, and follows it to the point of its intersection by the 32nd degree of east longitude; from which point it strikes direct to the point of confluence of the northern and southern branches of the River Kilambo, and thence follows that river till it enters Lake Tanganyika.

The course of the above boundary is traced in general accordance with a map of the Nyasa-Tanganyika Plateau, officially prepared for the British Government in 1889.

3. To the west by a line which, from the mouth of the River Kilambo to the 1st parallel of south latitude, is conterminous with the Congo Free State.

The sphere in which the exercise of influence is reserved to Great Britain is bounded—

1. To the south by the above-mentioned line running from the mouth of the River Umba to the point where the 1st parallel of south latitude reaches the Congo Free State. Mount Mfumbiro is included in the sphere.

2. To the north by a line commencing on the coast at the north bank of the mouth of the River Juba; thence it ascends that bank of the river, and is conterminous with the territory reserved to the influence of Italy in Gallaland and Abyssinia, as far as the confines of Egypt.

3. To the west by the Congo Free State, and by the western watershed of the basin of the Upper Nile.

Art. II

In order to render effective the delimitation recorded in the preceding Article, Germany withdraws in favour of Great Britain her Protectorate over Witu. Great Britain engages to recognize the sovereignty of the Sultan of Witu over the territory extending from Kipini to the point opposite the Island of Kwyhoo fixed as the boundary in 1887.

Germany also withdraws her Protectorate over the adjoining coast up to Kismayu, as well as her claims to all other territories on the mainland, to the north of the River Tana, and to the Islands of Patta and Manda.

Art. III

In South-west Africa the sphere in which the exercise of influence is reserved to Germany is bounded—

1. To the south by a line commencing at the mouth of the Orange River, and ascending the north bank of that river to the point of its intersection by the 20th degree of east longitude.

2. To the east by a line commencing at the above-named point, and following the 20th degree of east longitude to the point of its intersection by the 22nd parallel of south latitude, it runs eastward along that parallel to the point of its intersection by the 21st degree of east longitude; thence it follows that degree northward to the point of its intersection by the 18th parallel of south latitude; it runs eastward along that parallel till it reaches the River Chobe; and descends the centre of the main channel of that river to its junction with the Zambezi, where it terminates.

It is understood that under this arrangement Germany shall have free access from her Protectorate to the Zambezi by a strip of territory which shall at no point be less than 20 English miles in width.

The sphere in which the exercise of influence is reserved to Great Britain is bounded to the west and north-west by the above-mentioned line. It includes Lake Ngami.

The course of the above boundary is traced in general accordance with a Map officially prepared for the British Government in 1889.

The delimitation of the southern boundary of the British territory of Walfish Bay is reserved for arbitration, unless it shall be settled by the consent of the two Powers within two years from the date of the conclusion of this Agreement.

The two Powers agree that, pending such settlement, the passage of the subjects and the transit of goods of both Powers through the territory now in dispute shall be free; and the treatment of their subjects in that territory shall be in all respects equal. No dues shall be levied on goods in transit. Until a settlement shall be effected, the territory shall be considered neutral.

Art. IV

In West Africa—

1. The boundary between the German Protectorate of Togo and the British Gold Coast Colony commences on the coast at the marks set up after the negotiations between the Commissioners of the two countries of the 14th and 28th July, 1886; and proceeds direct northwards to the 6° 10′ parallel of north latitude; thence it runs along that parallel westwards till it reaches the left bank of the River Aka; ascends the mid-channel of that river to the 6° 20′ parallel of north latitude; runs along that parallel westwards to the right bank of the River Dchawe or Shavoe; follows that bank of the river till it reaches the parallel corresponding with the point of confluence of the River Deine with the Volta; it runs along that parallel westward till it reaches the Volta; from that point it ascends the left bank of the Volta till it arrives at the neutral zone established by the Agreement of 1888, which commences at the confluence of the River Dakka with the Volta.

Each Power engages to withdraw immediately after the conclusion of this Agreement all its officials and employés from territory which is assigned to the other Power by the above delimitation.

2. It having been proved to the satisfaction of the two Powers that no river exists on the Gulf of Guinea corresponding with that marked on Maps as the Rio del Rey, to which reference was made in the Agreement of 1885, a provisional line of demarcation is adopted between the German sphere in the Cameroons and the adjoining British sphere, which, starting from the head of the Rio del Rey Creek, goes direct to the point, about 9° 8′ of east longitude, marked "Rapids" in the British Admiralty Chart.

Art.V

It is agreed that no Treaty or Agreement, made by or on behalf of either Power to the north of the River Benué, shall interfere with the free passage of goods of the other Power, without payment of transit dues, to and from the shores of Lake Chad.

All Treaties made in territories intervening between the Benué and Lake Chad shall be notified by one Power to the other.

Art. VI

All the lines of demarcation traced in Articles I to IV shall be subject to rectification by agreement between the two Powers, in accordance with local requirements.

It is specially understood that, as regards the boundaries traced in Article IV, Commissioners shall meet with the least possible delay for the object of such rectification.

Art.VII

The two Powers engage that neither will interfere with any sphere of influence assigned to the other by Articles I to IV. One Power will not in the sphere of the other make acquisitions, conclude Treaties, accept sovereign rights or Protectorates, nor hinder the extension of influence of the other.

It is understood that no Companies nor individuals subject to one Power can exercise sovereign rights in a sphere assigned to the other, except with the assent of the latter.

Art. VIII

The two Powers engage to apply in all the portions of their respective spheres, within the limits of the free zone defined by the Act of Berlin of 1885, to which the first five Articles of that Act are applicable at the date of the present Agreement, the provisions of those Articles according to which trade enjoys a complete freedom; the navigation of the lakes, rivers, and canals, and of the ports on those waters, is free to both flags; and no differential treatment is permitted as regards transport or coasting trade; goods, of whatever origin, are subject to no dues except those, not differential in their incidence, which may be levied to meet expenditure in the interest of trade; no transit dues are permitted; and no monopoly or favour in matters of trade can be granted.

The subjects of either Power will be at liberty to settle freely in their respective territories situated within the free trade zone.

It is specially understood that, in accordance with these provisions, the passage of goods of both Powers will be free from all hindrances and from all transit dues between Lake Nyasa and the Congo State, between Lakes Nyasa and Tanganyika, on Lake Tanganyika, and between that lake and the northern boundary of the two spheres.

Art. IX

Trading and mineral Concessions, and rights to real property, held by Companies or individuals, subjects of one Power, shall, if their validity is duly established, be recognized in the sphere of the other Power. It is understood that Concessions must be worked in accordance with local laws and regulations.

Art. X

In all territories in Africa belonging to, or under the influence of, either Power, missionaries of both countries shall have full protection. Religious toleration and freedom for all forms of divine worship and religious teaching are guaranteed.

Art. XI

Great Britain engages to use all her influence to facilitate a friendly arrangement, by which the Sultan of Zanzibar shall cede absolutely to Germany his possessions on the mainland comprised in existing Concessions to the German East African Company, and their dependencies, as well as the Island of Mafia.

It is understood that His Highness will, at the same time, receive an equitable indemnity for the loss of revenue resulting from such cession.

Germany engages to recognize a Protectorate of Great Britain over the remaining dominions of the Sultan of Zanzibar, including the Islands of Zanzibar and Pemba, as well as over the dominions of the Sultan of Witu, and the adjacent territory up to Kismayu, from which her Protectorate is withdrawn. It is understood that if the cession of the German coast has not taken place before the assumption by Great Britain of the Protectorate of Zanzibar, Her Majesty's Government will, in assuming the Protectorate, accept the obligation to use all their influence with the Sultan to induce him to make that cession at the earliest possible period in consideration of an equitable indemnity.

Art. XII

1. Subject to the assent of the British Parliament, the sovereignty over the Island of Heligoland, together with its dependencies, is ceded by Her Britannic Majesty to His Majesty the Emperor of Germany.

2. The German Government will allow to all persons natives of the territory thus ceded the right of opting for British nationality by means of a declaration to be made by themselves, and, in the case of children under age, by their parents or guardians, which must be sent in before the 1st January, 1892.

3. All persons natives of the territory thus ceded, and their children born before the date of the signature of the present Agreement, are free from the obligation of service in the military and naval forces of Germany.

4. Native laws and customs now existing will, as far as possible, remain undisturbed.

5. The German Government binds itself not to increase the Customs Tariff at present in force in the territory thus ceded until the 1st January, 1910.

6. All rights to property which private persons or existing Corporations have acquired in Heligoland in connection with the British Government are maintained; obligations resulting from them are transferred to His Majesty the Emperor of Germany. It is understood that the above term, "rights to property," includes the right of signalling now enjoyed by Lloyd's.

7. The rights of British fishermen with regard to anchorage in all weathers, to taking in provisions and water, to making repairs, to transhipment of goods, to the sale of fish, and to the landing and drying of nets, remain undisturbed.

British Notification of the Niger Coast Protectorate,
13 May 1893*

FOREIGN OFFICE, MAY 13, 1893

With reference to the notification in the "London Gazette" of the 18th October 1887, respecting the British Protectorate of the Niger districts, and to certain agreements entered into between the British and German Governments,

*British and Foreign State Papers, LXXXV, 1203.

it is hereby notified, for public information, that the portion of the Protectorate under the administration of Her Majesty's Commissioner and Consul-General will, from the date of this notification, form a separate Protectorate, under the name of the "Niger Coast Protectorate," and will cease to be known as the "Oil Rivers Protectorate."

The eastern limit of the line of coast of the Niger Coast Protectorate is defined in the Agreement between the British and German Governments of the 14th April, 1893.

Statement of Imperial Principles by "the Founder of Nigeria,"
Sir George Goldie, 1898* [In 1897 Goldie had abolished slavery
in all territories controlled by the Royal Niger Company.]

If, in the year of grace when Her Majesty was born, a traveller had combined in a single volume his experiences on the Nile and Niger, the incongruity of the subjects would have then appeared almost as great as though the rivers had been the Ganges and St. Lawrence. We now know that the vast regions between the Nile and the Niger are so closely connected by unity of religious faith and by internal commerce, that political events on the one stream react upon the other; we recognise that the Nile and Niger questions are not disconnected, but are two sides of a single question—that of the Sudan.

Between these great rivers of East and West Africa lie regions of the breadth of the entire continent of Europe, regions which were, in 1819, altogether unknown and believed to be but sparsely inhabited. It was not until Major Denham and Captain Clapperton, in 1823–25, and Dr. Barth, in 1849–55, explored this vast area on behalf of the British Government, that the civilised world recognised that this heart of Africa was no barren desert. They found that it was filled with populous and organised States, that it possessed a fertile soil and intelligent and industrious inhabitants; but they did not sufficiently recognise—and this discovery was reserved for our days—that the considerable civilisation of the Sudan could make no further progress, that this lost thirtieth of the human race could have no adequate connection through commerce with the outer world, until a sound basis was substituted for that on which the social system in those regions has hitherto rested.

No student of history can, indeed, assert that the institution of slavery in its customary forms is an absolute barrier to intellectual progress and the creation of wealth. Greece, Rome and the United States of America have afforded a sufficient answer to that extreme view. Nor can the slave *trade* be such a barrier, if the word be confined to its usual and proper meaning of buying and

*Goldie, "Introduction" in Vandeleur, *Campaigning on the Upper Nile and Niger,* as reprinted in Wellesley, *Goldie,* 165–81.

selling of slaves; for this has been the natural course in all ages in all slave-holding countries; while the capture of slaves in war has proved, at any rate, preferable to the more ancient practice of killing all prisoners.

The radical vice of the Sudan, the disease which, until cured, must arrest all intellectual and material progress, is the general, constant, and intense prevalence of slave-*raiding*. It is not possible, in a brief preface, to present any adequate picture of a system under which considerable towns disappear in a night and whole tracts of country are depopulated in a single dry season—not as a result of war, but as the normal method of the rulers for collecting their human cattle for payment of tribute to their suzerains or for sale to distant parts of the continent. Much has been written on this extraordinary subject. It may suffice to refer the reader to Canon Robinson's *Hausa Land,* and to Sir Harry Johnson's *Autobiography of a Slave,* which, though presented in the form of fiction, is an under-statement of the facts. But perhaps a more vivid picture is given in *The Life and Travels of Dorugu,* dictated by himself, a translation of which appears in Dr. Schoen's *Magana Hausa,* published by the Society for Promoting Christian Knowledge. Dorugu was a native of the Niger Sudan, who was ultimately brought to London by Dr. Barth. The merit of his story lies in its artlessness and brevity. His childhood is largely filled with sudden flights into the forest or hills to escape the slave-raiders. His family rebuild their burnt farmhouses, or change their homes with philosophic equanimity like that of vine cultivators on the slopes of a volcano. The simplicity with which Dorugu relates the fears and dangers of his boyhood shows that to him they seemed as inevitable as measles and school to an English boy. At last he is caught in his turn; his parents, brothers and sisters, for whom he evidently had a strong affection, vanish suddenly and entirely out of his life, and he himself becomes one of the millions of pieces of human currency which pass from one Sudanese State to another.

At first sight it seems impossible to reconcile this universal and continual slave-raiding in times of peace with the considerable civilisation and complex political organisation of the Sudanese States. The system probably originated from the great demand for negro slaves that has existed from time immemorial amongst the lighter coloured races of mankind. The docility of the negro, combined with his intelligence and capacity for work, must have given him a special value in the slave markets of antiquity, as in those of modern days. The growth of Mohammedanism, with its polygamous institutions, during the eight centuries after the Hegira, gave an immense impulse to the export slave trade of the Sudan to Asia, Europe and North Africa. At the commencement of the sixteenth century the philanthropic efforts of Bishop Las Casas laid the foundations of the negro slave trade to the New World. Three centuries of this export trade on a large scale must have contributed to confirm and develop the old slave-raiding habits of the Sudan, though it seems unjust of certain writers to lay the entire blame on Christendom for a social canker which had existed in Africa for many hundreds of years, before Charles V, out of pure benevolence, permitted the import into St. Domingo of slaves from the Portuguese Guinea

Coast. But although the qualities of the negro and demand for his services by lighter coloured races in all ages account for the inception of the remarkable system of slave-raiding, the number of slaves exported has probably been insignificant compared with the number dealt with in the internal traffic of Negroland.

To understand this question properly, it must be remembered that the value of a slave is extremely small near his place of capture. His initial price is often lower than that of a sheep, which has less tendency to escape. As the slave is taken farther away from his home, his value rises rapidly; so that it is commercially a sound transaction to send a hundred slaves, say, from Bornu to Darfur, while bringing a hundred others from Darfur to Bornu. No doubt they have also a value as transport animals, but I venture to assert that this feature of the traffic has been over-estimated, especially as camels are plentiful in the northern regions, while horses and donkeys are largely used and might be cheaply bred to any extent throughout the Sudan. While, therefore, a well-planned system of Sudanese railways would have a considerable indirect effect on the internal slave trade, and consequently on slave-raiding, it would not, as generally believed, directly touch the root of the evil. This can only be eradicated by the same vigorous means which we employ in Europe for the prevention of crime and violence. It is, I fear, useless to hope that commerce with Europe will, by itself, suffice to alter a social system so deeply ingrained in the Sudanese mind; for the creation of commerce on a large scale is impossible until slave-raiding is abated.

Let me not be misunderstood as preaching a crusade of liberty against the Sudanese States. To this policy I am most strenuously opposed. Force must indeed underlie all social action, whether in Africa or Europe, whether in public life or in the more intimate relations of parent and child, school-master and pupil. But there is a wide difference between its necessity and constant display and its unnecessary use. The policemen of our towns have not their batons habitually drawn, though they do not hesitate to use them on occasions. There is probably no part of the world where diplomacy is more effective than Negroland, provided it is known that behind diplomacy is military power. There is certainly no part of the world where the maxim *Festina lente* is more applicable.

When, however, the application of force becomes absolutely necessary, it ought surely to be thorough and rapid. Yet last spring, after the completion of the operations described by Lieutenant Vandeleur in the latter half of this book, one of the most able and respected organs of public opinion in this country questioned the morality of "mowing down natives with artillery and Maxim guns." Now, these "natives" were the fighting organisation of great regions which they—though in a comparatively small minority—held down with a hand of iron, treating the less warlike inhabitants as cattle to be raided when wanted. The death of each Fulah killed at Bida secured the lives and liberty of scores of peaceful and defenceless natives. If Europe had no material interests to protect and develop in Africa, it would still have the same right, the same duty to extirpate slave-raiding that a man has to knock down a ruffian whom he sees maltreating a woman or child in the street.

While, however, this consideration should satisfy the consciences of persons interested in the welfare of the oppressed millions of Africa, the material importance of opening up the Sudan cannot be overlooked by any European State which subsists largely on its manufacturing and shipping interests. On this point it will be well for me to confine my remarks to the region lying between Lake Chad and the Niger, to which my studies of the last twenty years have been mainly directed. This region has been known of late under the name of the Niger Sudan. It comprises Bornu and the Fulah or Sokoto-Gando Empire, the greater and more valuable portion of which is mainly peopled by the civilised, commerce-loving, and industrious Hausas, who form about one-hundredth of mankind, and whose intellectual capacity H. M. Stanley has aptly emphasised by describing them as the "only Central African people who value a book."

In dealing with the value of the markets to be developed in the Niger Sudan, it is difficult to decide on how much must be said and what may be assumed as known. On the one hand, all geographers and many publicists are familiar with the fact that the region in question possesses populous towns and a fertile soil, and, most important of all, races whose industry is untiring, notwithstanding the discouraging and paralysing effects of insecurity of life, liberty, and property. They know that these races are possessed of high intelligence and considerable artistic skill, as displayed in their fine brass and leather work. They know that the early marriages in those latitudes, and the fecundity and vitality of the negro races, have, through countless generations, largely counteracted the appalling destruction of life resulting from slave-raiding, and that under reasonable conditions of security the existing population might soon be trebled and yet live in far greater material comfort than at present. They know, in short, that all that is needed to convert the Niger Sudan into an African India is the strong hand of a European protector. But, on the other hand, the general public and a considerable section of the press seem still inclined to confuse the Niger Sudan with the very different regions which border the Guinea Coast. The well-clad, intelligent and fairly civilised races of the interior are constantly referred to as half-naked and indolent savages; the fine country which forms three-fourths of the Niger Sudan is confounded with the swamps of the Niger Delta. It is not difficult to recognise how this delusion originated and is maintained. The Niger Sudan is separated from the civilisation of the Mediterranean regions by a thousand miles of the Sahara, which the Tuareg and other wandering tribes render well-nigh impassable. It is separated from the Guinea coast-line by a maritime belt, malarious in climate, and inhabited by lower races who have, perhaps, been gradually pushed seawards by the successive waves of higher races coming from the North. The vast majority of Englishmen—whether soldiers, officials, missionaries, or traders—who have visited West Africa have seen only the coast-line or, at most, the maritime belt, and their impressions of this small section of the continent have very naturally been accepted by uninformed readers as applicable to the vast *Hinterlands*. The difficulty of access to the Niger Sudan regions accounts amply for this important and valuable portion of the earth's surface having been cut off from outside inter-course for all practical purposes until the last quarter of the nineteenth century. The barriers which from time immemorial have separated the Sudanese races from the remainder of the human family have at last been effectually broken down, and it may be safely prophesied that within twenty years the union will be complete, provided vital errors of policy are avoided. The two principal dangers can hardly be too often urged, and I propose to deal with them briefly in turn.

Central African races and tribes have, broadly speaking, no sentiment of patriotism, as understood in Europe. There is therefore little difficulty in inducing them to accept what German jurisconsults term *Ober-Hoheit,* which corresponds with one interpretation of our vague term "Protectorate." But when complete sovereignty, or *Landes-Hoheit,* is conceded, they invariably stipulate that their local customs and system of government shall be respected. On this point they are, perhaps more tenacious than most subject races with whom the British Empire has had to deal; while their views and ideals of life are extremely difficult for an Englishman to understand. It is therefore certain that even an imperfect and tyrannical native African administration, if its extreme excesses were controlled by European supervision, would be, in the early stages, productive of far less discomfort to its subjects than well-intentioned but ill-directed efforts of European magistrates, often young and headstrong, and not invariably gifted with sympathy and introspective powers. If the welfare of the native races is to be considered, if dangerous revolts are to be obviated, the general policy of ruling on African principles through native rulers must be followed for the present. Yet it is desirable that considerable districts in suitable localities should be administered on European principles by European officials, partly to serve as types to which the native governments may gradually approx-imate, but principally as cities of refuge in which individuals of more advanced views may find a living, if native government presses unduly upon them; just as, in Europe of the Middle Ages, men whose love of freedom found the iron-bound system of feudalism intolerable, sought eagerly the comparative liberty of cities.

The second danger to be apprehended—a war of religions—will probably present itself to every thoughtful European. Fortunately for the Niger Sudan, Moslem fanaticism in this region has not the intensity of that now existing farther East—in Wadai, Darfur and the Nile provinces. Yet ill-advised legisla-tion, a careless administrative system, or a bad selection of officials, might well create an entirely different stage of things. Twenty-five to thirty years ago one was able to travel in the Egyptian Sudan without escort, and without even keeping watch at night. With what incredulity would one have then received a prophecy that only ten or fifteen years later that district would become a hotbed of Mohammedan fanaticism, and would be absolutely closed to Christendom for a long period of years! The danger in the Sudanese States is accentuated by the close connection between them, due not only to a common faith and similar modes of life, but also to the constant communications kept up by the Hausa trading caravans which radiate from Hausa land into distant parts of the continent. Prior to the Mahdin conquests, the pilgrim caravans from Central and Western Africa used to pass through Darfur to the Red Sea. I have travelled with no less than eight hundred Hausa pilgrims in a single caravan between Khartum and Suakin. The rise of Mahdism has temporarily diverted these pilgrim travellers northward from Lake Chad to the Mediterranean; but every part of the Sudan is still permeated by trading caravans constantly passing to and fro, and carrying news, almost always distorted and exaggerated, from one part of this vast region to another. About twelve years ago a placard issued by the late Mahdi was found posted in a street of Bida, no less than two thousand miles distant across country from Khartum; while one of the incidents that precipitated our war last year was the receipt of letters from the Khalifa at Omdurman by the Sultan of Sokoto and the Emirs of Nupe and other provinces of the Sokoto Empire, urging them to drive the Christians out of their country.

The similarity of the Sudan regions from east to west may be further illustrated by a striking fact of no little importance to the British Empire, and in which personally I take more interest than in the commercial development of the Sudan. Its entire northern belt, from Senegambia to the Red Sea, is inhabited by races at once capable of fighting and amenable to discipline. The value of the Sudanese regiments of the Egyptian army is widely known. Less has been heard, as yet, of the splendid qualities of the Hausa as a soldier when well officered. In the campaign described by Lieutenant Vandeleur, these qualities were fully proved. On the rapid and arduous march of seventeen days from Lokojá to Kabba, and thence to Egbon, and again on the march to Illorin, with serious scarcity of water, and at times shortness of rations, our troops were always good-tempered and cheerful; and, although in heavy marching order, would pick up and carry the seventy-pound loads of the porters who fell by the way. In camp their conduct was exemplary, while pillaging and ill-treatment of the natives were unknown. As to their fighting qualities, it is enough to say that, little over 500 strong, they withstood for two days 25,000 to 30,000 of the enemy; that, former slaves of the Fulahs, they defeated their dreaded masters; that, Mohammedans, they fought for their salt against their brethren of the faith; and finally, that though they had never before faced cavalry, they stood firm under charges *home* on to the faces of their squares, maintained perfect fire-discipline, and delivered their volleys as steadily as if on parade. Great Britain has had to rely too much of recent years on Indian troops for tropical climates. This is not a healthy condition of things, for many reasons. She may well find an independent source of military strength in the regions bordering the southern limits of the Great Sahara.

I have necessarily touched very briefly on the main features of the Nile and Niger question—one which must inevitably become better known in the early future. When the history of the Victorian age is written from a standpoint sufficiently removed to allow a just perception of proportion, the opening up of

Tropical Africa will probably stand out as a prominent feature of the latter half of that era. The fifty years that followed 1492 formed by no means the least interesting period in the domestic and international history of England, France, Germany or Spain, or in the history of freedom of human thought and action; yet no events of that half-century appear to us now more important than the discoveries of Columbus and the conquests of Cortes and Pizarro. The results of opening up Tropical Africa cannot, of course, be on a similar scale; yet it seems to me that they must be so great as to dwarf many contemporaneous questions which now occupy the public mind in a far higher degree.

The share that Great Britain may take in this movement depends on the condition of the national fibre. A statesman of the early Stuart period would have deemed it impossible that these little islands could control an empire such as that of the days of Chatham; while the Great Commoner himself might have felt misgivings could he have foreseen the Greater Britain of the Diamond Jubilee year. Yet the growing burden of empire has brought with it a more than equivalent accession of wealth, vigour and strength to maintain it; and, although it may be that the British Empire has now reached its zenith, and must gradually decline to the position of a second-rate power, we are not bound to accept such assertions without the production of more valid evidence than has yet been adduced in their support.

---

*Firsthand Account by Winston Churchill of the
Aftermath of the Battle of Omdurman, a Central
Event in Britain's Reconquest of the Sudan,
September 1898**

* * *

The night passed without misadventure, although continual firing and occasional volleys could be heard within the city; and neither the hardness of the ground nor the threatening noises could deprive the weary men of dreamless sleep. Early next morning orders reached the 21st Lancers to move round to the south side of Omdurman, and remain there in observation during the day.

It fell to my lot to be sent to make inquiries as to the condition and wants of the officers and men who had been wounded the day before, and whom we had not seen since they rode or were carried bleeding and in pain from the scene of the charge.

After some searching I found the barges which contained the wounded. In spite of circumstances they were all in good spirits. Colonel Rhodes was there, propped up against the railing of the barge, with a bullet through his shoulder, but brave and cheery as ever—the life and soul of the hospital, as formerly of

*Churchill, *The River War*, II, 201–14, 219–27.

the camp. Sentenced to death by the Boers, he had been shot by the Dervishes. Truly he has suffered many things at the hands of the low-grade races of Africa. But he has laughed and lived through all his misfortunes. Colonel Sloggett, who—I write judicially—was upon the whole the most popular officer with the Expeditionary Force, lay silent, but fully conscious, on an *angarib*. The bullet had entered his left breast above the heart, had traversed the lungs, and, passing completely through the body, found exit near his spine. It was said that he had only a few hours to live. His own knowledge of surgery confirmed the opinion of the others. He could not speak, but even in this dark hour he greeted me—a comparative stranger—with a bright smile of recognition. By what seems almost a miracle, he has since made a recovery as complete as any that would be possible from so terrible a shock. The distinguished part that he took in the action, and his ride across the dangerous ground, have been described. His services, not only in the final campaign but throughout the war, were duly recognised. His reputation as a medical officer was high. His friends are legion. The War Office, anxious to do justice to the Royal Army Medical Corps, determined to advise Her Majesty to confer the Distinguished Service Order on this gallant and accomplished doctor. Unfortunately, by a slight error they put down the wrong name on the list. Another received the coveted prize, and Colonel Sloggett has had to content himself with the universal respect and sympathy of his comrades-in-arms.

We had heard that Lieutenant Nesham had lost his left hand, and it was with relief that I learned that it might be saved. He told me of his return to camp from the field. He was bleeding terribly. Brinton, himself in like plight, had seen him; had managed, though his own arm was useless, to get a tourniquet from his pocket; and had made a soldier put it on Nesham's arm, explaining the method to the man. This had saved the subaltern's life. Otherwise, said the doctors, he would have bled to death. These are the sort of facts that brighten the picture of war with beautiful colours, till from a distance it looks almost magnificent, and the dark background and dirty brown canvas are scarcely seen.

Nothing of historic importance happened on the 3rd of September. The usual tidying-up that follows an action occupied the army and passed the hours. There were of course funerals, chiefly of soldiers who had died of their wounds. The others had been already interred. The long wail of the Dead March sounded, not for the first time, by the banks of the Nile, and a silent column of slow-pacing British soldiers accompanied a yet more silent row of bodies to their last resting-place. On an eminence which overlooks the hazy desert, the green trees of Khartoum, and the mud houses of Omdurman, and before which the majestic river sweeps with the cool sound of waters, a new churchyard appeared. The piles of reddish stones, and the protecting crosses which the living raised as a last tribute to those who had paid the bill for all the fun and glory of the game, will not, I think, be their only or their most enduring monument. The destruction of a state of society which had long become an anachronism—an insult as well as a danger to civilisation; the liberation of the great waterway; perhaps the foundation of an African India; certainly the settlement of a long dispute; these are cenotaphs which will scarcely be unregarded during the present generation.

The 4th of September—the anniversary of the French Republic—may become memorable for another great event. Detachments of officers and men from every regiment, British and Egyptian, were conveyed across the Nile in the gunboats and steamers to take part in the Gordon Memorial Service, and to witness the hoisting of the British flag amid the ruins of Khartoum. Personally I devoted leisure to repose. Nevertheless, the scene and ceremony were impressive. Surrounded by the soldiers he had directed with terrible and glorious effect, the successful General ordered the flags to be hoisted; and the little red flag of the Khedive and a great Union Jack—four times as big—were run up the staffs, while the officers saluted, the men presented arms, and the band played the Egyptian National Anthem and our own. Then the Sirdar called for three cheers for Her Majesty. Nor was the response without that subdued yet intense enthusiasm which stirs the sober and phlegmatic races of the North only on rare occasions. And there were some who cheered because of a victory over men; some in exultation of the conquest of territory; some that a heavy debt had been heavily paid; and others that the war was over and they would presently return home. But I would have raised my voice and helmet in honour of that persevering British people who—often affronted, often checked, often delayed—usually get their own way in the end.

The memorial service followed, and the solemn words of the English Prayer-book were read in that distant garden. More than thirteen years had passed since the decapitated trunk of the Imperial Envoy had been insulted by the Arab mob. The lonely man had perished; but his memory had proved a spell to draw his countrymen through many miles and many dangers, that they might do him honour and clear their own, and near his unknown grave, on the scene of his famous death, might pay the only tributes of respect and affection which lie within the power of men, however strongly they be banded together, however well they may be armed.

The bands played their dirge and Gordon's favourite hymn, 'Abide with me'; a gunboat on the river crashed out the salute, sending the live shells—for they had no blank ammunition—spinning away up the White Nile; the Highlanders piped a long lament; and thus the ceremony was duly fulfilled. Nine thousand of those who would have prevented it lay dead on the plain of Omdurman. Other thousands were scattered in the wilderness, or crawled wounded to the river for water. And if the British people had cared to indulge in the more indecent pleasures of triumph, they might reasonably have commanded the stonemason to bring his hammer and his chisel and cut on the pedestal of Gordon's statue in Trafalgar Square the sinister word 'Avenged!'

After the service was over the Sirdar turned and shook hands with his generals and principal officers, and each congratulated the other upon the fortunate termination of the long and difficult task. Major Snow produced his pint of champagne, which had lagged so long on its journey to Khartoum. With the assistance of a few friends who had passed, like the bottle and its owner, safely through the actions of Abu Klea and Abu Kru, and the battles of the Atbara and Omdurman, it was at last opened, and caused more enthusiasm than so small a quantity of wine could possibly have created unless assisted by the local circumstances.

Having defeated the enemy and taken his city, it was neither inappropriate nor unlikely that the conquerors should wish to examine the prize of war, and there were many visitors to Omdurman. The victorious army lay straggled along the river from the muddy waters of Khor Shambat to the suburbs of the town, a distance of nearly three miles. The southern end of the camp was already among the mud houses. Yet it was a ride of twenty minutes to the Great Wall. The road was as broad as Piccadilly and beaten level by much traffic. On both sides were mud houses. At the end the dome of the Mahdi's Tomb, much damaged by the shells, rose conspicuously.

About a quarter of a mile from this we reach on the left, as Baedeker would say, the wall of the city itself. As an obstacle the wall appears most formidable. The stones are well laid in regular courses, and the thickness is great. The officers who had toiled with the big 40-pounder guns all the way from Cairo eyed it with disappointed appetite. They had hoped to smash it to pieces. Unfortunately, the foolish people had opened their gates and prevented the fun. It was possible, however, to see the effect of the artillery on the water side. Here the gunboats had been at work at close and effective range. The results were remarkable. Great round holes had been made in the wall, which was perhaps eight feet thick. They were as neat and clean as if they had been punched in leather. There was no *débris*. A storming party would not have had to stumble over ruins of bricks and mortar. The impact of the shells had removed everything—disintegrated everything. The wind had blown the powder that remained away. Where there had been an obstacle, there was now an open doorway.

Within the wall were many horrible sights. Much killing and the paying-off of old scores had followed the downfall of the Khalifa's power and preceded the organisation of the new government. It had been a stormy interregnum. Dead bodies of men and women lay about the streets and in the narrow alleys. Some were the victims of the bombardment, some of the Maxim guns which had been used to clear the walls, but the greater number were a silent statement of the results of the continual firing we had listened to on the night of the battle.

The Khalifa's house, the Mahdi's Tomb, the Arsenal, and the Treasury were situated outside the great wall of Omdurman. The first is a building of some pretensions. The house itself was one-storeyed, but there was an annex which attained to the dignity of two rows of windows. I visited this first, climbing up a narrow but solid staircase which gave access to the upper room—an apartment about twenty feet square. What its contents may originally have been, it was impossible to say. The whole place was picked clean, and nothing had escaped the vigilant eye of the Soudanese plunderer. There was a hole in one of the walls, and floor and ceiling were spotted with scars. The shell which had caused the damage lay in splinters on the ground. The yellow sublimate of the Lyddite furred the interior surfaces of the pieces of iron with an evil-smelling powder. For the rest the room was bare.

From the windows a view might be obtained of the city. The whole prospect was revealed. Row after row, and line on line of mud houses extended on every side. The sight was not inspiring. The ugliness and universal squalor jarred unpleasantly on the eye and fancy. Yet we may imagine the Khalifa only a week before standing at this very window and looking over the homes of the thousands he ruled, proud of their numbers, confident of their strength, ignorant of their degradation. It was true Mahmud was prisoner and his army scattered. It was true the accursed infidels had crawled with their host to the south of Shabluka, so that they were but thirty miles away. It was true that their steamers and cavalry would be at the gates before many hours had passed. Of this, and all this, there was no doubt. But the battle was not fought yet. There were 50,000 faithful Dervishes ready to die or conquer for their dread Lord and for the successor of 'the expected Mahdi.' Surely they should prevail against the unbeliever, despite his big guns, his little guns, and all his iniquitous contrivances. Surely Allah would not let the True Faith perish or the Holy Shrine of his Mahdi be defiled. They would be victorious. They would kill this Egyptian rabble—he thought of ways and means—whose backs they had seen so often; and they would roll back to Cairo, as they had done before, the pestilent white men who had come from out of the unknown to annoy them and disturb their peace. And the Khalifa, soothed by such comfortable reflections, remembered that he had that day married a new wife, and turned his thoughts to the house he would build for her, when the bricks should be ferried across from the Khartoum ruins.

The rest of the Khalifa's house was practically uninjured by the shell-fire. It was an extremely good dwelling. The doorway gave access to a small central hall paved with black stone, and with rooms and offices opening out on each side. One of these contained a fine large bath, with brass taps for hot and cold water. The other chambers may have been used for sleeping, or eating, or study; but as they had been stripped of every stick of furniture, it was impossible to tell. The house had been, at any rate, the abode of one who must have possessed civilised qualities, since he was cleanly and showed some appreciation of the decencies of life.

From the Khalifa's house I repaired to the Mahdi's Tomb. The reader's mind is possibly familiar with its shape and architecture. It was much damaged by the shell-fire. The apex of the conical dome had been cut off. One of the small cupolas was completely destroyed. The dome itself had one enormous and several smaller holes smashed in it; the bright sunlight streamed through these and displayed the interior. Everything was wrecked. Still, it was possible to distinguish the painted brass railings round the actual sarcophagus, and the stone beneath which the body presumably lay. This place had been for more than ten years the most sacred and holy thing that the people of the Soudan knew. Their miserable lives had perhaps been brightened, perhaps in some way ennobled by the contemplation of something which they did not quite understand, but which they believed exerted a protecting influence. It had gratified that instinctive desire for the mystic which all human creatures possess, and which is perhaps the strongest reason for believing in a progressive destiny and a future state. By Sir H. Kitchener's orders the Tomb has been profaned and razed to the ground. The corpse of the Mahdi was dug up. The head was separated from the body, and, to quote the official explanation, 'preserved for future disposal'—a phrase which must in this case be understood to mean, that it was passed from hand to hand till it reached Cairo. Here it remained, an interesting trophy, until the affair came to the ears of Lord Cromer, who ordered it to be immediately reinterred at Wady Halfa. The limbs and trunk were flung into the Nile. Such was the chivalry of the conquerors!

Whatever misfortunes the life of Mohammed Ahmed may have caused, he was a man of considerable nobility of character, a priest, a soldier, and a patriot. He won great battles; he stimulated and revived religion. He founded an empire. To some extent he reformed the public morals. Indirectly, by making slaves into soldiers, he diminished slavery. It is impossible for any impartial person to read the testimony of such men as Slatin and Ohrwalder without feeling that the only gentle influence, the only humane element in the hard Mohammedan State, emanated from this famous rebel. The Greek missionary writes of 'his unruffled smile, pleasant manners, generosity, and equable temperament.' When the Christian priests, having refused to accept the Koran, were assailed by the soldiers and the mob and threatened with immediate death, it was the Mahdi who, 'seeing them in danger, turned back and ordered them to walk in front of his camel for protection.' When Slatin went to report the death of the unhappy French adventurer Olivier Pain, the Mahdi 'took it to heart much more than the Khalifa, said several sympathetic words, and read the prayers for the dead.' To many of his prisoners he showed kindness, all the more remarkable by comparison with his surroundings and with the treatment which he would have received had fortune failed him. To some he gave employment; to others a little money from the Beit-al-Mal, or a little food from his own plate. To all he spoke with dignity and patience. Thus he lived; and when he died in the enjoyment of unquestioned power, he was bewailed by the army he had led to victory and by the people he had freed from the yoke of the 'Turks.'

It may be worth while to examine the arguments of those who seek to justify the demolition of the Tomb. Their very enumeration betrays a confusion of thought which suggests insincerity. Some say that the people of the Soudan no longer believed in the Mahdi and cared nothing for the destruction of a fallen idol, and that therefore the matter was of little consequence. Others contend on the same side of the argument that so great was the Mahdi's influence, and so powerful was his memory, that though his successor had been overthrown his tomb would have become a place of pilgrimage, and that the conquering Power did not dare allow such an element of fanaticism to disturb their rule. The contradiction is apparent. But either argument is absurd without the contradiction. If the people of the Soudan cared no more for the Mahdi, then it was an act of Vandalism and folly to destroy the only fine building which might attract the traveller and interest the historian. It is a gloomy augury for the future of the Soudan that the first action of its civilised conquerors and present ruler should have been to level the one pinnacle which rose above the mud houses. If, on the other hand, the people of the Soudan still venerated the memory of the Mahdi—and more than 50,000 had fought hard only a week before to assert their respect and belief—then I shall not hesitate to declare that to destroy what was sacred and holy to them was a wicked act, of which the true Christian, no less than the philosopher, must express his abhorrence.

*   *   *

Another sight, besides the captured city, drew curious spectators. On the 5th of September, three days after the fight, I rode with Lord Tullibardine of the Egyptian cavalry, to examine the scene of battle. Our road lay by the *khor* whereat the victorious army had watered in the afternoon of the 2nd, and thence across the sandy, rock-strewn plain to the southern slopes of Surgham Hill. And so we came at once on to the ground over which the 21st Lancers had charged. Its peculiar formation was the more apparent at a second view. As we looked from the spot where we had wheeled into line and begun to gallop, it was scarcely possible to believe that an extensive *khor* ran right across what appeared to be smooth and unobstructed plain. An advance of a hundred yards revealed the trap, and displayed a long ditch with steeply sloping rocky sides, about four feet in depth and perhaps twenty feet wide. In this trench lay a dozen bodies of Dervishes, half-a-dozen dead donkeys, and a litter of goat-skin water-bottles, Dervish saddles, and broken weapons. The level ground beyond was sparsely spotted with corpses. Some had been buried where they fell by their friends in the city, and their places were indicated by little mounds of lighter-coloured earth. Half-a-dozen horses, stripped of saddles and bridles, made a brown jumble in the background. In the centre a red and white lance-pennon, flying from a stick, marked the grave of the fallen Lancers. And that was all. Yet the place may be remarkable. At any rate, a great many officers of all regiments and arms had been to visit it.

We rode on. We climbed the ridge of Surgham Hill, following almost the same route as that of the 'White Flag men' three days previously. At the crest of the ridge the village and the outline of the *zeriba* came into sight, and it was evident that we had now reached the spot where the Dervish column had come into the artillery fire. All over the ground—on the average three yards apart— were dead men, clad in the white and patched smocks of faithful Dervishes. Three days of burning sun had done their work. The bodies were swollen to almost gigantic proportions. Twice as large as living men, they appeared in every sense monstrous. The more advanced corpses hardly resembled human beings, but rather great bladders such as natives use to float down the Nile on. Frightful gashes scarred their limbs, and great black stains, once crimson, covered their garments. The sight was appalling. The smell redoubled the horror.

We galloped on. A strong, hot wind blew from the west across the great plain and hurried foul and tainted to the river. Keeping to windward of the thickest clusters, we picked our way, and the story of the fight unfolded itself. Here was where the artillery had opened on the swarming masses. Men had fallen in little groups of five or six to each shell. Nearer to the *zeriba*—about 1,000 yards from it—the musketry had begun to tell, and the dead lay evenly scattered about—one every ten yards. Two hundred yards further the full force of the fire—artillery, Maxims, and rifles—had burst on them. In places desperate rushes to get on at all costs had been made by devoted, fearless men. In such places the bodies lay so thickly as to hide the ground. Occasionally there were double layers of this hideous covering. Once I saw them lying three deep. In a space not exceeding a hundred yards square more than 400 corpses lay festering.

It is difficult to imagine the postures into which man, once created in the image of his Maker, had been twisted. It is not wise to try, for he who succeeds will ask himself with me: 'Can I ever forget?'

I have tried to gild war, and to solace myself for the loss of dear and gallant friends, with the thought that a soldier's death for a cause that he believes in will count for much, whatever may be beyond this world. When the soldier of a civilised Power is killed in action, his limbs are composed and his body is borne by friendly arms reverently to the grave. The wail of the fifes, the roll of the drums, the triumphant words of the Funeral Service, all divest the act of its squalor; and the spectator sympathises with, perhaps almost envies, the comrade who has found this honourable exit. But there was nothing *dulce et decorum* about the Dervish dead; nothing of the dignity of unconquerable manhood; all was filthy corruption. Yet these were as brave men as ever walked the earth. The conviction was borne in on me that their claim beyond the grave in respect of a valiant death was not less good than that which any of our countrymen could make. The thought may not be original; it may happily be untrue; it seemed certainly most unwelcome.

The incidents of the battle might be traced by the lines and patches of the slain. Here was where MacDonald's brigade, the three artillery batteries, and eight Maxim guns had repulsed the Khalifa's attack. A great heap of corpses lay round the spot where the Black Flag had been captured. There was where the brigade had faced about to meet Ali-Wad-Helu and Osman Sheikh-ed-Din. There, again, was where the Baggara cavalry had made their last splendid charge to certain death. The white-clad bodies of the men were intermingled with the brown and bay horses, so that this part of the field looked less white-speckled than the rest. They had ridden straight at the solid line of bayonets and in the teeth of the storm of projectiles. Every man had galloped at full speed, and when he fell he shot many lengths in front of his horse, rolling over and over—destroyed, not conquered, by machinery.

At such sights the triumph of victory faded on the mind, and a mournful feeling of disgust grew stronger. All this was bad to see, but worse remained; after the dead, the wounded. The officer or soldier who escapes from the field with a wound has a claim on his country. To the private it may mean a pension; to the officer a gratuity, perhaps a 'mention in despatches,' certainly advancement in his profession. The scar may even, when the sting has departed, be a source of pride—an excuse to re-tell the story. To soothe the pain there are anaesthetics; to heal the injury the resources of science are at hand. It was otherwise with the Dervish wounded.

There may have been wounded Dervishes among the heaps of slain. The atmosphere forbade approach. There certainly were many scattered about the plain. We approached these cautiously and, pistol in hand, examined their condition. Lord Tullibardine had a large water-bottle. He dismounted, and gave a few drops to each till it was all gone. You must remember that this was three days after the fight, and that the sun had beaten down mercilessly all the time. Some of the wounded were very thirsty. It would have been a grateful sight to see a large bucket of clear, cool water placed before each shaking, feverish figure. That, or a nameless man with a revolver and a big bag of cartridges, would have seemed merciful. The scenes were pathetic. Where there was a shady bush four men had crawled to die. Someone had spread a rag on the thorns to increase the shade. Three of the unfortunate creatures had attained their object; the fourth survived. He was shot through both legs. The bullet—a Martini-Henry bullet—had lodged in the right knee-cap. The whole limb was stiffened. We gave him a drink. You would not think such joy could come from a small cup of water. Tullibardine examined his injury. Presently he pulled out his knife, and after much probing and cutting extracted the bullet—with the button-hook. I have seen, and shall see perchance again, a man with a famous name worse employed.

Would the reader be further sickened with the horrors of the field? There was a man that had crawled a mile in three days, but was yet two miles from the river. He had one foot; the other remained behind. I wonder if he ever reached the water he had struggled so hard to attain! There was a man with both legs shattered; he had dragged himself along in a sitting posture, making perhaps four hundred yards a day. The extraordinary vitality of these poor wretches only prolonged their torments. So terrible were the sights and smells that the brain failed to realise the suffering and agony they proclaimed. As a man faints and his body refuses to suffer beyond a certain degree under torture, so the mind was unable to appreciate that an arrangement of line and colour lying on the ground was a human being, partly putrefied but still alive. Perhaps stern Nature, more merciful than stern civilisation, lent a kindly delirium. But I must record the fact that most of the men I saw were sane and capable of feeling every pang. And meanwhile they all struggled towards the Nile, the great river of their country, without which the invaders could never have come upon them, but which they nevertheless did not reproach. One man had reached it and lay exhausted, but content, on the bank. Another had attained the water and had died at its brim. Let us hope he had his drink first.

All this was three days after the action. Yet on the 9th of September, when a week had passed, there were still a few wounded who had neither died nor crawled away, but continued to suffer. How had they lived? It is not possible that they could have existed so long without food and water. The women and the disarmed population of Omdurman had been busy. Many hundreds not quite helpless had dragged themselves off and died all along the line of retreat. Those who were from the country round Omdurman had succour from their relations and neighbours; but it was bad for the man who had come from far and had no friends. The women would perhaps spare him a few drops of water—enough to help him through the day—but if he were a stranger, they would do no more.

Thus it was that these painful and shocking cases occurred, and it is not easy to see how they could have been prevented. The statement that 'the wounded Dervishes received every delicacy and attention' is so utterly devoid of truth that it transcends the limits of mendacity and passes into the realms of the ridiculous. I was impatient to get back to the camp. There was nothing to be gained by dallying on the field, unless a man were anxious to become quite callous, so that no imaginable misery which could come to human flesh would ever have moved him again. I may have written in these pages something of vengeance and of the paying of a debt. It may be that vengeance is sweet, and that the gods forbade vengeance to men because they reserved for themselves so delicious and intoxicating a drink. But no one should drain the cup to the bottom. The dregs are often filthy-tasting.

So as the haze deepened into the gloom of the night, and the uncertain outlines of the distant hills faded altogether from the view, we rode back to camp—'home to Omdurman,' and left the field of battle to its silent occupants. There they lie, those valiant warriors of a false faith and fallen domination; their only history preserved by their conquerors; their only monument, their bones—and these the drifting sand of the desert will bury in a few short years. Three days before I had seen them rise—eager, confident, resolved. The roar of their shouting had swelled like the surf on a rocky shore. The flashing of their blades had displayed their numbers, their vitality, their ferocity. They were confident in their strength, in the justice of their cause, in the support of their religion. Now only the heaps of corruption in the plain, and the fugitives dispersed and scattered in the wilderness, remained. The terrible machinery of scientific war had done its work. The Dervish host was scattered and destroyed. Their end, however, only anticipates that of the victors; for Time, which laughs at science, as science laughs at valour, will in due course contemptuously brush both combatants away.

Yet it may happen in some distant age, when a mighty system of irrigation has changed the desolate plain of Omdurman into a fertile garden, and the mud hovels of the town have given place to the houses, the schools, and the theatres of a great metropolis, that the husbandman, turning up a skull amid the luxuriant crop, will sapiently remark: 'There was aforetime a battle here.' Thus the event will be remembered.

* * *

Declaration by Great Britain and France Defining Their Respective Spheres of Influence in North Africa and Ending the Fashoda Crisis, 21 March 1899*

The Undersigned, duly authorized by their Governments, have signed the following Declaration: —

The IVth Article of the Convention of the 14th June, 1898, shall be completed by the following provisions, which shall be considered as forming an integral part of it:

1. Her Britannic Majesty's Government engages not to acquire either territory or political influence to the west of the line of frontier defined in the following paragraph, and the Government of the French Republic engages not to acquire either territory or political influence to the east of the same line.

2. The line of frontier shall start from the point where the boundary between the Congo Free State and French territory meets the water-parting between the watershed of the Nile and that of the Congo and its affluents. It shall follow in principle that water-parting up to its intersection with the 11th parallel of north latitude. From this point it shall be drawn as far as the 15th parallel in such manner as to separate, in principle, the Kingdom of Wadai from what constituted in 1882 the Province of Darfur; but it shall in no case be so drawn as to pass to the west beyond the 21st degree of longitude east of Greenwich (18° 40′ east of Paris), or to the east beyond the 23rd degree of longitude east of Greenwich (20° 40′ east of Paris).

3. It is understood, in principle, that to the north of the 15th parallel the French zone shall be limited to the north-east and east by a line which shall start from the point of intersection of the Tropic of Cancer with the 16th degree of longitude east of Greenwich (13° 40′ east of Paris), shall run thence to the south-east until it meets the 24th degree of longitude east of Greenwich (21° 40′ east of Paris), and shall then follow the 24th degree until it meets, to the north of the 15th parallel of latitude, the frontier of Darfur as it shall eventually be fixed.

4. The two Governments engage to appoint Commissioners who shall be charged to delimit on the spot a frontier-line in accordance with the indications given in paragraph 2 of this Declaration. The result of their work shall be submitted for the approbation of their respective Governments.

*Parliamentary Papers, 1899, CXII, Cmd. 9134, 2–3.

It is agreed that the provisions of Article IX of the Convention of the 14th June, 1898, shall apply equally to the territories situated to the south of the 14° 20′ parallel of north latitude, and to the north of the 5th parallel of north latitude, between the 14° 20′ meridian of longitude east of Greenwich (12th degree east of Paris) and the course of the Upper Nile.

Done at London, the 21st March, 1899.

(L.S.) Salisbury
(L.S.) Paul Cambon

Dispatch from the Foreign Office to the Treasury on the
Proposed Revocation of the Charter of the Royal Niger Company,
15 June 1899*

The Marquess of Salisbury has for some time past had under consideration the question of approaching the Royal Niger Company with a view to relieving them of their rights and functions of administration on reasonable terms. His Lordship has arrived at the opinion that it is desirable on grounds of national policy that these rights and functions should be taken over by Her Majesty's Government, now that the ratifications of the Anglo-French Convention of June 14th 1898, have been exchanged, and that the frontiers of the two countries have been clearly established in the neighbourhood of the territories administered by the Company. The state of affairs created by this Convention makes it incumbent on Her Majesty's Government to maintain an immediate control over the frontier and fiscal policy of British Nigeria such as cannot be exercised so long as that policy is dictated and executed by a Company which combines commercial profit with administrative responsibilities. The possibility of the early claim by the French Government to profit by the advantages in the Lower Niger which are secured to them by the Convention, makes it essential that an Imperial Authority should be on the spot to control the development of the policy which actuated Her Majesty's Government in granting those advantages, and to prevent the difficulties which would be sure to arise were the Company's officials alone to represent British interests.

There are, moreover, other cogent reasons for the step now contemplated. The West African frontier force, now under Imperial officers, calls for direct Imperial control; the situation created towards other firms by the commercial position of the Company which, although strictly within the rights devolving upon it by Char-

**Parliamentary Papers*, 1899, LXIII, Cmd. 9372, 3.

ter, has succeeded in establishing a practical monopoly of trade; the manner in which this commercial monopoly presses on the native traders, as exemplified by the rising in Brass, which called for the mission of enquiry entrusted to Sir John Kirk in 1895, are some of the arguments which have influenced his Lordship.

The question is not new to the Lords Commissioners, who at Lord Salisbury's suggestion, offered confidentially in November 1897, have had under consideration the terms on which the transfer could be made. Lord Salisbury does not therefore propose to enter into the financial aspect of the case, but would ask their Lordships to endeavour to come to an early settlement with the Company.

Dispatch from the High Commissioner of Northern Nigeria, F. D. Lugard, to the Colonial Secretary, Joseph Chamberlain, on Railroad Construction and Harbor Works, 11 May 1900**

I have the honor to acknowledge your despatch of March 6th, enclosing a report by Messrs. Coode and Son, relative to a scheme for spending £800,000 on harbour works at Lagos. In accordance with the last paragraph of your despatch I at once arranged to meet the Governor of Lagos at Illorin, as he happened to be in the neighbourhood of the frontier, and discussed the subject with him. I could not, of course, do so with Sir R. Moor, as he is in England.

2. Were the construction of the railway from the coast under discussion *ab initio*, there would, doubtless, be strong arguments for the selection of a port on which little expenditure would be needed, such as Warri or Sapeli, where there is no bar, and ocean-going vessels can find sufficient water at all times. But even in that case, it would have to be considered whether these ports were sufficiently healthy, and whether they afforded sufficient room for the expansion of a large township, and it would have to be noted that the railway would not run through a country as densely populated, or through so industrious a population as in the Lagos Protectorate, and that, instead of starting from a great trade centre like Lagos, everything would have to be created *de novo* at its sea-port.

3. The question, however, as it stands to-day, is that the line is practically complete to Ibadan. Thence to the Kaduna mouth is approximately a distance of 190 miles of fairly easy country, with two large towns *en route* (Ogbomosho and Illorin). On the other hand, the distance from Kaduna mouth to Warri, via Benin, is approximately 224 miles, and of this the southernmost portion appears to be a network of creeks which would require enormous bridging works, while the erection of preliminary workshops, sheds, &c., would again add to the cost.

Parliamentary Papers, 1906, LXXVIII, Cmd. 2787, 21-22.

It appears at least probable that the extra 34 miles (which would, of course, be added to by the route actually taken) plus the cost of bridging the creeks, and of establishing a railway base at Warri, would cost as much, or more than, the sum proposed to be expended on Lagos Harbour. I, of course, merely suggest this line of comparison, which can only be worth anything after a proper survey.

4. Admitting that the objective for a railway is Kano, and that the Lagos Railway cannot pay till it reaches the population of the Hausa States, the first question for decision is, the best point for a railway to cross the Niger. The line it should traverse in Northern Nigeria would appear to be somewhere along the Kaduna valley, tapping the trade of the great cities of Bida and Zaria. Instead of crossing opposite Bida, however, it may, for engineering reasons, be better that it should cross at any point higher up where the river has a firm and rocky bed, or even at Jebba, where a suspension bridge could be thrown across from the rocks on the south bank to the mid-river island, and thence to the rocks on the north bank. I submit that it would be of the greatest value in deciding the course that the railway should take that this point should first be settled by an expert.

5. Jebba is a place of little importance, and if it were considered that the railway should cross the Niger to east of the Kaduna mouth, so as to pass near Bida, and avoid bridging the Kaduna, the railway could be deflected westwards from Illorin to the neighbourhood of Egbom or Egbagi.

6. Looking to the development in the future of Nigeria as a whole (including Lagos) I am strongly of opinion that it would be of the greatest advantage to form a clear conception of the ultimate destination and course of the railway, and the point at which it should cross the Niger, so that existing plans might be based on a knowledge of what is to come hereafter. The selection of an administrative centre away from the unhealthy river valley—a point I hold to be of primary importance—would be influenced by this knowledge, and much might be done in preparation along the proposed course of the railway, by road-making, &c. These views I have frequently submitted for your consideration, and I would even go further, and suggest that not only should an expert railway survey be at once undertaken from the Niger to Kano, but that, if possible, a beginning should be made of the actual work, starting on the north bank at the point selected for the railway to cross. Material can be brought up in large cargo steamers at Niger flood.

7. I have not at present sufficient knowledge of the commercial prospects of these countries to offer any opinion worth consideration, as to the comparative merits of the schemes discussed by Messrs. Coode, or whether the prospective increase of revenue would warrant the adoption of the most expensive and thorough-going plan, but, in view of the projects now discussed in a serious spirit by eminent French authorities, *vide* article in *Revue des Deux Mondes*, of constructing a railway from Algeria to Timbuktu, and Chad, and the political importance attached to that project (in which, however, I do not wholly concur), I think the harbour of Lagos acquires a greater importance than that

merely resulting from trade expansion, and that hereafter it is possible that the Empire might have cause for regret if half measures only were adopted now.

8. The immediate commencement of a line from the Niger towards Kano would have an immense effect in stimulating trade and competition in this Protectorate. The cost of administration would, I believe, be reduced by the decreased roll of deaths and invalidings to England, and possibly by an increased length of the term of residential service, consequent on the better climate of the interior, while touch would be obtained with a country, the density of whose population is said to exceed that of any other country in the whole continent of Africa, and whose trading instincts are proverbial.

---

*Report of the Northern Nigeria Lands Committee
Recommending Changes in Land
Legislation, April 1910**

Terms of Reference

The terms in which the subject of our enquiry has been referred to us are: —
"To consider the evidence collected by Sir Percy Girouard, and any other evidence available as to the existing system of land tenure in Northern Nigeria; and to report (1) on the system which it is advisable to adopt, and (2) as to the legislative and administrative measures necessitated by its adoption."

Scope of Enquiry

We apprehend that the duty with which we are charged is to report as to the leading principles on which legislation affecting land in Northern Nigeria ought to be based, and by which the Government of the country in the exercise of their proper functions in relation to land ought to be guided, and that, in reporting on the "legislative and administrative measures" necessitated by the adoption of the principles which we recommend, it is not desired that we should do more than indicate where necessary the general line of action to which our conclusions point.

Proceedings of the Committee

We understand that the Colonial Office and the Government of Northern Nigeria attach much importance to an early decision on the points at issue. On this account, and owing to the fact that our colleagues, Mr. Temple and Captain Orr, are only available during the limited period of their furlough and to other circumstances, the time at our disposal has been somewhat short. We

Parliamentary Papers, 1910, XLIV, Cmd. 5102, iii, x–xi, xiv.

have, however, held thirteen meetings, in the course of which we have considered the evidence collected by Sir Percy Girouard in his two memoranda and their appendices, supplemented by the oral evidence of Sir Raymond Menendez, the late Chief Justice of Northern Nigeria, and of five experienced officers of the Political Department of Northern Nigeria, including our colleagues above mentioned. We have had before us also the various laws relating to land in force in the Protectorate and the memoranda on the subject of land, taxation and native revenue issued to his political officers by the late High Commissioner, Sir Frederick Lugard. Further it seemed of importance, as bearing upon the future development of the Protectorate, that we should be in possession of the views of firms and corporations possessing private industrial or commercial interests in the country with regard to questions affecting the occupation of land by Europeans for trading or other purposes. We accordingly invited the Niger Company, Limited, and Messrs. John Holt and Company (Liverpool) Limited, the two European firms who have been longest established on the Niger, and the British Cotton Growing Association, who, we understand, may be said to represent the interest of Lancashire in Northern Nigeria as a cotton-growing country, to send delegates to give evidence before us. Messrs. John Holt and Company and the British Cotton Growing Association responded to our invitation, and we have placed on record the views expressed on their behalf by Mr. John Holt and Sir Ralph Moor, K.C.M.G., respectively. The Niger Company elected not to give evidence.

* * *

(3) Application of Above Principles and Suggested Amendments of the Law

23. Apart from differences of phraseology, we find that the views expressed in the memoranda both by Sir F. Lugard and by Sir Percy Girouard are in substantial accord in laying down as the fundamental principle that the whole of the land of the Protectorate is under the control of the Crown. Whether it is necessary or desirable to distinguish between Crown Lands and Public Lands, and to lay down that the former are under the absolute ownership of the Crown and the latter under the administrative control of the Crown may well be doubted. It seems to us that when once the broad principle above stated is laid down such distinctions become unnecessary and may be misleading.

24. It seems better, we think, to approach the question from the point of view of the limitations which ought to be imposed by law or by administrative regulations and methods upon the general power of control over the lands inherent in the Government.

25. The principle governing the exercise of its power of control is the interest of the native population, by providing security for the use and enjoyment of the land now occupied by them and the reservation of sufficient land to provide for the requirements of the system of shifting cultivation and for the probable growth of native population. Second to this object the development of the country should be kept in view. This is dealt with in a subsequent part of our Report.

26. The question relating to the revenue to be derived by the Government from their control of the land of the Protectorate we deal with presently.

27. The first object of the Government is so to exercise its power of control of all lands as to secure to the native the undisturbed enjoyment of his occupation and use of land. No intermediate right to the land (nothing in the nature of a relation of mesne lord and tenant) is recognised. The native conception appears to be that each head of a family is entitled to the enjoyment of sufficient land within the limits of the village or other community to which he belongs for the support of his household. If the land he has occupied is exhausted he is entitled to permission to occupy fresh land. If he has no land, for instance, when he grows up and has a family of his own, he is entitled to permission to cultivate a new piece of land. It is the duty of the Government to protect the occupier from disturbance. His title to the enjoyment of land is that of a licensee of a Government, and he can only be deprived of his enjoyment by the Government. This is, as pointed out by Sir Frederick Lugard, a recognised consequence of conquest. Cases may occur where the Government for public purposes requires land actually occupied and cultivated. In that case the principle is that the occupier or licensee should have full compensation from the Government for the crops, buildings and improvements, though not for the land. According to native custom the right, if it may be so called, to dispossess the occupier for sufficient reason appears to be fully recognised, but the right to compensation is more precarious.

28. Probably the most important question is the method to be adopted with regard to the power of alienation: what restrictions should be placed on the power of the occupier of land to alienate his interest to a native or a non-native. It has already been pointed out that by "The Lands Proclamation, 1900," no land can be acquired by a non-native except by the consent of the Government. The evidence shows that in practice the transfer of the right of enjoyment to a native occupier also required the assent of the Chief. For the proper protection of the native it seems necessary that the consent of the Government should be required to any transfer of occupation and enjoyment from one native to another, and it seems that for this purpose legislation is necessary.

If anything in the nature of free alienation of the rights of enjoyment and use of land were recognised by law the whole of the land in all probability would within a very short time be heavily mortgaged.

29. It seems probable that questions of the right to occupy definite portions of land or houses are more likely to arise in thickly populated areas. For instance, should the law make any difference in respect of the occupation of land in urban and in rural districts? We should answer this question in the negative. It is quite possible that some system of land registration may be adopted in urban districts before it can be carried out in rural districts. But it seems important that the principles that all land is under the control of the Government and that legal security for the validity of any transfer of rights of occupation and enjoyment can only be given under a contract to which the

Government is a party should continue to be recognised in urban as well as in rural districts.

In urban and in rural districts there is a risk, especially as vacant land becomes filled up, that some sort of valuable title to bequeath and transfer land may grow up and be recognised by native law and custom; and this development of something akin to a proprietary right in land is a danger against which it is important to guard. It is difficult, if not impossible, to prevent it by legislation, but the variation of the assessment of both rural and urban holdings from year to year, which is in the administrative power of the Resident, should be so employed as to prevent as far as possible land from acquiring a marketable value other than that derived from the improvements made upon it.

*   *   *

40. As regards alienation of the right of use and enjoyment, we think it is essential that the Government should retain the power of preventing sales or mortgages without its assent. Every such transaction to which the Government has not assented should be void.

41. As regards succession, this we think may be left to the custom prevailing in the locality, but the person claiming either under a will, if any instrument in the nature of a will is recognised by custom, or as a representative of the deceased, should notify his claim to succeed.

42. It seems to us that if these simple and elementary provisions are laid down by Proclamation, the administration of the law may be left to the executive authorities and to the action of the tribunals, adopting and acting on native custom in so far as it is not inconsistent with the principles declared by Proclamation.

*   *   *

Speech by the Foreign Secretary, Sir Edward Grey, in the
House of Commons Advocating Closer Imperial Ties
with Germany, 27 November 1911*

*   *   *

One does not make new friendships worth having by deserting old ones. New friendships by all means let us make, but not at the expense of the ones we have. I desire to do all I can to improve the relations with Germany, as I shall presently show. But the friendships which we have have lasted now for some years, and it must be a cardinal point of improved relations with Germany that we do not sacrifice one of these, and what I desire—and what I hope it may be possible to have, though it may seem difficult at the present time—is that the improved relations may be such as will improve, not only ourselves, but those

*_Hansard_, 5.s., XXXII, 61-62.

who are our friends. We keep our friendships. We intend to retain them unimpaired, and the more we can do, so long as we can preserve that position, so much the better, and we shall endeavour to do it. That is an essential condition. Is the policy I have sketched out necessarily a bar to good relations with Germany? I do not believe it is. They say in Germany—I only take the opinions that are reported and as they appear in the Press in Germany—that it is part of our policy always to stand in Germany's way and object to Germany's expansion. It is unfortunate that the Morocco question has come up so often. But that is a special case by itself, where we have a special agreement and have special interests, to which we attach importance, which are set out in the agreement; but in my opinion—though I do not speak for more than myself personally when I say this—the wise policy for this country is to expand as little as possible, and certainly not further the African possessions.

I do not say that there are not—of course there are—certain parts of Africa lying absolutely contiguous to British possessions, especially to those of the Government of the Union of South Africa, which, if there were territorial changes, we could not see pass into other hands; and if there are great territorial changes there are no doubt other things close to British territory in the nature of frontier rectification. If there are to be changes brought about by the goodwill and negotiation with other Powers, then we are not an ambitious competing party, and, not being an ambitious competing party ourselves, if Germany has friendly arrangements to negotiate with other foreign countries, we are not anxious to stand in their way. I believe that is the wise policy for this country, and if it is the wise policy, not to go in for great schemes of expansion ourselves, then I think it would be diplomatically and morally wrong to indulge in a dog-in-the-manger policy with regard to others. I think, indeed, the House may see something of that sort in the recent negotiations.

*   *   *

Summary by the Former British Consul-General, Lord
Cromer, of Legislative and Legal Reforms in Egypt, July 1913*
[Formerly Sir Evelyn Baring, Cromer was
Consul-General from 1883 to 1907.]

During the six years which have elapsed since I left Cairo I have, for various reasons on which it is unnecessary to dwell, carefully abstained from taking any part in whatever discussions have arisen on current Egyptian affairs. If I now depart from the reticence which I have hitherto observed it is because there appears at all events some slight prospect that the main reform which is required to render the government and administration of Egypt efficient will be

*Cromer, "The Capitulations in Egypt," *The Nineteenth Century and After,* 1-10.

seriously considered. As so frequently happens in political affairs, a casual incident has directed public attention to the need of reform. A short time ago a Russian subject was, at the request of the Consular authorities, arrested by the Egyptian police and handed over to them for deportation to Russia. I am not familiar with the details of the case, neither, for the purposes of my present argument, is any knowledge of those details required. The nature of the offence of which this man, Adamovitch by name, was accused, as also the question of whether he was guilty or innocent of that offence, are altogether beside the point. The legal obligation of the Egyptian Government to comply with the request that the man should be handed over to the Russian Consular authorities would have been precisely the same if he had been accused of no offence at all. The result, however, has been to touch one of the most tender points in the English political conscience. It has become clear that a country which is not, indeed, British territory, but which is held by a British garrison, and in which British influence is predominant, affords no safe asylum for a political refugee. Without in any way wishing to underrate the importance of this consideration, I think it necessary to point out that this is only one out of the many anomalies which might be indicated in the working of that most perplexing political creation entitled the Egyptian Government and administration. Many instances might, in fact, be cited which, albeit they are less calculated to attract public attention in this country, afford even stronger ground for holding that the time has come for reforming the system hitherto known as that of the Capitulations.

Before attempting to deal with this question I may perhaps be pardoned if, at the risk of appearing egotistical, I indulge in a very short chapter of autobiography. My own action in Egypt has formed the subject of frequent comment in this country; Neither, assuredly, in spite of occasional blame, have I any reason to complain of the measure of praise—often, I fear, somewhat unmerited praise—which has been accorded to me. But I may perhaps be allowed to say what, in my own opinion, are the main objects achieved during my twenty-four-years' tenure of office. Those achievements are four in number, and let me add that they were not the results of a hand-to-mouth conduct of affairs in which the direction afforded to political events was constantly shifted, but of a deliberate plan persistently pursued with only such temporary deviations and delays as the circumstances of the time rendered inevitable.

In the first place, the tension with the French Government, which lasted for twenty-one years and which might at any moment have become very serious, was never allowed to go beyond a certain point. In spite of a good deal of provocation a policy of conciliation was persistently adopted, with the result that the conclusion of the Anglo-French Agreement of 1904 became eventually possible. It is on this particular feature of my Egyptian career that personally I look back with far greater pride and pleasure than any other, all the more so because, although it has, comparatively speaking, attracted little public attention, it was, in reality, by far the most difficult and responsible part of my task.

In the second place, bankruptcy was averted and the finances of the country placed on a sound footing.

In the third place, by the relief of taxation and other reforms which remedied any really substantial grievances, the ground was cut away from under the feet of the demagogues whom it was easy to foresee would spring into existence as education advanced.

In the fourth place, the Soudan, which had to be abandoned in 1884-85, was eventually recovered.

These, I say, are the things which were done. Let me now state what was not done. Although, of course, the number of Egyptians employed in the service of the Government was largely increased, and although the charges which have occasionally been made that education was unduly neglected admit of easy refutation, it is none the less true that little, if any, progress was made in the direction of conferring autonomy on Egypt. The reasons why so little progress was made in this direction were twofold.

In the first place, it would have been premature even to think of the question until the long struggle against bankruptcy had been fought and won, and also until, by the conclusion of the Anglo-French Agreement in 1904, the acute international tension which heretofore existed had been relaxed.

In the second place, the idea of what constituted autonomy entertained by those Egyptians who were most in a position to make their voices heard, as also by some of their English sympathisers, differed widely from that entertained by myself and others who were well acquainted with the circumstances of the country, and on whom the responsibility of devising and executing any plan for granting autonomy would naturally devolve. We were, in fact, the poles asunder. The Egyptian idea was that the native Egyptians should rule Egypt. They therefore urged that greatly increased powers should be given to the Legislative Council and Assembly originally instituted by Lord Dufferin. The counter-idea was not based on any alleged incapacity of the Egyptians to govern themselves—a point which, for the purposes of my present argument, it is unnecessary to discuss. Neither was it based on any disinclination gradually to extend the powers of Egyptians in dealing with purely native Egyptian questions. I, and others who shared my views, considered that those who cried 'Egypt for the Egyptians' on the house-tops had gone off on an entirely wrong scent because, even had they attained their ends, nothing approaching to Egyptian autonomy would have been realised. The Capitulations would still have barred the way to all important legislation and to the removal of those defects in the administration of which the Egyptians most complained. When the prominent part played by resident Europeans in the political and social life of Egypt is considered, it is indeed little short of ridiculous to speak of Egyptian autonomy if at the same time a system is preserved under which no important law can be made applicable to an Englishman, a Frenchman, or a German, without its detailed provisions having received the consent, not only of the King of England, the President of the French Republic, and the German Emperor, but also that of the President of the United States, the King of Denmark, and every other ruling Potentate in Europe. We therefore held that the only possible method by which the evils of extreme personal government could be averted, and by which the country could be provided with a workable legislative machine, was to include in the term 'Egyptians' all the dwellers in Egypt, and to devise some plan by which the European and Egyptian elements of society would be fused together to such an extent at all events as to render them capable of co-operating in legislative effort. It may perhaps be hoped that by taking a first step in this direction some more thorough fusion may possibly follow in the future.

As I have already mentioned, it would have been premature to deal with this question prior to 1904, for any serious modification of the regime of the Capitulations could not be considered as within the domain of practical politics so long as all the Powers, and more especially France and England, were pulling different ways. But directly that agreement was signed I resolved to take the question up, all the more so because what was then known as the Secret Agreement, but which has since that time been published, contained the following very important clause:

> In the event of their (His Britannic Majesty's Government) considering it desirable to introduce in Egypt reforms tending to assimilate the Egyptian legislative system to that in force in other civilised countries, the Government of the French Republic will not refuse to entertain any such proposals, on the understanding that His Britannic Majesty's Government will agree to entertain the suggestions that the Government of the French Republic may have to make to them with a view of introducing similar reforms in Morocco.

I was under no delusion as to the formidable nature of the obstacles which stood in the way of reform. Moreover, I held very strongly that even if it had been possible, by diplomatic negotiations with the other Powers, to come to some arrangement which would be binding on the Europeans resident in Egypt, and to force it on them without their consent being obtained, it was most undesirable to adopt anything approaching to this procedure. The European colonists in Egypt, although of course numerically far inferior to the native population, represent a large portion of the wealth, and a still larger portion of the intelligence and energy in the country. Moreover, although the word 'privilege' always rather grates on the ear in this democratic age, it is none the less true that in the past the misgovernment of Egypt has afforded excellent reasons why even those Europeans who are most favourably disposed towards native aspirations should demur to any sacrifice of their capitulary rights. My view, therefore, was that the Europeans should not be coerced but persuaded. It had to be proved to them that, under the changed condition of affairs, the Capitulations were not only unnecessary but absolutely detrimental to their own interests. Personally, I was very fully convinced of the truth of this statement, neither was it difficult to convince those who, being behind the scenes of government, were in a position to judge of the extent to which the Capitulations clogged progress in many very important directions. But it was more difficult to convince the general public, many of whom entertained very erroneous ideas as to the extent and nature of the proposed reforms, and could see nothing but the fact that it was intended to deprive them of certain privileges which they then possessed. It cannot be too distinctly understood that there never was—neither do I suppose there is now—the smallest intention of 'abolishing the Capitulations,' if by that term is meant a complete abrogation of all those safeguards against arbitrary proceedings on the part of the Government which the Capitulations are intended to prevent. Capitulations or no Capitulations, the European charged with a criminal offence must be tried either by European judges or an European jury. All matters connected with the personal status of any European must be judged by the laws in force in his own country. Adequate safeguards must be contrived to guard against any abuse of power on the part of the police. Whatever reforms are introduced into the Mixed Tribunals must be confined to comparatively minor points, and must not touch fundamental principles. In fact, the Capitulations have not to be abolished, but to be modified. An eminent French jurist, M. Gabriel Louis Jaray, in discussing the Egyptian situation a few years ago, wrote:

> On peut considérer comme admis qu'une simple occupation ou un protectorat de fait, reconnu par les Puissances Européennes, suffit pour mettre à néant les Capitulations, quand la réorganisation du pays est suffisante pour donner aux Européens pleine garantie de bonne juridiction.

I contend that the reorganisation of Egypt is now sufficiently advanced to admit of the guarantees for the good administration of justice, which M. Jaray very rightly claimed, being afforded to all Europeans without having recourse to the clumsy methods of the Capitulations in their present form.

In the last two reports which I wrote before I left Egypt I developed these and some cognate arguments at considerable length. But from the first moment of taking up the question I never thought that it would fall to my lot to bring the campaign against the Capitulations to a conclusion. The question was eminently one as to which it was undesirable to force the pace. Time was required in order to let public opinion mature. I therefore contented myself with indicating the defects of the present system and the general direction which reform should take, leaving it to those younger than myself to carry on the work when advancing years obliged me to retire. I may add that the manner in which my proposals were received and discussed by the European public in Egypt afforded good reason for supposing that the obstacles to be overcome before any serious reforms could be effected, though formidable, were by no means insuperable. After my departure in 1907, events occurred which rendered it impossible that the subject should at once come under the consideration of the Government, but in 1911 Lord Kitchener was able to report that the legislative powers of the Court of Appeal sitting at Alexandria had been somewhat increased. Sir Malcolm McIlwraith, the Judicial Adviser of the Egyptian Government, in commenting on this change, says:

> The new scheme, while assuredly a progressive step, and in notable advance of the previous state of affairs . . . can hardly be regarded, in its ensemble, as more than a temporary makeshift, and a more or less satisfactory palliative of the legislative impotence under which the Government has suffered for so long.

It is most earnestly to be hoped that the question will now be taken up seriously with a view to more drastic reform than any which has as yet been effected.

There is one, and only one, method by which the evils of the existing system can be made to disappear. The British Government should request the other Powers of Europe to vest in them the legislative power which each now exercises separately. Simultaneously with this request, a legislative Chamber should be created in Egypt for enacting laws to which Europeans will be amenable.

There is, of course, one essential preliminary to the execution of this pro-gramme. It is that the Powers of Europe, as also the European residents in Egypt, should have thorough confidence in the intentions of the British Govern-ment, by which I mean confidence in the duration of the occupation, and also confidence in the manner in which the affairs of the country will be adminis-tered.

As regards the first point, there is certainly no cause for doubt. Under the Anglo-French Agreement of 1904 the French Government specifically declared that 'they will not obstruct the action of government in Egypt by asking that a limit of time be fixed for the British occupation, or in any other manner.' Moreover, one of the last acts that I performed before I left Egypt in 1907 was to communicate to the British Chamber of Commerce at Alexandria a letter from Sir Edward Grey in which I was authorised to state that his Majesty's Government 'recognise that the maintenance and development of such reforms as have hitherto been effected in Egypt depend upon the British occupation. This consideration will apply with equal strength to any changes effected in the regime of the Capitulations. His Majesty's Government, therefore, wish it to be understood that there is no reason for allowing the prospect of any modifica-tions in that regime to be prejudiced by the existence of any doubt as to the continuance of the British occupation of the country.' It is, of course, conceiv-able that in some remote future the British garrison may be withdrawn from Egypt. If any fear is entertained on this ground it may easily be calmed by an arrangement with the Powers that in the event of the British Government wishing to withdraw their troops, they would previously enter into communica-tions with the various Powers of Europe with a view to re-establishing whatever safeguards they might think necessary in the interests of their countrymen.

As regards the second point, that is to say, confidence in the manner in which the administration of the country is conducted, I need only say that, so far as I am able to judge, Lord Kitchener's administration, although one of his mea-sures—the Five Feddan law—has, not unnaturally, been subjected to a good deal of hostile criticism, has inspired the fullest confidence in the minds of the whole of the population of Egypt, whether European or native. I cannot doubt that, when the time arrives for Lord Kitchener, in his turn, to retire, no brusque or radical change will be allowed to take place in the general principles under which he is now administering the country.

The rights and duties of any such Chamber as that which I propose, its composition, its mode of election or nomination, the degree of control to be exercised over it by the Egyptian or British Governments, are, of course, all points which require very careful consideration, and which admit of solution in a great variety of ways. In my report for the year 1906 I put forward certain suggestions in connexion with each of these subjects, but I do not doubt that, as the result of further consideration and discussion, my proposals admit of improvement. I need not now dwell on these details, important though they be. I wish, however, to allude to one point which involves a question of principle. I trust that no endeavour will for the present be made to create one Chamber, composed of both Europeans and Egyptians, with power to legislate for all the inhabitants of Egypt. I am strongly convinced that, under the present condition of society in Egypt, any such attempt must end in complete failure. It is, I believe, quite impossible to devise any plan for an united Chamber which would satisfy the very natural aspirations of the Egyptians, and at the same time provide for the Europeans adequate guarantees that their own legitimate rights would be properly safeguarded. I am fully aware of the theoretical objections which may be urged against trying the novel experiment of creating two Chambers in the same country, each of which would deal with separate classes of the community, but I submit that, in the special circumstances of the case, those objections must be set aside, and that one more anomaly should, for the time being at all events, be added to the many strange institutions which exist in the 'Land of Paradox.' Whether at some probably remote future period it will be possible to create a Chamber in which Europeans and Egyptians will sit side by side will depend very largely on the conduct of the Egyptians themselves. If they follow the advice of those who do not flatter them, but who, however little they may recognise the fact, are in reality their best friends—if, in a word, they act in such a manner as to inspire the European residents of Egypt with confidence in their judgment and absence of class or religious prejudice, it may be that this consummation will eventually be reached. If, on the other hand, they allow themselves to be guided by the class of men who have of late years occasionally posed as their representatives, the prospect of any complete legislative amalgamation will become not merely gloomy but practically hopeless. The true Egyptian patriot is not the man who by his conduct and language stimulates racial animosity in the pursuit of an ideal which can never be realised, but rather one who recognises the true facts of the political situation. Now, the dominating fact of that situation is that Egypt can never become autonomous in the sense in which that word is understood by the Egyptian nationalists. It is, and will always remain, a cosmopolitan country. The real future of Egypt, therefore, lies not in the direction of a narrow nationalism, which will only embrace native Egyptians, nor in that of any endeavour to convert Egypt into a British possession on the model of India or Ceylon, but rather in that of an enlarged cosmopolitanism, which, whilst discarding all the obstructive fetters of the cumbersome old international system, will tend to amalgamate all the inhabitants of the Nile Valley and enable them all alike to share in the government of their native or adopted country.

For the rest, the various points of detail to which I have alluded above present difficulties which are by no means insuperable, if—as I trust may be the case—the various parties concerned approach the subject with a real desire to arrive at some practical solutions. The same may be said as regards almost all the points to which Europeans resident in Egypt attach special importance, such, for instance, as the composition of criminal courts for trying Europeans, the regulation of domiciliary visits by the police, and cognate issues. In all these cases it is by no means difficult to devise methods for preserving all that is really worth keeping in the present system, and at the same time discarding those portions which seriously hinder the progress of the country. There is, however, one important point of detail which, I must admit, presents considerable practical difficulties. It is certain that the services of some of the European judges of the Mixed Tribunals might be utilised in constituting the new Chamber. Their presence would be of great use, and it is highly probable that they will in practice become the real working men of any Chamber which may be created. But apart from the objection in principle to confiding the making as also the administration of the law wholly to the same individuals, it is to be observed that, in order to create a really representative body, it would be essential that other Europeans—merchants, bankers, landowners, and professional men—should be seated in the Chamber. Almost all the Europeans resident in Europe are busy men, and the question will arise whether those whose assistance would, on general grounds, be of special value, are prepared to sacrifice the time required for paying adequate attention to their legislative duties. I can only say that I hope that sufficient public spirit is to be found amongst the many highly qualified European residents in Egypt of divers nationalities to enable this question to be answered in the affirmative.

It is, of course, impossible within the space allotted to me to deal fully on the present occasion with all the aspects of this very difficult and complicated question. I can only attempt to direct attention to the main issue, and that issue, I repeat, is how to devise some plan which shall take the place of the present Egyptian system of legislation by diplomacy. The late Lord Salisbury once epigrammatically described that system to me by saying that it was like the *liberum veto* of the old Polish Diet, 'without being able to have recourse to the alternative of striking off the head of any recalcitrant voter.' It is high time that such a system should be swept away and some other adopted which will be more in harmony with the actual facts of the Egyptian situation. If, as I trust may be the case, Lord Kitchener is able to devise and to carry into execution some plan which will rescue Egypt from its present legislative Slough of Despond, he will have deserved well, not only of his country, but also of all those Egyptian interests, whether native or European, which are committed to his charge.

DISSOLUTION OF THE EMPIRE
1914 − Present

DISSOLUTION OF THE EMPIRE
1914 – Present

COMMENTARY

Contrasting themes of advance and dissolution define post-1914 imperial history. On the one hand, the Commonwealth of Nations, the most comprehensive and rational expression of unity in British imperial history, matured. But of even greater force was the subsequent territorial decline of the British Empire, spurred on by the pressures of nationalism overseas and by Britain's loss of great-power status.

Institutionalized imperial union became a reality in the twentieth century via the mechanism of the Commonwealth. The unprecedented pressures of the First World War forged closer relations between Britain and her colonies. Although a preferential tariff scheme along the lines proposed by Joseph Chamberlain was not adopted until the 1930's, and although ambitious formulations for military union were never taken up, political and diplomatic ties solidified in the wartime setting. Imperial Conferences, summoned in 1917 and 1918, meshed the contributions of the several parts of the Empire. An Imperial War Cabinet consisting of representatives of the Dominion governments met with the British War Cabinet. And in this context an informal constitutional framework for Dominion partnership evolved. Canada, Australia, New Zealand, and South Africa, having already achieved *de facto* autonomy, were woven into a larger structure of union. Non-self-governing countries like India also achieved a more precise definition of their status.

The 1926 Report of the Imperial Relations Committee (known as the "Balfour Report") propounded a new theory of imperial union, that is, "autonomous communities within the British Empire, equal in status, in no way subordinate one to another in any aspect of their domestic or external relations." And during the ensuing decade the Statute of Westminster (1931) and the consequent adoption of a binding system of economic preferences gave the Commonwealth of Nations its permanent form. Financial relationships henceforth strengthened cultural and political ties.

Constructed at its core out of those British colonies which had secured responsible government, the Commonwealth of Nations has held together sufficiently well for over three decades, notwithstanding numerous shocks. Its emotional linkages are yet able to offer some resistance to increasing economic pressures. Given the fact of a circumscribed territorial context, it has continued to provide a diluted alternative to the polarity of a united Europe.

However, outside of the institutional and cultural frame provided by the Commonwealth, the post-1914 world has proven ungenial to the imperial ideal. The process of accreting colonial territory has totally reversed itself in the twentieth century. This was so despite important gains in Palestine, Iraq, and Transjordan, as a result of the break-up of Asiatic Turkey during the First World War. These three areas all subsequently gained independence (Palestine as Israel, 1948) and this process was paralleled throughout the Empire. Independence was achieved almost everywhere and in the idiosyncratic instances to the contrary, such as the "white settler" colony of Southern Rhodesia, virtual autonomy was secured. The British imperial writ ceased to circulate universally.

In India, a fertile laboratory for imperial ideas, independence was achieved by a slow, measured, and ultimately unsatisfactory process. Various reforms, including the constitutional changes of 1919 and 1935, pushed India to the brink of full-fledged Dominion status by the outbreak of war in 1939. But the complex territorial, religious, and political relationships on the Indian subcontinent retarded political advance. The sophisticated arrangements delineated by the India Government Act of 1935 remained partly unworkable. Self-government as an intermediate principle leading to independence was not unqualifiedly accepted by the British. Large segments of British opinion resisted comparatively minor concessions to Indian sensibilities, as epitomized by Winston Churchill's fateful resignation from the Conservative "Shadow Cabinet" in 1931. Bedevilling all aspects of the Indian question was the intractable web of Hindu-Moslem relationships. The 1947 division of the subcontinent into two nations, India and Pakistan, was, in retrospect, the British Government's single most tragic decision made in this part of the world. This labored birth was not propitious for the retention of close postimperial ties. As a result British influence in the Indian subcontinent has waned, notwithstanding Commonwealth allegiances. A similar failure occurred in Egypt where nominal independence lacking the substance of power was ceded as early as 1922. The strategic importance of the area as the locus of Britain's Middle Eastern strategy dictated entangling defense and other arrangements which were not discarded until the 1950's.

In other parts of the Empire, notably in Africa and Asia, independence became the recurrent motif in the aftermath of World War Two. Spectacular defeats at the hands of the Japanese between 1940 and 1942, as in the loss of Singapore, undermined the structure of British imperial rule. Postwar economic malaise in the teeth of rising nationalist demands added to the sense of loss. The Attlee Government (1945–1951), reflecting the obvious shifts of world power, took the first halting steps toward a policy of decolonization by granting independence to India, Pakistan, and Ceylon, all in 1947. But the significant breakthrough occurred a decade later with the concession of independence to Ghana (formerly the Gold Coast) in 1957. This unleashed a crescendo of independence agreements involving such emergent nations as Nigeria (1960), Cyprus (1960), Tanganyika (1961), and Kenya (1963).

However the process of decolonization is interpreted, its rapidity, often leaving a political vacuum in its wake, has represented a stunning loss of power for Britain. Confronted with the emergence of two superblocs and challenged by an effective "third force" nationalism, Britain has had to recognize the realities of her transformed imperial position to an even greater degree than is indicated by her concessions of independence. Her financial and institutional commitments have had to be decisively contracted and illusions of considerable political moment to be rapidly discarded.

The ill-fated Suez intervention of 1956 destroyed all surviving illusions of Britain's imperial position. Irrespective of the case for intervention (perhaps a stronger one than historians and committed contemporaries have been willing to concede) the *fact* of withdrawal in response to Russian and American pressures symbolized the finality of imperial autonomy. And in the ensuing fifteen years Conservative and Labor governments have both taken heed from this example. British influence has been substantially contracted and the critical decision taken by the Wilson Government in 1968 to eliminate a significant British presence east of Suez and in the Far East brought matters to a head. The Commonwealth of Nations, whose very existence is linked to the historic decision on the European Common Market, may face disintegration in the near future.

If the romance and glamour of an imperial tradition have begun to recede permanently into the past, history has not been entirely unkind to the British Empire. The overall imperial contribution, even by the standards of the twentieth century, has had many positive effects. The British Empire has made an imperishable contribution to world history.

DISSOLUTION OF THE OTTOMAN EMPIRE

*Sykes-Picot Agreement between Great Britain and France
Defining the Postwar Partition of Arabia, 16 May 1916**

1. France and Great Britain are prepared to recognise and uphold an independent Arab State or a Confederation of Arab States in the areas shown as (A) and (B) on the annexed map, under the suzerainty of an Arab Chief. France in area (A) and Great Britain in area (B) shall have a right of priority in enterprises and local loans. France in area (A) and Great Britain in area (B) shall alone supply foreign advisers or officials on the request of the Arab State or the Confederation of Arab States.

2. France in the Blue area and Great Britain in the Red area shall be at liberty to establish such direct or indirect administration or control as they may desire or as they may deem fit to establish after agreement with the Arab State or Confederation of Arab States.

3. In the Brown area there shall be established an international administration of which the form will be decided upon after consultation with Russia, and after subsequent agreement with the other Allies and the representatives of the Sharif of Mecca.

4. There shall be accorded to Great Britain
   (*a*) The ports of Haifa and Acre;
   (*b*) Guarantee of a specific supply of water from the Tigris and the Euphrates in area (A) for area (B).

His Majesty's Government, on their part, undertake that they will at no time initiate negotiations for the concession of Cyprus to any third Power without the previous consent of the French Government.

5. Alexandretta shall be a free port as regards the trade of the British Empire and there shall be no differentiation in treatment with regard to port dues or the extension of special privileges affecting British shipping and commerce; there shall be freedom of transit for British goods through Alexandretta and over railways through the Blue area, whether such goods are going to or coming from the Red area, area (A) or area (B); and there shall be no differentiation in treatment, direct or indirect, at the expense of British goods on any railway or of British goods and shipping in any port serving the areas in question.

Haifa shall be a free port as regards the trade of France, her colonies and protectorates, and there shall be no differentiation in treatment or privilege with regard to port dues against French shipping and commerce. There shall be freedom of transit through Haifa and over British railways through the Brown area, whether such goods are coming from or going to the Blue area, area (A)

*Antonius, *Arab Awakening,* 428-30.

or area (B), and there shall be no differentiation in treatment, direct or indirect, at the expense of French goods on any railway or of French goods and shipping in any port serving the areas in question.

6. In area (A), the Baghdad Railway shall not be extended southwards beyond Mosul, and in area (B), it shall not be extended northwards beyond Samarra, until a railway connecting Baghdad with Aleppo along the basin of the Euphrates will have been completed, and then only with the concurrence of the two Governments.

7. Great Britain shall have the right to build, administer and be the sole owner of the railway connecting Haifa with area (B). She shall have, in addition, the right in perpetuity and at all times of carrying troops on that line. It is understood by both Governments that this railway is intended to facilitate communication between Baghdad and Haifa, and it is further understood that, in the event of technical difficulties and expenditure incurred in the maintenance of this line in the Brown area rendering the execution of the project impracticable, the French Government will be prepared to consider plans for enabling the line in question to traverse the polygon formed by Banias-Umm Qais-Salkhad-Tall 'Osda-Mismieh before reaching area (B).

8. For a period of twenty years, the Turkish customs tariff shall remain in force throughout the Blue and Red areas as well as in areas (A) and (B), and no increase in the rates of duties and no alteration of *ad valorem* duties into specific duties shall be made without the consent of the two Powers.

There shall be no internal customs barriers between any of the areas mentioned above. The customs duties to be levied on goods destined for the interior shall be collected at the ports of entry and remitted to the Administration of the area of destination.

9. It is understood that the French Government will at no time initiate any negotiations for the cession of their rights and will not cede their prospective rights in the Blue area to any third Power other than the Arab State or Confederation of Arab States, without the previous consent of His Majesty's Government who, on their part, give the French Government a similar undertaking in respect of the Red area.

10. The British and French Governments shall agree to abstain from acquiring and to withhold their consent to a third Power acquiring territorial possessions in the Arabian Peninsula; nor shall they consent to the construction by a third Power of a naval base in the islands on the eastern seaboard of the Red Sea. This, however, will not prevent such rectification of the Aden boundary as might be found necessary in view of the recent Turkish attack.

11. The negotiations with the Arabs concerning the frontiers of the Arab State or Confederation of Arab States shall be pursued through the same channel as heretofore in the name of the two Powers.

12. It is understood, moreover, that measures for controlling the importation of arms into the Arab territory will be considered by the two Governments.

*Balfour Declaration, an Official Statement from the Foreign
Secretary, Arthur J. Balfour, to Lord Rothschild
Accepting the Principle of a Homeland for the
Jewish People, 2 November 1917**

I have much pleasure in conveying to you, on behalf of His Majesty's Government, the following declaration of sympathy with Jewish Zionist aspirations which has been submitted to, and approved by, the Cabinet.

"His Majesty's Government view with favour the establishment in Palestine of a national home for the Jewish people, and will use their best endeavours to facilitate the achievement of this object, it being clearly understood that nothing shall be done which may prejudice the civil and religious rights of existing non-Jewish communities in Palestine, or the rights and political status enjoyed by Jews in any other country."

I should be grateful if you would bring this declaration to the knowledge of the Zionist Federation.

---

*Treaty of Sevres between Great Britain, France, Italy,
and Turkey Establishing Mandates for Mesopotamia (Iraq)
and Palestine and Embodying Turkey's Renunciation of
Title to Egypt, 10 August 1920†*

* * *

Section VII. Syria, Mesopotamia, Palestine

Art. XCIV

The High Contracting Parties agree that Syria and Mesopotamia shall, in accordance with the fourth paragraph of Article 22, Part I (Covenant of the League of Nations), be provisionally recognised as independent States subject to the rendering of administrative advice and assistance by a Mandatory until such time as they are able to stand alone.

A Commission shall be constituted within fifteen days from the coming into force of the present Treaty to trace on the spot the frontier line described in

---

*Jewish Agency for Palestine, *Book of Documents Submitted to the General Assembly of the United Nations Relating to the Establishment of the National Home for the Jewish People*, A.
†*Parliamentary Papers*, 1920, LI, Cmd. 964, 26–29.

Article 27, II (2) and (3). This Commission will be composed of three members nominated by France, Great Britain and Italy respectively, and one member nominated by Turkey; it will be assisted by a representative of Syria for the Syrian frontier, and by a representative of Mesopotamia for the Mesopotamian frontier.

The determination of the other frontiers of the said States, and the selection of the Mandatories, will be made by the Principal Allied Powers.

Art. XCV

The High Contracting Parties agree to entrust, by application of the provisions of Article 22, the administration of Palestine, within such boundaries as may be determined by the Principal Allied Powers, to a Mandatory to be selected by the said Powers. The Mandatory will be responsible for putting into effect the declaration originally made on November 2, 1917, by the British Government, and adopted by the other Allied Powers, in favour of the establishment in Palestine of a national home for the Jewish people, it being clearly understood that nothing shall be done which may prejudice the civil and religious rights of existing non-Jewish communities in Palestine, or the rights and political status enjoyed by Jews in any other country.

The Mandatory undertakes to appoint as soon as possible a special Commission to study and regulate all questions and claims relating to the different religious communities. In the composition of this Commission the religious interests concerned will be taken into account. The Chairman of the Commission will be appointed by the Council of the League of Nations.

Art. XCVI

The terms of the mandates in respect of the above territories will be formulated by the Principal Allied Powers and submitted to the Council of the League of Nations for approval.

Art. XCVII

Turkey hereby undertakes, in accordance with the provisions of Article 132, to accept any decisions which may be taken in relation to the questions dealt with in this Section.

* * *

Section IX. Egypt, Soudan, Cyprus

1. —Egypt

Art. CI

Turkey renounces all rights and title in or over Egypt. This renunciation shall take effect as from November 5, 1914. Turkey declares that in conformity with the action taken by the Allied Powers she recognises the Protectorate proclaimed over Egypt by Great Britain on December 18, 1914.

Art. CII

Turkish subjects habitually resident in Egypt on December 18, 1914, will acquire Egyptian nationality *ipso facto* and will lose their Turkish nationality, except that if at that date such persons were temporarily absent from, and have not since returned to, Egypt they will not acquire Egyptian nationality without a special authorisation from the Egyptian Government.

Art. CIII

Turkish subjects who became resident in Egypt after December 18, 1914, and are habitually resident there at the date of the coming into force of the present Treaty may, subject to the conditions prescribed in Article 105 for the right of option, claim Egyptian nationality, but such claim may in individual cases be refused by the competent Egyptian authority.

Art. CIV

For all purposes connected with the present Treaty, Egypt and Egyptian nationals, their goods and vessels, shall be treated on the same footing, as from August 1, 1914, as the Allied Powers, their nationals, goods and vessels, and provisions in respect of territory under Turkish sovereignty, or of territory detached from Turkey in accordance with the present Treaty, shall not apply to Egypt.

Art. CV

Within a period of one year after the coming into force of the present Treaty persons over eighteen years of age acquiring Egyptian nationality under the provisions of Article 102 will be entitled to opt for Turkish nationality. In case such persons, or those who under Article 103 are entitled to claim Egyptian nationality, differ in race from the majority of the population of Egypt, they will within the same period be entitled to opt for the nationality of any State in favour of which territory is detached from Turkey, if the majority of the population of that State is of the same race as the person exercising the right to opt.

Option by a husband covers a wife and option by parents covers their children under eighteen years of age.

Persons who have exercised the above right to opt must, except where authorised to continue to reside in Egypt, transfer within the ensuing twelve months their place of residence to the State for which they have opted. They will be entitled to retain their immovable property in Egypt, and may carry with them their movable property of every description. No export or import duties or charges may be imposed upon them in connection with the removal of such property.

Art. CVI

The Egyptian Government shall have complete liberty of action in regulating the status of Turkish subjects in Egypt and the conditions under which they may establish themselves in the territory.

Art. CVII

Egyptian nationals shall be entitled, when abroad, to British diplomatic and consular protection.

Art. CVIII

Egyptian goods entering Turkey shall enjoy the treatment accorded to British goods.

Art. CIX

Turkey renounces in favour of Great Britain the powers conferred upon His Imperial Majesty the Sultan by the Convention signed at Constantinople on October 29, 1888, relating to the free navigation of the Suez Canal.

Art. CX

All property and possessions in Egypt belonging to the Turkish Government pass to the Egyptian Government without payment.

Art. CXI

All movable and immovable property in Egypt belonging to Turkish nationals (who do not acquire Egyptian nationality) shall be dealt with in accordance with the provisions of Part IX (Economic Clauses) of the present Treaty.

Art. CXII

Turkey renounces all claim to the tribute formerly paid by Egypt.

Great Britain undertakes to relieve Turkey of all liability in respect of the Turkish loans secured on the Egyptian tribute.

These loans are:

The guaranteed loan of 1855;

The loan of 1894 representing the converted loans of 1854 and 1871;

The loan of 1891 representing the converted loan of 1877.

The sums which the Khedives of Egypt have from time to time undertaken to pay over to the houses by which these loans were issued will be applied as heretofore to the interest and the sinking funds of the loans of 1894 and 1891 until the final extinction of those loans. The Government of Egypt will also continue to apply the sum hitherto paid towards the interest on the guaranteed loan of 1855.

Upon the extinction of these loans of 1894, 1891 and 1855, all liability on the part of the Egyptian Government arising out of the tribute formerly paid by Egypt to Turkey will cease.

2.—Soudan

Art. CXIII

The High Contracting Parties declare and place on record that they have taken note of the Convention between the British Government and the Egyptian Government defining the status and regulating the administration of the Soudan, signed on January 19, 1899, as amended by the supplementary Convention relating to the town of Suakin signed on July 10, 1899.

Art. CXIV

Soudanese shall be entitled when in foreign countries to British diplomatic and consular protection.

3.—Cyprus

Art. CXV

The High Contracting Parties recognise the annexation of Cyprus proclaimed by the British Government on November 5, 1914.

Art. CXVI

Turkey renounces all rights and title over or relating to Cyprus, including the right to the tribute formerly paid by that island to the Sultan.

Art. CXVII

Turkish nationals born or habitually resident in Cyprus will acquire British nationality and lose their Turkish nationality, subject to the conditions laid down in the local law.

"British Policy in Palestine," an Official Interpretation of the Balfour Declaration Issued by the British Government, June 1922*

The Secretary of State for the Colonies has given renewed consideration to the existing political situation in Palestine, with a very earnest desire to arrive at a settlement of the outstanding questions which have given rise to uncertainty and unrest among certain sections of the population. After consultation with the High Commissioner for Palestine the following statement has been drawn up. It summarises the essential parts of the correspondence that has already taken place between the Secretary of State and a Delegation from the Moslem Christian Society of Palestine, which has been for some time in England, and it states the further conclusions which have since been reached.

The tension which has prevailed from time to time in Palestine is mainly due to apprehensions, which are entertained both by sections of the Arab and by sections of the Jewish population. These apprehensions, so far as the Arabs are concerned, are partly based upon exaggerated interpretations of the meaning of the Declaration favouring the establishment of a Jewish National Home in Palestine, made on behalf of His Majesty's Government on 2nd November, 1917. Unauthorised statements have been made to the effect that the purpose in view is to create a wholly Jewish Palestine. Phrases have been used such as that Palestine is to become "as Jewish as England is English." His Majesty's Government regard any such expectation as impracticable and have no such aim in view. Nor have they at any time contemplated, as appears to be feared by the Arab Delegation, the disappearance or the subordination of the Arabic population, language or culture in Palestine. They would draw attention to the

Parliamentary Papers, 1922, XXIII, Cmd. 1700, 17–21.

fact that the terms of the Declaration referred to do not contemplate that Palestine as a whole should be converted into a Jewish National Home, but that such a Home should be founded *in Palestine*. In this connection it has been observed with satisfaction that at the meeting of the Zionist Congress, the supreme governing body of the Zionist Organisation, held at Carlsbad in September, 1921, a resolution was passed expressing as the official statement of Zionist aims "the determination of the Jewish people to live with the Arab people on terms of unity and mutual respect, and together with them to make the common home into a flourishing community, the upbuilding of which may assure to each of its peoples an undisturbed national development."

It is also necessary to point out that the Zionist Commission in Palestine, now termed the Palestine Zionist Executive, has not desired to possess, and does not possess, any share in the general administration of the country. Nor does the special position assigned to the Zionist Organisation in Article IV of the Draft Mandate for Palestine imply any such functions. That special position relates to the measures to be taken in Palestine affecting the Jewish population, and contemplates that the Organisation may assist in the general development of the country, but does not entitle it to share in any degree in its Government.

Further, it is contemplated that the status of all citizens of Palestine in the eyes of the law shall be Palestinian, and it has never been intended that they, or any section of them, should possess any other juridical status.

So far as the Jewish population of Palestine are concerned, it appears that some among them are apprehensive that His Majesty's Government may depart from the policy embodied in the Declaration of 1917. It is necessary, therefore, once more to affirm that these fears are unfounded, and that that Declaration, re-affirmed by the Conference of the Principal Allied Powers at San Remo and again in the Treaty of Sèvres, is not susceptible of change.

During the last two or three generations the Jews have recreated in Palestine a community, now numbering 80,000, of whom about one-fourth are farmers or workers upon the land. This community has its own political organs; an elected assembly for the direction of its domestic concerns; elected councils in the towns; and an organisation for the control of its schools. It has its elected Chief Rabbinate and Rabbinical Council for the direction of its religious affairs. Its business is conducted in Hebrew as a vernacular language, and a Hebrew press serves its needs. It has its distinctive intellectual life and displays considerable economic activity. This community, then, with its town and country population, its political, religious and social organisations, its own language, its own customs, its own life, has in fact "national" characteristics. When it is asked what is meant by the development of the Jewish National Home in Palestine, it may be answered that it is not the imposition of a Jewish nationality upon the inhabitants of Palestine as a whole, but the further development of the existing Jewish community, with the assistance of Jews in other parts of the world, in order that it may become a centre in which the Jewish people as a whole may take, on grounds of religion and race, an interest and a pride. But in order that this community should have the best prospect of free development and provide a full opportunity for the Jewish people to display its capacities, it is essential that it should know that it is in Palestine as of right and not on sufferance. That is the reason why it is necessary that the existence of a Jewish National Home in Palestine should be internationally guaranteed, and that it should be formally recognised to rest upon ancient historic connection.

This, then, is the interpretation which His Majesty's Government place upon the Declaration of 1917, and, so understood, the Secretary of State is of opinion that it does not contain or imply anything which need cause either alarm to the Arab population of Palestine or disappointment to the Jews.

For the fulfilment of this policy it is necessary that the Jewish community in Palestine should be able to increase its numbers by immigration. This immigration cannot be so great in volume as to exceed whatever may be the economic capacity of the country at the time to absorb new arrivals. It is essential to ensure that the immigrants should not be a burden upon the people of Palestine as a whole, and that they should not deprive any section of the present population of their employment. Hitherto the immigration has fulfilled these conditions. The number of immigrants since the British occupation has been about 25,000.

It is necessary also to ensure that persons who are politically undesirable are excluded from Palestine, and every precaution has been and will be taken by the Administration to that end.

It is intended that a special committee should be established in Palestine, consisting entirely of members of the new Legislative Council elected by the people, to confer with the Administration upon matters relating to the regulation of immigration. Should any difference of opinion arise between this committee and the Administration, the matter will be referred to His Majesty's Government, who will give it special consideration. In addition, under Article 81 of the draft Palestine Order in Council, any religious community or considerable section of the population of Palestine will have a general right to appeal, through the High Commissioner and the Secretary of State, to the League of Nations on any matter on which they may consider that the terms of the Mandate are not being fulfilled by the Government of Palestine.

With reference to the Constitution which it is now intended to establish in Palestine, the draft of which has already been published, it is desirable to make certain points clear. In the first place, it is not the case, as has been represented by the Arab Delegation, that during the war His Majesty's Government gave an undertaking that an independent national government should be at once established in Palestine. This representation mainly rests upon a letter dated the 24th October, 1915, from Sir Henry McMahon, then His Majesty's High Commissioner in Egypt, to the Sherif of Mecca, now King Hussein of the Kingdom of the Hejaz. That letter is quoted as conveying the promise to the Sherif of Mecca to recognise and support the independence of the Arabs within the territories proposed by him. But this promise was given subject to a reservation made in the same letter, which excluded from its scope, among other territories, the portions of Syria lying to the west of the district of Damascus. This reservation has always been regarded by His Majesty's Government as covering the vilayet of Beirut and the independent Sanjak of Jerusalem. The whole of Palestine west of the Jordan was thus excluded from Sir H. McMahon's pledge.

Nevertheless, it is the intention of His Majesty's Government to foster the establishment of a full measure of self-government in Palestine. But they are of opinion that, in the special circumstances of that country, this should be accomplished by gradual stages and not suddenly. The first step was taken when, on the institution of a civil Administration, the nominated Advisory Council, which now exists, was established. It was stated at the time by the High Commissioner that this was the first step in the development of self-governing institutions, and it is now proposed to take a second step by the establishment of a Legislative Council containing a large proportion of members elected on a wide franchise. It was proposed in the published draft that three of the members of this Council should be non-official persons nominated by the High Commissioner, but representations having been made in opposition to this provision, based on cogent considerations, the Secretary of State is prepared to omit it. The Legislative Council would then consist of the High Commissioner as President and twelve elected and ten official members. The Secretary of State is of opinion that before a further measure of self-government is extended to Palestine and the Assembly placed in control over the Executive, it would be wise to allow some time to elapse. During this period the institutions of the country will have become well established; its financial credit will be based on firm foundations, and the Palestinian officials will have been enabled to gain experience of sound methods of government. After a few years the situation will be again reviewed, and if the experience of the working of the constitution now to be established so warranted, a larger share of authority would then be extended to the elected representatives of the people.

The Secretary of State would point out that already the present Administration has transferred to a Supreme Council elected by the Moslem community of Palestine the entire control of Moslem religious endowments (Wakfs), and of the Moslem religious Courts. To this Council the Administration has also voluntarily restored considerable revenues derived from ancient endowments which had been sequestrated by the Turkish Government. The Education Department is also advised by a committee representative of all sections of the population, and the Department of Commerce and Industry has the benefit of the co-operation of the Chambers of Commerce which have been established in the principal centres. It is the intention of the Administration to associate in an increased degree similar representative committees with the various Departments of the Government.

The Secretary of State believes that a policy upon these lines, coupled with the maintenance of the fullest religious liberty in Palestine and with scrupulous regard for the rights of each community with reference to its Holy Places, cannot but commend itself to the various sections of the population, and that upon this basis may be built up that spirit of co-operation upon which the future progress and prosperity of the Holy Land must largely depend.

League of Nations Mandate for Palestine (Including the
Territory Known as Trans-Jordan) Signed at London,
24 July 1922*

The Council of the League of Nations:

Whereas the Principal Allied Powers have agreed, for the purpose of giving effect to the provisions of Article 22 of the Covenant of the League of Nations, to entrust to a Mandatory selected by the said Powers the administration of the territory of Palestine, which formerly belonged to the Turkish Empire, within such boundaries as may be fixed by them; and

Whereas the Principal Allied Powers have also agreed that the Mandatory should be responsible for putting into effect the declaration originally made on November 2nd, 1917, by the Government of His Britannic Majesty, and adopted by the said Powers, in favour of the establishment in Palestine of a national home for the Jewish people, it being clearly understood that nothing should be done which might prejudice the civil and religious rights of existing non-Jewish communities in Palestine, or the rights and political status enjoyed by Jews in any other country; and

Whereas recognition has thereby been given to the historical connection of the Jewish people with Palestine and to the grounds for reconstituting their national home in that country; and

Whereas the Principal Allied Powers have selected His Britannic Majesty as the Mandatory for Palestine; and

Whereas the mandate in respect of Palestine has been formulated in the following terms and submitted to the Council of the League for approval; and

Whereas His Britannic Majesty has accepted the mandate in respect of Palestine and undertaken to exercise it on behalf of the League of Nations in conformity with the following provisions; and

Whereas by the afore-mentioned Article 22 (paragraph 8), it is provided that the degree of authority, control or administration to be exercised by the Mandatory, not having been previously agreed upon by the Members of the League, shall be explicitly defined by the Council of the League of Nations;

Confirming the said mandate, defines its terms as follows:

Art. I

The Mandatory shall have full powers of legislation and of administration, save as they may be limited by the terms of this mandate.

Art. II

The Mandatory shall be responsible for placing the country under such political, administrative and economic conditions as will secure the establish-

*Parliamentary Papers, 1923, XXV, Cmd. 1785, 2–4, 8.

ment of the Jewish national home, as laid down in the preamble, and the development of self-governing institutions, and also for safeguarding the civil and religious rights of all the inhabitants of Palestine, irrespective of race and religion.

Art. III

The Mandatory shall, so far as circumstances permit, encourage local autonomy.

Art. IV

An appropriate Jewish agency shall be recognised as a public body for the purpose of advising and co-operating with the Administration of Palestine in such economic, social and other matters as may affect the establishment of the Jewish national home and the interests of the Jewish population in Palestine, and, subject always to the control of the Administration, to assist and take part in the development of the country.

The Zionist organisation, so long as its organisation and constitution are in the opinion of the Mandatory appropriate, shall be recognised as such agency. It shall take steps in consultation with His Britannic Majesty's Government to secure the co-operation of all Jews who are willing to assist in the establishment of the Jewish national home.

Art. V

The Mandatory shall be responsible for seeing that no Palestine territory shall be ceded or leased to, or in any way placed under the control of, the Government of any foreign Power.

Art. VI

The Administration of Palestine, while ensuring that the rights and position of other sections of the population are not prejudiced, shall facilitate Jewish immigration under suitable conditions and shall encourage, in co-operation with the Jewish agency referred to in Article 4, close settlement by Jews on the land, including State lands and waste lands not required for public purposes.

Art. VII

The Administration of Palestine shall be responsible for enacting a nationality law. There shall be included in this law provisions framed so as to facilitate the acquisition of Palestinian citizenship by Jews who take up their permanent residence in Palestine.

*   *   *

Art. XI

The Administration of Palestine shall take all necessary measures to safeguard the interests of the community in connection with the development of the country, and, subject to any international obligations accepted by the Mandatory, shall have full power to provide for public ownership or control of any of the natural resources of the country or of the public works, services and utilities established or to be established therein. It shall introduce a land system appropriate to the needs of the country, having regard, among other things, to the desirability of promoting the close settlement and intensive cultivation of the land.

The Administration may arrange with the Jewish agency mentioned in Article 4 to construct or operate, upon fair and equitable terms, any public works, services and utilities, and to develop any of the natural resources of the country, in so far as these matters are not directly undertaken by the Administration. Any such arrangements shall provide that no profits distributed by such agency, directly or indirectly, shall exceed a reasonable rate of interest on the capital, and any further profits shall be utilised by it for the benefit of the country in a manner approved by the Administration.

* * *

Art. XXII

English, Arabic and Hebrew shall be the official languages of Palestine. Any statement or inscription in Arabic on stamps or money in Palestine shall be repeated in Hebrew, and any statement or inscription in Hebrew shall be repeated in Arabic.

Art. XXIII

The Administration of Palestine shall recognise the holy days of the respective communities in Palestine as legal days of rest for the members of such communities.

Art. XXIV

The Mandatory shall make to the Council of the League of Nations an annual report to the satisfaction of the Council as to the measures taken during the year to carry out the provisions of the mandate. Copies of all laws and regulations promulgated or issued during the year shall be communicated with the report.

Art. XXV

In the territories lying between the Jordan and the eastern boundary of Palestine as ultimately determined, the Mandatory shall be entitled, with the consent of the Council of the League of Nations, to postpone or withhold application of such provisions of this mandate as he may consider inapplicable to the existing local conditions, and to make such provision for the administration of the territories as he may consider suitable to those conditions, provided that no action shall be taken which is inconsistent with the provisions of Articles 15, 16 and 18.

Art. XXVI

The Mandatory agrees that, if any dispute whatever should arise between the Mandatory and another Member of the League of Nations relating to the interpretation or the application of the provisions of the mandate, such dispute, if it cannot be settled by negotiation, shall be submitted to the Permanent Court of International Justice provided for by Article 14 of the Covenant of the League of Nations.

Art. XXVII
The consent of the Council of the League of Nations is required for any modification of the terms of this mandate.

Letter to the Times *from the Conservative Party Leader and Lord Privy Seal, Andrew Bonar Law, Criticizing Lloyd George's Handling of the Greek-Turkish Conflict (the "Chanak Crisis"), 6 October 1922*[*]

I have followed with the greatest anxiety recent events in the Near East, and the position at this moment seems to me very alarming. It would serve no useful purpose to criticise or even to consider the circumstances which have led me to the present situation; what is alone important is to find the right course of action to be taken now.

When the Greek forces were annihilated in Asia Minor and driven into the sea at Smyrna, it seems to me certain that, unless a decisive warning had at once been issued, the Turkish forces, flushed with victory, would have attempted to enter Constantinople and cross into Thrace. If they had been allowed to do so, what would have been the result?

In the first place, our withdrawal in such circumstances would have been regarded throughout the whole Musulman world as the defeat of the British Empire, and, although it may be true that the supposed pro-Greek sympathies of the British Government have alienated Musulmen feeling in India, the danger and trouble in India from that cause would be as nothing in comparison with the danger which would arise as a consequence of what would have been regarded as British impotence in the face of a victorious Turkish army.

Further, such an advance of the Turkish forces would probably have meant a repetition in Constantinople of the recent events in Smyrna; it would certainly have involved Thrace in horrors similar to those which have occurred in Anatolia, and the probability— indeed, I think it a certainty—of the renewal of war throughout the Balkans.

---

*Times, 6 October 1922

It was, therefore, undoubtedly right that the British Government should endeavour to prevent these misfortunes. It is not, however, right that the burden of taking necessary action should fall on the British Empire alone. The prevention of war and massacre in Constantinople and the Balkans is not specially a British interest; it is the interest of humanity. The retention also of the freedom of the Straits is not specially a British interest; it is the interest of the world. We are at the Straits and in Constantinople not by our own action alone, but by the will of the Allied Powers which won the war and America is one of these Powers.

What, then, in such circumstances ought we to do? Clearly the British Empire, which includes the largest body of Mahomedans in any State, ought not to show any hostility or unfairness to the Turks. In the agreement arranged with the Allies in Paris by Lord Curzon, proposals were made to the Turks which are certainly fair to them, and beyond these terms, in my opinion, the Allies ought not to go.

I see rumours in different newspapers, which I do not credit, that the French representative with the Kemdist forces has encouraged them to make impossible demands. The course of action for our government seems to me clear. We cannot alone act as the policemen of the world. The financial and social condition of this country makes that impossible. It seems to me, therefore, that our duty is to say plainly to our French Allies that the position in Constantinople and the Straits is as essential a part of the Peace settlement as the arrangement with Germany, and that if they are not prepared to support us there, we shall not be able to bear the burden alone, but shall have no alternative except to imitate the Government of the United States and to restrict our attention to the safeguarding of the more immediate interests of the Empire.

FORMATION OF THE BRITISH
COMMONWEALTH OF NATIONS

Minutes and Proceedings of the Imperial War Conference,
March – April 1917*

I. Resolutions Agreed to by the Conference

The following Resolutions were unanimously agreed to by the Conference:

*   *   *

II. Uniformity of Equipment

(Third Day; Monday, March 26th.) That this Conference, recognising the importance of assimilating as far as possible the military stores and equipment of the Imperial forces throughout the Empire, recommends that an expert Committee representative of the military authorities of the United Kingdom, the Dominions, and India be appointed as early as possible to consider the various patterns in use with a view to selecting standard patterns for general adoption as far as the special circumstances of each country admit.

III. Training of Ordnance Personnel

(Third Day; Monday, March 26th.) This Conference is of opinion that it is desirable that the ordnance personnel of the military organisations of the Empire should, as far as possible, be trained on the same methods and according to the same principles, and that to secure this end selected officers of the ordnance service from all parts of the Empire should be attached for adequate periods to the Imperial Ordnance Department.

IV. Naval Defence

(Fifth Day; Friday, March 30th.) That the Admiralty be requested to work out immediately after the conclusion of the War what they consider the most effective scheme of Naval Defence for the Empire for the consideration of the several Governments summoned to this Conference, with such recommendations as the Admiralty consider necessary in that respect for the Empire's future security.

V. Trade Commissioner Service

(Seventh Day; Wednesday, April 4th. . . .) That the Imperial War Conference welcomes the proposed increase of the Board of Trade service of Trade Commissioners and its extension throughout the British Empire in accordance with the recommendations of the Dominions Royal Commission, and recommends that the Governments concerned should co-operate so as to make that service as useful as possible to the Empire as a whole, especially for the promotion of Inter-Imperial Trade.

**Parliamentary Papers*, 1917–18, XXIII, Cmd. 8566, 4–7.

VI. Patents

(Seventh Day; Wednesday, April 4th.) The Imperial Conference commends the proposals of the Board of Trade in the Memorandum on Patents and Trade Marks to the careful consideration of the several constituent Governments of the Empire.

VII. Representation of India at future Imperial Conferences

(Eighth Day; Friday, April 13th. . . .) That the Imperial War Conference desires to place on record its view that the Resolution of the Imperial Conference of 20th April 1907 should be modified to permit of India being fully represented at all future Imperial Conferences, and that the necessary steps should be taken to secure the assent of the various Governments in order that the next Imperial Conference may be summoned and constituted accordingly.

VIII. Care of Soldiers' Graves

(Eighth Day; Friday, April 13th. . . .) The Conference, having considered the Minute addressed to the Prime Minister on the 15th March 1917 by His Royal Highness the Prince of Wales, concurs in the proposals made therein, and humbly prays His Majesty to constitute by Royal Charter an Imperial War Graves Commission for the purposes stated by His Royal Highness, and along the lines therein set forth as embodied in the draft charter submitted to the Conference. The Conference places on record its very deep appreciation of the generous action of the French Government in allotting in perpetuity the land in that country where our men are buried, and urges that similar arrangements should be made, if possible, in the terms of peace with all Governments—Ally, Enemy, or Neutral—for a similar concession in Gallipoli, Mesopotamia, Africa, and all other theatres of war. The Conference desires to record its grateful appreciation of the work already done by the Prince of Wales and his Committee in caring for the graves of those who have fallen in the common cause of the Empire, and its satisfaction that His Royal Highness has consented to become the President of the permanent Commission.

IX. Constitution of the Empire

(Ninth Day; Monday, April 16th. . . .) The Imperial War Conference are of opinion that the readjustment of the constitutional relations of the component parts of the Empire is too important and intricate a subject to be dealt with during the War, and that it should form the subject of a special Imperial Conference to be summoned as soon as possible after the cessation of hostilities.

They deem it their duty, however, to place on record their view that any such readjustment, while thoroughly preserving all existing powers of self-government and complete control of domestic affairs, should be based upon a full recognition of the Dominions as autonomous nations of an Imperial Commonwealth, and of India as an important portion of the same, should recognise the right of the Dominions and India to an adequate voice in foreign policy and in foreign relations, and should provide effective arrangements for continuous consultation in all important matters of common Imperial concern, and for such necessary concerted action, founded on consultation, as the several Governments may determine.

X. Naturalization

(Tenth Day; Wednesday, April 18th. . . .) The Conference recognises the desirability and importance of securing uniformity of policy and action throughout the Empire with regard to naturalization, and it is resolved that the proposals set forth in the Memorandum submitted by the Home Office be commended to the consideration of the respective Governments summoned to the Conference.

XI. Earl Grey's Scheme for a Dominion House in Aldwych

(Tenth Day; Wednesday, April 18th. . . .) The Conference, in expressing to Earl Grey its deep appreciation and warm thanks for the great interest that he has taken in the proposal to secure the Aldwych site, and to erect thereon a building suitable for the purposes of the Dominions, considers that it is not practicable to proceed with the proposal under existing conditions or in the immediate future.

XII. Care of Soldiers' Graves

(Eleventh Day; Monday, April 23rd. . . .) That the Imperial War Graves Commission be requested as soon as possible after their appointment and organization to prepare an estimate of the probable cost of carrying on the work entrusted to them and to submit the same to the Governments of the United Kingdom and Oversea Dominions with their recommendation as to the proportion that should be borne by each.

XIII. Imperial Mineral Resources Bureau

(Eleventh Day; Monday, April 23rd.) That it is desirable to establish in London an Imperial Mineral Resources Bureau, upon which should be represented Great Britain, the Dominions, India, and other parts of the Empire.

The Bureau should be charged with the duties of collection of information from the appropriate Departments of the Governments concerned and other sources regarding the mineral resources and the metal requirements of the Empire, and of advising from time to time what action, if any, may appear desirable to enable such resources to be developed and made available to meet the metal requirements of the Empire.

That the Conference recommends that His Majesty's Government should, while having due regard to existing institutions, take immediate action for the purpose of establishing such a Bureau, and should as soon as possible submit a scheme for the consideration of the other Governments summoned to the Conference.

XIV. Production of Naval and Military Material, Munitions, and Supplies

(Twelfth Day; Tuesday, April 24th.) That this Conference, in view of the experience of the present War, calls attention to the importance of developing an adequate capacity of production of naval and military material, munitions, and supplies in all important parts of the Empire (including the countries

bordering on the Pacific and Indian Oceans) where such facilities do not presently exist and affirms the importance of close co-operation between India, the Dominions, and the United Kingdom with this object in view.

XV. Double Income Tax

(Thirteenth Day; Wednesday, April 25th. . . .) The present system of Double Income Taxation within the Empire calls for review in relation—

(i)   to firms in the United Kingdom doing business with the Oversea Dominions, India, and the Colonies;

(ii) to private individuals resident in the United Kingdom who have capital invested elsewhere in the Empire, or who depend upon remittances from elsewhere within the Empire; and

(iii) to its influence on the investment of capital in the United Kingdom, the Dominions and India, and to the effect of any change on the position of British capital invested abroad.

The Conference, therefore, urges that this matter should be taken in hand immediately after the conclusion of the War, and that an amendment of the law should be made which will remedy the present unsatisfactory position.

XVI. Development and Control of Natural Resources

(Thirteenth Day; Wednesday, April 25th. . . .) Having regard to the experience obtained in the present War, this Conference records its opinion that the safety of the Empire and the necessary development of its component parts, require prompt and attentive consideration, as well as concerted action, with regard to the following matters: —

(1) The production of an adequate food supply and arrangements for its transportation when and where required, under any conditions that may reasonably be anticipated.

(2) The control of natural resources available within the Empire, especially those that are of an essential character for necessary national purposes, whether in peace or in war.

(3) The economical utilization of such natural resources through processes of manufacture carried on within the Empire.

The Conference commends to the consideration of the Governments summoned thereto the enactment of such legislation as may assist this purpose.

XVII. Control of Imports after the War from present Enemy Countries

(Thirteenth Day; Wednesday, April 25th. . . .) The Imperial War Conference consider it desirable, with a view to prevent dumping or any other mode of unfair competition from present enemy countries during the transition period after the War, that the several Governments of the Empire, while reserving to themselves freedom of action in any particular respect, take power to control the importation of goods originating in such countries into the Empire for a period of twelve months after the War.

*   *   *

XXI. Imperial Preference

(Fourteenth Day; Thursday, April 26th. . . .) The time has arrived when all possible encouragement should be given to the development of Imperial resources, and especially to making the Empire independent of other countries in respect of food supplies, raw materials, and essential industries. With these objects in view this Conference expresses itself in favour of:

(1) The principle that each part of the Empire, having due regard to the interests of our Allies, shall give specially favourable treatment and facilities to the produce and manufactures of other parts of the Empire.

(2) Arrangements by which intending emigrants from the United Kingdom may be induced to settle in countries under the British flag.

XXII. Reciprocity of Treatment between India and the Self-governing Dominions

(Fifteenth Day; Friday, April 27th. . . .) That the Imperial War Conference, having examined the Memorandum on the position of Indians in the Self-governing Dominions presented by the Indian representatives to the Conference, accepts the principle of reciprocity of treatment between India and the Dominions and recommends the Memorandum to the favourable consideration of the Governments concerned.

XXIII. Address to His Majesty the King

(Fifteenth Day; Friday, April 27th. . . .) That His Majesty the King be asked to receive the Members of the Imperial War Conference now in Session, who desire to present a humble address to His Majesty.

XXIV. Temptations of Oversea Soldiers

(Fifteenth Day; Friday, April 27th.) That the attention of the authorities concerned be called to the temptations to which our soldiers when on leave are subjected, and that such authorities be empowered by legislation or otherwise (1) to protect our men by having the streets, the neighbourhood of camps, and other places of public resort, kept clear, so far as practicable, of women of the prostitute class, and (2) to take any other steps that may be necessary to remedy the serious evil that exists.

XXV. Concluding Resolution

(Fifteenth Day; Friday, April 27th. . . .) The Members of the Conference representing India and the Oversea Dominions desire before they separate to convey to the Secretary of State for the Colonies their earnest and sincere appreciation of his labours in preparing for, and presiding over, the Conference.

They desire also to put on record their deep sense of gratitude for the many courtesies which they have received from the Prime Minister and the other members of His Majesty's Government, as well as for the generous hospitality which has been extended to them by the Government and people of the United Kingdom.

Report of the Inter-Imperial Relations Committee
Appointed by the Imperial Conference,
October 1926*
[*This famous "Balfour Formula" defined Dominion status within the*
Commonwealth of Nations.]

I.—Introduction

We were appointed at the meeting of the Imperial Conference on the 25th October, 1926, to investigate all the questions on the Agenda affecting Inter-Imperial Relations. Our discussions on these questions have been long and intricate. We found, on examination, that they involved consideration of fundamental principles affecting the relations of the various parts of the British Empire *inter se,* as well as the relations of each part to foreign countries. For such examination the time at our disposal has been all too short. Yet we hope that we may have laid a foundation on which subsequent Conferences may build.

II.—Status of Great Britain and the Dominions

The Committee are of opinion that nothing would be gained by attempting to lay down a Constitution for the British Empire. Its widely scattered parts have very different characteristics, very different histories, and are at very different stages of evolution; while, considered as a whole, it defies classification and bears no real resemblance to any other political organisation which now exists or has ever yet been tried.

There is, however, one most important element in it which, from a strictly constitutional point of view, has now, as regards all vital matters, reached its full development—we refer to the group of self-governing communities composed of Great Britain and the Dominions. Their position and mutual relation may be readily defined. *They are autonomous Communities within the British Empire, equal in status, in no way subordinate one to another in any aspect of their domestic or external affairs, though united by a common allegiance to the Crown, and freely associated as members of the British Commonwealth of Nations.*

A foreigner endeavouring to understand the true character of the British Empire by the aid of this formula alone would be tempted to think that it was devised rather to make mutual interference impossible than to make mutual co-operation easy.

Such a criticism, however, completely ignores the historic situation. The rapid evolution of the Oversea Dominions during the last fifty years has involved

**Parliamentary Papers,* 1926, XI, Cmd. 2768, 13–27.

many complicated adjustments of old political machinery to changing conditions. The tendency towards equality of status was both right and inevitable. Geographical and other conditions made this impossible of attainment by the way of federation. The only alternative was by the way of autonomy; and along this road it has been steadily sought. Every self-governing member of the Empire is now the master of its destiny. In fact, if not always in form, it is subject to no compulsion whatever.

But no account, however accurate, of the negative relations in which Great Britain and the Dominions stand to each other can do more than express a portion of the truth. The British Empire is not founded upon negations. It depends essentially, if not formally, on positive ideals. Free institutions are its life-blood. Free co-operation is its instrument. Peace, security, and progress are among its objects. Aspects of all these great themes have been discussed at the present Conference; excellent results have been thereby obtained. And, though every Dominion is now, and must always remain, the sole judge of the nature and extent of its co-operation, no common cause will, in our opinion, be thereby imperilled.

Equality of status, so far as Britain and the Dominions are concerned, is thus the root principle governing our Inter-Imperial Relations. But the principles of equality and similarity, appropriate to *status,* do not universally extend to function. Here we require something more than immutable dogmas. For example, to deal with questions of diplomacy and questions of defence, we require also flexible machinery—machinery which can, from time to time, be adapted to the changing circumstances of the world. This subject also has occupied our attention. The rest of this Report will show how we have endeavoured not only to state political theory, but to apply it to our common needs.

III.—Special Position of India

It will be noted that in the previous paragraphs we have made no mention of India. Our reason for limiting their scope to Great Britain and the Dominions is that the position of India in the Empire is already defined by the Government of India Act, 1919. We would, nevertheless, recall that by Resolution IX of the Imperial War Conference, 1917, due recognition was given to the important position held by India in the British Commonwealth. Where, in this Report, we have had occasion to consider the position of India, we have made particular reference to it.

IV.—Relations Between the Various Parts of the British Empire

Existing administrative, legislative, and judicial forms are admittedly not wholly in accord with the position as described in Section II of this Report. This is inevitable, since most of these forms date back to a time well antecedent to the present stage of constitutional development. Our first task then was to examine these forms with special reference to any cases where the want of adaptation of practice to principle caused, or might be thought to cause, inconvenience in the conduct of Inter-Imperial Relations.

(a.) The Title of His Majesty the King

The title of His Majesty the King is of special importance and concern to all parts of His Majesty's Dominions. Twice within the last fifty years has the Royal Title been altered to suit changed conditions and constitutional developments.

The present title, which is that proclaimed under the Royal Titles Act of 1901, is as follows: —"George V, by the Grace of God, of the United Kingdom of Great Britain and Ireland and of the British Dominions beyond the Seas King, Defender of the Faith, Emperor of India."

Some time before the Conference met, it had been recognised that this form of title hardly accorded with the altered state of affairs arising from the establishment of the Irish Free State as a Dominion. It had further been ascertained that it would be in accordance with His Majesty's wishes that any recommendation for change should be submitted to him as the result of discussion at the Conference.

We are unanimously of opinion that a slight change is desirable, and we recommend that, subject to His Majesty's approval, the necessary legislative action should be taken to secure that His Majesty's title should henceforward read:—"George V, by the Grace of God, of Breat Britain, Ireland and the British Dominions beyond the Seas King, Defender of the Faith, Emperor of India."

(b.) Position of Governors-General

We proceeded to consider whether it was desirable formally to place on record a definition of the position held by the Governor-General as His Majesty's representative in the Dominions. That position, though now generally well recognised, undoubtedly represents a development from an earlier stage when the Governor-General was appointed solely on the advice of His Majesty's Ministers in London and acted also as their representative.

In our opinion it is an essential consequence of the equality of status existing among the members of the British Commonwealth of Nations that the Governor-General of a Dominion is the representative of the Crown, holding in all essential respects the same position in relation to the administration of public affairs in the Dominion as is held by His Majesty the King in Great Britain, and that he is not the representative or agent of His Majesty's Government in Great Britain or of any Department of that Government.

It seemed to us to follow that the practice whereby the Governor-General of a Dominion is the formal official channel of communication between His Majesty's Government in Great Britain and His Governments in the Dominions might be regarded as no longer wholly in accordance with the constitutional position of the Governor-General. It was thought that the recognised official channel of communication should be, in future, between Government and Government direct. The representatives of Great Britain readily recognised that the existing procedure might be open to criticism and accepted the proposed change in principle in relation to any of the Dominions which desired it. Details were left for settlement as soon as possible after the Conference had completed its work, but it was recognised by the Committee, as an essential feature of any change or development in the channels of communication, that a Governor-General should be supplied with copies of all documents of importance and in general should be kept as fully informed as is His Majesty the King in Great Britain of Cabinet business and public affairs.

(c.) Operation of Dominion Legislation

Our attention was also called to various points in connection with the operation of Dominion legislation, which, it was suggested, required clarification.

The particular points involved were: —

(a.) The present practice under which Acts of the Dominion Parliaments are sent each year to London, and it is intimated, through the Secretary of State for Dominion Affairs, that "His Majesty will not be advised to exercise his powers of disallowance" with regard to them.

(b.) The reservation of Dominion legislation, in certain circumstances, for the signification of His Majesty's pleasure which is signified on advice tendered by His Majesty's Government in Great Britain.

(c.) The difference between the legislative competence of the Parliament at Westminster and of the Dominion Parliaments in that Acts passed by the latter operate, as a general rule, only within the territorial area of the Dominion concerned.

(d.) The operation of legislation passed by the Parliament at Westminster in relation to the Dominions. In this connection special attention was called to such Statutes as the Colonial Laws Validity Act. It was suggested that in future uniformity of legislation as between Great Britain and the Dominions could best be secured by the enactment of reciprocal Statutes based upon consultation and agreement.

We gave these matters the best consideration possible in the limited time at our disposal, but came to the conclusion that the issues involved were so complex that there would be grave danger in attempting any immediate pronouncement other than a statement of certain principles which, in our opinion, underlie the whole question of the operation of Dominion legislation. We felt that, for the rest, it would be necessary to obtain expert guidance as a preliminary to further consideration by His Majesty's Governments in Great Britain and the Dominions.

On the questions raised with regard to disallowance and reservation of Dominion legislation, it was explained by the Irish Free State representatives that they desired to elucidate the constitutional practice in relation to Canada, since it is provided by Article 2 of the Articles of Agreement for a Treaty of 1921 that "the position of the Irish Free State in relation to the Imperial Parliament and Government and otherwise shall be that of the Dominion of Canada."

On this point we propose that it should be placed on record that, apart from provisions embodied in constitutions or in specific statutes expressly providing for reservation, it is recognised that it is the right of the Government of each Dominion to advise the Crown in all matters relating to its own affairs. Consequently, it would not be in accordance with constitutional practice for advice to be tendered to His Majesty by His Majesty's Government in Great Britain in any matter appertaining to the affairs of a Dominion against the views of the Government of that Dominion.

The appropriate procedure with regard to projected legislation in one of the self-governing parts of the Empire which may affect the interests of other self-governing parts is previous consultation between His Majesty's Ministers in the several parts concerned.

On the question raised with regard to the legislative competence of members of the British Commonwealth of Nations other than Great Britain, and in particular to the desirability of those members being enabled to legislate with extra-territorial effect, we think that it should similarly be placed on record that the constitutional practice is that legislation by the Parliament at Westminster applying to a Dominion would only be passed with the consent of the Dominion concerned.

As already indicated, however, we are of opinion that there are points arising out of these considerations, and in the application of these general principles, which will require detailed examination, and we accordingly recommend that steps should be taken by Great Britain and the Dominions to set up a Committee with terms of reference on the following lines: —

To enquire into, report upon, and make recommendations concerning—
  (i.) Existing statutory provisions requiring reservation of Dominion legislation for the assent of His Majesty or authorising the disallowance of such legislation.
  (ii.) (a.) The present position as to the competence of Dominion Parliaments to give their legislation extra-territorial operation.
       (b.) The practicability and most convenient method of giving effect to the principle that each Dominion Parliament should have power to give extra-territorial operation to its legislation in all cases where such operation is ancillary to provision for the peace, order, and good government of the Dominion.
  (iii.) The principles embodied in or underlying the Colonial Laws Validity Act, 1865, and the extent to which any provisions of that Act ought to be repealed, amended, or modified in the light of the existing relations between the various members of the British Commonwealth of Nations as described in this Report.

(d.) Merchant Shipping Legislation

Somewhat similar considerations to those set out above governed our attitude towards a similar, though a special, question raised in relation to Merchant Shipping Legislation. On this subject it was pointed out that, while uniformity of administrative practice was desirable, and indeed essential, as regards the Merchant Shipping Legislation of the various parts of the Empire, it was difficult to reconcile the application, in their present form, of certain provisions of the principal Statute relating to Merchant Shipping, viz., the Merchant Shipping Act of 1894, more particularly Clauses 735 and 736, with the constitutional status of the several members of the British Commonwealth of Nations.

In this case also we felt that, although, in the evolution of the British Empire, certain inequalities had been allowed to remain as regards various questions of maritime affairs, it was essential in dealing with these inequalities to consider the practical aspects of the matter. The difficulties in the way of introducing any immediate alterations in the Merchant Shipping Code (which dealt, amongst other matters, with the registration of British ships all over the world) were fully appreciated and it was felt to be necessary, in any review of the position, to take into account such matters of general concern as the qualifications for registry as a British ship, the status of British ships in war, the work done by His Majesty's Consuls in the interest of British shipping and seamen, and the question of Naval Courts at foreign ports to deal with crimes and offences on British ships abroad.

We came finally to the conclusion that, following a precedent which had been found useful on previous occasions, the general question of Merchant Shipping Legislation had best be remitted to a special Sub-Conference, which could meet most appropriately at the same time as the Expert Committee, to which reference is made above. We thought that this special Sub-Conference should be invited to advise on the following general lines: —

> To consider and report on the principles which should govern, in the general interest, the practice and legislation relating to merchant shipping in the various parts of the Empire, having regard to the change in constitutional status and general relations which has occurred since existing laws were enacted.

We took note that the representatives of India particularly desired that India, in view of the importance of her shipping interests, should be given an opportunity of being represented at the proposed Sub-Conference. We felt that the full representation of India on an equal footing with Great Britain and the Dominions would not only be welcomed, but could very properly be given, due regard being had to the special constitutional position of India as explained in Section III of this Report.

(e.) Appeals to the Judicial Committee of the Privy Council

Another matter which we discussed, in which a general constitutional principle was raised, concerned the conditions governing appeals from judgments in the Dominions to the Judicial Committee of the Privy Council. From these discussions it became clear that it was no part of the policy of His Majesty's Government in Great Britain that questions affecting judicial appeals should be determined otherwise than in accordance with the wishes of the part of the Empire primarily affected. It was, however, generally recognised that, where changes in the existing system were proposed which, while primarily affecting one part, raised issues in which other parts were also concerned, such changes ought only to be carried out after consultation and discussion.

So far as the work of the Committee was concerned, this general understanding expressed all that was required. The question of some immediate change in the present conditions governing appeals from the Irish Free State was not pressed in relation to the present Conference, though it was made clear that the right was reserved to bring up the matter again at the next Imperial Conference for discussion in relation to the facts of this particular case.

V.—Relations with Foreign Countries

From questions specially concerning the relations of the various parts of the British Empire with one another, we naturally turned to those affecting their relations with foreign countries. In the latter sphere, a beginning had been made towards making clear those relations by the Resolution of the Imperial Conference of 1923 on the subject of the negotiation, signature, and ratification of treaties. But it seemed desirable to examine the working of that Resolution during the past three years and also to consider whether the principles laid down with regard to Treaties could not be applied with advantage in a wider sphere.

(a.) Procedure in Relation to Treaties

We appointed a special Sub-Committee under the Chairmanship of the Minister of Justice of Canada (The Honourable E. Lapointe, K.C.) to consider the question of treaty procedure.

The Sub-Committee, on whose report the following paragraphs are based, found that the Resolution of the Conference of 1923 embodied on most points useful rules for the guidance of the Governments. As they became more thoroughly understood and established, they would prove effective in practice.

Some phases of treaty procedure were examined however in greater detail in the light of experience in order to consider to what extent the Resolution of 1923 might with advantage be supplemented.

Negotiation. It was agreed in 1923 that any of the Governments of the Empire contemplating the negotiation of a treaty should give due consideration to its possible effect upon other Governments and should take steps to inform Governments likely to be interested of its intention.

This rule should be understood as applying to any negotiations which any Government intends to conduct, so as to leave it to the other Governments to say whether they are likely to be interested.

When a Government has received information of the intention of any other Government to conduct negotiations, it is incumbent upon it to indicate its attitude with reasonable promptitude. So long as the initiating Government receives no adverse comments and so long as its policy involves no active obligations on the part of the other Governments, it may proceed on the assumption that its policy is generally acceptable. It must, however, before taking any steps which might involve the other Governments in any active obligations, obtain their definite assent.

Where by the nature of the treaty it is desirable that it should be ratified on behalf of all the Governments of the Empire, the initiating Government may assume that a Government which has had full opportunity of indicating its attitude and has made no adverse comments will concur in the ratification of the treaty. In the case of a Government that prefers not to concur in the ratification of a treaty unless it has been signed by a plenipotentiary authorised to act on its behalf, it will advise the appointment of a plenipotentiary so to act.

Form of Treaty. Some treaties begin with a list of the contracting countries and not with a list of Heads of States. In the case of treaties negotiated under the auspices of the League of Nations, adherence to the wording of the Annex to the Covenant for the purpose of describing the contracting party has led to the use in the preamble of the term "British Empire" with an enumeration of the Dominions and India if parties to the Convention but without any mention of Great Britain and Northern Ireland and the Colonies and Protectorates. These are only included by virtue of their being covered by the term "British Empire." This practice, while suggesting that the Dominions and India are not on a footing of equality with Great Britain as participants in the treaties in question, tends to obscurity and misunderstanding and is generally unsatisfactory.

As a means of overcoming this difficulty it is recommended that all treaties (other than agreements between Governments) whether negotiated under the auspices of the League or not should be made in the name of Heads of States, and, if the treaty is signed on behalf of any or all of the Governments of the Empire, the treaty should be made in the name of the King as the symbol of the special relationship between the different parts of the Empire. The British units on behalf of which the treaty is signed should be grouped together in the following order: Great Britain and Northern Ireland and all parts of the British Empire which are not separate members of the League, Canada, Australia, New Zealand, South Africa, Irish Free State, India. A specimen form of treaty as recommended is attached as an appendix to the Committee's Report.

In the case of a treaty applying to only one part of the Empire it should be stated to be made by the King on behalf of that part.

The making of the treaty in the name of the King as the symbol of the special relationship between the different parts of the Empire will render superfluous the inclusion of any provision that its terms must not be regarded as regulating *inter se* the rights and obligations of the various territories on behalf of which it has been signed in the name of the King. In this connection it must be borne in mind that the question was discussed at the Arms Traffic Conference in 1925, and that the Legal Committee of that Conference laid it down that the principle to which the foregoing sentence gives expression underlies all international conventions.

In the case of some international agreements the Governments of different parts of the Empire may be willing to apply between themselves some of the provisions as an administrative measure. In this case they should state the extent to which and the terms on which such provisions are to apply. Where international agreements are to be applied between different parts of the Empire, the form of a treaty between Heads of States should be avoided.

Full Powers. The plenipotentiaries for the various British units should have Full Powers, issued in each case by the King on the advice of the Government concerned, indicating and corresponding to the part of the Empire for which they are to sign. It will frequently be found convenient, particularly where there are some parts of the Empire on which it is not contemplated that active obligations will be imposed, but where the position of the British subjects belonging to these parts will be affected, for such Government to advise the issue of Full Powers on their behalf to the plenipotentiary appointed to act on behalf of the Government or Governments mainly concerned. In other cases provision might be made for accession by other parts of the Empire at a later date.

Signature. In the cases where the names of countries are appended to the signatures in a treaty, the different parts of the Empire should be designated in the same manner as is proposed in regard to the list of plenipotentiaries in the preamble to the treaty. The signatures of the plenipotentiaries of the various parts of the Empire should be grouped together in the same order as is proposed above.

The signature of a treaty on behalf of a part of the Empire should cover territories for which a mandate has been given to that part of the Empire, unless the contrary is stated at the time of the signature.

Coming into Force of Multilateral Treaties. In general, treaties contain a ratification clause and a provision that the treaty will come into force on the deposit of a certain number of ratifications. The question has sometimes arisen in connection with treaties negotiated under the auspices of the League whether, for the purpose of making up the number of ratifications necessary to bring the treaty into force, ratifications on behalf of different parts of the Empire which are separate Members of the League should be counted as separate ratifications. In order to avoid any difficulty in future, it is recommended that, when it is thought necessary that a treaty should contain a clause of this character, it should take the form of a provision that the treaty should come into force when it has been ratified on behalf of so many separate Members of the League.

We think that some convenient opportunity should be taken of explaining to the other Members of the League the changes which it is desired to make in the form of treaties and the reasons for which they are desired. We would also recommend that the various Governments of the Empire should make it an instruction to their representatives at International Conferences to be held in future that they should use their best endeavours to secure that effect is given to the recommendations contained in the foregoing paragraphs.

(b.) Representation at International Conferences

We also studied, in the light of the Resolution of the Imperial Conference of 1923 to which reference has already been made, the question of the representation of the different parts of the Empire at International Conferences. The conclusions which we reached may be summarized as follows: —

1. No difficulty arises as regards representation at conferences convened by, or under the auspices of, the League of Nations. In the case of such conferences all members of the League are invited, and if they attend are represented separately by separate delegations. Co-operation is ensured by the application of paragraph I.1. (*c*) of the Treaty Resolution of 1923.

2. As regards international conferences summoned by foreign Governments, no rule of universal application can be laid down, since the nature of the representation must, in part, depend on the form of invitation issued by the convening Government.

> (*a.*) In conferences of a technical character, it is usual and always desirable that the different parts of the Empire should (if they wish to participate) be represented separately by separate delegations, and where necessary efforts should be made to secure invitations which will render such representation possible.
>
> (*b.*) Conferences of a political character called by a foreign Government must be considered on the special circumstances of each individual case.

It is for each part of the Empire to decide whether its particular interests are so involved, especially having regard to the active obligations likely to be imposed by any resulting treaty, that it desires to be represented at the conference, or whether it is content to leave the negotiation in the hands of the part or parts of the Empire more directly concerned and to accept the result.

If a Government desires to participate in the conclusion of a treaty, the method by which representation will be secured is a matter to be arranged with the other Governments of the Empire in the light of the invitation which has been received.

Where more than one part of the Empire desires to be represented, three methods of representation are possible: —

> (i.) By means of a common plenipotentiary or plenipotentiaries, the issue of Full Powers to whom should be on the advice of all parts of the Empire participating.
>
> (ii.) By a single British Empire delegation composed of separate representatives of such parts of the Empire as are participating in the conference. This was the form of representation employed at the Washington Disarmament Conference of 1921.
>
> (iii.) By separate delegations representing each part of the Empire participating in the conference. If, as a result of consultation, this third

method is desired, an effort must be made to ensure that the form of invitation from the convening Government will make this method of representation possible.

Certain non-technical treaties should, from their nature, be concluded in a form which will render them binding upon all parts of the Empire, and for this purpose should be ratified with the concurrence of all the Governments. It is for each Government to decide to what extent its concurrence in the ratification will be facilitated by its participation in the conclusion of the treaty, as, for instance, by the appointment of a common plenipotentiary. Any question as to whether the nature of the treaty is such that its ratification should be concurred in by all parts of the Empire is a matter for discussion and agreement between the Governments.

(c.) General Conduct of Foreign Policy

We went on to examine the possibility of applying the principles underlying the Treaty Resolution of the 1923 Conference to matters arising in the conduct of foreign affairs generally. It was frankly recognised that in this sphere, as in the sphere of defence, the major share of responsibility rests now, and must for some time continue to rest, with His Majesty's Government in Great Britain. Nevertheless, practically all the Dominions are engaged to some extent, and some to a considerable extent, in the conduct of foreign relations, particularly those with foreign countries on their borders. A particular instance of this is the growing work in connection with the relations between Canada and the United States of America which has led to the necessity for the appointment of a Minister Plenipotentiary to represent the Canadian Government in Washington. We felt that the governing consideration underlying all discussions of this problem must be that neither Great Britain nor the Dominions could be committed to the acceptance of active obligations except with the definite assent of their own Governments. In the light of this governing consideration, the Committee agreed that the general principle expressed in relation to Treaty negotiations in Section V (a) of this Report, which is indeed already to a large extent in force, might usefully be adopted as a guide by the Governments concerned in future in all negotiations affecting foreign relations falling within their respective spheres.

(d.) Issue of Exequaturs to Foreign Consuls in the Dominions

A question was raised with regard to the practice regarding the issue of exequaturs to Consuls in the Dominions. The general practice hitherto, in the case of all appointments of Consuls de Carrière in any part of the British Empire, has been that the foreign Government concerned notifies His Majesty's Government in Great Britain, through the diplomatic channel, of the proposed appointment and that, provided that it is clear that the person concerned is, in fact, a Consul de Carrière, steps have been taken, without further formality, for the issue of His Majesty's exequatur. In the case of Consuls other than those de Carrière, it has been customary for some time past to consult the Dominion Government concerned before the issue of the exequatur.

The Secretary of State for Foreign Affairs informed us that His Majesty's Government in Great Britain accepted the suggestion that in future any application by a foreign Government for the issue of an exequatur to any person who was to act as Consul in a Dominion should be referred to the Dominion Government concerned for consideration and that, if the Dominion Government agreed to the issue of the exequatur, it would be sent to them for counter-signature by a Dominion Minister. Instructions to this effect had indeed already been given.

(e.) Channel of Communication between Dominion Governments and Foreign Governments

We took note of a development of special interest which had occurred since the Imperial Conference last met, viz., the appointment of a Minister Plenipotentiary to represent the interests of the Irish Free State in Washington, which was now about to be followed by the appointment of a diplomatic representative of Canada. We felt that most fruitful results could be anticipated from the co-operation of His Majesty's representatives in the United States of America, already initiated, and now further to be developed. In cases other than those where Dominion Ministers were accredited to the Heads of Foreign States, it was agreed to be very desirable that the existing diplomatic channels should continue to be used, as between the Dominion Governments and foreign Governments, in matters of general and political concern.

*   *   *

Radio Broadcast by the Prime Minister, Stanley Baldwin,
on Empire Day, 24 May 1927

The keeping of an anniversary corresponds to some deep-felt want of human nature. Putting on one side anniversaries of religious importance, each with its peculiar significance and appeal, or of national importance, as Armistice Day, what family, from one end of the country to the other, does not cherish the memory of each birthday within its small circle? In what family is there not a day made sacred by the memory of a loved one no longer with them? And it is good for us in these busy days to be brought up sharply against anything that will make us think, if only for a minute or two, of something besides ourselves, our material welfare and our amusements. So to-day we are called to think of the British Empire and of our relation thereto; and it is fitting that Empire Day coincides with the anniversary of the birth of Her late Majesty Queen Victoria, for it was largely during her long and glorious reign that the British Empire as we know it to-day came into being.

*Baldwin, *Our Inheritance*, 71–76.

There has never been anything like the British Empire in the world before, and that is why the word Empire sometimes puzzles people. You associate it with Rome, Germany, Austria, Russia, and France at different periods of their history. You must rid yourself of all those associations, and try to think of it as an old word chosen to represent a new idea.

In our thought of Empire to-day there is nothing in the nature of flag-wagging or boasting of painting the map red. No! Only a sense of pride in the race from which we spring—a pride which makes us humble in our own eyes, and resolute to make ourselves as worthy as we may of the heritage and responsibilities which are ours.

Let us consider for a moment what we mean by heritage. We have been born into a community settled in a small island, dependent for our food supplies on the produce of countries overseas, and that food we pay for by exporting goods. In these circumstances there inevitably come times when the opportunities of many of our people are restricted, but for us alone are still opportunities denied to other nations. It is open to us to settle and work in any climate we may choose and in almost any part of the world, and find ourselves amongst people who speak our tongue, who obey our laws, who cherish the same ideals, and worship according to the rites familiar to us, who are subjects of the same Sovereign; and to this we must devote our best energies in the years to come—Tory, Liberal and Labour alike—to make our unity such a reality that men and women regard the Empire as one, and that it may become possible for them to move within its bounds to New Zealand, to Australia, to South Africa, to Canada, as easily and as freely as from Glasgow to London or Bristol to Newcastle. To build up the new nations overseas, for each one of them with ourselves to make her own peculiar contribution to the whole, and to make the whole a great force for righteousness in the world, that is not only the task of statesmen, but it is the task, if it is to be successful, which can only be accomplished by the conscious enthusiasm and participation of our people of all ranks and of all classes.

Last year we had the Imperial Conference of the Dominions and India. Let me remind you of another conference which is now being held in London this year for the first time, and of which you have been reading in the newspapers. I mean the conference of the Governors and principal officials of the Colonies, Protectorates, and Mandated Territories, which have a population of some fifty millions of peoples, infinite in their variety of language and culture, with a total trade already exceeding five hundred millions a year and increasing rapidly. In this group you have the oldest and youngest of our members. Barbados recently celebrated the tercentenary of British occupation, and only a few years ago Bermuda celebrated the three hundredth anniversary of its Legislature. The great tropical territories of Africa have been added to the Empire within the memory of living men, and Tanganyika, a mandated territory, is a legacy of the Great War. Here we have a direct responsibility which we no longer have in regard to our Dominions.

For centuries there has been no more difficult problem than the relationship of European and Asiatic and African races forming part of the same community. That there is a problem at all has scarcely been realised. For more than a century, for good or for ill, the ultimate responsibility for the administration of vast territories inhabited mainly by these indigenous races has rested upon us. We are indeed happy in the character of the men who are undertaking this work—political, religious, scientific—but we require a quickened conscience to impel a sufficient number of our best men to grapple with a task even yet so novel but fraught with infinite possibilities for the future. And what of India? What we call India is almost a world of its own, covering an area as large as the whole of Europe without Russia, containing over three hundred millions of human beings speaking one hundred and fifty tongues, with an ancient history and an ancient civilisation. Her position in the Empire has as yet been necessarily somewhat different from that of the Dominions, but some ten years ago it was declared that the aim of British policy was: "The progressive realisation of responsible Government in British India as an integral part of the Empire." Since then great strides towards that goal have been made and in all the joint activities of the British Commonwealth of nations India now plays her part, and in the fullness of time we look forward to seeing her in equal partnership with the Dominions.

We who have inherited this Empire are proud of it, and it is right that we should be proud. With our pride there should mingle gratitude to those who have gone before us, by whose efforts this Empire has grown.

In a world still suffering from the shock of war, the British Empire stands firm as a great force for good. Let us then to-day bear the Empire in our minds and in our prayers. It invites and requires some service of us all.

It stands in the sweep of every wind, by the wash of every sea, a witness to that which the spirit of confidence and brotherhood can accomplish in the world. It is a spiritual inheritance which we hold in trust not only for its members, but for all the nations which surround it. Let us see to it that we hand it on to our successors with untarnished glory.

Statute of Westminster, an Act Creating the British Commonwealth of Nations (22 Geo. V, c. 4), 11 December 1931*

Whereas the delegates of His Majesty's Governments in the United Kingdom, the Dominion of Canada, the Commonwealth of Australia, the Dominion of New Zealand, the Union of South Africa, the Irish Free State and Newfoundland, at Imperial Conferences holden at Westminster in the years of our Lord

*Public General Acts, 1932, 13–17.

nineteen hundred and twenty-six and nineteen hundred and thirty did concur in making the declarations and resolutions set forth in the Reports of the said Conferences:

And whereas it is meet and proper to set out by way of preamble to this Act that, inasmuch as the Crown is the symbol of the free association of the members of the British Commonwealth of Nations, and as they are united by a common allegiance to the Crown, it would be in accord with the established constitutional position of all the members of the Commonwealth in relation to one another that any alteration in the law touching the Succession to the Throne or the Royal Style and Titles shall hereafter require the assent as well of the Parliaments of all the Dominions as of the Parliament of the United Kingdom:

And whereas it is in accord with the established constitutional position that no law hereafter made by the Parliament of the United Kingdom shall extend to any of the said Dominions as part of the law of that Dominion otherwise than at the request and with the consent of that Dominion:

And whereas it is necessary for the ratifying, confirming and establishing of certain of the said declarations and resolutions of the said Conferences that a law be made and enacted in due form by authority of the Parliament of the United Kingdom:

And whereas the Dominion of Canada, the Commonwealth of Australia, the Dominion of New Zealand, the Union of South Africa, the Irish Free State and Newfoundland have severally requested and consented to the submission of a measure to the Parliament of the United Kingdom for making such provision with regard to the matters aforesaid as is hereafter in this Act contained:

Now, therefore, be it enacted by the King's most Excellent Majesty by and with the advice and consent of the Lords Spiritual and Temporal, and Commons, in this present Parliament assembled, and by the authority of the same, as follows: —

1. In this Act the expression "Dominion" means any of the following Dominions, that is to say, the Dominion of Canada, the Commonwealth of Australia, the Dominion of New Zealand, the Union of South Africa, the Irish Free State and Newfoundland.

2.— (1) The Colonial Laws Validity Act, 1865, shall not apply to any law made after the commencement of this Act by the Parliament of a Dominion.

(2) No law and no provision of any law made after the commencement of this Act by the Parliament of a Dominion shall be void or inoperative on the ground that it is repugnant to the law of England, or to the provisions of any existing or future Act of Parliament of the United Kingdom, or to any order, rule or regulation made under any such Act, and the powers of the Parliament of a Dominion shall include the power to repeal or amend any such Act, order, rule or regulation in so far as the same is part of the law of the Dominion.

3. It is hereby declared and enacted that the Parliament of a Dominion has full power to make laws having extra-territorial operation.

4. No Act of Parliament of the United Kingdom passed after the commence-

ment of this Act shall extend, or be deemed to extend, to a Dominion as part of the law of that Dominion, unless it is expressly declared in that Act that that Dominion has requested, and consented to, the enactment thereof.

5. Without prejudice to the generality of the foregoing provisions of this Act, sections seven hundred and thirty-five and seven hundred and thirty-six of the Merchant Shipping Act, 1894, shall be construed as though reference therein to the Legislature of a British possession did not include reference to the Parliament of a Dominion.

6. Without prejudice to the generality of the foregoing provisions of this Act, section four of the Colonial Courts of Admiralty Act, 1890 (which requires certain laws to be reserved for the signification of His Majesty's pleasure or to contain a suspending clause), and so much of section seven of that Act as requires the approval of His Majesty in Council to any rules of Court for regulating the practice and procedure of a Colonial Court of Admiralty, shall cease to have effect in any Dominion as from the commencement of this Act.

7.—(1) Nothing in this Act shall be deemed to apply to the repeal, amendment or alteration of the British North America Acts, 1867 to 1930, or any order, rule or regulation made thereunder.

(2) The provisions of section two of this Act shall extend to laws made by any of the Provinces of Canada and to the powers of the legislatures of such Provinces.

(3) The powers conferred by this Act upon the Parliament of Canada or upon the legislatures of the Provinces shall be restricted to the enactment of laws in relation to matters within the competence of the Parliament of Canada or of any of the legislatures of the Provinces respectively.

8. Nothing in this Act shall be deemed to confer any power to repeal or alter the Constitution or the Constitution Act of the Commonwealth of Australia or the Constitution Act of the Dominion of New Zealand otherwise than in accordance with the law existing before the commencement of this Act.

9.—(1) Nothing in this Act shall be deemed to authorise the Parliament of the Commonwealth of Australia to make laws on any matter within the authority of the States of Australia, not being a matter within the authority of the Parliament or Government of the Commonwealth of Australia.

(2) Nothing in this Act shall be deemed to require the concurrence of the Parliament or Government of the Commonwealth of Australia in any law made by the Parliament of the United Kingdom with respect to any matter within the authority of the States of Australia, not being a matter within the authority of the Parliament or Government of the Commonwealth of Australia, in any case where it would have been in accordance with the constitutional practice existing before the commencement of this Act that the Parliament of the United Kingdom should make that law without such concurrence.

(3) In the application of this Act to the Commonwealth of Australia the request and consent referred to in section four shall mean the request and consent of the Parliament and Government of the Commonwealth.

10.—(1) None of the following sections of this Act, that is to say, sections two, three, four, five and six, shall extend to a Dominion to which this section applies as part of the law of that Dominion unless that section is adopted by the Parliament of the Dominion, and any Act of that Parliament adopting any section of this Act may provide that the adoption shall have effect either from the commencement of this Act or from such later date as is specified in the adopting Act.

(2) The Parliament of any such Dominion as aforesaid may at any time revoke the adoption of any section referred to in subsection (1) of this section.

(3) The Dominions to which this section applies are the Commonwealth of Australia, the Dominion of New Zealand and Newfoundland.

11. Notwithstanding anything in the Interpretation Act, 1889, the expression "Colony" shall not, in any Act of the Parliament of the United Kingdom passed after the commencement of this Act, include a Dominion or any Province or State forming part of a Dominion.

12. This Act may be cited as the Statute of Westminster, 1931.

Ottawa Agreements Act, an Act Implementing a System of Preferential Tariffs for the Commonwealth of Nations (22 & 23 Geo. V, c. 53), 15 November 1932*

Most Gracious Sovereign,

We, Your Majesty's most dutiful and loyal subjects, the Commons in Parliament assembled, with a view to the giving of effect to the agreements made on the twentieth day of August, nineteen hundred and thirty-two, at the Imperial Economic Conference held at Ottawa (being the agreements set out in the First Schedule to this Act), and to the announcement made at that Conference on behalf of His Majesty's Government in the United Kingdom (being the announcement set out in Part VIII of the said Schedule), have freely and voluntarily resolved to give and grant unto Your Majesty the duties for which provision is hereinafter contained; and do therefore most humbly beseech Your Majesty that it may be enacted, and be it enacted by the King's most Excellent Majesty, by and with the advice and consent of the Lords Spiritual and Temporal, and Commons, in this present Parliament assembled, and by the authority of the same, as follows: —

1.— (1) With a view to the fulfilment of the agreements set out in the First Schedule to this Act (hereafter in this Act referred to as the "scheduled agreements") and the announcement set out in Part VIII of that Schedule, there shall be charged on the importation into the United Kingdom of goods of

*Public General Acts, 1932, 953–60.

the classes and descriptions specified in the first column of Part I of the Second Schedule to this Act, the duties of customs respectively specified in the second column of that part of that Schedule, subject to the provisions of Part II of that Schedule.

(2) If at any time the Treasury are satisfied with respect to any duty chargeable under this section that the duty can be repealed, or the rate thereof reduced, as regards goods of any class or description (whether being a class or description specified in Part I of the Second Schedule to this Act or a subsidiary class or description comprised in a class or description so specified) without contravening any of the scheduled agreements for the time being in force, the Treasury shall, unless it appears to them that the repeal or reduction would be inconsistent with the announcement aforesaid, by order direct that, as from such date as may be specified in the order, that duty, as the case may be, shall not be charged on goods of that class or description, or shall be charged thereon at such reduced rate specified in the order as appears to the Treasury to be the lowest rate at which the duty can be charged without contravening any of the scheduled agreements for the time being in force.

(3) If, at any time after an order has been made under the last foregoing subsection, the Treasury are satisfied that the reimposition, or the increase of the rate, of the duty specified in the order is necessary for the fulfilment of any of the scheduled agreements for the time being in force, the Treasury shall by order direct that, as from such date as may be specified in the order, the duty shall again be charged or, as the case may be, shall be charged at such increased rate specified in the order as appears to the Treasury to be the lowest rate at which the duty can be charged without contravening any of the scheduled agreements for the time being in force:

Provided that nothing in this subsection shall authorise any such duty to be charged on goods of any class or description at a rate higher than the rate specified in relation thereto in Part I of the Second Schedule to this Act.

(4) Subject to the provisions of this Act, the duties of customs chargeable on any goods under this section shall be charged in addition to any other duties of customs for the time being chargeable thereon or on any of the components thereof:

Provided that—

(a) nothing in this subsection shall affect the provisions of paragraph (a) of subsection (2) of section one of the Import Duties Act, 1932 (which exempts from the general ad valorem duty certain goods for the time being chargeable with a duty of customs by or under any enactment other than that Act); and

(b) while any goods are chargeable with duty under this section, any order in force under the Import Duties Act, 1932, at the date when those goods become so chargeable shall, if and so far as it imposes an additional duty on those goods, cease to have effect.

(5) Notwithstanding anything in the last foregoing subsection—

> (*a*) the Import Duties Advisory Committee may recommend, subject to and in accordance with section three of the Import Duties Act, 1932, that an additional duty ought to be charged on goods of any class or description for the time being chargeable with a duty of customs under this section, as if the duty chargeable under this section were the general ad valorem duty, and the Treasury may make an order under that section accordingly; and
>
> (*b*) the provisions of the enactments set out in Part III of the Second Schedule to this Act shall, subject to the provisions of that Part of that Schedule, apply for the purposes of this section as they apply for the purposes of the Import Duties Act, 1932:

Provided that this subsection shall not apply to goods which, immediately before they became chargeable with duty under this section, were exempt from the general ad valorem duty by virtue of the provisions of paragraph (*a*) of subsection (2) of section one of the said Act.

2.—(1) Neither the duties chargeable under the foregoing provisions of this Act nor the general ad valorem duty nor, subject as hereinafter provided, any additional duty shall be charged in the case of goods which are shown to the satisfaction of the Commissioners to have been consigned from any part of the British Empire and grown, produced or manufactured in any country the Government of which is a party to one of the scheduled agreements for the time being in force:

Provided that if at any time the Treasury are satisfied with respect to any such country that an additional duty chargeable on goods of any particular class or description can, without contravention of any of the scheduled agreements for the time being in force, be charged on goods of that class or description which are shown as aforesaid to have been consigned from a part of the British Empire and to have been grown, produced or manufactured in that country, the Treasury may by order direct that, as from such date as may be specified in the order, that duty shall be charged on such goods, either at the full rate or at such lower rate as may be so specified.

Any order made under this subsection may be varied or revoked by a subsequent order.

(2) For the purposes of the last foregoing subsection, any territory in respect of which a mandate of the League of Nations is being exercised by, or which is administered under the authority of, the Government of any country shall be treated as if it were a part of that country.

(3) In the case of goods which are shown to the satisfaction of the Commissioners to have been consigned from any part of the British Empire and grown, produced or manufactured in the Irish Free State, the duties chargeable under the foregoing provisions of this Act, or under any order made under section three of the Import Duties Act, 1932, by virtue of the foregoing provisions of this Act, shall not become chargeable until the earliest date on which no order

is in force by virtue of which duties are chargeable under the Irish Free State (Special Duties) Act, 1932, or such later date as may be fixed by resolution of the Commons House of Parliament.

(4) The duties chargeable under the foregoing provisions of this Act shall not be charged in the case of goods which are shown to the satisfaction of the Commissioners to have been consigned from any part of the British Empire and grown, produced or manufactured in any part of the British Empire to which section four of the Import Duties Act, 1932, does not apply.

(5) During the period of three years from the passing of this Act, or such further period as may be prescribed, any copper produced in any part of the British Empire but refined outside the British Empire, being copper to which this subsection applies, shall, subject to proof being given in the prescribed manner that it has been so produced and that it has been consigned from the country in which it was refined, be treated for the purposes of this section as if it had been consigned from a part of the British Empire.

This subsection applies to any kind of copper to which it is declared to apply by regulations made by the Board of Trade, after consultation with the Treasury, for the purposes of this subsection, and the expression "prescribed" in this subsection means prescribed by regulations made as aforesaid, and different regulations may be made with respect to different parts of the British Empire and different kinds of copper.

(6) Goods shown to the satisfaction of the Commissioners to have been consigned from the port of Beira in Portuguese East Africa and shown as aforesaid, by means of a certificate signed by a Customs officer in the service of the Government of Southern or Northern Rhodesia or of Nyasaland, to have been grown, produced or manufactured in Southern or Northern Rhodesia or Nyasaland, as the case may be, shall be treated for the purposes of this section and of section five of the Import Duties Act, 1932, as if they had been consigned from a part of the British Empire.

(7) The provisions of section six of, and the Third Schedule to, the Import Duties Act, 1932 (being supplementary provisions as to Imperial preference), shall apply for the purposes of this section as they apply for the purposes of sections four and five of that Act, as if references to any duty chargeable under that Act or any provision thereof included a reference to any duty chargeable under the foregoing provisions of this Act.

3. With a view to the fulfilment of the agreements set out in Parts II and IV of the First Schedule to this Act,—

(a) the duty of customs chargeable under section five of the Finance Act, 1927, on wine, not being an Empire product and not exceeding twenty-five degrees of proof spirit, shall be increased from three shillings per gallon to four shillings per gallon; and

(b) the duty of customs chargeable under the said section on wine not exceeding twenty-seven degrees of proof spirit, being an Empire product, shall be charged at a preferential rate representing the full rate of duty for the time being chargeable on wine not exceeding twenty-five degrees of proof spirit and not being an Empire product, reduced by two shillings per gallon:

Provided that—

(i) if at any time the Treasury are satisfied that none of the scheduled agreements for the time being in force would be contravened if the words "one shilling per gallon" were substituted in paragraph (b) of this subsection for the words "two shillings per gallon," the Treasury shall by order direct that that paragraph shall have effect as if those words were so substituted, so, however, that any such order shall be revoked if and when the Treasury are satisfied that any such agreement is being contravened by the order; and

(ii) in relation to wine produced or manufactured in a country the Government of which is party to one of the scheduled agreements, the said paragraph shall in any case have effect, at any time when that agreement is not in force, as if the said words were substituted as aforesaid.

4.—(1) With a view to the fulfilment of the Agreements set out in Parts I, IV, VI and VII of the First Schedule to this Act, subsection (1) of section seven of the Finance Act, 1926, (which provides for the stabilisation of rates of imperial preference) shall, in relation to the duties of customs chargeable on tobacco, have effect as if the period of ten years mentioned in that subsection were extended so as to expire on the nineteenth day of August, nineteen hundred and forty-two.

(2) With a view to the fulfilment of the Agreements set out in Parts VI and VII of the First Schedule to this Act, coffee (not kiln-dried, roasted or ground) being an Empire product, shall be charged with a duty of customs at a preferential rate representing the full rate of duty for the time being chargeable on such coffee, not being an Empire product, reduced by nine shillings and fourpence per hundredweight:

Provided that—

(a) if at any time the Treasury are satisfied that none of the scheduled agreements for the time being in force would be contravened if the words "two shillings and fourpence per hundredweight" were substituted in this subsection for the words "nine shillings and fourpence per hundredweight," the Treasury shall by order direct that this subsection shall have effect as if those words were so substituted, so, however, that any such order shall be revoked if and when the Treasury are satisfied that any such agreement is being contravened by the order; and

(b) in relation to coffee produced or manufactured in a country the Government of which is a party to one of the scheduled agreements, this subsection shall in any case have effect, at any time when that agreement is not in force, as if the said words were substituted as aforesaid.

(3) For the rates of drawback on coffee and mixtures of coffee and chicory specified in subsection (4) of section three of the Finance Act, 1924, there shall, if a duty of customs was paid on the coffee, or on the coffee or any part of the coffee contained in the mixture, as the case may be, at a preferential rate representing the full rate of duty reduced by nine shillings and fourpence per hundred-weight, be substituted the following reduced rates, that is to say: —

	£	s.	d.
Coffee, for every one hundred pounds.............		4	8

Mixtures of coffee and chicory—

	£	s.	d.
For every one hundred pounds of coffee contained in the mixture on which a duty of customs was paid as aforesaid.............		4	8
For every one hundred pounds of the other components of the mixture	The rate payable under the said subsection (4) for every one hundred pounds of the whole mixture,		

and so in proportion for any less quantity.

5.—(1) If at any time the Board of Trade are satisfied that any preferences granted by this Act in respect of any particular class or description of goods, being preferences granted in fulfilment of the agreement set out in Part I of the First Schedule to this Act, are likely to be frustrated in whole or in part by reason of the creation or maintenance, directly or indirectly, of prices for that class or description of goods through State action on the part of any foreign country, the Board of Trade may by order prohibit the importation into the United Kingdom of goods of that class or description grown, produced or manufactured in that foreign country.

(2) Any order made under this section shall be revoked by a subsequent order made in like manner if and when the Board of Trade are satisfied that the further operation of the order is no longer necessary to make effective or to maintain the preferences granted as aforesaid in respect of the class or description of goods to which the order relates.

(3) No order shall be made under this section except with the concurrence of the Treasury, given after consultation with any other Government Department which appears to the Treasury to be interested.

*   *   *

THE CONCEPT OF TRUSTEESHIP IN AFRICA

Report by Sir F. D. Lugard on the Amalgamation of Northern and
Southern Nigeria and Their Administration from 1912 to 1919
(Including a Discussion of Educational and Legal Reforms).
December 1919*

Part I.—Introduction and Preliminaries to Amalgamation

1. The general character of Nigeria. Geography, area, and climate.—Before dealing with the amalgamation of the two separate Governments of Northern and Southern Nigeria, it will perhaps serve a useful purpose if I sketch briefly the character of each country, and indicate the causes of their divergent forms of Administration and the reasons which led to the necessity of amalgamation.

The area of "Northern Nigeria" was about 255,700 square miles, that of "Southern Nigeria," including the Colony, being about 76,700 square miles. The former consisted for the most part either of open prairie and cultivation, or was covered by sparse and low forest of the deciduous "dry zone" type. The central portion—Zaria and Bauchi—forms a plateau varying from 2,000 to 4,500 ft. in altitude, with a bracing climate. The dry desert wind, the "Hamattan"—which prevails in the winter months causes the temperature to fall rapidly when the hot sun goes down, so that the nights, especially on the plateau, are often very cold. The rainfall is small, decreasing towards the confines of the Sahara, which forms the northern boundary.

Southern Nigeria, on the other hand, is situated in the zone of equatorial rainfall. A great part of the country is, or was till recently, covered by primeval forest. It is low-lying with the exception of the water parting, which traverses it from East to West, and divides the watershed of the Niger and Benue to the North from that towards the sea in the South. The southern portion is intersected by a network of salt-water creeks, bordered by mangrove swamp or vegetation so dense that it forms almost a wall of giant trees and undergrowth interlaced with creepers.

Horses, donkeys and vast herds—aggregating millions—of cattle, sheep, and goats flourish in the North, but animal life is scarce in the South, where the yam fields of a dense population cover every acre reclaimed from the grassless forests, which are infested with tsetse and other biting flies. There are, of course, exceptions to these generalities. Districts in the South from which the forest has disappeared tend to resemble the open character of the North, and there are districts in the North on the banks of the Niger and Benue which approximate to the characteristics of the South. These two great rivers are a

**Parliamentary Papers*, 1919, XXXVI, Cmd. 468, 5–12, 20–25, 59–66.

prominent geographical feature of the country. The Niger, flowing North and South, divides the Southern Protectorate roughly into halves. Some 250 miles from its mouth its course lies with a sharp inclination to the West, and the Benue, which joins it here, forms with it a continuous waterway of some 700 miles from the Cameroon frontier in the East to Jebba in the West, where the Niger, bending northwards again, is broken by rapids almost to the point where it first enters Nigeria from French territory. The Cross River in the extreme East is the only other river which is navigable by large steamers, with the exception of the creeks and the affluents of the Niger Delta.

2. *Ethnography, population, religions, etc.*—The population of the North— described 60 years ago by Barth as the densest in all Africa—had by 1900 dwindled to some 9 millions, owing to inter-tribal war, and, above all, to the slave raids of the Fulani. But these dreaded horsemen could not penetrate the forests of the South, where a population estimated at 7¾ millions (probably an over-estimate) found refuge. These tribes are of purer negro stock than the Hausas and other negroids of the North. Though in the more open areas they show themselves to be admirable agriculturists, many of the delta tribes live a semi-aquatic life in their canoes, fishing and collecting the abundant sylvan produce (especially of the oil palm), both for their own sustenance and for trade with the middlemen who carry it to the coast merchants.

From a very early date the influence of Islam had made itself felt in the North, and the religious revival of the early years of the nineteenth century had formed the motive for the Fulani conquests, which swept the country from Sokoto in the north-west to Yola, 1,000 miles to the East, and from the Sahara to the confines of the Equatorial Belt. The social and religious organisation of the Koran supplemented, and combined with, the pre-existing, and probably advanced, form of tribal administration handed down from the powerful Songhay Empire, which had extended from Chad to Timbuktu. The courts were served by judges erudite in Moslem law and fearless in its impartial application. The system of taxation was highly developed, and the form of Administration highly centralised.

A rapid deterioration had, however, followed the decay of the religious zeal which had prompted the Fulani *Jihad,* and at the time when the Administration was assumed by the Imperial Government in 1900 the Fulani Emirates formed a series of separate despotisms, marked by the worst forms of wholesale slave-raiding, spoliation of the peasantry, inhuman cruelty, and debased justice. The separate dynasty of Bornu on the Chad plain had fallen before the armies of Rabeh from Wadai, who at this time was looting and ravaging the country. The primitive Pagan races held their own in the inaccessible fastnesses of the mountainous districts of the plateau or in the forests bordering the Benue river. Others had come under the domination of the ruling race and lived a hard life.

The South was, for the most part, held in thrall by Fetish worship and the hideous ordeals of witchcraft, human sacrifice, and twin murder. The great Ibo race to the East of the Niger, numbering some 3 millions, and their cognate tribes had not developed beyond the stage of primitive savagery. In the West, the Kingdom of Benin—like its counterpart in Dahomey—had up to 1897 groaned under a despotism which revelled in holocausts of human victims for its Fetish rites. Further West the Yorubas, Egbas, and Jebus had evolved a fairly advanced system of Government under recognised rulers. The coast fringe was peopled by negro traders and middlemen, who had acquired a smattering of education in Mission schools, and who jealously guarded the approaches to the interior from the European merchant. In the principal towns (Lagos, Calabar, etc.) there were some few educated native gentlemen who practised as doctors, barristers, etc.

3. The advent of British Rule.—The British Government, which had maintained a Consul at Lagos since 1852, obtained the cession of the island in 1861 with the sole object of putting an end to the overseas slave traffic. In the following years the abandonment of all West African settlements was contemplated, and any extension of responsibilities with the interior was vetoed. It was not therefore until the "Scramble for Africa" which followed the Berlin Act of 1885 that any steps were taken to secure the coast line from Lagos to the Cameroons and to establish a claim to the hinterland as a British "sphere of influence." This area was then placed under the Consular jurisdiction of the Foreign Office (under the name of the Oil Rivers Protectorate), to whom also the Royal Niger Chartered Company, who were endeavouring to open up the districts bordering the Niger, were responsible. Colonial Office control remained limited to Lagos Colony. It was not until 1893-4 that, in consequence of friction with France, the Foreign Office was compelled to champion the cause of the Niger Company and to declare a Protectorate over the Niger territories. The Oil Rivers then became the Niger Coast Protectorate. With the advent of Mr. Chamberlain to the Colonial Office in 1895, British West Africa entered on a new era. British influence was extended into the Lagos hinterland. The "French crisis" was brought to a close by the Convention of June, 1898, and steps were taken to buy out the Charter of the Niger Company. This was completed on January 1st, 1900, and the Governments of Northern and Southern Nigeria were created. The former included all territory North of Lat. 7° 10′ (approx.) and the latter the old Niger Coast Protectorate, with the addition of such parts of the Company's territory as lay to the South of that line. Lagos formed a third Administration.

4. Character of British Administration.—The divergent conditions which I have described—geographical, ethnographical, and climatic—together with the very different manner in which the two countries had come under the direct control of the Crown, had, as was to be expected, profoundly influenced the form which British Administration took in each. The early Administrations in the South were confined to the Coast area, where a large revenue was at hand from the duties imposed on imported trade spirits—small though the duties were at that time. Access to the interior was the first desideratum, the creation of roads through the primeval "Bush," the clearing of waterways blocked with sudd, and, later, the creation of a port at Lagos and the commencement of a railway. Any coherent policy of Native Administration was well-nigh impossible in such circumstances, and the material was very unpromising except among the tribes in the hinterland of Lagos. Gradually the wall of opposition which barred access to the interior was broken down. Systematic penetration of the almost wholly unexplored country East of the Niger began in 1900, and in 1902 the Aro Fetish, whose ramifications extended throughout the eastern portion of the country—a cult of human sacrifice and slavery—was crushed by force of arms.

The inauguration of British rule in the North was in strong contrast. Here the Chartered Company, restricted by financial considerations, had been compelled to confine their depôts chiefly to the banks of the Niger and Benue Rivers. The very existence of any organised Government was threatened by the haughty insolence of the Fulani armies. The condition of Bornu—where the French had intervened—compelled immediate action. Nothing could be done until a force strong enough to cope with these powerful Emirates had been created.

The West African Frontier Force was raised in 1898–99, and on its return from its successful campaign in Ashanti, the task of dealing with the Moslem Emirates was undertaken, in 1902-3. Kontagora, the noted slave-raider, who had boasted that, like a cat with a mouse, he would "die with a slave in his mouth," was the first to be coerced. Nupe, who had also threatened the existence of the new Administration, followed. Bornu, overrun by Rabeh's army from the Egyptian Sudan, which in turn had been defeated in British territory by a French force, placed itself under the Government, and General Morland's force, *en route* thither, brought Bauchi under control, and its Emir was deposed in reprisal for his ruthless massacre of the people of Guaram. Zaria offered no opposition to peaceful occupation, but the murder of Captain Malony, Resident at Keffi, precipitated hostilities with Kano. The fall of this great city and that of Sokoto in March, 1903, was followed by the submission of the minor Emirates, and convinced those which had already submitted that their belief that the British would be exterminated by these powerful Emirs was vain.

When this had been accomplished, and the forces of disorder had been broken, the British Administration was faced with the insistent urgency of creating a new organisation and of developing a native policy without delay. The system evolved will be described in a later paragraph.

The necessity of securing means wherewith to carry on the Administration was no less insistent than the reorganisation of the Native Administration. There was no revenue to be got from spirits, which were wholly prohibited, while the cost of the large force necessary for the control of the country absorbed the greater part of the wholly inadequate grant from the Imperial Government.

5. Necessity for Amalgamation: (a) Finance.—Such in brief were the antecedents which had given to the North and South their divergent characteristics and policies. In 1906 a further step in amalgamation was effected in the South. Southern Nigeria and Lagos became one Administration under the title of the Colony and Protectorate of Southern Nigeria. From this date the material prosperity of the South increased with astonishing rapidity. The liquor duties—increased from 3s. in 1901 to 3s. 6d. in 1905—stood at 5s. 6d. a gallon in 1912, and afforded an ever-increasing revenue, without any diminution in the quantity imported. They yielded a sum of £1,138,000 in 1913.

The North, largely dependent on the annual grant from the Imperial Government, was barely able to balance its budget with the most parsimonious economy, and was starved of the necessary staff, and unable to find funds to house its officers properly. Its energies were concentrated upon the development of the Native Administration and the revenue resulting from direct taxation. Its distance from the coast (250 miles) rendered the expansion of trade difficult. Thus the anomaly was presented of a country with an aggregate revenue practically equal to its needs, but divided into two by an arbitrary line of latitude. One portion was dependent on a grant paid by the British taxpayer, which in the year before Amalgamation stood at £136,000, and had averaged £314,500 for the 11 years ending March, 1912.

6. (b) Railways.—To the financial dilemma there was now added a very pressing difficulty in regard to Railway policy and control. The North, to ensure the development of its trade and to secure its Customs duties, commenced a railway from Baro, a port on the Niger, to Kano in 1906. The South responded by pushing on the Lagos Railway to the frontier, and obtained the Secretary of State's sanction to carry it on in the North, to effect a junction with the Baro-Kano line at Minna. In the opinion of Sir John Eaglesome, Director of Railways, the line, when it reached the Northern Nigerian frontier at Offa, should have crossed the Niger at Pateji, traversing a well-populated country and tapping the great trade centre at Bida—thus avoiding the extremely costly and difficult bridge at Jebba, and the uninhabited country to the North of it—the distance to Minna being precisely the same. But no single railway policy had been possible, and the two outlets to the sea were now in acute competition. Major Waghorn, R.E., was sent out to report on the two railways, and to propose some system of joint use and control. He animadverted very strongly on the needless cost which had characterised the construction of the southern section of the Lagos line. It was full of sharp curves and dangerous gradients, which had to be rectified at an expenditure of £200,000. It was stated that the section to Ibadan, which presented no special difficulties, had cost two millions (over £15,000 a mile). Immediate unification of control with a view to checking extravagance was recommended. The advent of the railway, moreover, accentuated the need for a revision of the apportionment of Customs duties collected at the port. The growing divergence of administrative methods, as the interior became opened up in the South, also called for a common policy. In a long memorandum, dated May, 1905 (while still High Commissioner of Northern Nigeria), I advocated amalgamation, a policy supported by the then High Commissioner of Southern Nigeria and the Governor of Lagos, and there was increasing evidence that it could no longer be postponed.

7. *Decision to Amalgamate.*—Towards the close of 1911, Mr. (now Viscount) Harcourt, Secretary of State for the Colonies, invited me to undertake the task. I was at the time Governor of Hong Kong, having previously been High Commissioner of Northern Nigeria from its inauguration in 1900. I was therefore intimately acquainted with the method of Administration there, for the creation of which I had indeed been responsible. Reaching England in April, 1912, I was appointed Governor of the two separate Administrations simultaneously, and after spending several weeks in England, to acquaint myself with the current views on some important matters, I proceeded to Africa in September, 1912. I returned in the following March, and submitted my proposals for amalgamation in May. They were accepted in September, when I returned to Nigeria, and on January 1st, 1914, the new Government of Nigeria, as set up by fresh Letters Patent and other Instruments, was proclaimed.

8. *Nature of the Task.*—It was clear that so large a country as Nigeria, with an area of 332,400 square miles—of which the North and South were connected only by a single railway and the uncertain waterway of the Niger, while no lateral means of communication existed at all—must be divided into two or more dependent Administrations under the control of a Central Government. The first problem therefore which presented itself was the number of such Lieutenant-Governors, their powers, and relations to the various departments, together with the subordinate Administrative units throughout the country, and the control of such departments as the Railway and the Military Forces, which were common to the whole of Nigeria. The functions, and future constitutions, of the Executive and Legislative Councils, the unification of the Laws and the Regulations based upon them, and of the Executive "General Orders" and other instructions, the Judicial system, the methods of Taxation direct and indirect, and the disposal of the Revenue so as to benefit the country as a whole, without creating jealousy and friction, the assimilation of the policy of Native Administration—these, with many minor problems, had to be solved by any scheme of amalgamation which should have any prospect of permanency. In every one of these matters the systems of the two Governments differed essentially, as I shall show in discussing each in detail. The alarm and suspicion caused among the native population of the South by the appointment in England of a Committee to enquire into the question of land tenure added to the difficulty of the task. Amalgamation in my view was "not a mere political, geographical, or more especially a financial expression." I regarded it rather "as a means whereby each part of Nigeria should be raised to the level of the highest plane attained by any particular part." Thus regarded each of the two Administrations had much to learn from the other. The North—a younger Government—was capable of improvement in its departmental organisation, and backward both in the development of its material resources and of the facilities (such as roads) required for the purpose. The South required a better organisation of its Native Administration and of its judicial system.

Part II.—Method of Amalgamation
General Scheme. Division of the Country—Central Departments

9. Amalgamation, January 1st, 1914.—On January 1st, 1914, the former Governments of Southern and Northern Nigeria were formally amalgamated with some fitting ceremonial. After the oaths of office had been taken at each capital—Lagos and Zungeru—by the Governor-General, the Lieutenant-Governors, and the Chief Justice, etc., a Durbar was held on the great plain at Kano, which was attended by all the chief Moslem rulers from Sokoto to Chad, who met for the first time in common friendship to swear allegiance to His Majesty, and by representatives of the principal Pagan tribes. Though the retinue of the chiefs was necessarily limited by considerations of food supply, etc., it was estimated that not fewer than 30,000 horsemen took part in the picturesque display. Each in turn marched past and then gave the Salute of the Desert, charging at full gallop with brandished weapons. Nor was the gathering a mere ceremonial. Hereditary rivals met as friends. The Shehu of Bornu was the honoured guest of his quondam enemy, the Fulani Emir of Kano, and no friction or dispute for precedence among their somewhat turbulent following disturbed the harmony of this remarkable gathering, which undoubtedly had a very beneficial effect. A uniform time for Nigeria (viz., 7½° meridian)—half an hour fast of Greenwich—was established for railway and telegraphic convenience. A single weekly Gazette, with a supplement containing all ephemeral matter, superseded the former publications. The "General Orders" of the former Administrations were cancelled, and replaced as soon as possible by Standing Orders common to all Nigeria. The printed forms in use in all departments were revised and largely reduced. A new Colonial badge was introduced consisting of the interlaced triangles known as "Solomon's Seal."

10. The Governor-General.—The whole of Nigeria—the size of which approximates to one-third that of British India, with a population of 16 or 17 millions, the largest of the Crown Colonies and the Protectorates of the Empire—was placed under the control of a Governor-General, but it was intimated that the title was personal to myself. The Letters Patent and other Instruments setting up the new Government omitted the usual provision that when the Governor was absent from Nigeria his Deputy should administer the Government, for it had been decided that the Governor should spend four months of each year *on duty* in England. The object of this somewhat startling departure from precedent was to preserve continuity of Administration, to keep closer touch, by the personal presence of the Governor, with the Colonial Office and the commercial and other interests in England, and to give the Governor some time to carry through the heavy work of re-drafting laws, etc., while relieved of the onus of comparatively unimportant daily routine in Africa. He was when absent from Nigeria represented by a Deputy, fully empowered to deal with all matters of urgency, with whom he was in telegraphic communication. It was not desired to decrease the responsibility of "the man on the spot"—the change, as

Mr. Churchill expressed it, consisted rather of a definition of "the spot" due to the rapid means of transport and communication which steam and telegraphy had introduced. A room was provided at the Colonial Office for the use of the Governor and his Private Secretary and clerk.

The system served its purpose, and without it I doubt if the work could have been accomplished. It presented obvious difficulties, and the Secretary of State decided to cancel it in 1917. It demands only a brief reference here, as an integral part of the method by which amalgamation was carried out.

11. Duties of Governor.—The Governor directs the policy in regard to Native Administration, and with him rests the initiative in all legislation (by means of Ordinance, Regulations, or Orders in Council), which is of course exercised with the advice of the Executive Council, the approval (in accordance with the Royal Instructions) of all except temporary leases, and the direct control of the "Central" Departments (to which I shall presently refer). He alone corresponds with the Secretary of State, and all matters such as the promotion of European officers, and financial sanctions, which require such reference, are referred to him.

His personal office consists of a Political Assistant and a Private Secretary. The former is an officer ranking in seniority with a Secretary or Resident. In my own emphatic opinion, and that of both Lieutenant Governors, this post should be continuously held and by a Senior Officer. All confidential reports (including those on the Lieutenant Governors) and secret papers pass through his hands, and he is able to relieve the Governor of many interviews and to carry through many confidential matters, which could not be entrusted to a junior however able.

The Private Secretary is at present selected from among the juniors in the Secretariat. His time is very fully occupied with the office routine. Both appointments afford an excellent training for their holders. An extra junior is accordingly provided on the establishment of the Central Secretariat, and an extra subaltern as A.D.C. in the W.A.F.F.

12. Lieutenant Governors and the Division of the Country.—I recommended that the Administrative areas of Northern and Southern Nigeria should be placed under two Lieutenant Governors, without any territorial change, each with a Secretariat and departmental organisation, while those Departments which were practically indivisible, and whose functions were common to both, should be centralised under the direct control of the Governor-General assisted by a Central Secretariat. The small area which constitutes the Crown Colony (as opposed to the Protectorate) would form a separate Administration under an Administrator, sharing its departmental staff with the Southern Administration.

The two Administrations thus formed were called the Northern and Southern Provinces. The former had an area of 255,700 square miles and a population of approximately 9,000,000, the latter an area of 76,700 square miles and a reputed population of 7,750,000. The Colony comprised 1,335 square miles and a population of 154,000. It was for the first time properly demarcated and defined in the Letters Patent.

The separation of the Administration of the Colony from that of the Southern Provinces, though advisable during the transition period, could not be expected to work well so long as the headquarters of both were in the same place (Lagos), nor was there sufficient scope for an officer ranking next below a Lieutenant Governor, while the intimate connection between the Colony and Southern Province affairs caused an inevitable duplication of work, and rendered the demarcation of duties impossible. The post has therefore latterly remained in abeyance, the duties being merged in those of the Lieutenant Governor and the separate Secretariat abolished.

When the unification of the Laws, etc., had been completed in 1917, the boundaries of the Northern and Southern Provinces—drawn when the territory had not yet been explored, and depending on no geographical or ethnological features—were carefully revised so as no longer to bisect tribal units, except where by the usage of 17 years a fraction of a tribe had become incorporated with its neighbour.

13. Duties and Powers of Lieutenant Governors.—Central Departments.— Each Lieutenant Governor is (under the general control of the Governor-General) charged with the direct administration of the area to which he is appointed, submitting to the Governor-General any question which affects Nigeria as a whole, or which involves a ruling as to general policy or legislative action, or is otherwise of sufficient importance for reference. He also keeps the Governor-General informed on all matters. He submits his annual budget of Revenue and Expenditure for approval and incorporation in the general budget. He is not superseded by the presence of the Governor-General in his area of jurisdiction. To enable him to undertake these duties the statutory powers vested in the Governor by Ordinance are, as required, delegated by Gazette notice. Similarly the executive powers which a Lieutenant Governor is authorised to exercise are formally notified, in order that no confusion may arise.

Each Lieutenant Governor has a private secretary, a Secretariat and the various departments necessary to an Administration, *e.g.,* Political, Medical, Public Works, Forestry, Agriculture, Education, Police, Prisons and Mines—to which in the Southern Provinces are added Marine, Customs and Printing. The two former were for special reasons at first treated as Central (*see* paras. 34 and 35), but were later included in the Southern Provinces, to which their work is almost entirely confined.

The "Central" Departments, under the direct control of the Governor-General as being common to both, are the Railway (including the Colliery), the Military, the Audit, Treasury, Post and Telegraphs, Judicial and Legal (each Lieutenant Governor having a legal adviser) and the Survey. The heads of these Departments when on leave are replaced by an officer exercising their full powers. To these will be added this year a Geological Survey. In addition "a Director of the Medical and Sanitary Services" acts as Adviser to the

Governor-General, and superintends the Departments in both Administrations, without interfering with their departmental organization (*see* para. 36). A similar office is held by the "Director of Forests," while the "Director of Railways and Works" not only bears the same relation to the Public Works departments in the North and South, and to the "Open Lines" railway, but is directly responsible for all new construction, and advises on matters of Railway policy and extension and on Loan Works (*see* para. 37). No substitutes are required for these "Common Heads" when on leave.

14. Reasons for the Division.—Various other schemes of amalgamation had been put forward. They were all based on the principle of dividing the territory into a large number of units—from 4 to 7—each under the control of a high official responsible to the Governor-General. They were fully described in my original report, and there is no need to discuss them here.

My reasons for preferring the retention of the old boundaries—subject to modification later—were as follows: — (1). There appeared no adequate reason for creating a third Lieutenant Governorship, since the work and responsibility which had hitherto devolved upon the Governors of Northern and Southern Nigeria, would under the new scheme be considerably reduced by the transfer of all larger questions of policy, with legislation, regulations, general orders, and the control of all Central Departments to the Governor-General. (2). Each of the two former Administrations was under a separate body of laws, and the executive policy embodied in general orders and other instructions differed, as also did the conditions of service of both European and Native Staff. A territorial re-division which transferred portions of one Administration to the other, or included portions of each in a new Administration, would have been productive of chaos, and interminable appeals for "Rulings," at a moment when the inevitable pressure on the Central Government was greatest. It appeared to me incontestable that the unification of the laws, general orders and policy, and the adjustment of the finances, should precede the creation of any new Administration. Moreover, the multiplicity of Secretariats, and the reduplication of Departmental Heads, involved by the creation of a number of subordinate Administrations appeared to me to be an insuperable objection, involving unnecessary correspondence, duplication of work, and needless cost. Without such duplication the Lieutenant Governorships would become mere provinces, under a greatly overweighted and highly centralised Government. This would inevitably result (*inter alia*) in much delay, in a country of such vast distances and imperfect communications. It would in effect have been the adoption of the "provincial system" of Southern Nigeria (which is described in the next para.) rendered more than ever difficult by increased distances. The Governor-General would be tied to headquarters and the management of a large Secretariat. He would be unable to travel, and would have great difficulty in preserving uniformity of policy among the several Administrations, and little time to devote to larger questions of policy. Owing also to the system of leave in West Africa, the large powers vested in the Lieutenant Governors must have been exercised by others in their absence necessitating a very large number of men qualified to exercise high office. The simultaneous creation of 4 to 7 new Governments, the distribution from existing Secretariats of the records belonging to each, and the absence of buildings for public offices, would all add to the difficulty, and postpone effective amalgamation for many years. My conception on the other hand was that the office of Lieutenant Governor should be one of recognised executive responsibility, to which should be delegated many of the statutory and executive functions of the Governor-General by a process of decentralization.

15. Provincial Administration and Departmental Control.—Prior to Amalgamation Northern Nigeria had, for the purposes of Native Administration, been divided into 13 provinces under "Residents." Illorin and Kabba, two very small ones South of the Niger, were now amalgamated, and later Bassa and Muri were reorganised. The provinces of the North are now approximately as follows:

Name of Province.	Area in sq. miles.	Population.	Name of Province.	Area in sq. miles.	Population.
*Sokoto.......	35,400	1,262,300	Kontagora....	27,000	118,400
*Kano........	28,600	3,398,300	Illorin........	14,100	330,100
*Bornu........	32,800	679,700	Nassarawa....	17,900	582,600
*Bauchi.......	24,700	679,700	Munshi.......	17,000	471,000
*Zaria.........	9,850	390,300	Muri.........	15,600	407,800
Nupe.........	18,450	388,500	Yola.........	14,300	291,300

Total Area and Population.................... 255,700   9,000,000**

*First class. **Approximately 5,855,000 Moslems, 3,135,000 Pagans, and 10,000 Christians.

Southern Nigeria had comprised three "Divisions" under Provincial Commissioners—viz., the territories of the former Southern Nigeria east and west of the Niger, and the hinterland of Lagos. The Provincial Commissioners were charged with the supervision of all Departments in their Divisions, and were in fact, though not in name, Lieut.-Governors, but without adequate Secretariat assistance. As their duties increased the tendency for the Commissioners' Office to become a small Secretariat developed. The Provincial Commissioners, charged with much administrative and departmental work, found, they said, little time to supervise the District Staff, and the Governor and Colonial Secretary were quite out of touch with the administration of native affairs. Since the supervision of both the "District" and the Native Courts was in the hands of the Puisne Judges, the District Commissioners looked to them in a great part of their work. The District Commissioners were also largely employed in departmental duties connected with the Customs, Treasury and Public Works, which seriously interfered with their duties as Administrative Officers. All Departmental officers corresponded through the Provincial Commissioners, even on technical details—a system which involved delay and circumlocution, rendered the position of the Head of the Department most difficult, and deprived him of control. Stores were ordered from England by the Provincial Commissioners independently, with the result of extra cost and accumulations.

With the creation of Lieut.-Governors with definite areas of administration, and not merely as the *alter ego* of the Governor, the function of the Provincial Commissioner naturally expired. The Southern Protectorate was divided into nine Provinces, averaging considerably less than half the average size of Northern Provinces, but with an approximately equal population, each under a Resident (as in the Northern Provinces) and divided into three or more divisions under "District Officers" (1st and 2nd class) with their assistant District Officers, the number varying according to the size, population, and needs of each Province. The five most important in the Northern Provinces, and three in the Southern Provinces, are "1st class" under Residents of the 1st class. The area and population of the Provinces of the Southern Administration are as follows: —

Name of Province.	Area in sq. miles.	Population.	Name of Province.	Area in sq. miles.	Population.
*Oyo..........	14,872	1,027,000	Onitsha.......	7,519	1,342,000
*Owerri.......	7,613	1,272,000	Ondo.........	6,051	384,000
*Abeokuta.....	6,694	552,000	Benin........	8,799	567,000
Calabar......	6,248	871,000	Warri........	9,342	515,000
Ogoja........	8,211	1,066,000	*The Colony*....	1,335	154,000
Total Area and Population.....................				76,684	7,750,000

*First Class. British Cameroons area, 31,150 square miles. Population, 600,000 (?).

Since the beginning of 1916 the Cameroons occupied territory South of Lat. 7° 10' (18,000 square miles) has been added as a Province to the South, while the smaller areas in the North were absorbed in the Provinces of Yola and Bornu.

There are, therefore, 21 Provinces in Nigeria (exclusive of the Colony and the Cameroons) with an average area of 16,000 square miles and a population of about 800,000. The average Staff for the administration of these large units (reduced by over one-third during the War and by the Staff required for the Colony and Cameroons) is 12 officers (viz., 8 in the country and 4 on leave) inclusive of sick, vacancies, etc.

The Resident of a Province, as the senior Government official, is, generally speaking, responsible as such for the efficiency of the Public Service in his Province. He is, however, primarily concerned with the Native Administration, including the conduct of the Provincial and Native Courts. Control of his subordinates by the Head of each Department is now preserved. He delegates duties and responsibilities to them as may be necessary, and not to an Administrative officer, and conveys his professional and technical orders direct. If a difference should arise between the Resident and a Departmental officer it is referred to the Lieut.-Governor or to the Departmental Head, and if necessary eventually to the Governor-General.

Native Administration

16. Reason of Divergent Policy in the North and South.—It is a truism to observe that in a country possessing a native population of upwards of 16 millions, the policy of the Government and its methods of administration of the native races stands first in importance. It is the natural protector and the permanent trustee of the welfare of these races, while safeguarding the interests of the comparative handful of traders and missionaries who form the constantly changing European population, few of whom remain for very many years in the country. It is almost equally obvious that since the boundaries of North and South were, as I have already described, mere parallels of latitude, in many cases leaving part of a tribal area in one Administration and the remainder in the other, some uniformity in policy was highly desirable. At the time of Amalgamation, however, both policy and method were profoundly divergent.

This divergence was in part due to deliberate differences of Administrative method and organisation, in part due to the earlier history of each Government and the circumstances which had moulded its development under British rule, and in part to the characteristics of the people themselves. Southern Nigeria had been much longer under British rule. Its wealth in oleaginous produce had attracted large numbers of traders, chiefly British and German, whose influence had naturally been in the direction of material development of roads, waterways, and trade. Northern Nigeria, prior to the transfer from the Royal Niger Company in 1900, had practically no system of Native Administration, and the officials of the Chartered Company were unable to go far from the banks of the Niger and Benue. The interior was dominated by powerful Emirs, who commanded large armies. The initial task of the new Government had been to check slave-raids and constant warfare, and this could only be done by defeating the Emirs and imposing upon them the authority of Government. As a consequence the problem of Native policy and Administration was one which forced itself upon the Northern Government at the very beginning, whereas in the South the trader and the missionary were the pioneers, and it was only such events as the massacre at Benin, the outbreak at Brass, or the unavoidable necessity of dealing with such barbarous cults as that of the Aro fetish, with its wholesale human sacrifice and slavery, which compelled the Government to take strong action. The Southern Provinces were populated by tribes in the lowest stage of primitive savagery without any central organisation, except in the West where the Yorubas, Egbas, Benis and some minor allied tribes had developed a social organisation under paramount Chiefs, but, in the early years, they were still addicted to many barbarous rites. A great part of the North, on the other hand, had come under the influence of Islam, and the Hausa States and Bornu had an elaborate administrative machinery, though it had become corrupt and degraded. There remained, however, in the North a vast population of Pagans in a similar stage of savagery to those in the South.

*   *   *

The Courts of Law

44. The Former System.—The "Supreme Court," the "Provincial Courts," the "Native Courts" and the "Criminal Procedure" Ordinances of 1914 effected very important changes in the judicial system of the South, which was assimilated to that prevailing in the North, while no change of importance was made as regards the Colony. These changes curtailed the activities of the local Bar in certain directions, and have in consequence been the subject of much criticism, and of several petitions to the Secretary of State. Their intrinsic importance, moreover, justifies a full account, both of the alterations introduced, and of the effect which they have had.

(a) Supreme Court.—Under the pre-existing system the jurisdiction of the Supreme Court extended, for all practical purposes, throughout the old Protectorate of Southern Nigeria with limited powers ceded by treaty in Egba-land, [which was "independent" and where a "Mixed Court" existed] and also in Oyo, Jebu-Ode, and Ife. The rest of the old Lagos Protectorate was not subject to the jurisdiction of any British Court, or if subject no provision had been made for the exercise of any such jurisdiction. The Chief Justice and Puisne Judges sat at certain places, and visited on Assize the "District Courts" held by Political Officers, who sat as Commissioners of the Supreme Court and submitted to the Judges monthly their lists of cases. These lists operated as appeals and there was also an independent appeal. The procedure of these Courts was of course that of the Supreme Court.

45. (b) Native Courts.—The Native Courts of the former Southern Nigeria Protectorate exercised a jurisdiction concurrent with that of the Supreme Court, and had powers up to six months' imprisonment, and in civil suits up to £25 fine. (To the Native Courts of the Lagos Protectorate I shall refer later.)

The District Officer sat as President *ex officio,* and exercised in that capacity higher powers than he possessed as a Commissioner of the Supreme Court in his District Court. He passed sentence, but was largely relieved of responsibility, since the judgment was in theory that of the Native Chiefs, in whose name it was recorded. A large number of Native Chiefs were appointed as members and sat by rotation, but the Courts were without educative value to them, since they also were deprived of responsibility by the presence of the District Officer.

To each Court was attached a native clerk, who was supposed to keep full records, and since the Court was conducted in accordance with Supreme Court procedure, and apparently administered English law [modified by native custom in marriage cases, &c.], the clerk, a semi-educated person on a low salary, dominated the native chiefs in the absence of the District Officer, and exercised an undue authority in the issue of the processes of Court with its manifold printed forms. He was exposed to great temptation and not unnaturally often succumbed to it. Cases were reported in which the clerk had accepted bribes, tried cases himself, and even terrorised the Chiefs by publicly turning out any member whom he wished to disgrace. There were other and even worse charges in some cases, though many no doubt have done their duty to the best of their ability. Mr. Osborne, Chief Justice of Southern Nigeria, stated that in his opinion "the dishonesty of the Native Court clerks was the chief evil of the system." The fines and fees of Court were I believe in some cases the perquisite of the Native Judges, but in the Eastern and Central Divisions were credited to a Fund which amounted to a very large sum, and was at the disposal of the Provincial Commissioner. It was spent partly on sitting fees and salaries, partly on road making, &c. It was subject to no audit and did not appear in the Budget.

The Judges of the Supreme Court could transfer any case to another Native Court, to the District Court or to the Supreme Court. They were supposed to review the cases (as well as those of the District Courts), but it was impossible for them to discharge such a task, nor were the records kept by the Court Clerk adequate for the purpose.

The number of cases heard in these Native Courts was more than double the number heard in the Supreme, District and Police Courts combined. An appeal lay to the Supreme Court, and such appeals, prompted by native lawyers, naturally led to endless litigation among a very litigious and illiterate people, to the benefit of the lawyers and the ruin of the suitors.

At the time when Native Courts were first established in the old Southern Nigeria Protectorate, the tribal authority had already broken down, and had been succeeded by a complete collapse of native rule under the disintegrating influence of middlemen traders, and of the Aros. The latter are described as professional slave-traders who ruled by the terror of their *Juju*. The Native Courts no doubt did much to re-establish tribal authority, and their usefulness is shown by their growing influence and the number of cases with which they dealt. They had prepared the way for a further advance.

In the old Lagos Protectorate the Native Councils Ordinance purported to set up native tribunals, but it was practically a dead letter, and was never really brought into force except perhaps at Ibadan. In the small unimportant and neglected territories of Illesha and Ondo practically the old Native Courts continued to try cases under, or perhaps without supervision by, the District Commissioner, who as a matter of fact did not sit on the Native Council except perhaps in very important cases. "It is difficult to describe a system where in fact no system existed" says the Chief Justice (Sir E. Speed) from whose account I have quoted. The Native Councils exercised a complete jurisdiction, without appeal or revision, and were empowered to inflict sentences of death or of penal servitude without review by the Supreme Court or any judicial authority. Any interference with them was political not judicial, and some of the Chiefs who exercised these powers had very bad reputations. The Supreme Court had no jurisdiction, or at any rate exercised none in the Lagos Protectorate except under the agreements with Ibadan, Ife, and Jebu-Ode.

46. Description of Former System by Chief Justice.—The judicial system of Southern Nigeria as it existed prior to 1914 is described by the Chief Justice in his report of October, 1917 [*see* Appendix 3]. He pointed out that Assizes could only be held in a limited number of places. Cases must therefore be heard at great distances from the scene of action, and at infrequent intervals, so that prisoners were kept for long periods awaiting trial, and cases broke down owing to the absence of witnesses, who had often to be treated as prisoners themselves. Difficulties and friction with the Executive arose from actions at law prompted by lawyers' touts, involving decisions with regard to tribal boundaries already adjudicated after careful investigation by political officers, and finally district officers had, in consequence of the pressure on the Judges, often been entrusted with the full powers of the supreme Court regardless of qualification.

Not only was the jurisdiction of the Supreme Court limited by the Treaties in the Western Division, but throughout the Protectorate "its activities were circumscribed by the fact that its organisation was faulty. It was never adequately manned. The greater portion of the territory had been very recently brought under control, means of communication were limited or non-existent, and the Court was unprovided with the necessary equipment to enable it to perform the duties nominally imposed upon it by law. Its staff was so small, and its organisation so rudimentary, that outside the trading centres and coast towns its criminal jurisdiction was rarely exercised, and its civil jurisdiction was only invoked for the purpose of adjudicating upon disputes on land boundaries fostered by the large army of native lawyers attending in the Native Courts."

Speaking of the criminal jurisdiction of the Supreme Court, the Chief Justice writes: —"The greatest enemy to the efficient administration of the Criminal Law is delay, and delay is inherent in the Supreme Court system . . . A considerable proportion of the crime thus goes unpunished, and a further considerable proportion is inadequately punished, in order to avoid committal for trial, or remitted to Native Courts and tried without much reference to the principles of English justice." With regard to civil actions the late Chief Justice of Southern Nigeria (Mr. W. Osborne) had also expressed the view that the jurisdiction of the Supreme Court in civil cases in newly administered districts was a danger. The results were so bad that in 1911 an Order in Council had been passed depriving the Supreme Court of a large part of its jurisdiction in matters relating to land. (*See* Mr. Osborne's report in Appendix 3.)

47. Object and Nature of Changes in 1914.—It is evident from this brief summary that reform was urgently needed, and prior to my return to Nigeria in 1912 I had examined the whole question at the Colonial Office, with a view to extending to the South in its main essentials the system which I had set up in the North in 1900, and which had proved suitable there. Sir Edwin Speed, Chief Justice of Northern Nigeria, who had had long experience as Attorney-General in the South, and who became Chief Justice of Nigeria on amalgamation, undertook to draft the necessary legislation. Mr. Willoughby Osborne, Chief Justice of Southern Nigeria, was fully consulted while in England, and agreed with the drafts in principle. Sir E. Speed's object was "to evolve a system applicable to the whole country, with only such disturbance of existing conditions as was necessary in the interest of good government."

The considerations which presented themselves to him in making his recommendations are set out in his Report (*see* Appendix 3). Briefly they were that the Colony of Lagos (as distinct from the Protectorate) was in possession of a properly organised judicial system, which had for many years proved adequate and which no one with any local knowledge would have thought of disturbing, that the functions of the Supreme Court of Northern Nigeria could easily be performed by the Supreme Court of the Colony of Lagos with only a slight increase of staff; that the Provincial Court system, which had been in operation in Northern Nigeria for over 10 years [for five years of which he had himself revised the returns and confirmed the sentences] had proved itself an unqualified success.

With the object therefore both of reforming the judicial system of the South, and of establishing uniformity throughout Nigeria, the Northern system with some slight modification was adopted, and Provincial Courts were established throughout the Southern Provinces, together with Native Courts subject to strict supervision by Political Officers, and invested with a jurisdiction strictly limited in accordance with the capacity of the members. The jurisdiction of the Supreme Court was confined to the commercial centres, where alone it had been continuously and regularly exercised from the time when the territories were first administered, with due provision for whatever extension circumstances should appear to require. In addition to its original local jurisdiction the Supreme Court was constituted a Court of Appeal from the Provincial Courts in civil matters, and the widest possible powers of transfer thereto from the Provincial Courts were vested both in the Governor and the Chief Justice.

When introducing the Supreme Court Bill in March, 1914, I informed the Legislative Council that these Ordinances had been drafted more than a year previously by the Chief Justice of Northern Nigeria, and submitted for the comments of the Chief Justice of Southern Nigeria, whose valuable suggestions had been for the most part adopted, and in principle they had received the approval of the Secretary of State. They were, therefore, "the result of mature and careful consideration, with the highest technical and legal advice." They were supported almost unanimously by the officers of the longest judicial and legal experience in the country. Sir E. Speed wrote, "The Supreme Court system has been tried in the Southern Nigeria Protectorate, and has in my opinion proved a failure, . . . I have every confidence that these measures will secure a more efficient administration from a judicial as well as from an executive point of view."

48. The New System: (a) Supreme Court.—Under the new Ordinance the jurisdiction of the Supreme Court is limited territorially to the Colony, and certain defined areas in which a large number of non-natives and native foreigners reside, while it exercises a concurrent jurisdiction with the Provincial Court over all non-natives throughout Nigeria. The definition of a "non-native" was simultaneously revised and simplified. By a later arrangement Egbaland and Yorubaland were fully included under the jurisdiction of the Supreme and Provincial Courts, so that a single judicial procedure was established throughout the whole of Nigeria. Any case can at any time be transferred, with the consent of the Chief Justice, from a Provincial to the Supreme Court, on application by one of the parties, or by a Resident. Mr. Osborne desired to vest the power of transfer in the Governor only. Police and station magistrates, and any Political Officer exercising judicial functions within the "local limits" of the Supreme Court, does so as a Commissioner of that Court.

49. (b) Provincial Courts.—The Provincial Courts now set up in the South had been in successful operation for nearly 15 years in the North. The full powers of the Court, which are unlimited, are exercised only by the Resident of the Province in which it is constituted, and by such other officers as may from their qualifications be granted such powers by the Governor. All Political Officers are Commissioners of the Court with varying powers, and any other officer may be so appointed. Unofficials of standing may, in exceptional cases, be appointed Justices of the Peace, and thus also become Commissioners of the Court. The Court exercises jurisdiction over all classes of persons throughout the Province, except in those areas in which the Supreme Court has exclusive jurisdiction. All sentences in excess of six months' imprisonment, 12 strokes, or £50 fine, require confirmation by the Governor-General, who may reduce or modify the sentence, or order re-trial before the same or another Court. These powers of confirmation have, in practice, been delegated to Lieutenant-Governors, advised by their Legal Advisers (but *see* paragraph 53). In the Southern Provinces, however, for some time past the duty has been discharged by the Chief Justice, and in the Northern Provinces all capital sentences are reviewed and confirmed by him. Appeals in Civil Causes over £50 lie to the Supreme Court. No legal practitioner may appear before the Provincial Court, or in an appeal to the Supreme Court, except in the latter case, by leave of the Chief Justice or the presiding Judge when any legal point is in dispute.

50. Provincial Courts contrasted with the former System.—Contrasting the Provincial Court system with the system which it superseded in the Southern Provinces, the Chief Justice observed that it brings English justice practially to the door of everyone. The same law is administered by the same men who as Commissioners of the Supreme Court sat as District Court Judges, "the only difference being that the procedure is summary . . . and that *no* cases come automatically before the Judges of the Supreme Court."

Dealing with the objection that some of the Provincial Court Judges are not trained lawyers, he pointed out that under the new Ordinance the District Commissioners are "surrounded by safeguards which practically prevent any serious miscarriage of justice," that only the senior and experienced officers have unlimited jurisdiction, subject to review and confirmation, and that against the lack of legal training must be set knowledge of the locality and people, and an increasing knowledge of the language, while the free exercise of the power of transfer to the Supreme Court must not be ignored. The result of the new law is in fact greatly to curtail the independent powers of district officers, which are now granted according to qualification, while all important sentences must be confirmed. These officers have now to pass an examination in law, and also in the native language, and their promotion largely depends on their judicial work, which now comes under the purview of the Executive.

In reference to the complaint that the right to be represented by Counsel is denied in the Provincial Courts, the Chief Justice remarks that "every single officer political and judicial who has had any experience of districts recently brought under control has pronounced emphatically against it." He points out that when the Judicial Agreements with the Egba, Ibadan, and Oyo native authorities were negotiated, they insisted of their own accord on inserting a clause excluding lawyers from the Courts in their territories. He added various cogent reasons for their exclusion (*vide* Appendix 3). The late Chief Justice of Southern Nigeria, Mr. Willoughby Osborne, and many others of experience were also particularly insistent on the advisability of this exclusion, which he proposed should extend to all appeals from Provincial Courts heard in the Supreme Court. There can be no doubt that the appearance of Counsel in the District Courts—and even in Native Courts—under the old system, had led to the fomenting of litigation by lawyers' agents, especially in land cases, with disastrous results to the ignorant people who had spent their substance in bootless litigation.

51. (c) The New Native Courts.—The Native Courts set up under the new Ordinance were also modelled on the Northern Nigeria principle, but considerable changes were introduced. The Courts are of three types, and each Court exercises such powers as are accorded to it by the Warrant under which it is constituted. The powers are "graded" and the Court is described as of the A to D grade according to the powers vested in it.

(*a*) The "Judicial Council" is a Native Court usually of the A or B grade, presided over by a Paramount Chief with his principal officials as members, including as a rule in Moslem States an "Alkali" or other person learned in Moslem law. Under a separate instrument it is vested with executive powers by the Governor-General and forms the Head Chief's Council. Its judicial functions may be limited to quasi-political matters, such as land disputes, &c., or it may exercise a general jurisdiction, though ordinary criminal cases are left to the Alkali's Court.

(*b*) The second type is the single Judge Court, presided over in Moslem States by a trained "Alkali," and in Egbaland by a native with some judicial training. He may sit with native assistants or assessors. The powers vested in these Courts vary considerably, and there is usually a right of appeal from the district and market Courts to the Chief Native Court at the provincial capital.

(*c*) The third type consists of a number of petty chiefs, and is usually vested with very limited criminal jurisdiction, but more extensive civil powers for dealing with matrimonial, debt, trespass and petty assault cases. It is adapted to the primitive Pagan tribes, and in the Southern Province consists of as many as 20 or 30 members, who sit sometimes with a permanent President, but more often under the presidency of one or other by rotation, and are paid sitting fees when summoned to attend. The number of members is being steadily reduced, partly by the selection only of the most capable, and partly by the creation of additional Courts to serve more restricted areas. Most of the Courts in the Southern Provinces are of this type and exercise much less power than they formerly did.

The powers vested in the Native Courts are entrusted to the Chiefs (or Native Judges) themselves, closely supervised by the District Officer, who is not a member, but has access to them at all times, and may transfer any case at any stage to his own Court, or order a re-trial, or suspend or modify any sentence. The clerk is the servant, not the master, of the Court, which is conducted with as simple a procedure as possible, and deals with native law and custom only. His power is therefore greatly curtailed. The object in view is to educate the chiefs by giving them a sense of responsibility, and gradually to extend their powers as they show themselves to be qualified.

Courts of the A grade may inflict the death penalty, but these powers are restricted to a few Courts presided over by Alkali learned in Mohammedan law. The case is reviewed by the Resident, and before the sentence can be carried out it, of course, comes before the Governor in Council.

Natives who are either Government servants (in which term carriers and labourers are not included), or who are not ordinarily subject to the jurisdiction of Native Courts, and do not reside permanently in the Court's jurisdiction, are amenable to the jurisdiction of a Native Court, in civil cases only with their own consent or that of the Resident (who can only give his consent in certain circumstances), and in criminal cases, only with their own consent or that of the Lieut.-Governor. The Governor may also exempt any person, or class of persons, from the jurisdiction of any Court. These provisions are made to meet the case of native British subjects, or other aliens residing in the jurisdiction of the Court. Legal practitioners may not practise in Native Courts, the procedure of which is in no way modelled on that of the British Courts. They administer native law and custom only.

52. *Result of the Change.*—Such is the new system in contrast with the one it superseded. At the end of the year the Chief Justice was already able to write:—"The new judicial system, as far as I am able to judge, is a complete and unqualified success. I have heard no complaints as to the curtailment of the Supreme Court jurisdiction, and I am quite confident that no legitimate Civil business is being, or is likely to be, excluded, while crime is being, and will be, more rapidly and as satisfactorily tried as under the old system. There are now practically no arrears in either division—indeed, the success of the system has exceeded my most sanguine expectation."

A year later (January, 1916) he reported that the volume of business was equal to the previous average in both divisions of the Supreme Court and had been handled without any special effort, and without delay, other than that attributable to the parties, and there were no arrears. The whole of the arrears of the old Southern Nigeria Supreme Court had been cleared off. "That the work is up to the average, in spite of the fact that most of the land cases, which formerly almost filled the cause lists, have been withdrawn from the jurisdiction, amply justifies my original opinion that legitimate commercial business would soon compensate the profession for the loss of a class of work brought neither credit to the profession nor advantage to the public." He concludes, "the result of the first year's working has been to show that, for the first time in the history of the Colony and Protectorate, the Supreme Court has been adequately manned, arrears having been cleared off and business kept up to date without any outside assistance, and that an organisation has been brought into existence capable of meeting all reasonable demands which may be made upon it." "These words," he added later, "have been fully justified by the result of the second year's working."

In October, 1917, the Chief Justice again reported, at my request, on the working of the judicial system as a whole, which had now been in operation for three complete years. He was the better able to do so since he had for the previous nine months undertaken the duty of confirming sentences and revising the returns of the Southern Province, as he had previously done in the Northern Province for five years. Extracts from his report will be found in Appendix 3. Briefly, his opinion is that cases had been carefully and well dealt with, and that the Provincial Courts had proved themselves well adapted to the circumstances, on account of the simplicity and rapidity of their procedure. This was proved by the few transfers applied for, which were in almost every case at the instance of the Court itself, while the number of appeals were insignificant. (From Calabar, whence the loudest protests had emanated, there were only two appeals, both in land cases, and both were upheld.) In three and a quarter years leave to appeal was granted in eleven cases. There were 18 applications for transfer to the Supreme Court made by parties, of which 8 were refused. To facilitate appeals he had simplified the procedure.

Meanwhile the business of the Supreme Court has increased and has been dealt with without assistance or delay, in spite of the withdrawal of the land cases. The powers of confirmation had in the Southern Provinces been delegated to the Chief Justice instead of the Lieut.-Governor, and he expressed the view that this should be done in the Northern Provinces also, not because the Chief Justice was likely to take a different view from the Lieut.-Governor, but because it was possible that political officers might regard the Courts as an arm of the Executive, and they should be under purely judicial control.

He expressed a lack of confidence in the Native Courts except the higher tribunals in the Northern Provinces, but agreed that by British tradition the people were entitled to be trained to take part in their own administration, and the political staff could not possibly provide sufficient Courts to settle all petty disputes. He arrives at the conclusion that the new system has fully justified expectations, that the Northern Provinces have benefitted by a wider horizon, while in the Southern Provinces the Yorubas have for the first time had access to a British Court, and Government can effect by law what it previously could only do by political pressure. Elsewhere in the Southern Provinces the system is a great improvement, and is understood by the people; all who require, or have a traditional right, to resort to the Supreme Court can do so, and the necessary safeguards against oppression and corruption in the Native Courts have been maintained and strengthened. He concludes as follows: —"In conclusion I venture to express the opinion that the organisation of the Courts of the Colony and Protectorate, which has now stood the test of three years' working, has answered the expectations which were formed of it, is adequate for the needs of the community, and is capable of expansion and development, sufficient for any situation which can reasonably be anticipated for a considerable time to come."

It is also noteworthy that the number of convictions has very greatly increased since 1913, the reason given being that justice is now adequately enforced, whereas previously the difficulty and delay resulted in the condonation of crime.

*　*　*

Education

157. Position as regards Education.—Of the many problems which Amalgamation presented there was none comparable in importance and in urgency with that of education. The problem differs so profoundly in the North and South, not merely in its history, and the stage which had been reached, but in some respects in its very nature, that it is desirable to review briefly the conditions of each Administration separately.

(a) In Southern Nigeria.—In Southern Nigeria, of which the coast area had been open to European influence for upwards of half a century, there were (as might be expected) a very large number of schools, by the agency of which a great part of the coast population had attained a degree of education varying from a few barristers and doctors who had qualified in England, to the less than half educated school boys who, with a smattering of English and arithmetic, seek admission to the lower ranks of the clerical and other services. In 1913 the average attendance at Government schools in the South was about 4,600, and in assisted mission schools about 12,500. To these must be added a number of pupils vaguely estimated at from 20,000 to 30,000 in unassisted schools, which were not only under no control or inspection by Government, but of whose very numbers or existence the Government had no precise information.

Both Government and assisted schools were lamentably understaffed. With the exception of King's College, a small school for the sons of comparatively wealthy parents (average attendance 50)—the only Government schools which possessed a British instructor were at Warri and Bonny. The remainder of the European personnel of the Education Department consisted of inspectors who assessed the grant for assisted schools after an annual examination in set subjects. Nor was the personnel of the qualified native teaching staff in any way adequate. In Government schools it numbered 31 only, viz., one teacher to 148 pupils, in mission schools 1 to 91, in unassisted schools it was estimated at 1 to 800.

The cost of the Government schools was about £12,500, and of the grants to, and inspectorate of, assisted schools about £15,300. The net amount spent on education from revenue in the Southern Provinces and Colony in 1913 stood at £30,815, being 1.16 per cent of the ordinary revenue.

158. Government Schools in Southern Nigeria.—King's College, Lagos, with a staff of three British masters, afforded the highest and most expensive education for the sons of leading natives, or for boys of marked ability who had obtained scholarships. Some of its pupils completed their education in England, and entered the professions of law and medicine. It was not a boarding school. In the two boarding schools at Warri and Bonny, adult "apprentices" were associated with small boys, with bad results. They were under no indentures, and the Heads of Technical Departments found that their manual training had all to be begun afresh when they came to the workshops with power-driven machinery. The average attendance at these two schools in 1913 was 151 apprentices and 187 boys.

Three Moslem schools in the Colony, and 48 other elementary or primary schools under native instructors, where carpentry and agriculture, &c., were taught, completed the list of Government schools, with an average attendance of 4,200.

159. Non-Government Schools, Southern Nigeria.—The control by Government over education was only exercised to a very limited extent. Of the total number of pupils attending schools probably one-tenth were in Government schools, three-tenths in mission-assisted schools, in which the conditions of the grant code (which referred chiefly to examination subjects and buildings) had to be observed, and six-tenths in unassisted schools. These latter consisted of private venture schools and mission schools, which either had not qualified for, or did not desire to apply for, a grant, on the ground that the code was too rigid and presented gratuitous difficulties to the teaching of religion, which was the chief object of the mission schools.

Of the private venture schools there are, according to the reports of Residents, an enormous number which, in Mr. Fisher's words, are "frauds on the public," and are conducted for profit by half-educated boys and others who cannot read or write properly themselves. They are lacking in discipline and in loyalty to any constituted authority whatever, and the local chiefs find it very difficult to exercise any control over them. In some districts they are reported to be created as "outposts" by the minor missions and of no educational value. They are popular as the native considers that a "school" of any kind adds to the prestige of the village.

160. Results of Education: Southern Nigeria.—That the results of the system of education were, in the words of the Secretary of State, "generally admitted to have been very unsatisfactory" (and the same words are used by Mr. Carr (a native), Senior Inspector of Schools, after 22 years' service), is no reflection on the self-sacrifice and devotion of the missionaries, to whose efforts the country owes the existence of the class from which its supply of clerks to carry on the Administration are drawn. Some of these had done admirable work, notably the Church Missionary Society Training College at Oyo, and the Hope Waddell Institute at Calabar. But with the missions religious training was naturally the first object, towards which education was merely ancillary. That the system was at fault, as has since been admitted in India, does not detract either from the praise due to the work of the missionaries, or from the debt which the country owes to them.

It is, however, true that, with some notable exceptions, education seems to have produced discontent, impatience of any control, and an unjustified assumption of self importance in the individual. No doubt such results of the extension of education are not confined to Nigeria. The local press, inspired by a superficial and misdirected education, is, in the opinion of responsible and thoughtful natives, doing much "grievous harm" (Carr), especially among its clientèle of school-boy readers, by fomenting racial animosity, by its misrepresentation, and its invective against all Government action. This attitude is not one of recent origin. So long ago as 1882 a society had been formed in Lagos which was described by Sir G. Denton as "constituted for interference with political affairs in the hinterland, and capable of much misrepresentation and agitation." Its effect was to paralyse the efforts of the officer in charge of the Lagos "hinterland."

The situation had gone from bad to worse, and early in 1914 the late Mr. Sapara Williams, C.M.G., Senior Native Member of the Legislative Council, declared at a public meeting in Lagos, that the indiscipline and vanity of the young men produced by the schools had become so intolerable that parents were discussing the withdrawal of their sons. Something, he declared, must be done to rescue the rising generation from this deplorable state. Mr. Carr described them as ill-educated, unreliable and lacking self-control.

161. (b) Education in Northern Nigeria.—It was, as I have related elsewhere, only in 1903 that the Moslem States in the North were conquered, and access to them became possible. The task of organising an Administration absorbed all the energies of the small staff, while the natural suspicion and dislike with which the Christian Government was at first regarded by the Moslems rendered it inadvisable, even if it had been possible, to embark on any educational efforts at first. The earliest attempts to formulate a policy were made in 1905, but it was not till 1909 that Mr. Hans Vischer was able to form a small class of pupils at Kano, whose ages varied from 6 to 60. They were mostly sons of chiefs and men of influence, who had been brought from various provinces under pressure by Government. An industrial class was also formed by bringing artisans from Kano city, who plied their native trades and gave some instruction to pupils. The experiment was, however, regarded with intense suspicion and dislike by the Moslem chiefs, who thought they saw in it some deep-laid plan to subvert their religion; and the fact that Mr. Vischer had formerly been a missionary in Nigeria is said to have accentuated this fear.

Moreover, the obligation to send their sons to a distant province was very unpopular among the chiefs of outlying districts.

Towards the close of 1913 I was able to create two new schools (at Sokoto and Katsena), so that when Amalgamation took place there were, in all, three Government schools, with an average attendance of 354 pupils, all in the Moslem area. Meanwhile, many different missions had arrived to reinforce the efforts of the Church Missionary Society. They had opened altogether 43 schools, with a total attendance of about the same as that of the Government schools, and were almost entirely confined to the non-Moslem districts. No financial assistance had been given to these schools, and they were subject to no inspection or control by Government. Thus, at the time of Amalgamation the total number of pupils in Government or mission schools was between 700 and 800, out of a population of some nine millions.

Government did not interfere in the indigenous Koranic schools, in which reading and writing in the Arabic and Ajemi character, and memorising passages from the Koran formed the curriculum. They were estimated at some 25,000 with over a quarter of a million pupils. These Koranic schools had produced a literary class known as "Mallamai," learned in Arabic and the teachings of the Koran and commentaries, from whose ranks the officers of the Native Administration, the judges of the Native Courts, and the exponents of the creed of Islam were drawn. They are a very influential class, some of them very well read in Arabic literature and law, and deeply imbued with the love of learning.

162. The Language difficulty.—Throughout the Fulani Moslem States Hausa—a language easily acquired by the British staff—is spoken. In part of Bornu it is replaced by an Arabic dialect, and in Illorin by Yoruba. These languages have been reduced to writing in the Roman character, and much progress has been made in preparing text books. Hausa before the advent of the British was written in the Arabic or Ajemi character. Owing to his keen trading (and slaving) instincts the Hausa is ubiquitous, not merely in Nigeria, but throughout the Gold Coast and even as far as Sierra Leone and the Egyptian Sudan (in which pilgrims have settled). There is therefore hardly a Pagan village in which Hausa may not be heard, and it is the aim of the Administration to make it the *lingua franca* of the North except in Bornu and Illorin.

The intertribal wars and slave-raids, which constituted the early history of Nigeria, had resulted in fragments of tribes being herded together, so that to-day it is said that in one single province over sixty different languages have been identified. In Yola, Fulani (the original language of the conquering caste) is still spoken. Nupe is the language of a very large tribe, and Munshi is spoken by fully 10,000 people. Kanuri, the tongue of the aboriginal population of Bornu, is said to be impossible for a European to acquire. Some of these various languages have been studied, and reduced to writing by missionaries, but they present great difficulties and text books are not in existence. They will, no doubt, gradually be replaced by Hausa.

In the Southern Provinces, Yoruba, though a very difficult language, in which few Europeans have acquired fluency, is spoken (it is said) by three million people, and cannot be displaced. Ibo is said to be spoken by over two millions, but its dialects differ so greatly that for practical purposes they are separate languages, and the attempt to create a standard Ibo has so far had little success. For the rest there are said to be sixty-five different languages in the Southern Provinces, which have hitherto only been explored by the philologist or by an occasional missionary.

It will be realised how immensely these conditions complicate the problem of education, compared with Colonies in which there is a single vernacular with a literature of its own. In the circumstances the three languages, Hausa, Yoruba and Arabic (Shuwa dialect) should, I think, alone be recognised as media of instruction, and with this exception I venture to agree with Lord Kimberley that English must be the medium, and "though instruction in English must be given through the medium of the vernacular, instruction in the native languages may safely be left to the stimulus of self interest, and Government subsidies are not required for its encouragement." Mission schools naturally take a different view, since their aim is to teach pupils to read the Bible in the vulgar tongue. The education officers—and especially the native staff—must acquire sufficient knowledge of the vernacular to enable them to teach elementary-school pupils the language which will form the medium of their later instruction.

163. School Fees.—Another difficulty which presents itself in Africa is the value attached to child-labour, which manifests itself also in the kidnapping and enslaving of children. Parents, especially among the primitive tribes, are apt to consider that instead of paying school fees they should themselves be paid for allowing their children to attend school. On the other hand, the African is especially liable to undervalue what costs him nothing. I therefore attach much importance to the principle of school fees (not from a revenue point of view), and their payment is insisted on, even though they may be compounded under the guise of scholarships granted by Government or by the Native Administration.

164. Inadequate supply of Clerks, Teachers and Artisans.—The rapid expansion of the country, and in particular the development of railways, has created an enormous and an increasing demand for clerks, accountants, commercial agents, dispensers, dressers, sanitary and other inspectors, guards, stationmasters, and others with a good knowledge of English and accounting, and an increase in the supply has become a matter of vital and pressing necessity. There are about 2,500 posts under Government with salaries between £60 and £300 per annum, and about 2,000 from £24 to £60, with perhaps an additional 1,000 among commercial firms, aggregating in salaries about £500,-000 a year. Yet the number of candidates who succeed in passing the easy entrance examination for clerical appointments steadily decreases, and fell from 51 in 1910 to 17 only in 1914, and these figures include boys from other colonies. Mr. Carr estimates that the output of the secondary schools is from 200 to 300 at the most.

The result of this demand and inadequate supply has been not merely to raise the pay disproportionately to the qualifications of the candidates, but to tempt boys who can neither read nor write properly to leave school for lucrative employ, and withdraw them from parental discipline. (I have in paragraph 39 referred to a scheme of "Clerical Cadets" by which it is hoped to combat this evil.) The standard of the native official service was thus permanently lowered, and the majority of the candidates were unfitted for posts of responsibility.

The teaching profession, which could not (especially in mission schools) compete with the salaries offered to good clerks, was thus placed at so serious a disadvantage, that Mr. Carr was driven to advocate the wholesale importation of foreign teachers, who are, however, in any case, unobtainable. The attempt to introduce West Indians he admits to have had "no satisfactory results." The paucity of teachers had indeed become the chief difficulty alike in Government and in mission schools.

The demand for trained mechanics in the rapidly expanding industries was no less than that for the clerical class. It has been met on the whole with considerable success by agencies entirely dissociated from the Education Department or mission schools. The Railway, Marine, Public Works, Telegraphs, Survey and Printing Departments had for many years taken an increasing number of apprentices into their shops and establishments, and had trained them with much success. There were 500 apprentices in the shops at the end of 1916. The departments owed it, however, to the mission schools, that there was a class of young boys, with some rudiments of education, upon which they could draw. These departments had also now begun to feel the difficulty of obtaining suitable candidates.

165. The nature of the Problem.—Such was the nature of the problem, and such were the results achieved. In the South the rudiments of education were fairly widely distributed, if such a phrase is permissible when probably not more than one in every 180 children of school age had any sort of education whatever. Its results were evident in the decay of family and social discipline, and too often in discontent and hostility to any constituted authority, masquerading as racial or national patriotism, or as the vindication of rights unjustly ignored. In the North a well-defined student class looked eastwards for the language and literature of its classics, while the first small beginnings of modern teaching were groping their way amid suspicion and dislike.

The questions which demanded immediate solution were: —

(*a*) How to promote a better standard of discipline, self-control and integrity, combined with educational qualifications more adequate to the demands of the State and of commerce.

(*b*) How to increase the output so as to keep pace with the demand.

166. Objects of the New Code.—The New Ordinance, with its Regulations, which superseded the Grant Code, sought to lay down principles, alike for Government and for assisted schools, which it was hoped would in course of time produce better results. It was drafted early in 1914, and after circulation to all school managers was submitted to the Secretary of State in November of that year. After much delay it became law in December, 1916. It embodied the following general principles: —

(*a*) That the primary object of all schools should be the formation of character and habits of discipline; and that the grant in aid should be in part based on success in this direction.

(*b*) That the value of religion, irrespective of creed or sect, and the sanction and incentive it affords, should be recognised and utilised as an agent for this purpose, together with secular moral instruction.

(*c*) That the proportion of teachers to pupils should be adequate, and that they should be properly qualified, and their status improved, and made equal to that of clerks. Adequate grants must be given to assisted schools (from which Government and commercial clerks are also drawn) to enable them to pay adequate salaries to their staff.

(*d*) That educational agencies, whether controlled by Government or by missions, should co-operate with a common object, and as far as possible by similar methods of discipline and instruction.

(*e*) That continuation and evening classes, and institutions and classes for the training of teachers, should receive special encouragement.

(*f*) That Government should exercise some measure of control over all schools, even though not assisted by grants, and endeavour to bring them into line with the general policy.

(*g*) Finally, it was sought to adapt the teaching to the needs of the pupils, whether they were intending to qualify for clerical or other like service, or desired to become artisans and mechanics, or on the other hand had no desire to leave their village, and the pursuits their fathers had followed.

These principles are applicable to both North and South, in both of which there are large Pagan populations and large numbers of Mohammedans.

167. Education Ordinance, 1916.—The Ordinance set up Boards of Education in the North and South, of which the Lieutenant-Governor was President and the Director of Education a member. Their object was "to facilitate co-operation between Government and non-Government educational agencies— selected representatives of which would be given seats on the Board to ventilate and focus the difficulties which surround the problem of education in Africa, and to assist the Governor in solving those problems with the good will and assistance of those who have daily experience of the practical work of education." School Committees were also set up in every province which would include local chiefs of influence as members.

In order to check any tendency to set up rival schools in the same town, the Governor may exclude any new school from the Grant List, if he considers it superfluous on this account.

The Regulations prescribe that the grant to assisted schools should no longer be based on fixed percentages of marks obtained in an annual examination in certain set subjects, but should be awarded approximately as to 30 per cent. for tone, discipline, organisation and moral instruction, as to 20 per cent. for adequacy and efficiency of staff, as to 40 per cent. on the result of periodical examinations and general progress, and as to 10 per cent. for buildings, equipment and sanitation. Special grants are made for the teaching staff, for training institutes, and for residential pupils; the different grades of masters and teachers are defined in regard to their qualifications; the minimum requirements of staff in proportion to pupils are laid down; the subjects for instruction (with a new syllabus) are prescribed; and the grant of scholarships organised. The Ordinance anticipated the British Education Act in providing that every manager of a non-Government school must submit certain particulars annually to Government, and power to close a school in certain circumstances was added later.

In defending my proposal to introduce moral instruction, I wrote: "I conceive that if a short period daily be devoted to placing before children in an attractive way, the social and other incentives to gentlemanly conduct, the success which rewards self-control and industry, with similar lessons by the aid of illustration and anecdotal biography, it would form a valuable adjunct to the inculcation of the same ideals of right living as enforced by religious precept and sanction." Moral instruction forms an item in the ordinary curriculum and demonstrates the necessity of moral standards in social intercourse, and for success in secular affairs.

The draft Bill and Regulations were submitted to the criticism of managers of assisted schools, whose suggestions were as far as possible accepted, and the new code met with an almost unanimous approval.

168. Three types of Education required.—It was, of course, most desirable that Government should take the lead in the application of these principles to the education provided under its direct control. A clear distinction must, in the first place, be drawn between the three objects for which educational agencies are employed, viz., the literary training required for appointments in which a good knowledge of English and arithmetic is required; the technical and manual training of mechanics, and other workshop hands; and the teaching of crafts, and the very elementary schooling, suitable to those who purpose to live their own village life.

169. (a) Provincial Schools.—For the benefit of the first-class, from which the almost unlimited demand for teachers, clerks, accountants, &c., &c., must be met, it was proposed to set up at the capital of every province, a Government school, comprising in the Southern Provinces, and later on in the Northern

Provinces, all the "standards" of the code, with the object of not only increasing the output greatly, but of serving as a model. They would include an industrial class for the training of teachers for "rural schools" (*vide infra*). The ordinary curriculum of these schools would be reinforced by continuation and evening classes, in which more advanced teaching in school subjects would be given to pupils who had attained the highest standards. The instruction would include such special subjects as are not comprised in the curriculum of the school, and for which a sufficient number of candidates are forthcoming to form a class, such as agriculture, forestry, survey, &c., and in particular they would provide a "normal class" for the training of teachers in school method, and the imparting of knowledge.

In order that these schools should subserve the primary object of training character, and inculcating discipline, it is an essential feature of the new organisation that each should be under the continuous control of a British master, that the pupils should, as far as possible, be boarders, and that the school should be situated at some distance from the native town, so as to detach the boys from undesirable influences, and in order that the force of example and influence should be exerted in social intercourse and recreation, no less than in the class-room. Games are encouraged as conductive to health and manliness and ideas of fair play. The time of the pupils would not be wasted in manual or industrial training, which would be of no use to boys whose sole aim is a clerical or "literary" appointment. There would be an age limit, and a considerable number of free scholarships would be offered.

170. (b) Rural Schools.—For the third-class—the peasantry who do not seek either a literary education to qualify as clerks, &c., or a technical training for power-driven workshops, "rural schools" are provided. The pupils in these will not be boarders, and the head will be a native schoolmaster, but they will be affiliated to the central provincial school, which will supply the teaching staff and exercise such control as may be possible, in addition to the supervision of the Administrative staff, and the Inspectors of the Education Department. The number of these schools in a province is not limited. The education afforded will be restricted to the teaching of native arts and crafts, practical agriculture (and the marketing of produce), carpentry and blacksmithing, with elementary hygiene and local geography, colloquial English, and the rudiments of arithmetic, and in the Northern Provinces colloquial Hausa. Their object is to train character and promote habits of discipline, industry and truthfulness by moral and religious instruction (whether Christian or Moslem), and to fit the pupils for life in their own villages, and the improvement of the standard of that life. Promising pupils may obtain scholarships to the provincial school, or may, if they so desire, be indentured as apprentices.

171. (c) Technical Education.—The second-class, to which I have referred, includes those who seek a technical or manual training. Most of the openings for such boys are in the Railway, Marine, Public Works, or Printing Departments, where machinery driven by steam or electricity is used. Carpenters, no doubt, can earn a good living without a knowledge of power-driven lathes, but it is only in the large workshops that the making of high-class furniture and house-building can be efficiently taught. I have already said that the Government shops have long afforded very efficient instruction for apprentices, but many of these being illiterate could never make first-class workmen. Others had wasted several years in a manual training in schools which was adapted rather to village life, than as a serious preliminary to the education of a skilled mechanic.

The object in view is to improve the apprentice system. Boys who have passed the fourth or fifth standard in a provincial (or in a non-Government) school, will be accepted as apprentices, and trained in batches, their pay rising with each completed year of service, if passed as efficient. Instructors are provided in the shops, whose sole duty it is to train these apprentices. They will no longer be left to the casual attention of fellow workers. Opportunities will be afforded for their attendance at continuation classes, where they may improve their "literary" education, and also learn something of the theory of their profession and how to draw and work to scale plans. It is the desire of the Government to improve the status of the apprentice and artisan so that he may be recognised as being on the same social level as the clerk.

172. Application of the new principles in Southern Provinces.—The new system of inspection and award of grants to assisted schools has been in operation for two years with success. There were 32 new applications from mission schools which formerly preferred to forgo the grant rather than submit to the code, and I know of none which dissents from them. The Ordinance and Regulations have required practically no alteration since their publication, except to strengthen the control of Government over non-assisted schools.

King's College, Lagos, with its staff of three British masters, and the *esprit de corps* which animates the school, already conforms to the main principles, except that the pupils should be boarders, and it should have lower classes to feed its upper forms.

Unfortunately the demand made by the War for every available man who was not essential to the carrying on of the machinery of Government, has rendered it impossible to obtain the masters for the new provincial schools. The schools at Bonny and Warri will alone of existing schools become "Provincial Schools," the former being moved to the headquarters at Owerri, where, under the Resident's eye, it will be removed from the harmful influences of the past. The three Moslem schools in the Colony proper do not exactly fit into either of the designations. They may. later, be incorporated in one school with the characteristics of a provincial school, and the native staff improved by better teachers from the North. Many Moslem youths attend the Christian schools.

The remaining 46 Government schools are classed as "Rural." Their native teaching staff requires to be enlarged and improved. Under the supervision of the Inspectorate and of Residents, they will gradually conform to the new policy and system. Their number may be substantially reduced in view of mission activity, and the creation of the provincial schools. The improvements proposed in regard to apprentices will be gradually introduced. The new carpentry shop at Lagos has, under Mr. Peet, Director of Public Works, been an entire success. Furniture is made from local timber sawn in the Government mills for the whole of the Government requirements of Nigeria, and some very handsome articles have been produced from English designs, the workmanship of which rivals that of a first-class cabinet maker in England. The lathes are driven by electricity, and the apprentices are taught to undertake house construction, so that when they have served their articles they will be fully qualified in all branches. Admission to the school is eagerly sought.

The immediate needs are an increase of nine masters (including reliefs) for the provincial schools, and three more Inspectors for the increased work caused by the addition of many schools to the Assisted List, the more frequent inspection under the new system, and the reorganisation of the Government schools. These with the native staff and other expenses may add £8,000 to the cost of the Education Department of the South, a sum which is negligible in comparison to the importance of the object in view.

173. Application in Northern Provinces.—The British staff, numbering 26 in the Northern Provinces, is adequate for the provincial schools, but requires one or two Inspectors for the mission schools. The great difficulty here is to train native teachers, for it is of essential importance that these should be drawn from the local population, and that in the Moslem Provinces they should be Mohammedans. This task must take precedence of the training of clerks and others—urgently as these latter also are needed—for the Northern Province does not at present supply a single clerk or artisan for the Government service from its intelligent populations. The education also of the sons of chiefs, and of the officials of the Native Administration, is a matter of great importance.

The scope of the provincial schools in Pagan areas is at present limited to training teachers for the rural schools, and scribes for the local Native Courts. Moslem teachers are not employed in these schools. The medium of instruction in the lowest classes must of necessity be in the local vernacular, but Hausa, which is quickly learnt, will be substituted in the higher classes.

As it became possible to supply teachers from the ranks of the pupils in the existing schools, new schools were opened in different provinces, so that by the end of 1917 all but two provinces had a provincial school, while two additional schools were opened in the important emirates of Gando and Katsena, in the Sokoto and Kano Provinces. The total average attendance in 1916 was 750, with a native staff numbering 63. The number of pupils in each school is at present limited to 100.

The provincial schools are conducted on the principles described, but in deference to suspicion and prejudice in the Moslem States, it was at first impossible to give full effect to them. This attitude has of late been very notably altered, and the principal Emirs constantly visit the schools and show great interest in them. It is thus becoming possible gradually to convert them to boarding schools, and to remove them from the precincts of the city and township. Each school had a British master until the demands of the War led to the temporary withdrawal of many. A time is set apart for religious instruction (in the Moslem schools under a native "Limam"), and the formation of an Arabic class has tended greatly to popularise the schools. The study of English is popular, and it is interesting to note that it was selected in preference to Arabic by the pupils at Sokoto. Continuation classes are promoted, and each school has its Advisory Committee, of which the chief and the principal natives are members.

Owing to the backward state of education in the Northern Provinces these schools at present afford only a primary education, and the great need at the present moment is for a secondary boarding school for the training of teachers. It will be located near the Technical Institute (*see* below), and by the time that the provincial primary schools have developed into secondary schools it will be able to take its place as a Training Institute for teachers, and later still, in conjunction with the Technical Institute, it may become a general college for Nigeria, on the lines of the Gordon College at Khartoum, where the technical and literary pupils would be closely associated, and habits of industry, honesty, and discipline would be the keynote.

174. Rural Schools and Industrial Schools in Northern Provinces.—One or two rural schools have been opened in the Northern Provinces, but development in this important direction awaits a supply of teachers. The original class at Kano has now become the Kano Provincial School, while its industrial section is retained as a central industrial school, under control of the Native Administration, where native crafts are taught by native craftsmen. Its object is the preservation of indigenous art, and the improvement of native methods by improved tools. The native looms of Kano produce a cloth of great durability which Europeans (even ladies) like to wear. The tanned goat skins were famous as "Morocco leather" centuries ago. The dyes and the designs and execution of embroideries; and the architecture of the city are all worthy of preservation. A European instructor paid by Government supervises the school and also teaches carpentry, blacksmithing and brickmaking, and especially the construction of wheels and carts. To this school boys from all provinces are welcomed, and proportionate subscriptions are made by the various native Treasuries. At present it has one British and eleven native instructors, with about 100 pupils. A similar school will be opened in Bornu. The pupils are boarders, and these schools thus stand half way between the provincial and rural schools.

175. Technical Education: Northern Provinces.—Technical instruction awaits a supply of young men from the provincial schools, who have acquired a sufficient grounding to enable them to become qualified mechanics in Government shops.

The bequest made by the late Sir Alfred Jones has been assigned to the building of a Technical Institute, where apprentices will be trained under skilled tuition, and with the best appliances, in the use of European tools, and machinery driven by electricity. The plans are completed and the foundations finished, but the prohibitive cost of materials during the War, and still more, the lack of pupils, has delayed completion. It is situated about two miles from the Kaduna capital (on the side furthest from the native reservation), where electric power and water supply will be available, and it will be within a short distance of the great railway workshops at the junction, where practical demonstrations can be given. The pupils will not be associated with the artisans from the coast, who at present man the shops, since they profess a different religion, adopt a different dress, speak a different language, and their customs are different from those of the better-class Moslem youth, who, it is hoped, will be attracted to the institute. They will associate on equal terms with the pupils of the secondary school.

176. The Aliens' School: Northern Provinces.—A special need in the Northern Provinces is some provision for the education of the children of the large body of alien clerks and artisans. For their benefit a school has been opened at the capital.

177. Instructors from Khartoum.—With the kind assistance of Sir R. Wingate, the experiment is being made of bringing two or three teachers from Gordon College for the Arabic-speaking population of Bornu. They will come direct overland, and the Resident, Mr. Palmer, has himself proceeded to Khartoum to test the route. The Shuwa Arabs of Bornu are a particularly intelligent race, and if the experiment succeeds they may later provide teachers for other schools, and pupils for the Technical Institute.

178. Mission Schools: Northern Provinces.—At the end of 1917 there were 122 mission schools, with an average attendance of 1,876, chiefly confined to Pagan areas. They are not as yet subject to any inspection, for lack of an inspectorate, and none have come on the Assisted List. Some useful work has been accomplished by the missions in studying the grammar and reducing to writing various Pagan languages, and in some districts they have done admirable work.

179. Departmental Schools.—Either in the North or South, or in both, classes have been formed by the head of the department concerned—outside the purview of the Education Department—for instruction in survey, agriculture, forestry and veterinary work. The object is to train youths in these special subjects for service under the Native Administrations, and to select the more capable, should they desire it, for service in the department. Outside the Colony they will be affiliated to the provincial school of the province in which they are situated, so that they may prosecute their ordinary studies simultaneously with their special technical training. The survey schools, both in North and South, have done admirable work.

180. Cost of Education.—The net cost of education in Nigeria in 1916 was about 1.6 per cent. of the total ordinary revenue of the country, and 1.5 per cent. of the expenditure. If this were doubled it would still be an inadequate ratio, but the increase I propose would not bring the percentage up to 2 per cent. Looked at from no higher standpoint than the material requirements of Government, reform is called for by the imperious demands created by the expansion of the railways alone. The matter is of great urgency for there is no outside source from which the men required can be drawn. "In my judgment (I wrote) no efforts and no cost can be too great to introduce reforms, which shall have the result of producing a set of Government servants with high standards and with self-control, loyalty and integrity, and in producing a number sufficient to meet the demands of a rapidly growing country."

The cost per pupil in the Northern Provinces reached at the end of 1913 the abnormally high figure of £20. This will be steadily reduced as the schools fill up. The Native Treasuries now pay the native staff and the cost of school apparatus and buildings, and the school fees are credited to them. In 1916 the total expenditure on education in the Northern Provinces was £12,443 from revenue, and £5,325 by Native Administrations.

181. Effect of the War.—The demands of the War have fallen heavily upon the Education Department and a large proportion of the staff, especially in the Northern Provinces, have been continuously on active service. This has arrested progress, but the framework is now clearly laid down, and with the cessation of the War, and the provision of the staff required in the Southern Provinces, I trust that rapid progress will be made. Much progress can indeed be claimed even under these adverse circumstances, especially in the Northern Provinces.

*   *   *

*Government White Paper on Kenya Defining the
Concept of Responsibility for Africans, 1923**
*   *   *

Part II

1. General Statement of Policy

The general policy underlying any decision that may be taken on the questions at issue must first be determined. It is a matter for satisfaction that, however irreconcilable the views of the European and Indian communities in

**Parliamentary Papers*, 1923, XVIII, Cmd. 1922, 9–11.

Kenya on many points may be, there is one point on which both are agreed, namely, the importance of safeguarding the interests of the African natives. The African population of Kenya is estimated at more than 2½ millions; and according to the census of 1921, the total numbers of Europeans, Indians and Arabs in Kenya (including officials) were 9,651, 22,822 and 10,102 respectively.

Primarily, Kenya is an African territory, and His Majesty's Government think it necessary definitely to record their considered opinion that the interests of the African natives must be paramount, and that if, and when, those interests and the interests of the immigrant races should conflict, the former should prevail. Obviously the interests of the other communities, European, Indian or Arab, must severally be safeguarded. Whatever the circumstances in which members of these communities have entered Kenya, there will be no drastic action or reversal of measures already introduced, such as may have been contemplated in some quarters, the result of which might be to destroy or impair the existing interests of those who have already settled in Kenya. But in the administration of Kenya His Majesty's Government regard themselves as exercising a trust on behalf of the African population, and they are unable to delegate or share this trust, the object of which may be defined as the protection and advancement of the native races. It is not necessary to attempt to elaborate this position; the lines of development are as yet in certain directions undetermined, and many difficult problems arise which require time for their solution. But there can be no room for doubt that it is the mission of Great Britain to work continuously for the training and education of the Africans towards a higher intellectual moral and economic level than that which they had reached when the Crown assumed the responsibility for the administration of this territory. At present special consideration is being given to economic development in the native reserves, and within the limits imposed by the finances of the Colony all that is possible for the advancement and development of the Africans, both inside and outside the native reserves, will be done.

His Majesty's Government desire also to record that in their opinion the annexation of the East Africa Protectorate, which, with the exception of the mainland dominions of the Sultan of Zanzibar, has thus become a Colony, known as Kenya Colony, in no way derogates from this fundamental conception of the duty of the Government to the native races. As in the Uganda Protectorate, so in the Kenya Colony, the principle of trusteeship for the natives, no less than in the mandated territory of Tanganyika, is unassailable. This paramount duty of trusteeship will continue, as in the past, to be carried out under the Secretary of State for the Colonies by the agents of the Imperial Government, and by them alone.

2. Future Constitutional Evolution

Before dealing with the practical points at issue directly connected with the claims of Indians, it is necessary, in view of the declaration of policy enunciated above, to refer to the question of the future constitutional evolution of Kenya.

It has been suggested that it might be possible for Kenya to advance in the near future on the lines of responsible self-government, subject to the reservation of native affairs. There are, however, in the opinion of His Majesty's Government, objections to the adoption in Kenya at this stage of such an arrangement, whether it take the form of removing all matters affecting Africans from consideration in the Council, or the appointment of the Governor as High Commissioner for Native Affairs, or provision for a special veto by the Crown on local legislation which touches native interests; and they are convinced that the existing system of government is in present circumstances best calculated to achieve the aims which they have in view, namely, the unfettered exercise of their trusteeship for the native races and the satisfaction of the legitimate aspirations of other communities resident in the Colony.

His Majesty's Government cannot but regard the grant of responsible self-government as out of the question within any period of time which need now be taken into consideration. Nor, indeed, would they contemplate yet the possibility of substituting an unofficial majority in the Council for the Government official majority. Hasty action is to be strongly deprecated, and it will be necessary to see how matters develop, especially in regard to African representation, before proposals for so fundamental a change in the Constitution of the Colony can be entertained. Meanwhile, the administration of the Colony will follow the British traditions and principles which have been successful in other Colonies, and progress towards self-government must be left to take the lines which the passage of time and the growth of experience may indicate as being best for the country.

Report of the East Africa Commission Setting out Principles of Land Policy, April 1925*

* * *

Chapter III. Native Policy

General, Land, Native Production, Labour, Native Organisation, Education and Medical Services

(a) *General.* The Kenya White Paper of 1923, prepared by the Conservative Government of that year, laid down as the basis of our position in East Africa the duty of trusteeship for the native population under our control. It emphasised this by the use of the following phrase: —"As in the Uganda Protectorate so in the Kenya Colony the principle of Trusteeship for the Natives no less than in the Mandated Territory of Tanganyika is unassailable."

It therefore becomes necessary to define more precisely what is involved by this "Trusteeship."

Parliamentary Papers, 1924–25, IX, Cmd. 2387, 21–32.

During our tour of East Africa we were frequently told by Europeans, officials and unofficials alike, that the African native is a "child." Without questioning the truth of such a generalisation, it at any rate suggests that the position of the European race ruling in Africa is that of a guardian to a ward, and that our duty is to protect the interests of someone less capable of safeguarding his or her own interests, and to educate a less developed and less efficiently equipped people to become better equipped and more efficient. It is difficult to realise without seeing Africa what a tremendous impact is involved in the juxtaposition of white civilisation, with its command over material force, and its comparatively high and diversified social system, on the primitive people of Eastern Africa. The African native is confronted with a whole range of facts entirely beyond his present comprehension and he finds himself caught in a maelstrom of economic and cultural progress which in the majority of cases baffles him completely.

The status of trusteeship involves an ethical conception, that is to say, it imposes upon the trustee a moral duty and a moral attitude. This derives in part from the influence of Christianity upon Western civilisation, and in part from what is often claimed to be a specifically British conception, namely, that of "fair play for the weaker." Sentiment therefore enters, and rightly enters, into the consideration of the problem.

But trusteeship of this kind is not the only trusteeship which is exercised by the European in tropical Africa. As Sir Frederick Lugard has pointed out in his well-known book entitled "The Dual Mandate in British Tropical Africa," we are not only trustees for the development and advance in civilisation of the African, but we are also trustees for the world of very rich territories. This means that we have a duty to humanity to develop the vast economic resources of a great continent. There is no reason to suppose that these two trusteeships either should or do conflict. Having said this it should also be added that Government cannot restrict its conception of its duties to these two main considerations, it also has a duty to perform to those individuals and communities not of African race who by their courage and enterprise, and often at the instance and with the encouragement of Governments in the past, have made their homes, or at least the sphere of their life's work, in Africa. To be more precise, Government has equally a duty to perform to the Europeans and Asiatics engaged in work in Africa, be they settlers, merchants, civil servants, or missionaries. The ideal before Government is not merely that of holding the balance between a series of interests, native or non-native, but of serving the highest welfare of communities as a whole. In fact the development of the community sense is one of its paramount tasks.

We have already dealt with some of the contrasts between the conditions which obtain in East and West Africa. Without wishing to emphasise these contrasts we wish to stress the facts that economic and geographical conditions are different, that the natives are different, and that the presence of European settlements in the highland areas of East Africa is an existing reality which cannot be gone back upon even if it were desirable to do so.

To return to the question of native trusteeship, this duty has been regarded in the past as the special function of the agents of the Imperial Government and of the missionaries. But such a limitation is neither possible nor desirable. Britain will not be judged at the bar of history by the work of these two alone; the trusteeship lies really upon the shoulders of every man and woman of European race in Africa. It is in very truth a white man's burden, and all Europeans in Africa must share in the work.

In order to face these responsibilities certain misconceptions too long current in the public mind have got to be removed. The first of these is that the interests of non-native and native must necessarily conflict. In order to be pro-native it is not necessary to be anti-white. To be in favour of white settlement in such portions of Africa as are climatically suitable for European homes, it is not necessary to be anti-native. East Africa can only progress economically and socially on the basis of full and complete co-operation between all races. The white man's leadership in this co-operation is not due to any inherent right on account of the colour of his skin, but because, and only because, by his education and his moral and intellectual development and his command over natural forces, he is equipped for such leadership. The Europeans in East Africa have the position, and therefore the dangers and responsibilities, of any aristocracy.

In bringing Western civilisation and Western ideas into tropical Africa the missionaries were first in the field. Traders followed them; then Governments; and finally settlers. Without the work of the missions East Africa could not have advanced in the way that it has advanced in the last thirty or forty years. Their continuing efforts, both as pioneers in economic development and in the task of civilising the African, deserve unstinted recognition.

The main contribution of Government until recent years has been the introduction of inter-tribal peace, security for life and property, and the provision of Western standards of justice and criminal jurisdiction. These provisions, the first and paramount duties of all Governments, are often minimised and insufficient recognition is given to what they mean in tropical Africa, where, before the coming of European Government, inter-tribal warfare, raids, the supremacy of witchcraft, and the frequent arbitrary tyranny of the powerful were almost universally the rule. It is for the provision of these essential functions of Government that the native has been, and has rightly been, taxed. Of recent years the public conscience has increasingly demanded that these provisions alone do not finally satisfy the obligations of the State. It has become the duty of Government to make increasing provision for the further needs of the native population; such needs as medical services, schools, veterinary services, means of communication, and social and political organisation. The provision of all these further services can only be defrayed as and when the economic advance in the productivity and earning capacity of the native increases. The further development, therefore, of the conception of trusteeship is bound up with the economic advance of the individuals who compose the State. Only in proportion as the means of paying taxes increase and the native becomes capable of bearing, without hardship, further taxation, can all these things, the need of which is now universally recognised, be provided by Government.

(b) Land. As we have already stated, the economic resources of East Africa are almost entirely agricultural, and it is therefore to the better use of the soil of Africa that we must look for the means whereby any form of progress can be obtained. This consideration brings us at once to the question of the land, its ownership and its use. To attempt to consider the further economic development of Africa or the further progress of the natives without a careful examination of the land question is impossible.

The system of land tenure at present in vogue in East Africa is extremely varied; it may be said to fall into three main categories:

(1) Crown or public land.
(2) Land recognised as native land.
(3) Land alienated to non-natives either in freehold or leasehold title.

With certain notable exceptions the East African native has not in the past possessed the European idea of individual ownership of land. This was, in part, due to tribal custom, partly to nomadic habits, partly to the existence up to recent times of a superfluity of land (there being more land than there are people to use it). It is true, however, to say that in the main we found that the different tribes have historic claims, some of them comparatively recent, to the use by a tribe of certain specified areas. The boundaries of such tribal areas are sometimes quite clearly defined, in other cases they are vague, and in the old days before the coming of the white men they were the most frequent causes of inter-tribal wars. Above all it must be remembered that from time immemorial the more warlike pastoral tribes have continually raided and frequently dispossessed the agricultural tribes. This distinction between the purely pastoral tribes and the agricultural tribes must always be borne in mind in considering African system of land tenure. Among the agricultural tribes there is an undoubted tribal custom that the cultivator possesses an occupation title to the land he actually cultivates, of which he cannot easily be deprived. In some cases this occupation right is transmitted by different forms of hereditary claim, notably in the Bagishu district of Uganda and the neighbouring area of Kavirondo. In Kenya in a few cases this right is also transmitted by purchase, a system which obtains more particularly in the Kikuyu reserve in Kenya, and is locally known as the Gethaka system. Among the powerful pastoral tribes such as the Masai, individual rights are far more shadowy. Another factor to be borne in mind when considering East African land tenure is the character of the native agriculture. Over a great part of the area it is the custom of natives to cultivate a portion of ground for a few years only and then to move to vacant land, leaving land that was cultivated to go back to bush. Such a custom is bound up with the cultivation of purely annual crops. In the Kingdom of Buganda, however, the introduction at some remote period of the banana as the principal foodstuff of the whole population destroyed this custom. The banana is a permanent crop capable of cultivation on the same patch for many years in succession. Coffee is another example of a permanent crop which has affected native ideas of land tenure, and coffee is being increasingly cultivated by natives in different parts of the Uganda Protectorate, and still more in the Bukoba district of Tanganyika Territory. But, even apart from these economic causes which make for the disappearance of the old Bantu conceptions of land tenure, two other forces are operating in the direction of the creation of individual rights in land. First of these is the decay of tribal authority, due not so much to any deliberate policy on the part of the British administration as to the disappearance of the main buttress of the tribal system, namely, the necessity for organised military defence against neighbouring tribes. The second cause is contact with European civilisation and European ideas of land tenure. Both contact and imitation are tending to produce in Africa the "individual," where formerly the real unit was the family or tribe. There is now a career open to the individual who has hitherto had little chance of advancement unless he happened to belong to the tribal hierarchy by hereditary right. But the African native naturally imitates; and where the European is seen to acquire freehold or leasehold rights to land the more intelligent African is seeking to imitate his example. Such a movement is particularly noticeable among the natives of Kikuyu and Kavirondo. It is at this moment the subject of enquiry by an important Commission in Southern Rhodesia.

Looking to the future from the purely economic point of view, there can be little doubt that nomadic habits of the past, whether of pastoral or agricultural tribes, will be, and should be, stopped. Further, although tribal or communal conceptions of land tenure do not debar agricultural progress, taking the long view it is inevitable that the conception of fixity of tenure by families and by individuals is bound to grow, and is really necessary to the better use of the land. Progress in the direction of individual title to land by African natives has gone farthest, as would be expected, in the Kingdom of Buganda. Under the Uganda Agreement of 1900 between Sir Harry Johnston and the King and people of Buganda, all the land of the Kingdom was divided, half as Crown land to the British Government and half to the native government. The disposition of the half allotted to the native government was left largely to the Lukiko (native Council), but from the first included the recognition of freehold titles to land by the then existing native chiefs. The agreement originally contemplated the division of the native share into official lands set aside for the support of different members of the royal family and of the chiefs, known as the official mailos (to which we shall revert later), and the division of the rest of the land among approximately 1,000 native freeholders. In the actual distribution, however, it was found that not 1,000 but 3,000 native freeholders had to be provided for, and during the last 25 years, partly by sale and partly by bequest, this number has increased to over 7,000. To-day approximately one in every hundred of the population of the Kingdom of Buganda is a landlord possessing freehold title to his land. These freehold estates vary in size from the largest, which is approximately 50 square miles, down to small holdings of two or three acres. Under the Native Law of 1908 sale or bequest to non-natives is forbidden without the consent of the Lukiko and the Governor, and by a more recent resolution of the Lukiko this consent is now withheld in all cases. In the main, land passes by bequest to the family in the male line, the eldest son receiving by far the largest share. It is somewhat surprising to find this hereditary freehold right in a country where, with the exception of the royal house, the chieftainships, great and small, are non-hereditary. The ancient feudal system of Uganda is really an elaborate native civil service, the individual starting as a Matongoli chief or headman, over a few hundred families, then rising to the position of a Gombolola chief who has jurisdiction over between two and three thousand taxpayers, and finally to the position of a Saza or county chief. Of these last there are approximately 20 in the whole kingdom. All these administrators, for that is the correct way to describe them, are appointed by the native government, in agreement with the British Administration. All the Saza and Gombolola chiefs have official lands allotted for the support of whoever holds the office, in addition to any freehold land which the individual may own either within his jurisdiction or elsewhere. In the above sketch of the position in Uganda we have made no reference to the Butaka question, which will be dealt with in the chapter on Uganda.

In considering the question of land tenure and land rights in East Africa, the comparative sparseness of the population when compared with other territories inhabited by African natives must be borne in mind. The native population per square mile for different territories is seen from the following table: —

(1) Transkei (Cape Colony Native Reserve)	59	per square mile
(2) Nigeria	53	,, ,, ,,
(3) Gold Coast (Colony)	50	,, ,, ,,
(4) Basutoland	42.5	,, ,,
(5) Uganda	33	,, ,, ,,
(6) Nyasaland	31	,, ,, ,,
(7) Tanganyika Territory	11	,, ,, ,,
(8) Kenya	11	,, ,, ,,
(9) Northern Rhodesia	3	,, ,, ,,

In many parts of East Africa there are vast areas of good cultivable land either absolutely unoccupied or else so sparsely occupied that there is little or no chance of the land being put to any use at present. Even in Uganda, the most densely populated of the East African territories, one sees behind the comparatively narrow stretch of cultivation along the roads vast areas of elephant grass (a sure sign of good land) stretching for miles. With the exception of the north-eastern half of Kenya, which is deficient in rainfall, the area of absolutely useless land in East Africa is comparatively small. In examining the above table it must not be forgotten that nearly half the total area of Tanganyika Territory, a very considerable portion of North-Eastern Rhodesia, and parts of Nyasaland are depopulated on account of the presence of the tsetse fly. It may be said that nowhere in East Africa is the native population really congested. The areas which approach most nearly to congestion are in the southern portion of Nyasaland, in the Mwanza and North Tabora districts of Tanganyika Territory, in the Wachagga district on Mount Kilimanjaro, the Bagishu district of Uganda, and the Kavirondo and Kikuyu areas of Kenya. In all these areas the natives are primarily agricultural, though some are partly pastoral as well.

Purely pastoral tribes have in the main the most enormous areas, particularly the Masai. This celebrated tribe, which occupies most valuable land both in Kenya and in Tanganyika Territory, numbers not more than 50,000, of whom about 30,000 are in Kenya and 20,000 in Tanganyika Territory. The area reserved for them amounts to 14,639 square miles in Kenya and approximately 16,200 square miles in the Tanganyika Territory. None of the land is cultivated and they live entirely on and for their enormous herds of cattle, their sole diet being milk, raw blood, and meat. They rarely sell their cattle, though it is estimated that they own 585,000 cattle in Kenya and over 350,000 in the Tanganyika Territory. The quality of the cattle is inferior, and as they never castrate the bulls the stock is probably deteriorating. The customs of the tribes are primitive and barbaric in the extreme. Their women are loaded with great weights of iron and copper neckbands, arm bands and anklets. Few Masai women carry less than 30 pounds weight of irremovable metal ornaments throughout their lives. The tribe are rigidly conservative and look down upon their more progressive neighbours with contempt. They excelled as warriors and their social organisation is based on the maintenance of the able-bodied youth as a military caste. As this they are no longer required.

It is obvious that any attempt to lay down a single land policy for the Masai and for the cotton-growing, banana-eating Baganda is out of the question. Land policy must be varied in accordance with historical, social, and economic facts, and no one land policy or system of land tenure can be imposed. Further, land policy and land legislation are not static. They must be evolutionary. Africa is changing rapidly and each area, which is by no means co-terminous with the existing administrative boundaries, must be dealt with empirically. Into these varied conditions has come, in each of the East African territories, the European farmer or settler. In Nyasaland and Rhodesia, European land rights have been acquired in time past direct from native authorities, being subsequently confirmed by the British Government. Outside these two territories European rights in land in East Africa have been in the main acquired from the British Crown. Some Europeans have been granted freehold, some 999 years leasehold, some 99 years leasehold, and others leases for shorter periods. Freehold has generally been granted in Northern Rhodesia and Nyasaland. In Tanganyika Territory freehold was granted by the German Government and the title to the greater part of these freehold estates has passed to Europeans and Indians by purchase from the Custodian of Enemy Property. In Uganda European settlers obtain leases convertible into freehold title on British crown land. Since the war the British Government has only granted public land in Tanganyika Territory on the 99 years leasehold basis, and in Kenya on the 99 or 999 years basis.

The existence of white settlements in a country largely populated by natives has led to the classification of the land as: —

(1) Native areas, in which only natives and such bodies as missionary societies and traders under licence are allowed to acquire rights in land.

(2) European areas, divided into European farms where the land is cultivated by European farmers with the assistance of native labour.

(3) Doubtful areas where policy has been less defined.

In some quarters it is thought that the system of native and European reserves, for that is in effect what obtains, is bound up with the policy of industrial segregation, which has to-day so many advocates in the Union of South Africa on social and political grounds. The policy of industrial segregation does not obtain in East Africa. In fact, the trend of local European opinion seems wholly opposed to it. In South Africa it arises mainly from the existence of a European wage-earning class which is almost, if not entirely, absent in East Africa. In East Africa the native is actively encouraged to leave his reserve and become a skilled craftsman, and there is neither in practice nor in law anything in the nature of a colour bar in industry. In South Africa one never sees a native engine-driver or skilled mechanic, rarely even a native chauffeur. In East Africa an increasing number of engine-drivers, skilled mechanics, and chauffeurs are local African natives. In South Africa the native is limited in the building and carpentering trades to the less skilled work by a series of trade union rules. In East Africa, notably in Nyasaland and Kenya, work in these trades, that is ordinarily done by a European in South Africa, is done by the African native with ever-increasing efficiency.

The segregation of natives in large native reserves, into which few Europeans, other than Government officials, missionaries, and labour recruiters, ever penetrate, is held by some Europeans to be opposed to the agricultural progress of the natives themselves. One thing, however, seems to be clear, namely, that, accepting the reserve system as inevitable, in areas where there is a considerable European settlement it is essential in the interests of both native and non-native that there should be some clear definition of rights. There is probably no subject which agitates the native mind to-day more continuously than the question of their rights in land, both collectively as tribes and individually as owners or occupiers. In this disquiet they are actively supported in their claims by the missionary bodies of all denominations. Uncertainty in regard to future land policy is certainly the principal cause of disquiet among the natives, more particularly of Kenya and Nyasaland.

Although more appropriate to the chapter dealing with Kenya, the native land question in that Colony has become one of such general interest that we propose to deal with it in this general section of the report. At every meeting we had with the natives of Kenya Colony there was evidence of a feeling of insecurity as regards the tenure of their lands. The legal position appears to be that no individual native and no native tribe as a whole has any right to land in the Colony which can be recognised by the Courts. This position is summarised in an often quoted extract from a decision of the Kenya High Court in a Kikuyu land case in 1921: —

> In my view the effect of the Crown Lands Ordinance, 1915, and the Kenya (Annexation) Order in Council, 1920, by which no native rights were reserved, and the Kenya Colony Order in Council, 1921, as I have already stated, is clearly, *inter alia,* to vest land reserved for the use of the native tribe in the Crown. If that be so, then all native rights in such reserved land, whatever they were under the Gethaka system, disappeared, and the natives in occupation of such Crown land became tenants at will of the Crown of the land actually occupied.

This judgment is now widely known to Africans in Kenya, and it has become clear to them that, without their being previously informed or consulted, their rights in their tribal land, whether communal or individual, have "disappeared" in law and have been superseded by the rights of the Crown.

It is true that the Kenya Government cannot alienate land from a native reserve without the previous sanction of the Secretary of State for the Colonies, but for various reasons we are doubtful whether in the past this has provided adequate security.

In the first place, much remains to be done as regards gazetting reserves under the Crown Lands Ordinance, 1915. Two reserves, Kikuyu and Nyika, have been finally so gazetted, and 39 reserves, including all the Kavirondo, the Kenya, and the Wakamba reserves, can immediately be gazetted. Eleven others will then remain to be dealt with, containing an estimated population of 250,-000. There seems no reason why all the boundaries of reserved areas should not be completely settled at an early date.

In the second place, cases have occurred in the past where a Governor has alienated land from a native area, and has either not reported his action to the Secretary of State, or has reported it so long afterwards that it was not really practicable to reverse the action he had taken. An example of the latter class was the excision of a large area of the Nandi Reserve as a result of the ex-soldiers settlement scheme in 1919. When the reserves are finally gazetted there should be no danger of further excisions of this kind.

What we consider essential, both to satisfy the apprehensions of the natives and to ensure justice in the solution of this complex problem, is that representatives of native interests should without delay be given a legal status in regard to the tenure of native lands. In order to implement the White Paper of 1923, which so definitely affirms British trusteeship for natives, it seems necessary that a further instrument should be issued laying down the terms upon which the Crown holds native lands in Kenya, and the principles upon which the natives' estates should be managed on their behalf. As is pointed out in the judgment already quoted, the present position arises from the effect of Orders in Council, and it is a matter for legal consideration whether the new instrument which is required should not also have that form; but the exact form, whether an Order in Council or local Ordinance, can be considered later.

We discussed the whole question at a meeting in Nairobi with the late Governor, the Colonial Secretary, the Chief Native Commissioner, and other officials. As a result, a despatch has recently been received from Sir Robert Coryndon making definite proposals for meeting the difficulty. Generally, he proposed that, while the trust for the natives should remain vested in the Governor, there should be set up an Advisory Native Land Board in each native area, consisting of the Chief Native Commissioner as Chairman (with power to delegate his authority), the Senior Commissioner and District Commissioner, a representative of the Land and Survey Department, and such native representatives as the Government may appoint, these representatives to be, if possible, members of the local native Council. These Boards would arbitrate in native land disputes and advise the Government with regard to all questions affecting land in their area, and especially all projected leases or alienations of tribal land. Such proposals would be decided upon either by the Governor-in-Council or by the Secretary of State according to the area involved. Special arrangements would be made for considering any cases which were opposed by native representatives on the Advisory Board, and all such cases would require the prior approval of the Secretary of State.

Under the late Governor's proposals an Ordinance would give power to the Governor-in-Council to set apart land for the benefit of native tribes, and would prohibit the disposal of such land except as provided in the Ordinance. The land would be declared to be under the control and subject to the disposition of the Governor, and be held and administered for the use and common benefit of the natives, and no title to the occupation and use of any such land would be valid without the Governor's consent. Provision would be made for the temporary letting of portions of a native area for purposes beneficial to the inhabitants, but without the land ceasing to be part of the area.

Any such lease would bind the lessee to pay to the Governor compensation (which would be devoted by the Governor at his discretion to the benefit of the natives affected) for any damage caused to native individuals or communities in the exercise of the lessee's rights under the lease.

Such leases would not exceed 30 years, renewable at the lessee's option for a further period not exceeding 30 years, the Governor-in-Council reserving the right of re-assessment of rent at the expiration of each such period.

We have considered the Governor's proposals, but we fear that, as they stand, they would not completely allay the feeling of insecurity which now exists, and that it is necessary to set up a definite Trust Board, in which all native lands should be vested. It would, no doubt, be more satisfactory to the natives concerned if there were a separate Trust Board for each reserve, but, in view of the large number of reserves, and the small area of many of them, such an arrangement would be unwieldy. Subject to the safeguard afforded by the Governor's proposal of Advisory Boards in each reserve, we consider that one Trust Board would be sufficient for the whole country, and we suggest that it might consist of the Governor or Chairman, the Chief Native Commissioner, the three Senior Commissioners of the first class, two representatives of the natives (who, in the first instance, might be missionaries), and two representatives of the non-native unofficial population. These last four members would be nominated by the Governor. We suggest the presence of unofficial non-natives on the Trust Board in order to secure the maximum possible co-operation and confidence among all sections of the community.

We consider it necessary to add to the provisions proposed by the late Governor that the Government should have the right to acquire any native land required for a necessary public purpose, such as roads, railways, and Government stations, but that some compensation should be paid both to the tribe collectively and to any individual whose occupation of land is prejudiced. In addition, any monies paid as compensation or rent for dealings in native land would be received by the Trust Board and by them be handed over to the Native Trust Fund. It would have to be made clear that arbitration of disputes relating to the individual enjoyment of land in any reserve would be included in the functions of the local Advisory Boards.

It remains to consider whether any permanent alienation of native land should be allowed for non-Government purposes. Such alienations were apparently contemplated by the late Governor, but we cannot foresee any cases in which it would not be sufficient to grant a lease of the land, which would remain part of the reserve and revert to native use when it ceased to be employed for the purpose for which the lease was given.

We believe that, if this recognition of rights and these proposed safeguards were adopted in Kenya, a great deal of the present misunderstanding and unrest would be allayed and the solution of many other problems would be assisted. For instance, we are by no means certain that the present feeling among the natives of Kenya on the land question has not some effect on the labour problem.

We have dealt at some length with the land question in Kenya because it is in that territory that it assumes the greatest importance for the moment. It will, however, be necessary to deal with the land question in Nyasaland, and more particularly with native rights on land alienated in freehold title to European companies and individuals under the certificates of claim recognised by Sir Harry Johnston. This problem will be referred to in the chapter dealing with Nyasaland.

We understand that a general land law for the Uganda Protectorate outside the Buganda Kingdom has been prepared by the Uganda Government, and of this proposed Ordinance we saw a draft when in Entebbe. We consider that this draft Ordinance will require the careful attention of the new Governor. Some changes in the Tanganyika Land Ordinance and in its administration seem called for, which will be dealt with in the Tanganyika chapter. In regard to Northern Rhodesia we recommend that you should await the report of the Native Reserves Commission which has lately investigated the situation in the East Luangwa district under Sir Philip Macdonell before deciding what general land legislation should be introduced.

There is one further general question in connection with native land policy to which we desire to refer, namely, the demand that is sometimes put forward for the extension of a native reserve on account of the increase in native stock. Generally we endorse the principles laid down in the report of the Southern Rhodesia Native Reserves Commission of 1916 on this point. Because, owing to the cessation of tribal raids, native cattle, sheep and goats are no longer subject to the old wastage we do not consider that this fact alone entitles tribes to extensions of boundary. It is not in the interests of development or of the natives themselves that stock should be indefinitely increased. Further, as a tribe increases in numbers it should acquire the capacity for winning greater yields from the soil both for its own support and for its stock. Indefinite grazing—especially by goats which are in many parts of East Africa increasing quite unduly—is the most wasteful use of land, and leads in some cases to deterioration and desiccation of the soil. Above all it must be borne in mind that the grazing of stock is undertaken by natives not with a view to sale or real economic use of the stock, but largely for purchase of a plurality of wives and for the promotion in social standing in native eyes which larger stock owning brings. One of the regrettable features of East Africa is the present unwillingness of natives to dispose of their stock, but it is only fair to add that up to the present the market for native animal products has not been developed or assisted.

*   *   *

MOVEMENT TOWARD INDIAN INDEPENDENCE

Statement by the Colonial Secretary for India,
Sir Edwin Montagu, in the House of Commons
Outlining Constitutional Reforms for India,
20 August 1917*

MR. CHARLES ROBERTS asked the Secretary of State for India whether, in view of the Adjournment for the Recess, he is in a position to make any announcement as to the policy which the Government intend to pursue in India?

THE SECRETARY OF STATE FOR INDIA (Mr. Montagu): The Government of India have for some time been urging that a statement should be made in regard to Indian policy, and I am glad to have the opportunity, afforded by my hon. Friend's question, of meeting their wishes. The policy of His Majesty's Government, with which the Government of India are in complete accord, is that of the increasing association of Indians in every branch of the administration, and the gradual development of self-governing institutions, with a view to the progressive realisation of responsible government in India as an integral part of the British Empire. They have decided that substantial steps in this direction should be taken as soon as possible, and that it is of the highest importance, as a preliminary to considering what these steps should be, that there should be a free and informal exchange of opinion between those in authority at home and in India. His Majesty's Government have accordingly decided, with His Majesty's approval, that I should accept the Viceroy's invitation to proceed to India to discuss these matters with the Viceroy and the Government of India, to consider with the Viceroy the views of local governments, and to receive with him the suggestions of representative bodies and others.

I would add that progress in this policy can only be achieved by successive stages. The British Government and the Government of India, on whom the responsibility lies for the welfare and advancement of the Indian peoples, must be the judges of the time and measure of each advance, and they must be guided by the co-operation received from those upon whom new opportunities of service will thus be conferred, and by the extent to which it is found that confidence can be reposed in their sense of responsibility.

Ample opportunity will be afforded for public discussion of the proposals, which will be submitted in due course to Parliament.

* * *

---

*Hansard, 5.s., XCVII, 1695–96.

Government of India Act (Montagu-Chelmsford Reforms,
9 & 10 Geo. V, c. 101), 23 December 1919*

Whereas it is the declared policy of Parliament to provide for the increasing association of Indians in every branch of Indian administration, and for the gradual development of self-governing institutions, with a view to the progressive realisation of responsible government in British India as an integral part of the empire:

And whereas progress in giving effect to this policy can only be achieved by successive stages, and it is expedient that substantial steps in this direction should now be taken:

And whereas the time and manner of each advance can be determined only by Parliament, upon whom responsibility lies for the welfare and advancement of the Indian peoples:

And whereas the action of Parliament in such matters must be guided by the co-operation received from those on whom new opportunities of service will be conferred, and by the extent to which it is found that confidence can be reposed in their sense of responsibility:

And whereas concurrently with the gradual development of self-governing institutions in the Provinces of India it is expedient to give to those Provinces in provincial matters the largest measure of independence of the Government of India, which is compatible with the due discharge by the latter of its own responsibilities:

Be it therefore enacted by the King's most Excellent Majesty, by and with the advice and consent of the Lords Spiritual and Temporal, and Commons, in this present Parliament assembled, and by the authority of the same, as follows:

Part I. Local Governments

1.— (1) Provision may be made by rules under the Government of India Act, 1915, as amended by the Government of India (Amendment) Act, 1916 (which Act, as so amended, is in this Act referred to as "the principal Act")—

> (a) for the classification of subjects, in relation to the functions of government, as central and provincial subjects, for the purpose of distinguishing the functions of local governments and local legislatures from the functions of the Governor-General in Council and the Indian legislature;

**Public General Statutes*, LVII, 519-40.

(*b*) for the devolution of authority in respect of provincial subjects to local governments, and for the allocation of revenues or other moneys to those governments;

(*c*) for the use under the authority of the Governor-General in Council of the agency of local governments in relation to central subjects, in so far as such agency may be found convenient, and for determining the financial conditions of such agency; and

(*d*) for the transfer from among the provincial subjects of subjects (in this Act referred to as "transferred subjects") to the administration of the governor acting with ministers appointed under this Act, and for the allocation of revenues or moneys for the purpose of such administration.

(2) Without prejudice to the generality of the foregoing powers, rules made for the above-mentioned purposes may—

(i) regulate the extent and conditions of such devolution, allocation, and transfer;

(ii) provide for fixing the contributions payable by local governments to the Governor-General in Council, and making such contributions a first charge on allocated revenues or moneys;

(iii) provide for constituting a finance department in any province, and regulating the functions of that department;

(iv) provide for regulating the exercise of the authority vested in the local government of a province over members of the public services therein;

(v) provide for the settlement of doubts arising as to whether any matter does or does not relate to a provincial subject or a transferred subject, and for the treatment of matters which affect both a transferred subject and a subject which is not transferred; and

(vi) make such consequential and supplemental provisions as appear necessary or expedient:

Provided that, without prejudice to any general power of revoking or altering rules under the principal Act, the rules shall not authorise the revocation or suspension of the transfer of any subject except with the sanction of the Secretary of State in Council.

(3) The powers of superintendence, direction, and control over local governments vested in the Governor-General in Council under the principal Act shall, in relation to transferred subjects, be exercised only for such purposes as may be specified in rules made under that Act, but the Governor-General in Council shall be the sole judge as to whether the purpose of the exercise of such powers in any particular case comes within the purposes so specified.

(4) The expressions "central subjects" and "provincial subjects" as used in this Act mean subjects so classified under the rules.

Provincial subjects, other than transferred subjects, are in this Act referred to as "reserved subjects."

2.—(1) The provision in subsection (1) of section thirty of the principal Act, which gives power to local governments to raise money on real or personal estate within the limits of their respective governments by way of mortgage or otherwise, shall have effect as though that provision conferred a power on local governments to raise money on the security of their allocated revenues, and to make proper assurances for that purpose.

(2) Provision may be made by rules under the principal Act as to the conditions under which the power to raise loans on the security of allocated revenues shall be exercised.

(3) The provision in subsection (1) of section thirty of the principal Act, which enables the Secretary of State in Council with the concurrence of a majority of votes at a meeting of the Council of India to prescribe provisions or conditions limiting the power to raise money, shall cease to have effect as regards the power to raise money on the security of allocated revenues.

3.—(1) The presidencies of Fort William in Bengal, Fort St. George, and Bombay, and the provinces known as the United Provinces, the Punjab, Bihar and Orissa, the Central Provinces, and Assam, shall each be governed, in relation to reserved subjects, by a governor in council, and in relation to transferred subjects (save as otherwise provided by this Act) by the governor acting with ministers appointed under this Act.

The said presidencies and provinces are in this Act referred to as "governor's provinces" and the two first-named presidencies are in this Act referred to as the presidencies of Bengal and Madras.

(2) The provisions of section forty-six to fifty-one of the principal Act, as amended by this Act, shall apply to the United Provinces, the Punjab, Bihar and Orissa, the Central Provinces, and Assam, as they apply to the presidencies of Bengal, Madras, and Bombay: Provided that the governors of the said provinces shall be appointed after consultation with the Governor-General.

4.—(1) The governor of a governor's province may, by notification, appoint ministers, not being members of his executive council or other officials, to administer transferred subjects, and any ministers so appointed shall hold office during his pleasure.

There may be paid to any minister so appointed in any province the same salary as is payable to a member of the executive council in that province, unless a smaller salary is provided by vote of the legislative council of the province.

(2) No minister shall hold office for a longer period than six months, unless he is or becomes an elected member of the local legislature.

(3) In relation to transferred subjects, the governor shall be guided by the advice of his ministers, unless he sees sufficient cause to dissent from their opinion, in which case he may require action to be taken otherwise than in accordance with that advice: Provided that rules may be made under the principal Act for the temporary administration of a transferred subject where,

in cases of emergency, owing to a vacancy, there is no minister in charge of the subject, by such authority and in such manner as may be prescribed by the rules.

(4) The governor of a governor's province may at his discretion appoint from among the non-official members of the local legislature council secretaries, who shall hold office during his pleasure, and discharge such duties in assisting members of the executive council and ministers, as he may assign to them.

There shall be paid to council secretaries so appointed such salary as may be provided by vote of the legislative council.

A council secretary shall cease to hold office if he ceases for more than six months to be a member of the legislative council.

5.—(1) The provision in section forty-seven of the principal Act, that two of the members of the executive council of the governor of a province must have been for at least twelve years in the service of the Crown in India, shall have effect as though "one" were substituted for "two," and the provision in that section that the Commander-in-Chief of His Majesty's Forces in India, if resident at Calcutta, Madras, or Bombay, shall, during his continuance there, be a member of the governor's council, shall cease to have effect.

(2) Provision may be made by rules under the principal Act as to the qualifications to be required in respect of members of the executive council of the governor of a province in any case where such provision is not made by section forty-seven of the principal Act as amended by this section.

6.—(1) All orders and other proceedings of the government of a governor's province shall be expressed to be made by the government of the province, and shall be authenticated as the governor may by rule direct, so, however, that provision shall be made by rule for distinguishing orders and other proceedings relating to transferred subjects from other orders and proceedings.

Orders and proceedings authenticated as aforesaid shall not be called into question in any legal proceeding on the ground that they were not duly made by the government of the province.

(2) The governor may make rules and orders for the more convenient transaction of business in his executive council and with his ministers, and every order made or act done in accordance with those rules and orders shall be treated as being the order or the act of the government of the province.

The governor may also make rules and orders for regulating the relations between his executive council and his ministers for the purpose of the transaction of the business of the local government:

Provided that any rules or orders made for the purposes specified in this section which are repugnant to the provisions of any rules made under the principal Act as amended by this Act shall, to the extent of that repugnancy, but not otherwise, be void.

7.—(1) There shall be a legislative council in every governor's province, which shall consist of the members of the executive council and of members nominated or elected as provided by this Act.

The governor shall not be a member of the legislative council, but shall have the right of addressing the council, and may for that purpose require the attendance of its members.

(2) The number of members of the governor's legislative councils shall be in accordance with the table set out in the First Schedule to this Act; and of the members of each council not more than twenty per cent. shall be official members, and at least seventy per cent. shall be elected members:

Provided that—

(*a*) subject to the maintenance of the above proportions, rules under the principal Act may provide for increasing the number of members of any council, as specified in that schedule; and

(*b*) the governor may, for the purposes of any Bill introduced or proposed to be introduced in his legislative council, nominate, in the case of Assam one person, and in the case of other provinces not more than two persons, having special knowledge or experience of the subject-matter of the Bill, and those persons shall, in relation to the Bill, have for the period for which they are nominated all the rights of members of the council, and shall be in addition to the numbers above referred to; and

(*c*) members nominated to the legislative council of the Central Provinces by the governor as the result of elections held in the Assigned Districts of Berar shall be deemed to be elected members of the legislative council of the Central Provinces.

(3) The powers of a governor's legislative council may be exercised notwithstanding any vacancy in the council.

(4) Subject as aforesaid, provision may be made by rules under the principal Act as to—

(*a*) the term of office of nominated members of governors' legislative councils, and the manner of filling casual vacancies occurring by reason of absence of members from India, inability to attend to duty, death, acceptance of office, resignation duly accepted, or otherwise; and

(*b*) the conditions under which and manner in which persons may be nominated as members of governors' legislative councils; and

(*c*) the qualification of electors, the constitution of constituencies, and the method of election for governors' legislative councils, including the number of members to be elected by communal and other electorates, and any matters incidental or ancillary thereto; and

(*d*) the qualifications for being and for being nominated or elected a member of any such council; and

(*e*) the final decision of doubts or disputes as to the validity of any election; and

(*f*) the manner in which the rules are to be carried into effect:

Provided that rules as to any such matters as aforesaid may provide for delegating to the local government such power as may be specified in the rules of making subsidiary regulations affecting the same matters.

(5) Subject to any such rules, any person who is a ruler or subject of any State in India may be nominated as a member of a governor's legislative council.

8.— (1) Every governor's legislative council shall continue for three years from its first meeting:

Provided that—

(a) the council may be sooner dissolved by the governor; and

(b) the said period may be extended by the governor for a period not exceeding one year, by notification in the official gazette of the province, if in special circumstances (to be specified in the notification) he so think fit; and

(c) after the dissolution of the council the governor shall appoint a date not more than six months or, with the sanction of the Secretary of State, not more than nine months from the date of dissolution for the next session of the council.

(2) A governor may appoint such times and places for holding the sessions of his legislative council as he thinks fit, and may also, by notification or otherwise, prorogue the council.

(3) Any meeting of a governor's legislative council may be adjourned by the person presiding.

(4) All questions in a governor's legislative council shall be determined by a majority of votes of the members present other than the person presiding, who shall, however, have and exercise a casting vote in the case of an equality of votes.

9.— (1) There shall be a president of a governor's legislative council, who shall, until the expiration of a period of four years from the first meeting of the council as constituted under this Act, be a person appointed by the governor, and shall thereafter be a member of the council elected by the council and approved by the governor:

Provided that, if at the expiration of such period of four years the council is in session, the president then in office shall continue in office until the end of the current session, and the first election of a president shall take place at the commencement of the next ensuing session.

(2) There shall be a deputy-president of a governor's legislative council who shall preside at meetings of the council in the absence of the president, and who shall be a member of the council elected by the council and approved by the governor.

(3) The appointed president of a council shall hold office until the date of the first election of a president by the council under this section, but he may resign office by writing under his hand addressed to the governor, or may be removed from office by order of the governor, and any vacancy occurring

before the expiration of the term of office of an appointed president shall be filled by a similar appointment for the remainder of such term.

(4) An elected president and a deputy-president shall cease to hold office on ceasing to be members of the council. They may resign office by writing under their hands addressed to the governor, and may be removed from office by a vote of the council with the concurrence of the governor.

(5) The president and the deputy-president shall receive such salaries as may be determined, in the case of an appointed president, by the governor, and in the case of an elected president or deputy-president, by Act of the local legislature.

10.—(1) The local legislature of any province has power, subject to the provisions of this Act, to make laws for the peace and good government of the territories for the time being constituting that province.

(2) The local legislature of any province may, subject to the provisions of the subsection next following, repeal or alter as to that province any law made either before or after the commencement of this Act by any authority in British India other than that local legislature.

(3) The local legislature of any province may not, without the previous sanction of the Governor-General, make or take into consideration any law—

(a) imposing or authorising the imposition of any new tax unless the tax is a tax scheduled as exempted from this provision by rules made under the principal Act; or

(b) affecting the public debt of India, or the customs duties, or any other tax or duty for the time being in force and imposed by the authority of the Governor-General in Council for the general purposes of the government of India, provided that the imposition or alteration of a tax scheduled as aforesaid shall not be deemed to affect any such tax or duty; or

(c) affecting the discipline or maintenance of any part of His Majesty's naval, military, or air forces; or

(d) affecting the relations of the government with foreign princes or states; or

(e) regulating any central subject; or

(f) regulating any provincial subject which has been declared by rules under the principal Act to be, either in whole or in part, subject to legislation by the Indian Legislature, in respect of any matter to which such declaration applies; or

(g) affecting any power expressly reserved to the Governor-General in Council by any law for the time being in force; or

(h) altering or repealing the provisions of any law which, having been made before the commencement of this Act by any authority in British India other than that local legislature, is declared by rules under the principal Act to be a law which cannot be repealed or altered by the local legislature without previous sanction; or (*i*) altering or repealing any provision of an Act of the Indian Legislature made after the commencement of this act, which by the provisions of that Act may not be repealed or altered by the local legislature without previous sanction:

Provided that an Act or a provision of an Act made by a local legislature, and subsequently assented to by the Governor-General in pursuance of this Act, shall not be deemed invalid by reason only of its requiring the previous sanction of the Governor-General under this Act.

(4) The local legislature of any province has not power to make any law affecting any Act of Parliament.

11.—(1) Subsections (1) and (3) of section eighty of the principal Act (which relate to the classes of business which may be transacted at meetings of local legislative councils) shall cease to apply to a governor's legislative council, but the business and procedure in any such council shall be regulated in accordance with the provisions of this section.

(2) The estimated annual expenditure and revenue of the province shall be laid in the form of a statement before the council in each year, and the proposals of the local government for the appropriation of provincial revenues and other moneys in any year shall be submitted to the vote of the council in the form of demands for grants. The council may assent, or refuse its assent, to a demand, or may reduce the amount therein referred to either by a reduction of the whole grant or by the omission or reduction of any of the items of expenditure of which the grant is composed:
Provided that—

(*a*) the local government shall have power, in relation to any such demand, to act as if it had been assented to, notwithstanding the withholding of such assent or the reduction of the amount therein referred to, if the demand relates to a reserved subject, and the governor certifies that the expenditure provided for by the demand is essential to the discharge of his responsibility for the subject; and

(*b*) the governor shall have power in cases of emergency to authorise such expenditure as may be in his opinion necessary for the safety or tranquillity of the province, or for the carrying on of any department; and

(*c*) no proposal for the appropriation of any such revenues or other moneys for any purpose shall be made except on the recommendation of the governor, communicated to the council.

(3) Nothing in the foregoing subsection shall require proposals to be submitted to the council relating to the following heads of expenditure:

(i) contributions payable by the local government to the Governor-General in Council; and

(ii) interest and sinking fund charges on loans; and

(iii) expenditure of which the amount is prescribed by or under any law; and

(iv) salaries and pensions of persons appointed by or with the approval of His Majesty or by the Secretary of State in Council; and

(v) salaries of judges of the high court of the province and of the advocate-general.

If any question arises whether any proposed appropriation of moneys does or does not relate to the above heads of expenditure, the decision of the governor shall be final.

(4) Where any Bill has been introduced or is proposed to be introduced, or any amendment to a Bill is moved or proposed to be moved, the governor may certify that the Bill or any clause of it or the amendment affects the safety or tranquillity of his province or any part of it or of another province, and may direct that no proceedings or no further proceedings shall be taken by the council in relation to the Bill, clause or amendment, and effect shall be given to any such direction.

(5) Provision may be made by rules under the principal Act for the purpose of carrying into effect the foregoing provisions of this section and for regulating the course of business in the council, and as to the persons to preside over meetings thereof in the absence of the president and deputy-president, and the preservation of order at meetings; and the rules may provide for the number of members required to constitute a quorum, and for prohibiting or regulating the asking of questions on and the discussion of any subject specified in the rules.

(6) Standing orders may be made providing for the conduct of business and the procedure to be followed in the council, in so far as these matters are not provided for by rules made under the principal Act. The first standing orders shall be made by the governor in council, but may, subject to the assent of the governor, be altered by the local legislatures. Any standing order made as aforesaid which is repugnant to the provisions of any rules made under the principal Act, shall, to the extent of that repugnancy but not otherwise, be void.

(7) Subject to the rules and standing orders affecting the council, there shall be freedom of speech in the governors' legislative councils. No person shall be liable to any proceedings in any court by reason of his speech or vote in any such council, or by reason of anything contained in any official report of the proceedings of any such council.

12.—(1) Where a Bill has been passed by a local legislative council, the governor, lieutenant-governor or chief commissioner may, instead of declaring that he assents to or withholds his assent from the Bill, return the Bill to the council for reconsideration, either in whole or in part, together with any amendments which he may recommend, or, in cases prescribed by rules under the principal Act may, and if the rules so require shall, reserve the Bill for the consideration of the Governor-General.

(2) Where a Bill is reserved for the consideration of the Governor-General, the following provisions shall apply :—

(a) The governor, lieutenant-governor or chief commissioner may, at any time within six months from the date of the reservation of the Bill, with the consent of the Governor-General, return the Bill for further consideration by the council with a recommendation that the council shall consider amendments thereto:

(b) After any Bill so returned has been further considered by the council, together with any recommendations made by the governor, lieutenant-governor or chief commissioner relating thereto, the Bill, if re-affirmed with or without amendment, may be again presented to the governor, lieutenant-governor, or chief commissioner:

(c) Any Bill reserved for the consideration of the Governor-General shall, if assented to by the Governor-General within a period of six months from the date of such reservation, become law on due publication of such assent, in the same way as a Bill assented to by the governor, lieutenant-governor or chief commissioner, but, if not assented to by the Governor-General within such period of six months, shall lapse and be of no effect unless before the expiration of that period either—

(i) the Bill has been returned by the governor, lieutenant-governor or chief commissioner, for further consideration by the council; or

(ii) in the case of the council not being in session, a notification has been published of an intention so to return the Bill at the commencement of the next session.

(3) The Governor-General may (except where the Bill has been reserved for his consideration), instead of assenting to or withholding his assent from any Act passed by a local legislature, declare that he reserves the Act for the signification of His Majesty's pleasure thereon, and in such case the Act shall not have validity until His Majesty in Council has signified his assent and his assent has been notified by the Governor-General.

13.—(1) Where a governor's legislative council has refused leave to introduce, or has failed to pass in a form recommended by the governor, any Bill relating to a reserved subject, the governor may certify that the passage of the Bill is essential for the discharge of his responsibility for the subject, and thereupon the Bill shall, notwithstanding that the council have not consented thereto, be deemed to have passed, and shall, on signature by the governor, become an Act of the local legislature in the form of the Bill as originally introduced or proposed to be introduced in the council or (as the case may be) in the form recommended to the council by the governor.

(2) Every such Act shall be expressed to be made by the governor, and the governor shall forthwith send an authentic copy thereof to the Governor-General, who shall reserve the Act for the signification of His Majesty's pleasure, and upon the signification of such assent by His Majesty in Council, and the notification thereof by the Governor-General, the Act shall have the

same force and effect as an Act passed by the local legislature and duly assented to:

Provided that, where in the opinion of the Governor-General a state of emergency exists which justifies such action, he may, instead of reserving such Act, signify his assent thereto, and thereupon the Act shall have such force and effect as aforesaid, subject however to disallowance by His Majesty in Council.

(3) An Act made under this section shall, as soon as practicable after being made, be laid before each House of Parliament, and an Act which is required to be presented for His Majesty's assent shall not be so presented until copies thereof have been laid before each House of Parliament for not less than eight days on which that House has sat.

14. An official shall not be qualified for election as a member of a local legislative council, and, if any non-official member of a local legislative council, whether elected or nominated, accepts any office in the service of the Crown in India, his seat on the council shall become vacant:

Provided that for the purposes of this provision a minister shall not be deemed to be an official and a person shall not be deemed to accept office on appointment as a minister.

15.—(1) The Governor-General in Council may, after obtaining an expression of opinion from the local government and the local legislature affected, by notification, with the sanction of His Majesty previously signified by the Secretary of State in Council, constitute a new governor's province, or place part of a governor's province under the administration of a deputy-governor to be appointed by the Governor-General, and may in any such case apply, with such modifications as appear necessary or desirable, all or any of the provisions of the principal Act or this Act relating to governors' provinces, or provinces under a lieutenant-governor or chief commissioner, to any such new province or part of a province.

(2) The Governor-General in Council may declare any territory in British India to be a "backward tract," and may, by notification, with such sanction as aforesaid, direct that the principal Act and this Act shall apply to that territory subject to such exceptions and modifications as may be prescribed in the notification. Where the Governor-General in Council has, by notification, directed as aforesaid, he may, by the same or subsequent notification, direct that any Act of the Indian Legislature shall not apply to the territory in question or any part thereof, or shall apply to the territory or any part thereof subject to such exceptions or modifications as the Governor-General thinks fit, or may authorise the governor in council to give similar directions as respects any Act of the local legislature.

16.—(1) The validity of any order made or action taken after the commencement of this Act by the Governor-General in Council or by a local government which would have been within the powers of the Governor-General in Council or of such local government if this Act had not been passed, shall not be open to question in any legal proceedings on the ground that by reason of any provision of this Act or of any rule made by virtue of any such provision such order or action has ceased to be within the powers of the Governor-General in Council or of the government concerned.

(2) Nothing in this Act, or in any rule made thereunder, shall be construed as diminishing in any respect the powers of the Indian legislature as laid down in section sixty-five of the principal Act, and the validity of any Act of the Indian legislature or any local legislature shall not be open to question in any legal proceedings on the ground that the Act affects a provincial subject or a central subject, as the case may be, and the validity of any Act made by the governor of a province shall not be so open to question on the ground that it does not relate to a reserved subject.

(3) The validity of any order made or action taken by a governor in council, or by a governor acting with his ministers, shall not be open to question in any legal proceedings on the ground that such order or action relates or does not relate to a transferred subject, or relates to a transferred subject of which the minister is not in charge.

Part II. Government of India

17. Subject to the provisions of this Act, the Indian legislature shall consist of the Governor-General and two chambers, namely, the Council of State and the Legislative Assembly.

Except as otherwise provided by or under this Act, a Bill shall not be deemed to have been passed by the Indian legislature unless it has been agreed to by both chambers, either without amendment or with such amendments only as may be agreed to by both chambers.

18.—(1) The Council of State shall consist of not more than sixty members nominated or elected in accordance with rules made under the principal Act, of whom not more than twenty shall be official members.

(2) The Governor-General shall have power to appoint, from among the members of the Council of State, a president and other persons to preside in such circumstances as he may direct.

(3) The Governor-General shall have the right of addressing the Council of State, and may for that purpose require the attendance of its members.

19.—(1) The Legislative Assembly shall consist of members nominated or elected in accordance with rules made under the principal Act.

(2) The total number of members of the Legislative Assembly shall be one hundred and forty. The number of non-elected members shall be forty, of whom twenty-six shall be official members. The number of elected members shall be one hundred:

Provided that rules made under the principal Act may provide for increasing the number of members of the Legislative Assembly as fixed by this section, and may vary the proportion which the classes of members bear one to another, so, however, that at least five-sevenths of the members of the Legislative Assembly shall be elected members, and at least one-third of the other members shall be non-official members.

(3) The Governor-General shall have the right of addressing the Legislative Assembly, and may for that purpose require the attendance of its members.

20.—(1) There shall be a president of the Legislative Assembly, who shall, until the expiration of four years from the first meeting thereof, be a person appointed by the Governor-General, and shall thereafter be a member of the Assembly elected by the Assembly and approved by the Governor-General:

Provided that, if at the expiration of such period of four years the Assembly is in session, the president then in office shall continue in office until the end of the current session, and the first election of a president shall take place at the commencement of the ensuing session.

(2) There shall be a deputy-president of the Legislative Assembly, who shall preside at meetings of the Assembly in the absence of the president, and who shall be a member of the Assembly elected by the Assembly and approved by the Governor-General.

(3) The appointed president shall hold office until the date of the election of a president under this section, but he may resign his office by writing under his hand addressed to the Governor-General, or may be removed from office by order of the Governor-General, and any vacancy occurring before the expiration of his term of office shall be filled by a similar appointment for the remainder of such term.

(4) An elected president and a deputy-president shall cease to hold office if they cease to be members of the Assembly. They may resign office by writing under their hands addressed to the Governor-General, and may be removed from office by a vote of the Assembly with the concurrence of the Governor-General.

(5) A president and deputy-president shall receive such salaries as may be determined, in the case of an appointed president by the Governor-General, and in the case of an elected president and a deputy-president by Act of the Indian legislature.

21. Every Council of State shall continue for five years, and every Legislative Assembly for three years, from its first meeting:

Provided that—

(a) either chamber of the legislature may be sooner dissolved by the Governor-General; and

(b) any such period may be extended by the Governor-General if in special circumstances he so thinks fit; and

(c) after the dissolution of either chamber the Governor-General shall appoint a date not more than six months, or, with the sanction of the Secretary of State, not more than nine months after the date of dissolution for the next session of that chamber.

(2) The Governor-General may appoint such times and places for holding the sessions of either chamber of the Indian legislature as he thinks fit, and may also from time to time, by notification or otherwise, prorogue such sessions.

(3) Any meeting of either chamber of the Indian legislature may be adjourned by the person presiding.

(4) All questions in either chamber shall be determined by a majority of votes of members present other than the presiding member, who shall, however, have and exercise a casting vote in the case of an equality of votes.

(5) The powers of either chamber of the Indian legislature may be exercised notwithstanding any vacancy in the chamber.

22.—(1) An official shall not be qualified for election as a member of either chamber of the Indian legislature, and, if any non-official member of either chamber accepts office in the service of the Crown in India, his seat in that chamber shall become vacant.

(2) If an elected member of either chamber of the Indian legislature becomes a member of the other chamber, his seat in such first-mentioned chamber shall thereupon become vacant.

(3) If any person is elected a member of both chambers of the Indian legislature, he shall, before he takes his seat in either chamber, signify in writing the chamber of which he desires to be a member, and thereupon his seat in the other chamber shall become vacant.

(4) Every member of the Governor-General's Executive Council shall be nominated as a member of one chamber of the Indian legislature, and shall have the right of attending in and addressing the other chamber, but shall not be a member of both chambers.

23.—(1) Subject to the provisions of this Act, provision may be made by rules under the principal Act as to—

(a) the term of office of nominated members of the Council of State and the Legislative Assembly, and the manner of filling casual vacancies occurring by reason of absence of members from India, inability to attend to duty, death, acceptance of office, or resignation duly accepted, or otherwise; and

(b) the conditions under which and the manner in which persons may be nominated as members of the Council of State or the Legislative Assembly; and

(c) the qualification of electors, the constitution of constituencies, and the method of election for the Council of State and the Legislative Assembly (including the number of members to be elected by communal and other electorates) and any matters incidental or ancillary thereto; and

(d) the qualifications for being or for being nominated or elected as members of the Council of State or the Legislative Assembly; and

(e) the final decision of doubts or disputes as to the validity of an election; and

(f) the manner in which the rules are to be carried into effect.

(2) Subject to any such rules, any person who is a ruler or subject of any state in India may be nominated as a member of the Council of State or the Legislative Assembly.

24.— (1) Subsections (1) and (3) of section sixty-seven of the principal Act (which relate to the classes of business which may be transacted by the Indian legislative council) shall cease to have effect.

(2) Provision may be made by rules under the principal Act for regulating the course of business and the preservation of order in the chambers of the Indian legislature, and as to the persons to preside at the meetings of the legislative assembly in the absence of the president and the deputy president; and the rules may provide for the number of members required to constitute a quorum, and for prohibiting or regulating the asking of questions on, and the discussion of, any subject specified in the rules.

(3) If any Bill which has been passed by one chamber is not, within six months after the passage of the Bill by that chamber, passed by the other chamber either without amendments or with such amendments as may be agreed to by the two chambers, the Governor-General may in his discretion refer the matter for decision to a joint sitting of both chambers: Provided that standing orders made under this section may provide for meetings of members of both chambers appointed for the purpose, in order to discuss any difference of opinion which has arisen between the two chambers.

(4) Without prejudice to the powers of the Governor-General under section sixty-eight of the principal Act, the Governor-General may, where a Bill has been passed by both chambers of the Indian legislature, return the Bill for reconsideration by either chamber.

(5) Rules made for the purpose of this section may contain such general and supplemental provisions as appear necessary for the purpose of giving full effect to this section.

(6) Standing orders may be made providing for the conduct of business and the procedure to be followed in either chamber of the Indian legislature in so far as these matters are not provided for by rules made under the principal Act. The first standing orders shall be made by the Governor-General in Council, but may, with the consent of the Governor-General, be altered by the chamber to which they relate.

Any standing order made as aforesaid which is repugnant to the provisions of any rules made under the principal Act shall, to the extent of that repugnancy but not otherwise, be void.

(7) Subject to the rules and standing orders affecting the chamber, there shall be freedom of speech in both chambers of the Indian legislature. No person shall be liable to any proceedings in any court by reason of his speech or vote in either chamber, or by reason of anything contained in any official report of the proceedings of either chamber.

25.— (1) The estimated annual expenditure and revenue of the Governor-General in Council shall be laid in the form of a statement before both chambers of the Indian legislature in each year.

(2) No proposal for the appropriation of any revenue or moneys for any purpose shall be made except on the recommendation of the Governor-General.

(3) The proposals of the Governor-General in Council for the appropriation of revenue or moneys relating to the following heads of expenditure shall not be submitted to the vote of the legislative assembly, nor shall they be open to discussion by either chamber at the time when the annual statement is under consideration, unless the Governor-General otherwise directs—

(i) interest and sinking fund charges on loans; and
(ii) expenditure of which the amount is prescribed by or under any law; and
(iii) salaries and pensions of persons appointed by or with the approval of His Majesty or by the Secretary of State in Council; and
(iv) salaries of chief commissioners and judicial commissioners; and
(v) expenditure classified by the order of the Governor-General in Council as—
  (a) ecclesiastical;
  (b) political;
  (c) defence.

(4) If any question arises whether any proposed appropriation of revenue or moneys does or does not relate to the above heads, the decision of the Governor-General on the question shall be final.

(5) The proposals of the Governor-General in Council for the appropriation of revenue or moneys relating to heads of expenditure not specified in the above heads shall be submitted to the vote of the legislative assembly in the form of demands for grants.

(6) The legislative assembly may assent or refuse its assent to any demand or may reduce the amount referred to in any demand by a reduction of the whole grant.

(7) The demands as voted by the legislative assembly shall be submitted to the Governor-General in Council, who shall, if he declares that he is satisfied that any demand which has been refused by the legislative assembly is essential to the discharge of his responsibilities, act as if it had been assented to, notwithstanding the withholding of such assent, or the reduction of the amount therein referred to, by the legislative assembly.

(8) Notwithstanding anything in this section, the Governor-General shall have power, in cases of emergency, to authorise such expenditure as may, in his opinion, be necessary for the safety or tranquillity of British India or any part thereof.

26.—(1) Where either chamber of the Indian legislature refuses leave to introduce, or fails to pass in a form recommended by the Governor-General, any Bill, the Governor-General may certify that the passage of the Bill is essential for the safety, tranquillity or interests of British India or any part thereof, and thereupon—

(a) If the Bill has already been passed by the other chamber, the Bill shall, on signature by the Governor-General, notwithstanding that it has not been consented to by both chambers, forthwith become an Act of the Indian legislature in the form of the Bill as originally introduced or proposed to be introduced in the Indian legislature, or (as the case may be) in the form recommended by the Governor-General; and

(*b*) If the Bill has not already been so passed, the Bill shall be laid before the other chamber, and, if consented to by that chamber in the form recommended by the Governor-General, shall become an Act as aforesaid on the signification of the Governor-General's assent, or, if not so consented to, shall, on signature by the Governor-General, become an Act as aforesaid.

(2) Every such Act shall be expressed to be made by the Governor-General, and shall, as soon as practicable after being made, be laid before both Houses of Parliament, and shall not have effect until it has received His Majesty's assent, and shall not be presented for His Majesty's assent until copies thereof have been laid before each House of Parliament for not less than eight days on which that House has sat; and upon the signification of such assent by His Majesty in Council, and the notification thereof by the Governor-General, the Act shall have the same force and effect as an Act passed by the Indian legislature and duly assented to:

Provided that, where in the opinion of the Governor-General a state of emergency exists which justifies such action, the Governor-General may direct that any such Act shall come into operation forthwith, and thereupon the Act shall have such force and effect as aforesaid, subject, however, to disallowance by His Majesty in Council.

27.—(1) In addition to the measures referred to in subsection (2) of section sixty-seven of the principal Act, as requiring the previous sanction of the Governor-General, it shall not be lawful without such previous sanction to introduce at any meeting of either chamber of the Indian legislature any measure—

(*a*) regulating any provincial subject, or any part of a provincial subject, which has not been declared by rules under the principal Act to be subject to legislation by the Indian legislature; or

(*b*) repealing or amending any Act of a local legislature; or

(*c*) repealing or amending any Act or ordinance made by the Governor-General.

(2) Where in either chamber of the Indian legislature any Bill has been introduced, or is proposed to be introduced, or any amendment to a Bill is moved, or proposed to be moved, the Governor-General may certify that the Bill, or any clause of it, or the amendment, affects the safety or tranquillity of British India, or any part thereof, and may direct that no proceedings, or that no further proceedings, shall be taken by the chamber in relation to the Bill, clause, or amendment, and effect shall be given to such direction.

28.—(1) The provision in section thirty-six of the principal Act, imposing a limit on the number of members of the Governor-General's executive council, shall cease to have effect.

(2) The provision in section thirty-six of the principal Act as to the qualification of members of the council shall have effect as though the words "at the time of their appointment" were omitted, and as though after the word "Scotland" there were inserted the words "or a pleader of the High Court" and as though "ten years" were substituted for "five years."

(3) Provision may be made by rules under the principal Act as to the qualifications to be required in respect of members of the Governor-General's executive council, in any case where such provision is not made by section thirty-six of the principal Act as amended by this section.

(4) Subsection (2) of section thirty-seven of the principal Act (which provides that when and so long as the Governor-General's executive council assembles in a province having a governor the governor shall be an extraordinary member of the council) shall cease to have effect.

29.—(1) The Governor-General may at his discretion appoint, from among the members of the legislative assembly, council secretaries, who shall hold office during his pleasure and discharge such duties in assisting the members of his executive council as he may assign to them.

(2) There shall be paid to council secretaries so appointed such salary as may be provided by the Indian legislature.

(3) A council secretary shall cease to hold office if he ceases for more than six months to be a member of the legislative assembly.

Part III. Secretary of State in Council

30. The salary of the Secretary of State, the salaries of his under-secretaries, and any other expenses of his department may, notwithstanding anything in the principal Act, instead of being paid out of the revenues of India, be paid out of moneys provided by Parliament, and the salary of the Secretary of State shall be so paid.

31. The following amendments shall be made in section three of the principal Act in relation to the composition of the Council of India, the qualification, term of office, and remuneration of its members: —

(1) The provisions of subsection (1) shall have effect as though "eight" and "twelve" were substituted for "ten" and "fourteen" respectively, as the minimum and maximum number of members, provided that the council, as constituted at the time of the passing of this Act, shall not be affected by this provision, but no fresh appointment or reappointment thereto shall be made in excess of the maximum prescribed by this provision.

(2) The provisions of subsection (3) shall have effect as if "one-half" were substituted for "nine" and "India" were substituted for "British India."

(3) In subsection (4) "five years" shall be substituted for "seven years" as the term of office of members of the council, provided that the tenure of office of any person who is a member of the council at the time of the passing of this Act shall not be affected by this provision.

(4) The provisions of subsection (8) shall cease to have effect and in lieu thereof the following provisions shall be inserted:

"There shall be paid to each member of the Council of India the annual salary of twelve hundred pounds; provided that any member of the council who was at the time of his appointment domiciled in India shall receive, in addition to the salary hereby provided, an annual subsistence allowance of six hundred pounds.

Such salaries and allowances may be paid out of the revenues of India or out of moneys provided by Parliament."

(5) Notwithstanding anything in any Act or rules, where any person in the service of the Crown in India is appointed a member of the council before completion of the period of such service required to entitle him to a pension or annuity, his service as such member shall, for the purpose of any pension or annuity which would be payable to him on completion of such period, be reckoned as service under the Crown in India whilst resident in India.

32.—(1) The provision in section six of the principal Act which prescribes the quorum for meetings of the Council of India shall cease to have effect, and the Secretary of State shall provide for a quorum by directions to be issued in this behalf.

(2) The provision in section eight of the principal Act relating to meetings of the Council of India shall have effect as though "month" were substituted for "week."

(3) Section ten of the principal Act shall have effect as though the words "all business of the council or committees thereof is to be transacted" were omitted, and the words, "the business of the Secretary of State in Council or the Council of India shall be transacted, and any order made or act done in accordance with such direction shall, subject to the provisions of this Act, be treated as being an order of the Secretary of State in Council" were inserted in lieu thereof.

33. The Secretary of State in Council may, notwithstanding anything in the principal Act, by rule regulate and restrict the exercise of the powers of superintendence, direction and control, vested in the Secretary of State and the Secretary of State in Council, by the principal Act, or otherwise, in such manner as may appear necessary or expedient in order to give effect to the purposes of this Act.

Before any rules are made under this section relating to subjects other than transferred subjects, the rules proposed to be made shall be laid in draft before both Houses of Parliament, and such rules shall not be made unless both Houses by resolution approve the draft either without modification or addition, or with modifications or additions to which both Houses agree, but upon such approval being given the Secretary of State in Council may make such rules in the form in which they have been approved, and such rules on being so made shall be of full force and effect.

Any rules relating to transferred subjects made under this section shall be laid before both Houses of Parliament as soon as may be after they are made, and, if an Address is presented to His Majesty by either House of Parliament within the next thirty days on which that House has sat after the rules are laid before it praying that the rules or any of them may be annulled, His Majesty in Council may annul the rules or any of them, and those rules shall thenceforth be void, but without prejudice to the validity of anything previously done thereunder.

34. So much of section five of the principal Act as relates to orders and communications sent to India from the United Kingdom and to orders made in the United Kingdom, and sections eleven, twelve, thirteen, and fourteen of the principal Act, shall cease to have effect, and the procedure for the sending of orders and communications to India and in general for correspondence between the Secretary of State and the Governor-General in Council or any local government shall be such as may be prescribed by order of the Secretary of State in Council.

35. His Majesty may by Order in Council make provision for the appointment of a High Commissioner for India in the United Kingdom, and for the pay, pension, powers, duties, and conditions of employment of the High Commissioner and of his assistants; and the Order may further provide for delegating to the High Commissioner any of the powers previously exercised by the Secretary of State or the Secretary of State in Council, whether under the principal Act or otherwise, in relation to making contracts, and may prescribe the conditions under which he shall act on behalf of the Governor-General in Council or any local government.

*   *   *

*Report of the Indian Statutory Commission Recommending
Constitutional and Political Reforms in the Direction
of Self-Government (Simon Report), 27 May 1930**
[*This Report was for the most part not implemented.*]

*   *   *

Part XII.—General Survey and Conclusion

362. We have now reached the end of our task. By the terms of our Warrant
of Appointment, and by the provisions of the section on which it was based, we
have been required to survey the working of the existing system of government
in British India and to make recommendations for its amendment. In particular, we are directed to report "as to whether and to what extent it is desirable to
establish the principle of responsible government, or to extend, modify, or
restrict the degree of responsible government" now existing. The previous parts
of this volume give our detailed and considered answer to these questions. But
we realise how difficult it is, in dealing with matters so various and complicated, to present to those who may not be experts on the subject of the Indian
constitution, a clear picture of the main constitutional results which would be
achieved if our suggestions were incorporated into the existing system. We
propose, therefore, in this final chapter to point out the more important of the
changes which we recommend. What follows must not be treated as a summary
of this volume, for not only is it impossible in a brief survey to cover all its
contents, but a bald statement of conclusions would tend to mislead if it were
not accompanied by a consideration of the arguments which have led us to
reach them. We shall, therefore, add, at each point which we are going to
mention, the necessary references to earlier portions of our Report.

The Scope of our Proposals

363. British India at present has a constitution, based for the most part on
the Government of India Act, which includes (1) a Central Executive—the
Governor-General in Council; and a Central Legislature—the Council of State
and Legislative Assembly; and (2) nine Provincial Governments, each associated with a Provincial Council, and covering between them 97 per cent. of the
whole area. The balance is represented by the North-West Frontier Province
and other minor administrations. Our proposals touch every part of this constitution. We will venture to repeat words which we used in the first paragraph of
our former volume, when we wrote that we were entering upon our task "upon

**Parliamentary Papers*, 1930, XI, Cmd. 3569, 311–16.

the basis and assumption that the goal defined by Mr. Montagu represents the accepted policy to be pursued, and that the only proposals worthy to be considered are proposals conceived in the spirit of the announcement of 20th August, 1917, and inspired with the honest purpose of giving to it its due effect." We have kept this principle steadily in mind throughout the whole of our deliberations, and our recommendations are based upon it.

Outline of Provincial Changes

364. In the provinces, the main consequences of adopting our proposals would be as follows: —

The boundary now set up between departments of which Indian Ministers may take charge and departments from which they are excluded will be removed, and thus dyarchy will terminate.

The conduct of provincial administration as a whole will rest with a provincial Cabinet, the members of which will be chosen by the Governor. These Ministers, whether elected members of the legislature or not, will have joint responsibility for action and policy. The constitution of the provincial Cabinet will be elastic and, where and when the Governor considers it necessary, it will contain an official element.

The powers of the Governor for certain essential purposes, such as the protection of minorities, and of the civil service, will be defined, and will be exercised within the limits and under the conditions we have described.

Full powers of intervention in the event of a breakdown will remain in the hands of the Governor, subject to the direction of the Governor-General.

The Provincial Legislatures will be based upon a widened franchise—the extension we propose would treble the electorate and would include the admission of a larger number of women voters.

Certain important minorities will be adequately protected by the continuance of communal electorates unless and until agreement can be reached upon a better method.

The Depressed Classes will get representation by reservation of seats.

The Legislatures will be enlarged, and the constituencies reduced to a more manageable size. The Provincial Councils instead of being, as at present, purely legislative bodies, will acquire certain powers of recasting their own representative system, so that each province may advance to self-government on lines which are found to be best suited for its individual needs, subject always to securing that the vote of the majority shall not introduce constitutional changes which would prejudice minority rights.

The provinces will be provided with enlarged financial resources.

As for provincial areas, the question whether some redistribution is desirable will at once be taken up; such cases as those of Sind and the Oriya-speaking peoples will be the first to be considered.

Burma, which is admittedly not a natural part of British India, will be separated forthwith. Provision must be made without delay for framing its future constitution.

The administered areas of the North-West Frontier Province will now receive an advance in constitutional status represented by the creation of a local legislature, with powers which we have described. Both it and Baluchistan will acquire the right to representation at the Centre.

The complicated and interlacing systems of administration of the Backward Tracts will be revised, and such parts of these as remain excluded areas will come under the charge of the central administration.

Modifications at the Centre

365. We now pass to the Centre.

The Legislative Assembly, which should be called the "Federal Assembly," will be reconstituted on the basis of the representation of the Provinces and other areas in British India according to population. Members representing Governors' Provinces will be elected by the Provincial Councils by the method of proportional representation, which will ensure that members belonging to minority communities will be included in sufficient numbers in the Federal Assembly. Members will be returned from the North-West Frontier Province and other areas outside the Governors' Provinces by methods appropriate to each case. The official members of the Federal Assembly will consist of such members of the Governor-General's Council as sit in the Lower House, together with twelve other nominated officials.

The Council of State will continue with its existing functions as a body of elected and nominated members chosen in the same proportions as at present. Its members, who must have high qualifications, will, so far as they are elected, be chosen by indirect election carried out by provincial Second Chambers if such bodies are constituted, or, failing this, by the Provincial Councils.

The existing legislative and financial powers of the two Chambers of the Central Legislature will remain as at present, but the Federal Assembly will also have the special function of voting certain indirect taxes, collected by a central agency, the net proceeds of which will fall into a Provincial Fund for the purpose of being distributed amongst the different units represented in the Federal Assembly.

The Central Executive will continue to be the Governor-General in Council, but the Governor-General will henceforward be the authority who will select and appoint his Executive Councillors. Existing qualifications will remain, but will be laid down in statutory rules made under the new Government of India Act, so that when occasion arises to modify these conditions hereafter this may be done without passing a new Act of Parliament. But any modification in the statutory rules made for this purpose would require to be laid before both Houses of Parliament and the approval of both Houses expressed by resolution.

It is proposed that among the members of the Governor-General's Council should be one whose primary function it would be to lead the Federal Assembly. We have made other suggestions relating to the composition and character of the Governor-General's Council, and we propose that the Commander-in-chief should no longer be a member of it, or of the Central Legislature.

The Army

366. We have suggested for consideration a method by which, if agreement could be reached, the obstacle which the composition and functions of the Army in India present to the more rapid development of responsible government might be removed through treating the defence of India as a matter which should fall within the responsibilities of the Governor-General, advised by the Commander-in-Chief, as representing the Imperial authorities, instead of being part of the responsibilities of the Government of India in relation to the Central Legislature.

Civil Services, High Courts, India Office

367. As regards the Civil Services of India, the Security Services must continue to be recruited as All-India Services by the Secretary of State, and their existing rights must be maintained. These Security Services include the Indian Civil Service and the Indian Police Service. It is a matter for consideration whether the Irrigation Service and the Forest Service should not be similarly recruited. The privilege of premature retirement will be extended.

The rates of Indianisation laid down by the Lee Commission for the Security Services will be maintained.

In addition to the existing Public Service Commission, we intend that there should be established by Statute similar bodies covering the provincial and subordinate services in all the Provinces.

The High Courts will be centralised, and the expenses of the High Courts will become a central charge.

As regards the India Office, the Governor-General in Council will remain in constitutional theory under the superintendence, direction and control of the Secretary of State, and the extent to which this control is relaxed or falls into desuetude will depend upon further practice, and cannot be laid down in the Statute.

Apart from the Secretary of State's authority over the Governor-General in Council, he will exercise no control over Provincial Governments, save in so far as he does so in connection with the exercise of special powers vested in the Governor.

The functions and composition of the Council of India will be modified. Its size will be reduced, and the majority of its members should have the qualification of more recent Indian experience than is required at present. The Council will exist primarily as an advisory body, but independent powers will continue for (1) the control of Service conditions, and (2) the control of non-votable Indian expenditure.

Indian States

368. Lastly, for the purpose of promoting the closer association with British India of the Indian States in matters of common concern for India as a whole, we propose that the new Act should provide that it shall be lawful for the Crown to create a Council for Greater India, containing both representatives of the States and members representing British India. This Council would have consultative and deliberate functions in regard to a scheduled list of "matters of

common concern," together with such other subjects of common concern as the Viceroy from time to time certifies as suitable for consideration by the Council. We refer to Part VII of this volume for a more detailed account of the machinery and methods which we contemplate, and we put forward the proposals as designed to make a beginning in the process which may lead to the Federation of Greater India.

Conclusion

369. In writing this Report we have made no allusion to the events of the last few months in India. In fact, the whole of our principal recommendations were arrived at and unanimously agreed upon before these events occurred. We have not altered a line of our Report on that account, for it is necessary to look beyond particular incidents and to take a longer view.

Our object throughout has been to bring to the notice of the British Parliament and the British people such information as we are able to supply about the general conditions of the problem which now awaits solution, together with our considered proposals. We hope, at the same time, that our Indian fellow-subjects, after doing us the courtesy of studying the Report as a whole (for isolated sentences may give to any reader a wrong impression), will find that what we have put forward has been written in a spirit of genuine sympathy.

No one of either race ought to be so foolish as to deny the greatness of the contribution which Britain has made to Indian progress. It is not racial prejudice, nor imperialistic ambition, nor commercial interest, which makes us say so plainly. It is a tremendous achievement to have brought to the Indian sub-continent and to have applied in practice the conceptions of impartial justice, of the rule of law, of respect for equal civic rights without reference to class or creed, and of a disinterested and incorruptible civil service. These are essential elements in any state which is advancing towards well-ordered self-government. In his heart, even the bitterest critic of British administration in India knows that India has owed these things mainly to Britain. But, when all this is said, it still leaves out of account the condition essential to the peaceful advance of India, and Indian statesmanship has now a great part to play. Success can only be achieved by sustained goodwill and co-operation, both between the great religious communities of India which have so constantly been in conflict, and between India and Britain. For the future of India depends on the collaboration of East and West, and each has much to learn from the other.

We have grown to understand something of the ideals which are inspiring the Indian national movement, and no man who has taken part in working the representative institutions of Britain can fail to sympathise with the desire of others to secure for their own land a similar development. But a constitution is something more than a generalisation: it has to present a constructive scheme. We submit our Report in the hope that it may furnish materials and suggest a plan by means of which Indian constitutional reconstruction may be peacefully and surely promoted.

All of which we submit for Your Majesty's gracious consideration.

*Speech by Winston Churchill to the Indian Empire Society at the
Albert Hall Attacking British Concessions to India, 18 March 1931**
*[Churchill had resigned from the Conservative
"Shadow Cabinet" over this issue in January 1931.]*

I think it hard that the burden of holding and organising this immense meeting should be thrown upon the Indian Empire Society. One would have thought that if there was one cause in the world which the Conservative party would have hastened to defend, it would be the cause of the British Empire in India. One would have expected that the whole force of the Conservative party machine would have been employed for months past in building up a robust, educated opinion throughout the country, and in rallying all its strongest forces to guard our vital interests. Unhappily all that influence, and it is an enormous influence, has been cast the other way. The Conservative leaders have decided that we are to work with the Socialists, and that we must make our action conform with theirs. We therefore have against us at the present time the official machinery of all the three great parties in the State. We meet under a ban. Every Member of Parliament or Peer who comes here must face the displeasure of the party Whips. Mr. Baldwin has declared that the three-party collusion must continue, and in support of that decision he has appealed to all those sentiments of personal loyalty and partisan feeling which a leader can command. Is it not wonderful in these circumstances, with all this against us, that a few of us should manage to get together here in this hall to-night?

Our fight is hard. It will also be long. We must not expect early success. The forces marshalled against us are too strong. But win or lose, we must do our duty. If the British people are to lose their Indian Empire, they shall do so with their eyes open, and not be led blindfold into a trap. Already in our campaign we have had a measure of success. The movement and awakening of opinion in the Conservative party have already caused concern to our leaders. They feel they have to reckon with resolute forces in the party and far beyond it, who will not be easily quelled. Already they have rejected the plan of sending a three-party delegation out to India for which Lord Irwin pleaded so earnestly. For the moment, therefore, we have a breathing space. The Socialist and subversive enemy have been thrown into disarray by the breakdown of their scheme to entice the Conservatives out to India. They are arranging their forces for a renewed attack. Mr. Gandhi, their supreme hope, is to come to London, as soon as they can persuade him to come, and here in the centre of the Empire he will discuss with British ministers and politicians the best means for breaking it up. But by that time we shall be ready too. We shall not be taken by surprise,

*Churchill, *India*, 117–32.

as the country was during the Round Table Conference. We are not entirely defenceless or without means of expression. We have behind us the growing strength of Conservative opinion. We have the prospect at no great distance of a Conservative victory. Nothing will turn us from our path, or discourage us from our efforts; and by the time Mr. Gandhi has arrived here to receive the surrender of our Indian Empire, the Conservative party will not be so ready to have its name taken in vain.

What spectacle could be more sorrowful than that of this powerful country casting away with both hands, and up till now almost by general acquiescence, the great inheritance which centuries have gathered? What spectacle could be more strange, more monstrous in its perversity, than to see the Viceroy and the high officials and agents of the Crown in India labouring with all their influence and authority to unite and weave together into a confederacy all the forces adverse and hostile to our rule in India? One after another our friends and the elements on which we ought to rely in India are chilled, baffled and dismissed, and finally even encouraged to band themselves together with those who wish to drive us out of the country. It is a hideous act of self-mutilation, astounding to every nation in the world. The princes, the Europeans, the Moslems, the Depressed classes, the Anglo-Indians—none of them know what to do nor where to turn in the face of their apparent desertion by Great Britain. Can you wonder that they try in desperation to make what terms are possible with the triumphant Brahmin oligarchy?

I am against this surrender to Gandhi. I am against these conversations and agreements between Lord Irwin and Mr. Ghandi. Ghandi stands for the expulsion of Britain from India. Gandhi stands for the permanent exclusion of British trade from India. Gandhi stands for the substitution of Brahmin domination for British rule in India. You will never be able to come to terms with Gandhi. You have only to read his latest declarations, and compare them with the safeguards for which we are assured the official Conservatives will fight to the end, to see how utterly impossible agreement is. But let me tell you this. If at the sacrifice of every British interest and of all the necessary safeguards and means of preserving peace and progress in India, you came to terms with Gandhi, Gandhi would at that self-same moment cease to count any more in the Indian situation. Already Nehru, his young rival in the Indian Congress, is preparing to supersede him the moment that he has squeezed his last drop from the British lemon. In running after Gandhi and trying to build on Gandhi, in imagining that Mr. Ramsay Macdonald and Mr. Gandhi and Lord Irwin are going to bestow peace and progress upon India, we should be committing ourselves to a crazy dream, with a terrible awakening.

No! Come back from these perilous paths while time and strength remain. Study the report of your own statutory commission headed by Sir John Simon and signed unanimously by the representatives of all the three parties in the State. Let us take that as our starting-point for any extensions we may make of self-government in India. It is very wrong that the vast majority of Conservative electors throughout the country, and the vast majority of all those who are acquainted with and have practical experience of India, and of that enormous mass of patriotic people not attached to any party, should have these vital questions settled over their heads by an agreement or an understanding between the two front benches in the House of Commons, and have their future settled as if they were a lot of sheep. We are told that three-party unity must be preserved at all costs. What does that mean? Up to the present it has only meant one thing, namely, that the Conservative party has had to toe the Socialist line, and has been dragged at the Socialist tail. Here are these Socialists, maintained in office only on sufferance or by intrigue, expecting all other parties to serve them, and to dance to their tune. We are here to-night to say 'No, that shall not be.' We have a right to our own convictions; we are entitled to act in accordance with them. We will certainly make our faith apparent by every means in our power, and in every quarter of the land.

I repudiate the calumny which our opponents level at us that we have no policy for India but repression and force. Do not be deceived by these untruths. Do not be disquieted by exaggerations of the difficulty of maintaining order in India which are spread about for interested motives by the Socialist ministers and their allies. In the whole of the disturbances of the last year—except on the frontier—scarcely a British soldier has been required. Very few people have been killed or severely wounded in the rioting. But how did the most of them get hurt? They got hurt not by the Indian police, but in religious fights between Moslems and Hindus. The great body of expert opinion which is represented upon the Indian Empire Society will support me when I say that a calm, capable, determined Viceroy properly supported from home could maintain peace and tranquillity in India year after year with a tenth of the repressive measures which Lord Irwin in his misguided benevolence has been compelled to employ.

Neither is it true that we have no constructive policy. We take our stand upon views almost universally accepted until a few months ago. We believe that the next forward step is the development of Indian responsibility in the provincial governments of India. Efforts should be made to make them more truly representative of the real needs of the people. Indians should be given ample opportunities to try their hand at giving capable government in the provinces; and meanwhile the central Imperial executive, which is the sole guarantee of impartiality between races, creeds and classes, should preserve its sovereign power intact, and allow no derogation from its responsibility to Parliament. Is that Diehardism? That is the message of the Simon report, unanimously signed by the representatives of the three parties. That is the purport of the alternative scheme submitted a few months ago by the Viceroy himself.

After all, it opens immediately an immense and fertile field for Indian self-government. The provinces of India are great states and separate nations comparable in magnitude and in numbers with the leading powers of Europe. The responsible government of territories and populations as large as Germany, France, Poland, Italy or Spain is not a task unworthy of Indian capacity for self-government, so far as it has yet been displayed. It is a task the successful discharge of which would certainly not conflict with the ultimate creation of a federal system. On the contrary it is the indispensable preliminary without which no federation, desirable or undesirable, is possible. Why, the very word 'federal' signifies a *foedus* or treaty made between hitherto sovereign or autonomous states. All federations have arisen thus. In the United States of America, in Canada, in Australia, in South Africa, in every case the units have first been created. Why should these unpractised, unproved, unrepresentative, self-chosen groups of Indian politicians disdain the immense possibilities offered within the limits of the Statutory Commission's report, and demand an immediate setting up of an United States of India, with themselves in control, and the British army at their orders? Before a Federal system for India could be set up there must be first the self-governing constituent provinces; and, secondly, far greater, more real, more representative contact between the Indian political classes and the vast proletariat they aspire to rule. Even Europe cannot achieve such a united organisation. But what would be said of a scheme which handed the federal government of the United States of Europe over to political classes proportionately no larger than the inhabitants of Portugal, and no more representative of the needs and passions of a mighty continent than the inhabitants of a single city like Rome? Such are the follies we are forced to expose. We therefore resist upon the highest experience and authority the viewy hysterical megalomania of the Round Table Conference.

Why is it that the principles of Government and lessons of history which we have learnt in our experience with the great self-governing dominions, which we have learnt in Canada, in South Africa and in Ireland, apply only in a limited degree to India? It is because the problem of Indian government is primarily a technical one. In India far more than in any other community in the world moral, political and economic considerations are outweighed by the importance of technical and administrative apparatus. Here you have nearly three hundred and fifty millions of people, lifted to a civilisation and to a level of peace, order, sanitation and progress far above anything they could possibly have achieved themselves or could maintain. This wonderful fact is due to the guidance and authority of a few thousands of British officials responsible to Parliament who have for generations presided over the development of India. If that authority is injured or destroyed, the whole efficiency of the services, defensive, administrative, medical, hygienic, judicial; railway, irrigation, public works and famine prevention, upon which the Indian masses depend for their culture and progress, will perish with it. India will fall back quite rapidly through the centuries into the barbarism and privations of the Middle Ages. The question at stake is not therefore the gratification of the political aspirations towards self-government of a small number of intellectuals. It is, on the contrary, the practical, technical task of maintaining the peace and life of India by artificial means upon a much higher standard than would otherwise be possible. To let the Indian people fall, as they would, to the level of China, would be a desertion of duty on the part of Great Britain.

But that is not all. To abandon India to the rule of the Brahmins would be an act of cruel and wicked negligence. It would shame for ever those who bore its guilt. These Brahmins who mouth and patter the principles of Western

Liberalism, and pose as philosophic and democratic politicians, are the same Brahmins who deny the primary rights of existence to nearly sixty millions of their own fellow countrymen whom they call 'untouchable,' and whom they have by thousands of years of oppression actually taught to accept this sad position. They will not eat with these sixty millions, nor drink with them, nor treat them as human beings. They consider themselves contaminated even by their approach. And then in a moment they turn round and begin chopping logic with John Stuart Mill, or pleading the rights of man with Jean Jacques Rousseau.

While any community, social or religious, endorses such practices and asserts itself resolved to keep sixty millions of fellow countrymen perpetually and eternally in a state of sub-human bondage, we cannot recognise their claim to the title-deeds of democracy. Still less can we hand over to their unfettered sway those helpless millions they despise. Side by side with this Brahmin theocracy and the immense Hindu population—angelic and untouchable castes alike—there dwell in India seventy millions of Moslems, a race of far greater physical vigour and fierceness, armed with a religion which lends itself only too readily to war and conquest. While the Hindu elaborates his argument, the Moslem sharpens his sword. Between these two races and creeds, containing as they do so many gifted and charming beings in all the glory of youth, there is no intermarriage. The gulf is impassable. If you took the antagonisms of France and Germany, and the antagonisms of Catholics and Protestants, and compounded them and multiplied them ten-fold, you would not equal the division which separates these two races intermingled by scores of millions in the cities and plains of India. But over both of them the impartial rule of Britain has hitherto lifted its appeasing sceptre. Until the Montagu-Chelmsford reforms began to raise the question of local sovereignty and domination, they had got used to dwelling side by side in comparative toleration. But step by step, as it is believed we are going to clear out or be thrust out of India, so this tremendous rivalry and hatred of races springs into life again. It is becoming more acute every day. Were we to wash our hands of all responsibility and divest ourselves of all our powers, as our sentimentalists desire, ferocious civil wars would speedily break out between the Moslems and the Hindus. No one who knows India will dispute this.

But that is not the end. The Brahmins know well that they cannot defend themselves against the Moslems. The Hindus do not possess among their many virtues that of being a fighting race. The whole south of India is peopled with races deserving all earnest solicitude and regard, but incapable of self-defence. It is in the north alone that the fighting races dwell. Bengal, for instance, does not send from her forty-five million inhabitants any soldiers to the native army. The Punjabis, on the other hand, and the Pathans, together with the Ghurkas and the Sikhs, who are entirely exceptional sects of Hindus, all dwelling in the north, furnish three-quarters of the entire army in the time of peace, and furnished more than three-quarters of it in time of war. There can be no doubt therefore that the departure of the British from India, which Mr. Gandhi advocates, and which Mr. Nehru demands, would be followed first by a struggle in the North and thereafter by a reconquest of the South by the North, and of the Hindus by the Moslems. This danger has not escaped the crafty foresight of the Brahmins. It is for that reason that they wish to have the control of a British army, or failing that, a white army of janissaries officered, as Mr. Gandhi has suggested, by Germans or other Europeans. They wish to have an effective foreign army, or foreign-organised army, in order to preserve their dominance over the Moslems and their tyranny over their own untouchables. There, is the open plot of which we are in danger of becoming the dupes, and the luckless millions of Indians the victims.

It is our duty to guard those millions from that fate.

Let me just direct your attention once more upon these untouchables, fifty or sixty millions of them, that is to say more than the whole population of the British Isles; all living their lives in acceptance of the validity of the awful curse pronounced upon them by the Brahmins. A multitude as big as a nation, men, women and children deprived of hope and of the status of humanity. Their plight is worse than that of slaves, because they have been taught to consent not only to a physical but to a psychic servitude and prostration.

I have asked myself whether if Christ came again into this world, it would not be to the untouchables of India that he would first go, to give them the tidings that not only are all men equal in the sight of God, but that for the weak and poor and downtrodden a double blessing is reserved. Certainly the success of Christianity and missionary enterprise has been greater among the untouchables than among any other class of the Indian population. The very act of accepting Christianity by one of these poor creatures involves a spiritual liberation from this obsession of being unclean; and the curse falls from their minds as by a miracle. They stand erect, captains of their fate in the broad sunlight of the world. There are also nearly five million Indian Christians in India, a large proportion of whom can read and write, and some of whom have shown themselves exceptionally gifted. It will be a sorry day when the arm of Britain can no longer offer them the protection of an equal law.

There is a more squalid aspect. Hitherto for generations it has been the British policy that no white official should have any interest or profit other than his salary and pension out of Indian administration. All concession-hunters and European adventurers, company-promoters and profit-seekers have been rigorously barred and banned. But now that there is spread through India the belief that we are a broken, bankrupt, played-out power, and that our rule is going to pass away and be transferred in the name of the majority to the Brahmin sect, all sorts of greedy appetites have been excited, and many itching fingers are stretching and scratching at the vast pillage of a derelict Empire. I read in the *Times* newspaper, in the *Times* mind you, only last week of the crowd of rich Bombay merchants and millionaire millowners, millionaires on sweated labour, who surround Mr. Gandhi, the saint, the lawyer, Lord Irwin's dear colleague and companion. What are they doing there, these men, and what is he doing in their houses? They are making arrangements that the greatest bluff, the greatest humbug and the greatest betrayal shall be followed by the greatest ramp. Nepotism, back-scratching, graft and corruption in every form will be the handmaidens of a Brahmin domination. Far rather would I see every Englishman quit the country, every soldier, every civil servant embark at Bombay, than that we should remain clutching on to the control of foreign relations and begging for trading facilities, while all the time we were the mere cloak of dishonour and oppression.

If you were to put these facts, hard, solid indigestible facts, before Mr. Ramsay Macdonald, or Mr. Wedgwood Benn, or Sir Herbert Samuel, they would probably reply by pointing to the follies of Lord North in the American revolution, to the achievements of Lord Durham in Canada, or to what has happened in South Africa or in Ireland. All the Socialists and some of the Liberals, together with, I am sorry to say, the official Conservatives, have got these arguments on the tip of their tongue. They represent all of us and the millions who think with us, and the instructed Anglo-Indian administrators on whose advice we rely, as being mere dullards and reactionaries who have never been able to move with the age, or understand modern ideas. *We* are a sort of inferior race mentally deficient, composed principally of colonels and other undesirables who have fought for Britain. *They* are the sole possessors and monopolists of the spirit and of the message of our generation. But we do not depend on colonels—though why Conservatives should sneer at an honoured rank in the British army I cannot tell—we depend on facts. We depend on the private soldiers of the British democracy. We place our trust in the loyal heart of Britain. Our faith is founded upon the rock of the wage-earning population of this island which has never yet been appealed to, by duty and chivalry, in vain.

These great issues which arise from time to time in our history are never decided by the party caucuses. They are decided by the conscience and the spirit of the mass of the British people. It is upon the simple faith and profound unerring instinct of the British people, never yet found wanting in a crisis, that we must put our trust. We are deliberately trying to tell our story to the British masses, to the plain and simple folk to whom the fame of the British Empire is ever dear. In assailing the moral duty of Great Britain in India, the Socialist Government and all who aid and abet Mr. Ramsay Macdonald and his Socialist Government, or make their path smooth, will find they have stumbled upon a sleeping giant who, when he arises, will tread with dauntless steps the path of justice and of honour.

"Proposals for Indian Constitutional Reform," a White Paper
Embodying Further Acceptance of the Principle of
Responsible Government for India, March 1933*

1. The general principle underlying all these proposals is that all powers appertaining or incidental to the government of India and all rights, authority and jurisdiction possessed in that country—whether flowing from His Majesty's sovereignty over the territories of British India, or derived from treaty, grant, usage, sufferance or otherwise in relation to other territories—are vested in the Crown and are exercisable by and in the name of the King Emperor.

* * *

Part I. The Federation

General

2. The Federation of India will be a union between the Governors' Provinces and those Indian States whose Rulers signify their desire to accede to the Federation by a formal Instrument of Accession. By this Instrument the Ruler will transfer to the Crown for the purposes of the Federation his powers and jurisdiction in respect of those matters which he is willing to recognise as federal matters; and the powers and jurisdiction so transferred will thereafter be exercised on behalf of the Federation and in accordance with the provisions of the Constitution Act by the Governor-General, the Federal Legislature, the Federal Court (with an appeal therefrom to His Majesty in Council) and such other Federal organs as the Constitution Act may create. But in the case of every State which accedes, the powers and jurisdiction of the Federation in relation to that State and the subjects of its Ruler will be strictly co-terminous with the powers and jurisdiction transferred to the Crown by the Ruler himself and defined in his Instrument of Accession.

3. Except to the extent to which the Ruler of a State has transferred powers and jurisdiction, whether by his Instrument of Accession or otherwise—and, in the case of a State which has not acceded to the Federation, in all respects—the relations of the State will be with the Crown represented by the Viceroy, and not with the Crown represented by the Governor-General as executive head of the Federal Government. Accordingly, all powers of the Crown in relation to the States which are at present exercised by the Governor-General in Council, other than those which fall within the Federal sphere, will after Federation be exercised by the Viceroy as the Crown's representative.

*Parliamentary Papers, 1932–33, XX, Cmd. 4268, 38–65.

4. The Federation will be brought into existence by the issue of a Proclamation by His Majesty declaring that on a date to be appointed in the Proclamation the existing nine "Governors' Provinces," with Sind and Orissa (which will be constituted as new and separate Governors' Provinces), are to be united in a Federation of India with such Indian States as have acceded or may accede to the Federation; but the Proclamation will not be issued until—

   (a) His Majesty has received intimation that the Rulers of States representing not less than half the aggregate population of the Indian States and entitled to not less than half the seats to be allotted to the States in the Federal Upper Chamber, have signified their desire to accede to the Federation; and

   (b) Both Houses of Parliament have presented an Address to His Majesty praying that such a Proclamation may be issued.

5. The authority of the Federation will, without prejudice to the extraterritorial powers of the Federal Legislature (see paragraph 111), extend to the Governors' Provinces, to the acceding States (subject to the limitations mentioned in paragraph 3), and to those areas in British India which are administered by Chief Commissioners—namely, the Provinces of Delhi, Ajmer-Merwara, Coorg, British Baluchistan and the Andaman and Nicobar Islands. These Provinces (with one exception) will be directly subject to the jurisdiction of the Federal Government and Legislature.

In the case of British Baluchistan special provision will be made whereby the Governor-General will himself direct and control the administration of this Province (see paragraphs 57-58). Expenditure required for British Baluchistan will not be subject to the vote of the Federal Legislature, but will be open to discussion in both Chambers.

The Settlement of Aden is at present a Chief Commissioner's Province. The future arrangements for the Settlement are, however, under consideration, and accordingly no proposals in respect of it are included in this document.

The Federal Executive

6. The executive authority of the Federation, including the supreme command of the Military, Naval and Air Forces in India, will be exercisable on the King's behalf by a Governor-General holding office during His Majesty's pleasure, but His Majesty may appoint a Commander-in-Chief to exercise in relation to those Forces such powers and functions as may be assigned to him.

All executive acts will run in the name of the Governor-General.

7. The executive authority of the Federation will extend in relation to a State-member of the Federation only to such powers and jurisdiction falling within the Federal sphere as the Ruler has transferred to the King.

8. The Governor-General will exercise the powers conferred upon him by the Constitution Act as executive head of the Federation and such powers of His Majesty (not being powers inconsistent with the provisions of the Constitution Act) as His Majesty may be pleased by Letters Patent constituting the

office of Governor-General to assign to him. In exercising all these powers the Governor-General will act in accordance with an Instrument of Instructions to be issued to him by the King.

9. The draft of the Governor-General's Instrument of Instructions (including the drafts of any amendments thereto) will be laid before both Houses of Parliament, and opportunity will be provided for each House of Parliament to make to His Majesty representations for an amendment of, or addition to, or omission from, the Instructions.

10. The Governor-General's salary will be fixed by the Constitution Act, and all other payments in respect of his personal allowances, or of salaries and allowances of his personal and secretarial staff, will be fixed by Order in Council; none of these payments will be subject to the vote of the Legislature.

The Working of the Federal Executive

11. The Governor-General will himself direct and control the administration of certain Departments of State—namely, Defence, External Affairs and Ecclesiastical Affairs.

12. In the administration of these Reserved Departments, the Governor-General will be assisted by not more than three Counsellors, who will be appointed by the Governor-General, and whose salaries and conditions of service will be prescribed by Order in Council.

13. For the purpose of aiding and advising the Governor-General in the exercise of powers conferred upon him by the Constitution Act for the government of the Federation, other than powers connected with the matters mentioned in paragraph 11, and matters left by law to his discretion, there will be a Council of Ministers. The Ministers will be chosen and summoned by the Governor-General and sworn as Members of the Council and will hold office during his pleasure. The persons appointed Ministers must be, or become within a stated period, members of one or other Chamber of the Federal Legislature.

14. In his Instrument of Instructions the Governor-General will be enjoined *inter alia* to use his best endeavours to select his Ministers in the following manner, that is, in consultation with the person who, in his judgment, is likely to command the largest following in the Legislature, to appoint those persons (including so far as possible members of important minority communities and representatives of the States-members of the Federation) who will best be in a position collectively to command the confidence of the Legislature.

15. The number of Ministers and the amounts of their respective salaries will be regulated by Act of the Federal Legislature, but, until the Federal Legislature otherwise determines, their number and their salaries will be such as the Governor-General determines, subject to limits to be laid down in the Constitution Act.

The salary of a Minister will not be subject to variation during his term of office.

16. The Governor-General will, whenever he thinks fit, preside at meetings of his Council of Ministers. He will also be authorised, after consultation with

his Ministers, to make in his discretion any rules which he regards as requisite to regulate the disposal of Government business and the procedure to be observed in its conduct, and for the transmission to himself and to his Counsellors in the Reserved Departments, and to the Financial Adviser, of all such information as he may direct.

17. The Governor-General will be empowered, in his discretion, but after consultation with his Ministers, to appoint a Financial Adviser to assist him in the discharge of his "special responsibility" for financial matters—see next paragraph—and also to advise Ministers on matters regarding which they may seek his advice. The Financial Adviser will be responsible to the Governor-General and will hold office during his pleasure; his salary will be fixed by the Governor-General and will not be subject to the vote of the Legislature.

18. Apart from his exclusive responsibility for the Reserved Departments (paragraph 11) the Governor-General in administering the government of the Federation will be declared to have a "special responsibility" in respect of—

- (*a*) the prevention of any grave menace to the peace or tranquillity of India or any part thereof;
- (*b*) the safeguarding of the financial stability and credit of the Federation;
- (*c*) the safeguarding of the legitimate interests of minorities;
- (*d*) the securing to the members of the Public Services of any rights provided for them by the Constitution Act and the safeguarding of their legitimate interests;
- (*e*) the prevention of commercial discrimination;
- (*f*) the protection of the rights of any Indian State;
- (*g*) any matter which affects the administration of any Department under the direction and control of the Governor-General.

It will be for the Governor-General to determine in his discretion whether any of the "special responsibilities" here described are involved by any given circumstances.

19. If in any case in which, in the opinion of the Governor-General, a special responsibility is imposed upon him it appears to him, after considering such advice as has been given him by his Ministers, that the due discharge of his responsibility so requires, he will have full discretion to act as he thinks fit, but in so acting he will be guided by any directions which may be contained in his Instrument of Instructions.

20. The Governor-General, in administering the Departments under his own direction and control, in taking action for the discharge of any special responsibility, and in exercising any discretion vested in him by the Constitution Act, will act in accordance with such directions, if any, not being directions inconsistent with anything in his Instructions, as may be given to him by a principal Secretary of State.

21. The Governor-General's Instrument of Instructions will accordingly contain *inter alia* provision on the following lines: —

In matters arising in the Departments which you direct and control on your responsibility, or in matters the determination of which is by law committed to your discretion, it is Our will and pleasure that you should act in exercise of the powers by law conferred upon you in such manner as you may judge right and expedient for the good government of the Federation, subject, however, to such directions as you may from time to time receive from one of Our principal Secretaries of State.

In matters arising out of the exercise of powers conferred upon you for the purposes of the government of the Federation other than those specified in the preceding paragraph it is Our will and pleasure that you should, in the exercise of the powers by law conferred upon you, be guided by the advice of your Ministers, unless so to be guided would, in your judgment, be inconsistent with the fulfilment of your special responsibility for any of the matters in respect of which a special responsibility is by law committed to you; in which case it is Our will and pleasure that you should, notwithstanding your Ministers' advice, act in exercise of the powers by law conferred upon you in such manner as you judge requisite for the fulfilment of your special responsibilities, subject, however, to such directions as you may from time to time receive from one of Our principal Secretaries of State.

The Federal Legislature

General. 22. The Federal Legislature will consist of the King, represented by the Governor-General, and two Chambers, to be styled the Council of State and the House of Assembly, and will be summoned to meet for the first time not later than a date to be specified in the Proclamation establishing the Federation.

Every Act of the Federal Legislature will be expressed as having been enacted by the Governor-General, by and with the consent of both Chambers.

23. Power to summon, and appoint places for the meeting of, the Chambers, to prorogue them, and to dissolve them, either separately or simultaneously, will be vested in the Governor-General at his discretion, subject to the requirement that they shall meet at least once in every year and that not more than twelve months shall intervene between the end of one session and the commencement of the next.

The Governor-General will also be empowered to summon the Chambers for the purpose of addressing them.

24. Each Council of State will continue for seven years and each Assembly for five years, unless sooner dissolved.

25. A member of the Council of Ministers will have the right to speak, but not to vote, in the Chamber of which he is not a Member.

A Counsellor will be *ex officio* an additional member of both Chambers for all purposes except the right of voting.

The Composition of the Chambers. 26. The Council of State will consist, apart from the Governor-General's Counsellors, of not more than 260 members, of whom 150 will be elected from British India in the manner indicated in Appendix I, not more than 100 will be appointed by the Rulers of States, and not more than ten (who shall not be officials) will be nominated by the Governor-General in his discretion.

27. A member of the Council of State will be required to be at least 30 years of age (this age limit not, however, being applicable to the Ruler of a State) and a British subject or a Ruler or subject of an Indian State, and to possess certain prescribed property qualifications, or to have been at some previous date a member of the Indian Legislature or of the Federal Legislature, or to possess qualifications to be prescribed by the Government of the State or Province which he represents with a view to conferring qualification upon persons who have rendered distinguished public service.

28. Casual vacancies in the Council of State will be filled, in the case of a British Indian elected representative, by election (so long as communal representation is retained as a feature of the Constitution) by those members of the body by which he was elected who are members of the community to which the vacating member belongs, and in the case of an appointed or nominated member, by a fresh appointment or nomination.

29. The Assembly will consist, apart from the Governor-General's Counsellors, of not more than 375 members, of whom 250 will be elected to represent constituencies in British India in the manner indicated in Appendix II, and not more than 125 will be appointed by the Rulers of States.

30. A member of the Assembly will be required to be not less than 25 years of age and a British subject or a subject of an Indian State.

31. Casual vacancies in the Assembly will be filled, in the case of an elected member, by the same method as that prescribed in Appendix II for the election of the vacating member, and, in the case of an appointed member, by a fresh appointment by the person by whom the vacating member was appointed.

32. Only the Ruler of a State who has acceded to the Federation will be entitled to appoint, or take part in appointing, a member of either Chamber of the Federal Legislature, and any vacancies arising out of the operation of this restriction will for the time being remain unfilled.

33. Every member of either Chamber will be required to make and subscribe an oath or affirmation in the following form before taking his seat: —

In the case of a representative of a State: —

I, *A.B.*, having been appointed a member of this $\frac{\text{Council}}{\text{Assembly}}$ do solemnly swear (*or* affirm) that, saving the faith and allegiance I owe to *C.D.*, I will be faithful and bear true allegiance in my capacity as Member of this $\frac{\text{Council}}{\text{Assembly,}}$ to His Majesty the King Emperor of India, His heirs and successors, and that I will faithfully discharge the duty upon which I am about to enter.

In the case of a representative of British India: —

I, *A.B.*, having been $\frac{\text{elected}}{\text{nominated}}$ a member of this $\frac{\text{Council}}{\text{Assembly,}}$ do solemnly swear (*or* affirm) that I will be faithful and bear true allegiance to His Majesty the King Emperor of India, His heirs and successors, and that I will faithfully discharge the duty upon which I am about to enter.

34. The following disqualifications will be prescribed for membership of either Chamber: —

(*a*) in the case of elected members or of members nominated by the Governor-General, the holding of any office of profit under the Crown other than that of Minister;

(*b*) a declaration of unsoundness of mind by a competent Court;

(*c*) being an undischarged bankrupt;

(*d*) conviction of the offence of corrupt practices or other election offences;

(*e*) in the case of a legal practitioner, suspension from practice by order of a competent Court;

but provision will be made that the last two disqualifications may be removed by order of the Governor-General at his discretion;

(*f*) having an undisclosed interest in any contract with the Federal Government: provided that the mere holding of shares in a company will not by itself involve this disqualification.

35. A person sitting or voting as a member of either Chamber when he is not qualified for, or is disqualified from, membership will be made liable to a penalty of   in respect of each day on which he so sits or votes, to be recovered in the High Court of the Province 'or State which the person in respect of whom the complaint is made represents by suit instituted with the consent of a Principal Law Officer of the Federation.

36. Subject to the Rules and Standing Orders affecting the Chamber there will be freedom of speech in both Chambers of the Federal Legislature. No person will be liable to any proceedings in any Court by reason of his speech or vote in either Chamber, or by reason of anything contained in any official report of the proceedings in either Chamber.

37. The following matters connected with elections and electoral procedure, in so far as provision is not made by the Act, will be regulated by Order in Council: —

(*a*) The qualifications of electors;

(*b*) The delimitation of constituencies;

(*c*) The method of election of representatives of communal and other interests;

(*d*) The filling of casual vacancies; and

(*e*) Other matters ancillary to the above;

with provision that Orders in Council framed for these purposes shall be laid in draft for a stated period before each House of Parliament.

For matters other than the above connected with the conduct of elections the Federal Legislature will be empowered to make provision by Act. But until the Federal Legislature otherwise determines, existing laws or rules, including the law or rules providing for the prohibition and punishment of corrupt practices or election offences and for determining the decision of disputed elections, will remain in force, subject, however, to such modifications or adaptations to be made by Order in Council as may be required in order to adapt their provisions to the requirements of the new Constitution.

Legislative Procedure. 38. Bills (other than Money Bills, which will be initiated in the Assembly) will be introduced in either Chamber.

39. The Governor-General will be empowered at his discretion, but subject to the provisions of the Constitution Act and to his Instrument of Instructions, to assent in His Majesty's name to a Bill which has been passed by both Chambers, or to withhold his assent, or to reserve the Bill for the signification of the King's pleasure. But before taking any of these courses it will be open to the Governor-General to remit a bill to the Chambers with a Message requesting its reconsideration in whole or in part, together with such amendments, if any, as he may recommend.

No Bill will become law until it has been agreed to by both Chambers either without amendment or with such amendments only as are agreed to by both Chambers, and has been assented to by the Governor-General, or, in the case of a reserved Bill, until His Majesty in Council has signified his assent.

40. Any Act assented to by the Governor-General will within twelve months be subject to disallowance by His Majesty in Council.

41. In the case of disagreement between the Chambers, the Governor-General will be empowered, in any case in which a Bill passed by one Chamber has not, within three months thereafter, been passed by the other, either without amendments or with agreed amendments, to summon the two Chambers to meet in a joint sitting for the purpose of reaching a decision on the Bill. The members present at a Joint Session will deliberate and vote together upon the Bill in the form in which it finally left the Chamber in which it was introduced and upon amendments, if any, made therein by one Chamber and not agreed to by the other. Any such amendments which are affirmed by a majority of the total number of members voting at the Joint Session will be deemed to have been carried, and if the Bill, with the amendments, if any, so carried, is affirmed by a majority of the members voting at the Joint Session, it shall be taken to have been duly passed by both Chambers.

In the case of a Money Bill, or in cases where, in the Governor-General's opinion, a decision on the Bill cannot consistently with the fulfilment of his responsibilities for a Reserved Department or of any of his "special responsibilities" be deferred, the Governor-General will be empowered in his discretion to summon a Joint Session forthwith.

42. In order to enable the Governor-General to fulfil the responsibilities imposed upon him personally for the administration of the Reserved Departments and his "special responsibilities," he will be empowered at his discretion—

> (*a*) to present, or cause to be presented, a Bill to either Chamber, and to declare by Message to both Chambers that it is essential, having

regard to his responsibilities for a Reserved Department or, as the case may be, to any of his "special responsibilities," that the Bill so presented should become law before a date specified in the Message; and

(b) to declare by Message in respect of any Bill already introduced in either Chamber that it should for similar reasons become law before a stated date in a form specified in the Message.

A Bill which is the subject of such a Message will then be considered or reconsidered by the Chambers, as the case may require, and if, before the date specified, it is not passed by the two Chambers, or is not passed by the two Chambers in the form specified, the Governor-General will be empowered at his discretion to enact it as a Governor-General's Act, either with or without any amendments made by either Chamber after receipt of his Message.

A Governor-General's Act so enacted will have the same force and effect as an Act of the Legislature, and will be subject to disallowance in the same manner, but the Governor-General's competence to legislate under this provision will not extend beyond the competence of the Federal Legislature as defined by the Constitution.

43. It will be made clear by means of the enacting words of a Governor-General's Act, which will be distinguished from the enacting words of an ordinary Act (see paragraph 22), that Acts of the former description are enacted on the Governor-General's own responsibility.

44. Provision will also be made empowering the Governor-General in his discretion, in any case in which he considers that a Bill introduced, or proposed for introduction, or any clause thereof, or any amendment to a Bill moved or proposed, would affect the discharge of his "special responsibility" for the prevention of any grave menace to the peace or tranquillity of India, to direct that the Bill, clause or amendment shall not be further proceeded with.

Procedure With Regard to Financial Proposals. 45. A recommendation of the Governor-General will be required for any proposal in either Chamber of the Federal Legislature for the imposition of taxation, for the appropriation of public revenues, or any proposal affecting the public debt, or affecting, or imposing any charge upon, public revenues.

46. The Governor-General will cause a statement of the estimated revenue and expenditure of the Federation, together with a statement of all proposals for the appropriation of those revenues, to be laid, in respect of every financial year, before both Chambers of the Legislature.

The statement of proposals for appropriation will be so arranged as—

(a) to distinguish between those proposals which will, and those which will not (*see paragraph* 49) be submitted to the vote of the Legislature and amongst the latter to distinguish those which are in the nature of standing charges (for example, the items in the list in paragraph 49, marked†); and

(b) to specify separately those additional proposals (if any), whether under the votable or non-votable Heads, which the Governor-General regards as necessary for the discharge of any of his "special responsibilities."

47. The proposals for the appropriation of revenues, other than proposals relating to the Heads of Expenditure enumerated in paragraph 49, and proposals (if any) made by the Governor-General in discharge of his special responsibilities, will be submitted in the form of Demands for Grants to the vote of the Assembly. The Assembly will be empowered to assent or refuse assent to any Demand or to reduce the amount specified therein, whether by way of a general reduction of the total amount of the Demand or of the reduction or omission of any specific item or items included in it.

48. The Demands as laid before the Assembly will thereafter be laid before the Council of State which will be empowered to require, if a motion to that effect is moved on behalf of the Government and accepted, that any Demand which had been reduced or rejected by the Assembly shall be brought before a Joint Session of both Chambers for final determination.

49. Proposals for appropriations of revenues, if they relate to the Heads of Expenditure enumerated in this paragraph, will not be submitted to the vote of either Chamber of the Legislature, but will be open to discussion in both Chambers, except in the case of the salary and allowances of the Governor-General and of expenditure required for the discharge of the functions of the Crown in, and arising out of, its relations with the Rulers of Indian States.

The Heads of Expenditure referred to above are: —

(i) Interest, Sinking Fund Charges and other expenditure relating to the raising, service and management of loans;† expenditure fixed by or under the Constitution Act;† expenditure required to satisfy a decree of any Court or an arbitral award;

(ii) The salary and allowances of the Governor-General;† of Ministers;† of the Governor-General's Counsellors;† of the Financial Adviser;† of Chief Commissioners; of the Governor-General's personal and secretarial staff and of the staff of the Financial Adviser;

(iii) Expenditure required for the Reserved Departments; for the discharge of the functions of the Crown in and arising out of its relations with the Rulers of Indian States; or for the discharge of the duties imposed by the Constitution Act on a principal Secretary of State;

(iv) The salaries and pensions (including pensions payable to their dependants) of Judges of the Federal or Supreme Court or of Judicial Commissioners under the Federal Government; and expenditure certified by the Governor-General after consultation with his Ministers as required for the expenses of those Courts;

(v) Expenditure required for Excluded Areas and British Baluchistan;

(vi) Salaries and pensions payable to, or to the dependants of certain members of the Public Services and certain other sums payable to such persons (see Appendix VII, Part III).

The Governor-General will be empowered to decide finally and conclusively, for all purposes, any question whether a particular item of expenditure does or does not fall under any of the Heads of Expenditure referred to in this paragraph.

50. At the conclusion of the budget proceedings the Governor-General will authenticate by his signature all appropriations, whether voted or those relating to matters enumerated in paragraph 49; the appropriations so authenticated will be laid before both Chambers of the Legislature, but will not be open to discussion.

In the appropriations so authenticated the Governor-General will be empowered to include any additional amounts which he regards as necessary for the discharge of any of his special responsibilities, so, however, that the total amount authenticated under any Head is not in excess of the amount originally laid before the Legislature under that Head in the Statement of proposals for appropriation.

The authentication of the Governor-General will be sufficient authority for the due application of the sums involved.

51. The provisions of paragraphs 45 to 50 inclusive will apply with the necessary modifications to proposals for the appropriation of revenues to meet expenditure not included in the Annual Estimates which it may become necessary to incur during the course of the financial year.

Procedure in the Federal Legislature. 52. The procedure and conduct of business in each Chamber of the Legislature will be regulated by rules to be made, subject to the provisions of the Constitution Act, by each Chamber; but the Governor-General will be empowered at his discretion, after consultation with the President, or Speaker, as the case may be, to make rules—

(a) regulating the procedure of, and the conduct of business in, the Chamber in relation to matters arising out of, or affecting, the administration of the Reserved Departments or any other special responsibilities with which he is charged; and

(b) prohibiting, save with the prior consent of the Governor-General given at his discretion, the discussion of or the asking of questions on

(i) matters connected with any Indian State other than matters accepted by the Ruler of the State in his Instrument of Accession as being Federal subjects; or

(ii) any action of the Governor-General taken in his discretion in his relationship with a Governor; or

(iii) any matter affecting relations between His Majesty or the Governor-General and any foreign Prince or State.

In the event of conflict between a rule so made by the Governor-General and any rule made by the Chamber, the former will prevail and the latter will, to the extent of the inconsistency, be void.

Emergency Powers of the Governor-General in Relation to Legislation.
53. The Governor-General will be empowered at his discretion, if at any time he is satisfied that the requirements of the Reserved Departments, or any of the "special responsibilities" with which he is charged by the Constitution Act render it necessary, to make and promulgate such Ordinances as, in his opinion, the circumstances of the case require, containing such provisions as it would have been competent, under the provisions of the Constitution Act, for the Federal Legislature to enact.

An Ordinance promulgated under the proposals contained in this paragraph will continue in operation for such period, not exceeding six months, as may be specified therein; the Governor-General will, however, have power to renew any Ordinance for a second period not exceeding six months, but in that event it will be laid before both Houses of Parliament.

An Ordinance will have the same force and effect, whilst in operation, as an Act of the Federal Legislature; but every such Ordinance will be subject to the provisions of the Constitution Act relating to disallowance of Acts, and will be subject to withdrawal at any time by the Governor-General.

54. In addition to the powers to be conferred upon the Governor-General at his discretion in the preceding paragraph, the Governor-General will further be empowered, if his Ministers are satisfied, at a time when the Federal Legislature is not in session, that an emergency exists which renders such a course necessary, to make and promulgate any such Ordinances for the good government of British India, or any part thereof, as the circumstances of the case require, containing such provisions as, under the Constitution Act, it would have been competent for the Legislature to enact.

An Ordinance promulgated under the proposals contained in this paragraph will have, while in operation, the same force and effect as an Act of the Federal Legislature, but every such Ordinance—

(*a*) will be required to be laid before the Federal Legislature and will cease to operate at the expiry of six weeks from the date of the reassembly of the Legislature, unless both Chambers have in the meantime disapproved it by Resolution, in which case it will cease to operate forthwith; and

(*b*) will be subject to the provisions of the Constitution Act relating to disallowance as if it were an Act of the Federal Legislature; it will also be subject to withdrawal at any time by the Governor-General.

Provisions in the Event of a Breakdown in the Constitution. 55. The Governor-General will be empowered at his discretion, if at any time he is satisfied that a situation has arisen which renders it for the time being impossible for the government of the Federation to be carried on in accordance with the provisions of the Constitution Act, by Proclamation to assume to himself all such powers vested by law in any Federal authority as appear to him to be necessary for the purpose of securing that the government of the Federation shall be carried on effectively.

A Proclamation so issued will have the same force and effect as an Act of Parliament; will be communicated forthwith to a Secretary of State and laid before Parliament; will cease to operate at the expiry of six months unless, before the expiry of that period, it has been approved by Resolutions of both Houses of Parliament; and may at any time be revoked by Resolutions by both Houses of Parliament.

Chief Commissioners' Provinces

56. Each of the Provinces known as British Baluchistan, Delhi, Ajmer Merwara, Coorg and the Andaman and Nicobar Islands will be administered, subject to the provisions of the Constitution Act, by a Chief Commissioner who will be appointed by the Governor-General in his discretion to hold office during his pleasure.

57. Special provision will be made for British Baluchistan, whereby the Governor-General will himself direct and control the administration of that Province, acting through the agency of the Chief Commissioner.

58. Legislation required for British Baluchistan will be obtained in the following manner: —

No Act of the Federal Legislature will apply to the Province unless the Governor-General in his discretion so directs, and in giving such a direction the Governor-General will be empowered to direct that the Act, in its application to the Province, or any part thereof, is to have effect subject to such exceptions or modifications as he thinks fit.

The Governor-General will also be empowered at his discretion to make Regulations for the peace and good government of British Baluchistan and will be competent by any Regulations so made to repeal or amend any Act of the Federal Legislature which is for the time being applicable to the Province. Any such Regulation, on promulgation by the Governor-General in the official Gazette will have the same force and effect in relation to British Baluchistan as an Act of the Federal Legislature, and will, like such Acts, be subject to disallowance by His Majesty in Council.

The provisions of the preceding sub-paragraph will apply also to the Andaman and Nicobar Islands.

59. In the Chief Commissioners' Provinces the Chief Commissioner will have all such executive power and authority as may be necessary for the administration of the Province, and in the exercise of this power and authority he will (save in the case of British Baluchistan) be directly subordinate to the Federal Government.

60. The composition of the Coorg Legislative Council, as existing immediately before the establishment of the Federation, will continue unchanged, and special provisions will be made with regard to its legislative powers.

Part II. The Governors' Provinces

The Provincial Executive

61. A "Governor's Province" will be defined as meaning the Presidencies of Bengal, Madras and Bombay, and the Provinces known as the United Provinces, the Punjab, Bihar, the Central Provinces, Assam, the North-West Frontier Province, Sind, and Orissa.

62. In a Governor's Province the executive authority will be exercisable on the King's behalf by a Governor holding office during His Majesty's pleasure.

All executive acts will run in the name of the Governor.

63. The Governor will exercise the powers conferred upon him by the Constitution Act as executive head of the Provincial Government, and such powers of His Majesty (not being powers inconsistent with the provisions of the Act) as His Majesty may be pleased by Letters Patent constituting the office of Governor to assign to him. In exercising all these powers the Governor will act in accordance with an Instrument of Instructions to be issued to him by the King.

64. The draft of the Governor's Instrument of Instructions (including the drafts of any amendments thereto) will be laid before both Houses of Parliament, and opportunity will be provided for each House of Parliament to make to His Majesty any representation which that House may desire for any amendment or addition to, or omission from, the Instructions.

65. The Governor's salary will be fixed by the Constitution Act, and all other payments in respect of his personal allowances, or the salaries and allowances of his personal and secretarial staff, will be fixed by Order in Council; none of these payments will be subject to the vote of the Legislature.

Working of the Provincial Executive. 66. For the purpose of aiding and advising the Governor in the exercise of powers conferred on him by the Constitution Act for the government of the Province, except as regards matters left by law to his discretion and the administration of Excluded Areas, there will be a Council of Ministers. The Ministers will be chosen and summoned by the Governor and sworn as Members of the Council, and will hold office during his pleasure. Persons appointed Ministers must be, or become within a stated period, members of the Provincial Legislature.

67. In his Instrument of Instructions the Governor will be enjoined *inter alia* to use his best endeavours to select his Ministers in the following manner, that is, in consultation with the person who, in his judgment, is likely to command the largest following in the Legislature, to appoint those persons (including so far as possible members of important minority communities) who will best be in a position collectively to command the confidence of the Legislature.

68. The number of Ministers and the amounts of their respective salaries will be regulated by Act of the Provincial Legislature, but until the Provincial Legislature otherwise determines their number and salaries will be such as the Governor determines, subject to limits to be laid down in the Constitution Act.

The salary of a Minister will not be subject to variation during his term of office.

69. The Governor will whenever he thinks fit preside at meetings of his Council of Ministers. He will also be authorised, after consultation with his Ministers, to make at his discretion any rules which he regards as requisite to regulate the disposal of Government business, and the procedure to be observed in its conduct, and for the transmission to himself of all such information as he may direct.

70. In the administration of the government of a Province the Governor will be declared to have a special responsibility in respect of—

(a) the prevention of any grave menace to the peace or tranquillity of the Province or any part thereof;

(b) the safeguarding of the legitimate interests of minorities;

(c) the securing to the members of the Public Services of any rights provided for them by the Constitution and the safeguarding of their legitimate interests;

(d) the prevention of commercial discrimination;

(e) the protection of the rights of any Indian State;

(f) the administration of areas declared, in accordance with provisions in that behalf, to be partially excluded areas;

(g) securing the execution of orders lawfully issued by the Governor-General;

and the Governors of the North-West Frontier Province and of Sind will in addition be respectively declared to have a special responsibility in respect of—

(h) any matter affecting the Governor's responsibilities as Agent to the Governor-General in the Tribal and other Trans-border Areas; and

(i) the administration of the Sukkur Barrage.

It will be for the Governor to determine in his discretion whether any of the "special responsibilities" here described are involved by any given circumstances.

71. If in any case in which, in the opinion of the Governor, a special responsibility is imposed upon him, it appears to him, after considering such advice as has been given to him by his Ministers, that the due discharge of his responsibility so requires, he will have full discretion to act as he thinks fit, but in so acting he will be guided by any directions which may be contained in his Instrument of Instructions.

72. The Governor, in taking action for the discharge of any special responsibility or in the exercise of any discretion vested in him by the Constitution Act, will act in accordance with such directions, if any, not being directions inconsistent with anything in his Instructions, as may be given to him by the Governor-General or by a principal Secretary of State.

73. The Governor's Instrument of Instructions will accordingly contain *inter alia* provision on the following lines: —

> In matters, the determination of which is by law committed to your discretion, and in matters relating to the administration of Excluded Areas, it is Our will and pleasure that you should act in exercise of the

powers by law conferred upon you in such manner as you may judge right
and expedient for the good government of the Province, subject, however, to such directions as you may from time to time receive from Our
Governor-General or from one of Our principal Secretaries of State.

In matters arising out of the exercise of powers conferred upon you for
the purposes of the government of the Province other than those specified
in the preceding paragraph it is Our will and pleasure that you should in
the exercise of the powers by law conferred upon you be guided by the
advice of your Ministers, unless so to be guided would, in your judgment,
be inconsistent with the fulfilment of your special responsibility for any of
the matters in respect of which a special responsibility is by law committed to you; in which case it is Our will and pleasure that you should,
notwithstanding your Ministers' advice, act in exercise of the powers by
law conferred upon you in such manner as you judge requisite for the
fulfilment of your special responsibilities, subject, however, to such directions as you may from time to time receive from Our Governor-General
or from one of Our principal Secretaries of State.

The Provincial Legislature

General. 74. For every Governor's Province there will be a Provincial Legislature, consisting, except in the provinces of Bengal, the United Provinces and
Bihar, of the King, represented by the Governor, and of one Chamber, to be
known as the Legislative Assembly.

In the Provinces just named the Legislature will consist of His Majesty,
represented by the Governor, and of two Chambers, to be known respectively
as the Legislative Council and the Legislative Assembly.

But provision will be made enabling the Provincial Legislature at any time
not less than ten years after the commencement of the Constitution Act—

- (*a*) where the Legislature consists of two Chambers to provide by Act,
    which both Chambers separately have passed, and have confirmed
    by a subsequent Act passed not less than two years later, that it shall
    consist of one Chamber instead of two Chambers; and,
- (*b*) where the Legislature consists of one Chamber, to present an Ad-
    dress to His Majesty praying that the Legislature may be reconsti-
    tuted with two Chambers, and that the composition of, and method
    of election to, the Upper Chamber may be determined by Order in
    Council.

The Provincial Legislatures will be summoned to meet for the first time on
dates to be specified by Proclamation.

Every Act of a Provincial Legislature will be expressed as having been
enacted by the Governor, by and with the consent of the Legislative Assembly,
or, where there are two Chambers, of both Chambers of the Legislature.

75. Power to summon and appoint places for the meeting of the Provincial
Legislature, to prorogue it, and to dissolve it, will be vested in the Governor at
his discretion, subject to the requirement that it shall meet at least once in every
year, and that not more than twelve months shall intervene between the end of
one session and the commencement of the next. Where the Legislature consists

of two Chambers power to dissolve the Chambers will be exercisable in relation to either Chamber separately or to both simultaneously.

The Governor will also be empowered to summon the Legislature for the purpose of addressing it.

76. Each Legislative Assembly will continue for five years, and each Legislative Council, where such a Council exists, for seven years, unless sooner dissolved.

77. In the case of a Province having a Legislative Council a Member of the Council of Ministers will have the right to speak, but not to vote, in the Chamber of which he is not a member.

The Composition of the Provincial Legislature. 78. The Legislative Assembly of each Governor's Province will consist of the number of members indicated against that Province in Appendix III, Part I, who will be elected in the manner indicated in the same Appendix.

79. A member of a Provincial Legislative Assembly will be required to be at least 25 years of age and a British subject or a subject of an Indian State.

80. The Legislative Councils of Governors' Provinces will consist of the number of members indicated in Appendix III, Part II, who will be elected, or nominated by the Governor, as the case may be, in the manner indicated in the same Appendix.

81. A member of a Provincial Legislative Council will be required to be at least 30 years of age and a British subject or a subject of an Indian State.

82. Appropriate provision will be made for the filling of vacancies in a Provincial Legislature on the lines proposed for the Federal Legislature (*see paragraphs* 28 *and* 31).

83. Every member of a Provincial Legislature will be required to make and subscribe an oath or affirmation in the following form before taking his seat:

I, *A.B.*, having been $\frac{\text{elected}}{\text{nominated}}$ a member of this $\frac{\text{Council}}{\text{Assembly}}$ do solemnly swear (*or* affirm) that I will be faithful and bear true allegiance to His Majesty the King Emperor of India, His heirs and successors, and that I will faithfully discharge the duty upon which I am about to enter.

84. The following disqualifications will be prescribed for membership of a Provincial Legislature: —

(*a*) the holding of any office of profit under the Crown other than that of Minister;

(*b*) a declaration of unsoundness of mind by a competent Court;

(*c*) being an undischarged bankrupt;

(*d*) conviction of the offence of corrupt practices or other election offences;

(*e*) in the case of a legal practitioner, suspension from practice by order of a competent Court;

but provision will be made that this and the last preceding disqualification may be removed by order of the Governor in his discretion;

(*f*) having an undisclosed interest in any contract with the Provincial Government; provided that the mere holding of shares in a company will not by itself involve this disqualification.

85. A person sitting or voting as a member of the Provincial Legislature, when he is not qualified for, or is disqualified from, membership, will be made liable to a penalty of   in respect of each day on which he so sits or votes, to be recovered in the High Court of the Province by suit initiated with the consent of a principal Law Officer of the Provincial Government.

86. Subject to the rules and Standing Orders of the Legislature there will be freedom of speech in the Provincial Legislature. No person will be liable to any proceedings in any Court by reason of his speech or vote, or by reason of anything contained in any official Report of the proceedings.

87. In so far as provision is not made by the Act itself for the following matters connected with elections and electoral procedure, they will be prescribed by Order in Council under the Act:

(*a*) the qualifications of electors;
(*b*) the delimitation of constituencies;
(*c*) the method of election of representatives of communal and other interests;
(*d*) the filling of casual vacancies; and
(*e*) other matters ancillary to the above;
With provision that Orders in Council framed for these purposes shall be laid in draft for a stated period before each House of Parliament.

For matters connected with the conduct of elections for the Provincial Legislature other than the above each Provincial Legislature will be empowered to make provision by Act. But until the Provincial Legislature otherwise determines, existing laws or rules, including the law or rules providing for the prohibition and punishment of corrupt practices or election offences and for determining the decision of disputed elections, will remain in force; subject, however, to such modifications or adaptations to be made by Order in Council as may be required in order to adapt their provisions to the requirements of the new Constitution.

Legislative Procedure. NOTE.—The following paragraphs relating to legislative procedure are, with the exception of paragraph 91, framed, for the sake of brevity, to apply to unicameral Provincial Legislatures. Suitable modification of these provisions, for the purpose of adapting them to Legislatures which are bicameral would, of course, be made. In particular, provision would be made that in a bicameral Legislature, Bills (other than Money Bills, which will be initiated in the Legislative Assembly) will be introduced in either Chamber.

88. The Governor will be empowered at his discretion, but subject to the provisions of the Constitution Act and to his Instrument of Instructions, to assent in His Majesty's name to a Bill which has been passed by the Provincial

Legislature, or to withhold his assent, or to reserve the Bill for the consideration of the Governor-General. But before taking any of these courses it will be open to the Governor to remit a Bill to the Legislature, with a Message requesting its reconsideration in whole or in part, together with such amendments, if any, as he may recommend.

No Bill will become law unless it has been passed by the Legislative Assembly, with or without amendment, and has been assented to by the Governor, or in cases where the Constitution Act so provides, by the Governor-General; in the case of a Bill reserved for the consideration of the Governor-General, the Bill will not become law until the Governor-General (or, if the Governor-General reserves the Bill, His Majesty in Council) has signified his assent.

89. When a Bill is reserved by a Governor for the consideration of the Governor-General, the Governor-General will be empowered at his discretion, but subject to the provisions of the Constitution Act and to his Instrument of Instructions, to assent in His Majesty's name to the Bill, or to withhold his assent, or to reserve the Bill for the signification of the King's pleasure. He will also be empowered, if he thinks fit, before taking any of these courses, to return the Bill to the Governor with directions that it shall be remitted to the Legislature with a Message to the effect indicated in the preceding paragraph. The Legislature will then reconsider the Bill and if it is again passed with or without amendment it will be presented again to the Governor-General for his consideration.

If at the end of six months from the date on which a Bill is presented to the Governor-General, the Governor-General neither assents to it nor reserves it for the signification of the King's pleasure, nor returns it to the Governor, the Bill will lapse.

90. Any Act assented to by the Governor or by the Governor-General will within twelve months be subject to disallowance by His Majesty in Council.

91. In the case of a Province having a Legislative Council, the Governor will be empowered, in any case in which a Bill passed by one Chamber has not, within three months thereafter, been passed by the other, either without amendments or with agreed amendments, to summon the two Chambers to meet in a Joint Session for the purpose of reaching a decision on the Bill. The members present at a Joint Session will deliberate and vote together upon the Bill in the form in which it finally left the Chamber in which it was introduced and upon amendments, if any, made therein by one Chamber and not agreed to by the other. Any such amendments which are affirmed by a majority of the total number of the members voting at the Joint Session will be deemed to have been carried, and if the Bill, with the amendments, if any, so carried, is affirmed by a majority of the members voting at the Joint Session, it shall be taken to have been duly passed by both Chambers.

In the case of a Money Bill, or in cases where, in the Governor's opinion, a decision on the Bill cannot, consistently with the fulfilment of any of his "special responsibilities," be deferred, the Governor will be empowered at his discretion to summon a Joint Session forthwith.

92. In order to enable the Governor to discharge the "special responsibilities" imposed upon him, he will be empowered at his discretion—

(a) to present, or cause to be presented, a Bill to the Legislature, with a Message that it is essential, having regard to any of his "special responsibilities" that any Bill so presented should become law before a date specified in the Message; and

(b) to declare by Message in respect of any Bill already introduced in the Legislature that it should, for similar reasons, become law before a stated date in a form specified in the Message.

If, before the date specified, a Bill which is the subject of such a Message is not passed, or is not passed in the form specified, as the case may be, the Governor will be empowered at his discretion to enact it as a Governor's Act, either with or without any amendments made by the Legislature, after receipt of his Message.

A Governor's Act so enacted will have the same force and effect as an Act of the Provincial Legislature and will be subject to the same requirements in respect of the Governor-General's assent and to disallowance in the same manner as an Act of the Provincial Legislature, but the Governor's competence to legislate under this provision will not extend beyond the competence of the Provincial Legislature as defined by the Constitution.

93. It will be made clear by the enacting words of a Governor's Act, which will be distinguished from the enacting words of an ordinary Act (see paragraph 74), that Acts of the former description are enacted on the Governor's own responsibility.

94. Provision will also be made empowering the Governor, in any case in which he considers that a Bill introduced or proposed for introduction, or any clause thereof, or any amendment to a Bill moved or proposed, would affect the discharge of his "special responsibility" for the prevention of any grave menace to the peace or tranquillity of the Province, to direct that the Bill, clause or amendment shall not be further proceeded with.

Procedure with Regard to Financial Proposals. 95. A recommendation of the Governor will be required for any proposal in the Provincial Legislature for the imposition of taxation, for the appropriation of public revenues, or any proposal affecting the public debt of the Province or affecting or imposing any charge upon public revenues.

96. The Governor will cause a statement of the estimated revenues and expenditure of the Province, together with a statement of proposals for the appropriation of those revenues, to be laid in respect of every financial year before the Provincial Legislature, and, where the Legislature consists of two Chambers, before both Chambers.

The statement of proposals for appropriation will be so arranged as—

(a) to distinguish between those proposals which will, and those which will not (*see paragraph* 98), be submitted to the vote of the Legislature and amongst the latter to distinguish those which are in the nature of standing charges (for example the items in the list in paragraph 98, marked †); and

(*b*) to specify separately those additional proposals (if any), whether under the votable or non-votable Heads, which the Governor regards as necessary for the fulfilment of any of his "special responsibilities."

97. The proposals for the appropriation of revenues, other than proposals relating to the Heads of Expenditure enumerated in paragraph 98 and proposals (if any) made by the Governor in discharge of his special responsibilities, will be submitted, in the form of Demands for Grants, to the vote of the Legislative Assembly. The Assembly will be empowered to assent, or refuse assent, to any Demand or to reduce the amount specified therein, whether by way of a general reduction of the total amount of the Demand or of the reduction or omission of any specific item or items included in it.

98. Proposals for appropriations of revenues, if they relate to the Heads of Expenditure enumerated in this paragraph, will not be submitted to the vote of the Legislative Assembly, but, except in the case of the Governor's salary and allowances, will be open to discussion in the Assembly.

The Heads of Expenditure referred to above are: —

(i) Interest, Sinking Fund Charges and other expenditure relating to the raising, service and management of loans;† expenditure fixed by or under the Constitution Act;† expenditure required to satisfy a decree of any Court or an arbitral award;

(ii) The salary and allowances of the Governor;† of Ministers;† and of the Governor's personal or secretarial staff;

(iii) The salaries and pensions (including pensions payable to their dependants) of Judges of the High Court or Chief Court or Judicial Commissioners;† and expenditure certified by the Governor, after consultation with his Ministers, as required for the expenses of those Courts;

(iv) Expenditure debitable to Provincial revenues required for the discharge of the duties imposed by the Constitution Act on a principal Secretary of State;

(v) The salaries and pensions payable to, or to the dependants of, certain members of the Public Services and certain other sums payable to such persons (see Appendix VII, Part III).

The Governor will be empowered to decide finally and conclusively for all purposes any question whether a particular item of expenditure does, or does not, fall under any of the Heads of Expenditure referred to in this paragraph.

99. At the conclusion of the budget proceedings the Governor will authenticate by his signature all appropriations, whether voted or those relating to matters enumerated in paragraph 98; the appropriations so authenticated will be laid before the Legislature, but will not be open to discussion.

In the appropriations so authenticated the Governor will be empowered to include any additional amounts which he regards as necessary for the discharge of any of his special responsibilities, so, however, that the total amount authenticated under any Head is not in excess of the amount originally laid before the Legislature under that Head in the Statement of proposals for appropriation.

The authentication of the Governor will be sufficient authority for the due application of the sums involved.

100. The provisions of paragraphs 95 to 99 inclusive will apply with the necessary modifications to proposals for the appropriation of revenue to meet expenditure not included in the Annual Estimates which it may become necessary to incur during the course of the financial year.

101. Provision will be made that until the Provincial Legislature otherwise determines by a decision in support of which at least three-fourths of the members have voted, no proposal for the reduction in any Province (other than a reduction pro-rata with the general educational grant-in-aid) of an existing grant-in-aid on account of the education of the Anglo-Indian and domiciled European community will be deemed to have received the consent of the Legislature unless at least three-fourths of the members have voted in favour of the proposal.

Procedure in the Legislature. 102. The procedure and conduct of business in the Provincial Legislature will be regulated by rules to be made, subject to the provisions of the Constitution Act, by the Legislature. But the Governor will be empowered at his discretion, after consultation with the President or Speaker, as the case may be, to make rules regulating the procedure of, and the conduct of business in, the Chamber or Chambers in relation to matters arising out of, or affecting, any "special responsibility" with which he is charged by the Constitution Act.

In the event of conflict between a rule so made by the Governor and any rule made by a Chamber of the Legislature, the former will prevail and the latter will, to the extent of the inconsistency, be void.

Emergency Powers of the Governor in Relation to Legislation. 103. The Governor will be empowered at his discretion, if at any time he is satisfied that the requirements of any of the "special responsibilities" with which he is charged by the Constitution Act render it necessary, to make and promulgate such Ordinances as, in his opinion, the circumstances of the case require, containing such provisions as it would have been competent, under the provisions of the Constitution Act, for the Provincial Legislature to enact.

An Ordinance promulgated under the proposals contained in this paragraph will continue in operation for such period, not exceeding six months, as may be specified therein; the Governor will, however, have the power to renew any Ordinance for a second period not exceeding six months, but in that event it will be laid before both Houses of Parliament.

An Ordinance will have the same force and effect, whilst in operation, as an Act of the Provincial Legislature; but every such Ordinance will be subject to the provisions of the Constitution Act relating to disallowance of Acts and will be subject to withdrawal at any time by the Governor.

104. In addition to the powers to be conferred upon the Governor at his discretion in the preceding paragraph, the Governor will further be empowered, if his Ministers are satisfied, at any time when the Legislature is not in session, that an emergency exists which renders such a course necessary, to make and promulgate any such Ordinances for the good government of the Province or any part thereof as the circumstances of the case require, containing such provisions as, under the Constitution Act, it would have been competent for the Legislature to enact.

An Ordinance promulgated under the proposals contained in this paragraph will have, while in operation, the same force and effect as an Act of the Provincial Legislature, but every such Ordinance—

(a) will be required to be laid before the Provincial Legislature and will cease to operate at the expiry of six weeks from the date of the reassembly of the Legislature unless in the meantime the Legislature (or both Chambers, where two Chambers exist) has disapproved it by Resolution, in which case it will cease to operate forthwith; and

(b) will be subject to the provisions of the Constitution Act relating to disallowance as if it were an Act of the Provincial Legislature; it will also be subject to withdrawal at any time by the Governor.

Provisions in the Event of a Breakdown in the Constitution. 105. The Governor will be empowered at his discretion, if at any time he is satisfied that a situation has arisen which renders it for the time being impossible for the government of the Province to be carried on in accordance with the provisions of the Constitution Act, by Proclamation to assume to himself all such powers vested by law in any Provincial authority as appear to him to be necessary for the purpose of securing that the government of the Province shall be carried on effectively.

A Proclamation so issued will have the same force and effect as an Act of Parliament; will be communicated forthwith to the Governor-General and to a Secretary of State and laid before Parliament; will cease to operate at the expiry of six months unless before the expiry of that period it has been approved by Resolutions of both Houses of Parliament; and may at any time be revoked by Resolutions of both Houses of Parliament.

*   *   *

Speech by the Attorney-General, Sir Thomas Inskip, in the
House of Commons Defending the Government of
India Bill which Provided a New Constitutional Framework
for India, 5 June 1935* [*This Constitution was never fully put into effect.*]

The task of saying the last word on this Bill falls upon one who has, perhaps, almost less claim than any other speaker to have his voice heard upon the subject of India. So let me begin, at any rate, by saying one or two things with which everybody will agree, and perhaps I may thank the right hon. Gentleman for his reference to the Secretary of State and his colleagues. I want to join with my right hon. Friend the Member for Epping (Mr. Churchill)—and I wish there were more things on which I could agree with him—in what he said as to the services of our right hon. Friend, if I may so describe him, the Chairman of Committees, who has not merely helped us to arrange these Debates so that every question may be discussed, but has made probably a permanent contribution to our Parliamentary institutions. I hope that it will not be out of place if in these last moments I also pay a most sincere tribute to the Parliamentary draftsmen in their task of most unusual complexity, and to the civil servants whose efforts and wide knowledge have contributed so much to the success of these discussions.

There are two Amendments upon the Order Paper, and I am afraid that it is too much to suppose that those who put them down will not divide and will not go into the Lobby against the Bill. The right hon. Gentleman the Member for Darwen (Sir H. Samuel) described it as an unholy alliance. I should not have used that epithet myself. I would rather have described it as an uncomfortable alliance, because I am sure that each section of the opposition would be very much happier if the other were not in the Lobby.

MR. CHURCHILL: My right hon. and learned Friend speaks from experience.

THE ATTORNEY-GENERAL: My right hon. Friend must not display too much irritation at this comparatively early stage. At any rate, the combination has this useful effect of throwing light upon a feature which runs through the very intricate design of this Bill, and that is that the Bill grapples with difficulties. It is only when men have to face each other across the table in connection with this great problem of India, to hear each other's objections, to meet each other's points, and to answer each other's arguments, if they can, that they come down to solid earth. When they get away from the table and from the duty of preparing a Bill they are apt to moralise and theorise, and this Bill is the

Hansard, 5.s., CCCII, 2003–12.

answer of the practical man to the theorist represented by the ranks led by the right hon. Gentleman opposite. My Noble Friend made a somewhat long reference to-night to the Simon Report. He said one thing which he will allow me to describe as inaccurate, I hope that is a sufficiently mild term, when he said that the Simon Report had been abandoned in answer to clamour. It was not the plan that was eventually adopted for this simple reason, that it was displaced by, in the opinion of the Government, an even better plan. When my Noble Friend described the Simon Report as one to which he and his friends would give their whole-hearted support he very nearly forgot—he only remembered it just in time—that a cardinal feature of the Simon Report was the transfer of law and order to Provincial Governments. When my Noble Friend remembered it, just in time, he described it as a general proposition, whatever a general proposition may be. It was a feature of the recommendations of the Statutory Commission which could not be neglected when anybody was trying to make up his mind whether the report should be accepted or not.

Let me see where my noble Friend gets himself when he says that the report was abandoned in answer to clamour. His complaint is that this Bill is not wanted by anybody in India. If it be true that the clamour against the Simon Report to which he attaches himself was such as to compel the Government to abandon it, then it seems to follow that nobody wants the Simon Report any more than this Bill, and my noble Friend's argument about nobody wanting the Bill misses a great deal of its point. Is it true that nobody wants the Bill? I do not know. Let me assume for a moment that it is true; but it is only part of the truth. The people who do not want the Bill want not less but more than the Bill. If the people in India do not want the Government, they want my right hon. Friend still less.

So far as right hon. and hon. Gentlemen opposite are concerned, when they complain in their Amendment of the undue restrictions that are placed on the exercise of self-government they must have forgotten that the main safeguards embodied in this Bill were devised at a time when they were in power, when the first Round Table Conference was being held, and they seemed then to have given their assent to the proposition that it was necessary that peace and tranquillity, minorities, finance, commercial discrimination and the Services should all be the subject of special safeguards. I see the hon. Member for Caerphilly (Mr. Morgan Jones) shaking his head. Obviously, there is no time to-night to discuss the point in detail, but I say emphatically that, in germ, you will find in the discussions of the first Round Table Conference every one of the safeguards which I have mentioned this evening.

I will pass to the next criticism in the Amendment. It is said that this Bill provides for the entrenchment of wealth, privilege and reaction. The hon. and gallant Member for South-East Leeds (Major Milner) went so far as to say that it ensured the domination of the Princes for all time. In his closing sentences, his peroration led him to anticipate the advent to power of a Labour Government and to promise that the new Government would right the wrongs of the Bill courageously and fairly. That does not look as though the domination of the Princes were imposed upon India for all time. He must make up his mind what he wants to say.

MAJOR MILNER: I expressed a pious hope.

THE ATTORNEY-GENERAL: I agree that that is about the proper description of the prospects of the hon. and gallant Gentleman and his party. It is no good hon. Gentlemen opposite speaking of conditions in India as though they were precisely the same as in England.

DUCHESS OF ATHOLL: Hear, hear!

THE ATTORNEY-GENERAL: It is a mistake common to both oppositions, and I am glad to hear the Noble Lady cheer what I have said. The right hon. Gentleman the Member for Epping referred to what he described as the vices of the Bill—indirect election, small number of electors, primitive electoral machinery—

MR. CHURCHILL: The right hon. and learned Gentleman is thinking of the hon. Member for Bodmin (Mr. Isaac Foot).

THE ATTORNEY-GENERAL: No, I am not. When the right hon. Gentleman began his speech he dotted the i's and crossed the t's of what the hon. Member for Bodmin (Mr. Isaac Foot) said. He said that the hon. Member had set out in clear and striking fashion the criticisms that might be addressed to the Bill. My right hon. Friend adopted the criticisms, and made use of them for his own purposes. That is because the right hon. Gentleman assumes to believe that the conditions in India are such as require precisely the same democratic system as we enjoy in this country. On a previous occasion I called the attention of the House to the fact that Democracy may be expressed in many ways, in many forms and by many means, and that what is a democratic system in England must not necessarily be applied to India. They have their own conditions, and you have to recognise them. Autocratic government in Indian India is something that has to be reckoned with. It is no good hon. Gentlemen opposite waving it aside as though it were something indecent which must not be treated as a fact.

In this Bill we are facing the task of suiting to the conditions of India that which we have taught Indian people to cherish and desire in connection with the government of their own country. We have to make the best of the material that exists in India. I take leave to say that when the remarkable additions to the electorate are realised—I think they are between 25,000,000 and 30,000,-000 people—the facts that the electorate will be multiplied over four times and that there will be 6,000,000 women included in the 34,000,000 of electors, it will be conceded that the Bill is a step forward in applying Democracy to the new conditions in the Indian continent. [*Laughter.*] Hon. Gentlemen who oppose the Bill laugh, but that will not alter the fact that there has been a long succession of statements in this country to encourage the Indian people to have aspirations which, at some time or another, we are bound to satisfy, to respect and to treat with sympathy. The Government think that the Bill is a response to a demand which this country has itself created.

The hon. Member for Caerphilly was guilty, if he will allow me to say so, of an extravagance when he said that this Bill was fashioned to please ourselves rather than the Indian people. I conceive that the task of this House is neither to think primarily of pleasing ourselves nor of pleasing the Indian people; but surely we have to approve our own handiwork if it is to stand the test of Parliamentary discussion, and we have done, in pursuance of our duty, what I venture to think is the right thing and the best thing for India. If the hon. Gentleman meant to say that this Bill has been conceived with a view to the interest of this country, there are a hundred arguments that we have used which show that we have not thought merely of the interests of this country.

Reference has been made to the case of Lancashire. Did the hon. Gentleman think it was easy for us to stand up here, in answer to our friends from Lancashire, supporters of our policy, our colleagues, when they spoke in defence, as they thought, of the trade interests of that great industrial community? We resisted their demands because we thought that it was part of our duty, thinking of the interests both of India and of this country, to reject a policy that would place shackles upon the fiscal freedom of India, and to give to India the right, which has always been conceded, in the constitutional custom of our Empire, to a great community, to manage its own industrial and fiscal affairs. What would have been the Nemesis if we had acceded to the requests that were made on behalf of Lancashire? The boycott, of unhappy memory, was not prevented or brought to an end by force of arms or by domination; it was brought to an end because the people of India began to be satisfied that they were going to receive fair and honourable treatment. [HON. MEMBERS: "Oh!"] I have not the least doubt that I am right in what I am saying. That boycott could never have been ended by the display of military power. Hon. Members know that perfectly well.

MR. CHURCHILL: Utterly untrue. Rubbish.

THE ATTORNEY-GENERAL: There is not a person in this House, except possibly my right hon. Friend, who would dare to get up and say that it was a display of military force that led to the abandonment of the boycott in India. It was, as I have said, because of the sentiment and feeling of greater good will, and a desire to use other methods of attaining the end which both countries desired. I am bound, although my time is but short, to say that I did not quite understand the reference of my right hon. Friend the Member for Epping to the Privileges Report. He seemed to me to be rather like a litigant against whom judgment has been given and who frequents the courts in the hope of persuading somebody that he has a grievance.

MR. CHURCHILL: Your own Government have appointed this Committee. The Committee has reported, and the House can read the report.

THE ATTORNEY-GENERAL: All those litigants to whom I have referred are persuaded that they have a much better case than the court believes. I have not time to-night to reopen that discussion, upon which the House expressed a very clear opinion nearly a year ago. I was sorry, too, that my right hon. Friend gave an indication that he intended to carry on the fight after the Bill had been read the Third time. I much prefer the statements made by my hon. and gallant Friend the Member for Bournemouth (Sir H. Croft), my right hon. and gallant Friend the Member for Burton (Colonel Gretton), and the Noble Lord who spoke a few minutes ago. Perhaps I am more attracted, as I think the House is more attracted, by the promise they gave of co-operation in spite of their opinions, because of the fact that they have had a longer attachment to the Conservative party than my right hon. Friend.

VISCOUNT WOLMER: May I say that none of us was conscious of the slightest difference in what we expressed?

THE ATTORNEY-GENERAL: I can only say that all who heard the four speeches will be aware of the difference.

MR. CHURCHILL: You have got something to cheer at now.

THE ATTORNEY-GENERAL: I shall only be too delighted if there is no difference between what was said by the right hon. Gentleman and the Noble Lord. I hope that what the Noble Lord has said is a fact, because nothing could be more damaging to constitutional government than that when this House has ratified a particular proposal there should be carried on a sort of guerrilla warfare to embitter relations between this country and India. The right hon. Member for Epping has said that the Princes are not coming into this Federation. The Secretary of State has dealt with that matter on previous occasions. I am not going to attempt to deal with that particular piece of gratuitous folly. There is every reason to believe that the Princes are satisfied with the details which they now find in the Bill. If the right hon. Gentleman is so certain that they are not coming in he need not worry about it. There will be no Federation of India if he is right. I do not believe in this picture of India seething with hatred of Great Britain. There have been some manifestations of loyalty in India in quarters where it was least expected. The core of India is much more sound than some people would have us believe. There are reactionaries in India no doubt and they dislike the Bill because it threatens the ancient strongholds of tyranny and power. This Bill is a step forward on that road which will enable India to do for herself what we could never have done—to make the reforms which are desired by men of all parties. We have raised these aspirations, and we ought to satisfy them.

The right hon. Member for Epping referred in rather derisory terms to the faded flowers of Victorian Liberalism. He has spent 20 years of his otherwise virtuous life in offering them to anyone who would accept them. Now in spite of his attachment to the Conservative party, has he lost faith in the principles of Victorian democracy? He declared almost with glee that these principles are under a cloud in Europe. All that I can say is that they are not under a cloud in the British Empire. He said that we were handing over India to the lawyers and politicians. Well, I represent one class and my right hon. Friend represents the other. I see in this Bill a gift from the greatest majority which this country has ever known in the history of Parliament. It is a gift which we give willingly. My right hon. Friend the Member for Epping and the Noble Lord joined together in offering thanks to God that they were not associated with this Measure. I would rather join with other hon. Members in prayer that this gift may be divinely blessed for the enrichment of the British Empire and future of India instead of thanking God that I am perfectly right and everybody else is perfectly wrong. In this Bill we make a greater transfer of power than any country has ever made in the whole course of the history of the world, and we have made it voluntarily. There has been nothing in the way of compulsion. My right hon. Friend the Secretary of State declared yesterday that he was not depressed about the future of India. Unlike his opinion, my opinion is of no value, but there are some facts of the past that I cannot forget. We have established in India, as my hon. and gallant Friend the Member for Bourne-mouth (Sir H. Croft) truly said, the most efficient and benevolent administration ever known in the East. That has not happened without hazards being taken. Many times in the century and a half of constitutional government in India under this country these questions have been hotly debated in this House. Sometimes it has been difficult to arouse interest in them, sometimes party faction has embittered the controversies, and tragedy has sometimes filled the page of history. But somehow or other, at the end of every effort to do something fresh for India the genius of the British race for government has triumphed, and we have added another stone to the impregnable fortress where freedom is guarded. Why should we despair, as my right hon. Friend invited us to do to-night, when Parliament is bending itself once more to the task of devising something for India.

The right hon. Gentleman the Leader of the Opposition has asked me what we have to say as to the promise of Dominion status for India. If I have kept it until the last moment, it is because we have said, at length and in detail, in the course of these Debates all that there is to be said upon the subject. My right hon. Friend the Secretary of State, in the clearest possible terms in his speech introducing this Bill and moving the Second Reading, said that the Government had agreed upon the statement which embodied all that we wish to say, and all, I am sure, that the right hon. Gentleman would wish us to say, if he would rightly understand it. On that occasion my right hon. Friend the Secretary of State said :

> The Preamble of 1919 . . . is a clear statement of the purpose of the British people, and this Bill is a definite step, indeed a great stride forward, towards the achievement of that purpose. . . . Our policy is to do all that we can by sympathetic help and co-operation to enable India to overcome these difficulties and ultimately to take her place among the fully self-governing members of the British Commonwealth of Nations.
> [OFFICIAL REPORT, 6th February, 1935; cols. 1165–66, Vol. 297.]

The Leader of the Opposition asked whether this Bill was intended to be a step forward in the establishment of Dominion Status. I have given the right hon. Gentleman the answer in the words of my right hon. Friend the Secretary of State. Let him read again what was so carefully prepared and so deliberately said to this House on that occasion. This Bill has been meditated in conference, in committee, and now in council. While we have been meditating we are happy to think that India has become more settled and ready to take the gift which this House can give. We shall not be disloyal to the memories of the great men who have ruled India in the past. We shall be completing their work in the spirit of the best of those rulers.

Report by the Lord Privy Seal, Sir Stafford Cripps, to the House of Commons on His Mission to India, 23 April 1942 *

When it was announced by the Prime Minister that I was to go to India with the Cabinet's proposals, this House was good enough to express its hopes that the Mission might have a successful conclusion. That hope was, I know, shared by a great mass of the British people, by the Dominions and by a multitude of the friends of Great Britain and of India both in the United States of America and elsewhere. Unfortunately events have brought disappointment to these hopes, but I do not think that anyone in this country need feel regretful that the proposals were put forward or need blame His Majesty's Government or the British people for the unfortunate fact of failure to reach an agreement. Moreover, I should like to emphasise at the outset of what may, I fear, prove a rather long account of my Mission that, in my view, nothing but good will result both from the fact that the proposals were made and from the almost equally important fact that the War Cabinet sent one of its own number to discuss them in India with the leaders of Indian opinion. This method of presentation of the proposals has, I believe, demonstrated our sincerity of purpose.

Let me first say a word or two as to the background of my visit. Undoubtedly the moment was a difficult one, and a number of people have made the comment that it is a pity that something on the same lines was not done earlier. There is much in the relationships of this country to India that could be criticised, analysed and argued about, but I do not propose to embark upon any such argument, as it is far more profitable to spend the time available in an examination of the present and the future rather than in an attempt to allot blame for the past—that is a task which we can very well leave to the historians.

The moment was a difficult one, for three main reasons. First, because of the imminent approach of the enemy to the shores of India. The Japanese forces by

*Hansard, 5.s., CCCLXXIX, 826–43.

land, sea and air were almost at the gates of India, and in such circumstances many things that might have been usefully discussed and negotiated in more peaceful times could not be dealt with because there was an overriding need to do everything in our power to carry out our duty to defend India from the foreign invader. Second, owing to events in the Far Eastern theatre of war, accompanied by a highly skilled though grossly misleading propaganda from Axis sources, an atmosphere of defeatism and of anti-British sentiment was showing itself in certain sections of Indian opinion. The Indians were, too, uncertain of the future and of His Majesty's Government's view as to what that future would be. Third, with the approach of self-government or Dominion status as a reality, communal differences of view as to the form of government which would be suitable for the future India had tended to become more definitely crystallised, and especially the idea of two separate Indias, which, even two years ago was little more than a vague vision of certain extremists, had come to be the definite and accepted programme of the most powerful Moslem political organisation.

There were, of course, other factors in the situation, but these were the principal ones which increased the difficulties of obtaining any general understanding among the Indian peoples. It was the need for clarification of the situation and for the consolidation of Indian opinion in a favourable direction that impelled His Majesty's Government to decide that some positive step must be taken, and taken quickly. The objective and the hope of His Majesty's Government were that we might use these very difficulties of the occasion to bring together all the main leaders of Indian opinion for the double purpose of solving India's future and of reinforcing her defence against the invader that was threatening her shores. In order to accomplish this, two things were necessary: first, to give a clear and unequivocal promise as regards the future, and, second, to address an invitation to the various communal and political sections of Indian opinion to come together on the Viceroy's Executive Council for the immediate prosecution of the war in India. This invitation would have to be made upon the basis of the offer as to the future status of India.

In the circumstances of the communal situation in India at the present time, it must be borne in mind that the future is inevitably linked with the present, and I personally am quite confident that no more temporary arrangement could have been come to without some exposition of our future intentions. Had we attempted to deal only with the present, we should immediately have been met with a demand for clarification as to the future.

The difficulty of that communal situation has recently been emphasised by Mr. Gandhi in an article in "Harijan" of 19th April, where he makes the following statement:

> Attainment of independence is an impossibility till we have solved the communal tangle. We will never tackle this problem so long as either or both parties think that independence will or can come without any solution of the tangle. There are two ways of solving what has become insoluble, the royal way of non-violence or violence.

His Majesty's Government also had to deal with certain definite—and often conflicting—demands which had been voiced by the various leaders of important sections of Indian opinion. The Congress was known to have demanded repeatedly independence for India and a Constituent Assembly which should devise a new Constitution for the Indian people and, perhaps most important of all, a single Indian Government for the whole of India—British India and the Indian States together. The Moslem League, on the other hand, had adopted as the main plank of its programme the demand for Pakistan—a territory made up of the rather vague congeries of areas in which Moslems are in a majority. The more dispersed but still important minority of the depressed classes desired specific protection against the adverse effect of the caste system; while the Sikhs, that brave fighting race who have done and are doing so much to help Great Britain and the defence of India, desired some form of protection against the majority rule of another community. There were many other minorities, religious, racial or social, who equally asked for special treatment, either along the lines of that already accorded to them under the Act of 1935 or upon a more generous scale. Then, outside British India, were the Princes and their peoples, some of the Princes having special Treaty rights, arising in many cases over a century ago but the whole under the paramountcy of the King-Emperor.

Among those conflicting claims it was necessary for His Majesty's Government to act with the mind of an arbitrator and attempt to lay down some method by which the Indian peoples could determine their own future, a method that would be acceptable to as many shades of opinion as possible. It was, of course, wholly consistent with the trend of earlier declarations that if all sections of Indian opinion could agree upon some alternative method of self-determination, there would be no difficulty as to its acceptance by His Majesty's Government. In the past when it had been left to the Indian communities to agree upon some manner of deciding the future the British Government had been accused of relying upon the impossibility of agreement in order to perpetuate their own domination over India. It was, therefore, necessary to devise a scheme whereby the refusal of a large minority to co-operate would not hold up the majority in their attainment of self-government.

So much for the considerations upon which that part of the draft Declaration dealing with the future Constitution of India was based and which resulted in the form in which it was laid before the Indian leaders and in which it appears on page 4 of the White Paper. The second part of the draft Declaration—paragraph (e)—was to deal with the immediate period before the new Constitution could come into being. It was left in vague and general terms but was subject to one vital and precise reservation. The reason for this form was that it was desired to leave open for discussion the way in which participation by the Indian leaders "in the counsels of their country, of the Commonwealth and of the United Nations"—to use the words of the document—could be made most effective and immediate. The single express reservation was as to defence, and I will return to that point in detail, since it was one of the difficulties which arose in the course of the discussions in Delhi.

Let me now say a word about the manner of conducting these discussions. I was most anxious that there should be no suspicion whatever that His Majesty's Government were handpicking those whom I saw, and, consequently, I asked the main organisations themselves to appoint those whom they wished to meet me. This they did, and they mostly expressed the wish that I should not interview any other members of their Working Committees. Certain individuals I saw, such as Mr. Gandhi, Sir Taj Bahadur Sapru, Mr. Joshi and Mr. Jayakar, the present or past Prime Ministers of all the Provincial Governments, the Governors of the Provinces and, lastly, but by no means least, the members of the Viceroy's Executive Council. It was to this latter body that I first disclosed the details of the draft Declaration, immediately upon my arrival in India, and after seeing them each one individually, it was to the same body that I first announced the failure of agreement. His Majesty's Government are fully aware of the service that has been done by the members of the Viceroy's Executive and especially by those Indians who have represented the interests of their peoples in that body, and it was for that reason that I considered it necessary to go first and last to them. As the House will know, I kept the draft Declaration from publication for the first week of my stay in Delhi, during which time I submitted it to all the principal Indian representative leaders personally. It then became clear that its contents were becoming generally known, and it was considered better that it should be published, and this was done. The Indian Press were both helpful and fair, in that they gave the fullest publicity to all that I said to them at the Press conferences which I held every other day, while of course, at the same time, expressing their own views, often very forcibly.

It is worthy of note that the skilful and analytical minds of the Indians sometimes lead them to seek out and emphasise every point as to which there might be doubt, or disagreement, while they are apt to pass over the more uninteresting points as to which there is agreement. This sometimes gives the appearance of a much more keen and concentrated opposition than in fact exists. Upon the fundamental and vital point of their self-government and self-determination there was, I believe, no single case of disagreement, not excluding the representatives of the European community, whom I saw twice. Disagreement came upon the way in which that self-determination should be exercised and upon the transitory provisions for the government of India until the new Constitution could come into force. It must always be remembered that one legacy of the past is the unwillingness of any considerable section of Indian opinion to accept any British offer unless it is also accepted by at least one of the two principal bodies—Congress and the Moslem League. The state of internal opinion is such that unless there is to be a large measure of acceptance of an offer, no minority cares to lay itself open to the accusation of being the creature of British Imperialism. It was therefore to be anticipated, and we did anticipate, that there would either be a general acceptance or a general rejection of the draft Declaration.

Before I pass to the particular matters around which the discussions developed, I must make clear one other matter in relation to the negotiations.

When I was sent to India by the War Cabinet I was given full authority to arrive at a settlement within the terms of the draft Declaration. That is to say, its essentials had to be maintained, a matter which I myself regarded as of importance, as it was the one and only way in which a general discursive and endless discussion could be avoided. But I alone was responsible for what was put forward to Indian leaders by way of explanation or amplification of details in the draft Declaration. I naturally maintained the closest contact with the Viceroy. We met, in fact, every night during my stay and discussed the progress of events. I also maintained the closest contact with the Commander-in-Chief, and both of them were most helpful, but the responsibility for what was done was mine and was not theirs. There was a tendency in some Indian quarters to suggest that they were responsible for the difficulties over defence. Nothing could be further from the truth.

There is, perhaps, one other person to whom I should make reference so as to avoid any misunderstanding, since his name has been somewhat bandied about in the Press. It so happened by coincidence that while I was in New Delhi an Economic Mission arrived from the United States of America, headed by Colonel Louis Johnson, representing directly in that matter the President. He was entertained by the Viceroy at his house on his first arrival, and while he was there one of the Congress leaders asked to see him. After consulting with the Viceroy and in accordance with the latter's advice, he saw the Pandit Nehru and in a most helpful conversation ascertained what at that time seemed to be the difficulty in the way of a settlement. I also called upon Colonel Louis Johnson by way of courtesy on his arrival and gave him as accurate a picture of the situation as I could. Thereafter, on my suggestion, and in accordance with his own personal desire to be of any assistance that he could, he had other interviews which were of great help in clarifying the situation. At no time did he act otherwise than in a purely personal capacity, and he, like two or three of my good Indian friends, merely did his best to give what help he could to the parties. I am personally most grateful to him, and I am sure the leaders of Congress are similarly so. But I wish to make it abundantly clear that there was no question of any American intervention but only the personal help of a very able American citizen.

Let me now come to the difficulties that arose. These were mostly concentrated into my discussions and correspondence with Congress leaders. The Moslem League did not deliver to me their objections until after they knew the results of my negotiations with Congress. The questions outside the Congress objections which were raised by other sections of opinion I will deal with separately. The difficulties fell under three heads, as will be observed from a perusal of the final resolution of Congress and the letter from the Congress President of 10th April which appear respectively on pages 16 and 9 of the White Paper. First were those relating to the method of determining the new Constitution; second were those relating to defence; and third were those relating to the general form of the interim Government.

So far as the first category was concerned, there were three objections. First, to the use of the word "Dominion" and its definition in the opening paragraph of the draft Declaration. This was not a matter of prime importance. The claim of Congress had been, as we know, for independence, and they were afraid that their followers would attach undue importance to the apparent limitations included in the definition, though I think the leaders themselves appreciated that with the added words in Clause (*c*, II) of the draft Declaration—

> will not impose any restriction on the power of the Indian Union to decide in the future its relationship to the other Member States of the British Commonwealth—

it was made perfectly clear that India could, in fact, leave the British Commonwealth of Nations should the Indian Government under the new Constitution so decide. I pass, therefore, from that objection.

The second objection was a most substantial one. That was as to the right of non-accession of the Provinces after the new Constitution had been decided upon. In this relation I would ask hon. Members to study the two resolutions of Congress and the Moslem League and then to look at the draft Declaration. They will, I think, come to the conclusion that the draft Declaration does no more than Mr. Gandhi and other Congress leaders have constantly stated that they were prepared to do, that is, to keep open the issue of Pakistan, and they will also, I am sure, realise that the scheme of the draft Declaration is as fair a compromise as possible between the two extreme views. It was the duty of His Majesty's Government to find that agreement by compromise and not to give either party all of what they wanted and then force it upon the other. I do not personally believe that it is possible to find under existing circumstances a fairer solution of the problem, a solution which aims at and provides for a single united India but which admits that if in the last resort the parties cannot agree upon a form of Constitution which will enable them to work together, then the Moslems must be allowed in those Provinces where they can get a majority of the whole electorate to vote those Provinces out of the Union.

I should add one word of explanation as to the proposal which was made for effecting this non-accession and which does not appear in the document itself. The only ultimate test must be the wish of the actual majority of the adult male population in the Provinces—that is to say, a plebiscite. But it is not necessary to go to the trouble of a plebiscite where the result is a foregone conclusion. It was, therefore, suggested that every Province should pass in its Lower House a formal vote of accession to the new Union, but if there was a minority of 40 per cent. or more against that accession, then the minority should have the right to challenge a plebiscite, which should then determine the matter by a simple majority. I desire to emphasise once again that this whole scheme was no rigid and unchanging plan, since it was expressed to be open to the Indian communities to agree among themselves as to a better alternative.

The third and last objection under this head was as regards the position of the Indian States. Congress has for many years now interested itself in the lot of the people in the Indian States and has declared that in any new Constitution these people, as distinct from their autocratic rulers, must have a say. They therefore protested, not against the Indian States coming into the Constitution-making authority, but against their representatives being nominated by the rulers and not elected by the people. Unfortunately, in my view, representative institutions have not yet developed in the great majority of the Indian States, which must be dealt with as they are if they are to be brought into the Constitution-making authority. That participation, I believe, almost everyone desires, including indeed most of the States' rulers themselves.

His Majesty's Government would be only too glad to see as rapid a development of suitable representative institutions as is possible in all the Indian States, and if by the time a Constitution-making body came to be chosen there was machinery in the States by which popular representatives could be chosen, His Majesty's Government would be only too pleased. Already, as some hon. Members may know, a small beginning has been made in some States by more enlightened rulers and their Diwins, and I am certain this House would wish the British Administration in India to do all it can to encourage and expedite that development. But for the moment we can only deal with the situation as it exists historically. I need not trouble the House with all the complexities of the present constitutional position so far as the Indian States are concerned, since, under the draft Declaration, that position would have been altered only so far as alteration was necessary to adjust economic relationships with the new Indian Union or was caused by the action of the Indian States themselves in joining the new Union.

However, none of these three differences with the Congress Working Committee would have been decisive of a negative result. For though objecting and registering their protest, both Congress, the Moslem League and other bodies such as the Hindu Mahasabha, would have been prepared to co-operate upon the immediate situation despite the making of the Declaration of His Majesty's Government, and that is probably the most that one could expect in the circumstances. It would, in fact, have meant that the solution for self-determination laid down in the document would have then held the field with finality subject only to the various communities and bodies in India arriving at some alternative method by agreement.

There is one other matter with regard to the future that I must refer to, and that is the position of the minorities, such as the depressed classes, the Sikhs, the Indian Christians and others. Each one wished, and not unnaturally, to have some special and specific measure of protection included to cover its own case. But once self-determination had been promised to India as was proposed in the draft Declaration, it would be impossible for His Majesty's Government to impose terms in the new Indian Constitution. To do so would be the negation of self-determination. We have, however, in the past given undertakings to these minorities, but in none of the cases other than that of the Moslems could these promises be dealt with by such a device as non-accession. The minorities are not sufficiently localised or self-contained, even in the case of the Sikhs, to make that possible, assuming upon other grounds that it was desirable.

Some other solution, therefore, had to be found. I have not the slightest doubt that these minorities, all of whom would have been represented in the Constitution-making body, in accordance with their strength under the communal award, would have obtained ample protection under the Constitution from the majority. Indeed, the forces operating within that Constitution-making body would have tended very much in favour of the minorities. But in view of our pledges we could not leave the minorities to rely upon this alone. We, therefore, inserted the express clause as to a treaty covering minority protection which will be found in paragraph (c, II) of the draft Declaration. I should like to record here that neither Congress nor the Moslem League expressed the slightest objection to this method of treatment of the subject. The minorities themselves were, of course, unable to say at this stage what form of protection they wished for, since till the form of the new Constitution is known no one can state how within that form minorities can best be protected. That would have had to have been a matter for negotiation when the main lines of the Constitution had been decided upon. The minorities were all of them, I think, anxious to come into the temporary government had it been formed under the terms of the draft Declaration, despite their criticism of the scheme as a whole, as lacking more specific protection for their own interests.

I now pass to the second category of objection, that relating to defence. This is a matter which is far more complicated than might appear on the face of it, and one as to which there was a distinct division of opinion among Indians themselves. Upon one thing there was, I think, practical unanimity, and that was that the actual technical conduct of the war in India—the control of the Armed Forces for fighting purposes—must remain under the British Commander-in-Chief. Everyone realised that that was mere common sense, and so there was no difficulty with regard to it. The difference of opinion came when the responsibilities of the Government of India—as apart from those of His Majesty's Government—were considered. These latter—that is the direct responsibilities of His Majesty's Government—would have been quite satisfactorily dealt with by having a representative Indian on the War Cabinet and on the Pacific Council, both of which posts were offered to the Indian leaders. It was first sought to clarify the position as between His Majesty's Government's direct responsibilities and those of the Government of India by a rewording of the final draft of clause (e) in the form in which it now appears in the White Paper on page 5: The document says:

> During the critical period which now faces India and until the new Constitution can be framed His Majesty's Government must inevitably bear the responsibility for and retain control and direction of the defence of India as part of their world war effort, but the task of organising to the full the military, moral and material resources of India must be the responsibility of the Government of India with the co-operation of the peoples of India.

It was sought by those words to define as clearly as possible the division of responsibilities direct of His Majesty's Government and that of the Government of India. But there is another cross division of responsibilities which is much more difficult to define and separate out. The House will appreciate that since the last war the Commander-in-Chief in India has also held the post of Defence Member on the Viceroy's Executive Council, and his actual functions and activities are divided notionally between the two posts that he holds. In fact, the Defence Secretariat, the Defence Department and the Staff are, from the mere fact that they have a common chief—a single individual—all interlinked and interdependent in such a way as to make anything like a complete and detailed separation of the functions of the Commander-in-Chief from those of the Defence Minister a very long and complicated matter, and one which, if it were to be attempted at such a critical moment as this, would throw into chaos the whole defence organisation of India. Nevertheless I took the view—and in this the Viceroy and Commander-in-Chief agreed—that it would be difficult for the representative Indians on the Viceroy's Executive to rouse the people of India to their defence, unless they could say with justice that at least some part of that defence was the responsibility of a representative Indian, and so of the Indian peoples. That was the point that was stressed by practically everyone whom I interviewed, including the Europeans.

It was in the attempt to get over this very real difficulty that I spent a good deal of my time at New Delhi. Various suggestions were made, and several formulae were tried, until eventually that one was worked out which became the final suggestion, and that is the only one with which I need now deal. It will be found on page 8 of the White Paper, Document No. (8). Its object was quite simple: to allocate to the Commander-in-Chief, as War Member of the Viceroy's Executive, all those administrative functions under the Government of India that were vital to his efficient carrying on of the war—that is, the governmental relations of all his Staffs, his General Staff, his Naval Staff and his Air Staff—while at the same time leaving to a representative Indian other functions of the Defence Member roughly corresponding to the list on page 8 of the White Paper under the heading, Annex (I), together with a number of other very important functions, examples of which are given under Annex (II) on the same page, and which would, in fact, have made the new Defence Department one of the largest of all Departments in India. The House will, of course, realise that numerous other aspects of defence, such as civil defence, communications, labour and so on, are already in the hands of Indian Members of the Viceroy's Council and would, of course, have so continued, although the personages might have been changed.

It was impossible for His Majesty's Government to go further with safety— and no risk could be taken at such a moment as the present on so vital and immediate a matter as the defence of India. Moreover, I do not myself believe that the minorities who contain some of the finest fighting elements in India— such as the Punjaubi, Moslems and Sikhs—would have been prepared to consent at this stage to any further devolution of defence responsibilities. The question did not actually arise, as His Majesty's Government were not able to go any further, but from the attitude of those minorities I am confident they would not have consented to any further transfer in this field. I believe that this latest formula might have gained acceptance, and at one moment, as the House is aware, the Indian people seemed to think a satisfactory solution had been found. I myself feel pretty sure that had Congress leaders been able to accept finally the draft Declaration and enter the new Government they would, upon the question of defence, have been able to rally their Indian followers behind them.

But it was not upon this issue that the final break came, although it was no doubt to some undefined extent involved in the breakdown. The final question which was raised at my last and long meeting with the President of Congress and Pandit Nehru was as to the form of the temporary Government that should be in power until the end of the war and the coming into operation of the new Constitution. I had from the outset made it clear to all those whom I saw that it was not possible to make any constitutional changes except of the most insignificant kind prior to the new Constitution which would come into operation as a result of the labours of the Constitution-making Assembly. This fact had been accepted by everyone without discussion, and it was obvious that it was a practical impossibility to start upon the discussion and framing of a new Constitution at this present time, and that if such a discussion had been practicable and had been embarked upon, it would have occupied many months, during which nothing could have been done by way of forming a new Government. Not only so, but any such alteration now made would have been thought to prejudge the situation under the new Constitution, and that would no doubt have met with opposition for that reason. Therefore, any such step as recasting the Constitution at the present time was admittedly out of the question. This was made quite clear in my letter to the President of Congress, dated 17th April where I stated:

> As the Working Committee have fully understood, it is impossible to make any change in the existing Constitution during the period of hostilities.

At the same time His Majesty's Government were most anxious to make a reality of the offer under Clause (e) of the draft Declaration in any way that was practicable consistently with the existing Constitution. It is always possible in such circumstances by mutual understanding and with the co-operation of both sides to do much, especially when all are intent upon a common object so vital and all-embracing as the defence of India. The question as to the formation of a new Government, how the members of the Viceroy's Executive should be treated and how the business therein should be conducted, were, of course, essential matters for the Viceroy, who had to carry on the Government of India and not for me as a member of the War Cabinet on a visit to India. I therefore told the Congress leaders that the general principle of participation or co-operation was laid down in Clause (e) of the Declaration, which stated:

His Majesty's Government desire and invite the immediate and effective participation of the leaders of the principal sections of the Indian people in the counsels of their country.

but that the exact nature of its operation could only be decided as the result of discussions with the Viceroy, once Indian leaders had made up their minds that they could accept the draft Declaration upon other points. I stated that I was prepared to remain in India in such an event until the new Government was formed, so that I could, if necessary, give any help that was required, but that I was not prepared to bind the Viceroy to accept any particular arrangement for the conduct of his Executive. I informed them, after discussion with the Viceroy, that immediately they decided to accept he would call the principal leaders into consultation as to the formation of his new Government and that the only British members upon whom the scheme insisted were the Viceroy himself and the Commander-in-Chief. I also pointed out to them that, if the conditions offered by the Viceroy were such that they could not see their way to accept them, they would, of course, be free, as would any other individuals, to refuse to take office or, if they found they could not work in the Government, they would be free to resign, though naturally I hoped that such a situation would never in fact arise.

I see no other way myself in which the matter could have been arranged, but the Congress leaders, as is shown by their final letter, apparently felt that they would not have the wide powers which they thought necessary for their successful participation in the Government. As I pointed out in my broadcast on this subject from New Delhi, the position of complete power asked for by Congress—which was not demanded by any other section of opinion in India—would leave the matter in an impossible situation. The Executive Council, once chosen by the Viceroy, would not have been responsible to anyone but themselves, or, in a somewhat loose way perhaps, to their political or communal organisations, and there would have been no protection therefore for any of the minorities. I am quite confident that none of the minorities would have accepted such a position, and least of all the Moslems. It was on this issue that the final break came, followed, as I had expected, by a rejection by the Moslem League, for reasons the precise opposite of those stated by Congress, but all of them concerned with the future rather than with the present.

I regret, and His Majesty's Government regret, most profoundly that our efforts have failed. But do not let the House or the people of this country imagine that all the results of the War Cabinet's action and of my Mission are on the debit side. There is much, I think, on the credit side as well. First, there is the advantage which accrues from the methods which have been adopted in this case. Instead of a somewhat vague Declaration put out without previous consultation with leaders of Indian opinion, a precise and clear statement of a suggested solution has been discussed in India with all the Indian leaders by a member of the War Cabinet sent there for that particular purpose. And the fact that a member of the Cabinet was sent in the stressed circumstances of to-day has indicated the depth and genuineness of our desire to reach a settlement of our outstanding difficulties. Second, the content of the scheme has put beyond all possibility of doubt or question that we desire to give India self-government at the earliest practicable moment and that we wish her to determine for herself the form which that Government shall take. However great the criticism of detail may have been, no responsible Indian leader has challenged our sincerity upon that point. I think it would be accurate to say that this is the first time that such an assertion could be truly made, and it is a most important and significant fact for our future relationships. Third, the whole of the discussions have proceeded upon a basis of frank and mutual understanding and in an atmosphere of friendliness. Though the past is still perhaps too strong for complete confidence to have been established, I have the feeling that we have taken a step forward, especially so far as the younger elements in India are concerned, who are perhaps less influenced by the struggles and bitterness of the past than some of their older colleagues who still retain their leadership.

And, finally, the whole discussion upon the issue of defence has served to bring to the front the determination of the Indian peoples to defend their own country. Such statements as that made by Pandit Nehru, a man of great courage and determination, or the more recent attitude of Mr. Rajagopalachari must do much to influence Indian opinion. The representative of the Moslem League, Mr. Jinnah, and the leaders of other parties and communities, such as the Sikhs and the Mahrattas, have all of them expressed to me personally their readiness to stand with us in the defence of their country and to do their utmost to help in every way. It is unfortunate that they do not find themselves in a position to give that help as members of the Viceroy's Executive Council, but it is good to know that each in his own way is prepared to assist. We have been brought closer, I believe, to our Indian friends as fellow defenders of their country, but we are not yet so close as we would wish or even as is necessary for the most effective defence of India.

Looking back at this historical incident, an important incident in the history of both our countries, I feel no regret at the decisions taken by His Majesty's Government. I am convinced that they were just and that we have done all that we could in an admittedly difficult situation to bring about an agreement and a better understanding between the peoples of the two countries. It is, in fact, the past exercising its influence upon all parties that has proved too strong for us, and we must now leave the leaven of better understanding to work quietly towards an ultimate and satisfactory solution of the political problem. If we are to do this, let us at all costs forgo the transient satisfaction of blaming others and of encouraging those very antagonisms which have been a major part of our difficulty.

I stated when I left India that, in default of acceptance, the draft Declaration must be considered as being withdrawn. But this does not and cannot close the door to that closer co-operation which we desire to see in the defence of India or to the solution of the problem of self-government after the war. It means that His Majesty's Government have done their best to make their contribution to the solution of the problem both in the substance of the draft Declaration and in the method of its presentation to the Indian people. For the time being there is nothing further that we can do. We must be patient and open-minded, willing to consider any proposals upon which the Indian leaders can agree. But we must concentrate upon our duty to do our utmost for the defence of India, a task in which our great American Allies have generously come forward to offer their help, a help which we and the Indians alike welcome and appreciate. Many of the Indian leaders, too, will do their best to arouse the Indian peoples in their own defence, and I hope that by co-operation in defence we may move a step nearer to the solution of our problem.

Of this I am certain, that the Members of this House, the British people, and all well-wishers of democracy the world over will continue in the hope that through a successful resistance to the brutal aggression of Japan the Indian peoples will reach their goal of self-government and self-determination without internal strife and bitterness, and that thus India will emerge as a great equal of the free nations of the world able to make her full contribution to the future of a new civilisation after the victory of the Allied cause.

Statement by the Cabinet Mission to India and the Viceroy Recommending a Federal United Nation after Independence and Rejecting the Proposal for a Separate State of Pakistan, May 1946*

1. On the 15th March last, just before the despatch of the Cabinet Mission to India, Mr. Attlee, the British Prime Minister, used these words: —

> My colleagues are going to India with the intention of using their utmost endeavours to help her to attain her freedom as speedily and fully as possible. What form of Government is to replace the present regime is for India to decide; but our desire is to help her to set up forthwith the machinery for making that decision . . . .

> I hope that the Indian people may elect to remain within the British Commonwealth. I am certain that she will find great advantages in doing so . . . .

> But if she does so elect, it must be by her own free will. The British Commonwealth and Empire is not bound together by chains of external compulsion. It is a free association of free peoples. If, on the other hand, she elects for independence, in our view she has a right to do so. It will be for us to help to make the transition as smooth and easy as possible.

2. Charged in these historic words, we—the Cabinet Ministers and the Viceroy—have done our utmost to assist the two main political parties to reach agreement upon the fundamental issue of the unity or division of India. After prolonged discussions in New Delhi we succeeded in bringing the Congress and

Parliamentary Papers, 1945–46, XIX, Cmd. 6821, 2–6, 8–9.

the Muslim League together in conference at Simla. There was a full exchange of views and both parties were prepared to make considerable concessions in order to try to reach a settlement, but it ultimately proved impossible to close the remainder of the gap between the parties and so no agreement could be concluded. Since no agreement has been reached, we feel that it is our duty to put forward what we consider are the best arrangements possible to ensure a speedy setting up of the new constitution. This statement is made with the full approval of His Majesty's Government in the United Kingdom.

3. We have accordingly decided that immediate arrangements should be made whereby Indians may decide the future constitution of India, and an interim Government may be set up at once to carry on the administration of British India until such time as a new constitution can be brought into being. We have endeavoured to be just to the smaller as well as to the larger sections of the people; and to recommend a solution which will lead to a practicable way of governing the India of the future, and will give a sound basis for defence and a good opportunity for progress in the social, political and economic field.

4. It is not intended in this statement to review the voluminous evidence which has been submitted to the Mission; but it is right that we should state that it has shown an almost universal desire, outside the supporters of the Muslim League, for the unity of India.

5. This consideration did not, however, deter us from examining closely and impartially the possibility of a partition of India; since we were greatly impressed by the very genuine and acute anxiety of the Muslims lest they should find themselves subjected to a perpetual Hindu-majority rule. This feeling has become so strong and widespread amongst the Muslims that it cannot be allayed by mere paper safeguards. If there is to be internal peace in India it must be secured by measures which will assure to the Muslims a control in all matters vital to their culture, religion, and economic or other interests.

6. We therefore examined in the first instance the question of a separate and fully independent sovereign state of Pakistan as claimed by the Muslim League. Such a Pakistan would comprise two areas; one in the North-West consisting of the provinces of the Punjab, Sind, North-West Frontier, and British Baluchistan; the other in the North-East consisting of the provinces of Bengal and Assam. The League were prepared to consider adjustment of boundaries at a later stage, but insisted that the principle of Pakistan should first be acknowledged. The argument for a separate state of Pakistan was based, first, upon the right of the Muslim majority to decide their method of government according to their wishes, and, secondly, upon the necessity to include substantial areas in which Muslims are in a minority, in order to make Pakistan administratively and economically workable.

The size of the non-Muslim minorities in a Pakistan comprising the whole of the six provinces enumerated above would be very considerable as the following figures show: --

North-Western Area—

	Muslim.	Non-Muslim.
Punjab	16,217,242	12,201,577
North-West Frontier Province	2,788,797	249,270
Sind	3,208,325	1,326,683
British Baluchistan	438,930	62,701
	22,653,294	13,840,231
	62.07 per cent.	37.93 per cent.

North-Eastern Area—

	Muslim.	Non-Muslim.
Bengal	33,005,434	27,301,091
Assam	3,442,479	6,762,254
	36,447,913	34,063,345
	51.69 per cent.	48.31 per cent.

The Muslim minorities in the remainder of British India number some 20 million dispersed amongst a total population of 188 million.

These figures show that the setting up of a separate sovereign state of Pakistan on the lines claimed by the Muslim League would not solve the communal minority problem; nor can we see any justification for including within a sovereign Pakistan those districts of the Punjab and of Bengal and Assam in which the population is predominantly non-Muslim. Every argument that can be used in favour of Pakistan can equally, in our view, be used in favour of the exclusion of the non-Muslim areas from Pakistan. This point would particularly affect the position of the Sikhs.

7. We, therefore, considered whether a smaller sovereign Pakistan confined to the Muslim majority areas alone might be a possible basis of compromise. Such a Pakistan is regarded by the Muslim League as quite impracticable because it would entail the exclusion from Pakistan of (a) the whole of the Ambala and Jullundur divisions in the Punjab; (b) the whole of Assam except the district of Sylhet; and (c) a large part of Western Bengal, including Calcutta, in which city the percentage of the Muslim population is 23.6 per cent. We ourselves are also convinced that any solution which involves a radical partition of the Punjab and Bengal, as this would do, would be contrary to the wishes and interests of a very large proportion of the inhabitants of these provinces. Bengal and the Punjab each has its own common language and a long history and tradition. Moreover, any division of the Punjab would of necessity divide the Sikhs, leaving substantial bodies of Sikhs on both sides of the boundary. We have therefore been forced to the conclusion that neither a larger nor a smaller sovereign state of Pakistan would provide an acceptable solution for the communal problem.

8. Apart from the great force of the foregoing arguments there are weighty administrative, economic and military considerations. The whole of the trans-

portation and postal and telegraph systems of India have been established on the basis of a United India. To disintegrate them would gravely injure both parts of India. The case for a united defence is even stronger. The Indian Armed Forces have been built up as a whole for the defence of India as a whole, and to break them in two would inflict a deadly blow on the long traditions and high degree of efficiency of the Indian Army and would entail the gravest dangers. The Indian Navy and Indian Air Force would become much less effective. The two sections of the suggested Pakistan contain the two most vulnerable frontiers in India and for a successful defence in depth the area of Pakistan would be insufficient.

9. A further consideration of importance is the greater difficulty which the Indian States would find in associating themselves with a divided British India.

10. Finally, there is the geographical fact that the two halves of the proposed Pakistan state are separated by some seven hundred miles and the communications between them both in war and peace would be dependent on the goodwill of Hindustan.

11. We are therefore unable to advise the British Government that the power which at present resides in British hands should be handed over to two entirely separate sovereign states.

12. This decision does not, however, blind us to the very real Muslim apprehensions that their culture and political and social life might become submerged in a purely unitary India, in which the Hindus with their greatly superior numbers must be a dominating element. To meet this the Congress have put forward a scheme under which provinces would have full autonomy subject only to a minimum of central subjects, such as foreign affairs, defence and communications.

Under this scheme provinces, if they wished to take part in economic and administrative planning on a large scale, could cede to the centre optional subjects in addition to the compulsory ones mentioned above.

13. Such a scheme would, in our view, present considerable constitutional disadvantages and anomalies. It would be very difficult to work a central executive and legislature in which some ministers, who dealt with compulsory subjects, were responsible to the whole of India while other ministers, who dealt with optional subjects, would be responsible only to those provinces who had elected to act together in respect of such subjects. This difficulty would be accentuated in the central legislature, where it would be necessary to exclude certain members from speaking and voting when subjects with which their provinces were not concerned were under discussion. Apart from the difficulty of working such a scheme, we do not consider that it would be fair to deny to other provinces, which did not desire to take the optional subjects at the centre, the right to form themselves into a group for a similar purpose. This would indeed be no more than the exercise of their autonomous powers in a particular way.

14. Before putting forward our recommendations we turn to deal with the relationship of the Indian States to British India. It is quite clear that with the

attainment of independence by British India, whether inside or outside the British Commonwealth, the relationship which has hitherto existed between the Rulers of the States and the British Crown will no longer be possible. Paramountcy can neither be retained by the British Crown nor transferred to the new government. This fact has been fully recognised by those whom we interviewed from the States. They have at the same time assured us that the States are ready and willing to co-operate in the new development of India. The precise form which their co-operation will take must be a matter for negotiation during the building up of the new constitutional structure and it by no means follows that it will be identical for all the States. We have not therefore dealt with the States in the same detail as the provinces of British India in the paragraphs which follow.

15. We now indicate the nature of a solution which in our view would be just to the essential claims of all parties and would at the same time be most likely to bring about a stable and practicable form of constitution for All-India.

We recommend that the constitution should take the following basic form: —

(1) There should be a Union of India, embracing both British India and the States, which should deal with the following subjects: foreign affairs, defence, and communications; and should have the powers necessary to raise the finances required for the above subjects.

(2) The Union should have an executive and a legislature constituted from British Indian and States representatives. Any question raising a major communal issue in the legislature should require for its decision a majority of the representatives present and voting of each of the two major communities as well as a majority of all the members present and voting.

(3) All subjects other than the Union subjects and all residuary powers should vest in the provinces.

(4) The States will retain all subjects and powers other than those ceded to the Union.

(5) Provinces should be free to form groups with executives and legislatures, and each group could determine the provincial subjects to be taken in common.

(6) The constitutions of the Union and of the groups should contain a provision whereby any province could by a majority vote of its legislative assembly call for a reconsideration of the terms of the constitution after an initial period of ten years and at ten-yearly intervals thereafter.

16. It is not our object to lay out the details of a constitution on the above programme but to set in motion machinery whereby a constitution can be settled by Indians for Indians.

It has been necessary, however, for us to make this recommendation as to the broad basis of the future constitution because it became clear to us in the course of our negotiations that not until that had been done was there any hope of getting the two major communities to join in the setting up of the constitu-tion-making machinery.

* * *

23. While the constitution-making proceeds the administration of India has to be carried on. We attach the greatest importance therefore to the setting up at once of an interim Government having the support of the major political parties. It is essential during the interim period that there should be the maximum of co-operation in carrying through the difficult tasks that face the Government of India. Besides the heavy tasks of day-to-day administration, there is the grave danger of famine to be countered, there are decisions to be taken in many matters of post-war development which will have a far-reaching effect on India's future and there are important international conferences in which India has to be represented. For all these purposes a government having popular support is necessary. The Viceroy has already started discussions to this end and hopes soon to form an interim government in which all the portfolios, including that of War Member, will be held by Indian leaders having the full confidence of the people. The British Government, recognising the significance of the changes, will give the fullest measure of co-operation to the Government so formed in the accomplishment of its tasks of administration and in bringing about as rapid and smooth a transition as possible.

24. To the leaders and people of India, who now have the opportunity of complete independence, we would finally say this. We and our Government and countrymen hoped that it would be possible for the Indian people themselves to agree upon the method of framing the new Constitution under which they will live. Despite the labours which we have shared with the Indian parties and the exercise of much patience and goodwill by all, this has not been possible. We, therefore, now lay before you proposals which, after listening to all sides and after much earnest thought, we trust will enable you to attain your indepen-dence in the shortest time and with the least danger of internal disturbance and conflict. These proposals may not, of course, completely satisfy all parties, but you will recognise with us that, at this supreme moment in Indian history, statesmanship demands mutual accommodation and we ask you to consider the alternative to the acceptance of these proposals. After all the efforts which we and the Indian parties have made together for agreement, we must state that, in our view, there is small hope of a peaceful settlement by the agreement of the Indian parties alone. The alternative would, therefore, be a grave danger of violence, chaos and even civil war. The gravity and duration of such a distur-bance cannot be foreseen, but it is certain that it would be a terrible disaster for many millions of men, women and children. This is a possibility which must be regarded with equal abhorrence by the Indian people, our own countrymen and the world as a whole. We therefore lay these proposals before you in the profound hope that they will be accepted and operated by you in the spirit of accommodation and goodwill in which they are offered. We appeal to all who have the future good of India at heart to extend their vision beyond their own

community or interest to the interests of the whole 400 millions of Indian people.

We hope that the new independent India may choose to be a member of the British Commonwealth. We hope, in any event, that you will remain in close and friendly association with our people. But these are matters for your own free choice. Whatever that choice may be, we look forward with you to your ever-increasing prosperity among the greatest nations of the world and to a future even more glorious than your past.

Statement of Policy by the Prime Minister, Clement Attlee,
*Outlining a Timetable for Indian Independence, 20 February 1947**

I desire to make a statement on Indian policy.

It has long been the policy of successive British Governments to work towards the realisation of self-government in India. In pursuance of this policy an increasing measure of responsibility has been devolved on Indians and today the civil administration and the Indian Armed Forces rely to a very large extent on Indian civilians and officers. In the constitutional field the Acts of 1919 and 1935 passed by the British Parliament each represented a substantial transfer of political power. In 1940 the Coalition Government recognised the principle that Indians should themselves frame a new constitution for a fully autonomous India, and in the offer of 1942 they invited them to set up a Constituent Assembly for this purpose as soon as the war was over.

His Majesty's Government believe this policy to have been right and in accordance with sound democratic principles. Since they came into office, they have done their utmost to carry it forward to its fulfilment. The declaration of the Prime Minister of 15th March last which met with general approval in Parliament and the country, made it clear that it was for the Indian people themselves to choose their future status and constitution and that in the opinion of His Majesty's Government the time had come for responsibility for the Government of India to pass into Indian hands.

The Cabinet Mission which was sent to India last year spent over three months in consultation with Indian leaders in order to help them to agree upon a method for determining the future constitution of India, so that the transfer of power might be smoothly and rapidly effected. It was only when it seemed clear that without some initiative from the Cabinet Mission agreement was unlikely to be reached that they put forward proposals themselves.

These proposals, made public in May last, envisaged that the future constitution of India should be settled by a Constituent Assembly composed, in the

Hansard, 5.s., CDXXXIII, 1395–98.

manner suggested therein, of representatives of all communities and interests in British India and of the Indian States.

Since the return of the Mission an Interim Government has been set up at the Centre composed of the political leaders of the major communities exercising wide powers within the existing constitution. In all the Provinces Indian Governments responsible to Legislatures are in office.

It is with great regret that His Majesty's Government find that there are still differences among Indian Parties which are preventing the Constituent Assembly from functioning as it was intended that it should. It is of the essence of the plan that the Assembly should be fully representative.

His Majesty's Government desire to hand over their responsibility to authorities established by a constitution approved by all parties in India in accordance with the Cabinet Mission's plan, but unfortunately there is at present no clear prospect that such a constitution and such authorities will emerge. The present state of uncertainty is fraught with danger and cannot be indefinitely prolonged. His Majesty's Government wish to make it clear that it is their definite intention to take the necessary steps to effect the transference of power into responsible Indian hands by a date not later than June, 1948.

This great sub-continent now containing over 400 million people has for the last century enjoyed peace and security as a part of the British Commonwealth and Empire. Continued peace and security are more than ever necessary today if the full possibilities of economic development are to be realised and a higher standard of life attained by the Indian people.

His Majesty's Government are anxious to hand over their responsibilities to a Government which, resting on the sure foundation of the support of the people, is capable of maintaining peace and administering India with justice and efficiency. It is therefore essential that all parties should sink their differences in order that they may be ready to shoulder the great responsibilities which will come upon them next year.

After months of hard work by the Cabinet Mission a great measure of agreement was obtained as to the method by which a constitution should be worked out. This was embodied in their statements of May last. His Majesty's Government there agreed to recommend to Parliament a constitution worked out, in accordance with the proposals made therein, by a fully representative Constituent Assembly. But if it should appear that such a constitution will not have been worked out by a fully representative Assembly before the time mentioned in paragraph 7, His Majesty's Government will have to consider to whom the powers of the Central Government in British India should be handed over, on the due date, whether as a whole to some form of central Government for British India or in some areas to the existing Provincial Governments, or in such other way as may seem most reasonable and in the best interests of the Indian people.

Although the final transfer of authority may not take place until June, 1948, preparatory measures must be put in hand in advance. It is important that the efficiency of the civil administration should be maintained and that the defence of India should be fully provided for. But inevitably, as the process of transfer proceeds, it will become progressively more difficult to carry out to the letter all the provisions of the Government of India Act, 1935. Legislation will be introduced in due course to give effect to the final transfer of power.

In regard to the Indian States, as was explicitly stated by the Cabinet Mission, His Majesty's Government do not intend to hand over their powers and obligations under paramountcy to any Government of British India. It is not intended to bring paramountcy, as a system, to a conclusion earlier than the date of the final transfer of power, but it is contemplated that for the intervening period the relations of the Crown with individual States may be adjusted by agreement.

His Majesty's Government will negotiate agreements in regard to matters arising out of the transfer of power with the representatives of those to whom they propose to transfer power.

His Majesty's Government believe that British commercial and industrial interests in India can look forward to a fair field for their enterprise under the new conditions. The commercial connection between India and the United Kingdom has been long and friendly, and will continue to be to their mutual advantage.

His Majesty's Government cannot conclude this statement without expressing on behalf of the people of this country their goodwill and good wishes towards the people of India as they go forward to this final stage in their achievement of self-government. It will be the wish of everyone in these islands that, notwithstanding constitutional changes, the association of the British and Indian peoples should not be brought to an end; and they will wish to continue to do all that is in their power to further the well-being of India.

This concludes the statement on policy.

*   *   *

Speech by Harold Macmillan in the House of Commons on the
Second Reading of the Indian Independence Bill,
10 July 1947*

In the absence from this Debate today, for reasons which are universally regretted, of my right hon. Friend the Member for Woodford (Mr. Churchill), to whom the Prime Minister has paid a most graceful tribute, it has fallen to my lot to voice the views of the Opposition on this memorable occasion. We all deplore that at such a time the House should be deprived of the wise guidance and vast experience of the Leader of the Opposition, based upon so long and devoted a service to the Crown, and fortified by his supreme gifts of exposition

*Hansard, 5.s., CDXXXIX, 2462–74.

and eloquence. In these circumstances, I can only ask the indulgence of my fellow Members. The Second Reading of this Bill in the Imperial Parliament in the year of grace, 1947, is an important and, indeed, a historic moment. There is no Member of the House, whatever may be his views or party affiliations, who can fail to be moved by the last stage in this unique story. If I may be allowed to say so without impertinence, I should like to congratulate the Prime Minister on the lucidity, moderation and dignity with which he has performed his formidable task.

For over 300 years, as the Prime Minister reminded the House, there has been a close association between Great Britain and India. The British connection with India falls into four major divisions. From the middle of the seventeenth century to the middle of the eighteenth century, the aims of the British were purely those of traders. They had no aspirations to military power or territorial aggrandisement, but the gradual decay of the Mogul Empire from within, and the anarchy which followed, forced the British to take up arms in their own defence, and by a series of strange and dramatic episodes, they found themselves at last, almost unwittingly, in the seat of Empire. The next period was that of strategic conflict, arising from European rivalries. The political history of the British in India begins in the eighteenth Century with the French wars in the Carnatic. Between 1745 and 1748 the French almost drove the British out of India. After the Treaty of Aix-la-Chapelle only Madras was left to us. In the next 12 years, by the genius of Clive, the French were expelled, and British authority firmly and finally established. From Clive's second governorship the third phase in this long story begins.

The theme of trade and conquest are now succeeded by the new dominant motives of administration and expansion. Administrative reforms in the hands of Hastings, Bentinck, Metcalfe and many others began to build up those processes by which the hearts of the conquered population were gradually won over to venerate, as well as obey, their alien rulers. The policy of expansion was, at the same time, pressed too ruthlessly. I think it is now clear that the Mutiny of 1857 was largely the result of Lord Dalhousie's policy. At any rate, after a life of nearly two and a half centuries, the fate of the Company was sealed. In 1858 this House passed an Act for the better government of India. For the next 50 years the Indian scene is dominated by the skill and devotion of its administrators, following the broad purposes of 19th century idealism at its best. In that period immense progress was made in every field.

During those years was built up that devoted body of soldiers and civilians who have served India so well, and who are still India's loyal friends. Never, in the long course of history, has an alien nation given so much of its best. Service in India became a family tradition and affection for India a legacy from father to son. Nor should we think only of those who rose to great distinction. To humble members of these services, administrative and technical, to the collector, the commissioner, the health officer, the famine officer, the police, the judiciary, to all these, both British and Indian people owe an immeasurable debt. By the achievement of this period of our rule in India, the British stand justified. Much will be left in the material sense—railways, dams, irrigation schemes, health services and the like—but perhaps the greatest contribution which the British genius has made has been the sense of equal justice, incorruptible and unchangeable, carried out equally for Hindu and for Muslim, for the poor as for the rich, the humble as for the exalted. This has set a standard of equity unrivalled in the history of the world.

Then, as the Prime Minister reminded us, at the turn of the century, and especially dating from the Morley-Minto reforms, comes the last of these great periods, the preparation for self-government. To this task, British Government and British people conscientiously set their hand. We may say that it is unique in the history of the world that a ruling nation should voluntarily and deliberately prepare to surrender its authority on so large a scale. This policy, as the Prime Minister said, has been agreed by all parties. The story of two generations has been the steady determination on the part of various Governments at home and of the Government of India, to prepare the way for Indian self-government.

As early as the '90's the first councils were formed with Indian membership; the long history of various reforms has been the evolution upon this steady purpose. It has been followed, regardless of misunderstanding and obloquy, both in India and, less justifiably, at home and abroad; but in spite of all recriminations, it has been steadfastly pursued by the British people as a whole. Perhaps some of those who have so long maligned the British purpose at home and abroad may stand ashamed today. On this purpose there has never been any division among British parties. The methods, not the objective, have been the matter of dispute.

Finally, at the time of the so-called Cripps Mission in 1942, the Conservative and Liberal, as well as the Socialist, Members of the Churchill Government, were in agreement with the broad proposition to offer self-government to India. We asked, however, two essential conditions. First, that there should be agreement between the two major parties in India, Hindu and Muslim. Second, that Dominion status, as the phrase goes or, as I am content to say, Commonwealth membership, should be a reality and not a mere legal fiction. It should not be used to change from one day to the next from membership of the Commonwealth to complete severance of the link; but a fair and reasonable trial should be made on both sides, so that the advantages and the disadvantages to India of membership of the Commonwealth might be properly tested and in India, races, religions and parties be able to consider coolly where their interest and affections lay.

During the war, no agreement could be reached. After the war, the Cabinet Mission, in spite of good will, failed to reach an agreement, or rather, reached a form of agreement so equivocal and slender, that it was immediately repudiated on all sides. The Prime Minister said, perhaps truly, that it is unprofitable to go back to the past, but I must, in justice, remind the House that during all this time the Conservative Party maintained a most considerate reticence. We have not pressed debate unduly; we have not in any way incommoded the efforts of the Government and great as were, and are, our apprehensions, we restrained our criticism. The plan of the Cabinet Mission failed. The various interpretations of the scheme reached such a point of confusion as to make it generally unacceptable and unworkable.

A new situation was then created by the Government announcement of 20th February last. This decision to leave India by a fixed date in 1948, whether or not proper arrangements had been made for the transference of power, seemed to us an abdication of duty. We opposed it, upon two grounds. First, because the fixation of a date seemed to us an improper method for dealing with so great a question; it indicated a certain levity towards the immense responsibilities we had. Second, we felt that it was inconceivable that the British should in fact bring the story of over 250 years to an abrupt end without being certain that proper provisions were made, if not for the discharge of our obligations, at least for the continuance of orderly government. It was not, therefore, the mere fixation of the date to which we objected, but the abandonment of duty without any clear scheme by which the obligations we were unable to fulfil could be firmly placed upon other shoulders. Many difficulties sprang from that fateful decision. It made it almost certain that the two main parties in India would fail to reach any joint agreement, except an agreement to differ. It destroyed, for the present at any rate, all hope of preserving the unity of India.

Perhaps the greatest contribution which the British connection has made to India is to preserve, indeed to create, the political and economic unity of that vast medley of religious, races and peoples who inhabit the sub-continent which we call India. To the long series of devoted public servants who have given their lives to India, it would always have been felt a terrible disaster if that unity had been disintegrated. Somehow to maintain it, at the same time as making provision for complete Indian self government, was the underlying problem that was partially solved by the Act of 1935.

The decision of the present Government to leave India at a fixed date shattered, once and for all, the hope of unity. The only question which arose was whether the partition of India, now clearly necessary, could be achieved by peaceful methods or not. Partition which seems so easy a word to us Europeans, accustomed to minor groupings and small populations, is no clean-cut solution of age-long problems and processes. Enormous minorities will remain, however successful may be the work of the Boundary Commissions, on either side of the many frontiers. There is the possibility of Indian irredentism on an immense scale. Trieste, Trentino, Ireland, Poland, Czechoslovakia, and all the other minority problems of the world fade into insignificance compared to these. Moreover, there are other peoples, neither Muslim nor orthodox Hindu, in large numbers and of warlike character, who have a long tradition of loyalty to the Crown, who will be separated and divided, for instance, the Sikhs. Therefore partition, superficially attractive, like so many other superficially attractive remedies, has within it its own inherent dangers. The partition of the

Punjab fills us with apprehension, and partition of Bengal is a most delicate and dangerous undertaking. Nevertheless, we can only repeat, with satisfaction, that peaceful partition is better than civil war.

At this point, in a confused and dangerous situation, we must pay tribute to the work of the Viceroy. His efforts have radically altered and improved an almost desperate situation. He has been able to secure that partition should take place under conditions which reduce as much as possible the danger of a clash. The frightful blood bath which seemed to threaten India is, at the moment of our departure, at any rate, avoided. Immense as are the technical difficulties of making a fair distribution of assets, tangled as may be the problem of arranging that Pakistan should be in every sense a viable State, grave as are the dangers of India not being merely partitioned, but ultimately Balkanised, serious as may be our apprehensions as to the unworkability of the whole process, yet we on this side of the House must not endanger, but must welcome, a plan which avoids the most pressing and immediate dangers. It is largely the character and personality of Lord Mountbatten which has achieved this happy result, and to him we pay our tribute.

At the same time, we must hope with the Prime Minister that in this partition are also the seeds of some form of future unity, at least of co-operation. The common services, transport, aviation, and the like, must be arranged to serve Pakistan and Hindustan and the States. A joint foreign policy and a joint system of defence seem inevitable if the peninsula is effectively to resist foreign aggression. It is to be remarked that very swiftly following these disturbing movements has come a claim from a foreign Power for annexation of an Indian Province. This has been immediately repulsed by His Majesty's Government and the Government of India, at least up to 15th August. But, after 15th August, it will only be if the two Dominions stand shoulder to shoulder that the whole weight of the Empire can be available for their common protection. It is indeed good news that a Joint Defence Council has been agreed for the preliminary purpose of dividing the Army. I trust that that council may develop into an instrument of strategic defence.

I pass now to the second benefit which, in what seemed a black situation, the Viceroy has been able to obtain. That is the condition which my right hon. Friend the Member for Woodford and his supporters insisted upon at the time of the Cripps Mission of 1942, which we have always held to be an indispensable condition if the long process towards self-government is to be carried out honourably and smoothly; that is, the willingness of the Indian States, Pakistan and Hindustan, to remain within the ambit of the British Commonwealth of Nations with, of course, all the freedoms of the Statute of Westminster. I must here frankly say that my right hon. and hon. Friends and I do not much like the Title of this Bill, "Indian Independence Bill," the more so because I understand that it is a phrase which does not result from any Indian request, but is due to the sole initiative of British draftsmen. This phrase seems to us to dwell too much on one aspect of the Commonwealth system, for it is the peculiar glory of the free nations which comprise the British Commonwealth that they are both independent and inter-dependent. Of course, in a sense every Dominion is independent; Dominion status implies complete autonomy, complete freedom, complete sovereignty, but that freedom, that autonomy and that sovereignty are exercised in an undefinable and almost mystical union, within the circle of the Crown, of all the nations of the Commonwealth by which and through which they mutually defend their mutual rights and interests. I would say that there are many nations in the world today which nominally have this position of independence and freedom, but which cannot in fact exercise it. I wish the nations of Europe had independence and the inter-dependence equal to the nations of the Commonwealth.

Into our free association, therefore, we gladly welcome the new States of India and Pakistan. Let them make no mistake. We believe that experience will show them how great are the advantages. We do not seek to hold them against their will, for the obligations of the members to each other in voluntary co-operation may be very heavy. Nor must it be disguised that the decision—and I think it is a wise and statesmanlike decision—of the leaders of the Congress Party and Muslim League, to remain at this stage within the Commonwealth is one which places on us and all other members of the Commonwealth prospective and potential burdens which it would be wise not to ignore. It places upon us, for instance, moral obligations for defence, to carry out which effectively I am not sure how far we have provided ourselves with the effective material instruments. It is a melancholy fact that inevitably the process of dividing the present Indian Army, in order later to rebuild it into two armies, will create for years to come a serious weakening in the defence of India. It is, therefore, all the more important that the new Dominions should rapidly range themselves with the general body of the United Nations.

If we recognise the two major advantages of this agreement between the Muslim League and Congress and the decision of their leaders to remain within the British system of Commonwealths, we must not disguise from ourselves upon how slender a foundation the whole fabric rests. We cannot but have many apprehensions and misgivings as to the practical outcome of the future. Moreover, there are other serious considerations which weigh deeply with my right hon. Friends and hon. Friends. It is a rule of statesmanship, sometimes, alas, more honoured in the breach than in the observance, that in order to meet agreeable accommodation with interested parties with whom you may have been in conflict, it is not wise, indeed it is morally unjustifiable, to forget obligations to those who have long given you their trust and confidence. We have great obligations in India. The Muslims have been provided for; but we have also obligations to the many minorities in British India—the Anglo-Indians, the Sikhs, the millions of the depressed classes, primitive tribes and much else.

This House has always been much moved in particular by the problem of the Scheduled Classes. Dr. Ambadkar's name is welcomed and deeply respected here. We had hoped in the structure of a new constitutional Bill provision might have been made for their protection. That, of course, it would be beyond our power to secure enforcement after we have severed our direct connection with India must be admitted; but the fact that provision had been made in the Bill in black and white, open for all to read and backed by opinion throughout the world, would at least have given to the minorities some sense of security. I would, therefore, express the hope that the Indian political leaders should announce publicly that they personally will do their utmost to see that the new Constitutions provide a liberal treatment for the weaker communities within their States.

We have also obligations to all members of the services in India, civil or military, covenanted or non-covenanted, British or Indian, who have given the best part of their lives to the service of the Crown and whose loyalty to India is undoubted. Many of them feel anxious about their future and about the security of their pensions, provident funds and conditions of service. We were very glad to hear from the Prime Minister, and we welcome the statement made on behalf of the present Indian authorities, that they will recognise these obligations, but nothing can relieve the overriding obligation that rests upon us as well.

I come next to the States. Their destiny is not even mentioned in this Bill, except negatively. All treaties and agreements in force at the date of the passing of this Act between His Majesty and the rulers of Indian states, all functions exercisable by His Majesty at that date with respect to Indian States, all obligations of His Majesty existing towards Indian States or the rulers thereof, and all powers, rights, authority or jurisdiction exercisable by His Majesty, all agreements or treaties between His Majesty and any person having authority in the tribal areas—all these, are unilaterally dissolved and abrogated. What a long story is ended by the final words of this chapter. What memories of comradeship or conflict, of wonderful loyalties, of battle and peace, of victories gained in common—above all of the firm and devoted association with the glorious reigns of the Empress Victoria the Great and succeeding Emperors.

Clause 7, which I have summarised, sounds like the final end, but I cannot believe that is the only message which will go from this House to the Indian States. We warmly approve the decision of His Majesty's Government to resist the pressure to transfer paramountcy to the successor governments. They have been very wise in that. I was glad to hear, or think I heard, the Prime Minister say that the States were to be absolutely free in their choice as to whether or not they should join one or other of the new Constituent Assemblies; whether they should subsequently join one or other of the Dominions as they emerge from the Constituent Assemblies, or whether, finally, they will declare themselves free and independent sovereign authorities. I trust that this is true not only in words but in fact, because there have been disturbing rumours reaching us of a good deal of moral and even physical pressure which has been exercised, perhaps by misunderstanding of some of the official statements made in India or elsewhere.

It must not be forgotten that the partition of India on what was largely and what is, indeed, still a religious basis throws a heavy strain upon the States. For

they have always, and successfully, resisted the development within their territories of bitter communal strife. This explains the hesitation of some of them, at
any rate, in allying themselves with one or other of the two new Dominions
which are partitioned not on a geographical, not on an economical, but purely
on a religious foundation. I hope, therefore, that before the end of this Debate
the Government may be able to clarify the position a little further. They have
said that the States are to have freedom of choice. I hope that they will make it
clear that if it should prove that any of the great States, the important States,
are unable to find a satisfactory method of association with one or other of the
new Dominions, His Majesty's Government will be willing and ready to enter
into satisfactory relations with them. Surely, the flexible instrument of British
constitutional development, on which the Prime Minister rightly congratulated
us, is capable of finding a suitable formula of association by which their loyalty
and devotion to the Crown may find a new expression in harmonious association with the British Commonwealth, and with the United Nations.

As the Prime Minister stated in his concluding review, this Bill is not, of
course, a Bill to make a Constitution for British India. It is, to use his own
phrase, an enabling Bill. It brings into being two Dominions and it transforms
the present Constituent Assembly and the new Pakistan Assembly into bodies
that will be both constituent and legislative. It throws upon these organs the
task of framing their own constitution. It states nothing as to many vital
questions, the judiciary, the railways, the monetary system and a host of other
matters. It makes no provision in the Bill itself as to the arrangement for
settling the complicated problems of all Indian services and assets which will
have to be divided between the two Dominions. As drawn up, the Bill merely
contemplates providing the Governor-General, should the two Dominions
agree, with the formal right under Clause 9 to make all such necessary orders
and provisions as to resolve the great problems, the host of problems, which
must arise from these tremendous constitutional changes.

I have not been able yet quite to fit in what we have been told today as to
the recommendations for the new Governor-General with the provisions of
Clause 9. I cannot help feeling that it was drawn on a somewhat different plan.
Nevertheless, as I think the House must understand, this is really the legal
technical machinery in order to provide that agreements that are reached
should be made legally effective, and we must depend now on the good will and
good sense of the two Dominions through two Governments, supported and
advised by the Governor-General, to reach agreeable arrangements and implement them by the provisions of this Clause. I, for one, if I may be allowed to
say so, am very glad indeed to hear that the Viceroy has decided that it is his
duty to accept the post which has been offered, because I think that on the
Viceroy staying in India in whatever may be his capacity—Lord Mountbatten
being present in India—a great deal of the hope which we have of fair and
good arrangements depends.

Since this is not a constitutional but an enabling Bill, we do not propose to
treat the conduct of the Bill in this House as we would if it were a comprehen-

sive constitutional Measure. We shall not attempt to move the many Amendments which would be necessary to clothe it with the detail and the elaboration of a constitutional act. We shall, therefore, be content, although with considerable Debate, to regard the Committee stage as primarily one of elucidation and explanation of the meaning, purpose and effect of the various Clauses.

Parliament was informed a year ago of the Government's intentions, which we regarded as an abdication of their duty. This Bill is better than that, for it throws upon the Indian people now the major obligation of a great task. How are we to balance good and ill and how are we to make an evaluation of the position? Hon. and right hon. Gentlemen on this side of the House are not responsible for the developments which have taken place since the fall of the Coalition Government in the last two years. We have had great apprehensions and misgivings, but we fully recognise that there is in this Measure an opportunity better than that in existence a few months ago. To this salutary change the personality of the Viceroy has much contributed. This opportunity which, if it is grasped and exploited, may be of benefit not only to India but to Great Britain, because I believe that underlying the bitter conflicts between the politically minded classes in India and the Government, there is still a close and even intimate association of our people and the peoples of India which is the product of long association, and which cannot and indeed ought not to disappear. It may even be strengthened in the years that lie ahead.

I began by tracing, however cursorily, the various phases of the British connection with India. By this Bill the political phase comes finally to an end. His Majesty's Government will no longer be responsible for the administration of India. Yet so intertwined are the roots of British and Indian life for nearly 300 years that I believe the association of Britain with India, and of India with Britain and with the Commonwealth has in it still the hope of a fruitful, prosperous and honourable relationship. Let us, therefore, at this moment first remember with trust and pride those British officials, civil and military, and those British people in commerce and industry, who have served India well for so long a period. So well have they served her that they have always been able to call to their aid deep affection and loyalty from the Indians with whom they have worked. They have sometimes been the butt of foolish criticism from their compatriots and from foreigners. Today, let us forget all that and pay grateful tribute to their memory.

Let us pray that in this new sphere that is to begin the association between the British and Indian peoples on a new basis may be productive of great good to both. The English language is a permanent element in Indian life. Indian education, both in the humanities and science, is intimately linked with British institutions. The British system of justice is a lasting gift to India. In these and in intimate and sympathetic pursuits of the ethical and moral traditions of both elements, the pooling of technical knowledge and the free association of commercial interests, above all, in the great family of nations which comprise the British Commonwealth, let us hope that out of the darkness and uncertainty of recent years we may yet be destined to follow together in friendly comradeship, the road of co-operation and progress.

CONFLICT IN THE MIDDLE EAST

Treaty of Alliance between Great Britain and Egypt
Granting Independence to Egypt, 26 August 1936*

Art. I

The military occupation of Egypt by the forces of His Majesty The King and Emperor is terminated.

Art. II

His Majesty The King and Emperor will henceforth be represented at the Court of His Majesty the King of Egypt and His Majesty the King of Egypt will be represented at the Court of St. James's by Ambassadors duly accredited.

Art. III

Egypt intends to apply for membership to the League of Nations. His Majesty's Government in the United Kingdom, recognising Egypt as a sovereign independent State, will support any request for admission which the Egyptian Government may present in the conditions prescribed by Article 1 of the Covenant.

Art. IV

An alliance is established between the High Contracting Parties with a view to consolidating their friendship, their cordial understanding and their good relations.

Art. V

Each of the High Contracting Parties undertakes not to adopt in relation to foreign countries an attitude which is inconsistent with the alliance, nor to conclude political treaties inconsistent with the provisions of the present treaty.

Art. VI

Should any dispute with a third State produce a situation which involves a risk of a rupture with that State, the High Contracting Parties will consult each other with a view to the settlement of the said dispute by peaceful means, in accordance with the provisions of the Covenant of the League of Nations and of any other international obligations which may be applicable to the case.

Art.VII

Should, notwithstanding the provisions of Article 6 above either of the High Contracting Parties become engaged in war, the other High Contracting Party will, subject always to the provisions of Article 10 below, immediately come to his aid in the capacity of an ally.

Parliamentary Papers, 1936, XXVII, Cmd. 5720, 4–17.

The aid of His Majesty the King of Egypt in the event of war, imminent menace of war or apprehended international emergency will consist in furnishing to His Majesty The King and Emperor on Egyptian territory, in accordance with the Egyptian system of administration and legislation, all the facilities and assistance in his power, including the use of his ports, aerodromes and means of communication. It will accordingly be for the Egyptian Government to take all the administrative and legislative measures, including the establishment of martial law and an effective censorship, necessary to render these facilities and assistance effective.

Art. VIII

In view of the fact that the Suez Canal, whilst being an integral part of Egypt, is a universal means of communication as also an essential means of communication between the different parts of the British Empire, His Majesty the King of Egypt, until such time as the High Contracting Parties agree that the Egyptian Army is in a position to ensure by its own resources the liberty and entire security of navigation of the Canal, authorises His Majesty The King and Emperor to station forces in Egyptian territory in the vicinity of the Canal, in the zone specified in the Annex to this Article, with a view to ensuring in co-operation with the Egyptian forces the defence of the Canal. The detailed arrangements for the carrying into effect of this Article are contained in the Annex hereto. The presence of these forces shall not constitute in any manner an occupation and will in no way prejudice the sovereign rights of Egypt.

It is understood that at the end of the period of twenty years specified in Article 16 the question whether the presence of British forces is no longer necessary owing to the fact that the Egyptian Army is in a position to ensure by its own resources the liberty and entire security of navigation of the Canal may, if the High Contracting Parties do not agree thereon, be submitted to the Council of the League of Nations for decision in accordance with the provisions of the Covenant in force at the time of signature of the present treaty or to such other person or body of persons for decision in accordance with such other procedure as the High Contracting Parties may agree.

Annex to Article VIII

1. Without prejudice to the provisions of Article 7, the numbers of the forces of His Majesty The King and Emperor to be maintained in the vicinity of the Canal shall not exceed, of the land forces, 10,000, and of the air forces, 400 pilots, together with the necessary ancillary personnel for administrative and technical duties. These numbers do not include civilian personnel, *e.g.*, clerks, artisans and labourers.

2. The British forces to be maintained in the vicinity of the Canal will be distributed (*a*) as regards the land forces, in Moascar and the Geneifa area on the south-west side of the Great Bitter Lake, and (*b*) as regards the air forces, within 5 miles of the Port Said–Suez railway from Kantara in the north, to the junction of the railway Suez–Cairo and Suez–Ismailia in the south, together

with an extension along the Ismailia–Cairo railway to include the Royal Air Force Station at Abu Sueir and its satellite landing grounds; together with areas suitable for air firing and bombing ranges, which may have to be placed east of the Canal.

3. In the localities specified above there shall be provided for the British land and air forces of the numbers specified in paragraph 1 above, including 4,000 civilian personnel (but less 2,000 of the land forces, 700 of the air forces and 450 civilian personnel for whom accommodation already exists), the necessary lands and durable barrack and technical accommodation, including an emergency water supply. The lands, accommodation and water supply shall be suitable according to modern standards. In addition, amenities such as are reasonable, having regard to the character of these localities, will be provided by the planting of trees and the provision of gardens, playing fields, &c., for the troops, and a site for the erection of a convalescent camp on the Mediterranean coast.

4. The Egyptian Government will make available the lands and construct the accommodation, water supplies, amenities and convalescent camp, referred to in the preceding paragraph as being necessary over and above the accommodation already existing in these localities, at its own expense, but His Majesty's Government in the United Kingdom will contribute (1) the actual sum spent by the Egyptian Government before 1914 on the construction of new barracks as alternative accommodation to the Kasr-el-Nil Barracks in Cairo, and (2) the cost of one-fourth of the barrack and technical accommodation for the land forces. The first of these sums shall be paid at the time specified in paragraph 8 below for the withdrawal of the British forces from Cairo and the second at the time for the withdrawal of the British forces from Alexandria under paragraph 18 below. The Egyptian Government may charge a fair rental for the residential accommodation provided for the civilian personnel. The amount of the rent will be agreed between His Majesty's Government in the United Kingdom and the Egyptian Government.

5. The two Governments will each appoint, immediately the present treaty comes into force, two or more persons who shall together form a committee to whom all questions relating to the execution of these works from the time of their commencement to the time of their completion shall be entrusted. Proposals for, or outlines of, plans and specifications put forward by the representatives of His Majesty's Government in the United Kingdom will be accepted, provided they are reasonable and do not fall outside the scope of the obligations of the Egyptian Government under paragraph 4. The plans and specifications of each of the works to be undertaken by the Egyptian Government shall be approved by the representatives of both Governments on this committee before the work is begun. Any member of this committee, as well as the Commanders of the British forces or their representatives, shall have the right to examine the works at all stages of their construction, and the United Kingdom members of the committee may make suggestions as regards the manner in which the work

is carried out. The United Kingdom members shall also have the right to make at any time, while the work is in progress, proposals for modifications or alterations in the plans and specifications. Effect shall be given to suggestions and proposals by the United Kingdom members, subject to the condition that they are reasonable and do not fall outside the scope of the obligations of the Egyptian Government under paragraph 4. In the case of machinery and other stores, where standardization of type is important, it is agreed that stores of the standard type in general use by the British forces will be obtained and installed. It is, of course, understood that His Majesty's Government in the United Kingdom may, when the barracks and accommodation are being used by the British forces, make at their own expense improvements or alterations thereto and construct new buildings in the areas specified in paragraph 2 above.

6. In pursuance of their programme for the development of road and railway communications in Egypt, and in order to bring the means of communications in Egypt up to modern strategic requirements, the Egyptian Government will construct and maintain the following roads, bridges and railways: —

(A)—*Roads.*
(i) Ismailia–Alexandria, via Tel-el-Kebir, Zagazig, Zifta, Tanata, Kafr-el-Zayat, Damanhour.
(ii) Ismailia–Cairo, via Tel-el-Kebir and thence continuing along the Sweet Water Canal to Heliopolis.
(iii) Port Said–Ismailia–Suez.
(iv) A link between the south end of the Great Bitter Lake and the Cairo–Suez road about 15 miles west of Suez.

In order to bring them up to the general standard of good-class roads for general traffic, these roads will be 20 feet wide, have bye-passes round villages, &c., and be made of such material as to be permanently utilisable for military purposes, and will be constructed in the above order of importance. They will comply with the technical specifications set out below which are the ordinary specifications for a good-class road for general traffic.

Bridges and roads shall be capable of carrying a double line of continuous columns of either heavy four-wheeled mechanical transport, six-wheeled mechanical transport or medium tanks. With regard to four-wheeled vehicles, the distance between the front axle of one vehicle and the rear axle of the vehicle next ahead shall be calculated at 20 feet, the load on each rear axle to be 14 tons, on each front axle to be 6 tons and the distance between axles 18 feet. With regard to six-wheeled vehicles, the distance between the front axle of one vehicle and the rear axle of that next ahead shall be calculated to be 20 feet, between rear axle and middle axle to be 4 feet and between middle axle and front axle 13 feet; the load on each rear and middle axle to be 8.1 tons and on each front axle to be 4 tons. Tanks shall be calculated for as weighing 19.25 tons, to be 25 feet over all in length and to have a distance of 3 feet between the front of one tank and the rear of the next ahead; the load of 19.25 tons to be carried by tracks which have a bearing of 13 feet upon the road or bridge.

(B)—*Railways.*
(i) Railway facilities in the Canal Zone will be increased and improved to meet the needs of the increased garrison in the zone and to provide facilities for rapid entrainment of personnel, guns, vehicles and stores according to the requirements of a modern army. His Majesty's Government in the United Kingdom are hereby authorised to make at their own expense such subsequent additions and modifications to these railway facilities as the future requirements of the British forces may demand. Where such additions or modifications affect railway lines used for general traffic, the permission of the Egyptian Government must be obtained.
(ii) The line between Zagazig and Tanta will be doubled.
(iii) The Alexandria –Mersa Matruh line will be improved and made permanent.

7. In addition to the roads specified in paragraph 6 (A) above, and for the same purposes, the Egyptian Government will construct and maintain the following roads: —

(i) Cairo south along the Nile to Kena and Kus;
(ii) Kus to Kosseir;
(iii) Kena to Hurghada.

These roads and the bridges thereon will be constructed to satisfy the same standards as those specified in paragraph 6 above.

It may not be possible for the construction of the roads referred to in this paragraph to be undertaken at the same time as the roads referred to in paragraph 6, but they will be constructed as soon as possible.

8. When, to the satisfaction of both the High Contracting Parties, the accommodation referred to in paragraph 4 is ready (accommodation for the forces retained temporarily at Alexandria in accordance with paragraph 18 below not being included) and the works referred to in paragraph 6 above (other than the railways referred to in (ii) and (iii) of part (B) of that paragraph) have been completed, then the British forces in parts of Egypt other than the areas in the Canal Zone specified in paragraph 2 above and except for those maintained temporarily at Alexandria, will withdraw and the lands, barracks, aircraft landing grounds, seaplane anchorages and accommodation occupied by them will be vacated and, save in so far as they may belong to private persons, be handed over to the Egyptian Government.

9. Any difference of opinion between the two Governments relating to the execution of paragraphs 3, 4, 5, 6, 7 and 8 above will be submitted to the decision of an Arbitral Board, composed of three members, the two Governments nominating each a member and the third being nominated by the two Governments in common agreement. The decision of the Board shall be final.

10. In order to ensure the proper training of British troops, it is agreed that the area defined below will be available for the training of British forces: (a)

and (*b*) at all times of the year, and (*c*) during February and March for annual manoeuvres: —

(*a*) West of the Canal: From Kantara in the north to the Suez –Cairo railway (inclusive) in the south and as far as longitude 31 degrees 30 minutes east, exclusive of all cultivation;

(*b*) East of the Canal as required;

(*c*) A continuation of (*a*) as far south as latitude 29 degrees 52 minutes north, thence south-east to the junction of latitude 29 degrees 30 minutes north and longitude 31 degrees 44 minutes east and from that point eastwards along latitude 29 degrees 30 minutes north.

11. Unless the two Governments agree to the contrary, the Egyptian Government will prohibit the passage of aircraft over the territories situated on either side of the Suez Canal and within 20 kilometres of it, except for the purpose of passage from east to west or *vice versa* by means of a corridor 10 kilometres wide at Kantara. This prohibition will not, however, apply to the forces of the High Contracting Parties or to genuinely Egyptian air organisations or to air organisations genuinely belonging to any part of the British Commonwealth of Nations operating under the authority of the Egyptian Government.

12. The Egyptian Government will provide when necessary reasonable means of communication and access to and from the localities where the British forces are situated and will also accord facilities at Port Said and Suez for the landing and storage of material and supplies for the British forces, including the maintenance of a small detachment of the British forces in these ports to handle and guard this material and these supplies in transit.

13. In view of the fact that the speed and range of modern aircraft necessitate the use of wide areas for the efficient training of air forces, the Egyptian Government will accord permission to the British air forces to fly wherever they consider it necessary for the purpose of training. Reciprocal treatment will be accorded to Egyptian air forces in British territories.

14. In view of the fact that the safety of flying is dependent upon provision of a large number of places where aircraft can alight, the Egyptian Government will secure the maintenance and constant availability of adequate landing grounds and seaplane anchorages in Egyptian territory and waters. The Egyptian Government will accede to any request from the British air forces for such additional landing grounds and seaplane anchorages as experience may show to be necessary to make the number adequate for allied requirements.

15. The Egyptian Government will accord permission for the British air forces to use the said landing grounds and seaplane anchorages, and in the case of certain of them to send stocks of fuel and stores thereto, to be kept in sheds to be erected thereon for this purpose, and in case of urgency to undertake such work as may be necessary for the safety of aircraft.

16. The Egyptian Government will give all necessary facilities for the passage of the personnel of the British forces, aircraft and stores to and from the

said landing grounds and seaplane anchorages. Similar facilities will be afforded to the personnel, aircraft and stores of the Egyptian forces at the air bases of the British forces.

17. The British military authorities shall be at liberty to request permission from the Egyptian Government to send parties of officers in civilian clothes to the Western Desert to study the ground and draw up tactical schemes. This permission shall not be unreasonably withheld.

18. His Majesty the King of Egypt authorises His Majesty the King and Emperor to maintain units of his forces at or near Alexandria for a period not exceeding eight years from the date of the coming into force of the present treaty, this being the approximate period considered necessary by the two High Contracting Parties—

    (*a*) For the final completion of the barrack accommodation in the Canal zone;

    (*b*) For the improvement of the roads—

        (i) Cairo –Suez;
        (ii) Cairo –Alexandria via Giza and the desert;
       (iii) Alexandria –Mersa Matruh;

        so as to bring them up to the standard specified in part (A) of paragraph 6;

    (*c*) The improvement of the railway facilities between Ismailia and Alexandria, and Alexandria and Mersa Matruh referred to in (ii) and (iii) of part (B) of paragraph 6.

The Egyptian Government will complete the work specified in (*a*), (*b*) and (*c*) above before the expiry of the period of eight years aforesaid. The roads and railway facilities mentioned above will, of course, be maintained by the Egyptian Government.

19. The British forces in or near Cairo shall, until the time for withdrawal under paragraph 8 above, and the British forces in or near Alexandria until the expiry of the time specified in paragraph 18 above, continue to enjoy the same facilities as at present.

Art. IX

The immunities and privileges in jurisdictional and fiscal matters to be enjoyed by the forces of His Majesty The King and Emperor who are in Egypt in accordance with the provisions of the present treaty will be determined in a separate convention to be concluded between the Egyptian Government and His Majesty's Government in the United Kingdom.

Art. X

Nothing in the present treaty is intended to or shall in any way prejudice the rights and obligations which devolve, or may devolve, upon either of the High Contracting Parties under the Covenant of the League of Nations or the Treaty for the Renunciation of War signed at Paris on the 27th August, 1928.

Art. XI

1. While reserving liberty to conclude new conventions in future, modifying the agreements of the 19th January and the 10th July, 1899, the High Contracting Parties agree that the administration of the Sudan shall continue to be that resulting from the said agreements. The Governor-General shall continue to exercise on the joint behalf of the High Contracting Parties the powers conferred upon him by the said agreements.

The High Contracting Parties agree that the primary aim of their administration in the Sudan must be the welfare of the Sudanese.

Nothing in this article prejudices the question of sovereignty over the Sudan.

2. Appointments and promotions of officials in the Sudan will in consequence remain vested in the Governor-General, who, in making new appointments to posts for which qualified Sudanese are not available, will select suitable candidates of British and Egyptian nationality.

3. In addition to Sudanese troops, both British and Egyptian troops shall be placed at the disposal of the Governor-General for the defence of the Sudan.

4. Egyptian immigration into the Sudan shall be unrestricted except for reasons of public order and health.

5. There shall be no discrimination in the Sudan between British subjects and Egyptian nationals in matters of commerce, immigration or the possession of property.

6. The High Contracting Parties are agreed on the provisions set out in the Annex to this Article as regards the method by which international conventions are to be made applicable to the Sudan.

Annex to Article XI

1. Unless and until the High Contracting Parties agree to the contrary in application of paragraph 1 of this Article, the general principle for the future shall be that international conventions shall only become applicable to the Sudan by the joint action of the Governments of the United Kingdom and of Egypt, and that such joint action shall similarly also be required if it is desired to terminate the participation of the Sudan in an international convention which already applies to this territory.

2. Conventions to which it will be desired that the Sudan should be a party will generally be conventions of .a technical or humanitarian character. Such conventions almost invariably contain a provision for subsequent accession, and in such cases this method of making the convention applicable to the Sudan will be adopted. Accession will be effected by a joint instrument, signed on behalf of Egypt and the United Kingdom respectively by two persons duly authorised for the purpose. The method of depositing the instruments of accession will be the subject of agreement in each case between the two Governments. In the event of its being desired to apply to the Sudan a convention which does not contain an accession clause, the method by which this should be effected will be the subject of consultation and agreement between the two Governments.

3. If the Sudan is already a party to a convention, and it is desired to

terminate the participation of the Sudan therein, the necessary notice of termination will be given jointly by the United Kingdom and by Egypt.

4. It is understood that the participation of the Sudan in a convention and the termination of such participation can only be effected by joint action specifically taken in respect of the Sudan, and does not follow merely from the fact that the United Kingdom and Egypt are both parties to a convention or have both denounced a convention.

5. At international conferences where such conventions are negotiated, the Egyptian and the United Kingdom delegates would naturally keep in touch with a view to any action which they may agree to be desirable in the interests of the Sudan.

Art. XII

His Majesty The King and Emperor recognises that the responsibility for the lives and property of foreigners in Egypt devolves exclusively upon the Egyptian Government, who will ensure the fulfilment of their obligations in this respect.

Art. XIII

His Majesty The King and Emperor recognises that the capitulatory régime now existing in Egypt is no longer in accordance with the spirit of the times and with the present state of Egypt.

His Majesty the King of Egypt desires the abolition of this régime without delay.

Both High Contracting Parties are agreed upon the arrangements with regard to this matter as set forth in the Annex to this Article.

Annex to Article XIII

1. It is the object of the arrangements set out in this Annex: —

   (i)   To bring about speedily the abolition of the Capitulations in Egypt with the disappearance of the existing restrictions on Egyptian sovereignty in the matter of the application of Egyptian legislation (including financial legislation) to foreigners as its necessary consequence;

   (ii) To institute a transitional régime for a reasonable and not unduly prolonged period to be fixed, during which the Mixed Tribunals will remain and will, in addition to their present judicial jurisdiction, exercise the jurisdiction at present vested in the Consular Courts.

At the end of this transitional period the Egyptian Government will be free to dispense with the Mixed Tribunals.

2. As a first step, the Egyptian Government will approach the Capitulatory Powers as soon as possible with a view to (*a*) the removal of all restrictions on the application of Egyptian legislation to foreigners, and (*b*) the institution of a transitional régime for the Mixed Tribunals as provided in paragraph 1(ii) above.

3. His Majesty's Government in the United Kingdom, as the Government of a Capitulatory Power and as an ally of Egypt, are in no way opposed to the arrangements referred to in the preceding paragraph and will collaborate actively with the Egyptian Government in giving effect to them by using all their influence with the Powers exercising capitulatory rights in Egypt.

4. It is understood that in the event of its being found impossible to bring into effect the arrangements referred to in paragraph 2, the Egyptian Government retains its full rights unimpaired with regard to the capitulatory régime, including the Mixed Tribunals.

5. It is understood that paragraph 2 (*a*) involves not merely that the assent of the Capitulatory Powers will be no longer necessary for the application of any Egyptian legislation to their nationals, but also that the present legislative functions of the Mixed Tribunals as regards the application of Egyptian legislation to foreigners will terminate. It would follow from this that the Mixed Tribunals in their judicial capacity would no longer have to pronounce upon the validity of the application to foreigners of an Egyptian law or decree which has been applied to foreigners by the Egyptian Parliament or Government, as the case may be.

6. His Majesty the King of Egypt hereby declares that no Egyptian legislation made applicable to foreigners will be inconsistent with the principles generally adopted in modern legislation or, with particular relation to legislation of a fiscal nature, discriminate against foreigners, including foreign corporate bodies.

7. In view of the fact that it is the practice in most countries to apply to foreigners the law of their nationality in matters of "statut personnel," consideration will be given to the desirability of excepting from the transfer of jurisdiction, at any rate in the first place, matters relating to "statut personnel" affecting nationals of those Capitulatory Powers who wish that their Consular authorities should continue to exercise such jurisdiction.

8. The transitional régime for the Mixed Tribunals and the transfer to them of the jurisdiction at present exercised by the Consular Courts (which régime and transfer will, of course, be subject to the provisions of the special convention referred to in Article 9) will necessitate the revision of existing laws relating to the organisation and jurisdiction of the Mixed Tribunals, including the preparation and promulgation of a new Code of Criminal Procedure. It is understood that this revision will include amongst other matters: —

(i) The definition of the word "foreigner" for the purpose of the future jurisdiction of the Mixed Tribunals;

(ii) The increase of the personnel of the Mixed Tribunals and the Mixed Parquet, which will be necessitated by the proposed extension of their jurisdiction;

(iii) The procedure in the case of pardons or remissions of sentences imposed on foreigners and also in connection with the execution of capital sentences passed on foreigners.

Art. XIV

The present treaty abrogates any existing agreements or other instruments whose continued existence is inconsistent with its provisions. Should either High Contracting Party so request, a list of the agreements and instruments thus abrogated shall be drawn up in agreement between them within six months of the coming into force of the present treaty.

Art. XV

The High Contracting Parties agree that any difference on the subject of the application or interpretation of the provisions of the present treaty which they are unable to settle by direct negotiation shall be dealt with in accordance with the provisions of the Covenant of the League of Nations.

Art. XVI

At any time after the expiration of a period of twenty years from the coming into force of the treaty, the High Contracting Parties will, at the request of either of them, enter into negotiations with a view to such revision of its terms by agreement between them as may be appropriate in the circumstances as they then exist. In case of the High Contracting Parties being unable to agree upon the terms of the revised treaty, the difference will be submitted to the Council of the League of Nations for decision in accordance with the provisions of the Covenant in force at the time of signature of the present treaty or to such other person or body of persons for decision in accordance with such procedure as the High Contracting Parties may agree. It is agreed that any revision of this treaty will provide for the continuation of the Alliance between the High Contracting Parties in accordance with the principles contained in Articles 4, 5, 6 and 7. Nevertheless, with the consent of both High Contracting Parties, negotiations may be entered into at any time after the expiration of a period of ten years after the coming into force of the treaty, with a view to such revision as aforesaid.

Art. XVII

The present treaty is subject to ratification. Ratifications shall be exchanged in Cairo as soon as possible. The treaty shall come into force on the date of the exchange of ratifications, and shall thereupon be registered with the Secretary-General of the League of Nations.

In witness whereof the above-named plenipotentiaries have signed the present treaty and affixed thereto their seals.

Agreed Minute

The United Kingdom and Egyptian Delegations desire at the moment of signature to record in a minute certain points of interpretation of the provisions of the Treaty of Alliance upon which they are agreed.

These points are as follows: —

(i) It is of course understood that the facilities provided for in Article 7 to be furnished to His Majesty The King and Emperor include the sending of British forces or reinforcements in the eventualities specified in that Article.

(ii) With reference to Article 7, it is understood that as a result of the provisions of Article 6, there will have been mutual consultation between the two Governments in the case of a risk of a rupture. In the case of an apprehended international emergency, the same principle of mutual consultation applies.

(iii) The "means of communication" referred to in the second sentence of Article 7 include telecommunications (cables, telegraphs, telephones and wireless).

(iv) Amongst the military, administrative and legislative measures referred to in the third sentence of Article 7 are included measures under which the Egyptian Government, in the exercise of their powers as regards radio-electric communications, will take into account the requirements of the W/T stations of the British forces in Egypt, and will continue to co-operate with the British authorities to prevent any mutual interference between British and Egyptian W/T stations, and measures providing for the effective control of all means of communications referred to in that Article.

(v) The words "Geneifa area" in paragraph 2 (a) of the Annex to Article 8 mean: along the shore of the Great Bitter Lake from a point 3 kilometres North of Geneifa Station to a point 3 kilometres South-East of Fayid Station to a depth of 3 kilometres from the shore of the lake.

(vi) With reference to paragraph 2 (b) of the Annex to Article 8, it is understood that the exact sites in the area therein referred to where the air forces will be located will be defined as soon as possible.

The Royal Air Force Depot at present situated at Aboukir will also be transferred to this area not later than the date of the withdrawal of the British forces from Cairo under paragraph 8.

(vii) With reference to paragraph 3 of the Annex to Article 8, it is understood (a) that British barrack accommodation includes married quarters for officers and for a proportion of the other ranks, (b) that though the site of the convalescent camp cannot be definitely fixed at the moment, El Arish might possibly prove suitable, and (c) that the Egyptian Government, in pursuance of the policy which it has already taken in hand for the benefit of the inhabitants of those areas, will take all reasonable sanitary measures for the combating of malaria in the areas adjacent to those where the British forces are situated.

(viii) With reference to paragraph 6 of the Annex to Article 8, it is understood that, with regard to road No. (iii), the Egyptian Government will, unless they are able to make arrangements with the Suez Canal Company for the use of this road by the British and Egyptian forces and for the improvement of those sections which are not already up to this standard so as to satisfy the conditions laid down in paragraph 6, construct an entirely new road connecting these places.

(ix) With reference to paragraph 12 of the Annex to Article 8, it is understood that the number of the detachment referred to shall be limited to the minimum strictly necessary to handle and guard this material.

(x) With reference to paragraph 13 of the Annex to Article 8, it is under-stood that flying will take place for training purposes mostly over desert areas, and that populated areas will only be flown over where necessity so demands.

(xi) With reference to paragraph 2 of the Egyptian Note relating to military matters, it is of course understood that the cost of the Military Mission will be defrayed by the Egyptian Government, and that the words "proper training" in this paragraph include training in British military colleges and academies.

(xii) Paragraph 2 of the Egyptian Note relating to military matters only applies to persons who are already at the time members of the Egyptian armed forces.

(xiii) The word "equipment" in paragraph 3 of the Egyptian Note relating to military matters, means all such stores as it is desirable for forces acting together to have as a common pattern. It does not include articles of clothing or articles of local production.

(xiv) With reference to paragraph 1 of Article 11, it is agreed that the Governor-General shall furnish to His Majesty's Government in the United Kingdom and the Egyptian Government an annual report on the administration of the Sudan. Sudan legislation will be notified directly to the President of the Egyptian Council of Ministers.

(xv) With reference to paragraph 2 of Article 11, it is understood that, while the appointment of Egyptian nationals to official posts in the Sudan must necessarily be governed by the number of suitable vacancies, the time of their occurrence and the qualifications of the candidates forthcoming, the provisions of this paragraph will take effect forthwith on the coming into force of the Treaty. The promotion and advancement of members of the Sudan Service shall be irrespective of nationality up to any rank by selection in accordance with individual merits.

It is also understood that these provisions will not prevent the Governor-General occasionally appointing to special posts persons of another nationality when no qualified British subjects, Egyptian nationals or Sudanese are avail-

(xvi) With reference to paragraph 3 of Article 11, it is understood that, as the Egyptian Government are willing to send troops to the Sudan, the Gover-nor-General will give immediate consideration to the question of the number of Egyptian troops required for service in the Sudan, the precise places where they will be stationed and the accommodation necessary for them, and that the Egyptian Government will send forthwith, on the coming into force of the Treaty, an Egyptian military officer of high rank whom the Governor-General can consult with regard to these matters.

(xvii) With reference to Article 11, as it has been arranged between the Egyptian Government and His Majesty's Government in the United Kingdom that the question of the indebtedness of the Sudan to Egypt and other financial questions affecting the Sudan shall be discussed between the Egyptian Ministry of Finance and the Treasury of the United Kingdom, and as such discussions have already commenced, it has been considered unnecessary to insert in the Treaty any provision in regard to this question.

(xviii) With regard to paragraph 6 of the Annex to Article 13, it is under-stood that questions relating to this declaration are not subjects for the appreciation of any Courts in Egypt.

Signed in duplicate at London this 26th day of August, 1936.

> *Anthony Eden,*
> His Majesty's Principal Secretary of
> State for Foreign Affairs
> *Moustapha el-Nashas,*
> President of the Egyptian Council of
> Ministers

Official Statement of Policy Accepting the Principle of the Partition of Palestine between Arabs and Jews, July 1937*

His Majesty's Government in the United Kingdom, by direction of His Majesty, have considered the unanimous Report of the Palestine Royal Commission. They find themselves in general agreement with the arguments and conclusions of the Commission.

2. As is fully recognised by the Commissioners in their historical survey, His Majesty's Government and their predecessors, since the obligations of the Mandate were accepted, have taken the view, which the tenor of the Mandate itself implies, that their obligations to Arabs and Jews respectively were not incompatible, on the assumption that in the process of time the two races would so adjust their national aspirations as to render possible the establishment of a single commonwealth under a unitary government.

3. In spite of many discouraging experiences during the past seventeen years, His Majesty's Government have based their policy on this expectation, and have taken every opportunity of encouraging co-operation between Arabs and Jews. In the light of experience and of the arguments adduced by the Commission they are driven to the conclusion that there is an irreconcilable conflict between the aspirations of Arabs and Jews in Palestine, that these aspirations cannot be satisfied under the terms of the present Mandate, and that a scheme of partition on the general lines recommended by the Commission represents the best and most hopeful solution of the deadlock. His Majesty's Government propose to advise His Majesty accordingly.

4. His Majesty's Government therefore propose to take such steps as are necessary and appropriate, having regard to their existing treaty obligations under the Covenant of the League of Nations and other international instru-

*Parliamentary Papers, 1936–37, XIV, Cmd. 5513, 2–3.

ments, to obtain freedom to give effect to a scheme of partition, to which they earnestly hope that it may be possible to secure an effective measure of consent on the part of the communities concerned.

5. Pending the establishment of such a scheme, His Majesty's Government have no intention of surrendering their responsibility for peace, order and good government throughout Palestine. They are in general agreement with the Commission's recommendations in the matter of public security. If serious disorders should again break out, of such a nature as to require military intervention, the High Commissioner will delegate powers in respect of the whole country, under the Palestine (Defence) Orders-in-Council, to the General Officer Commanding the military forces.

6. In the immediate future, while the form of a scheme of partition is being worked out, His Majesty's Government propose that, as an interim measure, steps should be taken to prohibit any land transactions which might prejudice such a scheme. Further, since the period of the current labour schedule expires at the end of July and some provision must be made for the ensuing period, they propose that a total Jewish immigration in all categories of 8,000 persons shall be permitted for the eight months' period August 1937 to March 1938, provided that the economic absorptive capacity of the country is not exceeded.

7. In supporting a solution of the Palestine problem by means of partition, His Majesty's Government are much impressed by the advantages which it offers both to the Arabs and the Jews. The Arabs would obtain their national independence, and thus be enabled to co-operate on an equal footing with the Arabs of neighbouring countries in the cause of Arab unity and progress. They would be finally delivered from all fear of Jewish domination, and from the anxiety which they have expressed lest their Holy Places should ever come under Jewish control. The Arab State would receive financial assistance on a substantial scale both from His Majesty's Government and from the Jewish State. On the other hand, partition would secure the establishment of the Jewish National Home and relieve it from any possibility of its being subjected in the future to Arab rule. It would convert the Jewish National Home into a Jewish State with full control over immigration. Its nationals would acquire a status similar to that enjoyed by the nationals of other countries. The Jews would at last cease to live a "minority life," and the primary objective of Zionism would thus be attained. Under the proposed Treaties the rights of minorities in both States would be strictly guaranted. Above all, fear and suspicion would be replaced by a sense of confidence and security, and both peoples would obtain, in the words of the Commission, "the inestimable boon of peace."

"Palestine: Statement of Policy," a White Paper
Limiting Jewish Immigration into Palestine, May 1939

In the Statement on Palestine, issued on 9th November, 1938, His Majesty's Government announced their intention to invite representatives of the Arabs of Palestine, of certain neighbouring countries and of the Jewish Agency to confer with them in London regarding future policy. It was their sincere hope that, as a result of full, free and frank discussion, some understanding might be reached. Conferences recently took place with Arab and Jewish delegations, lasting for a period of several weeks, and served the purpose of a complete exchange of views between British Ministers and the Arab and Jewish representatives. In the light of the discussions as well as of the situation in Palestine and of the Reports of the Royal Commission and the Partition Commission, certain proposals were formulated by His Majesty's Government and were laid before the Arab and Jewish delegations as the basis of an agreed settlement. Neither the Arab nor the Jewish delegations felt able to accept these proposals, and the conferences therefore did not result in an agreement. Accordingly His Majesty's Government are free to formulate their own policy, and after careful consideration they have decided to adhere generally to the proposals which were finally submitted to, and discussed with, the Arab and Jewish delegations.

2. The Mandate for Palestine, the terms of which were confirmed by the Council of the League of Nations in 1922, has governed the policy of successive British Governments for nearly 20 years. It embodies the Balfour Declaration and imposes on the Mandatory four main obligations. These obligations are set out in Articles 2, 6 and 13 of the Mandate. There is no dispute regarding the interpretation of one of these obligations, that touching the protection of and access to the Holy Places and religious buildings or sites. The other three main obligations are generally as follows: —

(i) To place the country under such political, administrative and economic conditions as will secure the establishment in Palestine of a national home for the Jewish people, to facilitate Jewish immigration under suitable conditions, and to encourage, in co-operation with the Jewish Agency, close settlement by Jews on the land.

(ii) To safeguard the civil and religious rights of all the inhabitants of Palestine irrespective of race and religion, and, whilst facilitating Jewish immigration and settlement, to ensure that the rights and position of other sections of the population are not prejudiced.

(iii) To place the country under such political, administrative and economic conditions as will secure the development of self-governing institutions.

Parliamentary Papers, 1938–39, XXVII, Cmd. 6019, 2–12.

3. The Royal Commission and previous Commissions of Enquiry have drawn attention to the ambiguity of certain expressions in the Mandate, such as the expression "a national home for the Jewish people", and they have found in this ambiguity and the resulting uncertainty as to the objectives of policy a fundamental cause of unrest and hostility between Arabs and Jews. His Majesty's Government are convinced that in the interests of the peace and well-being of the whole people of Palestine a clear definition of policy and objectives is essential. The proposal of partition recommended by the Royal Commission would have afforded such clarity, but the establishment of self-supporting independent Arab and Jewish States within Palestine has been found to be impracticable. It has therefore been necessary for His Majesty's Government to devise an alternative policy which will, consistently with their obligations to Arabs and Jews, meet the needs of the situation in Palestine. Their views and proposals are set forth below under the three heads, (I) The Constitution, (II) Immigration, and (III) Land.

I.—The Constitution

4. It has been urged that the expression "a national home for the Jewish people" offered a prospect that Palestine might in due course become a Jewish State or Commonwealth. His Majesty's Government do not wish to contest the view, which was expressed by the Royal Commission, that the Zionist leaders at the time of the issue of the Balfour Declaration recognised that an ultimate Jewish State was not precluded by the terms of the Declaration. But, with the Royal Commission, His Majesty's Government believe that the framers of the Mandate in which the Balfour Declaration was embodied could not have intended that Palestine should be converted into a Jewish State against the will of the Arab population of the country. That Palestine was not to be converted into a Jewish State might be held to be implied in the passage from the Command Paper of 1922 which reads as follows: —

> Unauthorised statements have been made to the effect that the purpose in view is to create a wholly Jewish Palestine. Phrases have been used such as that "Palestine is to become as Jewish as England is English". His Majesty's Government regard any such expectation as impracticable and have no such aim in view. Nor have they at any time contemplated . . . . .the disappearance or the subordination of the Arabic population, language or culture in Palestine.They would draw attention to the fact that the terms of the (Balfour) Declaration referred to do not contemplate that Palestine as a whole should be converted into a Jewish National Home, but that such a Home should be founded *in Palestine.*

But this statement has not removed doubts, and His Majesty's Government therefore now declare unequivocally that it is not part of their policy that Palestine should become a Jewish State. They would indeed regard it as contrary to their obligations to the Arabs under the Mandate, as well as to the assurances which have been given to the Arab people in the past, that the Arab population of Palestine should be made the subjects of a Jewish State against their will.

5. The nature of the Jewish National Home in Palestine was further described in the Command Paper of 1922 as follows: —

> During the last two or three generations the Jews have recreated in Palestine a community, now numbering 80,000, of whom about one-fourth are farmers or workers upon the land. This community has its own political organs; an elected assembly for the direction of its domestic concerns; elected councils in the towns; and an organisation for the control of its schools. It has its elected Chief Rabbinate.and Rabbinical Council for the direction of its religious affairs. Its business is conducted in Hebrew as a vernacular language, and a Hebrew press serves its needs. It has its distinctive intellectual life and displays considerable economic activity. This community, then, with its town and country population, its political, religious and social organisations, its own language, its own customs, its own life, has in fact "national" characteristics. When it is asked what is meant by the development of the Jewish National Home in Palestine, it may be answered that it is not the imposition of a Jewish nationality upon the inhabitants of Palestine as a whole, but the further development of the existing Jewish community, with the assistance of Jews in other parts of the world, in order that it may become a centre in which the Jewish people as a whole may take, on grounds of religion and race, an interest and a pride. But in order that this community should have the best prospect of free development and provide a full opportunity for the Jewish people to display its capacities, it is essential that it should know that is is in Palestine as of right and not on sufferance. That is the reason why it is necessary that the existence of a Jewish National Home in Palestine should be internationally guaranteed, and that it should be formally recognised to rest upon ancient historic connection.

6. His Majesty's Government adhere to this interpretation of the Declaration of 1917 and regard it as an authoritative and comprehensive description of the character of the Jewish National Home in Palestine. It envisaged the further development of the existing Jewish community with the assistance of Jews in other parts of the world. Evidence that His Majesty's Government have been carrying out their obligation in this respect is to be found in the facts that, since the statement of 1922 was published, more than 300,000 Jews have immigrated to Palestine, and that the population of the National Home has risen to some 450,000, or approaching a third of the entire population of the country. Nor has the Jewish community failed to take full advantage of the opportunities given to it. The growth of the Jewish National Home and its achievements in many fields are a remarkable constructive effort which must command the admiration of the world and must be, in particular, a source of pride to the Jewish people.

7. In the recent discussions the Arab delegations have repeated the contention that Palestine was included within the area in which Sir Henry McMahon, on behalf of the British Government, in October, 1915, undertook to recognise and support Arab independence. The validity of this claim, based on the terms of the correspondence which passed between Sir Henry McMahon and the Sharif of Mecca, was thoroughly and carefully investigated by British and Arab representatives during the recent conferences in London. Their Report, which has been published, states that both the Arab and the British representatives endeavoured to understand the point of view of the other party but that they

were unable to reach agreement upon an interpretation of the correspondence. There is no need to summarise here the arguments presented by each side. His Majesty's Government regret the misunderstandings which have arisen as regards some of the phrases used. For their part they can only adhere, for the reasons given by their representatives in the Report, to the view that the whole of Palestine west of Jordan was excluded from Sir Henry McMahon's pledge, and they therefore cannot agree that the McMahon correspondence forms a just basis for the claim that Palestine should be converted into an Arab State.

8. His Majesty's Government are charged as the Mandatory authority "to secure the development of self-governing institutions" in Palestine. Apart from this specific obligation, they would regard it as contrary to the whole spirit of the Mandate system that the population of Palestine should remain for ever under Mandatory tutelage. It is proper that the people of the country should as early as possible enjoy the rights of self-government which are exercised by the people of neighbouring countries. His Majesty's Government are unable at present to foresee the exact constitutional forms which government in Palestine will eventually take, but their objective is self-government, and they desire to see established ultimately an independent Palestine State. It should be a State in which the two peoples in Palestine, Arabs and Jews, share authority in government in such a way that the essential interests of each are secured.

9. The establishment of an independent State and the complete relinquishment of Mandatory control in Palestine would require such relations between the Arabs and the Jews as would make good government possible. Moreover, the growth of self-governing institutions in Palestine, as in other countries, must be an evolutionary process. A transitional period will be required before independence is achieved, throughout which ultimate responsibility for the Government of the country will be retained by His Majesty's Government as the Mandatory authority, while the people of the country are taking an increasing share in the Government, and understanding and co-operation amongst them are growing. It will be the constant endeavour of His Majesty's Government to promote good relations between the Arabs and the Jews.

10. In the light of these considerations His Majesty's Government make the following declaration of their intentions regarding the future government of Palestine: —

(1) The objective of His Majesty's Government is the establishment within ten years of an independent Palestine State in such treaty relations with the United Kingdom as will provide satisfactorily for the commercial and strategic requirements of both countries in the future. This proposal for the establishment of the independent State would involve consultation with the Council of the League of Nations with a niew to the termination of the Mandate.

(2) The independent State should be one in which Arabs and Jews share in government in such a way as to ensure that the essential interests of each community are safeguarded.

(3) The establishment of the independent State will be preceded by a transitional period throughout which His Majesty's Government will retain responsibility for the government of the country. During the transitional period the people of Palestine will be given an increasing part in the government of their country. Both sections of the population will have an opportunity to participate in the machinery of government, and the process will be carried on whether or not they both avail themselves of it.

(4) As soon as peace and order have been sufficiently restored in Palestine steps will be taken to carry out this policy of giving the people of Palestine an increasing part in the government of their country, the objective being to place Palestinians in charge of all the Departments of Government, with the assistance of British advisers and subject to the control of the High Commissioner. With this object in view His Majesty's Government will be prepared immediately to arrange that Palestinians shall be placed in charge of certain Departments, with British advisers. The Palestinian heads of Departments will sit on the Executive Council, which advises the High Commissioner. Arab and Jewish representatives will be invited to serve as heads of Departments approximately in proportion to their respective populations. The number of Palestinians in charge of Departments will be increased as circumstances permit until all heads of Departments are Palestinians, exercising the administrative and advisory functions which are at present performed by British officials. When that stage is reached consideration will be given to the question of converting the Executive Council into a Council of Ministers with a consequential change in the status and functions of the Palestinian heads of Departments.

(5) His Majesty's Government make no proposals at this stage regarding the establishment of an elective legislature. Nevertheless they would regard this as an appropriate constitutional development, and, should public opinion in Palestine hereafter show itself in favour of such a development, they will be prepared, provided that local conditions permit, to establish the necessary machinery.

(6) At the end of five years from the restoration of peace and order, an appropriate body representative of the people of Palestine and of His Majesty's Government will be set up to review the working of the constitutional arrangements during the transitional period and to consider and make recommendations regarding the constitution of the independent Palestine State.

(7) His Majesty's Government will require to be satisfied that in the treaty contemplated by sub-paragraph (1) or in the constitution contemplated by sub-paragraph (6) adequate provision has been made for: —

(*a*) the security of, and freedom of access to, the Holy Places, and the protection of the interests and property of the various religious bodies.

(*b*) the protection of the different communities in Palestine in accordance with the obligations of His Majesty's Government to both Arabs and Jews and for the special position in Palestine of the Jewish National Home.

(*c*) such requirements to meet the strategic situation as may be regarded as necessary by His Majesty's Government in the light of the circumstances then existing.

His Majesty's Government will also require to be satisfied that the interests of certain foreign countries in Palestine, for the preservation of which they are at present responsible, are adequately safeguarded.

(8) His Majesty's Government will do everything in their power to create conditions which will enable the independent Palestine State to come into being within ten years. If, at the end of ten years, it appears to His Majesty's Government that, contrary to their hope, circumstances require the postponement of the establishment of the independent State, they will consult with representatives of the people of Palestine, the Council of the League of Nations and the neighbouring Arab States before deciding on such a postponement. If His Majesty's Government come to the conclusion that postponement is unavoidable, they will invite the co-operation of these parties in framing plans for the future with a view to achieving the desired objective at the earliest possible date.

11. During the transitional period steps will be taken to increase the powers and responsibilities of municipal corporations and local councils.

II.—Immigration

12. Under Article 6 of the Mandate, the Administration of Palestine, "while ensuring that the rights and position of other sections of the population are not prejudiced," is required to "facilitate Jewish immigration under suitable conditions." Beyond this, the extent to which Jewish immigration into Palestine is to be permitted is nowhere defined in the Mandate. But in the Command Paper of 1922 it was laid down that for the fulfilment of the policy of establishing a Jewish National Home

it is necessary that the Jewish community in Palestine should be able to increase its numbers by immigration. This immigration cannot be so great in volume as to exceed whatever may be the economic capacity of the country at the time to absorb new arrivals. It is essential to ensure that the immigrants should not be a burden upon the people of Palestine as a whole, and that they should not deprive any section of the present population of their employment.

In practice, from that date onwards until recent times, the economic absorptive capacity of the country has been treated as the sole limiting factor, and in the letter which Mr. Ramsay MacDonald, as Prime Minister, sent to Dr. Weizmann in February 1931 it was laid down as a matter of policy that economic absorptive capacity was the sole criterion. This interpretation has been supported by resolutions of the Permanent Mandates Commission. But His Majesty's Government do not read either the Statement of Policy of 1922 or the letter of 1931 as implying that the Mandate requires them, for all time and in all circumstances, to facilitate the immigration of Jews into Palestine subject only to consideration of the country's economic absorptive capacity. Nor do they find anything in the Mandate or in subsequent Statements of Policy to support the view that the establishment of a Jewish National Home in Palestine cannot be effected unless immigration is allowed to continue indefinitely. If immigration has an adverse effect on the economic position in the country, it should clearly be restricted; and equally, if it has a seriously damaging effect on the political position in the country, that is a factor that should not be ignored. Although it is not difficult to contend that the large number of Jewish immigrants who have been admitted so far have been absorbed economically, the fear of the Arabs that this influx will continue indefinitely until the Jewish population is in a position to dominate them has produced consequences which are extremely grave for Jews and Arabs alike and for the peace and prosperity of Palestine. The lamentable disturbances of the past three years are only the latest and most sustained manifestation of this intense Arab apprehension. The methods employed by Arab terrorists against fellow-Arabs and Jews alike must receive unqualified condemnation. But it cannot be denied that fear of indefinite Jewish immigration is widespread amongst the Arab population and that this fear has made possible disturbances which have given a serious setback to economic progress, depleted the Palestine exchequer, rendered life and property insecure, and produced a bitterness between the Arab and Jewish populations which is deplorable between citizens of the same country. If in these circumstances immigration is continued up to the economic absorptive capacity of the country, regardless of all other considerations, a fatal enmity between the two peoples will be perpetuated, and the situation in Palestine may become a permanent source of friction amongst all peoples in the Near and Middle East. His Majesty's Government cannot take the view that either their obligations under the Mandate, or considerations of common sense and justice, require that they should ignore these circumstances in framing immigration policy.

13. In the view of the Royal Commission, the association of the policy of the Balfour Declaration with the Mandate system implied the belief that Arab hostility to the former would sooner or later be overcome. It has been the hope of British Governments ever since the Balfour Declaration was issued that in time the Arab population, recognizing the advantages to be derived from Jewish settlement and development in Palestine, would become reconciled to the further growth of the Jewish National Home. This hope has not been fulfilled. The alternatives before His Majesty's Government are either (i) to seek to

expand the Jewish National Home indefinitely by immigration, against the strongly expressed will of the Arab people of the country; or (ii) to permit further expansion of the Jewish National Home by immigration only if the Arabs are prepared to acquiesce in it. The former policy means rule by force. Apart from other considerations, such a policy seems to His Majesty's Government to be contrary to the whole spirit of Article 22 of the Covenant of the League of Nations, as well as to their specific obligations to the Arabs in the Palestine Mandate. Moreover, the relations between the Arabs and the Jews in Palestine must be based sooner or later on mutual tolerance and goodwill; the peace, security and progress of the Jewish National Home itself require this. Therefore His Majesty's Government, after earnest consideration, and taking into account the extent to which the growth of the Jewish National Home has been facilitated over the last twenty years, have decided that the time has come to adopt in principle the second of the alternatives referred to above.

14. It has been urged that all further Jewish immigration into Palestine should be stopped forthwith. His Majesty's Government cannot accept such a proposal. It would damage the whole of the financial and economic system of Palestine and thus affect adversely the interests of Arabs and Jews alike. Moreover, in the view of His Majesty's Government, abruptly to stop further immigration would be unjust to the Jewish National Home. But, above all, His Majesty's Government are conscious of the present unhappy plight of large numbers of Jews who seek a refuge from certain European countries, and they believe that Palestine can and should make a further contribution to the solution of this pressing world problem. In all these circumstances, they believe that they will be acting consistently with their Mandatory obligations to both Arabs and Jews, and in the manner best calculated to serve the interests of the whole people of Palestine, by adopting the following proposals regarding immigration: —

(1) Jewish immigration during the next five years will be at a rate which, if economic absorptive capacity permits, will bring the Jewish population up to approximately one-third of the total population of the country. Taking into account the expected natural increase of the Arab and Jewish populations, and the number of illegal Jewish immigrants now in the country, this would allow of the admission, as from the beginning of April this year, of some 75,000 immigrants over the next five years. These immigrants would, subject to the criterion of economic absorptive capacity, be admitted as follows:—

(a) For each of the next five years a quota of 10,000 Jewish immigrants will be allowed, on the understanding that a shortage in any one year may be added to the quotas for subsequent years, within the five year period, if economic absorptive capacity permits.

(b) In addition, as a contribution towards the solution of the Jewish refugee problem, 25,000 refugees will be admitted as soon as the High Commissioner is satisfied that adequate provision for their maintenance is ensured, special consideration being given to refugee children and dependants.

(2) The existing machinery for ascertaining economic absorptive capacity will be retained, and the High Commissioner will have the ultimate responsibility for deciding the limits of economic capacity. Before each periodic decision is taken, Jewish and Arab representatives will be consulted.

(3) After the period of five years no further Jewish immigration will be permitted unless the Arabs of Palestine are prepared to acquiesce in it.

(4) His Majesty's Government are determined to check illegal immigration, and further preventive measures are being adopted. The numbers of any Jewish illegal immigrants who, despite these measures, may succeed in coming into the country and cannot be deported will be deducted from the yearly quotas.

15. His Majesty's Government are satisfied that, when the immigration over five years which is now contemplated has taken place, they will not be justified in facilitating, nor will they be under any obligation to facilitate, the further development of the Jewish National Home by immigration regardless of the wishes of the Arab population.

III.—Land

16. The Administration of Palestine is required, under Article 6 of the Mandate, "while ensuring that the rights and position of other sections of the population are not prejudiced", to encourage "close settlement by Jews on the land", and no restriction has been imposed hitherto on the transfer of land from Arabs to Jews. The Reports of several expert Commissions have indicated that, owing to the natural growth of the Arab population and the steady sale in recent years of Arab land to Jews, there is now in certain areas no room for further transfers of Arab land, whilst in some other areas such transfers of land must be restricted if Arab cultivators are to maintain their existing standard of life and a considerable landless Arab population is not soon to be created. In these circumstances, the High Commissioner will be given general powers to prohibit and regulate transfers of land. These powers will date from the publication of this statement of policy and the High Commissioner will retain them throughout the transitional period.

17. The policy of the Government will be directed towards the development of the land and the improvement, where possible, of methods of cultivation. In the light of such development it will be open to the High Commissioner, should he be satisfied that the "rights and position" of the Arab population will be duly preserved, to review and modify any orders passed relating to the prohibition or restriction of the transfer of land.

18. In framing these proposals His Majesty's Government have sincerely

endeavoured to act in strict accordance with their obligations under the Mandate to both the Arabs and the Jews. The vagueness of the phrases employed in some instances to describe these obligations has led to controversy and has made the task of interpretation difficult. His Majesty's Government cannot hope to satisfy the partisans of one party or the other in such controversy as the Mandate has aroused. Their purpose is to be just as between the two peoples in Palestine whose destinies in that country have been affected by the great events of recent years, and who, since they live side by side, must learn to practise mutual tolerance, goodwill and co-operation. In looking to the future, His Majesty's Government are not blind to the fact that some events of the past make the task of creating these relations difficult; but they are encouraged by the knowledge that at many times and in many places in Palestine during recent years the Arab and Jewish inhabitants have lived in friendship together. Each community has much to contribute to the welfare of their common land, and each must earnestly desire peace in which to assist in increasing the well-being of the whole people of the country. The responsibility which falls on them, no less than upon His Majesty's Government, to co-operate together to ensure peace is all the more solemn because their country is revered by many millions of Moslems, Jews and Christians throughout the world who pray for peace in Palestine and for the happiness of her people.

Speech by the Colonial Secretary, A. Creech Jones, in the
House of Commons on the Second Reading of the
*Palestine Independence Bill, 10 March 1948**

I beg to move, "That the Bill be now read a Second time."

This Bill is necessary to make provision for certain matters arising out of the termination of His Majesty's Government of Palestine. On 29th November the General Assembly of the United Nations recommended the adoption of a plan for the partition of Palestine with an economic union. That plan provided for the termination of the Mandate "as soon as possible but in any case not later than 1st August, 1948." The Bill accordingly provides that on a day to be appointed by His Majesty the jurisdiction of His Majesty in Palestine shall cease and His Majesty's Government will no longer be responsible for the government of Palestine. The day to be appointed, as has already been announced, will be 15th May of this year. As the House is aware, it will not be possible to withdraw all our Forces by that day, but they will be withdrawn by 1st August at the latest.

The Government of Palestine as we know it today will cease to exist on 15th May, and any contracts made by that Government will automatically terminate

Hansard, 5.s., CDXLVIII, 1246–61.

on that date, for example, contracts with public officers. The authority for the administration of Palestine after 15th May will, in accordance with the United Nations Resolution of 29th November, be the United Nations Palestine Commission. The partition plan gives the Commission authority to issue "necessary regulations." As I have said, His Majesty will have no jurisdiction in Palestine after 15th May, and any decision of His Majesty in Council after that day cannot be enforced. It necessarily follows that proceedings before the Privy Council must abate. A similar provision, I believe, was endorsed by the House in the Burma Independence Act. I understand, however, that it is likely that all pending cases from Palestine lodged with the Judicial Committee before the introduction of this Bill will be disposed of by 15th May.

The British Forces still in Palestine after that date will be in the position of armed forces in foreign territory. There is no exact precedent for the Palestine situation however. While I am advised that under international law the Forces will possess the necessary rights to protect themselves, and will have the powers required to secure their withdrawal, we have thought it right to give in the Bill express protection from proceedings in a British court in respect of acts done in good faith and in the executing of duty for the protection and withdrawal from Palestine of His Majesty's Forces or stores or other property. The troops in Palestine will merely carry out measures necessary for their safe withdrawal and the withdrawal of their stores. The action of our Forces will be limited to whatever may be required for the withdrawal and protection of themselves and their stores.

Immunity has also been conferred on the civil Government in respect of acts done for peace, order and good government in Palestine before the appointed day, or for the purpose of, or in connection with the termination of His Majesty's jurisdiction. The civil Government have, of course, been acting in accordance with the laws of Palestine and will continue so to act as far as is possible. But I am sure the House will appreciate that in the increasingly disturbed state of the country and in circumstances of extreme difficulty, which are entirely without precedent, it will not be possible for the Palestine Government to proceed in every way, and to leave every duty done, as if they were administering a peaceful country and an orderly population. We are not in the position of knowing what acts may be necessary in the increasing disorder in Palestine up to 15th May. After then the position is still more uncertain. The provisions are based on those of the Indemnity Act, 1920. It is for these reasons that it is proper to confer immunity from vexatious actions upon the officers of that Government.

The Bill also repeals Acts of Parliament having application to Palestine, but leaves them to continue in force as part of the domestic law of Palestine. Enactments specifically repealed relate to the raising of loans by the Palestine Government and their guarantee by the Treasury. There is one outstanding loan and the guarantee of that by the Treasury will continue. Clause 3 also repeals any enactments which have been applied to Palestine as a mandated territory. The Acts will, however, be repealed only so far as concerns the law of the United Kingdom, and are left to continue in force as part of the law of Palestine. Whether or not they will continue in force for long, will, of course, depend on the successor authorities, who will be able to alter them at their own will.

There are other transitional provisions, including power by Order in Council to transfer any funds or other property of the Government of Palestine which may be required to meet that Government's obligations. Thus the funds and other movable property vested in or belonging to the Government of Palestine can be vested in appropriate authorities here. Immovable property will, of course, be left to the successor authorities except such as is vested in a Government Department here, such as the War Office.

Regarding Palestine assets and liabilities generally, we are at present negotiating with the United Nations Commission in New York about them. Our object is to hand over the general assets of the Government to the successor authorities on their undertaking to meet liabilities. It may be that we shall be unable to complete satisfactory arrangements until well after 15th May, or possibly not at all. Accordingly we are taking power in this Bill to transfer to appropriate authorities here the funds and other movable property of the Palestine Government. They will be held until satisfactory arrangements can be made for meeting the obligations of the Palestine Government or for meeting liabilities falling due for settlement here, such as amounts due for payment under contracts placed on behalf of the Palestine Government by the Crown Agents for the Colonies, or such matters as retirement and superannuation benefits.

Power is also sought to adapt the Acts relating to superannuation so as to avoid any break in the service of officers of the Palestine Government which would otherwise be caused by that Government coming to an end. This is the only provision in the Bill which will impose any charge on public funds, but I understand that it will be small. I should add that this becomes necessary as the service of the officers with the Palestine Government terminates on 15th May. The House has already been informed that the expatriate officers have the assurance of His Majesty's Government that they will receive the compensation and statutory benefit to which they are entitled on the terms which have been intimated to them, while the local Palestinian staff are similarly guaranteed the payments due to them until such time as successor authorities have emerged capable of taking over this liability.

MR. PICKTHORN (Cambridge University): I do not complain about the right hon. Gentleman reading upon this occasion, but merely in order to try to understand him I would ask him to read a little slower. When a speech is read it is much harder to follow than the speech which is not read.

MR. CREECH JONES: The point I was making was that in regard to superannuation rights an announcement has already been given to the House as to what benefits will be given to the Palestinian staff as well as to those members of the Colonial Service who are concerned.

It is fitting that I should refer now to several points which emerge from the Amendments on the Order Paper.

MR. IVOR THOMAS (Keighley): Before my right hon. Friend leaves the provisions of the Bill itself, would he say whether it would be possible, under Clause 3, to sequestrate property now belonging to the Government of Palestine in order to meet the terms of compensation which he said, in an answer given to me about a week ago, were definitely promised to the Palestine Administration and the Police Force? His Majesty's Government have undertaken that they will be met, although they take the view that they should be met by the successor authorities.

MR. CREECH JONES: That is a matter among the financial arrangements with the successor authorities, which are now being discussed with the United Nations Palestine Commission. Until those negotiations have finished, I am not able to make a statement.

MR. SYDNEY SILVERMAN (Nelson and Colne): Will my right hon. Friend say whether, supposing that all these things are some day agreed upon, he will then need to come to the House for another Bill?

MR. CREECH JONES: I do not think that is desirable, and I also think that the powers asked for in this Bill are sufficiently wide.

There are protests that the Bill fails to make provision for the independence of Jewish and Arab States in Palestine as provided by the United Nations decision. I should point out that the future form of government to be established in Palestine is not a matter for His Majesty's Government but for the United Nations Assembly. On termination of our exercise of an international Mandate it was proper that that international authority should determine the new form of government which Palestine should enjoy. The Resolution of the Assembly provides that independent Arab and Jewish States shall be established by the United Nations Commission. There is nothing in this Bill which will prevent that. Indeed an act of the United Kingdom could not establish these independent States. Their recognition is a matter for international agreement, and cannot be done in a Bill designed to terminate the jurisdiction of His Majesty in Palestine.

It is also protested that the Bill makes no provision for the orderly transfer of His Majesty's jurisdiction to the United Nations Commission. It is assumed that acts for the orderly transfer of jurisdiction should be written into an Act of Parliament. What the Bill does is to leave the legal position straight, that is, to leave Palestine law in a form for the successor Government authority to take over. Moreover, the High Commissioner in Palestine has, by order in Council, been given power to make such legal provision as will be appropriate in preparation for the withdrawal of His Majesty's Government, thus leaving a body of law in a suitable state for the Commission to administer.

With the concurrence of the Commission, these powers are being exercised, for example, to transfer to municipal authorities certain administrative functions now exercised by the central Government. I repeat that the Bill makes the way clear for the establishment of the successor authority in Palestine and for the United Nations to take up its task. It places no impediment in the way of the United Nations Commission assuming the tasks required of it by the Assembly's Resolution. It terminates His Majesty's jurisdiction and everything that can be done by legislation is done to leave the house in order for the incoming tenant.

I understand that our policy in respect to Palestine is thought to undermine the authority of the United Nations organisation. I should like to meet this criticism. Presumably, it is based on our attitude to the Mandate and future government of Palestine; on our alleged non-co-operative attitude to the United Nations Commission; and on our refusal to enter into fuller commitments in Palestine should forces be called for to impose the Assembly's plan for Palestine.

The question of our attitude to the Mandate, which proved in practice both self-contradictory and unworkable, and of the reference of the Palestine question to the United Nations, has been debated in the House, and I need not explain further the principles of the Government's policy. There is no substantial body of opinion which believes that the Mandate should not be terminated. We gave full notice to the United Nations of our intention that in the absence of a settlement between Jews and Arabs we must plan for the withdrawal of the civil administration and military forces. That decision was welcomed by the United Nations.

We accepted the twelve general recommendations of the United Nations Special Committee which went to Palestine, and we contributed from our knowledge and experience to all the committees established by the United Nations for the study of the problem. We made it clear that we could not be responsible for implementing or enforcing any policy determined by the United Nations, nor could we carry responsibility for any changes through an indefinite transition period until Palestine attained independence. The Assembly accepted that position, and resolved that: "The Mandate for Palestine should terminate as soon as possible but in any case not later than 1st August, 1948." In this respect, therefore, our policy fully accords with the views of the United Nations. But it is alleged that since the resolution of the Assembly we have pursued a non-co-operative attitude with the United Nations Commission. I should point out that in the discussion on partition in the autumn we left no doubt as to our position in the future affairs of Palestine.

We made it plain that the success of any plan in Palestine depended on Arab and Jewish co-operation, that implementation must be an essential part of any plan, and that if an attempt were made to impose a policy which one or other community vigorously opposed, the means of enforcement was an important aspect of implementation. As for ourselves, we had asked for the judgment of an international opinion on the future government of Palestine, we had refused to prejudice discussion by promoting any plans of our own or urging any interests we may have in Palestine, and we had made it clear that we would not oppose the judgment. Indeed, both the Foreign Secretary and myself said to the

House in December that His Majesty's Government accepted the conclusion of the United Nations as to the future government of Palestine. Since the last Debate in this House we have acted in accordance with the policy we announced.

After the November meeting of the Assembly we told that body that it was essential to set up the United Nations Palestine Committee without delay. At once we sent our experts to New York in order that the fullest knowledge should be made available to the Commission. We have supplied the Commission with considerable information and discussed many problems with them concerning the withdrawal and orderly transfer of administration, and we have brought to their notice numerous matters which must be dealt with if they are to assume effective authority in Palestine. In this respect His Majesty's Government have been fully co-operative, though we have refrained from actions which would involve implementation of the United Nations policy. We have dealt with such matters as communications, the future personnel of the administration, the continuing food supply of Palestine and certain problems relating to the economy of the country; and we have submitted a considerable number of other problems which must be determined by the Commission at an early date.

The Commission have also asked us about our attitude to certain of the recommendations of the Assembly's Resolution. We have been unable, on grounds of security in Palestine, to make a port available to the Jews from 1st February for immigration of men and arms. We could not thus surrender our authority over a part of Palestine, while still retaining responsibility for law and order in the country, particularly when the surrender of a port would involve the heavy task of meeting increased Arab resistance. The consequence of such a step could not be faced at a time when we were evacuating our own Forces, and preparing for the transfer of our authority. We felt, for similar security reasons, that our plan for withdrawing our Forces and administration must not be compromised by allowing other areas to pass outside our control before the termination of the Mandate.

We were asked also whether we could agree to allow the Provisional Councils of the two successor States to recruit armed militias from their residents, leaving political and military control to the Commission. We have made it clear that we could not permit any authority other than our own to exercise governmental functions in Palestine before the end of the Mandate. To allow the recruitment of militias would involve two distinct authorities in the country at one time, one of them taking steps to implement the United Nations plan. Further, such a procedure could not fail to increase immeasurably the possibility of grave disturbances while the Mandate still ran. The suggestion did not take account of the realities of the situation. The possible result of an attempt to form a representative militia for the proposed Jewish State, which includes some 400,000 Arabs in its area, when the Arabs were strongly resisting the implementation of the partition plan, should be apparent to everybody. The objections to this step, of course, apply with even greater force to the Jewish request that the Commission should immediately start to establish a purely

Jewish militia for the Jewish State, with full training facilities and the acquisition of the necessary equipment and stores.

There was also a difference of view as to the time when the Commission should arrive in Palestine. Again, all the evidence appeared overwhelming that it was most inadvisable that the Commission should overlap with the mandatory administration for more than a very brief period, since, in view of the declared attitude of the Arabs, it was apparent that the arrival of the Commission would be the signal for increased disorder. We informed the Commission of the grave difficulties involved, and while their staff have already begun to take up their work in Palestine, they themselves will work on the numerous vital matters which can be settled in New York, and which can only be agreed and settled in calm conditions—far different from those likely to be found in Palestine.

I have frankly stated these difficulties, because we are told by various people that this inability to meet these parts of the Resolution of the Assembly is symptomatic of our non-co-operative attitude to the United Nations Commission. I say emphatically that the grave position in Palestine, and the security needs, alone account for the decisions His Majesty's Government took on the matters I have mentioned. In all this discussion by our critics there has been little comprehension of the problems confronting the administration and the Services in Palestine. Until 15th May we have a heavy and complicated responsibility in Palestine. It involves the carrying on of the administration in conditions of outrage and civil violence—almost civil war—at a time when that administration has to wind up its work, make arrangements for the transfer of Services and authority, and provide copious information to the United Nations, when its staffs are depleted and working with difficulty, and when the Services are packing and withdrawing as well as deployed to deal with disorder and outrages. It is important that the problem of our administration and Services should be appreciated as much as the problem of the United Nations Commission itself. I would only add that the situation in Palestine has tragically deteriorated since the Assembly Resolution. Consequently, the Assembly's plan, conceived as it was in conditions of strong partiality, has, in some respects, proved impracticable and unworkable.

The distinguished Chairman of the Palestine Commission has told the Security Council that many of these points which I have already mentioned are really irrelevant to the basic problem of applying the Assembly's Resolution. He indicated clearly that Arab and Jewish co-operation is a fundamental necessity, and that that co-operation is not forthcoming. Given the most perfect conditions, the scheme is hardly workable in many important respects; in any case, the co-operation which is required cannot be expected in the case of a plan to be imposed by force. The Commission therefore reached the conclusion that a non-Palestinian security force is essential for the protection of the Commission on its arrival and for assisting it in carrying out the terms of the Assembly's plan.

The British representatives on the Security Council, while pointing out the gravity of the situation in Palestine and the urgency of the matter, have maintained the view before the Council that this country cannot commit itself further in respect of Palestine, and that our Forces must be withdrawn and our civil administration end on the announced date. We decline to be parties in the implementation and enforcement of a scheme which is calculated inevitably to involve the Forces of the United Kingdom in a prolonged stay in Palestine, and the coercion by force of a considerable section of the population to a plan which they are determined actively to resist. I do not believe, after our bitter and tragic experience, that the British public would tolerate any new commitments in Palestine.

I want to emphasise, however, that we do not want to see our work in Palestine during the past 25 years undone; and that we have tried by our negotiations to secure an orderly transfer of authority and responsibility. It will interest the House to know that with a view to helping to that end the Government of Palestine are doing their utmost to facilitate the operation of essential services by local authorities after 15th May. They are creating and extending the powers of municipal and local councils and giving them new authority in respect to finance and the control of services. Municipal police forces are being formed in Jaffa and in 18 other medium sized Arab towns. A country wide scheme for the enrolment of armed special constables to police Arab villages is being initiated. These forces will be part of the Palestine Police Force until transfer to local authorities. Efforts to recruit a civil police force in Jerusalem, of Jews and Arabs, are also being made.

Certain water supplies have already been handed to local authorities for custody and operation. Arrangements have also been made to transfer responsibility for social welfare and remand homes. Plans for handing over Arab schools to the management of local authorities are in train, and it is hoped to supply a six months stock of drugs and dressings to treatment centres and to persuade medical practitioners to maintain these centres. The Government farm is to be maintained by Acre Municipality. In this and in other ways we are trying to get orderly conditions which can be maintained after the 15th May.

I have referred to the conflict and outrages which have been so distressing a feature of the Palestine scene in recent months, and which have caused such grievous loss to British families here as well as to decent Jews and Arabs, and women and children, in Palestine itself. We have been charged by both sides with favouring one or the other in this terrible trouble. I can find no evidence to sustain the baseless innuendoes and charges one often reads and hears. No side can excuse, and no one attempt to justify, the outrages by armed groups in either community.

The security Forces have had a desperately difficult task and they, with all our administrative and technical officers and officials, are entitled to our most generous appreciation in the anxious work and the enduring strain which they have experienced. They have tried to draw no distinction between Jews and Arabs in their action to suppress the activities of those obviously guilty of assault and violence. It has not been our policy to remove from the inhabitants of Palestine those weapons which can be regarded as necessary for defence on our departure. No searches for arms are being carried out, but where it is clear that arms have been, or are likely to be, used for offensive purposes, the security Forces in their exercise of impartial duty, confiscate such weapons.

We deeply deplore the fact that certain Arab bands have crossed the frontiers and dispersed themselves among the Arab villages. It is too often forgotten, however, how difficult it is, in the existing circumstances in Palestine, to control all the frontiers; how much patrolling has been done and how many Arab arms have been confiscated; how many bands of Arabs have been repulsed and how we have defended Jewish settlements. His Majesty's representatives in the Arab States which appear to be concerned have left the Arab Governments in no doubt of the serious view which His Majesty's Government take of these incursions from their territories into Palestine.

There are many other matters to which reference should be made—

MR. WARBEY (Luton): Can my right hon. Friend say how many public protests have been made to Arab Governments in respect of these incursions?

MR. CREECH JONES: That I cannot answer, but we have made our protests, and representations have been made to the Arab States which we believe to have been involved.

There are many other matters to which some reference should be made in any statement concerning the termination of our responsibilities in Palestine under the Mandate. We have a formidable agenda of matters still awaiting the attention of the Palestine Commission—problems concerning communications, posts, municipal and local council powers, prisoners, medical services and many other things. His Majesty's Government have assumed that after 15th May the United Nations Palestine Commission will be exercising the functions of Government in Palestine. Whether that is possible now, no one at the moment dare say.

MR. R. A. BUTLER (Saffron Walden): The right hon. Gentleman has made a very important statement. He has been referring throughout to the successor authority, but his last statement is to the effect that it may not be possible for this authority to take control on 15th May. What does he propose in that event?

MR. CREECH JONES: The British Mandate terminates on 15th May. Our civil administration, therefore, comes to an end. We have tried to create the conditions whereby orderly life can continue in Palestine, by creating local security forces and transferring powers to local councils, and to Jewish and Arab groups, in order that much of the normal life and many of the services of the country can continue. It is possible that the Palestine Commission of United Nations may find itself unable to proceed to Palestine because suitable arrangements have not been made, either by the Security Council or by other organs of the United Nations, for it to take up its duties there.

As I have said, no one can foresee precisely what the future of the Palestine Commission will be, but on withdrawal the mandatory administration will take whatever steps it can to hand over the assets of the Government of Palestine and to provide for the meeting of that Government's obligations. The United Nations Commission will, in the circumstances contemplated, be the effective authority in Palestine—

MR. PICKTHORN: The effective authority?

MR. CREECH JONES: In the circumstances contemplated under the partition recommendation.

MR. PICKTHORN: Will be the effective authority?

MR. CREECH JONES: As the situation is at the moment. Obviously, if the Commission is unable to take up its duties, we shall be confronted with a different and new situation.

It is contemplated that an overall financial agreement will be negotiated with the Commission covering the question of the transfer of assets of the Palestine Government and the acceptance of the liabilities properly incurred by that Government. Immovable assets in Palestine will be left to the successor authorities in the areas where they are situated, and arrangements will be made before our departure from Palestine to hand over to the Commission as trustee for the ultimate Government or Governments in Palestine all stores and other movable property belonging to the Palestine Government.

Certain of the proper liabilities of the Palestine Government will fall to be met in this country; for instance, the payment of leave salaries and retirement benefits of British staff of the Palestine Government who have been withdrawn to this country, of amounts due under contracts for the supply of stores to the Palestine Government, and of amounts due to the Ministry of Food for procurement of food supplies for Palestine. On the other hand, certain liquid and other assets of the Palestine Government are held here; for instance, monies invested by the Crown Agents on behalf of the Palestine Government. It is the intention to cover the question of meeting these liabilities and disposal of these assets in our negotiations with the United Nations Commission. All these matters can be covered by an appropriate Order in Council under Clause 3 (4, a) of the Bill.

Turning again to the Security Council—which, I may say, has failed to endorse the Resolution of the Assembly and did not find a sufficient number of members willing to accept the recommendations of the Assembly on 29th November in respect to the partition plan—unofficial and informal talks between the permanent members of the Security Council are now going on. We have agreed, not to serve as a member of that group, but to supply any information in our power; but the meetings are for the purpose of considering what advice to give to the Security Council in a week's time regarding the situation in Palestine and what guidance should be offered to the Palestine Commission with a view to implementing the partition plan of the Assembly. The House clearly knows that His Majesty's Government are unwilling to enter into new commitments in Palestine or to participate in implementing the resolution of the United Nations. The question whether a threat to peace, necessitating armed force or other means of restraint, exists in Palestine, has not yet been considered by the Security Council.

I would like to say a word in regard to the position of Jerusalem and the Holy Places. The trusteeship Council concluded its consideration yesterday of the constitution for the City of Jerusalem, including an area round the City proper and Bethlehem, in accordance with the general directions of the Assembly. I need not, at this point, outline the proposed constitution. It is suggested that a Legislative Council, a Council of Administration and an independent Supreme Court should be set up. The Trusteeship Council was also instructed to appoint a Governor. There has been some delay, and that appointment has not yet been made, although many of us have tried to bring home to the body the importance of a very early appointment. In the work of the Trusteeship Council we have made, as a nation and a Power, a very important contribution to this problem; but we have been obliged to point out the security danger which exists between 15th May, when our civil administration ceases, and 1st October when it is anticipated that the statute will become effective. The Governor's responsibility for the Holy Places has been specially emphasised in the Statute, under which provision has to be made by him for a "Special"—that is, non-Arab and non-Jew—police force, a security force working under the instructions of the Governor, whose function will be the protection of the Holy Places.

SQUADRON-LEADER FLEMING (Manchester, Withington): Will that come into operation on 15th May?

MR. CREECH JONES: What is provided for on that date is the British withdrawal. October 1st is the date when the new order begins in Jerusalem, and there is a gap between the withdrawal of the civil administration on 15th May and the date when the new order comes into operation. I myself have particularly directed the attention of the Palestine Commission to the risks of a gap between 15th May and 1st October, and the importance of speedy action by the Palestine Commission to meet that situation. We have also done our utmost to secure the appointment of the Governor and have offered facilities in regard to the recruitment of volunteers for the Special Police Force which he may require.

The immediate prospects in Palestine are not bright. Our concern is deep for the well-being of the people of both communities, the violence committed day after day and the unaccommodating spirit that is abroad. We have done all possible to preserve authority and respect for law, to reduce violence, to see the work achieved by Britain maintained and conditions created for an orderly and effective transfer of authority. We fervently endorse the appeal made by the United Nations that the peoples concerned should cease their acts of destruction and that no States should add fuel to the fire already burning. Many harsh and wicked things have been said about the men and women who have laboured in the discharge of our international obligations. We remember the sacrifices they have made, and we thank those who have served and those who are still serving.

We withdraw now with profound disappointment, conscious, however, that, whatever lapses we may have been guilty of—and mistakes are made by everybody—we have given, as a nation, much to Palestine and to the two communities there. We hope our friendship will not be dissolved by the experiences of recent years. The British people have given much in fulfilment of their international responsibilities. They should not be asked, to endure more. It is now for others to find and implement the solution which has eluded us. We pray that they will. We make the United Nations the fundamental principle in our international policy, and we have co-operated fully with it in this matter of Palestine. But terrorism has found its Nemesis in the attitude of the British people to this problem. With confidence, I ask the House to give this Bill a Second Reading.

SIR PATRICK HANNON (Birmingham, Moseley): May I ask the right hon. Gentleman a question before he sits down? The safety and security of the Holy Places is of profound consequence to the people of this country. What is the means of recruitment for the special Police Force, and will it be under the personal control of the Governor?

MR. CREECH JONES: The position is that this is the Security Force of the Governor, and it will not be controlled at all by any legislative body or other Council which is created in Jerusalem. It will be the Security Force of the Governor, who will be entirely responsible for it, as well as for its recruitment and everything else. It will be a non-Arab, non-Jewish organisation. We have urged the appointment right away of the Governor because we are anxious that the security force should come into being without delay. There is a large number of men in Palestine, some of whom have been members of the police force, who are prepared to offer their services as volunteers in this particular security force for the protection of the Holy Places.

Debate in the House of Commons on the Proposed Anglo-Egyptian Agreement for the Suez Canal Zone, 28 July 1954*

MR. ANTHONY EDEN: With your permission, Mr. Speaker, and that of the House, I should like to make a statement on Egypt in answer to Questions Nos. 5, 11 and 2.

I am glad to be able to tell the House that we have reached agreement in principle with the Egyptian Government on the future of the Suez Canal Zone

*Hansard, 5.s., DXXXI, 495–504.

Base. The full texts of the Heads of Agreement and of the Annex on the organisation of the Base will be circulated in the OFFICIAL REPORT and will also be made available as a White Paper this evening. Meanwhile, I should like to give a short summary of their provisions.

The Heads of Agreement provide that those parts of the Base which we require shall be kept in efficient working order and capable of immediate use in the event of an armed attack by an outside Power on Egypt, or on any member of the Arab League, or on Turkey. If such an attack takes place, Egypt will afford to the United Kingdom the necessary facilities to place the Base on a war footing and to operate it effectively.

In the event of the threat of an attack on any of the countries I have mentioned there will be immediate consultation between the United Kingdom and Egypt.

The installations we are retaining are required to assist in the supply and maintenance of Her Majesty's Forces in the Middle East in peace. They will also hold certain war reserves. They will be operated by civilian labour through firms, British or Egyptian, under contract to Her Majesty's Government in the United Kingdom. These contractors will be afforded by the Egyptian Government all the facilities which they require for their work. Her Majesty's Government will also have the necessary facilities for the inspection of these installations.

The Heads of Agreement have been initialled by my right hon. Friend the Secretary of State for War, to whom Her Majesty's Government are much indebted for the decisive part he played in the final stages of these difficult discussions. [An HON. MEMBER: "The next resignation."] Negotiations for a formal Agreement will now begin.

Our forces will be withdrawn from the Canal Zone within a period of 20 months from the date of the signature of the formal Agreement.

That Agreement will last for seven years from the date of signature. There is provision for consultation between the parties during the last year of its duration as to what arrangements are necessary on its conclusion.

The Agreement will also include a clause recognising the economic, commercial and strategic importance of the Suez Canal, and will express the determination of both parties to uphold the 1888 Convention guaranteeing freedom of navigation.

There is also a clause providing for overflying, landing and servicing facilities for aircraft under R.A.F. control.

There will be many points of detail to be worked out in the drafting of the Agreement itself.

It is the conviction of Her Majesty's Government that this Agreement will preserve our essential requirements in this area in the light of modern conditions. We are convinced that in the Middle East as elsewhere our defence arrangements must be based on consent and co-operation with the peoples concerned. [An HON. MEMBER: "What about Cyprus?"] I would like to take this opportunity to reaffirm the intention of Her Majesty's Government to abide by the terms of the Tripartite Declaration of 25th May, 1950, relating to peace and stability between the Arab States and Israel.

I have discussed this point with the French and the United States Governments and find them both equally determined to uphold that Declaration.

It is our hope that it will now be possible to establish our relations with Egypt on a new basis of friendship and understanding. Her Majesty's Government believe that this is also the intention of the Egyptian Government. The Agreement should thus contribute to a reduction of tension throughout the Middle East as a whole.

Following are the texts:

HEADS OF AGREEMENT

It is agreed between the Egyptian and British Delegations that with a view to establishing Anglo-Egyptian relations on a new basis of mutual understanding and firm friendship, and taking into account their obligations under the United Nations Charter, an agreement regarding the Suez Canal Base should now be drafted on the following lines.

2. The agreement will last until the expiry of seven years from the date of signature. During the last twelve months of this period the two Governments will consult together to decide what arrangements are necessary upon the termination of the agreement.

3. Parts of the present Suez Canal Base will be kept in efficient working order in accordance with the requirements set forth in Annex 1 and capable of immediate use in accordance with the following paragraph.

4. (i) In the event of an armed attack by an outside Power on Egypt, on any country which at the date of signature of the present agreement is a party to the Treaty of Joint Defence between Arab League States or on Turkey, Egypt will afford to the United Kingdom such facilities as may be necessary in order to place the Base on a war footing and to operate it effectively. These facilities will include the use of Egyptian ports within the limits of what is strictly indispensable for the above-mentioned purposes.

(ii) In the even of a threat of an attack on any of the above-mentioned countries, there shall be immediate consultation between the United Kingdom and Egypt.

5. The organisation of the Base will be in accordance with Annex 1 attached.

6. The United Kingdom will be accorded the right to move any British material into or out of the Base at its discretion. There will be no increase above the level of supplies to be agreed upon without the consent of the Egyptian Government.

7. Her Majesty's forces will be completely withdrawn from Egyptian territory according to a schedule to be established in due course within a period of twenty months from the date of signature of this agreement. The Egyptian Government will afford all necessary facilities for the movement of men and material in this connexion.

8. The agreement will recognise that the Suez Maritime Canal, which is an integral part of Egypt, is a waterway economically, commercially

and strategically of international importance, and will express the determination of both parties to uphold the 1888 Convention guaranteeing the freedom of navigation of the Canal.

9. The Egyptian Government will afford overflying, landing and servicing facilities for notified flights of aircraft under R.A.F. control. For the clearance of any flights the Egyptian Government will extend most favoured nation treatment.

10. There will be questions of detail to be covered in the drafting of the agreement including the storage of oil, the financial arrangements necessary, and other detailed matters of importance to both sides. These will be settled by friendly agreement in negotiations which will begin forthwith.

ANNEX 1
Organisation of the Base

Her Majesty's Government shall have the right to maintain certain agreed installations and to operate them for current requirements. Should Her Majesty's Government decide at any time no longer to maintain all these installations they will discuss with the Egyptian Government the disposal of any installation which they no longer require. The approval of the Egyptian Government must be obtained for any new construction.

2. Following the withdrawal of Her Majesty's forces the Egyptian Government will assume responsibility for the security of the base and of all equipment contained therein, or in transit on Egyptian territory to and from the base.

3. Her Majesty's Government will conclude contracts with one or more British or Egyptian commercial firms for the up-keep and operation of the installations referred to in paragraph 1 and the maintenance of the stores contained in these installations. These commercial firms will have the right to engage British and Egyptian civilian technicians and personel; the number of the British technicians employed by these commercial firms shall not exceed a figure which shall be agreed upon in the detailed negotiations. These commercial firms will have also the right to engage such local labour as they may require.

4. The Egyptian Government will give full support to the commercial firms referred to in paragraph 3 to enable them to carry out these tasks and will designate an authority with whom the contractors can co-operate for the discharge of their duties.

5. The Egyptian Government will maintain in good order such installations, public utilities, communications, bridges, pipe-lines and wharves, etc. as will be handed over to it according to agreement between the two Governments. The commercial firms referred to in paragraph 3 will be afforded such facilities as may be required in their operations.

6. Her Majesty's Government will be afforded facilities for the inspection of the installations referred to in paragraph 1 and the work being carried out therein. To facilitate this personnel shall be attached to Her Majesty's Embassy in Cairo. The maximum number of such personnel will be agreed between the two Governments.

MR. ATTLEE: In view of the fact that we are to have a debate tomorrow, I do not think it would be proper for me to ask many questions, but I should like to ask one: in view of the statements which were made by the present Prime Minister on the absolute necessity of having troops in Egypt for the defence of the Suez Canal and the violent language which he used when any proposal was put forward from this side of the House for withdrawal from Egypt, may I ask whether this agreement has the Prime Minister's consent?

THE PRIME MINISTER (SIR WINSTON CHURCHILL): I am convinced that it is absolutely necessary.

MR. ASSHETON: Is my right hon. Friend aware that the news which he has given us will be a great shock to millions of Her Majesty's subjects all over the Commonwealth and is also a matter of very grave concern to many of his own supporters?

MR. EDEN: I really cannot accept what my right hon. Friend has just said, that it will be a shock to Her Majesty's subjects all over the Commonwealth. That is a statement which I do not possibly endorse. For one thing, I do not think that any Member of this House is entitled to speak for the Commonwealth as a whole. I must add that the Commonwealth Governments have been kept in the fullest touch with every stage of these discussions, and I have no reason whatever to believe that the Commonwealth Governments endorse the views which my right hon. Friend has just expressed.

MR. H. MORRISON: May I ask the right hon. Gentleman whether his statement with regard to the Suez Canal means that there is now to be effective, free facilities for the transit of shipping through the Suez Canal, including shipping destined for Israel. Secondly, is he satisfied that the interests of Israel have been adequately safeguarded? Thirdly, is it the case that the information which he has now given to the House was first of all given to a committee of the Conservative Party upstairs?

MR. EDEN: I have done nothing improper so far as the committee upstairs is concerned. I have as much right to speak to the members of my party as the right hon. Gentleman has to speak to his. I found the experience agreeable, as I trust that he always does. In reply to the right hon. Gentleman's question about Israel, we have, of course, had very much in mind the question of relations between Egypt and Israel. The position about the Canal, as the right hon. Gentleman knows well, does not arise out of the Agreement of 1936, of which this is a replacement, but under the Suez Canal Convention of 1888.

MR. SHINWELL *rose—*

MR. EDEN: Perhaps the right hon. Gentleman will allow me to answer this important question. The position about the Suez Canal arises under the Suez Canal Convention of 1888 and, as the right hon. Gentleman knows, the trouble has arisen as a result of the war between the Arab States and Israel. It is the wish of the whole House to try to reduce tension between the Arab States and Israel, and I would ask the House to judge for itself whether we shall be better able to use that influence if we have an agreement with Egypt or not.

MR. SPEAKER: I should like to remind the House that we are to have a debate tomorrow.

MR. MANUEL: Not for the back benchers.

MR. SPEAKER: The hon. Member for Central Ayrshire (Mr. Manuel) should not take such a gloomy view. While questions to elucidate some facts are useful, I do ask hon. Members to refrain from anticipating the debate tomorrow.

MR. SHINWELL: I am rising on what, I hope, is a point of order; you, Sir, will advise me whether it is a correct point of order or not. It is this. It is already intimated that there is agreement on both sides that the debate will have the Closure applied, or at any rate it will be suspended or adjourned, at seven o'clock tomorrow. We shall therefore have a very short debate, and, in these circumstances, would it not be in order to ask one or two supplementary questions to elucidate the facts?

MR. SPEAKER: I do not think that what the right hon. Gentleman has said differs from what I tried to say. The expression of strong opinions is debate, but asking Questions to obtain facts is quite another thing.

MR. SHINWELL: In order to elucidate the facts so that hon. Members may be properly informed when the debate takes place tomorrow, may I ask the right hon. Gentleman two questions bearing on his statement? One is this—whether, pending the formal Agreement to which he referred, arising out of the present Agreement, is it intended to supply arms to Egypt? The second point I wish to put is this—whether the tripartite Agreement to which he has referred does not make it clear, beyond any possibility of doubt, that no arms will be supplied to any of the Arab States unless there is a firm assurance that they will not commit an act of aggression against any other State in the Middle East?

MR. EDEN: There is nothing whatever in this Agreement which compels Her Majesty's Government or permits Her Majesty's Government to supply arms to Egypt. That, of course, is a position which would have to be related, as the right hon. Gentleman quite rightly said, in its general context to the engagements we all have under the 1950 tripartite Agreement.

MR. LEWIS: On a point of order. You stated, Mr. Speaker, that, in view of the fact that there is to be a debate tomorrow, there perhaps would not be the necessity to have too many supplementary questions. May I draw to your attention the fact that a number of my hon. Friends on this side of the House intend to take part in the debate on the Motion concerning the Adjournment of the House for the Summer Recess? In view of the fact that that time will of necessity come out of the hours already suggested by the Leader of the House for the debate on Egypt, which is to end at seven o'clock, is it not a fact that the debate on that Motion concerning the Adjournment may go on until four, five or six o'clock, which will mean that we shall have only one hour's debate tomorrow on Egypt, and that, by the time the Front Benchers have spoken, the back benchers will have no time at all? I therefore again ask you to make some arrangement so that the rights of back benchers are protected in this matter.

MR. SPEAKER: To some extent back benchers have their rights in their own hands, and if there is a long debate on the Motion for the Adjournment, that, of course, may take up time, but we must see how we get on. I cannot anticipate.

MISS WARD: On a point of order. May I ask whether I should be in order in suggesting that there are back-bench Members on this side of the House as well as on the other side?

MR. SPEAKER: I think that the whole House is conscious of that fact.

MR. ANTHONY GREENWOOD: On a point of order. May I respectfully draw your attention, Mr. Speaker, to the fact that so far no back bencher on either side has had an opportunity of asking any supplementary question on this issue of Egypt?

MR. A. HENDERSON *rose*—

HON. MEMBERS: Oh.

MR. SPEAKER: The right hon. Gentleman had a question on the Order Paper for answer today. He was promised an answer in a statement after Questions.

MR. HENDERSON: May I ask whether it is intended to continue the alliance between the two countries which was established under Article 4 of the 1936 Treaty?

MR. EDEN: This will be a new instrument, when it is negotiated, which will take the place of the 1936 Treaty.

MR. P. WILLIAMS: The right hon. Gentleman mentioned in his statement the Suez Canal Convention of 1888. Is there as yet any indication at all from the Egyptian Government that they will even consider re-establishing freedom of the Canal?

MR. EDEN: The respect in which there is interference with the Canal or prohibition of the passage of goods through the Canal arises from the Israel-Arab war and the failure to settle their armistice. It is in that context that Egypt has stopped the passage of certain strategic goods to Israel. The whole House wants to try to reduce tension and to get a final settlement between the Arabs and the Israelis. I ask my hon. Friend whether it is not a good idea to start improving our relations with Egypt and making that a better foundation.

MR. PAGET: Is the Foreign Secretary aware of the general satisfaction that the Prime Minister has at last recognised the necessity of this measure? In what respects are the present Heads of Agreement worse than those which were available to us two years ago? Are they in any respect better?

MR. EDEN: Comparisons are always odious. Our hope is that this arrangement with the Government now established in Egypt is one which can develop in real friendship between the two countries. At least, I hope that the House will give it a real chance to do so.

MR. PATRICK MAITLAND: For our guidance in studying the White Paper, can my right hon. Friend say whether these terms are more gentle towards Egypt than those offered by his predecessors in office and by himself earlier on?

MR. EDEN: I much regret that I have not had time to make that comparison. I have not negotiated this arrangement on the basis of finding whether this or that was better or less better than anything offered before. What I have tried to do was to reach an arrangement which I thought was fair and reasonable between the two countries and which I was justified in putting before this House.

MR. S. SILVERMAN: While I fully endorse the Foreign Secretary's view that the interests of Israel will gain more by an improvement of general relations in the Middle East than by a continuance of their present or past relationship, will the Foreign Secretary nevertheless bear in mind that the attack by Egypt on Israel, out of which, the right hon. Gentleman rightly says, the present prohibition of passage through the Suez Canal arises, was itself an act of completely unprovoked aggression? Was any reference made during the discussions to the continued existence of this infringement of the arrangements with regard to the Suez Canal and free passage through it?

MR. EDEN: This is a subject which has been fully discussed on a number of occasions between us and the Egyptian Government. I should be quite willing to go into it in the debate tomorrow, but I do not think that I should deal further with it now.

MAJOR LEGGE-BOURKE: In view of the fact that any treaty along the lines now proposed would depend upon the stability of the Egyptian Government, and since the Egyptian Government's stability will depend very largely upon its economic stability, will the Foreign Secretary say whether, in addition to this Canal arrangement, Her Majesty's Government propose to try to negotiate a trade treaty with Egypt, and if so, when they propose to begin?

MR. EDEN: One of the results of this arrangement should be to improve our commercial relations with Egypt, which would assuredly be of benefit to both countries. It is also our hope that the increased resulting stability in the Middle East will be of benefit economically as a whole. It may be that other countries may also be able to do something to help economically.

MR. WIGG: The Foreign Secretary referred to the movement of troops from the Canal Zone as a withdrawal. Will he kindly say at what date that word came into use in the Foreign Office and was accepted by his party, remembering that the Prime Minister used the word "scuttle" repeatedly?

MR. EDEN: The hon. Member may prefer "redeployment"; I do not mind.

SEVERAL HON. MEMBERS rose—

MR. SPEAKER: Order. This is becoming a debate.

*Speech by the Minister of State for Foreign Affairs,
Anthony Nutting, in the House of Commons in Defense
of Britain's Middle Eastern Policy, Particularly Its
Reliance upon the Baghdad Pact, 7 March 1956**

I think it was clear on Monday last that the House heard with a sense of deep regret the statement by my right hon. Friend the Prime Minister about the dismissal of General Glubb and two other senior British officers of the Arab Legion.

British officers have had a long, proud and happy association with the Arab Legion since it was founded by Peake Pasha in 1920 to preserve order in the newly created State of Transjordan. General Glubb himself has been with the Legion since 1930 and has commanded it since 1939, a record of 26 years of devoted service to the Arab cause. Under his command the Legion has expanded from a small body of about 1,500 men into a well-equipped and well-trained force of some 21,000, and, may I add, one of the most effective and efficient fighting forces in the whole of the Middle East.

As the House well knows, this growth and development have been due very largely to the devoted and untiring service of General Glubb. As my right hon. Friend made plain on Monday last, General Glubb and his two fellow British officers deserved better of the country they had served than abrupt and discourteous dismissal at 24 hours notice. If I may say so with respect, it is right that the House should, at the earliest opportunity, debate the situation which has arisen, for not only are British officers involved, but very substantial sums of British money are voted yearly to support the Arab Legion, and the House will wish to consider these issues in the context of our future relations with Jordan and against the wider background of the situation in the Middle East.

Her Majesty's Government have not only contributed British officers to the Legion in fulfillment of their obligations under the 1948 Anglo-Jordan Treaty, which was made by the previous Government; they have largely been responsible for its equipment and for giving it financial support amounting to more than £60 million during the last nine years. In addition, we are pledged under the Treaty to come to Jordan's aid if she is attacked. We have maintained air and ground forces in Jordan to provide for her defence. We have therefore fulfilled the spirit and the letter of our obligations to Jordan.

I regret to say that the summary dismissal by the Jordan Government of General Glubb and the other British officers, without consultation with Her Majesty's Government, can hardly be said to fulfil the spirit of Jordan's obligations to us. The provisions of the Treaty cannot be fulfilled unless there is full

Hansard, 5.s., DXLIX, 2111–21.

and continuous consultation between Jordan and the United Kingdom on all matters essential to the effective defence of Jordan.

However, in the event, the Jordan Government did not see fit to consult us and summarily dismissed General Glubb from his post as Chief of the General Staff together with Brigadier Hutton and Colonel Sir Patrick Coghill, respectively Chief of Staff and Director-General of Intelligence. In addition, they relieved of their command one British brigade commander and seven British unit commanders.

The Jordan Government have, it is true, since stated that they wish to preserve their link with Britain under the Treaty and the presence of British officers in the Legion. Nevertheless, a state of uncertainty exists for the remaining British officers as a result of the treatment received by those who have been dismissed. As my right hon. Friend told the House, it would be wrong for those officers who held executive command to be left in the uncertain position where they hold responsibility without the authority to carry it out. I am sure, therefore, the House will feel that Her Majesty's Government acted correctly in asking that all those who were still in executive commands should be relieved of them.

Meanwhile, it is no secret that one of the essential elements in our co-operation with Jordan has been the maintenance of the Arab Legion as an effective defence force. The effect upon the Legion's efficiency of these sudden changes in its command may well be serious. That is one of the most important factors which Her Majesty's Government must weigh in considering their future policy and relationship with Jordan. It has always been our purpose to train as many Arab officers as possible to take on positions of responsibility, but there are still few who have the necessary experience to take over the higher commands. For this reason we must have grave doubts about the effect of the recent changes in command on the effectiveness of the Legion as a fighting force.

As my right hon. Friend made clear on Monday, the Government do not underestimate the gravity of the situation which has arisen. We are consulting with our Allies, and the House will not expect me to announce new decisions before these consultations have been completed. There are many grave issues which are thrown up by these changes in Jordan, issues which affect a wider situation than that of Jordan itself, and which must in consequence be judged against the wider background of the whole Middle East area.

This is no doubt the setting in which the House will wish to discuss these matters.

No one can deny that we are facing a difficult and troublesome phase in our relations with Arab national feeling. The causes of this lie partly in history but have been aggravated by the bitterness of Arab hostility towards Israel. We shall not find a quick remedy for these ills, more especially as there are third parties pouring poison into the wounds and doing their best to increase hostility against all that we stand for. In face of this, our best and wisest course is to show ourselves reliable, consistent, patient but yet firm in the policy—[*Laugh-*

ter.]—I repeat firm in the policy of seeking and extending co-operation with the Middle East States in the things that matter—the defence of their security and the development of their life and their resources.

It has recently been suggested from the benches opposite that Her Majesty's Government should get themselves a new policy for the Middle East. What new policy have the Opposition in mind? Our policy is based on the Bagdad Pact and the Tripartite Declaration. In the debate on the Bagdad Pact in April of last year, the right hon. Member for Lewisham, South (Mr. H. Morrison), speaking then officially on behalf of the Opposition, made it quite clear to the House that the Bagdad Pact was the right policy in existing circumstances. He voiced no criticism of the Pact, and at the end of the debate there was on Division on the Motion which approved—I repeat approved—our accession to the Pact.

Yet, speaking the other day from the Opposition Front Bench, the right hon. Member for Blyth (Mr. Robens) made it quite clear that, in his view, we should dismantle the Pact, which, he said, constituted a major danger to peace in the Middle East. This is a surprising change of front, and, what is far more important, I submit to the House, very dangerous doctrine indeed. I want to make it perfectly clear that we stand firm and four-square by the Bagdad Pact, and that we have no intention whatsoever of abandoning our friends who have joined in it with us. Our every interest and theirs—political, strategic and economic—make it imperative that we should stand together, as we do and as we shall continue to do, in the defence of the Middle East against aggression from without.

At the same time, we intend to use the economic institutions of the Pact to promote trade, technical assistance and development. The Bagdad Pact countries have already embarked upon plans for development on which their Governments are spending over £300 million a year—plans which include communications, agriculture and land use, joint development projects, technical education and the peaceful uses of atomic energy. It is the declared intention of these countries to increase the efficiency of this development through economic co-operation, the sharing of technical knowledge and the improvement of technical education.

We recognise that we have an important part to play in all this development, and this is fully understood and welcomed by our Middle Eastern Allies. [An HON. MEMBER: "Who are they?"] Our Allies under the Bagdad Pact. I noticed that the right hon. Member for Blyth, in the same speech the other day, said that the Bagdad Pact—and I quote his own words—

> . . . provoked, as might have been expected, the equally mischievous and dangerous Soviet intervention in the Middle East.—[OFFICIAL REPORT, 27th February, 1956; Vol. 549, c. 853.]

This, of course, is complete and arrant nonsense. [*Interruption.*] If the hon. Member will bide his time in patience, he will get the argument. If the right hon. Gentleman and his hon. Friend the Member for Nelson and Colne (Mr. S. Silverman) really think that Soviet policy, which is nothing if not long-term in its preparation and execution, is determined by reflex reactions of this kind, then they must think that Soviet politicians are much simpler and more nervous folk than we do.

The fact of the matter is that this Soviet move was a calculated and carefully planned action to stir up trouble in the Middle East and to undermine Western influence. What is more, to those who say that the Bagdad Pact constitutes a major danger to peace in the Middle East, I must say categorically that the opposite is the truth. It is proving an effective instrument for the defence of the Middle East, and if hon. Members opposite do not believe that, let them spend a few hours each week listening to what Radio Moscow has to say on the subject.

Having said that we stand by our friends in the Bagdad Pact, I want to make it equally clear that it is the intention of Her Majesty's Government to stand firm in the Persian Gulf, where a combination of old friendships and new resources imposes upon us a clear duty and responsibility. On that point, let there be no doubt that we shall take any steps that are necessary to sustain our position and our friends the Rulers of the Persian Gulf States.

One of the most remarkable phenomena of the post-war world has been the expansion of oil production in the Middle-East. The importance of this to British industry and to full employment in this country cannot be exaggerated. In Kuwait alone, the output of oil has increased from 28 million tons in 1951 to 53 million tons in 1955, and the approximate value of this oil has risen from £110 million to £200 million in 1955. Across the Gulf in Iran, another impressive story of expansion has unfolded. Over the past twelve months, the quantity of crude oil produced for export has risen from 3 million tons to 15 million tons, and its total value from £15 million to £75 million. That in twelve months.

But, of course, oil is not the whole of the story. We have granted a £10 million credit to Iran, and with the opening up of trade relations which followed the oil agreement in 1954, trade between our two countries has expanded very considerably indeed. In Iraq, oil production has increased over the last four years from 7 million tons to 33 million tons, and its total value from £35 million to £168 million. We are taking a large share in the development programme of that country, which will help to raise the standard of living and bring prosperity to Iraq and Britain alike.

I think it well to portray this encouraging side of the picture, and the House will see from what I have said that not all the Middle Eastern scene is dark and gloomy and full of frustrated endeavour. It will also, not, however, have escaped the attention of the House that all those thriving and rapidly de-veloping States of which I have spoken are allied to Britain by close ties of one form or another.

MR. E. SHINWELL (Easington): That is what you said about Jordan.

MR. NUTTING: I must now turn to the more difficult part of the area—the Arab-Israeli scene. Anybody standing in my place today would dearly like to have some encouraging news to give to Parliament about this, but I must frankly admit that, while our efforts continue to try to bring about an Arab-Israel settlement—and my right hon. and learned Friend the Foreign Secretary is in particular engaged in this search during his Middle Eastern tour—there is, alas, no progress that I can record.

The Government are often urged by the Opposition to bring about peace between Jew and Arab, but whether it be a final peace settlement or whether it be just the maintenance of an uneasy peace on the existing borders, the House must realise that this is not a job which we can carry out alone. We are only one of the three Powers that signed the Tripartite Declaration, and we are only one of the United Nations on whom responsibility falls for keeping the peace. We have fulfilled, and we will continue to fulfil, our obligation under the Tripartite Declaration. We are consulting with the Secretary-General of the United Nations about whether the machinery for truce supervision can be improved and, if necessary, expanded.

We have repeatedly said that we will support General Burns in any expansion of the Truce Supervisory Organisation that he considers necessary. My right hon. Friend, the House will recall, speaking in the debate on 24th January, threw out the idea of some additional measures to increase the preventive effect of the existing United Nations machinery. These ideas, too, are being examined by the Secretary-General in consultation with General Burns.

We are sometimes told that the Tripartite Declaration is not enough and that we must give a treaty guarantee to Israel within her present borders. That proposition has come many times from the benches opposite. But I often wonder whether hon. Gentlemen, when they suggest this, have fully thought out the implications of such a step. It would be committing this country to the permanent recognition of a frontier which is not agreed—[HON. MEMBERS: "No."]—a frontier which results from an armistice and not from a peace treaty, a frontier which is bitterly opposed by all the Arab States.

MR. ANTHONY GREENWOOD (Rossendale): Jordan's frontier.

MR. NUTTING: Jordan's frontier, precisely. The existing armistice—

MR. ALFRED ROBENS (Blyth): Absolute nonsense—the right hon. Gentleman needs a better brief.

MR. NUTTING: The right hon. Gentleman might perhaps keep his more abusive comments for his own speech, which I understand is to follow. I shall, of course, listen to the right hon. Gentleman with the greatest courtesy and attention. I hope that he will extend to me the same courtesy. We are being asked by the Opposition to guarantee a frontier which is bitterly opposed by all the Arab States.

MR. R. H. S. CROSSMAN (Coventry, East): Do I understand that the right hon. Gentleman is telling us that an alliance with Israel would mean guaranteeing her frontiers?

MR. NUTTING *indicated assent.*

MR. CROSSMAN: But we have made an alliance with Western Germany in which we are not committed to treat the present partition line as her frontier. I cannot understand why the right hon. Gentleman should say that we cannot ally ourselves with Israel without committing ourselves to the armistice line as a final frontier.

MR. NUTTING: I say that the Government cannot be expected to follow a course and to give a guarantee which would amount, in effect, to recognition in perpetuity to the existing armistice line. [HON. MEMBERS: "Why?"] In our opinion it would, in effect, be the biggest step we could take away from a peace settlement. It is one thing to say—and here I come to deal more fully with the point raised by the hon. Member for Coventry, East (Mr. Crossman)—that we would oppose the alteration of a truce line by force, because that would mean a fresh outbreak of war. It is quite another to say that we would recognise in perpetuity and undertake to maintain a frontier about which the parties are in violent disagreement—

MR. R. T. PAGET (Northampton) *rose*—

MR. NUTTING: Perhaps the hon. and learned Gentleman will let me finish. We have said, and I repeat, that we have always been ready to guarantee an agreed settlement and the United States have taken exactly the same line. If the Opposition say they are not asking for recognition in perpetuity of the existing armistice line but want a guarantee of this existing armistice line, that is precisely what the Tripartite Declaration lays down, and that is precisely the obligation to which we are committed and which we have declared repeatedly we shall fulfil.

MR. PAGET: What we on this side are wondering is this. Our Jordan Treaty guarantees this very line from one side—why should we not also guarantee it from the other.

MR. SYDNEY SILVERMAN (Nelson and Colne): What is the trouble?

MR. NUTTING: The existing armistice lines are guaranteed by the Tripartite Declaration. The hon. Gentleman asked what is the trouble, and I ask him what is the trouble, because I am being continually asked to give further guarantees.

MR. SILVERMAN *rose*—

MR. SHINWELL: The right hon. Gentleman will forgive me, but I think that he is missing the point. There may be some confusion—I admit to being confused myself because of what he said. Earlier he said that we have the 1948 Treaty with Jordan, and that that Treaty provided, among other things, for protection for Jordan in the event of aggression. I am within the recollection of the House. Surely a similar treaty with Israel, affording Israel protection in the event of aggression, would not be going any further than do the provisions of the Treaty with Jordan.

MR. NUTTING: The existing armistice lines, the existing boundaries—whatever the right hon. Gentleman likes to call them—are guaranteed, are upheld by the Tripartite Declaration, and we are bound to take action, both within and without the United Nations in fulfillment of the obligations under that Declaration. I cannot see what guarantee of the existing situation could be firmer.

MR. HERBERT MORRISON (Lewisham, South): What I cannot follow is this. If the Tripartite Declaration so to speak protects these frontiers, or whatever we may like to call them—including the frontier of Jordan, as I presume it does—why did we need the special Treaty with Jordan to supplement that guarantee? [HON. MEMBERS: "You did it."] I know we did it—I quite agree. Nevertheless the right hon. Gentleman is defending the position as it is, and if it be the case that it is right to have a separate Treaty and a specific guarantee in the case of Jordan, how can it be wrong to have a separate treaty and a specific guarantee in the case of Israel?

MR. NUTTING: The right hon. Gentleman has asked me why we concluded the Anglo-Jordan Treaty in 1948—[HON. MEMBERS: "No."]—And why we did not conclude a treaty with Israel. He was in power in those days and not us. [HON. MEMBERS: "Answer the question."] If hon. Gentlemen opposite would give me half a chance I would try to answer.

MR. JAMES CALLAGHAN (Cardiff, South-East): Yes, answer the question and let us get on with it.

MR. NUTTING: In any case, Mr. Speaker, I think that the right hon. Gentleman has his history a little wrong. The Anglo-Jordan Treaty was made in 1948—the Tripartite Declaration in 1950. But why is it suggested that the Tripartite Declaration is such an ineffective affair? I do not pretend that it pleases everyone, but the fact is that this Declaration—and the declared intention of its signatories to carry it out—has prevented the further outbreak of war between Jew and Arab. That is, after all, what the Tripartite Declaration was intended to do, and in that it has succeeded for the last six years. That is why the right hon. Gentleman's Government made it and why we uphold and fulfil it today.

During the Washington visit my right hon. Friends the Prime Minister and the Foreign Secretary discussed the Middle East at considerable length with the President and Mr. Dulles. They agreed that there was now increased danger in the Palestine situation and, accordingly, made arrangements for immediate consultations between the Tripartite Powers on the nature of the action which we should take in the event of the use or threat of force to violate the present boundaries. These consultations are now taking place in Washington.

I should not leave the Arab-Israel question without saying a word about arms deliveries. Our policy on this has been frequently stated in the House, and I can assure the House that, despite all the difficulties which have confronted the Tripartite Powers in keeping a check on deliveries, a balance of strength has been maintained up to date. We have never sought to deny that the recent Communist arms deal with Egypt may in due course upset this balance.

But we do not believe that that situation has yet arrived and in any case, we and our allies are convinced that the safety and security of Israel does not lie in entering upon an arms race in the Middle East. This might well end up with Israel being surrounded by hostile neighbours, all of them armed to the teeth. The safety and security of Israel must be found in establishing normal relations with her neighbours. That is one of several reasons why we consider a settlement so imperative and why we shall continue to concentrate on that and refrain from doing anything liable to jeopardise or endanger the peace.

I hope the House will accept from this account of what is being done that we and our American Allies are taking every step that is open to us to strengthen the inevitably uneasy peace which exists between Israel and her Arab neighbours. It would be idle to pretend that the events of the last few days may not have their effect upon our ability to discharge our manifold obligations, but I hope it will not go out from this House today that Her Majesty's Government have neither policy nor position in the Middle East. That would be a completely false picture. Our policy is based on the Bagdad Pact and the Tripartite Declaration. The first, apart from its economic values, is an effective shield against aggression from without. The second has proved an effective guardian of the peace within.

We stand by our obligations. We offer genuine help, friendship and cooperation to all nations in that area. Wherever and whenever necessary, we shall strengthen and fortify our vital interests and build up those who are our true friends. Whatever the setbacks and whatever the disruptive forces which may be ranged against us, we shall continue with a policy of building on strength, confident that this will bring eventual stability and peace to the whole of the Middle East.

Speech by the Leader of the Labour Party, Hugh Gaitskell, in the House of Commons Criticizing the Government's Middle Eastern Policies, 7 March 1956*

I am surprised and disappointed that the Prime Minister did not decide to open the debate himself. It seems to me that if he had something new to tell us it should have been told to us at the beginning of the debate. If, on the other hand, he has nothing new to say, all I can say is that many hon. Members on all sides of the House will be extremely disappointed that in this very difficult and dangerous situation Her Majesty's Government have still not decided what action they shall take.

*Hansard, 5.s., DXLIX, 2121–36.

In the circumstances, the Prime Minister gave the Minister of State an almost impossible task. Of the right hon. Gentleman's speech, I think it might be said that it made up in emphasis what it lacked in substance. The only point of importance that he mentioned was the possibility of a pact with Israel, and on that, and on his remarks alongside it regarding the Tripartite Declaration, I can only say that he left most of us confused and failing to understand the logic of his argument. Perhaps I might pursue this matter a little further now.

The right hon. Gentleman said that we could not have a pact or alliance with Israel because it would imply that we were permanently guaranteeing the existing frontiers. Of course, as he has said—I am glad that he said it again—we are in fact guaranteeing the existing armistice lines against aggression from either side. That, I think, is not in dispute. Furthermore, we have at the moment with Jordan an alliance which binds us to go to her help if she is attacked—if she is attacked across those armistice lines. My right hon. and hon. Friends have asked, very pertinently, why, if we have an alliance with Jordan which binds us to go to her assistance in the event of aggression against the existing frontiers, should we not equally have an alliance with Israel. To that the right hon. Gentleman gave, I am afraid, no satisfactory answer whatever.

I will return a little later on to the question of Arab-Israel relations. There are many other things about the Middle Eastern situation to which I should also like to refer in my speech.

I was glad that the Minister of State paid a tribute to General Glubb. Although the debate takes place as a result of his dismissal by the King of Jordan, I should like to say that in any remarks that we may make about the Government's policy we certainly do not wish in any sense to belittle his achievements. I had the pleasure of meeting him three years ago, and I was impressed by his moderation, wisdom and calmness. It certainly is no fault of his that he has found himself in this situation.

One of the features of this situation which is rather remarkable is the degree of unanimity in the British Press about the significance and probable consequences of General Glubb's dismissal. Almost every newspaper has drawn attention to three consequences. First, it is agreed, I believe, that it increases the danger of war between the Arab States and Israel either because a planned operation against Israel may be more likely now or that frontier incidents will be less under control. The reason why there has been such general agreement on this is that we know—I would certainly bear this out—that General Glubb and his fellow officers have exercised a restraining influence upon the Arab Legion and upon the policy of Jordan. I can vouch for that because the Foreign Secretary of Israel himself told me that three years ago.

Secondly, I do not think it is in dispute that for the past 18 months or so the Arab Legion has been actively engaged—very properly engaged—in trying to prevent infiltration and aggression from the Jordan side of the frontier, and has attempted, I think with some success, to exercise control over the Jordan National Guard.

The third reason why I think we must recognise that it increases the danger of war between Jordan and the Arab States, on the one side, and Israel, on the other, is that it is evident from what has been said in Jordan that this was indeed one of the most important reasons for the public demand for the removal of General Glubb. I notice that since then a certain event has taken place. It was reported in *The Times* of 6th March that:

> Members of the permanent bureau of Palestine refugees . . . were received in audience by King Hussein and asked him to conscribe in the Arab Legion all capable young men among the 900,000 refugees in Jordan to fight for the restoration of Palestine under his Majesty's banner and the banners of the newly reformed Arab Legion. The King promised to grant them their wish.

In those circumstances, we must also agree that the prospect of a settlement between the Arab States and Israel, which in our opinion was always extremely remote, is now even gloomier and less probable.

We must further recognise that if the Arab Legion was, as I would hold that it was, a restraining influence under General Glubb's command, the change in the situation must surely affect our whole attitude to the subsidy which maintains that Legion. There is now a very real danger if the subsidy continues that we shall find ourselves subsidising the maintenance of a force which might well go into action against Israel in circumstances in which we have to go to the defence and assistance of Israel. That is plainly a highly contradictory position.

The fact of the matter is that, although in effect we spoke as though the Arab Legion was part of our defence against the danger of attack from the north-east, nevertheless I do not think anybody who knew the Legion—I had the pleasure of meeting some of its officers and seeing their encampments and so on—could possibly say that it was particularly interested in any possible aggression from the north-east. The Arab officers have always looked to the west against Israel, and now, without the restraint of British officers, that must be enormously aggravated.

The second consequence is that there has been a severe blow to our prestige in the Middle East, and, indeed, to the prestige of the whole of the Western Alliance. I do not say that prestige is necessarily important for its own sake, but there is no denying that it can be a very powerful ally to a policy. What one means when one says that the prestige of Britain and her Allies is lowered by this event is that a number of our enemies—or those who profess to call themselves our enemies—are heartened by it and our friends are discouraged. In that part of the world, as indeed in others, we cannot ignore the tendency which exists in many countries to go to the side which they think is going to win. If they think Britain is going to lose there will be many people who will be quick to get out of the British camp. That is the particular danger which follows the loss of prestige.

The third consequence of these events in Jordan, to which I am surprised the Minister of State made no reference, is a very serious setback to the policy of the Bagdad Pact. The Bagdad Pact, about which I will say more in a moment, has undoubtedly become a big bone of contention in the Middle East. It has been opposed and attacked by Egypt, Saudi-Arabia and Syria. There is no doubt that a consequence of the dismissal of General Glubb is to make it extremely probable—to put it no higher—that Jordan will now go into the anti-Bagdad Pact camp and line up with Egypt and Saudi-Arabia. Since the Government have rightly declared that they base their policy, firstly on the hope of an Arab-Israel settlement and, secondly, on the Bagdad Pact, it is undeniable, as I said the other day, that these events must be regarded as constituting a major setback to our policy—I mean the policy of Her Majesty's Government. Indeed, I think those words, if anything were an understatement.

It accordingly becomes clear, surely, that we must have a reassessment of our whole policy in the Middle East. That I take to be the real purpose of this debate. Before considering exactly what we should do, I think it is as well to ask the question, why has this happened? Was it something which was fortuitous and could not have been anticipated or expected? We would say no. We would say that in our view the events which have taken place, whilst partly inherent in the situation, were nevertheless also the direct result of the policy of Her Majesty's Government in that part of the world.

Why do I say they were partly inherent in the existing situation? It is for this reason. I think one must admit that the peculiar arrangement under which the Arab Legion was led by British officers, financed by Great Britain and wholly under British control—the subsidies being paid not to the Jordan Treasury but to the Arab Legion office—could certainly not continue very much longer. I would add that a situation in which the whole of the Jordan people in consequence regarded General Glubb virtually as the dictator of the country was also something which was wholly inconsistent with the rise of Arab nationalism and the resentment in those countries against foreign domination, direct or indirect.

The fact is that the situation has now so changed in that part of the world that I do not think any of the Arab peoples are going any longer to tolerate a semi-colonial status. One must add in this case that the position was profoundly affected in Jordan itself when the rest of Palestine was transferred to Jordan and, in consequence, the population was more than doubled—doubled by an influx of refugees who are bitterly hostile to Israel and, rightly or wrongly, also hostile to Great Britain. But I do say that the termination of the arrangement—had the position been understood—could have been carried out very differently and without the loss of prestige which has occurred.

As to the policy of Her Majesty's Government, I do not say that there was any single event which one could pick out as the sole cause which led to this pretty disastrous situation, but I think there were a number of things which led to it. In particular, I am bound to say—contrary to what the Minister of State said—that I think the Bagdad Pact, in a way which I shall explain, has itself contributed very materially to this development.

The doctrine of the Northern Tier Alliance, if it were a voluntary agreement between Turkey, Iraq, Pakistan and Persia, is not one which I would oppose in principle. It is a defensive agreement, and we have defensive agreements in the West. Perhaps this will explain the misunderstanding which was evident in the mind of the right hon. Gentleman when he criticised my right hon. Friend. It is not the Northern Tier Agreement as such which we think has done harm. What we do think has done harm has been the attempt by Her Majesty's Government to convert this into a whole Middle Eastern policy.

I need not quote from the Prime Minister or the Minister of State, because they have repeatedly said that this should be the foundation of Middle Eastern defence as a whole. The Minister of State repeated this afternoon that the economic aspects of the Bagdad Pact are enormously important. They will not deny that they have made this the whole pivot of their policy. Why has that been dangerous? It has been dangerous because by so doing they have, first, provoked violent opposition from other Arab States, from the States which we can describe in this situation as being neutral or neutralist.

Secondly, it equally provoked very violent opposition from Jordan itself when an attempt was made—I will come to that in detail in a moment—to force her into the Pact. I think it was disastrous to pursue that policy of trying, as it were, to bring every Arab State in, particularly because that was done without the United States being a member of the Pact. As far as our relations with Saudi Arabia are concerned, that was an obvious gap in the whole policy.

Whatever the Prime Minister may say about what the Egyptians ought to think about this, the fact is that they have opposed the Bagdad Pact from the start, because they regarded it as an attempt to maintain Britain's power in the whole Arab world, which they resented, and because they regarded it as an attempt to do this through the influence and power of Iraq, the chief rival to Egypt in the Arab League. Saudi Arabia, of course, has been opposed to the Pact as well, and, as I have tried to imply, has been free to make as much trouble as she liked; and she has made a good deal of trouble with the dollars which she earns from selling oil to America.

Finally, the attempt to force Jordan in was doomed to failure. We have never had from the Government the full story of General Templer's visit and I hope that this evening, even if we are to have no new policy, some confusions and obscurities about the past may be cleared up by the Prime Minister. I should like to ask whether it is true, as my hon. Friend the Member for Coventry, East (Mr. Crossman) alleged in the last Middle East debate and as has been stated in the Press, that General Templer went out there with instructions to offer a very substantial increase in the Arab Legion without any guarantee that it would be under British control, in return for Jordan joining the Bagdad Pact.

What was, in fact, offered? What conditions, if any, were laid down? Who decided to send General Templer, the Chief of the Imperial General Staff and the highest ranking officer in the Army, to Jordan in circumstances which, if they had wanted to negotiate, were such that one would have supposed it wiser to send a less prominent personality? What was the Foreign Office advice on the probability or possibility that the Jordan Government would accept any such offer? All I can say is that whoever was advising the Government on this matter was advising extraordinarily badly.

I dare say that hon. Members will recall the questions which were put to the Joint Under-Secretary of State for Foreign Affairs on 21st December. After the Joint Under-Secretary's statement, my right hon. Friend the Member for Blyth (Mr. Robens) said:

> Does not this show the whole bankruptcy of the Middle East policy of the Government? Does it not show that the optimistic references made in the Middle East debate in this House only a few days ago were wide of the mark? Is it really the case that the Bagdad Pact and the arrangements by General Templar to get Jordan to accept the Bagdad Pact have gone so badly and the preparatory work done so wrongly, that instead of having a country that will support the Bagdad Pact we shall have a situation in which we are trying to thrust the Bagdad Pact down the throats of the Jordan people. . . .

I think those were very pertinent questions, but the Joint Under-Secretary of State blustered and objected that this was all very unfair and, indeed, reckless and irresponsible. All I can say is that his own closing remark in that passage was perhaps a classic. He said: ". . . what is now happening in Jordan will pass over."—[OFFICIAL REPORT, 21st December, 1955; Vol. 547, cc. 2038-40.]

If this ill-judged, ill-informed and badly carried out attempt to continue what was in essence a paternalistic policy, without the force and drive of unity with America to carry it through, has been one aspect of the Government's policy, then the other has been appeasement of Arab opinion over the Israel question.

I do not wish to go over the whole ground of the last debate, but I must briefly remined the House of our point of view. We take the view that the Prime Minister's Guildhall speech, with its implication of substantial concessions by Israel and its encouragement, accordingly, of Arab hopes, was a grave error. We say, secondly, that the announcement of the then Foreign Secretary when he was in Bagdad that "Britain was not going to try to outbid the Russians in providing arms for Egypt nor would she try to balance deliveries by increasing the supply of arms to Israel"—set alongside the Prime Minister's statement the following day,—"the right hon. Gentleman is perfectly right in saying that we should try to maintain a balance of arms",—was a contradiction giving the impressions of utter confusion to the world as a whole.

I say, thirdly, that the reliance on the arms race argument is one which we cannot accept, and it is one which frankly I regard as quite unworthy of the present Government. I will tell the right hon. Gentleman why. Nobody wants an arms race if it can be prevented by a general agreement to limit arms. That is what we are endeavouring to bring about; all of us would like to see it done internationally.

If the Government had come along and said, "Now that the Russians are supplying arms to Egypt we will try to get a general agreement to limit arms everywhere in that part of the world," it would have been logical; but merely to say that we will deprive one side of the opportunity of purchasing arms when the other side is free to go on getting as much as it likes and to defend that on the ground that we do not want to participate in an arms race reminds me of nothing else but the nonintervention agreement in Spain.

The real reason of course—and I do not know why the Government do not say so—for which they have refused to allow Israel to purchase so far even the quantities of arms necessary for her defence is fear of Arab resentment. That is the real reason and I venture to say that that kind of weakness makes no impression upon the Arab peoples.

Either we stand by the Tripartite Agreement—and in that case we are bound to allow Israel enough arms for self-defence, for that is laid down in the Agreement—or we do not. If we intend to stand by it, we must make our position abundantly plain to the Arab States and give up this policy of trying to appease them by our policy towards Israel.

In the last debate I put forward some suggestions as to what might be done. I will only mention them briefly, because there are other aspects to the debate. We believe that the Tripartite Agreement must be upheld, and I was very glad to hear the right hon. Gentleman today specifically mention it. I must say that on the last three or four occasions we have had to drag out of the Government a declaration of that kind. [HON. MEMBERS: "No."] It is all in the columns of HANSARD, and hon. Members know that it is true.

Secondly, we say that if we intend to carry out the Tripartite Agreement we must allow Israel the arms to balance those received by Egypt from Czechoslovakia. Today the right hon. Gentleman says he is not quite sure and that perhaps it might upset the balance. The Foreign Secretary has gone much further than that; he said that it will upset the balance and that there is no doubt about it. If we are to be told that it has not yet upset the balance, it makes us wonder when the right hon. Gentleman thinks it will upset the balance. How many more MiG. fighters have to be delivered to Egypt? Have we to wait for another year or two until Egypt has built up an overwhelming force before we try to maintain the balance?

The third point which we repeat is, as my right hon. Friend the Member for Blyth stressed in his speech on the last occasion, that we believe that a more effective frontier force of some kind could be used, and we still hold fast absolutely by our proposals for long-term settlement, including the settling of the refugees, including compensation, including frontier adjustments, including the ending of the economic boycott.

Finally, we repeat that we do not think this problem of the Middle East as a whole can be solved without bringing the Russians into it in some way. After all, this is already a United Nations affair and Russia is a member of the Security Council.

The last chance, it seems to me, of retrieving the situation occurred in the talks at Washington just after the debate to which I have referred. At that stage, positive plans could and should have been made following the talks with General Eisenhower and Mr. Dulles. But, in fact, nothing whatever has emerged from the Washington talks. There is no agreement on the very difficult, but very vital issue of the conflicting, and, indeed, fierce opposition between the British and American oil companies in Saudi Arabia and the Protectorates.

Secondly, not a word has come from the Prime Minister or anyone else about the balance of arms and what is to be done about it. Presumably, after the extraordinary contradictions to which I have referred, the right hon. Gentleman came to the conclusion that the least said about the subject the better.

Thirdly, as to the Tripartite Declaration, all that we are told is that consultations are going on. There has been a need for consultations ever since the announcement of the Czechoslovak arms deal last September. In a clever reply, the Foreign Secretary was able to tell us that, of course, there was an immediate meeting of the Tripartite Powers. It is not enough to have meetings and consultations unless some decisions are taken, and we are still waiting for them. I should have thought that when the Prime Minister referred to the necessity of consulting our Allies about events in Jordan, he might perhaps have pointed out, or reminded us, that these consultations were already taking place in Washington. I should have thought that by now at least we could have heard something of the outcome.

The fact is that the policy which led up to the present situation has, in our view, been ill-informed, ill-prepared and has managed, rather remarkably, to be both weak and yet provocative at the same time. It has landed us in discredit and danger.

I now turn, as we must, to future policy. I should like to begin with some fairly general observations. There are some hon. Members opposite, I know, who, exasperated by what they regard as a series of retreats in the Middle East, wish to reimpose our will on that part of the world by force over the whole area. They are those who particularly regret our evacuation from Abadan and Suez and who are most insistent that we should in no circumstances give up Cyprus. I understand their feelings. But emotion in this matter is not a very good guide.

I must say to them that although we ourselves are profoundly worried about the Middle Eastern situation, we cannot go their way for three reasons. First, because that kind of policy is not one for which we at present, even if we wanted to pursue it, have adequate forces. Certainly we have not without the U.S.A. and there is no hope, in my view, that the U.S.A. will join with us in a policy of this kind. Secondly, I think that this policy fails to recognise the tremendous force of nationalism and indeed anti-Westernism which is thrown up and has grown up in the Middle East and which, let us beware of it, will be driven directly into Communism, as it has been, for instance, in Indo-China, if we persist in trying to apply semi-colonial policies in that part of the world.

MR. JULIAN AMERY (Preston, North): How does the right hon. Gentleman think that the obligation under the Tripartite Agreement on which he very rightly, in my view, puts general emphasis can be carried out if we are not in a position of strength in Cyprus and elsewhere?

MR. GAITSKELL: It has always been our view and, so far as I know, the view of the Government that it was perfectly possible to meet the demands of the Cypriots for self-determination while retaining military bases in Cyprus. I should be very surprised indeed if the Colonial Secretary were to tell the House that he had been negotiating with Archbishop Makarios on any other basis.

The third reason why we cannot accept the views of the hon. Member for Preston, North (Mr. J. Amery) and others is that we feel that those views inevitably involve us in a conflict with international law and the United Nations. The plain fact of the matter is—and I am taking the case of Abadan now—that if we had put troops in Persia to maintain our hold in Abadan we should have been arraigned as aggressors before the United Nations. Of course, as my right hon. Friend the Member for Lewisham, South (Mr. H. Morrison) rightly pointed out the other day, the Government continued the policy, which we were driven to for that reason—if we like to put it that way—of waiting for an eventual agreement with Persia which we are all glad was reached without actually taking military action against her. That is why, as I say, we cannot accept the view of the hon. Gentleman and his hon. Friends.

In deciding policy, I suggest that we must first of all settle exactly what is our real interest in the Middle East and what our commitments are there. I would say that there were three things in particular which must be accepted as commitments or interests of an overriding character. The first is our commitment under the Tripartite Declaration which, I repeat in case there is any misunderstanding, is a declaration to go to the help of whichever side is attacked. It is an undertaking to guarantee those temporary armistice frontiers. Also, too, it carries with it the essential condition that we maintain the balance of arms to the two sides.

Reference has already been made to the possibility of an alliance with Israel, and I must say that we do not see that there is anything inconsistent with that and the Tripartite Declaration. I think that this is something to which the Government should give serious consideration in the light of the latest development. I will not pursue it further.

Our second interest—and it is an interest—is, of course, the supply of oil. It is no use denying the fact that we are very completely dependent on oil in that part of the world. This is a "must" so far as we are concerned. We cannot survive without it. But what precisely is the danger here? We get nearly 50 per cent. of our oil from Kuwait, some from Persia and some from Iraq. Oil is in these three territories and in Saudi Arabia. I think that we make a mistake if we jump to the conclusion that the Arab States with these oil reserves will be so desperately anxious to sell them to anyone else. The whole of their apparatus, their pipelines, refineries and everything else, are directed to selling to the existing Western countries.

I do not believe that, short of a big political change in that part of the world, the danger that we should be cut off from oil is nearly so great. That is why, when the hon. Gentleman talks as if we have to maintain military power in that part of the world to a greater extent than we do at the moment in order to safeguard the oil, I am afraid I cannot accept that conclusion.

MR. AMERY: I am glad that the right hon. Gentleman has given me an opportunity of disagreeing, because the earlier part of what he said was so good. Is it not the case that if we had not had physical force in the region of Buraimi we should have had to pay dollars for any oil that was extracted?

MR. GAITSKELL: Of course, if we have no Anglo-American understanding about the oil in that part of the world, that may be so. I go further and concede this to the hon. Gentleman. We are talking now about the sheikdoms of the Persian Gulf. I would say that the Government, in view of the situation that exists, had better look pretty hard to the position at Kuwait where we get nearly 50 per cent. of our oil.

The third objective, which I think we must all accept, is that we cannot accept that these territories with their oil reserves, which are very important to us, should come under Russian control. I say that quite emphatically. This is a vital interest of ours. I do not believe, however, that the Arab Governments are in the least anxious to allow the Communists to come in and control their territories. For these reasons—the three which I have given—we certainly cannot clear out and wash our hands of the whole area. It is far too important for us, and we could not trust Russia to keep out of it if we disappeared. I concede that. But I would say to hon. Members opposite that, first of all, it would probably be agreed that the United States should have, and has, exactly the same three objectives that we have, and therefore it should not be difficult to reach agreement with her on Middle Eastern policy.

Secondly, and in a sense this is repeating what I said in answer to the hon. Member for Preston, North, I do not believe that to achieve these objectives we have to have military forces disposed everywhere and have to continue semi-colonial policies everywhere. The plain fact is that the attempt to do this is a handicap today. Finally, it is not necessary in order to achieve these objectives— precisely because we are in a stronger position than is sometimes suggested—to take sides or to intervene in the rivalries between the different Arab States. We would do best, while standing firm on the question of Israel, to concentrate as far as the rest of the Middle East is concerned, on economic aid rather than on military force.

I come to the question which follows these basic considerations. What should our immediate policy be? Should we, for instance, reinforce our troops in Jordan? I take the view that we should do that only if it is necessary to protect British lives. I strongly urge the Government not to attempt by military force to impose a policy on Jordan. If the Jordan Government wish to break their alliance with us and to link up with Egypt and the neutralist *bloc,* they should be allowed to do so.

Secondly, we must have—and I hope that they have already begun— immediate talks with Jordan about the position under the Treaty. It would be unwise to repudiate the Treaty. It has not been broken technically by the dismissal of General Glubb, but it would be impossible to continue with the subsidy in the new situation. It may be that the money—and it is quite a substantial sum—could instead be made available for economic development and the settlement of Arab refugees as part of the general settlement.

MR. F. A. BURDEN (Gillingham) *rose*—

MR. GAITSKELL: I am sorry, but I do not want to go on for too long.

A third essential, surely, is to settle the ridiculous and absurd dispute between the British and American oil companies. It is really so ridiculous, because we all know that they are interlocked. Therefore, the way in which they are playing against each other in that part of the world is quite absurd. In fact, I should like to see a wider plan emerge from discussions between the companies under which both the Arab Governments concerned and the oil companies would subscribe to a large fund for the economic development of the whole area, and not only the oil-bearing territory.

Fourthly, the ban on arms for Israel must now be lifted. The situation is really far too dangerous as the new development has occurred in Jordan. It does not mean any spectacular sale of arms, but it means, at any rate, that Israel should be allowed to buy the necessary weapons in terms of quality with which she can match, if need be, the new arms which Egypt is now obtaining. In plain fact, it means Centurion tanks, which she was never given although Egypt has had them from us, and also modern fighters.

Fifthly, there is a lot to be said for Britain and America making a declaration of Middle Eastern policy on the lines which I have tried to indicate saying what our attitude is. We must be quite firm about Israel. Apart from that, we should say that we have no wish whatever to stifle or restrain Arab Nationalist sentiment, and are only too anxious to help the economic development of the area. We must not just make that declaration. We must do a great deal more about our propaganda, including our radio propaganda in that part of the world. I do not see why the station in Cyprus is not used for that purpose. I should have thought it quite effective. When Marshal Bulganin and Mr. Khrushchev come here in April, I hope that the Government will take the opportunity of talking about the Middle Eastern situation with them.

Before the Prime Minister went to Washington, I warned him that we were genuinely critical of the Government's Middle Eastern policy and that we could not support him in this if that policy continued. We hoped that Washington would produce a change. It has not done so. There has been nothing—just inaction. What has happened in Jordan confirms our view that the Government's policies were wrong and dangerous, and for this reason I have not hesitated to criticise the Government today.

I recognise that it is the duty of the Opposition to be constructive. I may not have carried all with me, but I have tried to show what can be done and I ask the Prime Minister to take these proposals seriously. Looking at the state of the world, and in particular the condition of the Western alliance, one cannot today but feel anxious and gloomy. There are signs of division and separation and public arguments and a general loss of that unity which existed when N.A.T.O. was first created.

It is never easy for democracies to work together with the same unity as totalitarian régimes, but that is a reason for trying very hard to achieve unity. There is a desperate need at the moment for a lead which will both rally the democratic forces and restore unity and yet at the same time give the reassurance which we must give to the uncommitted countries that our policies are progressive and peaceful. I hope that the Government will give that lead or else make way for one that can and will.

Message from the Prime Minister, Sir Anthony Eden, to President Dwight Eisenhower on the Suez Crisis, 6 September 1956*

Thank you for your message and writing thus frankly.

There is no doubt as to where we are agreed and have been agreed from the very beginning, namely that we should do everything we can to get a peaceful settlement. It is in this spirit that we favoured calling the twenty-two-power conference and that we have worked in the closest co-operation with you about this business since. There has never been any question of our suddenly or without further provocation resorting to arms, while these processes were at work. In any event, as your own wide knowledge would confirm, we could not have done this without extensive preparation lasting several weeks.

This question of precautions has troubled me considerably and still does. I have not forgotten the riots and murders in Cairo in 1952, for I was in charge here at the time when Winston was on the high seas on his way back from the United States.

We are both agreed that we must give the Suez committee every chance to fulfil their mission. This is our firm resolve. If the committee and subsequent negotiations succeed in getting Nasser's agreement to the London proposals of the eighteen powers, there will be no call for force. But if the committee fails, we must have some immediate alternative which will show that Nasser is not going to get his way. In this connection we are attracted by Foster's suggestion, if I understand it rightly, for the running of the canal by the users in virtue of their rights under the 1888 Convention. We heard about this from our Embassy in Washington yesterday. I think that we could go along with this, provided that the intention was made clear by both of us immediately the Menzies mission finishes its work. But unless we can proceed with this, or something very like it, what should the next step be?

You suggest that this is where we diverge. If that is so I think that the divergence springs from a difference in our assessment of Nasser's plans and intentions. May I set out our view of the position.

In the nineteen-thirties Hitler established his position by a series of carefully

*Eden, *Full Circle*, 518–21.

planned movements. These began with occupation of the Rhineland and were followed by successive acts cf aggression against Austria, Czechoslovakia, Poland and the West. His actions were tolerated and excused by the majority of the population of Western Europe. It was argued either that Hitler had committed no act of aggression against anyone, or that he was entitled to do what he liked in his own territory, or that it was impossible to prove that he had any ulterior designs, or that the Covenant of the League of Nations did not entitle us to use force and that it would be wiser to wait until he did commit an act of aggression.

In more recent years Russia has attempted similar tactics. The blockade of Berlin was to have been the opening move in a campaign designed at least to deprive the Western powers of their whole position in Germany. On this occasion we fortunately reacted at once with the result that the Russian design was never unfolded. But I am sure that you would agree that it would be wrong to infer from this circumstance that no Russian design existed.

Similarly the seizure of the Suez Canal is, we are convinced, the opening gambit in a planned campaign designed by Nasser to expel all Western influence and interests from Arab countries. He believes that if he can get away with this, and if he can successfully defy eighteen nations, his prestige in Arabia will be so great that he will be able to mount revolutions of young officers in Saudi Arabia, Jordan, Syria and Iraq. (We know that he is already preparing a revolution in Iraq, which is most stable and progressive.) These new Governments will in effect be Egyptian satellites if not Russian ones. They will have to place their united oil resources under the control of a united Arabia led by Egypt and under Russian influence. When that moment comes Nasser can deny oil to Western Europe and we here shall all be at his mercy.

There are some who doubt whether Saudi Arabia, Iraq and Kuwait will be prepared even for a time to sacrifice their oil revenues for the sake of Nasser's ambitions. But if we place ourselves in their position I think the dangers are clear. If Nasser says to them, "I have nationalized the Suez Canal. I have successfully defied eighteen powerful nations including the United States, I have defied the whole of the United Nations in the matter of the Israel blockade, I have expropriated all Western property. Trust me and withhold oil from Western Europe. Within six months or a year, the continent of Europe will be on its knees before you," will the Arabs not be prepared to follow this lead? Can we rely on them to be more sensible than were the Germans? Even if the Arabs eventually fall apart again as they did after the early Caliphs, the damage will have been done meanwhile.

In short we are convinced that if Nasser is allowed to defy the eighteen nations it will be a matter of months before revolution breaks out in the oil-bearing countries and the West is wholly deprived of Middle Eastern oil. In this belief we are fortified by the advice of friendly leaders in the Middle East.

The Iraqis are the most insistent in their warnings; both Nuri and the Crown Prince have spoken to us several times of the consequences of Nasser succeeding in his grab. They would be swept away.

[I then gave the President an account of three other warnings which we had received, each from a different Middle Eastern country; as the authors of these warnings are still alive, I do not propose to make their names public.]

The difference which separates us to-day [my message continued] appears to be a difference of assessment of Nasser's plans and intentions and of the consequences in the Middle East of military action against him.

You may feel that even if we are right it would be better to wait until Nasser has unmistakably unveiled his intentions. But this was the argument which prevailed in 1936 and which we both rejected in 1948. Admittedly there are risks in the use of force against Egypt now. It is, however, clear that military intervention designed to reverse Nasser's revolutions in the whole continent would be a much more costly and difficult undertaking. I am very troubled, as it is, that if we do not reach a conclusion either way about the canal very soon one or other of these Eastern lands may be toppled at any moment by Nasser's revolutionary movements.

I agree with you that prolonged military operations as well as the denial of Middle East oil would place an immense strain on the economy of Western Europe. I can assure you that we are conscious of the burdens and perils attending military intervention. But if our assessment is correct, and if the only alternative is to allow Nasser's plans quietly to develop until this country and all Western Europe are held to ransom by Egypt acting at Russia's behest it seems to us that our duty is plain. We have many times led Europe in the fight for freedom. It would be an ignoble end to our long history if we accepted to perish by degrees.

Statement by Sir Anthony Eden in the House of Commons on the
*Suez Crisis, 30 October 1956**

With your permission, Mr. Speaker, and that of the House, I will make a statement.

As the House will know, for some time past the tension on the frontiers of Israel has been increasing. The growing military strength of Egypt has given rise to renewed apprehension, which the statements and actions of the Egyptian Government have further aggravated. The establishment of a Joint Military Command between Egypt, Jordan and Syria, the renewed raids by guerillas, culminating in the incursion of Egyptian commandos on Sunday night, had all produced a very dangerous situation.

Five days ago news was received that the Israel Government were taking certain measures of mobilisation. Her Majesty's Government at once instructed

Hansard, 5.s., DLVIII, 1274-75.

Her Majesty's Ambassador at Tel Aviv to make inquiries of the Israel Minister for Foreign Affairs and to urge restraint.

Meanwhile, President Eisenhower called for an immediate tripartite discussion between representatives of the United Kingdom, France and the United States. A meeting was held on 28th October, in Washington, and a second meeting took place on 29th October.

While these discussions were proceeding, news was received last night that Israel forces had crossed the frontier and had penetrated deep into Egyptian territory. Later, further reports were received indicating that paratroops had been dropped. It appears that the Israel spearhead was not far from the banks of the Suez Canal. From recent reports it also appeared that air forces are in action in the neighbourhood of the Canal.

During the last few weeks Her Majesty's Government have thought it their duty, having regard to their obligations under the Anglo-Jordan Treaty, to give assurances, both public and private, of their intention to honour these obligations. Her Majesty's Ambassador in Tel Aviv late last night received an assurance that Israel would not attack Jordan.

My right hon. and learned Friend the Foreign Secretary discussed the situation with the United States Ambassador early this morning. The French Prime Minister and Foreign Minister have come over to London at short notice at the invitation of Her Majesty's Government to deliberate with us on these events.

I must tell the House that very grave issues are at stake, and that unless hostilities can quickly be stopped free passage through the Canal will be jeopardised. Moreover, any fighting on the banks of the Canal would endanger the ships actually on passage. The number of crews and passengers involved totals many hundreds, and the value of the ships which are likely to be on passage is about £50 million, excluding the value of the cargoes.

Her Majesty's Government and the French Government have accordingly agreed that everything possible should be done to bring hostilities to an end as soon as possible. Their representatives in New York have, therefore, been instructed to join the United States representative in seeking an immediate meeting of the Security Council. This began at 4 p.m.

In the meantime, as a result of the consultations held in London today, the United Kingdom and French Governments have now addressed urgent communications to the Governments of Egypt and Israel. In these we have called upon both sides to stop all warlike action by land, sea and air forthwith and to withdraw their military forces to a distance of 10 miles from the Canal. Further, in order to separate the belligerents and to guarantee freedom of transit through the Canal by the ships of all nations, we have asked the Egyptian Government to agree that Anglo-French forces should move temporarily—I repeat, temporarily—into key positions at Port Said, Ismailia and Suez.

The Governments of Egypt and Israel have been asked to answer this communication within 12 hours. It has been made clear to them that, if at the expiration of that time one or both have not undertaken to comply with these requirements, British and French forces will intervene in whatever strength may be necessary to secure compliance.

I will continue to keep the House informed of the situation.

Speech by the Foreign Secretary, Selwyn Lloyd, in the House of Commons in Defence of Britain's Military Intervention in Suez, 5 December 1956*

I beg to move,

> That this House supports the policy of Her Majesty's Government as outlined by the Foreign Secretary on 3rd December, which has prevented hostilities in the Middle East from spreading, has resulted in a United Nations Force being introduced into the area, and has created conditions under which progress can be made towards the peaceful settlement of outstanding issues.

I want to try to deal with certain matters which have been raised in the House about the past events and, first, with the questions which have been asked about the alleged collusion. I repeat the Answer which I gave to the House on 31st October:

> Every time any incident has happened on the frontiers of Israel and the Arab States we have been accused of being in collusion with the Israelis about it. That allegation has been broadcast from Radio Cairo every time. It is quite wrong to state that Israel was incited to this action by Her Majesty's Government. There was no prior agreement between us about it.—[OFFICIAL REPORT, 31st Oct., 1956; Vol. 558, c. 1573.]

HON. MEMBERS: Knowledge.

MR. LLOYD: It is true that we were well aware of the possibility of trouble. I would remind hon. Members of what had been happening during the months of September and October, because it is very frequently forgotten. I am not going to read out a list of every incident that took place on the Israel-Jordan frontier, but they had mounted in seriousness until, on 25th September, in an Israeli reprisal raid on Husan, about 39 Jordanians had been killed, and on 10th October, in an Israeli reprisal raid on a police post, 48 Jordanians had been killed. That last reprisal was the heaviest that had ever been mounted.

These are the two principal incidents. I have a long list with me of occasions from 10th September onwards, when, at one time, the Israelis were condemned by the Armistice Commission and, at other times, the Jordanians were condemned. There had been a steadily mounting state of tension on that frontier up to that last incident in which, as I have said, 48 Jordanians were killed. That, without doubt, had created a very serious situation.

Hansard, 5.s., DLXI, 1254–68.

There had been incidents in August on the Israeli-Egyptian frontier and then there had been a period of quiet, but Fedayeen raids began again in October. On 20th October a number of Israeli soldiers had been killed and on 24th and 28th October further raids had taken place.

Two other events occurred during the end of October. On 21st October a general election took place in Jordan, as a result of which a more extreme Parliament had been elected. By "more extreme" I mean one with greater hostility towards Israel. Then, on 24th October, that election had been followed by a move of considerable import for Israel, in the formation of the Syrian-Egyptian-Jordanian joint command under the Egyptian Commander-in-Chief.

It therefore looked at that time as though, after Egypt had been protected by the Russian veto in the Security Council of 13th October, that there would be a resumption of active hostility by Egypt and her associates against Israel. That was the background at that date. Then, on 26th October, we heard from our representative in Tel Aviv—

Mr. ANEURIN BEVAN (Ebbw Vale): I cannot quite follow this. What does the right hon. and learned Gentleman mean by "protected by the Russian veto"? In respect of what?

Mr. LLOYD: The right hon. Gentleman will recollect that the first part of the Resolution was unanimously carried. [HON. MEMBERS: "What Resolution?"] The Resolution dealing with the future of the Canal.

Mr. WILLIAM WARBEY (Ashfield): What has that to do with it?

Mr. LLOYD: If the hon. Member asks me that question he should examine how much knowledge he has. If he does not realise that a very important ingredient in this matter was Israel's feeling about what was going to happen over the future of the Canal, I despair even of him.

Mr. PHILIP NOEL-BAKER (Derby, South) rose—

Mr. LLOYD: I really must ask right hon. and hon. Members to allow me to put the point of view I am putting forward on this extremely important matter.

Mr. BEVAN: I am very sorry indeed to interrupt again, and I am grateful to the right hon. and learned Gentleman for giving way, but I should like to follow him on this matter. He said that Egypt had been protected by the Russian veto. We should like to know in what respect Egypt was protected.

Mr. LLOYD: In respect of Part II of the Resolution of that date. Part II of the Resolution of that date dealt with the future of the Canal, the 18-Power proposals or the equivalent. Because that Resolution was vetoed at that time it looked less likely that there was going to be an acceptable settlement of the Canal problem, in particular a settlement which would give Israel a right of passage for her ships. That was the matter which affected the Israeli point of view.

On 26th October, we heard from our representative in Tel Aviv—

Mr. Noel-Baker *rose*—

Hon. Members: Order.

Mr. Lloyd: On 26th October, we heard from our representative in Tel Aviv of the Israeli mobilisation. It was not known then whether it was partial or total, and instructions were sent on 27th October to Her Majesty's Ambassador at Tel Aviv to make representations to Israel on the matter. He pointed out that if there were an Israeli attack on Jordan, the United Kingdom would be bound to intervene in accordance with the Anglo-Jordan Treaty. He also urged restraint on Israel in other directions because it was quite obvious that if Israel did attack one of the other Arab countries there was the possibility of Jordan becoming involved and a difficult situation being created for the United Kingdom.

That was quite apart from the risk of general war which would have resulted from any such attack. Those were the facts, that was the extent of our knowledge. There was a critical and deteriorating situation which I believe anyone in possession of the facts would realise was likely to lead to something pretty drastic at any time.

Mr. Denis Healey (Leeds, East) *rose*—

Hon. Members: Sit down.

Mr. Lloyd: I have a somewhat long speech to make and I think we shall get through it more quickly if I am not interrupted so much.

The right hon. Gentleman the Member for Derby, South (Mr. P. Noel-Baker) raised two questions on Monday. The first dealt with negotiations about the Canal settlement. I have checked my recollection on that matter. The position is that after our talks in New York—by that I mean the private talks with the Secretary-General, the Foreign Ministers of France and Egypt and myself—the Egyptian Foreign Minister stayed on in New York for some days and further discussions took place between him and the Secretary-General. It was on 19th October that the Secretary-General made a tentative suggestion for a meeting in Geneva on 29th October.

We pointed out, in fact I made the point in a public speech in this country on 20th October, that Egypt had been asked, in the Security Council Resolution, promptly to make known their proposals for a settlement. The onus was upon them and, so far as we were concerned, we were ready to meet with a representative of Egypt as soon as Egyptian proposals had been put forward in accordance with Part II of the Anglo-French Resolution before the Security Council. I stated that in answer to the suggestion of the Secretary-General. I think partly because I had said that, and in an endeavour to produce the basis for such a meeting, the Secretary-General on 24th October sent a letter to the Egyptian Foreign Minister, a copy of which is in the records of the United Nations.

That was on 24th October; by 29th October there had been no reply from the Egyptian Foreign Minister to that letter. Therefore, on that date there was no basis for a meeting in Geneva on 29th October.

MR. P. NOEL-BAKER: I am much obliged to the Foreign Secretary for giving way. Is it not also a fact that Egypt proposed a meeting in Geneva on 29th October, which, obviously, must have been on the basis of the letter from the Secretary-General, as the proposal was made after he had read it?

MR. LLOYD: The point is that we had said quite definitely we would not agree to a meeting until, in accordance with the Part II of the Security Council Resolution, proposals had been put forward for us to consider. That was the position clearly understood and it was not until 2nd November—in answer to a supplementary question I said 3rd November, but I was wrong—that the Egyptians accepted the Secretary-General's memorandum as a basis for negotiation.

The next matter raised by the right hon. Member related to the cease-fire. The Egyptians, on 2nd November, did accept the Resolution for a cease-fire on the condition that operations were discontinued by the other three countries. On 3rd November, the Israeli Government handed to the Secretary-General an *aide memoire* containing the text of a declaration about Israel agreeing to an immediate cease-fire provided that a similar answer was forthcoming from Egypt.

It also included some observations on the questions then before the Emergency Special Session. That *aide memoire* was immediately followed by a letter on 4th November asking for clarification of five questions. The Secretary-General again got into touch with the Egyptian Government, as I understand, and received an answer on 4th November stating that Egypt was ready to bring to a halt all hostile military action in the area by 20.00 hours that night.

On 5th November, in the afternoon, the Secretary-General made a communication to our Permanent Representative stating that the Government of Egypt had, on 4th November, accepted the request for a cease-fire without any attached conditions and that the Government of Israel had handed in a clarification of its first reply to the request by the Secretary-General for a cease-fire, stating that in the light of Egypt's declaration of willingness to accept a cease-fire Israel confirmed its readiness to agree to a cease-fire.

The Secretary-General went on to say that the conditions for a cease-fire seemed, by those two communications, to be satisfied. That matter was considered by the Cabinet here on the morning of 6th November and Sir Pierson Dixon, because of that, handed to the Secretary-General a notification of the intention of Her Majesty's Government to order a cease-fire at midnight that night.

MR. P. NOEL-BAKER: In other words, what I said the other day was perfectly accurate. Both sides had accepted the cease-fire before we made our landings on 5th November, and, in spite of that, we went on with our offensive until midnight on 6th November.

MR. LLOYD: The right hon. Member should have waited for just a moment.

In the question he put to me last Monday, he left out from the chain of events which he described the communication of 4th November from the Israeli Government which put into doubt the question whether or not they had accepted a cease-fire. They put that into doubt—[*Interruption*]. There really is no dispute about this among those who are prepared to be fair-minded on this matter. It was in doubt as far as we were concerned, it was obviously in doubt as far as the Secretary-General was concerned, and in consequence of that he made his further communication to us on 5th November.

In my statement last Monday I claimed that certain results had flowed from the action of Her Majesty's Government, that we had stopped the war and prevented it spreading. That was greeted with a certain amount of hilarity by most hon. Members of the Opposition. As I listened, I could not help being reminded of the statement of the Leader of the Opposition on a previous occasion about the premature ending of hostilities. Is it the view of the Opposition that our action did not stop the war spreading through the Middle East? There is silence.

MR. HEALEY: The right hon. and learned Gentleman used a rather equivocal phrase when he said that we warned the Israelis on 29th October against action in other directions. Can he tell the House whether, at any time after 27th October, we warned the Israelis unequivocally against an attack on Egypt? If we did not, the whole case of the Government falls to the ground.

MR. LLOYD: The hon. Member has, very cleverly, tried to put another question to the question on which I gave way. [HON. MEMBERS: "Answer."] I will answer the question. Her Majesty's Ambassador in Tel Aviv warned the Israeli Government to use restraint and warned of the dangers if restraint were not used. If the hon. Member thinks that that does not cover the question of hostilities against Egypt, he should examine the matter again.

MR. BEVAN: The right hon. and learned Gentleman asked a question and his Friends behind him took it up. I understand the question—the last sentence he uttered—to be what would we have done to prevent—[HON. MEMBERS: "No."]

MR. LLOYD: May I repeat my question? Do the Opposition still dispute our contention that our action stopped the war spreading through the Middle East?

MR. BEVAN: If the right hon. Gentleman will glance over what he has read in the last five minutes he will see that Her Majesty's Government connived at the war.

MR. LLOYD: That is very clever, but it is not an answer to my question. It is now quite plain that Her Majesty's Opposition are not prepared to face up to the question which I put, because they know quite well, in their heart of hearts, that what I have stated is the truth.

However, to fortify the conclusion which apparently they have reached, I do not think that I can do better than call in evidence a witness possibly more likely to convince them—the Commander-in-Chief of the Egyptian Army. He said, on 30th November, in a statement broadcast by Cairo Radio, that Egypt was bound by military agreements with Saudi Arabia, Jordan, Syria and the Yemen. In his capacity as Commander-in-Chief of the Joint Arab Forces he issued instructions on the evening of 29th October to put into effect plans prepared to meet an Israeli attack. In consequence of those instructions, various military movements began. After the Anglo-French communication to Egypt on 30th October, he went on to say, the Egyptian Government decided not to involve the other Arab States in military operations. Orders were issued to commanders of joint forces to avoid taking part in military operations. I believe that that statement proves conclusively the accuracy of our claim that our action prevented the spread of hostilities and is, in fact, its basic justification. It is not easy to say how far the spread of hostilities would have gone, or in what the Middle East and the whole world might ultimately have been involved.

I also claimed, on Monday, that our action had revealed the extent of Soviet penetration into the area. That, again, was received with a certain amount of hilarity by hon. Members opposite. What are the facts about that? We had known of substantial sales to Egypt of Soviet arms. Before the operation they had been reckoned to be of the value of about £150 million.

MR. LESLIE HALE (Oldham, West): What did we send?

MR. LLOYD: As a result of the information now in our possession, it appears that Egypt had received 50 I.L. 28s, 100 M.I.G.s, 300 medium and heavy tanks, more than 100 self-propelled guns, 200 armoured personnel carriers, 500 pieces of artillery and a great variety of other military equipment, including rocket launchers, bazookas, plastic mines, small arms, radar, wireless, etc., 2 destroyers, 4 minesweepers, 20 motor torpedo boats and a number of smaller vessels. There was also the probability, or the possibility, that some small submarines were to be provided. It would appear that Egypt was being equipped by the Soviet Union for full-scale military operations.

As far as our deliveries of arms are concerned, they represent, as every hon. Member who knows anything about it recognises, only a trickle. That has been gone into before, and I am quite prepared to go into it again. This was the equipment by the Soviet Union of Egypt for full-scale military operations.

Certain information has been published from Israeli sources since these operations. They state that in Sinai they captured 1,500 military vehicles, more than 60 armoured personnel carriers, more than 250 pieces of artillery, 30 T.34 tanks, a number of self-propelled guns, 200 Czech anti-tank guns, and 7,000 tons of ammunition. This equipment was captured in a campaign which involved about one-third of the Egyptian Army. It takes no account of other Soviet equipment. In particular, we know that the 60 Josef Stalin heavy tanks were held back from the final battle in Sinai.

Another interesting factor is that much of the 7,000 tons of ammunition was for a type of Soviet gun none of which was captured in Sinai.

MR. R. R. STOKES (Ipswich): What good was it?

MR. LLOYD: I should have thought that even the right hon. Gentleman would have drawn the conclusion that the guns were to follow. I agree that the ammunition would have been no use without the guns.

We are told that great quantities of arms and equipment are still scattered throughout the desert. Some of the rifles and machine guns found were of the latest Soviet *bloc* models and were still packed in the grease in which they arrived.

In addition to these large dumps of ammunition there was a very curious find—over 1 million blankets. The Egyptian Army consisted, before the operation, of about 80,000 men. One wonders what was the purpose of these very large deliveries of equipment of one sort and another.

MR. STOKES: May I ask a question?

MR. LLOYD: I have not yet finished.

In our own restricted operations in Port Said, about 30 self-propelled Soviet guns were found, together with a considerable variety of other Soviet equipment. Large numbers of expert technicians had been sent from behind the Iron Curtain to Egypt. We believe that at least 1,000 technicians and instructors had come to Egypt for essential servicing and training. In addition, Egyptians had been sent to Czechoslovakia, Poland and the Soviet Union for technical training.

MR. STOKES: This is very important. Will the Foreign Secretary say whether the amount of arms we discovered in the shape of heavy tanks and armoured vehicles was more than sufficient to arm more than four or five brigades? Does he say that it was more than that?

MR. LLOYD: I agree with the right hon. Gentleman that it is a very important matter. Our information is that the amount of equipment found was far more than necessary to equip the Egyptian Army.

The broad outline of much of this was known to us or guessed by us before the operation took place. What has happened as a result of that operation is that the magnitude of the Soviet penetration has been revealed. It had permeated every branch of the Egyptian armed forces, and, as Egypt is a military dictatorship, that meant that the Communist influence was in a position to have a dominating effect upon events. However right hon. and hon. Members opposite may try to get out of the matter, those are the facts of the situation which have been disclosed by our action.

I also claimed in my statement on Monday that a third result of our intervention had been the action taken by the United Nations. Some sensitivity has been shown to our claim that it was our action which forced the formation of the United Nations Emergency Force. I do not see how anyone can believe that this Force could have been created without our action—[*Interruption.*]—or without the suggestion put forward by my right hon. Friend the Prime Minister in the House.

I will repeat to the House what I said to the General Assembly of the United Nations, on the Middle East, when I spoke in the debate on Friday week:

> Over the past few years the United Nations, whether in the Assembly or the Security Council, has completely failed so far as the Middle East is concerned, either to keep the peace or to procure compliance with its own resolutions, or to pave the way for a settlement.

I said that in saying that I was not criticising—I was stating the fact. And that is known to right hon. Gentlemen opposite, who were in office before us, at a time when they had responsibility. Nevertheless, that is the record of the United Nations. I do not say that it was the United Nations' fault. We may very well say that it was the fault of member States, or of a conglomeration of member States but, in fact, United Nations progress in those matters had been blocked in that period.

I believe that it is that reason, the failure of the United Nations over those years, which is the basic reason for the events of 29th and 30th October. I believe that a solid advantage which has resulted from this action is the existence in Egypt of this United Nations Force to keep the peace. I believe that it is the desire of the great majority of the countries that this Force should be effective, that it should discharge its functions, and should be an element creating conditions under which a final settlement may be possible.

I would add only this about the atmosphere of the United Nations as I saw it a fortnight ago. It was disturbing to note the comparative indifference about the situation in Hungary which was displayed by some of the countries which were most ready to condemn us.

I do not propose to say any more to the House today about the clearance arrangements for the Canal, or the basis of negotiations for a long-term settlement, because I dealt with those fully in my statement on Monday.

I want to come now, if I may, to the question of Anglo-American relations. The effect of these events upon Anglo-American relations has been much discussed. I do not think that it is profitable to talk in detail about the past. There have been differences of opinion, and I can assure the House that neither country thinks that it is the only one which believes that it has cause for complaint. There have been differences in the past, and I think it would be idle to attempt to disguise that fact. But I believe that what we now have to consider is the future, and upon what basis we can seek to co-operate in the Middle East.

MRS. JEAN MANN (Coatbridge and Airdrie) *rose—*

MR. LLOYD: In a speech which I made in New York, to the English-Speaking Union, on 26th November—

MRS. MANN: Before the right hon. and learned Gentleman goes on, would he explain why he kept it so very quiet from his great friend and ally, "Ike"?

MR. LLOYD: I am not quite certain of the point of the hon. Lady's intervention. I think that the differences of opinion about action in the Middle East were very well known to many members of the Administration on that side of the Atlantic.

As I say, I do not think it profitable to seek to recriminate—I do not think that that is the right word—to be critical about the past.

What, I think, is much more important, is to see whether we can create an effective basis for working together in the future. I do not believe that an acute difference necessarily makes it more difficult to associate together in the future. It may do a great deal to clear the air, and make possible closer alliance in the future, but the point is: upon what basis should we seek to co-operate?

In the speech which I made in New York to the English-Speaking Union, on 26th November, I indicated five points as a possible basis for this co-operation in the future. First, the prevention of further hostilities between Israel and the Arab States, and the fullest support of the United Nations Force to that end.

Secondly, the restoration of a permanent system for the Suez Canal, securing the international rights under the 1888 Convention, and in accordance with the six principles, unanimously adopted by the Security Council last October.

Thirdly, the procurement of a permanent settlement between Israel and the Arab States which will include a just settlement of the problems of the unfortunate victims of the events of the past eight years—the Arab refugees.

Fourthly, the strengthening of the Bagdad Pact.

Fifthly, the tackling of the economic problems of the area with imagination and foresight so that there may be a steady lifting of the standards of living throughout the area as a whole. That seems to me to be a statement of the objectives upon which co-operation could well be based in the future.

I do not think that a statement reportedly approved personally by the President and by Mr. Dulles, and released by the State Department on the evening of 3rd December, has been adequately noticed in this country, because of the difference in the time of release. That statement, after welcoming the Anglo-French decision announced on Monday, went on to say:

> The United States has repeatedly said, during this crisis in the Middle East that the United Nations cannot rightfully or prudently stop merely with maintaining peace. Under its Charter it is obligated to deal with the basic sources of international friction and conflicts of interest. Only in this way can it attain the Charter's goal of peace with justice. In keeping with this obligation the United States will continue fully to support the measures required to make the United Nations Force adequate and effective for its mission. In carrying out his plan for this purpose, the Secretary-General can count on the unstinting co-operation of the United States.
>
> As the United Nations Force replaces those of the United Kingdom and France, the clearance of the Canal becomes imperative. Every day of delay in restoring the Canal to normal use is a breach of the 1888 Treaty, and a wrong to the large number of nations throughout the world whose economies depend so heavily on its reliable operation. The United Nations and the interested States should, we believe, promptly direct their attention to the underlying Middle East problems.

The United States Government considers it essential that arrangements be worked out without delay to ensure the operation of the Canal in conformity with the six principles approved by the resolution of the Security Council of 13th October, 1956. The United States is equally determined, through the United Nations and in other useful ways, to assist in bringing about a permanent settlement of the other persistent conflicts which have plagued the Middle East over recent years.

Repeatedly, we have made clear our willingness to contribute for the purpose of bringing stability and a just peace to this area. The present crisis is a challenge to all nations to work to this end.

The House will notice that in the five points which I set forth in my speech to the English-Speaking Union, I mentioned the Bagdad Pact. In addition to the statement that I have just read out, I would remind the House of what the United States Government have said about the Bagdad Pact: "The United States reaffirms its support for the collective efforts of those nations"—that is, the Bagdad countries—"to maintain their independence. A threat to the territorial integrity or political independence of the members, would be viewed by the United States with the utmost gravity." It is well known that the view of Her Majesty's Government is that it was a step forward when the United States became a member of the Economic Committee. I think that that pronouncement is perhaps rather more important than some hon. Members who laugh at it may think.

MR. M. PHILIPS PRICE (Gloucestershire, West): Would the Secretary of State bear in mind that the Government of Iraq have said that they will not come to the Bagdad Pact if we are there? How does the right hon. and learned Gentleman propose to deal with that situation?

MR. LLOYD: I think that that situation had better be allowed to work itself out. I am disappointed at the hon. Member for Gloucestershire, West (Mr. Philips Price) who, I know, is a very sincere supporter of friendship between us and the Arab countries and who, I think, will be as anxious as anyone to see that the Bagdad Pact should develop and strengthen. I believe that what the hon. Gentleman has drawn attention to is a purely temporary phase.

I have been in close contact with the member Governments of the Bagdad Pact. I believe that this statement of the United States is of major importance, and I think that better service would have been done to the cause of restoring the situation of friendship between the Arab countries and ourselves if the hon. Gentleman had welcomed what I said without pointing out the other matter.

I believe that the Bagdad Pact will grow in strength with our membership, and, as I was going on to say, I hope that the United States will pass on from its membership of the Economic Committee, beyond its declaration to which I have referred today, to full membership of that Pact.

There is another matter, and that is the question of closer association between the countries of Western Europe. There is, I think, another line of development which becomes clear in consequence of what has happened in the Middle East and in consequence of the present situation in the United Nations. That is the need for a more efficient basis for co-operation between the nations of Western Europe. I believe that this can be achieved without impairing either our association with the Commonwealth or our alliance with the United States, and without creating new institutions. I go at the weekend to the meetings of the Western European Union and the North Atlantic Treaty Organisation with those considerations very much in mind.

I maintain—it has been my belief throughout and it is still my conviction—that out of this situation certain definite advantages have been achieved. [*Laughter.*] I really do not think that right hon. and hon. Members opposite do their country a service in seeking to make out that this whole business has been a disastrous failure, as in the words of their Amendment. I believe that what we did was right. I believe that we stopped a war. I believe—and, for once, an extraordinary fact, hon. Members opposite were almost reduced to silence—that I proved, by my quotation from the Egyptian Commander-in-Chief, that we stopped the war from spreading in the Middle East.

I believe that we have now given this United Nations Force a task of the greatest responsibility. Those who criticise us so vocally and glibly—

MR. WILLIAM ROSS (Kilmarnock): Which side?

MR. LLOYD: —forget what would have been the consequences of inactivity. They forget completely the dangers which are existent in the area. They forget completely the steady deterioration which was taking place. They forget completely the mounting risk of war between Israel and the Arab States. They shut their eyes to all those things. We have shown in this country our will to act in a situation of crisis, and it is now for us all, I suggest, to bend our energies to see that the United Nations grasps this opportunity.

---

*Speech by Aneurin Bevan in the House of
Commons Denouncing the Suez Intervention,
5 December 1956**

I beg to move, to leave out from "House" to the end of the Question and to add instead thereof:

> recognising the disastrous consequences of Her Majesty's Government's policy in the Middle East, calls upon Her Majesty's Government to take all possible steps to restore Commonwealth unity, recreate confidence between our allies and ourselves and strengthen the authority of the United Nations as the only way to achieve a lasting settlement in the Middle East.

The speech to which we have just listened is the last of a long succession that the right hon. Gentleman the Secretary of State for Foreign Affairs has made to

*Hansard, 5.s., DLXI, 1268–83.

the House in the last few months and, if I may be allowed to say so, I congratulate him upon having survived so far. He appears to be in possession of vigorous health, which is obviously not enjoyed by all his colleagues, and he appears also to be exempted from those Freudian lapses which have distinguished the speeches of the Lord Privy Seal, and therefore he has survived so far with complete vigour.

However, I am bound to say that the speech by the right hon. Gentleman to-day carries the least conviction of all.

MR. CYRIL OSBORNE (Louth): The right hon. Gentleman wrote that before he heard the speech.

MR. BEVAN: I have been looking through the various objectives and reasons that the Government have given to the House of Commons for making war on Egypt, and it really is desirable that when a nation makes war upon another nation it should be quite clear why it does so. It should not keep changing the reasons as time goes on. There is, in fact, no correspondence whatsoever between the reasons given today and the reasons set out by the Prime Minister at the beginning. The reasons have changed all the time. I have got a list of them here, and for the sake of the record I propose to read it. I admit that I found some difficulty in organising a speech with any coherence because of the incoherence of the reasons. They are very varied.

On 30th October, the Prime Minister said that the purpose was, first, "to seek to separate the combatants"; second, "to remove the risk to free passage through the Canal."

The speech we have heard today is the first speech in which that subject has been dropped. Every other statement made on this matter since the beginning has always contained a reference to the future of the Canal as one of Her Majesty's Government's objectives, in fact, as an object of war, to coerce Egypt. Indeed, that is exactly what hon. and right hon. Gentlemen opposite believed it was all about. [*Interruption.*] Hon. Members do not do themselves justice. One does not fire in order merely to have a cease-fire. One would have thought that the cease-fire was consequent upon having fired in the first place. It could have been accomplished without starting. The other objective set out on 30th October was "to reduce the risk . . . to those voyaging through the Canal."—[OFFICIAL REPORT, 30th October, 1956; Vol. 558, c. 1347.]

We have heard from the right hon. and learned Gentleman today a statement which I am quite certain all the world will read with astonishment. He has said that when we landed in Port Said there was already every reason to believe that both Egypt and Israel had agreed to cease fire.

THE MINISTER OF DEFENCE (MR. ANTONY HEAD) *indicated dissent.*

MR. BEVAN: The Minister shakes his head. If he will recollect what his right hon. and learned Friend said, it was that there was still a doubt about the Israeli reply. Are we really now telling this country and the world that all these calamitous consequences have been brought down upon us merely because of a doubt? That is what he said.

Surely, there was no need. We had, of course, done the bombing, but our ships were still going through the Mediterranean. We had not arrived at Port Said. The exertions of the United Nations had already gone far enough to be able to secure from Israel and Egypt a promise to cease fire, and all that remained to be cleared up was an ambiguity about the Israeli reply. In these conditions, and against the background of these events, the invasion of Egypt still continued.

In the history of nations, there is no example of such frivolity. When I have looked at this chronicle of events during the last few days, with every desire in the world to understand it, I just have not been able to understand, and do not yet understand, the mentality of the Government. If the right hon. and learned Gentleman wishes to deny what I have said, I will give him a chance of doing so. If his words remain as they are now, we are telling the nation and the world that, having decided upon the course, we went on with it despite the fact that the objective we had set ourselves had already been achieved, namely, the separation of the combatants.

As to the objective of removing the risk to free passage through the Canal, I must confess that I have been astonished at this also. We sent an ultimatum to Egypt by which we told her that unless she agreed to our landing in Ismailia, Suez and Port Said, we should make war upon her. We knew very well, did we not, that Nasser could not possibly comply? Did we really believe that Nasser was going to give in at once? Is our information from Egypt so bad that we did not know that an ultimatum of that sort was bound to consolidate his position in Egypt and in the whole Arab world?

We knew at that time, on 29th and 30th October, that long before we could have occupied Port Said, Ismailia and Suez, Nasser would have been in a position to make his riposte. So wonderfully organised was this expedition—which, apparently, has been a miracle of military genius—that long after we had delivered our ultimatum and bombed Port Said, our ships were still ploughing through the Mediterranean, leaving the enemy still in possession of all the main objectives which we said we wanted.

Did we really believe that Nasser was going to wait for us to arrive? He did what anybody would have thought he would do, and if the Government did not think he would do it, on that account alone they ought to resign. He sank ships in the Canal, the wicked man. What did hon. Gentleman opposite expect him to do? The result is that, in fact, the first objective realised was the opposite of the one we set out to achieve; the Canal was blocked, and it is still blocked.

The only other interpretation of the Government's mind is that they expected, for some reason or other, that their ultimatum would bring about disorder in Egypt and the collapse of the Nasser regime. None of us believed that. If hon. Gentleman opposite would only reason about other people as they reason amongst themselves, they would realise that a Government cannot possibly surrender to a threat of that sort and keep any self-respect. We should not, should we? If somebody held a pistol at our heads and said, "You do this or we fire", should we? Of course not. Why on earth do not hon. Members opposite sometimes believe that other people have the same courage and independence as they themselves possess? Nasser behaved exactly as any reasonable man would expect him to behave.

The other objective was "to reduce the risk . . . to those voyaging through the Canal."

That was a rhetorical statement, and one does not know what it means. I am sorry the right hon. Gentleman the Prime Minister is not here. I appreciate why he is not here, but it is very hard to reply to him when he is not in the House, and I hope hon. Members opposite will acquit me of trying to attack him in his absence.

On 31st October, the Prime Minister said that our object was to secure a lasting settlement and to protect our nationals. What do we think of that? In the meantime, our nationals were living in Egypt while we were murdering Egyptians at Port Said. We left our nationals in Egypt at the mercy of what might have been merciless riots throughout the whole country, with no possibility whatever of our coming to their help. We were still voyaging through the Mediterranean, after having exposed them to risk by our own behaviour. What does the House believe that the country will think when it really comes to understand all this?

On 1st November, we were told the reason was "to stop hostilities" and "prevent a resumption of them."—[OFFICIAL REPORT, 1st November, 1956; Vol. 558, c. 1653.]

But hostilities had already been practically stopped. On 3rd November, our objectives became much more ambitious "to deal with all the outstanding problems in the Middle East."—[OFFICIAL REPORT, 3rd November, 1956; Vol. 558, c. 1867.]

In the famous book "Madame Bovary" there is a story of a woman who goes from one sin to another, a long story of moral decline. In this case, our ambitions soar the farther away we are from realising them. Our objective was, "to deal with all the outstanding problems in the Middle East." After having outraged our friends, after having insulted the United States, after having affronted all our friends in the Commonwealth, after having driven the whole of the Arab world into one solid phalanx, at least for the moment, behind Nasser, we were then going to deal with all the outstanding problems in the Middle East.

MR. GILBERT LONGDEN (Hertfordshire, South-West): As this is going on the record, and as the Prime Minister is not here, I hope that the right hon. Gentleman will be fair enough not deliberately to mislead the House, as I am sure he would not wish to, but the Prime Minister never said that we alone could deal with all the problems of the Middle East. What the Prime Minister said on 1st November was:

> We do not seek to impose by force a solution on the Israel-Egypt dispute, or the Suez Canal dispute, or any other dispute in the area.—[OFFICIAL REPORT, 1st November, 1956; Vol. 558, c. 1653.]

He said that if the United Nations would send forces to relieve us no one would be better pleased than we.

MR. BEVAN: The hon. Gentleman need not worry; I will deal with that quite soon; I am coming to that quite quickly. This is a new alibi. It was only a few weeks ago in this House that hon. and right hon. Gentlemen opposite sneered at every mention of the United Nations. We will deal with that.

The next objective of which we were told was to ensure that the Israeli forces withdrew from Egyptian territory. That, I understand, is what we were there for. We went into Egyptian territory in order to establish our moral right to make the Israelis clear out of Egyptian territory. That is a remarkable war aim, is it not? In order that we might get Israel out, we went in. To establish our case before the eyes of the world, Israel being the wicked invader, we, of course, being the nice friend of Egypt, went to protect her from the Israelis, but, unfortunately, we had to bomb the Egyptians first.

On 6th November, the Prime Minister said:

> The action we took has been an essential condition for . . . a United Nations Force to come into the Canal Zone itself.—[OFFICIAL REPORT, 6th November, 1956; Vol. 559, c. 80.]

That is one of the most remarkable claims of all, and it is one of the main claims made by right hon. and hon. Members opposite. It is, of course, exactly the same claim which might have been made, if they had thought about it in time, by Mussolini and Hitler, that they made war on the world in order to call the United Nations into being. If it were possible for bacteria to argue with each other, they would be able to say that of course their chief justification was the advancement of medical science.

As *The Times* has pointed out, the arrival of the United Nations Force could not be regarded as a war aim by the Government; it called it, "an inadvertance." That is not my description; it is *The Times.* It was a by-product of the action not of Her Majesty's Government but of the United Nations itself.

Let me ask hon. Members opposite to listen to this case. The right hon. and learned Gentleman was spending most of his time in America trying to persuade the United States—that is after we were in Egypt—to make the control of the Canal one of the conditions of our withdrawal. On Thursday last he himself said here:

> I mention these facts to the House because, obviously, the build-up of this force must have an important relationship to a phased withdrawal of our own and the French troops. There are, however, other important matters to be considered, such as the speedy clearance of the Canal, and negotiation of a final settlement with regard to the operation of the Canal.—[OFFICIAL REPORT, 29th November, 1956; Vol. 561, c. 582.]

On every single occasion—and hon. Members opposite expected this—when he went upstairs to tell his hon. Friends that he had come back empty-handed, what did they say? Why did we start this operation? We started this operation in order to give Nasser a black eye—if we could to overthrow him—but, in any case, to secure control of the Canal.

Viscount Hinchingbrooke (Dorset, South): To stop the war.

Mr. Bevan: I have been dealing with that; the hon. Gentleman must catch up.

The United Nations Force was in Egypt as a result of a Resolution of the United Nations for the purposes of the Charter. All along, the United States and all the other nations attached to the United Nations resolutely refused to allow the future of the Canal to be tied up with the existence of the Force. But the right hon. and learned Gentleman, in order to have some trophy to wave in the faces of his hon. Friends, wanted to bring from across the Atlantic an undertaking which would have destroyed the United Nations, because if the United Nations had agreed that the future of the Canal should also be contingent upon the withdrawal of British troops, then the United Nations Force would no longer have been a United Nations Force but an instrument of the rump of the United Nations, that is, the Western Powers.

I put it again to the right hon. and learned Gentleman that if hon. Members opposite had succeeded in what they wanted to do, they would have ruined the United Nations, because the very essence of the United Nations Force is that it is not attempting to impose upon Egypt any settlement of the Canal.

Mr. Anthony Fell (Yarmouth): It is a police force.

Mr. Bevan: I hope that hon. Members opposite will realise that the argument is a really serious one. It was seen to be so serious by the United States that, despite what I believe to be the desire on the part of a very large number of Americans to help us in these difficulties, it was clear to President Eisenhower, as it should be clear to anybody, that a settlement of that sort was bound to be resented by the whole of the Arab world and Egypt. It was bound to be resented by the Commonwealth because it would make it appear that Her Majesty's Government were using the United Nations to obtain an objective that we set ourselves as far back as last August. Therefore, if the right hon. and learned Gentleman had succeeded, if the future of the Canal had been tied up with our withdrawal, the United Nations Force in Egypt would no longer have been a police force for the world, but would have been a means of coercing Egypt to accept our terms about the Canal.

Mr. Fell: Surely the right hon. Gentleman would find it very difficult to imagine a United Nations Force that could, in fact, be a successful police force unless under certain circumstances it had the right to infringe—

Mr. Bevan: The hon. Member is not meeting my point. The point that the Government spokesmen are making here and in the country is that they have been responsible for calling the United Nations Force into existence. My answer is that by attaching to the United Nations Force a persistent attempt to secure the future of the Canal in order to satisfy hon. Members opposite they are, in fact, sabotaging the United Nations.

Mr. K. Zilliacus (Manchester, Gorton): Is it not a fact that the Government voted against the Security Council Resolution calling the General Assembly and then abstained on the vote creating the United Nations Force?

MR. BEVAN: This, of course, is known to hon. Members in all parts of the House. They may have their own explanations for it, but I was not anxious to add to the burden of my argument. That fact is known. Of course, the Government did not support the United Nations Force—we all know that. Nevertheless, in this retrospective exercise that we are having from the other side of the House, it is possible for us to deal with the seriousness of the whole case.

The right hon. and learned Gentleman is sufficiently aware of the seriousness of it to start his speech today with collusion. If collusion can be established, the whole fabric of the Government's case falls to the ground, and they know this. It is the most serious of all the charges. It is believed in the United States and it is believed by large numbers of people in Great Britain that we were well aware that Israel was going to make the attack on Egypt. In fact, very few of the activities at the beginning of October are credible except upon the assumption that the French and British Governments knew that something was going to happen in Egypt.

Indeed, the right hon. and learned Gentleman has not been frank with the House. We have asked him over and over again. He has said, "Ah, we did not conspire with France and Israel." We never said that the Government might have conspired. What we said was that they might have known about it. The right hon. and learned Gentleman gave the House the impression that at no time had he ever warned Israel against attacking Egypt. Even today, he hinged the warning we gave to Jordan on the possibility of the other Arab States being involved in any attack on Jordan.

We understand from the right hon. and learned Gentleman that at no time did the Government warn Israel against an attack on Egypt. If we apprehend trouble of these dimensions—we are not dealing with small matters—if we apprehend that the opening phases of a third world war might start or turn upon an attack by Israel on anyone, why did we not make it quite clear to Israel that we would take the same view of an attack on Egypt as we took of an attack on Jordan?

The fact is that all these long telephone conversations and conferences between M. Guy Mollet, M. Pineau and the Prime Minister are intelligible only on the assumption that something was being cooked up. All that was left to do, as far as we knew from the facts at that time, was to pick up negotiations at Geneva about the future of the Canal, as had been arranged by the United Nations. But all the time there was this coming and going between ourselves and the French Government.

Did the French know? It is believed in France that the French knew about the Israeli intention. If the French knew, did they tell the British Government? We would like to know. Did M. Guy Mollet, on 16th October, tell the British Prime Minister that he expected that there was to be an attack on Egypt? Every circumstantial fact that we know points to that conclusion. For instance, Mr. Ben Gurion, the Israeli Prime Minister, had already made it clear in the *Knesset* on several occasions that Israel regarded Egypt as the real enemy, and not Jordan. Therefore, a warning not to attack Jordan was not relevant. At the same time, many Israelis were saying that at last Israel had got a reliable friend.

What happened? Did Marianne take John Bull to an unknown rendezvous? Did Marianne say to John Bull that there was a forest fire going to start, and did John Bull then say, "We ought to put it out," but Marianne said, "No, let us warm our hands by it. It is a nice fire"? Did Marianne deceive John Bull or seduce him?

Now, of course, we come to the ultimate end. It is at the end of all these discussions that the war aim of the Government now becomes known. Of course, we knew it all the time. We knew where they would land. After this long voyaging, getting almost wrecked several times, they have come to safe harbour. It was a red peril all the time. It was Russia all the time. It was not to save the Canal. The hon. Member who interjected has been deceived all the time. It was not the Canal, it was the red peril which they had unmasked. The Government suspected it before, said the right hon. and learned Gentleman, about the arms to Egypt. We on this side knew it—we did not suspect it—but the right hon. and learned Gentleman suspected it, so he said, at the very time when he was informing the House that he thought there was a proper balance of arms between Egypt and Israel.

What will the Israelis think of this when they read the right hon. and learned Gentleman's words, or are we to understand that the Israelis have got as many arms as the Egyptians have? We understand that they were fully armed all the time, because the right hon. and learned Gentleman suspected that the Egyptians had these arms.

I am not in the least surprised by this situation. That the Russians have provided these arms to the Egyptians we accept—of course they did. It is a curious thing—I may be frivolous, but I am not frightened by it—and I will tell the House why. The Russians have a habit, curiously enough, it seems to me, of not knowing what is happening in other nations. They do not even know what is happening in Poland or Hungary, and it does not seem to have occurred to the Russians that there was no military advantage in providing weapons that the Egyptians could not use.

The fact of the matter is that these great modern weapons are practically useless in the hands of backward nations. [HON. MEMBERS: "There were the volunteers."] But there were no volunteers. Do not, however, let hon. Members push the argument too far. I am not for one moment seeking to justify the Russian supply of arms to Egypt. I think it was a wicked thing to do and I think it is an equally wicked thing for us to supply arms. That area is much too combustible, far too inflammatory. This is now the end of 1956, when very many things have happened in the Middle East, when it is more dangerous than ever. I think that the Russians ought not to have done it and I will say further that I think that Nasser ought not to have invited them.

It seems to me—and here I probably shall carry hon. Members opposite with me—that Nasser has not been behaving in the spirit of the Bandoeng Conference which he joined, because what he did was not to try to reduce the temperature of the cold war: what he did was to exploit it for Egyptian purposes. Therefore, Nasser's hands are not clean by any means. I have said this before. I said it in Trafalgar Square. We must not believe that because the Prime Minister is wrong Nasser is right. That is not the view on this side of the House.

What has deeply offended us is that such wrongs as Nasser has done and such faults as he has have been covered by the bigger blunders of the British Government. That is what vexes us. We are satisfied that the arts of diplomacy would have brought Nasser to where we wanted to get him, which was to agree about the free passage of ships through the Canal, on the civilised ground that a riparian nation has got no absolute rights over a great waterway like the Canal. That is a principle which has been accepted by India and by America and by most other nations. We have never taken the position that in the exercise of sovereign rights Egypt has the right to inflict a mortal wound upon the commerce of the world.

MR. OSBORNE: Will not the right hon. Gentleman agree that six years of patient negotiation had not caused Nasser to allow the passage of Israeli ships?

MR. BEVAN: Do not let hon. Members now bring to the forefront of the argument the fact that Egypt had not been allowing Israeli ships to go through the Canal. If they thought so much of the seriousness of that, why did they not even invite Israel to the conference? It is not good enough to bring these things forward all the time as though they were the main objectives. Of course, we take the view that Egypt should permit the ships of all nations to pass through the Canal, and we hope that that objective will still be insisted upon. We are satisfied that those objectives could have been realised by negotiation. Not only have they not been realised by the action taken by the Government, but the opposite has been realised.

It had been clear to us, and it is now becoming clear to the nation, that for many months past hon. Members opposite have been harbouring designs of this sort. One of the reasons why we could not get a civilised solution of the Cyprus problem was that the Government were harbouring designs to use Cyprus in the Middle East, unilaterally or in conjunction with France. Whenever we put in this House Questions to the right hon. Gentleman asking him why he did not answer whether he wanted a base on Cyprus or Cyprus as a base, he answered quite frankly that we might want to activate the base on Cyprus independently of our allies. That was the answer. Well, we have activated it—and look at us. We have had all these murders and all this terror, we have had all this unfriendship over Cyprus between ourselves and Greece, and we have been held up to derision in all the world merely because we contemplated using Cyprus as a base for going it alone in the Middle East. And we did go it alone. Look at the result.

Was it not obvious to hon. Members opposite that Great Britain could not possibly engage in a major military adventure without involving our N.A.T.O.

allies? Was it not very clear, if we did contemplate any adventure at all, that it would have to be in conjunction with them? No. It is a sad and bitter story. We hope that at least one beneficial byproduct of it will be a settlement of the Cyprus question very soon indeed.

Now I would conclude by saying this. I do not believe that any of us yet—I say any of us yet—have realised the complete change that has taken place in the relationship between nations and between Governments and peoples. These were objectives, I do beg hon. Members to reflect, that were not realisable by the means that we adopted. These civil, social and political objectives in modern society are not attainable by armed force.

Even if we had occupied Egypt by armed force we could not have secured the freedom of passage through the Canal. It is clear that there is such xenophobia, that there is such passion, that there is such bitter feeling against Western imperialism—rightly or wrongly: I am not arguing the merits at the moment—among millions of people that they are not prepared to keep the arteries of European commerce alive and intact if they themselves want to cut them. We could not keep ships going through the Canal. The Canal is too easily sabotaged, if Egypt wants to sabotage it. Why on earth did we imagine that the objectives could be realised in that way in the middle of the twentieth century?

VISCOUNT HINCHINGBROOKE: Would the right hon. Gentleman apply the same argument to Germany at the end of the last war? It seems to me that the Germans showed great willingness to open the Kiel Canal.

MR. BEVAN: That is not really a parallel at all. The noble Lord does not face the argument. We should be imposing our will upon Egypt against the bitter opposition of the whole population there.

VISCOUNT HINCHINGBROOKE: Not necessarily.

MR. BEVAN: It is necessarily so. If the noble Lord does not understand that, then he is in the eighteenth and not even the nineteenth century.

Exactly the same thing is true of the Russians in Hungary. The Russians in Hungary are attempting to achieve civil, social and political objectives by tanks and guns, and the Hungarian people are demonstrating that it cannot be done.

The social furniture of modern society is so complicated and fragile that it cannot support the jackboot. We cannot run the processes of modern society by attempting to impose our will upon nations by armed force. If we have not learned that we have learned nothing. Therefore, from our point of view here, whatever may have been the morality of the Government's action—and about that there is no doubt—there is no doubt about its imbecility. There is not the slightest shadow of doubt that we have attempted to use methods which were bound to destroy the objectives we had, and, of course, this is what we have discovered.

I commend to hon. Members, if they have not seen it, a very fine cartoon in *Punch* by Illingworth and called "Desert Victory." There we see a black, ominous, sinister background and a pipeline broken, pouring oil into the desert sands. How on earth do hon. Members opposite imagine that hundreds of miles of pipeline can be kept open if the Arabs do not want it to be kept open? It is not enough to say that there are large numbers of Arabs who want the pipeline to be kept open because they live by it.

It has been proved over and over again now in the modern world that men and women are often prepared to put up with material losses for things that they really think worth while. It has been shown in Budapest, and it could be shown in the Middle East. That is why I beg hon. Members to turn their backs on this most ugly chapter and realise that if we are to live in the world and are to be regarded as a decent nation, decent citizens in the world, we have to act up to different standards than the one that we have been following in the last few weeks.

I resent most bitterly this unconcern for the lives of innocent men and women. It may be that the dead in Port Said are 100, 200 or 300. If it is only one, we had no business to take it. Do hon. Members begin to realise how this is going to revolt the world when it passes into the imagination of men and women everywhere, and in this country, that we, with eight million here in London, the biggest single civilian target in the world, with our crowded island exposed, as no nation in the world is exposed, to the barbarism of modern weapons, we ourselves set the example.

We ourselves conscript our boys and put guns and aeroplanes in their hands and say, "Bomb there." Really, this is so appalling that human language can hardly describe it. And for what? The Government resorted to epic weapons for squalid and trivial ends, and that is why all through this unhappy period Ministers—all of them—have spoken and argued and debated well below their proper form—because they have been synthetic villains. They are not really villains. They have only set off on a villainous course, and they cannot even use the language of villainy.

Therefore, in conclusion, I say that it is no use hon. Members consoling themselves that they have more support in the country than many of them feared they might have. Of course they have support in the country. They have support among many of the unthinking and unreflective who still react to traditional values, who still think that we can solve all these problems in the old ways. Of course they have. Not all the human race has grown to adult state yet. But do not let them take comfort in that thought. The right hon. Member for Woodford (Sir W. Churchill) has warned them before. In the first volume of his *Second World War,* he writes about the situation before the war and he says this:

> Thus an Administration more disastrous than any in our history saw all its errors and shortcomings acclaimed by the nation. There was however a bill to be paid, and it took the new House of Commons nearly ten years to pay it.

MR. CHARLES IAN ORR-EWING (Hendon, North): Was not that after appeasement?

MR. BEVAN: No, this was before. In any case, the words are apposite. It will take us very many years to live down what we have done. It will take us many years to pay the price. I know that tomorrow evening hon. and right hon. Members will probably, as they have done before, give the Government a vote of confidence, but they know in their heart of hearts that it is a vote which the Government do not deserve.

Speech by the Prime Minister, Harold Wilson, in the House of Commons on the Arab-Israeli War, 5 June 1967*

The tone in which the right hon. Member for Kinross and West Perthshire (Sir Alex Douglas-Home) has spoken has been in harmony with the tone adopted right through the debate. The gravity with which the whole House has approached this debate has shown that it was right, as the right hon. Gentleman the Leader of the Opposition said, for the Government to propose that our pre-arranged Parliamentary programme should be altered so that the whole House could express its concern about the situation which developed with such dramatic and startling speed during the Recess.

The debate has been inevitably serious and sombre, but it has been more than that: it has been constructive and it has been determined. I do not propose tonight to go over the ground which was so fully covered by my right hon. Friend this afternoon. His analysis and interpretation have been widely recognised by the House as fair and judicious, and there has been a general desire in the speeches which have followed to support him in keeping the international temperature down, so far as that is possible in this situation. So I shall not attempt to go over the same ground, whether the events of the past three or four weeks, or the wider historical setting in which my right hon. Friend placed this present confrontation.

I think that I am summing up the mood of the House today and the vast majority of speeches—although, as the right hon. Gentleman said, there have been two or three on both sides which have taken a line different from this—when I say that there is no attempt to take sides, either in terms of support, or in terms of condemnation. The whole House feels—and in this I take account of the very serious and constructive approach of so many who have spoken—that, as the right hon. Gentleman has just said, Britain has an important role to play in securing peace and in securing an honourable negotiated settlement. I think that it has been recognised throughout the debate that that role can best be fulfilled not on the basis of dramatic declarations but on patient diplomacy, seeking to influence others and, as occasion offers, to influ-

Hansard, 5.s., DCCXLVII, 199–212.

ence others to take initiatives which in other circumstances we might have felt it right to take ourselves.

For this reason, and again following my right hon. Friend, while there is a great deal which all of us on this Bench would like to say, as the Leader of the Opposition and the right hon. Gentleman very fairly recognised, there are things which are best not said if we want to get the result which we want.

What we have today is not conflict but confrontation, not a breach of the peace but a deep and dangerous threat to peace. This confrontation and the dangers which it presents are on two levels. As so many hon. and right hon. Gentlemen have said, including the Leader of the Opposition, there is first confrontation along hundreds of miles of land frontier between Israel and Arab countries. Aircraft and naval units are in a state of instant readiness. Indeed, one of the great dangers last weekend was the fears of one side of a pre-emptive strike by the other.

Nor is it solely Israel and Egypt, or Israel on the one hand and Egypt and Syria on the other. Arab States which have been deeply divided on ideological grounds and grounds of national interest one with another have suddenly made common cause, burying, for the moment at least, their differences in new-found unity directed against their old enemy, Israel. In some respect—and this adds to the dangers—this confrontation has all the dangers and characteristics of a holy war.

It is not only for that reason that this confrontation is so dangerous. In the past, wars have been threatened and wars have been fought between sovereign States who, recognising one another's existence and recognising one and another's right to exist, nevertheless had deep differences of national interest or imagined national interest, claims on territory, or claims of persecution of ethnic minorities, or whatever it might be, and those feelings have led to war. But the characteristic of this situation is the declared aim of one side not to win concessions from the other. Their demand is that Israel should cease to exist—indeed has never existed.

But there is a still deeper danger which every speaker in the debate has recognised. The Leader of the Opposition—I made the same point outside the House—felt that if we are to seek in any sense an historical analogy—there have been references to Munich, Suez and the rest—that analogy is to be found, not in the events of 1956 or anywhere in the history of the Middle East, but in the Cuba confrontation of 1962. I think that both of us are right in feeling that even that analogy is not complete. The Cuban situation was dramatically described at the time, rightly, as an eyeball-to-eyeball confrontation of the two super-Powers, with all the dangers that that confrontation presented of a thermo-nuclear holocaust.

As both the opening speakers and most of those who have followed have made clear today, the statements, commitments and postures of powerful outside countries with a vital interest in the Middle East suggest that a local conflict, disastrous and brutal though that would be, might quickly escalate into a still more tragic war whose consequences could engulf the whole world. But there are, as I think we all recognise, important differences from the Cuba situation—differences on the favourable side. There is, I think, the clear desire and determination on all sides to urge restraint and to prevent the first fatal step from being taken by either side.

No one will doubt the sincerity with which the United States, we ourselves and France have urged the maximum restraint during this past week, whatever provocation might have been thought to exist. Equally, I fully accept—indeed my right hon. Friend the Foreign Secretary was given evidence of this on his visit to Moscow last week—the sincerity of the Soviet Union in desiring and urging restraint at this critical time. Here at least we have common ground which, despite all disappointments—disappointments about the fate of the French President's proposal for four-Power talks—could provide a basis for co-operation and consultation between the four great Powers to help all concerned to work their way towards a negotiated and honourable settlement. We have urged—and I was glad that the Leader of the Opposition supported this today—that the United Nations presents, or might present, the right forum for quadripartite co-operation of this kind to begin. I am less sure that the right hon. Gentleman was right in suggesting that such co-operation might be more productive or perhaps easier to get off the ground if the aim of the four-Power talks at the United Nations were to be an attack on wider world problems, including, as I suspect he had in mind, dangers in the Far East as well as the Middle East. I should like to feel that this was so and was right.

We for our part have proved that we are as anxious to secure an end to the fighting in Vietnam and to get the parties there to the conference table as we are to prevent fighting in the Middle East and get the parties there to the conference table. We shall continue to pursue peace in Vietnam with all the energy and imagination of which we are capable. Nothing that has happened in the Middle East in the last two or three weeks has made that less urgent. But to widen the area of peace-keeping, as I thought the right hon. Gentleman was perhaps suggesting, might lead to delay in dealing with the desperately critical and urgent situation in the Middle East. Indeed, it might even provide opportunities for delay for those who might welcome them.

While we must hope and feel that we now have a short breathing space— that view has been expressed on both sides today—and while every minute of that short breathing space must be used to work for peace—while that must be our hope—time is certainly not on the side of peace.

That brings us to the other difference from the Cuba situation. Cuba, dangerous though it was—the right hon. Gentleman made the same point this afternoon—was a situation uniquely within the control of the two nuclear protagonists. Either of them had it in its power to call a halt to the actions on the high seas which were bringing war nearer. One could have called the ships back and the other could have dropped the proposals for the quarantine. In the end, it was the supreme statesmanship of both sides, the give and take, which meant that action was taken on both sides and that the danger was averted.

In the Middle East crisis, however, the great Powers which are concerned, and, indeed, who are committed by their statements, are not in complete control of the situation because the action of countries on the spot, those to whom commitments have been made—on the Arab side, not necessarily one country—or a dangerous border incident coming from either side—either of these things could trigger off conflagration and involve the great Powers.

I want now to turn to what has been the central theme of the debate, as it is the central theme of the danger which we face, and that is the central theme of the search for peace. This is the threat to the right of innocent passage through the Straits of Tiran. I say "the threat to the right of innocent passage" because up to this moment the Straits remain open. Hon. Members who have talked of reopening the Straits rather than keeping them open, which, I think, is the right phrase, could perhaps tend to overstate the present position and thereby possibly make a solution just that bit more difficult.

Hon. Member after hon. Member from my right hon. Friend the Foreign Secretary onwards has stressed that the ten years since the time when Mr. Hammarskjoeld negotiated the settlement that led to the withdrawal of the Israeli troops from the Sharm el Sheikh area and the debate which followed in the General Assembly in March, 1957, have been years of free movement through the Straits.

Again, and I know that the right hon. Gentleman will not object to my making the point, while that was, as he suggested, partly due to the stationing of the U.N.E.F. force in Sharm el Sheikh that was not the only reason for continued freedom of passage because, quite apart from what happened to the battery there, as recent events have made plain, shipping could have been interfered with in other ways whoever held the battery, but it was not interfered with.

The position of Her Majesty's Government about the freedom of passage I made clear about a week ago in a speech in the country, and this was repeated by my right hon. Friend this afternoon. It repeated the statement that was made on behalf of Britain in the General Assembly debate ten years ago. It remains our position, and the Government today have been encouraged by the very wide support given to it by right hon. and hon. Members in all parts of the House.

It is through the United Nations that, in the first instance, we shall seek to secure acceptance of the principle that was laid down. It is through the United Nations that, in the first instance, we shall seek to get effective agreement on the part of all concerned to see that that principle continues to hold good and that the right of the international waterway is maintained.

Here again, I very much agreed with the right hon. Member for Kinross and West Perthshire when he expressed agreement with my right hon. Friend that this problem is best looked at, not as a special localised problem, but as part of a much wider internationally-agreed conception of the freedom of passage through international waterways.

Doubts have been thrown this evening on the question of whether there is a legal right of free passage. Those who have the duty of advising Her Majesty's

Government in this matter are in no doubt whatever that this is an international waterway, and that the right of free passage for innocent vessels through that waterway does not derive in any sense from the agreement registered by Mr. Hammarskjoeld in 1957, or from anything that was said at the General Assembly in that year, that this right is a right inherent in the situation of the Straits as part of a much wider international agreement. My right hon. Friend made clear that, with the present deep division within the Security Council, there can be no guarantee that a satisfactory arrangement will be concluded and made effective.

Perhaps here I should reply to the point with which the right hon. Gentleman the Leader of the Opposition asked me to deal. He took up the words of my right hon. Friend today about what our attitude would be in the event of a failure to secure an equitable settlement. The words which my right hon. Friend used were these:

> We could not be satisfied with a situation in which a numerical majority are satisfied with an inequitable settlement which will merely ensure that an Arab-Israel war is inevitable sooner or later.

The right hon. Gentleman asked whether, given such a situation, that implied an intention to use the veto or, if not, what other action might be appropriate.

This is not the right moment at which to anticipate what will happen, and I am sure that the right hon. Gentleman will agree that it would be unwise and perhaps unhelpful if I were now to try and forecast either the situation which might arise or what the appropriate action might be in any particular circumstances. We might be faced at the Security Council, for example, with a situation where the hopes of an equitable settlement were frustrated by a veto used against such a settlement. We might face a situation where there was a majority in favour but not an adequate majority in terms of the requirements of Security Council procedures. We might face a situation where there was no majority at all. Again, we might face a situation where there was general agreement on a resolution, but on a resolution which did not go far enough to secure the right objective, in which case we should have to try again. That is what my right hon. Friend had in mind.

At this stage, it is impossible also to forecast, whatever present disappointments there have been about the fate of the proposals of the President of France for four-Power talks, what prospects there might be of discussion between the four great Powers in this context, which has been proposed, which so far has fallen on stony ground, but which will be pressed with the very warmest support from Her Majesty's Government.

What my right hon. Friend was urging, with very strong support from all parts of the House, was that, as I have said, time not being on the side of peace, it is our duty to extend our diplomatic activity beyond what we are now trying to do in the Security Council; for example, as he said, by our contacts with other maritime countries which share with us a vital interest in the freedom of the seas.

While, so far as the Security Council is concerned, our position has been made clear in New York and while we shall continue to press it there, above all, I feel that our decision was right to consult with other like-minded nations—and here I am thinking of the maritime nations—about the issuing of a clear declaration by the international maritime community that the Gulf of Aqaba is an international waterway and that the Straits of Tiran do provide an international waterway into which and through which the vessels of all nations have a right of passage. For the same reason as my right hon. Friend said, if our other diplomatic efforts did not produce the desired results and such a declaration of itself failed to secure the right of innocent passage to which we and other maritime nations attach such importance, we should be failing in our duty if we were not now consulting with those concerned about the situation which would then arise and what action would then be appropriate to ensure that the objective which we have in mind is fulfilled.

As to the attitude of the international maritime community to the problem of maintaining freedom of passage through the Straits of Tiran, we are, of course, in consultation with them. The right hon. Gentleman mentioned a number of those whom he and we might feel would be particularly concerned, but I would like to remind the House, as my right hon. Friend did this afternoon, of the very clear declarations made by practically the whole international maritime community when the matter was debated in the General Assembly on 1st March, 1957.

The statement of the representative of Her Majesty's then Government has been repeated a number of times today, and I shall not weary the House with it again. There was the statement of the United States Government, and indeed the public declaration of the then President of the United States, which was quoted in the General Assembly. There was the statement of the French Government, which I think puts this so clearly that it would be right to remind the House that it said:

> The French Government considers that the Gulf of Aqaba, by reason partly of its breadth and partly of the fact that its shores belong to four different States, constitutes international waters. Consequently it believes that, in conformity with international law, freedom of navigation should be ensured in the Gulf through the Straits which give access to it. In these circumstances no nation has the right to prevent the free and innocent passage of ships, whatever their nationality or type.

The representative of Italy said:

> As far, in particular, as free navigation in the Gulf of Aqaba and the Straits of Tiran are concerned, I do not need to restate here that we consider that the Gulf of Aqaba is an international waterway and that no nation has a right to prevent free and innocent passage in the Gulf of Aqaba and through the Straits giving access thereto.

The Netherlands Government said that they were

> in full agreement with the statements made by Israel, the United States, France and a number of other countries to the effect that passage through the Straits of Tiran should be free, open and unhindered for the ships of all nations.

The Australian representative said:

> Let me now turn to the issue of the Gulf of Aqaba. In this case, we have a gulf of importance to the commerce and shipping of at least two States—Israel and Jordan—and bounded by the territories of four States, Israel, Jordan, South Arabia and Egypt. I think no one could fairly deny that the Gulf of Aqaba is part of the seas where the principle of the freedom of maritime communication applies—a principle.

The Australian delegate went on to say "which the International Court of Justice, in its judgment of 9 April, 1949 on the Corfu Channel case characterised as one of 'certain general and well-recognised principles'." I think that that is what the right hon. Gentleman had in mind a few moments ago.

The New Zealand Government, Norway, Denmark—I could go on, but I do not intend to weary the House because the whole world maritime community was saying these very things in 1957. I think it is therefore right, and it seems to enjoy the support of the House as a whole, that we should be working with the rest of the world maritime community to secure a declaration of the kind to which my right hon. Friend referred this afternoon.

The House will not expect me to say more about what we will do, or what we feel it will be right to do, if, first, action through the Security Council proves ineffective, or the mere issuing of a declaration fails to maintain the freedom of passage through these Straits. All of us here recognise that time is not on our side, and I think it is recognised that one of the significant facts which has so far prevented action of a kind which could have escalated in a way which we all know it could, indeed one of the significant facts which I believe last weekend prevented such action being taken, with all the dread consequences which would have followed, has been the assertion of the obvious concern of ourselves and other maritime nations about the continued right of free passage through this as through other international waterways, and I think it right to say to the House that if this concern had not been expressed as strongly as it has been, it is very doubtful whether there would have been sufficient confidence last weekend to have averted what might have become a general conflagration.

Because of that, and because of the concern which has been expressed so clearly, time is not on our side in working out the necessary arrangements. We may have a few weeks, as the right hon. Gentleman said, or even a month or two. None of us can be certain about that. Therefore, I believe that we have a very strong sense of urgency, and I believe that the House appreciates that sense of urgency.

As my right hon. Friend made clear and as has been said by hon. Members on both sides of the House, we shall do everything in our power to secure the effective presence of an appropriate United Nations agency or agencies to help maintain the peace in the area. As we all recognise and have said, they did so successfully in the past. It would be wrong at this stage to speculate about the precise duties which will be assigned to such a United Nations presence, but certainly, as has again been said by hon. Members on both sides, we are right to press that Israel as well as the Arab countries must accept a United Nations presence on their soil.

When the right hon. Gentleman the Leader of the Opposition made his comments on the precipitate decision to withdraw United Nations peacekeeping force and, indeed, when the right hon. Member for Kinross and West Perthshire said what he did in pretty strong terms about the precipitate withdrawal and the acceptance, without consultation, of that demand, I believe that what they said was absolutely right, and we fully support their account and their criticism of this decision.

The Leader of the Opposition asked what possible consequences or implications this might have for Cyprus. I will come to that in detail in a moment. I certainly agree with the implication contained in a number of speeches, including that of the right hon. Member for Kinross and West Perthshire, that this decision could have very far-reaching consequences for the United Nations as a whole, in a wider sphere, if we are not able in a very short time to repair the damage that has been done—and damage has been done, and it was done very much against the very strong pressure and insistence of the British delegation there, which wanted to have full consultation in the way the right hon. Gentleman suggested.

This situation has no bearing on the circumstances in which the Cyprus peace-keeping operation was set up. That was set up not by the General Assembly but, as the right hon. Gentleman remembers very well, by a Security Council resolution which requires a confirming resolution every six months. We are the major contributors to that force, as the right hon. Gentleman knows, and even if no more were done on such an occasion than was done in the case of the Sinai force we should have the right of consultation there, because there were some informal consultations with the countries who had troops in Sinai.

But this is not the point here, because if the Government of Cyprus requested that the forces be withdrawn Britain could and should demand that the question be debated by the Security Council, because the Security Council set it up and also because such a withdrawal of that force would be rightly regarded— indeed, this has been underlined by the events of the last two or three weeks— as a major threat to peace. We could therefore ourselves request, and would request, a meeting of the Security Council. Therefore, in terms of a parallel between the two cases, the unfortunate and regrettable decision in the case of Sinai has no governing influence on what would happen in the case of Cyprus.

The right hon. Gentleman criticised this withdrawal, but it was not only Britain; other countries were with us in pressing that there should be full consultation and a full generalised discussion by those whose authority it was and under whose authority the original force had been sent out. Here I think particularly of Canada, whose forces have co-operated in maintaining this lonely vigil for these many years.

To sum up, I feel that this debate has been undeniably useful, not only in stating the views of the great majority of hon. Members—and I believe that they are the views of the great majority of hon. Members—but also in helping to emphasise, from a vastly confused and tortured situation, those issues to which Her Majesty's Government and all others who are concerned in the search for peace should now give priority.

I emphasise again that we are not concerned in this debate or in the actions which follow—and I think the House is not concerned—with taking sides or apportioning blame. However visionary this may seem in such a dangerous situation, what we must seek to do is not only to avoid the dangers of a tragic war, which would be tragic enough in all conscience even if confined to those who now only glower at one another across Middle Eastern frontiers. Many of us here who have visited one or another of many Middle Eastern countries in recent years can imagine the tragedy of the destruction that would follow, not only in loss of life but of treasured possessions and buildings and historic treasures of the countries in question.

Even if so limited, it would be tragic enough, but, as we have all emphasised, it is the danger of a war more horrible because of the dangers of escalation. Visionary as I have called it and visionary though it may seem, what we must seek to do in this situation is not merely to avoid war but to create the conditions of peace. A number of hon. Members have made their contribution to what we call conditions for a lasting peace rather than concentrating on things which must be done urgently to stop war breaking out.

One condition of a lasting peace must be the recognition that Israel has the right to live. As my hon. Friend reminded us, it has been for nearly twenty years a member country of the United Nations, entitled to the respect and protection of the United Nations. Whatever the bitterness that rules today, there are wise men in Israel and there are wise men in Arab countries, however difficult it may be for them to become articulate, who recognise not only the need for co-existence but also the immense opportunities for peaceful co-operation which exist once man-made barriers, based on primeval hostility, can be broken down.

There are some, we know, in Arab countries who argue that with all the poverty and hunger in the Middle East, poverty which there is still, despite the new but inequitably shared riches which oil has brought, and which is still the lot of the great majority of people in the Middle East, the cutting off of an initially fertile area and its designation as a home for large numbers of refugees from vast areas of the world is a provocative act and one which inevitably condemns the rest of the area to continued poverty.

But this is entirely to misconceive the problem of poverty in the Middle East. Wise men, Arabs and Jews alike, conscious of what has been achieved in this small country, which is one of the classic prototypes of successful economic development, conscious of what has been done particularly in irrigation and the transformation of desert into fertile areas, these men know how much could be achieved in a total Middle Eastern war on poverty and hunger if political differences could be set aside.

Commonwealth and other countries in Africa and Asia have good reason to know what Israeli technical assistance means, based as it is not on the expertise of an established advanced industrial country, with all the irrelevancies which are sometimes provided in the form of technical assistance from advanced countries, but on their own recent experience in developing a primitive and under-developed area. They have come through this way, and they have made mistakes. They know what mistakes to avoid. But they have also had tremendous successes.

The tragedy for the Middle East is not that the Israelis are occupying a small part of the vast cultivable area; it is that political hostilities on both sides and, above all, perhaps the wasteful deployment on both sides on arms and military expenditure of a prodigious amount—a scale that cannot be afforded—of resources which should be devoted to economic developments, it is these things, the continuing bitter hostility and this wasteful use of resources on arms one against another which has stood in the way of the economic and social development of millions upon millions of people.

In putting on record my feeling about the constructive way in which the whole House has approached this debate, I feel that it is right to interpret this debate as a mandate to Her Majesty's Government by every means in our power to continue with all who are working with us in the search for peace, as we are working with them, but in a wider sense, to use this opportunity today, if opportunity be given, having peered into the abyss as we have, to turn the threat of military war into the reality of total war in the Middle East against man's most ancient enemies of poverty, hunger and disease.

THE END OF EMPIRE

*Communications between Prime Minister Winston Churchill,
General Wavell, and General Percival on the Fall of
Singapore, 10–13 February 1942* [Singapore surrendered
to the Japanese on 15 February 1942.]*

Prime Minister to General Wavell
10 Feb. 42

I think you ought to realise the way we view the situation in Singapore. It was reported to the Cabinet by the C.I.G.S. that Percival has over 100,000 men, of whom 33,000 are British and 17,000 Australian. It is doubtful whether the Japanese have as many in the whole Malay peninsula, namely, five divisions forward and a sixth coming up. In these circumstances the defenders must greatly outnumber Japanese forces who have crossed the straits, and in a well-contested battle they should destroy them. There must at this stage be no thought of saving the troops or sparing the population. The battle must be fought to the bitter end at all costs. The 18th Division has a chance to make its name in history. Commanders and senior officers should die with their troops. The honour of the British Empire and of the British Army is at stake. I rely on you to show no mercy to weakness in any form. With the Russians fighting as they are and the Americans so stubborn at Luzon, the whole reputation of our country and our race is involved. It is expected that every unit will be brought into close contact with the enemy and fight it out. I feel sure these words express your own feeling, and only send them to you in order to share your burdens.   *   *   *

General Wavell to General Percival
13 Feb. 42

You must all fight it out to the end as you are doing. But when everything humanly possible has been done, some bold and determined personnel may be able to escape by small craft and find their way south to Sumatra through the islands. Any such small craft with sandbag protection and mounting an automatic or small gun such as two-pounder would be valuable also in defending Sumatra rivers.

*Churchill, The Hinge of Fate, 100, 104.

General Percival to General Wavell
13 Feb. 42

Enemy now within 5000 yards of sea-front, which brings whole of Singapore town within field artillery range. We are also in danger of being driven off water and food supplies. In opinion of commanders troops already committed are too exhausted either to withstand strong attack or to launch counter-attack. We would all earnestly welcome the chance of initiating an offensive, even though this would only amount to a gesture, but even this is not possible, as there are no troops who could carry out this attack. In these conditions it is unlikely that resistance can last more than a day or two. My subordinate commanders are unanimously of the opinion that the gain of time will not compensate for extensive damage and heavy casualties which will occur in Singapore town. As Empire overseas is interested, I feel bound to represent their views. There must come a stage when in the interests of the troops and civil population further bloodshed will serve no useful purpose. Your instructions of February 10 are being carried out, but in above circumstances would you consider giving me wider discretionary powers?

Burma Independence Act (11 Geo. VI, c. 3), 10 December 1947*

Be it enacted by the King's most Excellent Majesty, by and with the advice and consent of the Lords Spiritual and Temporal, and Commons, in this present Parliament assembled and by the authority of the same, as follows: —

1.—(1) On the appointed day, Burma shall become an independent country, neither forming part of His Majesty's dominions nor entitled to His Majesty's protection.

(2) In this Act, the expression "the appointed day" means the fourth day of January, nineteen hundred and forty-eight.

(3) The suzerainty of His Majesty over the part of Burma known as the Karenni States shall lapse as from the appointed day, and with it all treaties and agreements in force between His Majesty and the rulers of the Karenni States, all functions exercisable by His Majesty with respect to the Karenni States, all obligations of His Majesty towards the Karenni States or the rulers thereof, and all powers, rights, authority or jurisdiction exercisable by His Majesty in or in relation to the Karenni States by treaty, grant, usage, sufferance or otherwise.

2.—(1) Subject to the provisions of this section, the persons specified in the First Schedule to this Act, being British subjects immediately before the appointed day, shall on that day cease to be British subjects:

Public General Statutes, LXXXV, pt. 2, 1938-41.

Provided that a woman who immediately before the appointed day is the wife of a British subject shall not cease by virtue of this subsection to be a British subject unless her husband ceases by virtue of this subsection to be a British subject.

(2) A person who by virtue of subsection (1) of this section ceases to be a British subject on the appointed day and is immediately before that day domiciled or ordinarily resident in either—

(*a*) any part of the United Kingdom;

(*b*) any of the Channel Islands;

(*c*) the Isle of Man;

(*d*) Newfoundland;

(*e*) any colony;

(*f*) any territory in respect of which a mandate from the League of Nations was accepted by His Majesty, being a territory under the sole administration of His Majesty's Government in the United Kingdom;

(*g*) any territory administered under the trusteeship system of the United Nations, being a territory under the sole administration of His Majesty's Government in the United Kingdom;

(*h*) any British protectorate;

(*i*) any British protected state outside Burma; or

(*k*) any other place outside Burma in which, by treaty, capitulation, grant, usage, sufferance or other lawful means, His Majesty has jurisdiction over British subjects,

may, by a declaration made before the expiration of the two years beginning with the appointed day to such person and in such manner as may be prescribed, elect to remain a British subject, and if he so elects, the provisions of subsection (1) of this section (including the proviso thereto) shall be deemed never to have applied to or in relation to him or, except so far as the declaration otherwise provides, any child of his who is under the age of eighteen years at the date of the declaration:

Provided that a declaration under this subsection shall be of no effect unless it is registered in the prescribed manner in pursuance of an application made within, or within the prescribed period after the expiration of, the said two years.

In this subsection, the expression "prescribed" means prescribed by regulations of the Secretary of State or of such Government, authority or person as may be authorised in that behalf by the Secretary of State, and different provision may be made under this subsection for different classes of cases.

(3) A person who by virtue of subsection (1) of this section ceases to be a British subject on the appointed day, not being such a person as is mentioned in subsection (2) of this section, shall, if on that day he neither becomes, nor becomes qualified to become, a citizen of the independent country of Burma for which provision is made by section one of this Act, have the like right of

election as is provided for by subsection (2) of this section, and the said subsection (2) shall have effect accordingly.

(4) If provision is made by the law of any part of His Majesty's dominions not mentioned in subsection (2) of this section for the exercise by any persons, being persons domiciled or ordinarily resident in that part of His Majesty's dominions or in any territory administered by the Government thereof, of a right to elect not to cease to be British subjects on the appointed day by reason of Burma becoming an independent country on that day, then, so far as is necessary to give effect under the law of the United Kingdom to the results flowing under the law of that part of His Majesty's dominions from the exercise of the right of election, the provisions of subsection (1) of this section shall be deemed never to have applied to or in relation to, or to or in relation to the children of, the persons who duly exercise that right.

(5) Save as provided in this section, no person who is a British subject immediately before the appointed day shall cease to be a British subject by reason of Burma ceasing on that day to be part of His Majesty's dominions.

(6) The exercise by a person of any such right of election as is referred to in subsection (2), subsection (3) and subsection (4) of this section shall not render unlawful anything done before the date of the election which would have been lawful if the election had not been made.

3.— (1) Notwithstanding any of the provisions of this Act, the enactments relating to customs (including the enactments relating to customs in the Isle of Man) shall, on and after the appointed day, have effect, until such date as may be specified by His Majesty by Order in Council, as if Burma were part of His Majesty's dominions:

Provided that His Majesty may by Order in Council direct that, as from a specified date, all goods or goods of specified classes or descriptions shall be charged under the said enactments either as if the preceding provisions of this section had not passed or at such rates as may be specified in the Order, not being rates higher than would have been chargeable if the said provisions had not passed.

(2) Any Order in Council made under this section may be revoked or varied by a subsequent Order in Council made thereunder.

(3) Any Order in Council made under this section shall be laid before both Houses of Parliament after it is made and if, within a period of forty days beginning with the day on which any such Order is so laid before it, either House of Parliament presents an Address to His Majesty praying that the Order may be revoked, His Majesty may revoke the Order accordingly, but without prejudice to the making of a new Order.

(4) In reckoning the said period of forty days, no account shall be taken of any time during which Parliament is dissolved or prorogued, or during which both Houses are adjourned for more than four days.

(5) Section one of the Rules Publication Act, 1893 (which requires notice to be given of a proposal to make statutory rules) shall not apply to any Order in Council made under this section.

4.—(1) Any appeal to His Majesty in Council from any court in Burma which is pending on the appointed day shall abate on that day.

(2) No proceedings shall be brought in any court on or after the appointed day against the Secretary of State in any such case as is mentioned in section one hundred and thirty-three of the Government of Burma Act, 1935, and any proceedings brought by or against the Secretary of State by virtue of that section which are pending immediately before the appointed day shall abate on that day so far as the Secretary of State is concerned.

(3) Nothing in this Act shall affect the jurisdiction of the High Court in England or the Court of Session in Scotland under the Indian and Colonial Divorce Jurisdiction Acts, 1926 and 1940, as respects decrees or orders made in Burma which, before the appointed day, have been registered in those Courts respectively under those Acts:

Provided that—

> (a) notwithstanding anything in those Acts, the said Courts may entertain applications for the modification or discharge of orders notwithstanding that the person on whose petition the decree for dissolution was pronounced is resident in Burma; and
>
> (b) no regard shall be had to any order made in Burma on or after the appointed day modifying or discharging any decree or order made before the appointed day.

*   *   *

Statement by the Prime Minister, Clement Attlee, in the
House of Commons on the State of Emergency in Malaya, 13 April 1948*

Mr. Skinnard asked the Prime Minister whether, in view of the representations received by His Majesty's Government from the Government of Malaya, he will give an assurance that His Majesty's Government have no intention of relinquishing their responsibilities there.

The Prime Minister (Mr. Attlee): Yes, Sir. His Majesty's Government have no intention of relinquishing their responsibilities in Malaya until their task is completed. The purpose of our policy is simple. We are working, in co-operation with the citizens of the Federation of Malaya and Singapore, to guide them to responsible self-government within the Commonwealth. We have no intention of jeopardising the security, well-being and liberty of these peoples, for whom Britain has responsibilities, by a premature withdrawal.

*Hansard, 5.s., CDLXIII, 2815.

MR. SKINNARD: Is my right hon. Friend aware of the satisfaction that will be felt, not only by the whole House, but in Malaya and in this country, at the nature of his answer?

MR. GALLACHER: Shooting down women—is that his responsibility?

Speech by a Labour Party Spokesman, James Griffiths, in the House of Commons on the Malayan Crisis, 17 July 1952*

*   *   *

I leave Kenya and Africa and turn my attention to some aspects of the situation in Malaya. Four years have gone by since guerilla warfare and terrorism came to Malaya. The people of Malaya have lived for those four years under daily and nightly terror. When it is remembered that before the four years 1948 to 1952 during which this guerilla warfare has been proceeding there was a period of years during which Malaya was occupied ruthlessly by the Japanese, one realises that for a very long time the people of Malaya have lived under a very great strain.

I want to pay my tribute to all those who live and work and serve and endure in Malaya, without seeking to mention any particular group or any particular kind of service. I was privileged to visit Malaya over two years ago, and the Secretary of State was there recently. One has to go there to realise the setting. Here is a country in which the jungle is at everybody's back garden and people live in conditions where, at any moment of any day, and particularly of any night after darkness comes round about seven o'clock and the blinds are drawn, there may be an attack or an ambush.

I pay my tribute to all those who are living in Malaya and who are enduring these trials with so much fortitude and bravery. I hope that there is unanimous agreement in this Committee that we are resolved to stamp out terrorism in Malaya. Questions are put to me sometimes at meetings in this country asking why we do not leave Malaya. Implicit in those questions sometimes is the idea that if we left Malaya and our boys came home, freedom would follow in that country.

There would be nothing of the kind. It would be the imposition on the people of a ruthless minority rule. I begin, therefore, by saying that it is our duty to stamp out terrorism; and I say now what I said as a Minister—and I am sure that the present Minister will re-affirm it today—that we are determined to carry on until terrorism is stamped out. The problem is not whether we are agreed on that but how it is to be done.

The first thing which it is important for us to convey to the country and to people outside this country is that what we are confronted with in Malaya is not

*Hansard, 5.s., DIII, 2352–57.

a national upsurge representing the people, but a movement sponsored, led and inspired by the Communists in order to try to secure control of the country. It is generally estimated that there are 5,000 to 6,000 guerilla fighters in the jungle who hide by day and ambush by night.

One of the apparently unchanging factors in the situation in Malaya in the last four years is that, as far as I know—and if the Secretary of State has other information, no doubt he will tell us—there has been no increase in the number of guerillas; and although there have been casualties, no one will say that there has been a substantial decrease in the number. They are able to replace their casualties from their supporters in the country.

I have heard varying estimates of the number of those willing to support them out of a population of somewhere between 5 million and 6 million. It is important to remember these figures for the sake of proportion. They number from 10,000 to the highest estimate I have heard mentioned of 50,000. It is right to say—and I believe it from my experience when I was in the country and from what I learned as Secretary of State—that this movement does not have the support of the vast mass of the people.

In those circumstances, what are the problems? The first problem is that of protecting the people from the terrorists. When I was in Malaya two years ago, the major proposal to that end was the plan designed by Sir Harold Briggs and fully supported by Sir Henry Gurney. I should like to pay my tribute to the memory of Sir Henry Gurney and also to the work of Sir Harold Briggs. That plan was for the re-settling of from 450,000 to 500,000 squatters who had settled in Malaya and who were living, in a sense, outside the orbit of government altogether.

That is an immense problem. I saw it in process of being solved and the Secretary of State has seen it more recently. I believe that up to now, within a period of two and a half years, about 450,000 squatters in Malaya have been re-settled. The settlements are of varying character. The best are very good, but quite frankly some are such as to make one anxious, worried, and apprehensive.

It has been a major operation. I hope that the Secretary of State will be able to tell us whether this settlement scheme is now complete and what are the conditions in the villages and communities in which these people have been re-settled. I hope that he will be able to tell us also whether one problem, which we saw looming ahead when re-settlement had been completed, is on the way to solution.

That problem relates to the question of the future security of tenure of these people in areas to which we and the Government of Malaya, as part of policy, have moved them, taking them away from the lands which they had made their own and had cultivated. It is very important for us to realise that this movement creates a problem. These people want to know whether they are re-settled with a reasonable degree of security of tenure to enable them to build their lives in the future.

This is not only a military problem. I expect that the Secretary of State has received deputations, as I did, from people in this country and, indeed, occasionally from people in Malaya who put forward this view. A good many think that they have the short answer to the problem. They have said that all that was required was to put the country under martial law and then everything would be all right. I have said already that part of the problem is to protect the people from the terrorists. But another part is how to invoke the willing co-operation of the millions of people in Malaya who do not support the terrorists, who are sometimes terrorised by them but who, so far, whatever may be the reasons, do not give us their active co-operation on this problem.

THE SECRETARY OF STATE FOR THE COLONIES (MR. OLIVER LYTTELTON): I think that the right hon. Gentleman should know that neither the Commander-in-Chief nor any civil authority, or any official authority, has ever suggested to me the imposition of martial law. I want to make that quite clear.

MR. GRIFFITHS: I can assure the right hon. Gentleman that such representations were made to me.

MR. LYTTELTON: Not officially.

MR. GRIFFITHS: By delegations and deputations. I am not going to be drawn into saying by whom, but I assure the right hon. Gentleman that they were made.

This problem is the problem of invoking the aid of the population. Very frankly, my own view is that it is absolutely essential that if we are to invoke the aid of the people then, at the same time as we deal with the military aspect of the problem, we must deal with the economic, social and political problems. We cannot dissociate the economic, social and political problems of this area from the military problem. We have a dual task which is to beat the terrorists and to start building now for the future of Malaya. We have to work rapidly towards self-government in Malaya.

I should like the Secretary of State and hon. Members who give their time and thought to this problem to consider what I am about to say. We are going to win this battle, I am sure; and the sooner the better. When we have won it there will be an irresistible demand for self-government in Malaya. Make no mistake about that. The demand is growing. The war itself will add impetus, drive and urgency to it. We have to prepare Malaya so that there are the appropriate institutions which can make it into a democracy. That is what we have to work at.

I should like to deal briefly with some aspects of this problem and to ask some questions about it. The first problem we have to solve is the problem of citizenship. Here we have 5½ million people. The effective political power is almost completely in the hands of the Malayans. The Chinese have no political authority and neither have the Indians. I should like to pay tribute to the work the Commissioner for South-East Asia, Mr. MacDonald, has done in his efforts to get agreement on the terms of citizenship. We marked an advance. There was an agreement upon the terms of a Bill to extend citizenship and to bring more Chinese and Africans into citizenship in Malaya.

I am told that that Bill which had been agreed upon is being held up and is not yet operative because some of the separate States are still proving obstructive. I ask the Secretary of State whether any of the States are still holding it up. If they are, I should like him to say which States they are. It is vitally important not only for the future of Malaya but for the immediate situation that this Bill should be put forward. It is criminal stupidity for any of the States to get in the way of this modest advance towards building a Malayan nation.

I come to the question of elections. I discussed this matter with the late Sir Henry Gurney when he was High Commissioner. I knew how his mind was working. I knew that tentative—I emphasise the word "tentative"—plans had been made. They could not be anything but tentative in view of the position in Malaya. The tentative plan which he had was to hold municipal elections last year or this year in some of the principal towns. Those elections having been held, he planned to follow that up by holding State elections in 1953, leading up to Federal elections in 1954.

I should like to ask the Secretary of State whether that plan is still adhered to and if so, the municipal elections having taken place, since the plan envisaged State elections within about a year or 18 months, whether he can say what arrangements are being made for elections within the States. As it was also agreed that elections for the Federal Legislative Council should take place after an interval of 18 months, have any arrangements been made for them?

* * *

Official Memorandum by the British Government
Summarizing the Constitutional Stages toward
Self-Government for the Sudan, 17 February 1953*
[The Sudan received its independence on
1 January 1956.]

I

Condominium rule in the Anglo-Egyptian Sudan began with the signature in January, 1899, of the "Agreement between Her Britannic Majesty's Government and the Government of the Khedive of Egypt relative to the future administration of the Sudan". This agreement, and a minor amending agreement signed the following July, are commonly called the "Condominium Agreements". The preamble to the main agreement reads as follows: —

> Whereas certain provinces in the Sudan which were in rebellion against the authority of His Highness the Khedive have now been reconquered by the joint military and financial efforts of Her Britannic Majesty's Government and the Government of His Highness the Khedive;

*Parliamentary Papers, 1952–53, XXX, Cmd. 8767, 3–11.

And whereas it has become necessary to decide upon a system for the administration of, and for the making of, laws for the said reconquered provinces, under which due allowance may be made for the backward and unsettled condition of large portions thereof, and the varying requirements of different localities;

And whereas it is desired to give effect to the claims which have accrued to Her Britannic Majesty's Government, by right of conquest, to share in the present settlement and future working and development of the said system of administration and legislation. . . .

The agreement goes on to say: —

Article 2. The British and Egyptian flags shall be used together, both on land and water, throughout the Sudan. . . .Article 3. The supreme military and civil command in the Sudan shall be vested in one officer, termed the "Governor-General of the Sudan". He shall be appointed by Khedivial Decree on the recommendation of Her Britannic Majesty's Government, and shall be removed only by the Khedivial Decree, with the consent of Her Britannic Majesty's Government.

Article 4. Laws, as also Orders and Regulations, with the full force of law, for the good government of the Sudan, and for regulating the holding, disposal and devolution of property of every kind therein situate, may from time to time be made, altered, or abrogated by Proclamation of the Governor-General. Such Laws, Orders and Regulations may apply to the whole or any named part of the Sudan, and may, either explicitly or by necessary implication, alter or abrogate any existing Law or Regulation.

During the years which followed, the administration set up under this agreement carried out the work of pacification and consolidation. Ordered government was extended over the whole territory of the Sudan, and the country gradually recovered from the devastation and chaos in which the Anglo-Egyptian reconquering army under Lord Kitchener had found it in 1898.

After the world war of 1914-18, however, the Sudan was affected by the nationalist ferment in Egypt. The Egyptian nationalist movement, whilst demanding independence for Egypt and the end of the British Protectorate reasserted the Egyptian claim to the Sudan as an integral part of Egyptian territory, and included the Sudan in its demand for the elimination of British influence. The policy of His Majesty's Government at this time was summed up in the statement that:

they have contracted heavy moral obligations by the creation of a good system of administration; they cannot allow that to be destroyed; they regard their responsibilities as a trust for the Sudan people; there can be no question of their abandoning the Sudan until their work is done.

His Majesty's Government recognised Egypt as "an independent sovereign state" in the Declaration of 1922. In this Declaration, the Sudan was included amongst the four subjects which were:

absolutely reserved to the discretion of His Majesty's Government until such time as it may be possible to free discussion and friendly accommodation on both sides to conclude agreements in regard thereto between His Majesty's Government and the Government of Egypt.

In the repeated attempts which followed to negotiate a full settlement of relations between Britain and Egypt, the Sudan time and again proved to be the most intractable of the matters on which the two Governments sought "friendly accommodation", and when a Treaty of Alliance was eventually signed in 1936, the provisions relating to the Sudan were essentially an agreement to maintain the *status quo,* with certain modifications in Egypt's favour, and to reserve the Egyptian claim on the issue of central importance. Article 11 (1) of the Treaty stated:

> While reserving liberty to conclude new conventions in future, modifying the agreements of the 19th January and the 10th July, 1899, the High Contracting Parties agree that the administration of the Sudan shall continue to be that resulting from the said agreement. The Governor-General shall continue to exercise on the joint behalf of the High Contracting Parties the powers conferred upon him by the said agreements.
>
> The High Contracting Parties agree that the primary aim of their administration in the Sudan must be the welfare of the Sudanese.
>
> Nothing in this article prejudices the question of sovereignty over the Sudan.

It was also provided that the Governor-General, in making appointments to posts for which qualified Sudanese were not available, should select suitable candidates of British and Egyptian nationality; and that, in addition to Sudanese troops, both British and Egyptian troops should be placed at the disposal of the Governor-General for the defence of the Sudan. (Since the disturbances of 1924 there had been no Egyptian troops stationed in the Sudan.)

II

In the meantime, the Sudan Government had built up in the Sudan an administration generally regarded as a model in the enlightened government of dependent territories. They had brought the Sudan through the successive crises of the 1914-18 war (when their ranks were cruelly depleted for service elsewhere), the political crisis of the nineteen twenties, and the economic crisis of the nineteen thirties. From the first task of establishing orderly government, they had gone on to the second of making the Sudan economically independent (chiefly through the Gezira Cotton Scheme which earned world-wide tributes). New generations of Sudanese had grown up, educated to take their place in the Government service; and the Sudan was now ready for the next stage, the creation of representative institutions through which they should gradually assume control of the government of their own country, and decide for themselves on their own future.

The Second World War caused some delay, but in 1944, the Governor-General promulgated a law setting up an Advisory Council for the Northern Sudan. The Council was thirty strong, of whom twenty-nine were Sudanese. In 1946, a "Sudan Administration Conference"—with a majority of Sudanese members—was convened to study the question of how to associate the

Sudanese more closely with the central Government. The following year another important step was taken. In the Southern Provinces, which are inhabited by peoples sharply distinguished in race, creed, and culture from the Moslem North, development had been much slower; and no final decision had ever been taken on the eventual political future of these provinces. In 1947, however, a conference was called at which representatives of the South discussed their future with Northern Sudanese, and decided that their lot should be thrown in with the Northern Provinces, as partners in a united Sudan.

These various constitutional changes in the Sudan had been carried out by the Governor-General in the exercise of his "supreme military and civil command" and his power to make "laws for the good government of the Sudan". There had, however, been a background to them of strain in Anglo-Egyptian relations, which necessarily had a disturbing effect in the Sudan. The body of Sudanese opinion favouring eventual independence showed continual anxiety lest His Majesty's Government's negotiations with Egypt should lead to the acceptance of Egyptian claims to the unity of the Nile Valley; whilst those favouring union with Egypt refused their co-operation in constitutional developments. All this hampered progress within the Sudan; and in His Majesty's Government's post-war negotiations with Egypt, the Sudan again proved to be the most ineluctable point of difference.

Anxiety in the Sudan caused Mr. Bevin to make the following statement to the House of Commons on 26th March, 1946: "His Majesty's Government consider that no change should be made in the status of the Sudan as a result of treaty revision, until the Sudanese have been consulted through constitutional channels."

Negotiations in London later that year led to the initialling of the "Sidki-Bevin" Protocol, according to which:

> The policy which the High Contracting Parties undertake to follow in the Sudan within the framework of the unity between the Sudan and Egypt under the common Crown of Egypt will have for its essential objectives to assure the well-being of the Sudanese, the development of their interests and their active preparation for self-government and consequently the exercise of the right to choose the future status of the Sudan.

After his return to Egypt, however, the Egyptian Prime Minister, Ismail Sidki Pasha, made it clear in public that by unity of Egypt and the Sudan under the Egyptian Crown, he meant permanent unity; an interpretation which was confirmed by his successor M. Fahmi Nokrashi Pasha. It proved impossible to find an agreed interpretation of this formula which would safeguard ultimate Sudanese freedom of choice. On this rock, the negotiations foundered early in 1947.

In the meantime, the recommendations of the Sudan Administration Conference, and the decision on the future of the Southern provinces, had taken shape, and in November, 1947 the Governor-General addressed a note to the United Kingdom and Egyptian Governments embodying his proposals for the next stage of constitutional development: the setting up of a Legislative Assembly with an elected majority—including representatives from the South—and an Executive Council with a Sudanese majority. Ultimate authority was reserved to the Governor-General, though in the event the arrangements worked so smoothly that his reserved powers were never used.

In their reply, the Egyptian Government criticised the manner and the content of the proposed constitutional changes. His Majesty's Government were, however, anxious to persuade the Egyptian Government to co-operate and promulgation of the Legislative Assembly and Executive Council Ordinance was delayed for several months whilst the Egyptian Government were persuaded to enter discussions upon it. A provisional agreement was reached between His Majesty's Ambassador in Cairo and the Egyptian Foreign Minister which would have given the Egyptian Government the right to nominate two members to the Executive Council. The agreement was, however, repudiated by the Egyptian Government and the Ordinance was promulgated in June, 1948 without Egypt's blessing. In consequence, the elections to the Legislative Assembly the following autumn were boycotted by pro-Egyptian groups in the Sudan.

In 1950 and 1951, the British and Egyptian Governments were once more engaged in conversations to reach a general settlement of the questions outstanding between them. These finally issued in the Four Power Proposals of 13th October, 1951, concerning Egyptian participation in a Middle East Command; at the same time, His Majesty's Government made a number of proposals to meet the Egyptian point of view on the Sudan. They included:

> (a) An international commission to reside in the Sudan, watching over the constitutional development of the country and tendering advice to the Co-domini.
> (b) A joint Anglo-Egyptian statement of the common principles with regard to the Sudan.
> (c) An agreed date to be fixed for the attainment of self-government by the Sudanese as a first step on the way to the choice by the Sudanese of their final status.

By the time these proposals were made, however, the Egyptian Government had already passed legislation as a result of which, in the Egyptian Government's view: "Any intervention by the English in the affairs of the Sudan must cease immediately and there will remain only the natural unity which has bound Egypt and the Sudan from time immemorial."

This quotation is extracted from a note in which the Egyptian Government informed His Majesty's Government of their decision, made public on October 8th, 1951, to pass legislation purporting to proclaim King Farouk to be King of Egypt and the Sudan, to abrogate the Condominium Agreements and the 1936 Treaty, and to set up a constitution for the Sudan which would have made the Sudanese subject to Egypt in matters of foreign affairs, defence, finance, and currency.

III

The action of the Egyptian Government caused considerable confusion and uncertainty among the Sudanese. A Constitutional Amendment Commission had been set up in March 1951 to consider the next steps. The Commission consisted entirely of Sudanese, except for their British chairman (His Honour Mr. Justice R. C. Stanley-Baker), and for the first time it had been possible to get together the representatives of all sections of opinion, including those with leanings towards some form of union with Egypt, with the exception of the extreme Ashigga. By October their work was almost complete; but as a result of events in Egypt there were resignations from the Commission and, on the advice of the chairman, the Commission was dissolved. On November 15th, the Secretary of State for Foreign Affairs made a statement in the House of Commons, reaffirming that His Majesty's Government

> ... regard the Governor-General and the present Sudan Government as fully responsible for continuing the administration of the Sudan. ...
> His Majesty's Government will give the Governor-General their full support for the steps he is taking to bring the Sudanese rapidly to the stage of self-government as a prelude to self-determination. ...

Although the Constitutional Amendment Commission was dissolved before it had made its report, its work had been sufficiently advanced for the Sudan Government to draft, in the form of an amendment to the 1948 Legislative Assembly and Executive Council Ordinance, "An Order to provide for full Self-Government in the Sudan". The Legislative Assembly approved this draft in April 1952, and, in accordance with the procedure laid down for constitutional changes in the Legislative Assembly Ordinance, it was submitted to the Governments of the United Kingdom and Egypt by the Governor-General in May 1952. (Appendices 2 and 3.)

Between February and June 1952, there were fresh conversations between Her Majesty's Government and the Egyptian Government under Neguib el Hilali Pasha designed to pave the way for negotiations for a general settlement. Hilali Pasha made it a condition of the resumption of negotiations that Her Majesty's Government and his Government should agree on a preliminary "formula". In a despatch to Her Majesty's Ambassador in Cairo of 30th April, 1952, the Secretary of State for Foreign Affairs wrote: "The Egyptian Prime Minister has made it clear that he must make agreement over a formula on defence dependent upon agreement on one from the Sudan. The formula over the Sudan appears to present greater difficulties."

The formula which Her Majesty's Government were prepared to accept ran thus:

> The Egyptian Government having declared that His Majesty King Farouk holds the title of King of Egypt and the Sudan, Her Majesty's Government reaffirm that they would accept either the unity of Egypt and the Sudan under the Egyptian Crown or any other status for the Sudan provided that it resulted from the exercise of the right of the Sudanese people freely to decide their future status, which right is recognised and

accepted by both Governments. Her Majesty's Government realise that there are differences of opinion between the two Governments as to the question of the King's title during the interim period before self-determination. They therefore also declare that they are ready to enter into immediate consultation with the Sudanese in regard to this matter, in order to ascertain whether any solution is possible which is agreeable to the Sudanese and consistent with the pledges given by Her Majesty's Government to them.

Hilali Pasha was unable to accept this formula and no further progress could be made in these conversations.

IV

In May Her Majesty's Government received the draft Self-Government Statute. Under the terms of the 1948 Ordinance, it could be brought into force by the Governor-General, provided that both Governments did not object within six months of the date of its submission. Her Majesty's Government had made it clear that they would support the Governor-General's policy, and preparations had been made in the Sudan for the holding of elections in November and December. In accordance with the policy consistently followed by Her Majesty's Government in the past of seeking to associate their Co-dominus in constitutional progress for the Sudan, Her Majesty's Ambassador in Cairo was instructed in September, 1952, to approach the Egyptian Prime Minister and to inform him that Her Majesty's Government intended in the near future to give their approval to the draft Statute, and to express the hope that it would be possible to reach agreement on some constructive Anglo-Egyptian approach to the subject. He was instructed to suggest that the Egyptian Government should join in an international commission on which the Sudanese and the British and Egyptian Governments would be represented, under the chairmanship of a national of a State not directly interested in the Sudan. This commission would supervise elections to be held under the Statute and report to the two Governments on them. He was to stress that the immediately urgent problem was to get over the "preliminary hurdle" of the elections. Thereafter Her Majesty's Government would hope to agree on some machinery for associating Egypt with them in ordering Sudanese affairs in the interim period between the bringing into force of the Constitution and the exercise of self-determination by the Sudanese. One way would be to maintain the international commission in being after the elections: discussion of this would, however, be facilitated by the existence of a Sudanese Parliament and a Sudanese Government.

Her Majesty's Ambassador spoke to General Neguib in this sense on 24th September, 1952. General Neguib's response was encouraging, and he asked for time in which to study Her Majesty's Government's suggestions. On 22nd October, Mr. Eden told the House of Commons that Her Majesty's Government had informed the Acting Governor-General of the Sudan of their consent to his making the Proclamation necessary to bring the draft Self-Government Statute into force. (Appendix 4.) He added: —"The views of the Egyptian

Government have not yet been received. I hope that they may be in time for consideration by Her Majesty's Government and the Sudan Government before the Statute is brought into effect."

In the meantime, various Sudanese parties had been invited to send delegations to Egypt for discussions, and, towards the end of October, it was announced that agreement had been reached between the Egyptian Government and the representatives of these parties. On 2nd November, the Egyptian Government presented to Her Majesty's Government a note which set out the Egyptian Government's proposals for the manner in which the United Kingdom and Egyptian Governments could co-operate in constitutional development in the Sudan. (Appendix 5.)

The most striking features of the Egyptian Government's note, which was repeated in the agreements with the Sudanese "Independence parties" (the Umma and the Socialist Republican Party) were the following. The Egyptian Government agreed that a period of self-government should begin immediately in the Sudan; that it should be followed by self-determination; that in the meantime sovereignty should be reserved for the Sudanese; and that during the interim period self-government should be on the basis of the draft Statute submitted by the Governor-General. This was a new turn in the unhappy record of attempts to reach agreement with Egypt about the Sudan. As Mr. Eden told the House of Commons on 12th February, 1953: "It completely changed the situation. Whereas hitherto we had been unable to find any basis for negotiations, from that moment there was good reason to hope that we could reach agreement."

The Egyptian Government's proposals, however, included a number of suggestions which involved radical changes in the carefully prepared Statute, drawn up on the basis of the recommendations made by the Sudanese Constitutional Amendment Commission, and approved by the Legislative Assembly. Some of these had been accepted by the Sudanese political parties in the agreements which they had signed; but there were important differences.

An especial source of difficulty was that the Self-Government Statute contained a number of provisions designed to reassure the population of the relatively backward Southern provinces that their interests would not suffer through the transfer of power to an all-Sudanese government. They were to have approximately one-quarter of the seats in the two Houses of Parliament; at least two members of the Council of Ministers; and, in addition, Article 100 of the Statute gave the Governor-General special powers to veto legislation, and to make orders with the force of law, to protect their interests.

The Egyptian Government's note proposed to remove these special powers altogether (see Appendix 5 (Appendix B, "Article 88")). A similar proposal was contained in the agreement made by the Egyptian Government with the Umma Party; but in the agreement made with the Socialist Republican Party a special appendix explained why it was necessary that Article 100 should remain.

The most important of the remaining provisions in the Egyptian note were that there should be an International Commission to supervise the elections; a separate International Commission which would be required to give approval to decisions of the Governor-General taken in the exercise of certain of his powers (Appendix A); and a "Sudanisation" Committee to speed up the Sudanisation of Government posts "in order to provide a free and neutral atmosphere for Sudanisation". The transitional period was "not to exceed three years" subject to the completion of Sudanisation.

Foreseeing that discussion of this and other proposals, which did not affect the elections, would lead to delay, Her Majesty's Ambassador on instructions again suggested to General Neguib on 20th November that the two Governments should agree on the conditions under which elections were to be held. There was broad agreement on these conditions, and once a Sudanese Parliament and Government had come into existence, it would be possible for them to participate in the discussion of matters which were of primary concern to themselves. In the meantime discussion could continue on other matters, and if agreement was not reached, the Sudanese Government and Parliament could be left to decide.

General Neguib indicated, however, that his Government preferred to reach agreement on all the matters in their note first. It was by this time clear that a current of opinion was now running in the Sudan in favour of an agreement which would end the long period of uncertainty caused by the differences between Her Majesty's Government and the Egyptian Government on the future of the Sudan. The "pro-independence" groups, who in the past had followed the course of Anglo-Egyptian discussions with anxiety and suspicion were now eager that the new mood in Egypt should not be allowed to pass; and that the opportunity of securing agreement, based on self-determination for the Sudan, should be seized. In these circumstances, it seemed to Her Majesty's Government that it would be worth while accepting a certain amount of delay and they therefore embarked on what proved to be a complicated negotiation to reach agreement on the amendments to be made in the Statute and also on the arrangements for the eventual exercise by the Sudanese of self-determination.

The eagerness of the political parties in the Northern Sudan to reach agreement was underlined on 10th January when they signed, with a representative of the Egyptian Government, an agreement covering various points of difficulty which had arisen in the negotiations (Appendix 6). In this agreement, the Socialist Republican Party accepted the removal from the Statute of the Governor-General's special powers to protect the South (Article 100), and agreed that it should be replaced by a formula in the Anglo-Egyptian agreement giving the Governor-General the right to refer to the Co-domini legislation which he considered unfair to any of the various provinces of the Sudan (Appendix 6, Article 1).

In the meantime, sufficient progress had been made in the Anglo-Egyptian discussions for Her Majesty's Ambassador to present to the Egyptian Government, on 12th January, a draft Agreement incorporating the considerable range of matters on which agreement had been reached. A reply to this was received from the Egyptian Government on 2nd February. In the course of discussions during the following week, Her Majesty's Ambassador at Cairo was able to narrow the remaining area of difference and it was possible to instruct him to sign on 12th February the Agreement published in this White Paper (Appendix 8).

V

The new Agreement establishes for the Sudanese the right to self-determination (Preamble) to be exercised after a transitional period of self-government (Article 1), during which sovereignty is reserved for the Sudanese (Article 2); and provides the machinery by which the condominium is to be wound up at all stages of this process. An international commission, on which the Sudanese, the United Kingdom, Egypt and the United States are represented, with an Indian chairman, will supervise the elections of the first Sudanese Parliament (Article 7 and Annex II). A second international commission, on which the Sudanese, the United Kingdom and Egypt are represented, with a Pakistani chairman, remain during the whole period of self-government and the Governor-General will exercise his discretionary powers with the aid of this Commission (Articles 3 and 4, Annex I). A third body called the "Sudanisation Committee" on which the Sudanese, the United Kingdom and Egypt are represented, will have the task of completing the "Sudanisation" of various Government posts in order to "provide a free and neutral atmosphere" for self-determination (Article 8 and Annex III). When the Sudanese Parliament passes a resolution expressing its desire for self-determination, elections will be held for a Constituent Assembly which will draw up a new Constitution, and decide on the future status of the Sudan (Articles 10 to 13). The process of self-determination, including arrangements designed to secure a "free and neutral atmosphere" will be subject to international supervision (Article 10). Various amendments to be made in the draft Statute are listed in Annex IV.

The major points of difficulty which had arisen during the negotiations were the questions of the Governor-General's special responsibility for the Southern provinces; replacement of British officials by Sudanese; and the reference of provisions of the Agreement to the Sudanese Parliament.

In spite of the agreements made by the Sudanese parties, Her Majesty's Government were unwilling to see the removal from the Statute of the Governor-General's special responsibility for the South, without the southern population (who were not parties to the agreements) expressing their views. Under the Agreement, the Article remains, though it is enlarged into a special responsibility to ensure fair treatment to all the various provinces of the Sudan. His powers under this Article are, however, to be exercised with the approval of the International Commission set up under Article 4 of the Agreement. The Southern population are also, of course, to have their quarter of the membership of the Houses of Parliament and their minimum of two Ministers in the Government.

The concern of the Egyptian Government on the subject of Sudanisation was lest British administrative officials remaining in the Sudan might influence the choice of the Sudanese against union with Egypt. Her Majesty's Government, on the other hand, maintained that the decision whether or not to retain the British officials ought to rest with the Sudanese themselves, and that their right to have self-determination should not be dependent upon the removal of all British officials. Under the Agreement, the Sudanisation Committee set up "to ensure a free and neutral atmosphere for self-determination" will report in the first instance to the Sudanese Council of Ministers, and the final decision on what is necessary to ensure a "free and neutral atmosphere" will, with the other arrangements to secure the impartiality of the elections to the Constituent Assembly, be subject to international supervision. (Article 10.)

In the event, the Egyptian Government were unwilling to agree to the inclusion in the Agreement of a protocol declaring that the Sudanese Parliament should be free to discuss the main provisions of the Agreement. The Secretary of State for Foreign Affairs, however, made it clear in his statement in the House of Commons on 12th February that in the opinion of Her Majesty's Government due consideration should be given to any views expressed by the Sudanese Parliament. The Sudanese Parliament is, of course, able under Article 101 of the Statute to discuss any of the contents of the Statute and to propose any constitutional amendments.

The Agreement now signed sets the scene for the final stages of Her Majesty's Government's task in the Sudan. From the summary given above it will be clear that a number of threads have run unbroken through British policy: the government of the Sudan in the interests of the Sudanese; the preparation of the Sudanese to take over responsibility for the government of their country and to decide their own future status; and agreement with the Egyptian Co-dominus on the manner of fulfilling this policy.

With the new Constitution, the Sudanese have in their hands the instrument through which will be fulfilled the pledge that they would be consulted about their future status. Whatever the decision is to be, it must be of vital importance to the Sudan that her people should live in harmony with the people of Egypt, their next neighbours, and it can only be in their best interests that the Egyptian Government are now formally associated with Her Majesty's Government in this pledge.

Speech by a Labour Party Spokesman, Reginald Paget,
in the House of Commons on the Mau Mau
Uprising in Kenya, 31 March 1953*

I beg to move, "That this House do now adjourn."

We have now to discuss what is perhaps the most shocking event that has occurred in the history of our Commonwealth and Empire. I say that advisedly, because at the time of the Indian Mutiny—an event which seems most comparable with this massacre—India was not part of our Commonwealth and Empire. It is perhaps significant that, as a result of the Indian Mutiny, we altered the Government of India.

What happened on this occasion? At about nine o'clock on Thursday there was a diversionary attack by lorry-conveyed members of the Mau Mau on a police station some 20 miles from Uplands. This attack, which dispersed the defending forces, was carried out with resolution. The police post was stormed and arms, including machine guns, were captured, as well as ammunition. About an hour after this attack no fewer than three columns converged simultaneously upon the settlement at Uplands. Their arrival was timed to coincide with the absence of the male population on Home Guard patrols. Those patrols had probably been diverted by the original attack on the police station.

This second attack demonstrated discipline. It was a selective attack upon the houses of the families of the Home Guard and of the servants of the Government. Those houses were burnt down and the women and children ruthlessly massacred. Anyone who was concerned with Commando operations will realise the organisational difficulty of bringing three converging columns to a perfectly synchronised attack, which is what occurred on this occasion. This operation was on a military scale and argues highly competent central direction and planning. Since that occurrence, screening of the local inhabitants has taken place. Apparently local people have identified a large number of men who are said to have taken part in this attack.

As a lawyer I am always suspicious of "That is the man" evidence. I shall have something to say later about police methods adopted in Kenya. I shall not be altogether convinced even if this identification is corroborated by a quota of confessions. I find it hard to believe that an organisation which carried out and controlled this attack could leave the—I almost used the word "troops"—the people which it used for this purpose, to be collected and screened in that immediate locality. An organisation which could carry out an operation of that kind could also have carried out their evacuation to the Mau Mau hide-outs.

---

*Hansard, 5.s., DXIII, 1108-14.

It is now for us to consider the causes of what occurred and how they may be met. As the Secretary of State for the Colonies agreed at Question time, this is a new situation calling for new action. We have first to consider where the responsibility lies. I would say, first, that we cannot lay the responsibility upon the Kikuyu. The whole justification of our presence in that Colony, as in any other Colony, is that the Kikuyu are irresponsible; that they are people incapable of governing themselves; that they require protection and guidance. It is never for the protector and guide to place the blame for what goes wrong upon the colonial people, any more than it is right that a parent or a schoolmaster should place upon his children the blame for mischief which he ought to have controlled.

I would say first that the responsibility lies upon the white settlers. They have been a governing class. They have failed to secure the loyalty of their servants, their tenants and their retainers. For a governing class to fail to secure that loyalty is a formidable indictment. I would say next that responsibility lies upon the Government of Kenya. Mau Mau came suddenly and unexpectedly on the Government, which argues a shocking failure in their intelligence service.

At one time it was said that there was difficulty in finding in the whole Colony two people who could speak the language of the Kikuyu. These facts, ignorance of what was happening among the Kikuyu and ignorance of their language, argues a regrettable lack of interest in these people who are our wards.

Thirdly, I say that responsibility rests in some measure upon the Minister. Though I consider it to be a false impression. He has in this House created an impression of indifference to African interests and African liberties—[HON. MEMBERS: "Nonsense."] I say that may be a mistaken impression, but it is an impression which has been created, and which has done great harm in Africa. We understand the right hon. Gentleman better than do the Africans. It has perhaps been an error in manners, but it has resulted in serious consequences.

Finally, I would mention failure to make economic provision for the people. I agree with the right hon. Gentleman in believing that the primary cause of Mau Mau is a failure in personal relations, while not going so far as he does in saying that economic causes are irrelevant. So much for the causes of Mau Mau. But what are the causes of its growth, which has been so alarming that they can now carry out this military operation?

Mau Mau began last summer with sporadic attacks on cattle. By September there were murders. By 20th October, when the right hon. Gentleman made a statement in the House, it had reached, as he recognised, the proportions of a national resistance movement. He than said of it that its purpose was to destroy all authority save its own. That is as good a definition as I can give of a national resistance movement.

What have we done? Since then we have made almost every mistake available to an occupying or colonial Power faced with a national resistance movement. I recall a conversation which I had with a very experienced and, as I thought, wise German commander. He talked to me about resistance movements, and his success had a grim tribute paid to it in the transportation of the population of the Crimea to Siberia, which occurred afterwards when the Soviet forces came back.

What he said was, "Hitler was always saying to us 'You must make the inhabitants more frightened of you than of the guerillas.' I believe that that is profoundly wrong. Terror is the coin of the guerilla. The purpose of the guerilla is to create chaos and anarchy, and terror is the foundation of chaos and anarchy. As one creates terror so does one build up what the guerilla is seeking to create. The only answer to a resistance movement is to obtain the support of the people, and we can do that only if we provide protection for those who support us, and if we provide them with justice and the means of living when they are under our protection."

If those maxims are correct, then since October we have done almost exactly the opposite. We have failed to protect the Africans who support us. Chief after chief has been killed. There was Chief Waruhiu, who had been threatened. There was Chief Nderi. We failed to protect one chief even in hospital, so that the Mau Mau could kill him there. There was a councillor of the Council of Nairobi who, having asked for police protection and having been refused it, was killed in the streets of Nairobi. Finally, there was this massacre which occurred while the local Home Guard were out, and when no steps at all had been taken to protect their helpless dependents.

We have failed. We have allowed the Mau Mau to demonstrate their power and our impotence. That is the first failure. The second is our failure to appeal to African opinion. The right hon. Gentleman said at Question time that African leaders are not forbidden to address their followers—

THE SECRETARY OF STATE FOR THE COLONIES (MR. OLIVER LYTTELTON): I am sorry to interrupt this travesty of what I said. I did not say anything of the kind. I said that the Kenya Government would sympathetically consider any application by an African leader to address a meeting, but no such application has been received. The hon. and learned Gentleman would do well to confine himself to the facts.

MR. PAGET: What else was I saying? I said that at Question time the right hon. Gentleman had said that African leaders were not forbidden to address their followers, and that applications would be favourably considered. What use is that? Here are men who risk their lives if they attack Mau Mau. Is it enough to say that applications to do so will be favourably considered? It was the Government's duty to make every effort to persuade them to do so, to build up an alternative African leadership to Mau Mau, instead of adopting an attitude in which they did everything in their power to discredit the Africans who would help. They treat them in this sort of manner.

Instead of trying to bring people round to their support they have done everything to antagonise them. They have gone in for collective punishment in a situation which was not like that in Malaya. General Templer went in for collective punishment in Malaya in a situation which he controlled. The Government have gone in for collective punishment in a situation which they did not control and in which they could not protect. That is the one way to antagonise a population and make them enemies.

Finally, we have indulged in what I think can only reasonably be described as a competitive terror in this area. I wish to refer to some of the ordinances which have been issued. One provided:

> Any person who . . . fails to stop after being challenged by an authorised officer, may be arrested by force, which force may, if necessary to effect arrest, extend to voluntarily causing death.

Authorised officers are:

> . . . any administrative officer, any forest officer, any game officer, any subordinate officer within the meaning of the Wild Animals Protection Ordinance . . .

Included are special constables who, without police training, have been enrolled from among the youngsters. They are men who I have heard reported from two sources have been heard in the bars of Nairobi hotels swanking about how many Kukes they have "potted." That has been the attitude of undisciplined police who have been causing terror.

I should like to read a letter which was published in the "South London Press" from a detective named Tony Cross. He was a detective in the Streatham force and he is now a member of the Kenya Police Force. In a letter to his former colleagues he said that he polices 30 square miles in the heart of the Kikuyu country and that he inherited 50 prisoners without records of their crimes. He says:

> As to Mau Mau activities we have three home guard sections each about 50 strong and they go out and bring in the information. Some are pretty good, and we go out and raid and knock a few off. Don't ask me why . . . just because the home guard say they are bad men. Anyway, after persuasion they usually confess something. I inspect all prisoners and if they are a bit dubious I refuse to have them. The next morning I am usually called to a dead body, and proceed normally.

> If you are on patrol and find some men hiding in the bush you call on them to stop and if they don't they are shot or rather shot at. These boys are rotten shots, so I grab the first bloke's rifle and have a go. Compared with coppering in London, this really shakes you. There seem to be no judge's rules, cautions, etc., but I am gradually getting some proper policing. I am sure that all this Gestapo stuff never got anybody anywhere.

That is a letter from a member of the Kenya police who had served as a detective in the London police. I agree with him. These Gestapo methods, as has been proved by one resistance movement after another throughout Europe, get nowhere in face of this sort of problem.

I have not previously intervened in debates about Kenya. My grandfather was a distinguished colonial governor. I have been brought up in an atmosphere of government, with an intense feeling, which he felt and which was the basis of our Colonial Service, of responsibility for the protection of the natives whom we govern, and also in the profound belief that the man on the spot should be supported until the time came for him to be removed. I intervene now because I think that time has come. The Government have failed and they should be removed.

The Kenya constitution ought to be suspended. Until we establish a new Government we shall not gain the confidence of the people. That Government, by their weakness, their failure and their irresponsibility, as evidenced by their police methods, have lost the confidence of the people. We shall not regain that confidence until we substitute for that Government strong government.

I would urge upon the Government to recall General Templer from Malaya. The nut there seems to have been just about cracked, and the situation is in hand. Let them bring General Templer, who has proved himself in Malaya, to Kenya. Give him the power. Let him have political officers. Tell him not merely to pacify the country, which is essential, but also to build up there a proper foundation for an effective Government.

Let his instructions include the Devonshire Declaration made by the Government of 1923, which is to this effect:

> Primarily, Kenya is an African territory, and His Majesty's Government think it necessary definitely to record their considered opinion that the interests of the African natives must be paramount, and that if and when those interests and the interests of immigrant races should conflict, the former should prevail.

Let that be given to General Templer or whoever is sent, and placed in his instructions.

Tell him to start with a clean sheet, to form a new Government and to make it strong; and, by their resolution, by their justice and by their interest in all native populations that have been neglected, let them re-win for Britain the confidence of the people, who have to trust us. The Government, I feel, should go. They have allowed Mau Mau to build themselves up to a size when they could carry out this operation. This is the time for drastic, quick action, and it must mean a new Government.

Speech by the Colonial Secretary, Oliver Lyttelton, in the House of Commons on the Mau Mau Uprising in Kenya, 31 March 1953*

The thanks of the House are due to the right hon. Gentleman the Member for Smethwick (Mr. Gordon Walker) for the temperate tone of his speech, so sharply in contast with those of the hon. and learned Gentleman the Member for Northampton (Mr. Paget) and the hon. Member for Eton and Slough (Mr. Fenner Brockway). My first task should be not only to assure the House about

*Hansard, 5.s., DXIII, 1155–64.

our objectives in Kenya, but to try, as far as I can to show that those objectives are common to all hon. Members in every part of the House.

Some criticism has been made of my lack of sympathy. The hon. and learned Gentleman was at it again and he talked about me ignoring the progressive movements in the Colonies. I am not going to attempt to meet that. It is quite untrue and hon. and right hon. Gentlemen opposite can go on saying it as long as they like. I can say with the utmost sincerity that what we are trying to do in Kenya is to build a society of all races, to raise the economic conditions of the country, including wages, and to see that all races co-operate together in the country where they can go on living and educating their children as they wish, as, indeed, they can in Kenya. That is our objective and let no one have any doubt about it.

But it does this objective no good whatever to make the kind of malicious, mischievous and intemperate speech such as that delivered by the hon. and learned Gentleman the Member for Northampton. He threw the blame chiefly on the white settlers in Kenya. The white settlers there are under great pressure at the moment. We want to see this whole situation dealt with calmly and I will try to do it in that spirit. I have very few notes and if I miss any point which hon. and right hon. Gentlemen opposite want me to take up I hope they will interrupt me.

I think that the main tenor of the debate is designed to show that Government policy in Kenya is now in rags and tatters, that it has failed and we have to retrace our steps. The right hon. Gentleman the Member for Smethwick used the phrase that we must regain the initiative from Mau Mau. That is not at all the kind of phraseology that I should use. Let us go back and see what the facts are. On 28th January I used these words in the House:

> There is evidence that the area under Mau Mau influence is being reduced. These developments, and the closer policing of the Kikuyu districts, have, however, driven some of the Mau Mau leaders to more desperate measures, and the danger of savage attacks by gangs may even for a time increase.—[OFFICIAL REPORT, 28th January, 1953; Vol. 510; c. 1014.]

I spoke of what had been happening; that the area of Mau Mau activities had been compressed and that the leaders had been driven, by such measures as combing the edges of the bamboo forests and closer policing of the Kikuyu areas, to take these new measures and to resort, not to sporadic assassinations but to more or less organised raids and so forth, by large bodies of men. That is what has happened. This is—

MR. PAGET *rose*—

MR. LYTTELTON: I really cannot give way. [HON. MEMBERS: "Oh."] I allowed the hon. and learned Gentleman a great deal of latitude. He made a most intemperate speech and has done a great deal of harm. He must at any rate let me develop the first part of my argument before I give way. I will give way later. No, I will give way now.

MR. PAGET: All I was wanting to ask the right hon. Gentleman was whether he was claiming that the fact that sporadic crime had now developed into the major military operation of which Mau Mau were capable was an improvement. That is what he seemed to be saying.

MR. LYTTELTON: Nothing of the kind. I only said that the compression of this terrible Mau Mau into an area of Kenya and closer policing were following a very common mathematical formula and causing these particular activities to be much more intense than they were. That is what has happened.

Nearly every argument that has been used this afternoon, and some of the arguments of the hon. and learned Gentleman, I heard about Malaya. The hon. and learned Gentleman had only one constructive suggestion to make in his speech, and that was to move General Templer from Malaya, to cancel the Constitution of Kenya in every respect, and to set General Templer in sole authority over all these matters. The hon. and learned Gentleman coupled that argument with the rather peculiar one that the Government was rather too authoritarian and he actually read a number of extracts from the regulations, of the drastic nature of which he complained. I ought not to devote very much time to the hotch-potch of inconsistencies which he delivered.

There was one other thing he said. He referred to the Mau Mau movement as "a national resistance movement." Could anything be more fantastic when, as a matter of fact, out of the whole population of Kenya only one-quarter are Kikuyu and out of the 1,250,000 Kikuyu, or thereabouts, a very large proportion are loyal? A very large proportion of those who have taken the Mau Mau oath have done so under intimidation. To describe this as "a national resistance movement" and to relate that term and all that it means to us to what happened on Thursday is unworthy both of the intentions of the hon. and learned Gentleman and of his profession.

What we want to do is to build a common society in which inter-racial co-operation is raised to the greatest point that we can. Of course, these are difficult matters. It is very difficult at this moment, when Europeans are under great pressure and live under conditions of terrible strain; when nobody knows, when the dogs begin to bark at night, what will happen. There is great difficulty in bringing them in. We have the great difficulty in getting co-operation from the Africans because they themselves, as the figures will show, are rent by intestine strife.

It is customary for hon. Gentlemen to describe the inhabitants of Kenya as just "Africans," but do hon. Members think it is easy to get co-operation among the Masai, the Luo and the Kikuyu at this moment? Has it ever occurred to them that the term "African" is entirely misused in this context? They say "Asian." Are they not aware that it is very difficult to bring the Asians together, the Hindu and Moslem populations? These vague phrases—"Let us bring all the races together now"—are a little difficult.

MR. J. GRIFFITHS: Surely the Secretary of State knows that all the races, including the Asians, such as the Hindus and Mohammedans, are all represented on the Legislative Council.

MR. LYTTELTON: The Moslems are solidly behind the Government of Kenya at present. But let us have no argument about our objectives. What I have to think of, what Her Majesty's Government and the Government of Kenya have to think of, is what we are going to do now. With all due deference, all the speeches to which I have listened show a complete lack of reality. We have to deal with the threat now. I heard all these arguments over Malaya and yet the previous Government allowed the Malayan situation to get into an almost irretrievable position, not from lack of good intentions—they were full of those.

All their intentions over the long-term problems of Malaya—racial co-operation and internal government—I share, but one must have more than good intentions in this world. We have first to deliver freedom from fear to the inhabitants and, in doing that, we have to make it quite clear that they are fighting for something. There I agree entirely with what the right hon. Gentleman the Member for Smethwick has been saying. They have to see an objective, an ideal for which they are struggling, but our first duty is to deliver peace and order. We must do that. No suggestion that has been made this evening impinges on the immediate problem, which is, first, how are we to protect the loyal Kikuyu, secondly, how are we to build up racial co-operation in the present circumstances, and, thirdly, how we are to suppress what is a terrorist organisation.

MR. JOHN DUGDALE (West Bromwich) *rose*—

MR. LYTTELTON: I have a very short time. I did not interrupt many of the speeches.

MR. PAGET: The right hon. Gentleman does not seem to have anything to say.

MR. LYTTELTON: I have a good deal to say. I did not interrupt many of the speeches—

MR. DUGDALE: The right hon. Gentleman invited interruptions.

MR. LYTTELTON: I am entitled to a hearing on this occasion. What are we going to do now? The only constructive suggestion, other than the general ones I have mentioned, is that we ought to bring the responsible African leaders into play. There, again, the phrases used are completely misleading, because that is exactly what we are doing. What do hon. Members opposite think of those Africans who, all over the Kikuyu areas, are leading the resistance groups— now I am using the correct phrase—against the Mau Mau? Those are the responsible African leaders and everything they are doing is being helped by the Government. I have messages from them here with which I will not trouble the House, but these are the men who are doing it.

The responsible African leaders to whom the right hon. Gentleman the Member for Llanelly (Mr. J. Griffiths) was referring were, of course, one or two political leaders. What has happened over them is that time and again they have been told by the Government that if they would define the constituencies or the meetings which they wished to address, security arrangements would be

GREAT BRITAIN: THE SPAN OF EMPIRE

made if it were possible. Not surprisingly—I am not throwing a brick at them—those applications have not been made.

The right hon. Gentleman seemed to imply that we are deterring these African leaders from getting into touch with their people. I have a recent telegram here, about three weeks old, saying that Mr. Mathu had been offered the opportunity of addressing his constituents in the Kikuyu reserve and he may yet do so. Arrangements have been made for himself and one other to tour the settled areas of the Southern Rift Valley to talk to Kikuyu labour on European farms. The object of this is to try to dissuade them from the voluntary movement back to the reserves. They have just returned from such a visit.

I must make it clear that I could not approve, nor does the Kenya Government ask me to do so, of an unlimited right of assembly in these circumstances. The only result of that would be inevitably a large increase in the number of murders. I do not quite know what line the hon. and learned Member would take then. So utterly unrealistic is the approach to all this that the solution of an incident last Thursday is put forward of making assembly unlimited and without check.

But I give this pledge to the hon. and learned Gentleman. If any African leader wishes to address his constituents, the Government of Kenya will do their very best to make conditions under which that is possible. That has been the condition for many weeks, but we are dealing with a community in which very great risks have to be run.

My duty, for the remaining quarter of an hour, is to tell the House where we are on restoring peace and law and order, which, I think, is our first duty. Does any right hon. or hon. Gentleman opposite disagree with that?

MRS. WHITE: The right hon. Gentleman was not present while I made a few remarks. The tenor of some of the remarks, from this side of the House, at any rate, was precisely that the Government in Kenya are not effectively dealing with the very problem of law and order and that there is, therefore, lack of confidence both among the settlers in Kenya in their own Government and in this House.

MR. LYTTELTON: The hon. Lady is exactly making my point. I hope, therefore, I am correct in assuming that in the remaining short time the House would wish me to address myself to what we are doing to restore law and order.

I have already tried to say that we have common objectives. The point to which I shall address myself now, and with which, I think, the Opposition agree, is that we must attempt to restore law and order, which means also the protection of the loyal Kikuyu.

The duty of Her Majesty's Government, of course, is to be satisfied that the resources and organisation are adequate; and I say, in parenthesis, that we must be satisfied that they are being employed for the right objects. The military forces are, at present, about 5,000 or 6,000 and, as the House knows, are being reinforced by two battalions, a brigade headquarters and also an infantry brigade signal headquarters. In all these matters of an incoherent impalpable sort of war, the matter of communication is prime. The result of these reinforcements will not only be two further battalions who must be used, not only in offensive operations against the Mau Mau, but also in defensive operations of trying to protect what I may call, for want of a better word, the loyalists.

In addition to that, we want a very much better system of communications and, therefore, the extra brigade headquarters and the signal headquarters troop will attend to that. The plan is to have a brigade headquarters at Nyeri for the Central Provinces and one at Nakuru for the Rift Valley. I mention this because the reinforcements were a result of the visit of the Chief of the Imperial General Staff, his appreciation coinciding with our own that the movement was becoming more violent because it was being compressed. Therefore, we think that these reinforcements are necessary. The object of the extra reinforcements is to be able at one and the same time to carry out active operations against the Mau Mau gangs and also to provide extra defence for the loyal Kikuyu.

There are in Kenya altogether 12,000 police, of which about 8,000 are regulars and 4,000 are reserves. Thirty-five new police stations have been established and 150 police posts are being built, of which 50 are now occupied. This, again, is part of a policy to try to police these areas more closely; not in the main to hunt down gangs, but to provide protection for the loyal Kikuyu.

I must say a word about the Home Guard and how they are armed. The right hon. Member was particularly concerned about this question, as we are. I say, quite frankly, that no Home Guard we can organise or arm can be expected to act without full aid from both the military and the police. If we tried to form such a force we would fail. I say, equally frankly, that we must arm them as well as we can, but it will have to be done gradually. If we armed the Home Guard, which has just been formed, for instance, with automatic weapons—which I think an hon. Member mentioned—we would run the risk that, with the lack of training in the Home Guard those weapons would fall into the hands of Mau Mau.

That is not a risk any hon. Member opposite, or on this side of the House, would wish to run. So we must aim at building up the Home Guard and equipping them with better and better equipment as their training warrants. In the early part of their training the Home Guard tend to be vulnerable. We will use all our endeavours to see that they are protected as well as our forces can ensure that and reinforcements will help them.

As the House probably knows, the whole of the intelligence system has been reorganised as a result of a visit by Sir Percy Sillitoe, last November. He has left behind an officer, Mr. Macdonald, who has done most devoted work in the field of intelligence. To prove that the Mau Mau have not wrested the initiative from the Government but rather the opposite, I would point out that the kind of information which is coming forward has greatly improved. A trickle is beginning and, of course, in all this type of guerrilla warfare or para-military operations intelligence is valuable. It is almost impossible to conduct a campaign to restore law and order unless it is backed by every effective intelligence and it has not been effective. It was not effective and it is not easy to improve on that in a short time.

In the last few minutes I wish to go back to where I began about these objectives. We all had the advantage of talking to Mr. Michael Blundell last week. There is no doubt that his ideas are extremely liberal and his intentions in all these matters are such that we can all support. He sees, as I do, the necessity of trying to get together as early as possible another racial conference which the right hon. Member promised, a promise from which I do not resile in any way. I do not want it to come together at a time when I know from information that it would be likely to fail. I believe, as the right hon. Member said, that the horror of this last incident has possibly given us a new opportunity of looking forward to such a conference and I again pledge myself to this extent: if I thought there was any chance of useful results and not merely further quarrelling emerging from such a conference. I would do my best to see that it was called together.

The right hon. Member asked a question about an article concerning suspicions of their Kikuyu labourers and squatters entertained by some Europeans. It is no good supposing—[Interruption.] I hope I am not interrupting the conversation on the Front Bench opposite. Perhaps, having moved a Motion of censure, the hon. and learned Member is deciding whether to divide the House. The terms on which the hon. and learned Member for Southampton moved and the hon. Member for Eton and Slough supported the Motion were in the form of a vote of censure and it would be curious if they did not divide the House. Perhaps we shall hear about that later.

I was dealing with the suspicion which the European employer is said to entertain against his Kikuyu squatter. That we cannot help. The most effective way of doing it was by this method, which the hon. Member for Eton and Slough condemns, of having cards containing the photograph of the man and his previous employer and place of employment. That has been very much criticised, but the object is to try to restore the confidence of employers that when they take on someone new they are not taking on a Mau Mau terrorist. It appears to me to be a simple measure to meet the very point which the right hon. Gentleman was ventilating when he read out the rather moving words of the lady in East Africa.

With the extra reinforcements we have, and the reorganisation of the police and intelligence service we can look forward to compressing and containing this terror. I do not take such a gloomy view about the immediate future as do some hon. Members opposite. I make no prophecies. It will require a much less impalpable situation to make any such promise. We cannot even talk about the numbers of the Kikuyu who are infected by this disease. All these things are difficult to assume. But I am sure that we are getting better information; that we are building up an increasing number of resistance groups. They receive a set-back because of such occurrences as the ghastly incident of last Thursday and we must do everything we can.

It is a matter of military and police organisation and intelligence to prevent those who are beginning to believe in our good intentions for the future of Kenya from being murdered in their beds, or what is worse, having their wives and children murdered while they are out trying to defend the cause of law and order.

I fear that some of the things which have been said will do no good in Kenya. That remark does not apply, as I need hardly say, to what was said by the right hon. Gentleman the Member for Llanelly or by his right hon. Friend the Member for Smethwick. In all these debates on Kenya hon. Gentlemen opposite have paid lip-service to the cause of suppressing terrorism and have then proceeded to exacerbate the situation, as did the hon. and learned Member for Northampton, by intemperate remarks and criticisms of the settlers and the Kenya Government, and, so far as possible, of Her Majesty's Government.

We shall get this terror down. We shall restore peace, not with the object of one race or another dominating the situation in Kenya, but so that Kenya may be built up by all races and have a prosperous and a peaceful future.

Official Statement by the Colonial Office on the Suspension of the Constitution of British Guiana, 9 October 1953*

Her Majesty's Government have decided that the constitution of British Guiana must be suspended to prevent Communist subversion of the Government and a dangerous crisis both in public order and in economic affairs. The necessary Order-in-Council will shortly be laid before Parliament and an independent commission of inquiry appointed to report on what has happened and to recommend a revised constitution.

The faction in power have shown by their acts and their speeches that they are prepared to go to any lengths, including violence, to turn British Guiana into a Communist State. The Governor has therefore been given emergency powers and has removed the portfolios of the party Ministers. Armed forces have been landed to support the police and to prevent any public disorder which might be fomented by Communist supporters. These measures are being announced to the people of British Guiana in a broadcast by the Governor.

Her Majesty's Government are quite satisfied that the elected Ministers and the party were completely under the control of a Communist clique. There is no doubt whatever that Dr. Jagan, Mrs. Jagan, Rory Westmaas, and Sidney King, to name the ringleaders, are closely associated with international Communist organizations such as the World Federation of Trade Unions, the World Federation of Democratic Youth, the World Peace Council, and the Women's International Democratic Federation.

Times, 10 October 1953.

It is well known that these organizations are used for indoctrinating support-ers in all parts of the world and as a cloak for concerting Communist plans. From the actions and public statements of these extremists, it is clear that their objective was to turn British Guiana into a totalitarian State subordinate to Moscow and a dangerous platform for extending Communist influence in the western hemisphere.

Ministers have used their official positions in the trade unions and their influence as Ministers to provoke and encourage a stoppage of work in the sugar industry for political purposes, without regard to the real interests of the workers.

They deliberately spread the stoppage of work to other industries, including the services essential to the life of the community, which it was their duty as Ministers to protect. They then attempted to gain their political ends in the trade unions by legislation and to set aside the rules of the House to get this passed at once. They incited large and unruly crowds to attend meetings of the House of Assembly seeking to intimidate the opposition members with threats and abuse.

They have conducted an assiduous campaign to undermine the loyalty and discipline of the police force and have proposed to establish what they term people's police.

They have persistently intruded into the sphere of the public service in an attempt to subject it to their political control; as part of this campaign they have attacked the Public Service Commission set up to ensure the freedom of the public service from political interference and pressure and have announced their intention to abolish it.

Ministers have promoted the formation of a Communist political youth organization, the Pioneer Youth League, and have sought to undermine the position and influence of the established youth movements, such as the Boy Scouts and Girl Guides. The Minister of Education has announced his intention to remove churches from their present participation in the educational system of the country and to revise the curriculum and text-books of schools with the evident objective of indoctrinating the children of the country with their politi-cal views.

Ministers have sponsored a British Guiana branch of the Communist-inspired Peace Committee. Both personally and through their agents they have engaged in the dissemination of Communist subversive propaganda and initiated and directed subversive activities. They have set up a committee which supports Communist terrorists in Malaya and deliberately foments racial hatred.

In these and other directions Ministers have deliberately used their powers, not to further the interests of the whole community, but to pervert the constitu-tion and secure totalitarian control over all aspects of the social, cultural, and economic life of British Guiana. Among other things they are seeking to turn the workers of British Guiana and their unions into the political tool of an extremist clique.

These events have already done serious harm. Moderate opinion in the territory is alarmed at the turn events have taken, as was marked by the recent resolution passed by the State Council. There can be no doubt that in the present circumstances no business will undertake further capital development in the territory nor is there any hope of bringing the technical assistance from abroad that is so badly needed for economic development. This could only lead, and lead soon, to mass unemployment.

It has become clear to her Majesty's Government that the Ministers have no intention of making the constitution work, that on the contrary their sole object is to seize control of the whole life of the territory and to run it on totalitarian lines. They have clearly shown that they are prepared to use violence and to plunge the State into economic and social chaos to achieve their ends. Their next attempt to demonstrate their power might have been disastrous to the territory.

These are the reasons why steps were taken to vest in the Governor full control of the Government of the colony and the necessary emergency powers to ensure law and order. As soon as the necessary legal steps can be taken the present constitution will be suspended and an interim Government set up with which the Guianese will be fully associated.

The commission of inquiry will be set up in due course by the Secretary of State to inquire into the events in British Guiana which have led to this check in the political advance of the colony and to make recommendations for a revised constitution.

The damage which this Communist plot has done to the economic and social life of the community must be repaired as quickly as possible. The Governor will take vigorous steps forthwith to restore the economic position of the country, to ensure the rapid development of its resources, and to accelerate the improvement in housing and other social services.

The Governor is announcing that he will hasten to carry out the recommendations of the International Bank report which has been available in the territory for some time and which is to be published shortly.

The Bank's recommendation to set up a British Guiana credit corporation, which will provide credits for agriculture, industry, forestry, fisheries, and rural and urban housing, will be carried out as soon as possible. In this and other ways it is hoped that the social and economic progress of the territory will be resumed.

This action in British Guiana is not because of any change in the policy of her Majesty's Government of encouraging political advance, reaffirmed by the Secretary of State when he took office: the action has been taken to meet the danger which hangs over the colony and is designed solely to protect the life and liberty of the people of British Guiana.

*Report of the Conference on British Caribbean Federation Held in
London, February 1956**
[*A British Caribbean Federation was in existence from 1958 to1962.*]

I. Introduction

The 1956 Conference on British Caribbean Federation is the culmination of
nearly eleven years' consideration of the question of closer political association in
the region, which was first formally put to West Indian Governments as a result
of a despatch dated 14th March, 1945, from Colonel Oliver Stanley, then
Secretary of State for the Colonies.

2. West Indian Legislatures declared themselves in favour of considering the
formulation of a political plan for closer association and the Governments
concerned accordingly sent delegates in 1947 to a Conference at Montego Bay
in Jamaica, at which a resolution recognising the desirability of a political
federation was recorded and it was recommended, with the subsequent endorse-
ment of Legislatures, that a Standing Closer Association Committee (S.C.A.C.)
should be set up composed of delegates of Legislatures. The Report of this
Committee (Col. No. 255), published in 1950, provided not only a detailed
examination of the implications of federation but a statement of faith in its
economic and political necessity and a provisional scheme for a federal constitution based on the Australian pattern i.e. with residual powers remaining with
the constituent units. Accepted by the Legislatures of Barbados, Jamaica, the
Leeward Islands, Trinidad and Tobago, and the Windward Islands, this scheme
formed the basis of the Plan for a British Caribbean Federation (Cmd. 8895)
which was drawn up by the London Conference of 1953 and subsequently
adopted by all the Legislatures which sent delegates to that Conference.

3. In accordance with the decision of West Indian Legislatures to accept the
Federal Plan, the Secretary of State for the Colonies announced on the 2nd
February, 1955, that Her Majesty's Government would proceed with the next
steps towards a Federation and accordingly set up three Commissions, headed
by Sir Sydney Caine, K.C.M.G., Sir Hilary Blood, G.B.E., K.C.M.G., and Sir
Allan Chalmers Smith, M.C., to examine respectively the fiscal, civil service
and judicial aspects of Federation. The Reports of the three Commissions,
which were at work in the West Indies throughout the summer and early
autumn of 1955, were published early in January, 1956 (Cmd. Nos. 9618,
9619, and 9620 respectively). In the meantime a Conference, convened in
Trinidad in March, 1955, under the Chairmanship of Lord Lloyd, Parliamentary Under-Secretary of State for the Colonies, urged Her Majesty's Government to proceed with the greatest possible speed with the completion of prelimi-

Parliamentary Papers, 1955–56, XII, Cmd. 9733, 3–7, 12–13.

nary measures to enable the Federation to be established and unanimously reached agreement on the measures to be adopted towards facilitating and controlling the movement of persons within a British Caribbean Federation. They recorded their conclusions in a Report (Col. No. 315) which was subsequently adopted by all the Legislatures concerned.

4. During eleven years, therefore, the issues of Federation have been the subject of four committees or Commissions and three Conferences, and have been before the Legislatures of the Caribbean territories on no less than five occasions in the course of which agreement has been reached on the form the British Caribbean Federation is to take.

II. The Conference

5. The Secretary of State convened the present Conference to take final decisions on the major outstanding issues concerning Federation and to agree on suitable machinery for settling all minor and less controversial issues and for taking the necessary administrative steps prior to the establishment of the Federation itself. The Conference took as its basis the agreed Federal Plan, and the Plan, together with the Reports of the London Conference of 1953, the Trinidad Conference of 1955 and the three Commissions referred to in paragraph 3, constituted the documents before the Conference.

6. The Conference met from the 7th to the 23rd February, 1956, in Lancaster House, London, under the Chairmanship of the Right Hon. Alan Lennox-Boyd, M.P., Secretary of State for the Colonies. It was attended by delegates from the Governments of Antigua, Barbados, Dominica, Grenada, Jamaica, Montserrat, St. Kitts, Nevis and Anguilla, St. Lucia, St. Vincent Trinidad and Tobago, and the United Kingdom. Observers were sent by the Governments of British Guiana and British Honduras, which had reached no final decision on participation in the Federation but which had interest in various regional developments associated with the Federation. A list of those taking part is given in Appendix I.

7. In his opening address to the Conference, Mr. Lennox-Boyd drew attention to the long way which had been travelled along the road to Federation. Referring to the purpose of the Conference to take final decisions within the framework of the agreed Federal Plan, without the necessity for further reference back to Legislatures, Mr. Lennox-Boyd said that he was prepared, subject to the Conference reaching agreement on all substantial points, to seek leave to introduce an enabling Bill into the United Kingdom Parliament at an early date and hoped that it would be possible to pass it through all stages in both Houses before the summer of 1956. Such an Act would enable the constitutional instruments of the Federation to be embodied in an Order of Her Majesty in Council which would provide for the establishment of the Federation, including the appointment of a Governor-General and the holding of Federal elections at a date to be decided. He reiterated the intention of Her Majesty's Government to do all in its power to further the wishes of the West Indies in regard to Federation.

8. Mr. Lennox-Boyd went on to refer to the future of the Federation. Pointing out how Federation would facilitate the eventual achievement of self-government within the Commonwealth, he drew attention to the implications of that status. Self-government meant something more than the formal relinquishment by Her Majesty's Government in the United Kingdom of constitutional powers of control. It meant that a country must be able to stand on its own feet economically and financially, that it could finance its own administration and that it was able and prepared to assume responsibility for its own defence and its own international relations to the extent that either was involved by its geographical or international standing. On the other hand, in these days no country was independent in the sense of being entirely self-contained and self-sufficient. Mutual help was one of the great principles of the Commonwealth and there was no reason why one member or group of members should not help other members with their economic development, perhaps on the lines of the Colombo Plan. Nor would self-government preclude arrangements for intra-Commonwealth commerce of which the Commonwealth Sugar Agreement was an example. Unlike the situation where a state relied for its existence on outside help, there was nothing derogatory to a country's dignity in accepting the help of other partners to improve its economic situation and develop its resources to the general advantage of the partnership. The Commonwealth was an association of free nations, each of which was independent in the sense outlined. Membership of the Commonwealth was a matter for all members to consider, but delegates could be assured that when the British Caribbean Federation Government felt in due course ready to assume the responsibilities and obligations involved, it would find Her Majesty's Government in the United Kingdom glad to sponsor its admission to full Commonwealth membership.

9. In reply the Caribbean delegates and observers thanked Her Majesty's Government for the support they had always given to the concept of Federation and expressed their determination to bring the Conference to a successful conclusion. They regretted the delays with which Federation had met, but hoped that the eleven years which had passed since Colonel Oliver Stanley's despatch—years during which the Units themselves had all made remarkable constitutional progress—had not been wasted, and that the Federation, the constitution of which they now intended to agree, would be laid on sound foundations, politically and economically.

III. Constitutional Matters

10. We agree that the Plan for a British Caribbean Federation put forward by the London Conference in April, 1953, and subsequently endorsed by the Legislatures of all the territories concerned, shall be the basis for the Federal Constitution, subject to the variations set out below.

11. The preamble to the Constitution shall include a recital to the effect that all persons in the Federation shall continue to enjoy the free exercise of their

respective modes of religious worship. The preamble shall also contain a recital in respect of customs union which is set out in full in Chapter IV.

12. We agree that the following item shall be inserted in the Exclusive Legislative List: "The establishment, maintenance and regulation of Federal agencies for the purpose of advising or otherwise assisting any Government, person or authority." (It will be understood that the advice or assistance of these agencies will only be made available at the request of any Government, person or authority concerned.)

13. We agree that the proposals for amending the Federal Constitution in the 1953 Plan shall be varied in the following manner:

(*a*) The Constitution shall be amendable by Order in Council as proposed in paragraph 78 of the S.C.A.C. Report, subject to the deletion of the provision in that paragraph for a referendum and to the substitution therefor of the provisions in paragraph 92 (3) of the 1953 Plan. The guarantees included in the 1953 Plan with regard to the numerical representation of Units in the Federal Legislature will not, therefore, be altered in any way.

(*b*) A special clause shall be added to the Constitutional instruments to provide for the entry of other territories to the Federation. This is to provide in particular for the possible accession at a later date of British Guiana and British Honduras. We desire to place on record our view that the way should be made as easy as possible for them to join the Federation. We therefore agree that the terms of admission of new members should be agreed between Her Majesty's Government, the Federal Government and the applicant, and that the approval of Units under paragraph 92 (3) of the 1953 Plan should not be required in the case of an amendment of the constitution to admit British Guiana or British Honduras if no change in the numerical representation of existing Units in the Federal Legislature is involved. An amendment to admit any other territory, however, would be subject to the full provisions of paragraph 92 (3), should their accession involve their having representation in the Federal Legislature.

14. We agree that paragraph 52 (ii) of the 1953 Plan regarding the constitution of the Council of State shall be deleted and that the Council of State shall not contain the three official members. The Governor-General shall, however, nominate three officials, selected by him, who will have the right to attend all meetings of the Council and to take part in its discussions. The Secretary of State gave an assurance that the need for the attendance of the officials would be reviewed from time to time and agreed that at such time as the Governor-General concluded that their attendance was no longer required, the right of attendance might be allowed to fall into desuetude or should be withdrawn from the Constitution.

15. We agree that the Governor-General shall consult Unit Governors before making appointments to the Federal Senate, and we suggest that a direction to this effect should be included in the Royal Instructions to the Governor-General. We also agree that the three Federal senators shall be appointed to the Council of State by the Governor-General on the recommendation of the Prime Minister of the Federation and not, as proposed in the 1953 Plan, by the Governor-General in Council.

16. We have considered the question of reserved powers under the proposed Federal Constitution and have agreed as follows: —

(a) With regard to the Reservation of Bills, we agree that the proviso to paragraph 42 (2) of the 1953 Plan and the whole of paragraph 43 shall be omitted. The effect of this is to make general the power of the Governor-General to reserve bills instead of specifying the particular categories of bills in respect of which the power might be exercised.

(b) With regard to legislation by Order in Council, we agree that an addition shall be made to paragraph 45 (3) to make clear, what has always been the intention, that no Order in Council made under paragraph 45 (1) (c) may provide for the raising of revenue in excess of what it will be permissible for the Federal Government itself to raise under the Constitution, due account being taken of any revenue already raised by that Government.

17. We agree that the provision of the S.C.A.C. Report (Clauses 10 (2) and 22 (2) of the Consolidated Recommendations) with regard to membership of the Legislative or Executive bodies of the Units and the Federal Legislature shall be restored—i.e. the ban on duality of membership shall be reinstated. The period within which a member of a Unit Legislative or Executive body shall be required to resign after becoming a member of the Federal Legislature shall, however, be three months and not four weeks as provided in the S.C.A.C. Report. We note that Clauses 11 and 23 of the Consolidated Recommendations in the S.C.A.C. Report (which relate to the tenure of their seats by members of the Federal Legislature) do not provide that a member of the Federal Legislature who becomes a member of the Legislature or Executive Council of a Unit shall vacate his seat in the Federal Legislature. We agree that this omission should be rectified and that the exact provision necessary should be a matter for the Standing Federation Committee.

18. The Fiscal Commissioner assumed in paragraph 12 of his Report that in the initial phase no substantial executive services would be transferred from Units to the Federation. Under the 1953 Plan, however, certain non-revenue producing services relating to defence matters, immigration, emigration and deportation were included in the Exclusive Legislative List and would have to be transferred to the Federation immediately. As this may not be practicable, we agree that the Constitution shall provide that where, immediately before the coming into force of the Constitution, the legislature of any Unit has power to

make laws relating to a matter included in the Exclusive Legislative List, that power shall not cease until a notification is published by the Governor-General in the Official Gazette of the Unit concerned. Until that date, such a matter shall be deemed to be included in the Concurrent Legislative List.

19. We consider that the following common or joint services are among those which are likely to need to be co-ordinated by the Federal authorities rather than through a continuance of separate contributions from Unit governments: —

(i)   University College of the West Indies
(ii) Student services in the United Kingdom, United States of America and Canada
(iii) Intra-regional shipping
(iv) Miscellaneous contributions.

We regard the University College of the West Indies as a matter for the Exclusive Legislative List, though higher education in general, including professional and technological training, will be included in the Concurrent Legislative List.

20. We also agree that the Legislative List shall be amended to take account of the recommendations of the 1955 Trinidad Conference on Movement of Persons within the Federation.

21. We agree that, as external affairs are on the Exclusive Legislative List, it will be necessary for the Federal Government to assume responsibility for group membership or associate membership of any international organisation in which some or all of the Federated Colonies at present participate.

22. In order to clarify the meaning of the item "External Affairs" in the Exclusive Legislative List, we agree that this item shall be expanded to read as follows: —

> External affairs, that is to say such external relations (not being relations between the United Kingdom and any unit) as may from time to time be entrusted to the Federation by Her Majesty's Government in the United Kingdom.

We further agree that, though the Federal Legislature shall be able to enact legislation for implementing treaties on any matter, it may be very inconvenient if Unit Legislatures are unable to pass legislation for implementing treaties in regard to concurrent and residual matters. We accordingly agree that a clause shall be inserted in the constitutional instrument enabling Unit Legislatures to do this.

23. We agree that Federal elections shall be held as soon as practicable after the 1st January, 1958, and in any event not later than the 1st March, 1958.

* * *

VII. Post Conference Machinery

49. We considered the work that must be carried out between the end of the Conference and the appointment of a Governor-General and recognise that it falls under two main heads—Constitutional and Administrative.

50. On the constitutional side, a complete draft constitution will have to be agreed and this will involve decisions on points of detail not covered by the 1953 Plan or the conclusions of the present Conference. We were told that a draft could be prepared in the Colonial Office to be ready for consideration by the Standing Federation Committee in November or December, 1956.

51. The administrative work consists of the measures that will have to be taken, both before the appointment of a Governor-General and between his appointment and the elections for the first Federal Legislature, to ensure that when the elections have been held there will be in existence an administrative machine to carry out the business of the Government. This entails such things as the selection of key officers and the setting up of skeleton Departments at an early stage, the acquisition of buildings, including housing, for the temporary Federal Capital, the drafting of Laws, Regulations and Standing Orders for the Federal Assembly, etc., arrangements for meeting expenditure on the pre-Federal measures and for permanent public services, and other matters.

52. In our present session we have settled all the major issues relating to the constitution. We agree that:—

(i) The British Caribbean delegations to the Conference shall continue as a standing body to carry out the functions set out in paragraphs 50 and 51 above. It will remain in being until the Federal elections result in the setting up of a full Federal Government.

(ii) For the purpose of its functions under sub-paragraph (i) above it shall be known as a Standing Committee of the Federation of the British Caribbean (or Standing Federation Committee).
Its Chairman shall be the Comptroller for Development and Welfare as Commissioner for the Preparation of the Federal Organisation, until the appointment of the Governor-General of the Federation. When the Governor-General is appointed, it will be constitutionally appropriate that he shall be formally responsible for the steps still remaining before Federal elections, but the Standing Federation Committee will no doubt continue to operate as a body advisory to the Governor-General, in which case he will then preside over it.

(iii) The British Caribbean composition of the Standing Federation Committee will be the same as that of the Conference i.e., a total of 16 exclusive of the Chairman and drawn from the territories concerned in the proportions, Barbados 3, Jamaica 3, the Leeward Islands 3 (1 each for Antigua, St. Kitts, Nevis and Anguilla, and Montserrat), Trinidad and Tobago 3, and the Windward Islands 4 (1 each for Dominica, Grenada, St. Lucia and St. Vincent). Governments will from time to time appoint to represent them the individuals they consider most appropriate. Decisions will be taken when necessary by a simple majority of votes cast, with one vote for each of the 16 British Caribbean representatives and a casting vote for the Chairman. British Guiana will be entitled to send 2 Observers and British Honduras 1 Observer, on the same basis as that on which they have attended the present Conference, i.e., that on matters on which they are directly concerned, such as the Federal Supreme Court, they are regarded as full members, and that on other issues confined to the Federation itself their status is that of Observers only.

53. The Committee will be responsible as set out above for reaching agreement on questions arising out of the drafting of the constitution, and on the draft constitution itself. It will also set in motion and supervise the administrative work outlined in paragraph 51, and it will be responsible for settling the number, responsibilities and salaries of the posts to be filled before the Federal Government comes into being. The Secretary of State will be responsible for the provisional appointment of members of the Public Service Commission, and for the provisional appointment of officers to the posts in question subject, as appropriate, to consultation with the Public Service Commission. All such appointments will be subject to the confirmation of the Governor-General.

* * *

Ghana Independence Act, an Act Providing Independence for the Gold Coast (5 & 6 Eliz. II, c. 6), 7 February 1957*

Be it enacted by the Queen's most Excellent Majesty, by and with the advice and consent of the Lords Spiritual and Temporal, and Commons, in this present Parliament assembled, and by the authority of the same, as follows: —

1. The territories included immediately before the appointed day in the Gold Coast as defined in and for the purposes of the Gold Coast (Constitution) Order in Council, 1954, shall as from that day together form part of Her Majesty's dominions under the name of Ghana, and—

(a) no Act of the Parliament of the United Kingdom passed on or after the appointed day shall extend, or be deemed to extend, to Ghana as part of the law of Ghana, unless it is expressly declared in that Act that the Parliament of Ghana has requested, and consented to, the enactment thereof;

(b) as from the appointed day, Her Majesty's Government in the United Kingdom shall have no responsibility for the government of Ghana or any part thereof;

(c) as from the appointed day, the provisions of the First Schedule to this Act shall have effect with respect to the legislative powers of Ghana:

3240 GREAT BRITAIN: THE SPAN OF EMPIRE

Provided that nothing in this section other than paragraphs (a) to (c) thereof shall affect the operation in any of the territories aforesaid of any enactment, or any other instrument having the effect of law, passed or made with respect thereto before the appointed day.

2. As from the appointed day, the British Nationality Act, 1948, shall have effect—

(a) with the substitution in subsection (3) of section one thereof (which provides for persons to be British subjects or Commonwealth citizens by virtue of citizenship of certain countries) for the words "and Ceylon" of the words "Ceylon and Ghana";

(b) as if in the British Protectorates, Protected States and Protected Persons Order in Council, 1949, the words "Northern Territories of the Gold Coast" in the First Schedule thereto and the words "Togoland under United Kingdom Trusteeship" in the Third Schedule thereto were omitted:

Provided that a person who, immediately before the appointed day, was for the purposes of the said Act and Order in Council a British protected person by virtue of his connection with either of the territories mentioned in paragraph (b) of this section shall not cease to be such a British protected person for any of those purposes by reason of anything contained in the foregoing provisions of this Act, but shall so cease upon his becoming a citizen of Ghana under any law of the Parliament of Ghana making provision for such citizenship.

3.— (1) No scheme shall be made on or after the appointed day under the Colonial Development and Welfare Acts, 1940 to 1955, wholly or partly for the benefit of Ghana.

(2) Any scheme in force under the said Acts immediately before the appointed day which was made solely for the benefit of Ghana or any part thereof shall cease to have effect on that day without prejudice to the making of payments in pursuance of that scheme on or after that day in respect of any period falling before that day; and, so far as practicable, no part of any sums paid out of moneys provided by Parliament for the purposes of any other scheme made under those Acts before that day shall be employed in respect of any period falling on or after that day for the benefit of Ghana.

(3) Nothing in the two foregoing subsections shall restrict the making of, or the employment of sums paid out of moneys provided by Parliament for the purposes of, any scheme under the said Acts with respect to a body established for the joint benefit of Ghana and one or more of the following territories, that is to say, the Federation or any Region of Nigeria, Sierra Leone and the Gambia, in a case where Ghana has undertaken to bear a reasonable share of the cost of the scheme.

(4) Without prejudice to the continuance of any operations commenced by the Colonial Development Corporation in any part of Ghana before the appointed day, as from that day the expression "colonial territories" in the

Overseas Resources Development Acts, 1948 to 1956, shall not include Ghana or any part thereof.

4.—(1) Notwithstanding anything in the Interpretation Act, 1889, the expression "colony" in any Act of the Parliament of the United Kingdom passed on or after the appointed day shall not include Ghana or any part thereof.

(2) As from the appointed day, the expression "colony" in the Army Act, 1955, and the Air Force Act, 1955, shall not include Ghana or any part thereof, and in the definitions of "Commonwealth force" in subsection (1) of section two hundred and twenty-five and subsection (1) of section two hundred and twenty-three respectively of those Acts and in section eighty-six of the Naval Discipline Act as amended by the Revision of the Army and Air Force Acts (Transitional Provisions) Act, 1955, for the words "or Ceylon" there shall be substituted the words "Ceylon or Ghana".

(3) Any Order in Council made on or after the appointed day under the Army Act, 1955, or the Air Force Act, 1955, providing for that Act to continue in force beyond the date on which it would otherwise expire shall not operate to continue that Act in force beyond that date as part of the law of Ghana.

(4) As from the appointed day, the provisions specified in the Second Schedule to this Act shall have effect subject to the amendments respectively specified in that Schedule, and Her Majesty may by Order in Council, which shall be subject to annulment in pursuance of a resolution of either House of Parliament, make such further adaptations in any Act of the Parliament of the United Kingdom passed before this Act, or in any instrument having effect under any such Act, as appear to her necessary in consequence of section one of this Act; and any Order in Council made under this subsection may be varied or revoked by a subsequent Order in Council so made and, though made after the appointed day, may be made so as to have effect from that day:

Provided that this subsection shall not extend to Ghana as part of the law thereof.

5.—(1) This Act may be cited as the Ghana Independence Act, 1957.

(2) In this Act, the expression "the appointed day" means the sixth day of March, nineteen hundred and fifty-seven, unless before that date Her Majesty has by Order in Council appointed some other day to be the appointed day for the purposes of this Act.

Schedules

First Schedule Legislative Powers of Ghana

1. The Colonial Laws Validity Act, 1865, shall not apply to any law made on or after the appointed day by the Parliament of Ghana.

2. No law and no provision of any law made on or after the appointed day by the Parliament of Ghana shall be void or inoperative on the ground that it is repugnant to the law of England, or to the provisions of any existing or future Act of the Parliament of the United Kingdom, or to any order, rule or

regulation made under any such Act, and the powers of the Parliament of Ghana shall include the power to repeal or amend any such Act, order, rule or regulation in so far as it is part of the law of Ghana.

3. The Parliament of Ghana shall have full power to make laws having extra-territorial operation.

4. Without prejudice to the generality of the foregoing provisions of this Schedule, sections seven hundred and thirty-five and seven hundred and thirty-six of the Merchant Shipping Act, 1894, shall be construed as though reference therein to the legislature of a British possession did not include reference to the Parliament of Ghana.

5. Without prejudice to the generality of the foregoing provisions of this Schedule, section four of the Colonial Courts of Admiralty Act, 1890 (which requires certain laws to be reserved for the signification of Her Majesty's pleasure or to contain a suspending clause) and so much of section seven of that Act as requires the approval of Her Majesty in Council to any rules of court for regulating the practice and procedure of a Colonial Court of Admiralty shall cease to have effect in Ghana.

6. Notwithstanding anything in the foregoing provisions of this Schedule, the constitutional provisions shall not be repealed, amended or modified otherwise than in such manner as may be specified in those provisions.

In this paragraph, the expression "the constitutional provisions" means the provisions for the time being in force on or at any time after the appointed day of the Gold Coast (Constitution) Orders in Council, 1954 to 1956, and of any other Order in Council made before that day, or any law, or instrument made under a law, of the Parliament of Ghana made on or after that day, which amends, modifies, re-enacts with or without amendment or modification, or makes different provision in lieu of, any of the provisions of any such Order in Council or of any such law or instrument previously made.

* * *

Federation of Malaya Independence Act (5 & 6 Eliz. II, c. 60),
31 July 1957*

Be it enacted by the Queen's most Excellent Majesty, by and with the advice and consent of the Lords Spiritual and Temporal, and Commons, in this present Parliament assembled, and by the authority of the same, as follows: —

1.— (1) Subject to the provisions of this section, the approval of Parliament is hereby given to the conclusion between Her Majesty and the Rulers of the Malay States of such agreement as appears to Her Majesty to be expedient for

**Public General Acts*, 1957, 986–89.

the establishment of the Federation of Malaya as an independent sovereign country within the Commonwealth.

(2) Any such agreement as aforesaid may make provision—

(a) for the formation of the Malay States and of the Settlements of Penang and Malacca into a new independent Federation of States under a Federal Constitution specified in the agreement, and for the application to those Settlements, as States of the new Federation, of State Constitutions so specified;

(b) for the termination of Her Majesty's sovereignty and jurisdiction in respect of the said Settlements, and of all other Her power and jurisdiction in and in respect of the Malay States or the Federation as a whole, and the revocation or modification of all or any of the provisions of the Federation of Malaya Agreement, 1948, and of any other agreements in force between Her Majesty and the Rulers of the Malay States.

(3) Any such agreement shall be conditional upon the approval of the new Federal Constitution by enactments of the existing Federal Legislature and of each of the Malay States; and upon such approval being given Her Majesty by Order in Council may direct that the said Federal and State Constitutions shall have the force of law within the said Settlements, and, so far as She has jurisdiction in that behalf, elsewhere within the Federation, and may make such other provision as appears to Her to be necessary for giving effect to the agreement.

(4) Any Order in Council under this section shall be laid before Parliament after being made.

(5) In this Act "the appointed day" means such day as may be specified by Order in Council under this section as the day from which the said Federal Constitution has the force of law as aforesaid.

2.—(1) On and after the appointed day, all existing law to which this section applies shall, until otherwise provided by the authority having power to amend or repeal that law, continue to apply in relation to the Federation or any part thereof, and to persons and things in any way belonging thereto or connected therewith, in all respects as if no such agreement as is referred to in subsection (1) of section one of this Act had been concluded:

Provided that—

(a) the enactments referred to in the First Schedule to this Act shall have effect as from the appointed day subject to the amendments made by that Schedule (being amendments for applying in relation to the Federation certain statutory provisions applicable to Commonwealth countries having fully responsible status within Her Majesty's dominions);

(b) Her Majesty may by Order in Council make such further adaptations in any Act of the Parliament of the United Kingdom passed before the appointed day, or in any instrument having effect under any such Act, as appear to Her necessary or expedient in consequence of the agreement referred to in subsection (1) of section one of this Act;

(c) in relation to the Colonial Development and Welfare Acts, 1940 to 1955, this subsection shall have effect only so far as may be necessary for the making of payments on or after the appointed day in pursuance of schemes in force immediately before that day and in respect of periods falling before that day;

(d) nothing in this section shall be construed as continuing in force any enactment or rule of law limiting or restricting the legislative powers of the Federation or any part thereof.

(2) An Order in Council made under this section shall be subject to annulment in pursuance of a resolution of either House of Parliament.

(3) An Order in Council made under this section may be varied or revoked by a subsequent Order in Council so made and may, though made after the appointed day, be made so as to have effect from that day.

* * *

3.— (1) Her Majesty may by Order in Council confer on the Judicial Committee of the Privy Council such jurisdiction in respect of appeals from the Supreme Court of the Federation as appears to Her to be appropriate for giving effect to any arrangements made after the appointed day between Her Majesty and the Head of the Federation for the reference of such appeals to that Committee.

(2) An Order in Council under this section may determine the classes of cases in which, and the conditions as to leave and otherwise subject to which, any such appeal may be entertained by the said Committee, and the practice and procedure to be followed on any such appeal, and may in particular make such provision with respect to the form of the report or recommendation to be made by the Committee in respect of any such appeal, and the transmission to the Head of the Federation of such reports or recommendations, as appears to Her Majesty to be appropriate having regard to the said arrangements.

(3) Except so far as otherwise provided by Order in Council under this section, and subject to such modifications as may be so provided, the Judicial Committee Act, 1833, shall apply in relation to appeals under this section as it applies in relation to appeals to Her Majesty in Council.

(4) Arrangements made in pursuance of this section may apply to any appeal to Her Majesty in Council, or any application for leave to bring such an appeal, which is pending on the appointed day; but except as aforesaid nothing in this Act shall be construed as continuing in force any right of appeal to Her Majesty in Council from any court in the Federation.

* * *

*Official Declaration by the British Government on the Establishment
of the Republic of Cyprus Signed at London, 17 February 1959**
*[The independence of the Republic of Cyprus was
proclaimed at Nicosia on 16 August 1960.]*

The Government of the United Kingdom of Great Britain and Northern Ireland, having examined the documents concerning the establishment of the Republic of Cyprus, comprising the Basic Structure for the Republic of Cyprus, the Treaty of Guarantee and the Treaty of Alliance, drawn up and approved by the Heads of the Governments of Greece and Turkey in Zurich on February 11, 1959, and taking into account the consultations in London from February 11 to 16, 1959, between the Foreign Ministers of Greece, Turkey and the United Kingdom
Declare:

A. That, subject to the acceptance of their requirements as set out in Section B below, they accept the documents approved by the Heads of the Governments of Greece and Turkey as the agreed foundation for the final settlement of the problem of Cyprus.

B. That, with the exception of two areas at

(a) Akrotiri—Episkopi—Paramali, and

(b) Dhekelia—Pergamos—Ayios Nikolaos—Xylophagou, which will be retained under full British sovereignty, they are willing to transfer sovereignty over the Island of Cyprus to the Republic of Cyprus subject to the following conditions:

(1) that such rights are secured to the United Kingdom Government as are necessary to enable the two areas as aforesaid to be used effectively as military bases, including among others those rights indicated in the Annex attached, and that satisfactory guarantees are given by Greece, Turkey and the Republic of Cyprus for the integrity of the areas retained under British sovereignty and the use and enjoyment by the United Kingdom of the rights referred to above;

(2) that provision shall be made by agreement for:

(i) the protection of the fundamental human rights of the various communities in Cyprus;

(ii) the protection of the interests of the members of the public services in Cyprus;

(iii) determining the nationality of persons affected by the settlement;

(iv) the assumption by the Republic of Cyprus of the appropriate obligations of the present Government of Cyprus, including the settlement of claims.

**British and Foreign State Papers*, CLXIV, 1–3.

C. That the Government of the United Kingdom welcome the draft Treaty of Alliance between the Republic of Cyprus, the Kingdom of Greece and the Republic of Turkey and will co-operate with the Parties thereto in the common defence of Cyprus.

D. That the Constitution of the Republic of Cyprus shall come into force and the formal signature of the necessary instruments by the parties concerned shall take place at the earliest practicable date and on that date sovereignty will be transferred to the Republic of Cyprus.

Selwyn Lloyd
Alan Lennox-Boyd

Annex

The following rights will be necessary in connexion with the areas to be retained under British sovereignty:

(*a*) to continue to use, without restriction or interference, the existing small sites containing military and other installations and to exercise complete control within these sites, including the right to guard and defend them and to exclude from them all persons not authorised by the United Kingdom Government;

(*b*) to use roads, ports and other facilities freely for the movement of personnel and stores of all kinds to and from and between the above-mentioned areas and sites;

(*c*) to continue to have the use of specified port facilities at Famagusta;

(*d*) to use public services (such as water, telephone, telegraph, electric power, &c.);

(*e*) to use from time to time certain localities, which would be specified, for troop training;

(*f*) to use the airfield at Nicosia, together with any necessary buildings and facilities on or connected with the airfield to whatever extent is considered necessary by the British authorities for the operation of British military aircraft in peace and war, including the exercise of any necessary operational control of air traffic;

(*g*) to overfly the territory of the Republic of Cyprus without restriction;

(*h*) to exercise jurisdiction over British forces to an extent comparable with that provided in Article VII of the Agreement regarding the Status of Forces of Parties to the North Atlantic Treaty, in respect of certain offences committed within the territory of the Republic of Cyprus;

(*i*) to employ freely in the areas and sites labour from other parts of Cyprus;

(*j*) to obtain, after consultation with the Government of the Republic of Cyprus, the use of such additional small sites and such additional rights as the United Kingdom may, from time to time, consider technically necessary for the efficient use of its base areas and installations in Cyprus.

Speech by the Prime Minister, Harold Macmillan, to the
South African Parliament ("Winds of Change" Speech),
3 February 1960*

It is a great privilege to be invited to address members of both Houses of the Union Parliament. It is a unique privilege to do so in 1960, just half a century after the Parliament of the Union came to birth. I am especially grateful to your Prime Minister, Dr. Verwoerd, who invited me to visit your country and arranged for me to address you here to-day.

It is fitting that my tour of Africa should culminate in the Union Parliament in the town so long Europe's gateway to the Indian Ocean and the East. I am most grateful to your Government for all the trouble they have taken in making the arrangements, which have enabled me to see so much in so short a time. Wherever we have gone in town or in country, we have been received in a spirit of friendship and affection which has warmed our hearts, and we value this the more because we know that it is an expression of your good will, not only to ourselves but to all the people of Britain.

It is, as I have said, a special privilege for me to be here in 1960, when you are celebrating the golden wedding of the Union. At such a time it is natural and right that you should pause to take stock of your position—to look back at what you have achieved and to look forward to what lies ahead.

In the 50 years of their nationhood the people of South Africa have built a strong economy founded on healthy agriculture and thriving and resilient industries.

During my visit I have been able to see something of your mining industry, on which the prosperity of your country is so firmly based. I have seen your Iron and Steel Corporation, and visited your Council for Scientific and Industrial Research at Pretoria. These two bodies, in their different ways, are symbols of a lively forward-looking and expanding economy.

I have seen the great city of Durban, with its wonderful port, and the skyscrapers of Johannesburg standing where 70 years ago there was nothing but open veldt. I have seen, too, the fine cities of Pretoria and Bloemfontein.

No one could fail to be impressed by the immense material progress which has been achieved. That all this has been accomplished in so short a time is a striking testimony to the initiative, energy, and skill of your people.

We in Britain are proud of the contribution we have made to this remarkable achievement. Much of it has been financed by British capital. According to a recent survey made by the Union Government, nearly two-thirds of oversea investment outstanding in the Union at the end of 1956 was British.

* *Times,* 4 February 1960.

But that is not all. We have developed trade between us to our common advantage, and our economies are now largely interdependent. You export to us raw materials and food—and, of course, gold—and we in return send you consumer goods and capital equipment. We take a third of all your exports and we supply a third of all your imports.

This broad traditional pattern of investment and trade has been maintained in spite of changes brought about by the development of our two economies. It gives me great encouragement to reflect that the economies of both our countries, while developing rapidly have yet remained interdependent and capable of sustaining one another. Britain has always been your best customer and, as your new industries develop, we believe we can be your best partners, too.

In addition to building this strong economy within your own borders, you have also played your part as an independent nation in world affairs. As a soldier in the First World War, and as a Minister in Sir Winston Churchill's Government in the Second, I know personally the value of the contribution which your forces made to victory in the cause of freedom. I know something, too, of the inspiration which General Smuts brought to us in Britain in our darkest hours. Again, in the Korean crisis, you played your full part.

Thus, in testing times of war and aggression, your statesmen and your soldiers have made their influence felt far beyond the African continent. In the period of reconstruction, when Dr. Malan was your Prime Minister, your resources greatly assisted the recovery of the sterling area in the post-war world.

Now, in the no less difficult task of peace, your leaders in industry, commerce, and finance continue to be prominent in world affairs.

To-day, your readiness to provide technical assistance to the less well-developed parts of Africa is of immense help to the countries which receive it. It is also a source of strength to your friends in the Commonwealth and elsewhere in the western world.

You are collaborating in the work of the Commission for Technical Cooperation in Africa South of the Sahara, and now in the United Nations Economic Commission for Africa. Your Minister of External Affairs intends to visit Ghana later this year. All this proves your determination, as the most advanced industrial country of the continent, to play your part in the new Africa of to-day.

As I have travelled through the Union I have found everywhere, as I expected, a deep preoccupation with what is happening in the rest of the African continent. I understand and sympathize with your interest in these events, and your anxiety about them.

Ever since the break-up of the Roman Empire one of the constant facts of political life in Europe has been the emergence of independent nations. They have come into existence over the centuries in different shapes with different forms of government. But all have been inspired with a keen feeling of nationalism, which has grown as nations have grown.

In the twentieth century, and especially since the end of the war, the processes which gave birth to the nation-states of Europe have been repeated all over the world. We have seen the awakening of national consciousness in peoples who have for centuries lived in dependence on some other power.

Fifteen years ago this movement spread through Asia. Many countries there, of different races and civilizations, pressed their claim to an independent national life.

To-day, the same thing is happening in Africa. The most striking of all the impressions I have formed since I left London a month ago is of the strength of this African national consciousness. In different places it may take different forms but it is happening everywhere. The wind of change is blowing through the continent.

Whether we like it or not, this growth of national consciousness is a political fact. We must all accept it as a fact. Our national policies must take account of it.

Of course, you understand this as well as anyone. You are sprung from Europe, the home of nationalism. And here in Africa you have yourselves created a full nation—a new nation. Indeed, in the history of our times yours will be recorded as the first of the African nationalisms.

And this tide of national consciousness which is now rising in Africa is a fact for which you and we and the other nations of the western world are ultimately responsible.

For its causes are to be found in the achievements of western civilization in pushing forward the frontiers of knowledge, applying science in the service of human needs, expanding food production, speeding and multiplying means of communication and, above all, spreading education.

As I have said, the growth of national consciousness in Africa is a political fact and we must accept it as such. I sincerely believe that if we cannot do so, we may imperil the precarious balance of east and west on which the peace of the world depends.

The world to-day is divided into three great groups. First, there are what we call the western Powers. You in South Africa and we in Britain belong to this group, together with our friends and allies in other parts of the Commonwealth, in the United States of America, and in Europe.

Secondly, there are the Communists—Russia and her satellites in Europe and China, whose population will rise by 1970 to the staggering total of 800 million. Thirdly, there are those parts of the world whose people are at present uncommitted either to Communism or to our western ideas. In this context we think first of Asia and of Africa.

As I see it, the great issue in this second half of the twentieth century is whether the uncommitted peoples of Asia and Africa will swing to the east or to the west. Will they be drawn into the Communist camp? Or will the great experiments in self-government that are now being made in Asia and Africa, especially within the Commonwealth, prove so successful, and by their example so compelling, that the balance will come down in favour of freedom and order and justice?

The struggle is joined and it is a struggle for the minds of men. What is now on trial is much more than our military strength or our diplomatic and administrative skill. It is our way of life.

The uncommitted nations want to see before they choose. What can we show them to help them choose aright? Each of the independent members of the Commonwealth must answer that question for itself.

It is the basic principle for our modern Commonwealth that we respect each other's sovereignty in matters of internal policy. At the same time, we must recognize that, in this shrinking world in which we live to-day, the internal policies of one nation may have effects outside it. We may sometimes be tempted to say to each other, "Mind your own business." But in these days I would myself expand the old saying so that it runs, "Mind your own business, but mind how it affects my business, too."

Let me be very frank with you, my friends. What Governments and Parliaments in the United Kingdom have done since the war in according independence to India, Pakistan, Ceylon, Malaya, and Ghana, and what they will do for Nigeria and the other countries now nearing independence—all this, though we take full and sole responsibility for it, we do in the belief that it is the only way to establish the future of the Commonwealth and of the free world on sound foundations.

All this, of course, is also of deep and close concern to you, for nothing we do in this small world can be done in a corner or remain hidden. What we do to-day in West, Central, and East Africa becomes known to everyone in the Union, whatever his language, colour, or tradition.

Let me assure you in all friendliness that we are well aware of this, and that we have acted and will act with full knowledge of the responsibility we have to you and to all our friends. Nevertheless, I am sure you will agree that in our own areas of responsibility we must each do what we think right. What we think right derives from long experience, both of failure and success in the management of our own affairs.

We have tried to learn and apply the lessons of both. Our judgment of right and wrong and of justice is rooted in the same soil as yours—in Christianity and in the rule of law as the basis of a free society.

This experience of our own explains why it has been our aim, in countries for which we have borne responsibility, not only to raise the material standards of living but to create a society which respects the rights of individuals—a society in which men are given the opportunity to grow to their full stature, and that must in our view include the opportunity to have an increasing share in political power and responsibility; a society in which individual merit, and individual merit alone, is the criterion for man's advancement whether political or economic.

Finally, in countries inhabited by several different races, it has been our aim to find the means by which the community can become more of a community, and fellowship can be fostered between its various parts.

This problem is by no means confined to Africa, nor is it always the problem of the European minority. In Malaya, for instance, though there are Indian and

European minorities, Malays and Chinese make up the great bulk of the population, and the Chinese are not much fewer in numbers than Malays. Yet these two peoples must learn to live together in harmony and unity, and the strength of Malaya as a nation will depend on the different contributions which the two races can make.

The attitude of the United Kingdom Government towards this problem was clearly expressed by the Foreign Secretary, Mr. Selwyn Lloyd, speaking at the United Nations General Assembly on September 17, 1959. These are his words: —

> In those territories where different races or tribes live side by side, the task is to ensure that all the people may enjoy security and freedom and the chance to contribute as individuals to the progress and well being of these countries. We reject the idea of any inherent superiority of one race over another. Our policy therefore is non-racial. It offers a future in which Africans, Europeans, Asians, the peoples of the Pacific, and others with whom we are concerned, will all play their full part as citizens in the countries where they live and in which feelings of race will be submerged in loyalty to the new nations.

I have thought you would wish me to state plainly and with full candour the policy for which we in Britain stand.

It may well be that in trying to do our duty as we see it, we shall sometimes make difficulties for you. If this proves to be so, we shall regret it.

But I know that even so, you would not ask us to flinch from doing our duty. You, too, will do your duty as you see it.

I am well aware of the peculiar nature of the problems with which you are faced here in the Union of South Africa. I know the differences between your situation and that of most of the other states in Africa.

You have here some three million people of European origin. This country is their home. It has been their home for many generations. They have no other. The same is true of the Europeans in Central and East Africa.

In most other African states, those who have come from Europe have come to work, to contribute their skills, perhaps to teach, but not to make a home.

The problems to which you members of the Union Parliament have to address yourselves are very different from those which face the parliaments of countries with homogeneous populations. These are complicated and baffling problems. It would be surprising if your interpretation of your duty did not sometimes produce very different results from ours in terms of government policies and actions.

As a fellow member of the Commonwealth, it is our earnest desire to give South Africa our support and encouragement, but I hope you won't mind my saying frankly that there are some aspects of your policies which make it impossible for us to do this without being false to our own deep convictions about the political destinies of free men, to which in our own territories we are trying to give effect.

I think we ought as friends to face together—without seeking to apportion credit or blame—the fact that in the world of to-day this difference of outlook lies between us.

I said that I was speaking as a friend. I can also claim to be speaking as a relation. For we Scots can claim family connections with both great European sections of your population, not only with the English-speaking people but with Afrikaans-speaking as well.

This is a point which hardly needs emphasis in Cape Town, where you can see every day the statue of that great Scotsman, Andrew Murray. His work in the Dutch Reformed Church in the Cape, and the work of his son in the Orange Free State, was among Afrikaans-speaking people. There has always been a very close connexion between the Church of Scotland and the Church of the Netherlands. The Synod of Dort plays the same great part in the history of both. Many aspirants to the Ministry of Scotland, especially in the seventeenth and eighteenth centuries, went to pursue their theological studies in the Netherlands. Scotland can claim to have repaid the debt in South Africa. I am thinking particularly of the Scots in the Orange Free State. Not only the younger Andrew Murray, but also the Robertsons, the Frasers, the McDonalds— families which have been called the Free State clans who became burghers of the old Free State and whose descendants still play their part there.

But though I count myself a Scot, my mother was American, and the United States provides a valuable illustration of one of the main points which I have been trying to make in my remarks to-day. Its population, like yours, is a blend of many different strains, and over the years most of those who have gone to North America have gone there in order to escape conditions in Europe which they found intolerable.

It is not surprising, therefore, that for so many years a main objective of American statesmen, supported by the American public, was to isolate themselves from Europe, and with their great material strength and vast resources open to them this might have seemed an attractive and practicable course.

Nevertheless, in the two world wars of this century, they have found themselves unable to stand aside. Twice their manpower in arms has streamed back across the Atlantic to shed its blood in those European struggles from which their ancestors thought they would escape by emigrating to the new world. And when the second war was over, they were forced to recognize that in the small world of to-day isolationism is out of date and offers no assurance of security.

The fact is that in this modern world no country, not even the greatest, can live for itself alone. It has always been impossible for individual man to live in isolation from his fellows—in home, tribe, village, or city. To-day it is impossible for nations to live in isolation from one another. All nations are interdependent, one upon another, and this is generally realized throughout the western world. I hope in due course the countries of Communism will recognize it too.

It was certainly with that thought in mind that I took the decision to visit Moscow about this time last year. Russia has been isolationist in her time and still has tendencies that way, but the fact remains that we must live in the same world with Russia and we must find a way of doing so. I believe that the initiative which we took last year has had some success, although grave difficulties may arise. Nevertheless I think nothing but good can come out of extending contacts between individuals, contacts in trade and from the exchange of visitors.

The members of the Commonwealth feel particularly strongly the value of interdependence. They are as independent as any countries in this shrinking world can be, but they have voluntarily agreed to work together. I certainly do not believe in refusing to trade with people just because you dislike the way they manage their internal affairs at home. Boycotts will never get you anywhere.

Here I would like to say in parenthesis that I deprecate attempts which are being made in Britain to-day to organize a consumer boycott of South African goods. It has never been the practice of any Government in the United Kingdom, including a Labour Government, to undertake or support campaigns of this kind designed to influence the internal policies of another Commonwealth country.

They recognize that there may be differences between them in their institutions or in their internal policies, and membership does not imply either a wish to express a judgment on these matters or a need to impose a stifling uniformity.

It is, I think, a help that there has never been a question of any rigid constitution for the Commonwealth. Perhaps this is because we have got on well enough in the United Kingdom without a written constitution and tend to look suspiciously at them.

Whether that is so or not, it is quite clear that a rigid constitutional framework for the Commonwealth would not work. At the first of the stresses and strains which are inevitable in this period of history, cracks would appear in the framework and the whole structure would crumble. It is the flexibility of our Commonwealth institutions which gives them their strength.

In conclusion, may I say this. I have spoken frankly about the differences between our two countries in their approach to one of the great current problems with which each has to deal within its own sphere of responsibility. These differences are well known, they are matters of public knowledge— indeed, of public controversy. And I should have been less than honest if, by remaining silent on them, I had seemed to imply that they did not exist.

But differences on one subject, important though it is, need not and should not impair our capacity to cooperate with one another in furthering the many practical interests which we share in common. The independent members of the Commonwealth do not always agree on every subject. It is not a condition of their association that they should do so. On the contrary, the strength of our Commonwealth lies largely in the fact that it is a free association of independent sovereign States, each responsible for ordering its own affairs but cooperating in the pursuit of common aims and purposes in world affairs.

Moreover, these differences may be transitory. In time, they may be resolved. Our duty is to see them in perspective against the background of our long association.

Of this, at any rate, I am certain. Those of us, who, by the grace of the electorate, are temporarily in charge of affairs in my country and in yours have no right to sweep aside on this account the friendship that exists between our two countries. For that is the legacy of history. It is not ours alone to deal with as we wish.

We must face the differences. But let us try to see beyond them down the long vista of the future. I hope—indeed I am confident—that in another 50 years we shall look back on the differences that exist between us now as matters of historical interest.

For as time passes and one generation yields to another, human problems change and fade. Let us remember these truths. Let us resolve to build, not to destroy. And let us remember always that weakness comes from division, and strength from unity.

Nigeria Independence Act (8 & 9 Eliz. II, c. 55), 29 July 1960*

Be it enacted by the Queen's most Excellent Majesty, by and with the advice and consent of the Lords Spiritual and Temporal, and Commons, in this present Parliament assembled, and by the authority of the same, as follows: —

1.—(1) On the first day of October, nineteen hundred and sixty (in this Act referred to as "the appointed day"), the Colony and the Protectorate as respectively defined by the Nigeria (Constitution) Orders in Council, 1954 to 1960, shall together constitute part of Her Majesty's dominions under the name of Nigeria.

(2) No Act of the Parliament of the United Kingdom passed on or after the appointed day shall extend, or be deemed to extend, to Nigeria or any part thereof as part of the law thereof, and as from that day—

> (a) Her Majesty's Government in the United Kingdom shall have no responsibility for the government of Nigeria or any part thereof; and
>
> (b) the provisions of the First Schedule to this Act shall have effect with respect to legislative powers in Nigeria.

(3) Without prejudice to subsection (2) of this section, nothing in subsection (1) thereof shall affect the operation in Nigeria or any part thereof on and after the appointed day of any enactment, or any other instrument having the effect of law, passed or made with respect thereto before that day.

2.—(1) As from the appointed day, the British Nationality Acts, 1948 and 1958, shall have effect as if—

> (a) in subsection (3) of section one of the said Act of 1948 (which provides for persons to be British subjects or Commonwealth citizens

**Public General Acts*, 1960, 638–43.

by virtue of citizenship of certain countries) the word "and" in the last place where it occurs were omitted, and at the end there were added the words "and Nigeria";

(b) in the First Schedule to the British Protectorates, Protected States and Protected Persons Order in Council, 1949, the words "Nigeria Protectorate" were omitted:

Provided that a person who immediately before the appointed day is for the purposes of the said Acts and Order in Council a British protected person by virtue of his connection with the Nigeria Protectorate shall not cease to be such a British protected person for any of those purposes by reason of anything contained in the foregoing provisions of this Act, but shall so cease upon his becoming a citizen of Nigeria under the law thereof.

(2) Subject to the subsequent provisions of this section, any person who immediately before the appointed day is a citizen of the United Kingdom and Colonies shall on that day cease to be such a citizen if—

(a) under the law of Nigeria he becomes on that day a citizen of Nigeria; and

(b) he, his father or his father's father was born in any of the territories comprised in Nigeria.

(3) Subject to subsection (8) of this section, a person shall not cease to be a citizen of the United Kingdom and Colonies under the last foregoing subsection if he, his father or his father's father—

(a) was born in the United Kingdom or in a colony; or

(b) is or was a person naturalised in the United Kingdom and Colonies; or

(c) was registered as a citizen of the United Kingdom and Colonies; or

(d) became a British subject by reason of the annexation of any territory included in a colony.

(4) A person shall not cease to be a citizen of the United Kingdom and Colonies under subsection (2) of this section if he was born in a protectorate, protected state or United Kingdom trust territory, or if his father or his father's father was so born and is or at any time was a British subject.

(5) A woman who is the wife of a citizen of the United Kingdom and Colonies shall not cease to be such a citizen under subsection (2) of this section unless her husband does so.

(6) Subsection (2) of section six of the British Nationality Act, 1948 (which provides for the registration as a citizen of the United Kingdom and Colonies of a woman who has been married to such a citizen) shall not apply to a woman by virtue of her marriage to a person who ceases to be such a citizen under subsection (2) of this section, or who would have done so if living on the appointed day.

(7) Subject to the next following subsection, the reference in paragraph (b) of subsection (3) of this section to a person naturalised in the United Kingdom

and Colonies shall include a person who would, if living immediately before the commencement of the British Nationality Act, 1948, have become a person naturalised in the United Kingdom and Colonies by virtue of subsection (6) of section thirty-two of that Act (which relates to persons given local naturalisation before that commencement in a colony or protectorate).

(8) Any reference in subsection (3) or (4) of this section to a territory of any of the following descriptions, that is to say, a colony, protectorate, protected state or United Kingdom trust territory, shall, subject to the next following subsection, be construed as a reference to a territory which is of that description on the appointed day; and the said subsection (3) shall not apply to a person by virtue of any certificate of naturalisation granted or registration effected by the governor or government of a territory outside the United Kingdom which is not on that day of one of those descriptions.

(9) The protectorates of Northern Rhodesia and Nyasaland shall be excepted from the operation of any reference in subsection (4) or (8) of this section to a protectorate.

(10) Part III of the British Nationality Act, 1948 (which contains supplemental provisions) shall have effect for the purposes of subsections (2) to (9) of this section as if those subsections were included in that Act.

3.—(1) Notwithstanding anything in the Interpretation Act, 1889, the expression "colony" in any Act of the Parliament of the United Kingdom passed on or after the appointed day shall not include Nigeria or any part thereof.

(2) As from the appointed day—

>   (a) the expression "colony" in the Army Act, 1955, the Air Force Act, 1955, and the Naval Discipline Act, 1957, shall not include Nigeria or any part thereof: and
>
>   (b) in the definitions of "Commonwealth force" in subsection (1) of section two hundred and twenty-five and subsection (1) of section two hundred and twenty-three respectively of the said Acts of 1955, and in the definition of "Commonwealth country" in subsection (1) of section one hundred and thirty-five of the said Act of 1957—
>
> >   (i) the word "or" (being, in the said Acts of 1955, that word in the last place where it occurs in those definitions) shall be omitted; and
> >
> >   (ii) at the end there shall be added the words "or Nigeria".

(3) Any Order in Council made on or after the appointed day under either of the said Acts of 1955 providing for that Act to continue in force beyond the date on which it would otherwise expire shall not operate to continue that Act in force beyond that date as part of the law of Nigeria or any part thereof.

(4) As from the appointed day, the provisions specified in the Second Schedule to this Act shall have effect subject to the amendments respectively specified in that Schedule, and Her Majesty may by Order in Council, which shall be subject to annulment in pursuance of a resolution of either House of

Parliament, make such further adaptations in any Act of the Parliament of the United Kingdom passed before this Act, or in any instrument having effect under any such Act, as appear to Her necessary in consequence of section one of this Act; and any Order in Council made under this subsection may be varied or revoked by a subsequent Order in Council so made and, though made after the appointed day, may be made so as to have effect from that day:

Provided that this subsection shall not extend to Nigeria or any part thereof as part of the law thereof.

4.— (1) In relation to any person who at the date of the passing of this Act is serving in the naval forces of the Federation of Nigeria established by section three of the Nigeria (Constitution) Order in Council, 1954, the Overseas Service Act, 1958 (which authorises the Secretary of State to appoint officers to be available for civilian employment in the public service of an overseas territory in accordance with arrangements made by the Secretary of State with the government of that territory and to make provision as to superannuation in respect of officers so appointed) shall have effect as if service in those forces and service on or after the appointed day in the naval forces of Nigeria were civilian employment in the public service of that Federation or, as the case may be, of Nigeria.

(2) In relation to any person who, having served in the naval forces of the said Federation in accordance with arrangements made by the Secretary of State with the government of that Federation, has by reason of death or retirement ceased so to serve before the date of the passing of this Act, subsection (2) of section four of the said Act of 1958 (which authorises the Secretary of State to pay pensions to or in respect of persons who have served as officers to whom that Act applies) shall have effect as if that person were a person who has served as such an officer and as if those arrangements were such arrangements as are mentioned in subsection (1) of section one of that Act.

5.— (1) This Act may be cited as the Nigeria Independence Act, 1960.

(2) References in this Act to any enactment are references to that enactment as amended or extended by or under any other enactment.

Schedules

First Schedule Legislative Powers in Nigeria

1. The Colonial Laws Validity Act, 1865, shall not apply to any law made on or after the appointed day by any legislature established for Nigeria or any part thereof.

2. No law and no provision of any law made on or after the appointed day by any such legislature as aforesaid shall be void or inoperative on the ground that it is repugnant to the law of England, or to the provisions of any Act of the Parliament of the United Kingdom, including this Act, or to any order, rule or regulation made under any such Act, and, subject to paragraph 6 of this Schedule, the powers of any such legislature shall include the power to repeal or

amend any such Act, order, rule or regulation in so far as it is part of the law of Nigeria or any part thereof and in so far as it relates to matters within the legislative powers of that legislature.

3. Any such legislature as aforesaid shall have full power to make laws having extra-territorial operation, so far as those laws relate to matters within the legislative powers of that legislature.

4. Without prejudice to the generality of the foregoing provisions of this Schedule, sections seven hundred and thirty-five and seven hundred and thirty-six of the Merchant Shipping Act, 1894, shall be construed as though reference therein to the legislature of a British possession did not include reference to any such legislature as aforesaid.

5. Without prejudice to the generality of the foregoing provisions of this Schedule, section four of the Colonial Courts of Admiralty Act, 1890 (which requires certain laws to be reserved for the signification of Her Majesty's pleasure or to contain a suspending clause) and so much of section seven of that Act as requires the approval of Her Majesty in Council to any rules of court for regulating the practice and procedure of a Colonial Court of Admiralty shall cease to have effect in Nigeria.

6. Nothing in this Act shall confer on any such legislature as aforesaid any power to repeal, amend or modify the constitutional provisions otherwise than in such manner as may be provided for in those provisions.

In this paragraph, the expression "the constitutional provisions" means this Act, any Order in Council made before the appointed day which revokes the Nigeria (Constitution) Orders in Council, 1954 to 1960, and any law, or instrument made under a law, of any such legislature as aforesaid made on or after that day which amends, modifies, re-enacts with or without amendment or modification, or makes different provision in lieu of, any of the provisions of this Act, that Order in Council or any such law or instrument previously made.

* * *

Statement by the Commonwealth and Colonial Secretary, Duncan Sandys, in the House of Commons Outlining a Timetable for the Proposed Federation of Malaysia, 1 August 1962* [The Federation was dissolved in August 1965.]

With permission, I would like to make a statement about the proposed Federation of Malaysia.

The British and Malayan Governments have received and studied the Report of the Commission under the chairmanship of Lord Cobbold which visited North Borneo and Sarawak earlier this year to ascertain the views of the

Hansard, 5.s., DCLXIV, 584–90.

inhabitants on the proposal to create a Federation of Malaysia embracing Malaya, Singapore, Sarawak, North Borneo and Brunei. The Report is being published today and is now available in the Vote Office.

The two Governments are most grateful to the Commission for its valuable Report and have accepted almost all the recommendations on which the Commission was unanimous. The two Governments have noted, in particular, that the Commission was unanimously agreed that a Federation of Malaysia is in the best interests of North Borneo and Sarawak and that an early decision in principle should be reached.

In the light of this Report and of the agreement reached between the Government of Malaya and the Government of Singapore, the British and Malayan Governments have now decided in principle that, subject to the necessary legislation, the proposed Federation of Malaysia should be brought into being by 31st August, 1963.

To give effect to this decision, the two Governments intend to conclude, within the next six months, a formal agreement which, among other things, will provide for:

first, the transfer of sovereignty in North Borneo, Sarawak and Singapore by 31st August, 1963;

secondly, provisions governing the relationship between Singapore and the new Federation, as agreed between the Governments of Malaya and Singapore;

thirdly, defence arrangements as set out in the joint statement by the British and Malayan Governments dated 22nd November, 1961; and

fourthly, detailed constitutional arrangements, including safeguards for the special interests of North Borneo and Sarawak, to be drawn up after consultation with the Legislatures of the two territories.

These safeguards will cover such matters as religious freedom, education, representation in the Federal Parliament, the position of the indigenous races, control of immigration, citizenship and the State constitutions.

In order that the introduction of the new Federal system may be effected as smoothly as possible and with the least disturbance to existing administrative arrangements, there will be, after the transfer of sovereignty, a transition period, during which a number of the Federal constitutional powers will be delegated temporarily to the State Governments.

An Inter-Governmental Committee will be established as soon as possible, on which the British, Malayan, North Borneo and Sarawak Governments will be represented. Its task will be to work out the future constitutional arrangements and the form of the necessary safeguards for the two territories.

The Minister of State for the Colonies, Lord Lansdowne, who will be the Chairman of this Committee, and the Deputy Prime Minister of the Federation of Malaya, Tun Abdul Razak, will proceed shortly to Sarawak and North Borneo to conduct discussions.

In order to maintain the efficiency of the administration, the British and Malayan Governments are agreed on the importance of retaining the services of as many of the expatriate officials as possible. The Minister of State will discuss with the Governments of the territories and with the staff associations how this best can be done.

The British and Malayan Governments have informed the Sultan of Brunei of the agreement they have reached and have made it clear that they would welcome the inclusion of the State of Brunei in the new Federation.

MR. HEALEY: My right hon. and hon. Friends welcome the conclusion of an agreement to set up a federation which I think the great majority of hon. Members on both sides believe will be in the interests of the inhabitants of all the territories concerned. However, experience has taught us to be a little cautious about proposals for federation in Commonwealth and Colonial Territories. Will the right hon. Gentleman enlighten us on three particular issues referred to in his account of the agreement?

First, does the description of the agreement as being "in principle" mean that both parties to it are free to withdraw from it if they are dissatisfied with the course of negotiations before the Federation is actually set up? Secondly, is it the case that the Sultanate of Brunei is totally free to decide whether to join the Federation and that the Tunku of Malaya has decided that the Federation shall go forward whatever decision is taken by the Government of Brunei? Finally, is it intended that expatriate civil servants shall continue to administer the territories concerned until the end of the transitional period under the sovereignty of the local administration?

MR. SANDYS: First, when we say that the agreement has been decided "in principle", we intend that this shall, in fact, take place, but, as I made clear in my statement, before the process is complete, we have got to conclude a formal agreement which will set out all the various points which have been under discussion and which will be further discussed with the Legislatures of the two territories. Naturally, if we fail to reach agreement on what the treaty shall contain, which, I think, is extremely unlikely, it will break down. But, in view of the wide measure of agreement which we have already reached, I think that that is a most unlikely eventuality.

Secondly, the Sultan of Brunei has already declared publicly that he is in favour of the creation of the new Federation. I therefore think it unlikely that the issue raised by the hon. Gentleman will arise.

Thirdly, in regard to the transition period, it is the hope and wish—I thought that I had made this reasonably clear in my statement—that as many as possible of the expatriate officials shall continue to undertake the administration of the territories for as long as possible.

SIR J. BARLOW: I thank my right hon. Friend for his statement. While we all agree that this new idea of a greater Malaysia is a good thing, does he realise that the people of North Borneo and Sarawak are not universally in favour of this new proposal? Will my right hon. Friend take great care to ensure that there are proper safeguards for these two peoples, who are not so far advanced as those of Singapore and Malaya?

MR. SANDYS: The Commission, in its Report, which my hon. Friend will see, came to the conclusion that, provided adequate safeguards were secured, the majority of the people of these two territories are in favour of the proposed Federation. We recognise, of course, that the securing of proper safeguards to meet their special interests is of cardinal importance. That has been the major topic which we have been discussing during the past ten days with Malayan Ministers in London, and we shall continue to discuss the matter in further detail through the medium of the Inter-Governmental Committee to which I referred in my statement.

MR. GRIMOND: In welcoming the Minister's statement, may I ask him whether any of the unanimous recommendations of the Cobbold Commission which have not been accepted are major recommendations? Can he give the House any information on this point? Secondly, is the date of 31st August, 1963, a firm date? I take it that if all the preliminaries are concluded satisfactorily, that is a firm date for independence and federation.

MR. SANDYS: It would not be a good thing for me to try to summarise the points on which the Commission was not agreed. I would hope that the right hon. Gentleman will study that for himself.

I have stated that we have agreed in principle that the new Federation should be brought into being by 31st August, 1963; that is to say, a date not later than 31st August, 1963.

SIR K. PICKTHORN: Can my right hon. Friend assure us that any hopes placed in continued service by expatriates will not be endangered by their having any reason whatever themselves to lose confidence in their careers and in their treatment?

MR. SANDYS: That, of course, will be our intention in the talks which we are proposing to have with the staff associations in the two territories.

MR. CREECH JONES: Having had some responsibility for the separation of Singapore from Malaya and the inclusion of Sarawak in the Commonwealth, I should like to express my sincere congratulations to the Minister and to the Prime Ministers of Malaya and Singapore on the discussions which have taken place and my hope for the success of these arrangements in the future. I would only inform the Secretary of State, if I may, that this is a stage in the consummation of a policy which some of us ardently desired in the early days after the war.

MR. TURNER: Can my right hon. Friend assure the House that in the consultations that will take place in North Borneo and Sarawak, in addition to the Legislatures outside bodies will also be consulted about the safeguards?

MR. SANDYS: Yes, Sir. I have no doubt that the Inter-Governmental Committee will exercise wide discretion in deciding with whom it is appropriate to have consultations. The Cobbold Commission has, however, been over the whole of this ground and has consulted a whole variety of bodies in the two territories. Therefore, our primary task now is to consult the Legislatures of the two territories concerned.

MR. G. THOMAS: Will the inter-Governmental discussions on religious freedom in Sarawak ultimately be referred to this House in view of the deep anxiety which, as the Secretary of State will know, has been expressed by Christian communities in Sarawak at the prospect of an Islamic State?

MR. SANDYS: My belief is that when this matter is fully discussed with the peoples concerned, they will be satisfied—certainly, we want to be absolutely sure on this point—that there will be complete religious freedom in the two territories after the creation of the new Federation.

SIR C. OSBORNE: Will there be an opportunity to discuss the whole matter in this House before a final decision is taken? Secondly, did I understand my right hon. Friend correctly to say that one of the items was control of immigration? What degree of control will be exercised and who asked for control of immigration—the Malayan Government or the British Government?

MR. SANDYS: The control of immigration was one of the safeguards which was very much wanted by the peoples of the two territories. I think that they want a control of immigration much greater, perhaps, than this House would have approved in the discussion of a Bill earlier this Session. They are afraid, in particular, of large-scale immigration and land settlement which might affect the character and balance of the country.

As to a debate in this House, before the process can be completed legislation will, of course, be required.

---

*Statement by Duncan Sandys in the House of Commons Announcing Future Independence for Kenya, 2 July 1963**

With your permission, Mr. Speaker, and that of the House, I will now answer Question No. 54.

After the elections last May Kenya was given full internal self-government as a prelude to early independence. I have recently had consultations with Kenya Ministers about the further steps to be taken for the transfer of the remaining powers and I am publishing today as a White Paper a joint statement setting out our agreed conclusions.

In the last few weeks there has been an important new development, which has affected the constitutional arrangements to be made, and which has to be taken into account in the timing of Kenya's independence. I refer to the

*Hansard, 5.s., DCLXXX, 201–02.

decision of the Governments of Tanganyika, Uganda and Kenya to form an East African Federation, which, as I said in the House last week, is warmly welcomed by Her Majesty's Government.

The three East African Governments have already made substantial progress in working out the constitution for the proposed Federation, and it is their aim to bring it into being before the end of the year, in time to enable the new Federal State to be admitted to the United Nations in the forthcoming session. In order that Kenya's final decision to join this new association may be taken with the full authority and responsibility of a sovereign nation, it will be necessary for her to obtain independence shortly before the inauguration of the Federation.

In the light of these considerations, I propose to convene a conference in London towards the end of September to settle the final form of Kenya's constitution. Representatives of the Government and Opposition parties in the Legislature and of the European community will be invited to attend.

To enable the necessary forward planning to be undertaken, not only by the Kenya Government, but also by the Governments of the other East African countries concerned, Her Majesty's Government have informed the Government of Kenya that, subject to the necessary steps being completed in time, Kenya will be granted independence on 12th December.

Statement by the Former Minister of Defence for the Royal Navy,
Christopher Mayhew, in the House of Commons Outlining a Policy of
Disengagement from the Far East, 22 February 1966*

It is an old and generous custom of the House to permit a Minister who has resigned to explain his position in a personal statement. I am grateful to the House for this opportunity.

I begin by wishing my successor well. As he knows, it was my strongly expressed hope that he would succeed me. He has already earned, and will certainly continue to receive, the full confidence of the Navy and he can be sure that in what I have to say now I shall do my utmost not to make his difficult task more difficult still.

I am afraid that he will feel severely the loss of the advice and support of Admiral Luce, whose help to the Admiralty Board and to the Navy and to myself personally I would regard as irreplaceable. One would have thought it impossible that the Fleet's long-held respect for Admiral Luce could be enhanced, were it not for the announcement which we have just heard this afternoon.

*Hansard, 5.s., DCCXXV, 254–65.

Anyone who has had, as I have had, responsibility for the management of the Royal Navy will always feel proud and grateful. I left with profound regret. Nevertheless, as I propose to show, decisions on defence have been taken by colleagues whom I respect, and who have treated me with kindness, which leave me no alternative but to resign.

I shall try to show that the approach to the Defence Review has been mistaken, that the proposed cuts in resources are not matched by the proposed cuts in commitments and that the result will be strain on the Armed Forces, or dependence on the United States beyond what this House should accept.

The principal mistake in the handling of the Defence Review was commitment to a world role with a presence east of Suez, and also to a budget of £2,000 million, before the review began. This was a very strange thing to do. No previous studies have been made to find out whether the two aims were compatible. It was simply assumed that they were and throughout the review the assumptions were never seriously challenged.

The figure of £2,000 million was a purely artificial one, simply a statistical projection of the cost of defence in 1964–65 into 1969–70. After it had been laid down the overseas Departments earnestly studied what should be our minimum commitments in the 1970s and the Ministry of Defence earnestly studied what would be the most economical way of meeting those commitments and then both came up with the figure which the Treasury first thought of.

The fact is that we have only to look back over the years of administration of the previous Government to see that far stricter Treasury control was needed over our defence expenditure. Experience has now shown that there is danger in the opposite direction, too, in laying down a defence budget too early and too rigidly before working out its implications in foreign policy and defence. For one thing, it immediately inhibits any considerations of a budget of less than the stated sum. Surely, never in the whole history of public administration has a Department been offered money by the Treasury and not found the need for it. In practice, throughout the whole Defence Review no serious study has been given to a defence budget of less than £2,000 million related to reduced commitments.

The rigid fixing of the budget in advance placed a heavy strain on inter-Service relations. In the old days there was a dangerous tendency for the Services to gang up together and collectively present a demand for a defence budget in excess of their needs. This was bad, but, again, there is a danger in going to the opposite extreme, by rigidly fixing in advance a level compelling each Service to fight for its own vital interests by attacking the vital interests of the other Services. The result is that too little collective decision is given to the question whether the total sum is enough for the Armed Forces as a whole.

Not that the inter-Service rivalry was on anything like the scale that public opinion has been led to believe. It should be placed to the credit of the Admiralty Board that from the beginning to the end of the Defence Review it stoutly maintained that if we were to remain east of Suez we should need F111As for the job as well as carriers.

Now the sums of the defence review have been worked out and it is plain that £2,000 million is a bad figure for a defence budget—it is too small if we want to stay east of Suez and much too big if we do not. It lands us with an in-between presence east of Suez, which is still extremely expensive, especially in foreign currency, involves us in considerable risks, military and politically, and makes no equivalent contribution to our real national interest.

This, then, was the beginning of the trouble—a rigid laying down in advance of two incompatible objectives, a world role and the £2,000 million. The inevitable consequence followed, cuts in resources out of all proportion to cuts in commitments. The House will not want me to spell out in detail the cuts involved in the reduction of £400 million in the planned budget for 1969. The House should note that not all these things are specified in the defence White Paper.

In the case of the Navy, they are much wider than merely the cancellation of the CVA01 but they are not specified. The cuts apply to all three Services and amount to one-sixth of the total budget. Some of these reductions were to cut out waste. On the other hand, the cuts are overwhelmingly in the realm of equipment and weapons and not in the realm of administration, pay and pensions, which amount to one-half of the total budget. Thus, one-sixth of the total budget represents much more than one-sixth of the budget for arms weapons and equipment. It represents a very heavy cut indeed in military capabilities.

The most spectacular and controversial of the cuts was the cancellation of the new carrier. I would like to make it clear that my position throughout the defence review has been that if the Government insist on a world rôle east of Suez in the 1970s, then carriers are essential, and that my duty as Navy Minister was to fight for them.

At the same time, although not my direct personal responsibility, I did not hesitate to question whether we should adopt that rôle, whether that was the right rôle for Britain in the 1970s. As long ago as April, 1963, after visiting the Far East and the Gulf as deputy spokesman for the then Opposition on foreign affairs, I sent a report to the present Prime Minister expressing the same doubts about this rôle that I propose to express later on, and recommending a policy of gradual long-term disengagement. It seems to be perfectly logical and honourable to hold doubts about remaining east of Suez in the 1970s, but, at the same time, to say, as Navy Minister, that if the Government insist on remaining east of Suez in the 1970s, the Navy will need new carriers.

I will now like to explain the reasons why a viable carrier force is absolutely essential if we are to stay east of Suez in the 1970s and why the plan for carriers given in the White Paper will not work. The four major reasons why the carriers would be essential are these. First, they enable us to exercise air power in any part of the ocean and not merely within an agreed manageable range of a land-air base. Outside this agreed range only carriers can provide the air strike and air defence to protect naval shipping or an amphibious force, or replenishment ships or merchant ships, and so on. Any military operation involving the use of such shipping must have carrier support, either British or

American. That is agreed and no one disputes it. Outside of this range, without a carrier the Navy is unprotected. It is a "sitting duck" for any small country with a few Soviet bombers or missile patrol craft.

The second reason why carriers are essential if we are to stay east of Suez is that they provide essential reinsurance against the loss of a lang-air base. Land bases and carriers are both vulnerable. The most extensive analyses show that in Vietnam the carrier is less vulnerable and less expensive than the land-air base. Without the carrier one has all of one's eggs in one basket. Everything will depend on one air base. If it is sabotaged or mortared by guerrillas, one is left with no air cover at all.

The third reason why carriers are essential if we are to stay east of Suez is their deterrent power. This has been proved over and over again from practical experience and arises from the factors I have just mentioned. Phasing out the carriers will encourage our adversaries east of Suez at the very time that they will make it more difficult for us to cope with that challenge if it comes.

The fourth reason is that carriers are extremely flexible. They can provide air defence, ground attack and fulfil other functions which make them infinitely valuable for dealing with unpredictable occasions, as, again, has been shown in experience. Practically all our peace-keeping operations since the war were not, and could not have been, predicted.

Those, then, are the reasons why, if we must stay east of Suez in the 1970s, we are, in my view, morally obliged to do so with a viable Navy and a viable carrier force. The cost is stated in the White Paper to be £1,400 million. This is misleading, because some of the carriers' functions are essential and cannot be replaced by other means, which the White Paper points out. What the White Paper does not do is to cost the reprovisioning of the essential functions of the carrier. If that is done, the total cost of the carrier comes down to a small fraction of the £1,400 million; and that is a factor to be borne in mind.

The facts which I have stated are, I think, broadly agreed in the White Paper. The factor that the carriers are of vital importance and that some of their functions are irreplaceable is reflected in the statement in the White Paper that " . . . . we attach great importance to continuing the existing carrier force as far as possible into the 1970s". But it is the considered professional view of the Navy and the unanimous opinion of the Board that the carrier plan in the White Paper is unworkable. The Fleet Air Arm is already short of air crew. The cancellation of CVA01 is bound to be a heavy blow to the members of the Fleet Air Arm. We cannot help but expect a bad effect on recruiting and re-engagement. With the maximum financial incentives and the greatest possible support from the Royal Air Force it might be possible to prolong the death throes of the Fleet Air Arm by three, perhaps four, years, but into the mid-1970s, no; that is impossible.

Meanwhile, when the carriers are phased out, where is the protection for the Fleet and how can honourable men be expected to take the risk to be personally, directly responsible in the posts, for example, of First Sea Lord, or of Minister, for a plan which their most expert professional advisers tell them is unworkable? Suppose that it is possible to carry on the old fleet of carriers into the mid-1970s. There are still operational disadvantages; I will not detail them now.

I cannot feel that it is right that a nation which considers itself strong enough to take on a world rôle and to act as peacemaker and guardian over other nations thousands of miles away can, at the same time, say that it is too poor to afford the sailors with the ships and equipment that they need for the tasks they are ordered to carry out. All the same, it would be absurd to say—and the White Paper is right to stress this—that the phasing out of the carriers will be the end of the Navy. The Navy will remain an essential part of our national defence. It will continue to offer a fine and honourable career.

The White Paper lists the new ships and equipment which will come into service in the years ahead. By "new" I do not mean that they have been added to the programme. I mean that they have not been taken out of the programme. Of the 10 items listed, all except two have always been in our future programme. Moreover, as I have said, the White Paper does not specify the full range of cuts either in the Navy or in the other Services.

So much for the cuts in capability. What now of the cuts in commitments and the limitations on our military action east of Suez which are held to justify these very substantial cuts? The White Paper mentions Aden. But it also states that we intend to maintain our treaties with Libya and Malta and our commitments to N.A.T.O., S.E.A.T.O., CENTO, in the Gulf, in Gibraltar, in Hong Kong, in the island territories of the Atlantic, Indian and Pacific Oceans, in Cyprus and in Singapore. The undertaking to remain in Singapore as long as possible commits us to the defence of Malaysia and Singapore and may make more difficult and postpone the end of confrontation which is an essential assumption behind the Government's whole defence planning. The White Paper also notes our growing commitments in Africa.

We must note, too, that the power of our possible adversaries east of Suez is growing. As the White Paper points out, the arms race is continuing among smaller countries. Other countries are following the lead of Indonesia, which, with Soviet help, has made itself a formidable military proposition in only five years. Thus, all the time the challenge is growing, the task increases and our resources dwindle. It is quite plain that the defence policy set out in the White Paper will open up a vast gap in the 1970s between what the Service men are expected to do and what they are given to do the job with.

I come to the review's last line of defence: our allies—that is to say, the Americans—will help us out. This assumption is contained in the White Paper's statement that " . . . Britain will not undertake major operations of war except in co-operation with allies". I hope that the implications of this statement will be very fully studied. First, it involves distinguishing in advance between a major military operation and a minor one. We promise only to undertake minor military operations alone. But the distinction is an extremely difficult one to make in advance. For example, how can we be sure that a minor operation will not escalate into a major operation? This is, in fact, how most major operations usually begin. Vietnam began as a minor operation in a small country.

Nor can we be sure that the minor operations which we undertake alone do not escalate. How can we? What do we do if they do escalate? Either we can withdraw and leave in the lurch those whom we have gone to help, which would be dishonourable, or we can ask our troops to go on fighting, having provided them, as the White Paper's own admission makes clear, without the resources necessary to enable them to get victory, which would be more dishonourable still. Or—and this is the heart of the matter—we could run to the Americans for help. But this means, in practice, that before even a minor operation is undertaken by us alone we shall need to get the agreement of the Americans and to make contingency plans with them in case things go wrong.

In practice, I believe that, unless we were to take unacceptable risks, the White Paper policy would mean virtually taking no action at all on our own initiative, even if appealed to by those whom we are supposed to be supporting. If they appeal for our help, we shall stand idly by. Alternatively, we shall act with the consent and support, or promised support, of our vastly more powerful ally, the United States, and the more we act the more we shall depend on their support. We shall be acting not as a power in our own right, but as an extension of United States power—not as allies, but as auxiliaries of the United States.

Even this assumes that we have solved the operational and logistic difficulties of interrelating American military support and carrier support with our own forces. These practical difficulties have not yet been studied, nor has any suggestion been made that they should be studied. Nor is there any assurance that in a situation in which we might need American support it would be physically available. There would certainly be no American carriers available to us today.

More serious, however, are the political implications of what is proposed. How can we suppose that the Americans will always come to our aid and not ask us to come to their aid? They have come to the aid of the Australians with substantial military aid and, in return, quite naturally, the Australians have sent a battalion to Vietnam. In my view, the degree of military dependence involved in the Government's new plans would present serious problems even if there were solid political agreement with the Americans on the basic issues in the Far East.

But is that, in fact, true? In Europe, in the 1940s and 1950s, the situation was totally different. In a very minor way, I played a small part in helping the late Ernest Bevin to bring the Americans into an alliance in Europe at that time. But, of course, we and the Americans agreed about Stalin, and in that partnership there were European countries, too, with substantial military potential which helped as a counterweight to the overwhelming force, strength and influence of the United States.

Today in the Far East it is totally different. We do not agree with the United States about Communist China. We do not support the Formosan Government. We have a different emphasis in our interpretation of the problem of containing

Communism there. Moreover, in military terms we are virtually alone in an absurdly unequal relationship with the vast power of the United States.

I have been, and still am, a warm supporter of the present Anglo-American Alliance. I respect and admire the United States. It would, however, be in the interests of both countries that if we stay east of Suez we should do so with a force with a substantial degree of self-sufficiency—that is, not wholly dependent upon the United States; a force including both F111As and carriers, a force costing substantially more than £2,000 million.

Should we, however, find more than £2,000 million for defence? If we insist upon a world role, I am sure that we must. Had agreement been reached on this basis, my direct personal responsibility for the Navy would have been met and my personal position would, in my judgment, have been tolerable.

I am bound to say that I should still have had serious misgivings about a role so far beyond our economic strength. Surely, there would have been something totally incongruous about a nation performing a proud world rôle of peace-keeping on borrowed money with the sound of our gunfire drowned by the rattling of our collection boxes.

As I have explained, as has long been known to my friends, I have had doubts about this rôle east of Suez in itself. I seriously doubt whether, in the 1970s, with the growth of nationalism and racialism, any white nation, either alone or with others, can perform an effective peacekeeping task east of Suez. Already, the political and psychological obstacles to Western military deployment, let alone Western military action, in Asia and the Middle East are extremely strong. By the 1970s, they well have become crippling.

While we sympathise with the United States in the harrowing experience which they have in Vietnam, ought we not also to learn from it and to draw the lessons of it? Should we not clearly take note that for all their gigantic military effort, the United States have so far been unable to contain North Vietnam—not China, but North Vietnam? May it not be, therefore, in the 1970's that the first white-faced soldier, sailor or airman who sets foot on the mainland of Asia or the Middle East will automatically unite against himself and his Government the coloured people whom he has come to help? Indeed, would we not feel the same in their shoes?

There is no specific mention in the White Paper of the policy of containing China. Is this one of the objectives of our policy or not? If it is, it should be stated. If it is not, that should be made quite plain to the United States, the Australians and the New Zealanders. Meanwhile, since, I think, the Government are not committed to that policy, I will not state my serious misgivings about the policy of containing China on the narrow basis of two or three white nations.

Plainly, in the 1970s we shall still have some colonial responsibilities—for example, in Hong Kong—and also a moral commitment to the Australians and the New Zealanders to help in the defence of their territories. Apart from these things, however, we need have no commitment east of Suez in the 1970s, moral or otherwise, except as members of the United Nations.

That does not mean sudden or unilateral abandonment of obligations. We are not talking about this year or next year or even the year after. We are talking about the 1970s. It would be perfectly honourable and sensible for us now to decide to adjust ourselves to a changed world. In my view, it is no sign of vitality in a nation that it clings stubbornly to positions which it already holds. Indeed, not many years ago we criticised the French and the Dutch for a similar kind of stubbornness in the Far East.

A surer sign of vitality in a nation is an ability to take hard decisions to adapt ourselves to new circumstances. I should feel much greater faith in this country's future if we firmly decided now to withdraw over the years ahead from our increasingly exposed positions overseas.

The approach which I have suggested would make possible a defence budget below £1,800 million in 1969–70. This would help us immensely to put our own affairs in order. We should pay more attention to growing opportunities in Europe. We could extend our influence overseas out of the substantial saving of foreign currency which we could make.

If we decide to take some such course as this, now must be the moment to take the decision, because the Government's proposals to go east of Suez and to carry on east of Suez in this new joint basis will morally commit us to stay there for years and years to come. It is, in fact, a new commitment which we shall be taking on east of Suez. Therefore, if we are to decide this great matter, now is the moment to decide it and to make up our minds for ourselves.

The basic mistake of the Defence Review has been the classic crime of peacetime British Governments of giving the Armed Forces too large tasks and too few resources. The overseas Departments have laid down a proud defence role for Britain, the Treasury has laid down a humble defence budget for Britain, and the Service men "carry the can".

This has all happened before. It happened in 1939, when both parties were to blame. Admittedly, we then had a commitment that we could not possibly avoid, but then, again, we placed upon the Services a task far beyond the resources we had given them. I was myself a member of the first Territorial unit to land in France in September, 1939. We had field guns of an ancient design—converted 18-pounders. Equipped as we were, and trained as we were, we should never had been sent abroad on active service at all. Many of us had jobs which were quite unfamiliar to us. For several weeks, I was an officer's batman, and a very poor, patient officer he was.

Most of the men whom I knew then came back safely through Dunkirk. But more would have come back if they had had the tanks and air support which they needed and deserved, if they had not been let down by the nation, by Parliament and by their Service Ministers. I am convinced that the House will never allow that kind of thing to happen again.

Let us have a full and bold debate on all these great issues in the House and in the country, and God grant that we choose right for our nation.

*Statement by the Commonwealth Secretary, Herbert Bowden, in the
House of Commons Reaffirming British Rights to Gibraltar,
13 April 1967**

An Order was published in Madrid on 12th April establishing a zone in
which all flying will be prohibited, allegedly in accordance with Article 9 of the
Chicago Convention. This zone is in the immediate vicinity of Gibraltar.

The decree declared that the reason for the prohibition was "for the basic
reasons of national security". The decree is to take effect one month after its
notification to the International Civil Aviation Organisation.

The text of the decree and the charts attached to it will require careful study
to see whether the decree would have any practical effect on flights in and out
of Gibraltar. After this study, a further statement will be made.

We, of course, Mr. Speaker, intend to uphold to the full our right to use the
airfield at Gibraltar.

In view of this new development, which I greatly deplore, we have decided
to postpone the talks on Gibraltar which were due to be held with Spain in
London next week. The Spanish Ambassador has been informed.

As regards our general policy on Gibraltar, the House will know that the
Minister of State recently had discussions with the Governor, and with the
Chief Minister of Gibraltar and his deputy. At these talks complete agreement
was reached on the policy and course of action to be followed. But the House
will obviously not expect me to elaborate on this matter at this stage.

MR. MAUDLING: This is a very serious matter for Gibraltar. We on this side
welcome the Secretary of State's affirmation of the Government's determination
to protect the right of peaceful access to Gibraltar. As this danger has been well
known as a possibility for a long time to all concerned, what plans have the
Government made in advance to prepare against it?

MR. BOWDEN: Contingency planning is going on, and has been for some time.
It is regrettable that the Spanish Government, who could have used the talks
that should have taken place next week to discuss this position, did not do so,
but, two or three days before, made this announcement.

SIR G. DE FREITAS: Does my right hon. Friend agree that although we should
rely on international law in this matter, where our case is very strong, we
should also emphasise the fact that what Spain is presuming to do is to prevent
British aircraft from using British territory?

*Hansard, 5.s., DCCXLIV, 1375–78.

Mr. Bowden: Whether or not this proposal has any effect at all on flights into and out of Gibraltar, it is obviously the Spaniards' intention for it to do so, but, as I have already said, we propose to continue these flights.

Sir F. Bennett: Does the right hon. Gentleman recall that the last series of talks was preceded by a very similar act of harassment, and that many of us at that time warned of the danger of holding talks under duress? Will the Minister now take note that this is not a matter just for the present, but for the future, too?

Mr. Bowden: The question whether or not the talks should be resumed at a later date is a matter for us, and we shall have to watch developments. I would urge the House not to press me on the question of the position regarding flying rights over what are alleged to be Spanish territorial waters until we have had an opportunity to study the charts.

Mr. George Jeger: Is it not time that the Government reviewed their previous decision and decided to take reprisals against Spain?

Mr. Bowden: I do not think that the question of retaliation and reprisals arises at this stage.

Mr. Thorpe: Is it not a fact that the Spanish Government have to justify this claimed zoning before the Convention? If so, may we take it that Her Majesty's Government will be resisting this and instructing our personnel to do so?

Can the right hon. Gentleman say more about the postponed talks? Is it not a fact that this action was a deliberate attempt to get the talks cancelled? Since the case for Her Majesty's Government is a very strong one, does he not think that we should review the question of having talks even before this is settled?

Mr. Bowden: We have never agreed that we have infringed Spanish rights in flying in and out of Gibraltar.

On the question of talks, I think that we must see the charts first and what effect they have on the territorial waters before a decision is taken by Her Majesty's Government on whether there would be value in further talks.

Sir J. Langford-Holt: Will the right hon. Gentleman make clear what is involved? Am I right in assuming that it is not just the convenience of aircraft approaching Gibraltar, but of safety in landing and taking off?

Mr. Bowden: Of course, the question of safety in landing and taking off is being closely studied, but what the Spaniards intend under the Order, provided that it is upheld under the Convention, is to declare a prohibited area in which flights should not take place.

Mr. Luard: Is it the intention of Her Majesty's Government, if and when talks are reopened, to impose any conditions on the reopening of the talks?

Mr. Bowden: That is too hypothetical a point to decide at this stage. We must see the charts we expect from the Spanish Government and study them closely.

MR. WALL: Is the right hon. Gentleman aware that every time Anglo-Spanish talks have been initiated the Spanish Government have imposed new restrictions on Gibraltar which have been particularly designed to check the growing tourist trade to Gibraltar? Will he give an undertaking which can be heard by intending tourists that these restrictions will not be allowed to stop the tourist programme and people going to Gibraltar this year by air?

MR. BOWDEN: I certainly hope that people intending to take their holidays through Gibraltar into Spain this year will not defer their holidays, because flights by B.E.A. and B.U.A. will continue.

MR. ORME: Will my right hon. Friend inform the Spanish Government that Her Majesty's Government are prepared to take economic action against the Spanish Government, particularly in regard to tourism, which could greatly damage their economy? They ought to be warned of this.

MR. BOWDEN: No. I would prefer not to discuss retaliation at this stage. It is wrong to get into that sort of attitude. I have said that I hope the tourist trade will continue.

SIR A. V. HARVEY: Will the right hon. Gentleman give an assurance that if the Spanish Government come forward with a proposal to allow civil airliners but not military aircraft to operate he will have none of it? Will he give an assurance that Her Majesty's Government will not weaken on the assurance that he has given this afternoon?

MR. BOWDEN: It is our intention that both civil and military flights shall continue.

MR. E. L. MALLALIEU: In view of the fact that this latest action of the Spanish Government was probably a provocation which was intended to make the British Government withdraw from the talks, can my right hon. Friend be a little more forthcoming in giving the reasons why he thought it desirable to postpone them?

MR. BOWDEN: It is very difficult to continue these general talks, which have arisen from the United Nations resolution of 20th December and which could have included matters of this sort—the question of delimitation and drawing of areas of territorial waters round Gibraltar—when the Spanish Government have made an issue and a proclamation of this sort three or four days before they were to take place.

MR. HEATH: We welcome the Commonwealth Secretary's firm insistence that these flights, military and civil, shall continue. Can he volunteer a further statement to the House when he has had an opportunity of considering the charts and the legal implications?

MR. BOWDEN: Yes, Sir. I said that in my original reply.

*Speech by the Defence Secretary, Dennis Healey, in the House of
Commons Announcing the Proposed Withdrawal from Bases in Singapore
and Malaysia by the Mid-1970's, 27 July 1967**

I beg to move, That this House approves the Supplementary Statement on Defence Policy 1967, Command Paper No. 3357.

The Supplementary Statement on Defence Policy marks the end of a process which has taken three years continuous hard work. It does not mark the end of the Government's review of defence. On the contrary, the machinery which we have set up and developed over the last three years will enable the present Government and future Governments to keep every aspect of our defence policy permanently under review in order to ensure that the commitments which we undertake are still relevant to our political needs; that we have the weapons and forces needed to carry out these commitments; and that we are getting the best possible value for every £1 we spend for military purposes.

The process whose completion is marked by the present White Paper is a unique exercise, which, I hope, will not be repeated for many years. It is the first serious attempt by any British Government to bring our defence, foreign and economic policies into balance with one another not only in the current year or the years immediately ahead, but, so far as can be foreseen, over the next decade.

The programme which we inherited from the previous Administration involved spending 7 per cent. of our national product on defence for the following 10 years. It took no account of the impact of this rate of spending on our economy over a period when none of our European allies envisaged expenditure on anything like this scale. It was not related to any view of the way in which our foreign policy and the military commitments springing from it would develop over the years in question. Evidently, the previous Government did not believe these aspects of defence policy even worth considering.

The major exercise undertaken by the present Government has fallen into two phases. The first phase looked only to the end of this decade. We were concerned to lop £400 million off the Conservative Government's defence plans for the financial year 1969–70. The consequences of our work during this phase of the review were set out in the 1966 White Paper. We then showed how we planned to save over £300 million by getting better value for money, with no reduction in our ability to fulfil our commitments.

The savings here were real ones and were painful. They meant cancelling projects on which metal was being cut and men employed. They meant redun-

*Hansard, 5.s., DCCLI, 985–1013.

dancies, for example, in the Territorial Army. The House will recall that thousands of aircraft workers marched in the streets to protest on one issue; a Minister and a Chief of Staff resigned on another; and on one occasion the Government came within a hair's breadth of losing their majority in Parliament.

They were real cuts and painful ones, but, as a result, the nation has had £750 million more to spend on other purposes over the last three years than it would have had under the plans which the Conservatives had announced in office and continued to support in opposition.

Nevertheless, it was not possible, in February last year, to decide finally on how the remaining gap would be closed and the full £400 million saved on the 1969–70 defence budget. I told the House on 8th March, 1966:

> . . . we plan, when confrontation is brought to an end . . . that it must be a major objective to reduce the level of our forces in the Far East to that once planned by the previous Government before confrontation began; when we are able to reduce our deployment in the Far East to that level—we shall make further reductions in equipment and manpower which will save the additional £100 million.—[OFFICIAL REPORT, 8th March, 1966; Vol. 725. c. 2045–6.]

The right hon. Member for Wolverhampton, South-West (Mr. Powell) poured scorn on this statement, saying that the ending of confrontation was mere speculation, and that we could not rely on it ending before 1969. Of course, he was wrong, as in most of his predictions in the House in the last three years, as he was wrong in predicting, in the same speech, that the carrier force would collapse through a fall-off in recruiting to the Fleet Air Arm. As I hope he now knows, recruiting to the Fleet Air Arm is almost embarrassingly high; and confrontation came to an end only three months after he was suggesting that we could not count on it ending in the following three years.

The ending of confrontation last summer, and the progress which we have made towards revising N.A.T.O. strategy in the last 12 months, have made it possible for us to complete the first phase of the defence review by achieving our full target of £400 million saving in 1969–70. They have also made it possible for us to carry out the second phase of our defence review by looking well into the 1970s, so as to make even greater savings on the basis of commitments which will be reduced following major modifications in our foreign policy. As a result, we have been able to define the role of the Armed Services in the 1970s in a way which will ensure that, although reduced in size, they are able to carry out all their essential tasks in protecting the security of the nation and supporting our foreign policy.

I was glad to see from the foreign affairs debate last week that the Opposition Front Bench supports the Government in giving first priority to our defence policy in Europe. Here, the review of N.A.T.O. strategy is now well under way and the Alliance as a whole has gone far towards accepting the major principles which the present Government have been preaching for the last three years. We have often debated those principles and I will not repeat them now.

The most important outcome of the discussions in N.A.T.O. so far is a general agreement that the level of forces now maintained by N.A.T.O. is sufficient to make war in Europe highly improbable, and that it is neither necessary nor possible to plan on any substantial increase in those forces—though there is still work to be done in improving their efficiency and strengthening co-operation between their national components.

On the other hand, it is not possible to envisage a substantial reduction in N.A.T.O.'s present forces without either a major change in N.A.T.O.'s strategy or some progress towards agreement for reciprocal reductions on both sides of the Iron Curtain. This remains a major objective of our policy, but we cannot base our actions now on the assumption that it will be achieved by any given date. So we must assume that our contribution to N.A.T.O. will remain broadly of its present size.

At the same time, the N.A.T.O. countries now agree that the stability of the military situation in Europe is now such that any major change in Soviet policy is likely to be preceded by weeks or months of political warning. For this reason, it may be possible for N.A.T.O. countries which lose excessive foreign exchange through stationing their troops in Germany to hold some of them at home in normal circumstances, provided that they remain under N.A.T.O.'s command and are capable of returning rapidly in a crisis.

We are, therefore, proposing to withdraw one of the six brigades in B.A.O.R. to Britain in the New Year so as to save the foreign exchange costs involved in keeping it in Germany. As a result, and thanks to our success in negotiating the payment of £69 million in offset, seven-eighths of our stationing costs in Germany will be covered in the current year.

The House will remember that a few months ago the right hon. Member for Wolverhampton, South-West was lecturing us to the effect that we should be very lucky to obtain at the utmost one-half of our present stationing costs in offset. I do not blame him for his pessimism. His own Government got well under one-third in their last year of office—only £24 million. We have got seven-eighths—£69 million.

Mr. J. Enoch Powell (Wolverhampton, South-West): Will the right hon. Gentleman do me the kindness to refer to the occasion when I said that?

Mr. Healey: Yes. The occasion on which the right hon. Gentleman said that was during the debate on the White Paper in March this year. I will give him the precise column reference later in the debate, before I sit down.

We shall aim to do at least as well in future years as we have this year and thus to avoid the need for further redeployment. But, as the White Paper makes clear, there is little budgetary saving to be achieved from this type of redeployment. As I told the House over a year ago, the major budgetary savings must follow a reduction in our forces in the Far East. And this we were not able to begin negotiating until the end of confrontation last summer.

Our first step was to get our forces out of Borneo. By Easter this year we had reduced our overall manpower in the Far East by nearly 10,000. By next April we shall have reduced by 20,000, and in terms of British uniformed personnel and Gurkhas will be back to the pre-confrontation level. Considering the immense problems involved in moving and housing about 18,000 men and their families, this is not bad going for 18 months.

But, as the dust settled in South-East Asia following the end of confrontation, we found it possible and necessary to look further ahead. We have now agreed, after consultation with our allies in the area, that by some time in 1970–71 we should reduce those working in and for the Services in Malaysia and Singapore by a further 30,000—a total cut of 50 per cent. compared with the current level. The bulk of this reduction will fall on the Army.

We accept the view expressed a year ago by the right hon. Member for Kinross and West Perthshire (Sir Alec Douglas-Home) that

> our military contribution in this theatre of operations should be a balanced naval task force and air power, with the bias . . . tipped towards the sea and the naval task force—[OFFICIAL REPORT, 26th April, 1966; Vol. 727, c. 550.]

Of course, as the right hon. Gentleman must have been well aware, when he said those words, this will create some problems for Australia and New Zealand in relation to the Commonwealth Brigade, and these are problems on which consultations are now proceeding. But our view is fully shared by the Governments of Malaysia and Singapore themselves, and, after all, it is the Malaysian Defence Agreement which is the main reason for our presence.

Both Malaysia and Singapore are building up their own land forces. The Malaysian Army has already taken over the old British positions in Borneo with admirable smoothness and efficiency. The only threat which our Commonwealth partners do not feel confident of dealing with themselves by 1970 is the potential threat by air and sea. This we shall be fully capable of meeting with the forces that remain, and the House will probably have seen that the Deputy Prime Minister of Malaysia has publicly stated his satisfaction that this is so.

At the same time, we shall have progressively to alter our force declarations to S.E.A.T.O. contingency plans and in some cases increase the notice at which forces could be provided. I am glad to see that the right hon. Member for Kinross and West Perthshire agrees with us also on this. He pointed out on 4th March, 1965, that in S.E.A.T.O.

> each member has complete judgment about his own contribution . . . we should keep the necessary flexibility so that we can decide whether our contribution should be by sea or air or a combination of both.—[OFFICIAL REPORT, 4th March, 1965; Vol. 707, c. 1545.]

I only wish that the *Daily Telegraph* had taken note of that before it wrote its leading article this morning.

When we looked beyond 1970, it emerged that, once our presence in the Far East is reduced by one-half, once our commitments, particularly in S.E.A.T.O. are reduced, the sort of base facilities we maintain at present on the Asian mainland become very bad value for money indeed.

On the one hand, vast stockpiles of equipment require men to guard and maintain them and men to guard the men who guard them—plus houses, hospitals, schools, and so on, for their families—what the economists call a multiplier effect. In the second place, the equipment in the stockpiles needs duplicating at home so that the units which might use it can train efficiently, and the men who guard and maintain the base must also be duplicated at home so that they can be relieved after their tour of duty abroad.

A large fixed base just does not make sense, unless a large-scale war is in prospect in the area, particularly when the capability of air transport is growing and more and more equipment can be carried by air.

These were the practical factors of which we had to take account. There were no less important political factors, too. The United States has publicly announced that, once the Vietnam war is over, it wants no bases in Asia and is prepared to leave Vietnam. As we said in this year's Defence White Paper, we, too, must aim at a situation in which the local peoples can live at peace without the presence of external forces.

On a careful calculation of the likely trend of events, and after the most thorough consultation with our allies, we came to the conclusion that we should plan on winding up our bases in Malaysia and Singapore altogether in the middle 1970s. But we do plan to maintain thereafter a capability for military action in the area, and this has been welcomed by Australia and New Zealand, which have come to our aid in two world wars.

It is a capability which may be required not only by our political obligations, but also for peace-keeping under United Nations auspices.

MR. VICTOR GOODHEW (St. Albans): Will the Secretary of State give way?

MR. HEALEY: Yes.

MR. E. SHINWELL (Easington): Will my right hon. Friend give us some indication of the nature of the capability—

MR. GOODHEW: Mr. Speaker—

MR. SPEAKER: Order. I am bipartisan. We cannot have two interventions at once. Which one is it to be?

MR. SHINWELL: May I follow up the point, because it seems to be a very important one, of the capability to which my right hon. Friend refers and which is to be capable after we come out of Singapore and Malaysia? Can my right hon. Friend tell us what is its nature?

MR. HEALEY: Yes. It will consist mainly of on the spot amphibious forces, to which I shall refer later in my speech, but it will also be capable of being reinforced from the reserve forces in the United Kingdom, to which I shall also refer later in my speech. I now give way to the hon. Member of St. Albans (Mr. Goodhew).

MR. GOODHEW: I am grateful to the right hon. Gentleman. How does he reconcile what he has just said with the statement written into the United States

Congressional Record of 8th April, 1963, Col. 5513, by the Prime Minister when, at the National Press Club Luncheon in New York, he said:

> I believe it to be a mistake to evacuate key bases where we have the chance to remain. It is a hundred times easier for Britain to remain there even with a token force, than for us, still less the United States, to seek to enter if trouble breaks out.

How can the Secretary of State reconcile that statement with what he has just said?

MR. HEALEY: When the Prime Minister said that he did not mean that we should stay in a base that we do not need. We do not believe in staying in Aden, or in Singapore, or Malaysia once we have reduced our commitments and presence to the level we shall reduce them to by 1970, for the same reasons. I would have thought that that was obvious.

I think that the House will agree that this decision to wind up our bases in Singapore and Malaysia is without doubt the most important single decision in the White Paper, and it is a historic one. It was not possible to reach it earlier in view of the fact that confrontation ended less than 12 months ago, and we have needed to carry out the most prolonged and detailed consultations about our policy with our allies and partners in the Commonwealth.

As a result of this consultation, the Governments of Malaysia and Singapore—who are most directly concerned here—have accepted our decision and fully appreciate the reasons for it. I will not deny it faces them and us with some real problems of adjustment, but their reaction, to quote the *Straits Times,* on the spot, has been "realistic, sober and confident".

I believe that the overwhelming majority of opinion in Britain believes that it is the right decision, too. Even the Conservative Opposition have not chosen to contest it in principle. How could they, since their spokesman in another place set it as the right objective for Britain in his speech on the Defence White Paper last May?

I hope that the right hon. Member for Wolverhampton, South-West, who usually prefers to skulk behind his own verbal ambiguities and pedantic logic—chopping about the words that we use to describe our policies—will come out honestly and clearly this afternoon and tell us whether the Conservative Opposition think our decisions right or not.

If his only criticism, as he said on television last week, is that having taken our decision we should have tried to keep it dark from the House, from our allies, and from the rest of the world, my right hon. Friend will deal with that criticism when he winds up the debate.

MR. POWELL: Is the right hon. Gentleman purporting to quote what I said, or is he, as usual, making up words and attributing them to me? If not, will he quote the context?

MR. HEALEY: I regret that, again, I cannot at this moment quote the context, but I shall do so before I sit down.

As far as I can quote it from memory, when he was asked by Mr. George Ffitch whether he agreed that we should withdraw he replied, as he usually does, "That is not the real question. The question is whether we should have announced our intentions so long in advance", but I will do the right hon. Gentleman the courtesy of quoting his exact words before I sit down. I hope that the right hon. Gentleman will continue interrupting me in that way, because I have here other quotations which I am going to use. They are from versions produced by the Conservative Central Office.

I am certain that on Singapore and Malaysia the Government are right in announcing their intentions in the terms they have. I am equally certain that we are right not to attempt to fix, still less to announce, a date for a withdrawal from our positions in the Persian Gulf. At the moment, we are making a vital contribution towards stability in the Gulf, a contribution welcomed by the local States who are not yet in agreement on how to handle the situation if and when we should withdraw.

Perhaps I might tell the House a story. I remember President Nasser remarking to me in a conversation when I was still in opposition that our presence in the Gulf is like that of the Arab caretaker in the Church of the Holy Sepulchre in Jerusalem. As the House may know, the three Christian denominations which share the church in Jerusalem have never been able to agree with one another on which of them should be physically responsible for the building's security.

About 1,000 years ago they appointed an Arab family as caretaker, and its descendants are still performing that function. My only comment to President Nasser, when he drew that analogy, was that we had no intention of staying so long in the Gulf. But it would be equally wrong at this time to fix or announce a date for leaving.

By eliminating the wasteful duplication of men and equipment required for large fixed base facilities, by changing the size and composition of our forces in the Far East and reducing our commitments in parallel, we have been able to plan a substantial reduction in the size of all three Services and in the number of civilians who support them.

By the middle 'seventies, when our withdrawal from Singapore and Malaysia is complete, the Armed Forces will contain about 75,000 fewer men and women than today, and there will be 80,000 fewer civilians serving the forces. We shall achieve roughly half of this reduction by April, 1971.

The Opposition Amendment claims that these cuts will make it impossible for the Services to do their job. I suppose they are judging from their own experience, because the only time they made a big cut in the forces was when the hon. Member for Streatham (Mr. Sandys) hacked blindly at our military capability without any attempt to think the problem through—relying on Blue Streak instead of aircraft, for example. In his 1957 White Paper he envisaged Armed Services of 375,000 men—a cut of 47 per cent. on the level obtaining at the time.

But at that time our commitments were far bigger than they are today. We had the Baghdad Pact, the defence of Aden, and garrisons for British Colonies and Protectorates all over the word. The Conservative Government were still fighting to prevent Cyprus from gaining its independence, and they also had a major emergency to cope with in Malaya.

Then, when the right hon. Gentleman passed to the Commonwealth Office, he dumped a great load of new commitments on the forces he had cut—the South Arabian Federation and confrontation in the Far East—so that in 1964 our forces were over-stretched almost to breaking point.

The present Government have brought confrontation to a successful end; our last defence commitments in South Arabia will soon be over; and nearly all the colonial commitments we had when the Conservatives planned their massive cut in our forces are now ended. As I said, we are going to make substantial reductions in the force declarations to S.E.A.T.O. which were made by the Conservative Government, and our commitment to Malaysia will be carried out mainly with air and naval forces, as the Opposition recommended.

Yet we shall still have 350,000 British based adult males in the Services in April, 1971, only a fraction fewer than the previous Government planned against a background of far greater and still increasing commitments. The fact is that the policy I have outlined, and the reductions in our military commitments which have taken place or have been decided on, will relax the over-stretch from which our forces have suffered for so many years, and leave a larger reserve in Britain for dealing with the unforeseen contingencies.

The forces will be infinitely better able to carry out their tasks than when the Conservatives left power.

Sir Alec Douglas-Home (Kinross and West Perthshire): The right hon. Gentleman said that these defence reductions were the result of major alterations in foreign policy. I have not heard him name any major alterations in foreign policy. Indeed, the S.E.A.T.O. commitment is there, although he may not be able to fulfil it.

Mr. Healey: I hope that the right hon. Gentleman will reflect on what he said in 1965, and then withdraw that last remark. He made the point that we had the perfect right, and must exercise it, to reduce our force declarations to S.E.A.T.O., or change them whenever we wished to do so. Such a reduction or change constitutes a major change in foreign policy. The decision to leave Singapore and Malaysia has many important impacts on our foreign policy in that area, as I am sure the right hon. Gentleman would agree.

Sir Alec Douglas-Home: The right hon. Gentleman said that these reductions resulted from major changes in foreign policy. What he is now saying is that he has made reductions in the forces, and, therefore, the foreign policy has to be changed.

MR. HEALEY: With respect to the right hon. Gentleman, we have not made these reductions. They will be made over the next five to 10 years. The change in foreign policy has been made already, but the change in our commitments will be made progressively as our forces are reduced.

I will now explain how our plans will affect the individual Services. The Royal Navy will provide, through its Polaris submarines, Britain's contribution to N.A.T.O.'s strategic deterrent and will make a bigger contribution than any other European navy to N.A.T.O.'s shield forces in the Atlantic. Outside Europe, the Navy, in the 1970s, will have the main responsibility for maintaining Britain's military influence and her contribution towards keeping the peace.

MR. EMRYS HUGHES (South Ayrshire): Will the right hon. Gentleman confirm that we shall spend £370 million for four Polaris submarines, which is a much bigger sum than the Tory Government spent? How does he explain this?

MR. HEALEY: That figure is completely false. We have already spent the bulk of the capital expenditure involved in creating the Polaris force. The capital expenditure is substantially reduced, partly because we are cutting the force by one boat and partly for other reasons with which I will not bother the House, connected with the cost of the missiles in the United States. The cost of the four boats, which will be completed in about a year's time, will be under 1 per cent. of the defence budget and 0.001 per cent.—I may have this wrong—of the gross national product.

MR. EMRYS HUGHES: Those figures are wrong.

MR. HEALEY: My hon. Friend is mixing up the total cost of the programme since it began with the amount that still remains to be spent. The programme has been running now since 1963—for four years—and the bulk of the capital expenditure has already been committed.

We will keep our powerful amphibious forces, with the Royal Marine Commandos, in the Far East and they will be supported by destroyers, frigates and submarines. Our two largest aircraft carriers, "Eagle" and "Ark Royal", modernised and equipped with Phantom aircraft, will continue in service until the middle 'seventies. Such naval forces have special advantages in peace-keeping overseas through their flexibility. They can remain poised for long periods visible or invisible at will, and are a powerful deterrent to aggression.

As the carriers phase out in the middle 1970s three new classes of ship will be introduced—the new cruisers, Sea Dart destroyers and frigates, all equipped with missiles and helicopters. The functions now carried out by our aircraft carriers in protecting the Fleet at short range will continue to be mainly carried out by the Fleet itself; its helicopters will give it its own means of reconnaissance and attack against a surface as well as a submarine threat.

The longer range functions of the carrier will be carried out partly by the Fleet submarines and partly by aircraft of the Royal Air Force controlled by the new cruisers. If the right hon. Gentleman the Member for Wolverhampton, South-West is not satisfied with this, perhaps he will come clean and tell us whether the Conservative Opposition are now firmly committed to keep the carrier force going after the middle 1970s at a cost of up to £200 million a year and operating solely east of Suez.

I hope that the right hon. Gentleman, who has shilly-shallied and dodged this question repeatedly for the last two years, will tell us what he intends. If not, perhaps the right hon. Member for Barnet (Mr. Maudling) will do so. Otherwise, let the right hon. Member for Wolverhampton, South-West "belt up" on this issue.

SIR HARRY LEGGE-BOURKE (Isle of Ely): Will the right hon. Gentleman tell us where the aircraft which are supposed to be replacing the aircraft which hitherto would be flying off the decks of aircraft carriers will be based?

MR. HEALEY: Yes. Up to 1975 the aircraft will be based at Bahrein, Masirah, Gan, the Cocos Islands—and Australia if she is involved—and Singapore. After 1975 they will no longer be based on Singapore, but, as the White Paper makes clear, we are discussing the possibility of using facilities provided by the Australians in Northern Australia, and there is no reason why, should a particular emergency arise, we should not operate from bases in any allied country to whose help we come. We made it clear in the Defence Review two years ago that we depended on the readiness of our allies to provide the bases that we needed in such cases.

In the 1970s the main rôle of the Army will be in Europe, but with the withdrawal from Aden an additional brigade will be added to the Strategic Reserve for operations anywhere in the world. This force will be airportable with specialised training for a wide variety of rôles. Training overseas will be even more important than it is today, since more of the Army will be permanently stationed in Britain.

With the cuts in its commitments outside Europe, the Army will be reduced by 15,000 all ranks by April, 1971. As we say in the White Paper, this involves the disappearance of 17 major units. Many of these are regiments with long and distinguished histories. The necessity for their disappearance is particularly painful, but I am glad to say that we shall be able, like the Conservative Government in similar circumstances, to preserve time-honoured traditions and probably some famous regimental names through the merging of regimental identities in many cases.

The reorganisation of the infantry, about which I informed the House in May, will preserve the best features of the regimental tradition while ensuring that the Army is able to make the best and most economical use of its limited and expensive manpower.

MR. OSCAR MURTON (Poole): How can the right hon. Gentleman preserve the best regimental traditions if some regiments disappear completely and are not amalgamated?

MR. HEALEY: In those cases it will not be possible to preserve regimental traditions. The Conservative Government faced this problem sensibly after the cut which the right hon. Member for Streatham (Mr. Sandys) imposed, and there are now a large number of battalions in the British Army formed by merging famous regiments which continue to maintain the traditions of their regiments. I am glad to say that my contacts with such battalions during the last three years all over the world suggest that the mergers have been a complete success.

Some Members, I know, are concerned how the Gurkha Brigade will be affected by these new plans. *The Times* published a wise leader on this subject the other day, and I fully agree with what it said. Some further reductions in the Gurkha Brigade may be necessary when those already announced have been completed in 1969, but we must see how we go on this issue.

It would be a great mistake to take a final decision now, before we are clearer about the way in which our plans develop in detail. And of course, we should have to consult the Government of Nepal before deciding on any further reduction.

So far as the Royal Air Force is concerned, our new plans will be reflected in reductions in size rather than changes in shape. The Royal Air Force will continue to play its essential role in guarding the nation's security by long-range tactical strike and reconnaissance, and by the provision of air support and air defence for the Army and Navy at home and overseas. With a higher proportion of our forces in the United Kingdom, the Royal Air Force will provide the necessary strategic mobility, and flexibility with its transport aircraft always at a high level of operational readiness.

The Service is now engaged in a large-scale process of re-equipment with modern high-performance aircraft arising mainly from decisions taken by the Government two years ago. Twenty of the new Hercules transport aircraft are already in this country and the Phantoms are coming in next year.

The year 1969 will be a most important one. The Royal Air Force will then begin to receive P1127s and the F111. The maritime Comet—now known as Nimrod—and the Chinook heavy-lift helicopter are already coming into service. The only major unresolved equipment problem lies far ahead—it is that part of the tactical strike reconnaissance role which the V-bombers will cease to carry out after the middle 'seventies.

The main impact of our new plans here is that we can afford to give a higher priority to the requirements of the European theatre. This should make it easier to reach agreement with customers or collaborators among our other N.A.T.O. allies now that France has withdrawn from the A.F.V.G. project.

All three Services in the 1970s will require a degree of professional skill unsurpassed in any other profession, as well as the courage, enterprise and endurance which have been the hallmark of the fighting man throughout the ages. I would like to take this opportunity of paying a tribute to the fine way in which the Services have displayed these qualities under the pressures of recent years.

As the hon. and gallant Member for Winchester (Rear-Admiral Morgan Giles) wrote in a letter in today's *Daily Telegraph*—and I thank him for writing the letter: "The services will remain a stable and exciting career for any young man with these qualities in future."

REAR-ADMIRAL MORGAN GILES (Winchester): I thank the right hon. Gentleman, but it was *The Times*.

MR. HEALEY: If I may say so, even better.

MR. STANLEY R. McMASTER (Belfast, East): What proportion of our defence will depend on various types of nuclear weapons by the mid-'seventies?

MR. HEALEY: I do not quite know what the hon. Gentleman means by that question in that form, but the proportion of our defence expenditure which will go on nuclear weapons at that time will be below 1 per cent.

MR. McMASTER: I was not referring so much to expenditure as to the extent to which we will depend on nuclear weapons.

MR. HEALEY: That is a totally different question which it is difficult to answer in a moment. In Europe, which is the only theatre in which we have any expectation of using nuclear weapons, provided that our allies do as we do, our dependence on nuclear weapons will be very much as it is today; no greater and no less.

Perhaps I can take advantage of this natural break, so to speak, to remind the right hon. Member for Wolverhampton, South-West of the words he asked me to quote. [HON. MEMBERS: "Come on."] I assure the House that I have this information, but I will answer the other question first. In doing so, I apologise to the House for having to refer to the right hon. Gentleman by name. I must do so if I am to quote him accurately.

George Ffitch asked:

> Mr. Powell. Do you agree with the main theme of the White Paper that Britain should pull out of the Far East by the mid 1970s?

Then:

> Mr. Enoch Powell. I don't think it's so much a question of whether by the mid 1970s we have ceased to be present in force ashore on the mainland of Asia; I think it's a question of what you say about it now . . .

I will refresh the right hon. Gentleman's defective memory in respect of the other speech to which I referred. In the debate on 27th February last the right hon. Gentleman estimated that the total that we would get from Germany this year would be £12½ million, plus £31½ million. He said: "These two sums together, taking them at their utmost"—whatever he meant by that—"add up to £44 million—approximately half of the year's cost of the present strength of our forces in Germany." That was exactly what I had said the right hon. Gentleman said.

MR. POWELL *rose*—

MR. HEALEY: Delighted to give way.

MR. POWELL: The right hon. Gentleman alleged—and I am within the recollection of the House—that I said that we would be lucky if half the costs were recovered. The paragraph which he just quoted begins with the words: "So far as is known what has been achieved is as follows". I ended that paragraph by saying:

> If that is still the situation at the end of June, does that mean that half our forces will then be withdrawn from B.A.O.R.?—[OFFICIAL REPORT, 27th February, 1967; Vol. 742. c. 125.]

In other words, the right hon. Gentleman has, as usual, utterly falsified what I said.

MR. HEALEY: That is precisely the type of pedantic nit-picking about words for which the right hon. Gentleman has become famous throughout the world, during the last three years in defence debates. I have plenty more quotations with me and I will certainly quote the right hon. Gentleman.

As the White Paper makes clear, the great majority of the 75,000 reduction in our Services by the middle 'seventies will be achieved through normal wastage as men complete their engagements. Redundancies as such will average 2,500 to 3,000 a year, though they will not be evenly spread from year to year.

We aim to organise the rundown in such a way as to maintain or restore, where necessary, the career prospects for those who stay in the forces and to ensure that the forces have a proper balance of ranks, seniorities, ages and specialists. Applications will be invited from the appropriate categories to leave the Service early when redundancy is expected. There will have to be some compulsory redundancies and we aim to give at least six months' notice to all those affected. Compensation terms for those made redundant have already been circulated in detail within the Services.

I will give two examples. An R.A.F. squadron leader retired at the age of 40 with 19½ years' reckonable service will receive a lump sum of £3,417 in addition to his retired pay and terminal grant. An army warrant officer Class I (Technician) with 17 years' reckonable service will receive a lump sum of £11,364 in addition to his pension and terminal grant; he will also receive a credit of service for pension purposes which will give him additional pension and terminal grant to a capitalised value nearly equal to his lump sum. I think that the House will agree that this is fair and reasonable compensation.

We are also increasing resettlement facilities to meet the increased requirement and shall make greater use of the arrangements which already exist for attachment to civilian firms and organisations for resettlement training.

The immediate impact of redundancy will be small. During the next 12 months, the Army will lose about 350 officers and 600 soldiers, the R.A.F. about 500 officers—mainly in the general duties flying branch, and about 500 airmen air-crew. Because it has been short of manpower for some time, the Royal Navy is unlikely to have any redundancies until about 1970, and then not in all branches.

There is one point I should stress here. Surprising as it may appear at first sight, the requirement for new recruits will be only marginally affected by the rundown. About 40,000 Servicemen leave the Services every year in normal circumstances and have to be replaced. Thus, the annual redundancies we foresee will have only a marginal impact on the need for new recruits. In the case of a Service now short of men, like the Royal Navy, we shall continue to need the same number of recruits as we are getting today.

Moreover, recruiting staffs are having to operate in a hardening market. As the post-war bulge dies away the pool of young men in the relevant age groups is becoming smaller. Boys are tending to stay longer at school and, particularly in the technical arms, competition with industry grows fiercer year by year and the standard required by the Services rises year by year. Indeed, work we have been doing over the last 12 months suggests that manpower difficulties might well have compelled us to reduce Service ceilings even if there had not been sound political and economic reasons for doing so.

The reductions in Service manpower will be matched by corresponding reductions among civilians working for the Services. Of the 80,000 reductions we expect by the mid 'seventies, about 30,000 will be United Kingdom employees and 50,000 local entrants employed by the Ministry of Defence overseas. We shall, of course, have full consultations with the staff associations and trade unions as the rundown develops.

Mr. J. D. CONCANNON (Mansfield): I have already received two letters from constituents on this vital point. For members of the Army who are now ready for release or whose time has nearly expired, if they wish—or, perhaps, have already applied—to sign on for another stretch, perhaps of seven years, what is their position?

Mr. HEALEY: Those who wish to stay on will be given advice about whether they are running any risk of redundancy. This will be dealt with on an individual basis in the unit concerned. If my hon. Friend has any specific cases, I hope that he will write to me, whereupon I will do my best to advise him.

I turn to the economic consequences of this major reshaping of our military commitments and capabilities. We expect to remain at all times below the original Defence Review ceiling of £2,000 million a year, at 1964 prices. This means a reduction of more than £400 million in the Conservative programme for 1969–70.

In 1970–71 we expect our defence budget to be £1,900 million at constant prices, despite the high incidence of expenditure on new equipment in that year. In the middle 1970s, when withdrawal from Singapore and Malaysia is complete, we expect to be down to £1,800 million a year, although the equipment of our forces will then be far more efficient, sophisticated and expensive than it is today.

Mr. CHRISTOPHER MAYHEW (Woolwich, West): Will my right hon. Friend give way? This is quite a straightforward question. Does the 1975 budget of £1,800 million include provision for the continuance of our presence in the Persian

Gulf and for the continuance of our obligations under the Anglo-Malaysia Treaty?

MR. HEALEY: Yes. In both cases it includes it. I shall have a word to say in a moment about the foreign exchange effect of that. I wonder what guilt or embarrassment led my right hon. Friend to preface his remarks with that exordium.

Assuming a 3 per cent. annual rate of economic growth, this should represent under 5 per cent. of our G.N.P. compared with the 7 per cent. the Conservatives envisaged—putting us well in line with our major European allies. This is a massive contribution to strengthening our national economy and making valuable resources available for other purposes.

The achievement in reducing the strain of defence on our balance of payments will be even more dramatic. Our stationing costs in areas other than Germany will be reduced from £173 million this year to £120 million in 1970–71, and to £60 million or less by the mid-1970s—a total reduction of about two-thirds on the level today.

Under the Conservative Administration the impact of defence on our balance of payments was completely ignored. Hon. Members will search in vain in the Defence White Papers published during the lifetime of the previous Government for any statistics of overseas stationing costs. Yet, in fact, between 1957 and 1964 military expenditure overseas more than doubled. It increased from about £120 million to about £250 million.

But there is no sign that the long succession of right hon. Gentlemen opposite who were responsible for defence policy at that time ever noticed that increase. Perhaps the right hon. Member for Barnet (Mr. Maudling), will tell us whether he noticed it when, as Chancellor of the Exchequer, he gave us an £800 million deficit on the balance of payments, and if so, what he did about it. It would be interesting to have an answer to that question tonight.

We on this side of the House have done far better than even we originally planned. Our original target in the Defence Review was to cut our stationing costs by a quarter by the end of the decade. In fact, we have achieved more than that already. In round figures the stationing cost in 1964 was running at £275 million a year. From this had to be deducted the proceeds of the German offset agreement—only £24 million in 1964–65—giving a net cost of £250 million. In the current year our total stationing costs outside Germany are estimated at £173 million.

To this we have to add the £11 million net costs of our forces in Germany after the offset agreement of £69 million negotiated by my right hon. Friend the Minister of State at the Foreign Office. Thus, our total stationing costs on defence this year are only £184 million compared with about £250 million in the last year of the previous Government—a reduction of more than one quarter. And we shall have reduced this net total by two-thirds in the middle 1970s. Our foreign stationing costs will then be only a quarter of what they were when we assumed office.

Mr. WOODROW WYATT (Bosworth) *rose*—

Mr. HEALEY: With respect to my hon. Friend, I must get on.

We are asking the House to approve this White Paper because for the first time since the Second World War it brings Britain's foreign policy and defence policy into balance with one another, and with the nation's economic and social objectives at home. It builds a stable, long-term relationship between cost, commitments, and capabilities of defence. There is no evidence that the party opposite, whose Amendment we are also debating, ever attempted this when it was in office. It certainly never succeeded.

In opposition, the Conservatives have not even tried. They have shown a blind indifference to the economic cost of defence and are totally divided on the commitments which our defence forces should be capable of meeting. That is why, over the last three years, they have confined themselves to a dreary and pedantic nagging, and have steadfastly refused every invitation to tell us what they would do in our place.

Mr. McMASTER: Resign.

Mr. HEALEY: Even in Europe, although most of the Front Bench opposite seems to be in full agreement with the Government, the right hon. Member for Wolverhampton, South-West is still ploughing his lonely furrow. He is the only leading politician in the Western world who believes that we should be preparing ourselves to fight and win a large-scale conventional war in Europe. And he keeps insisting that Britain's defence policy must recognise the fact that Britain is insular as well as European.

On Saturday, 8th July, the right hon. Member told the faithful on Ripon race-course—a well chosen location—that "we must have the maritime capability appropriate to a nation which is not only European, but insular." He added: "and oceanic", for he likes to cover all his bets. He seems to be sliding back to the extra-ordinary view he held some time ago, when he said:

> The two great objects of British foreign policy ought to be to facilitate the defence by air/sea power alone of the British territories and to secure a stable balance of power in Europe without Britain.

If the right hon. Gentleman is not going back to that view which he once held, will he tell us precisely what he means by using the word "insular" in respect of our defence policy as he has been doing regularly in recent times?

Mr. POWELL *rose*—

Mr. HEALEY: The right hon. Gentleman will have his chance to speak in a moment.

Mr. POWELL: Will the right hon. Gentleman give the date of the article which he just quoted?

Mr. HEALEY: The article, which also said that we should support France in Vietnam so that France could reduce our burden in Europe, was in 1954. But if the right hon. Gentleman does not now mean by "insular" what he meant then, will he tell us, when he speaks, precisely what he means?

In the Middle East the split in the Conservative Party is a yawning chasm. Only the other day the right hon. Member for Wolverhampton, South-West seemed to be arguing that we should clear out altogether. He poured scorn on what he termed the so-called British presence in the Mediterranean and the Persian Gulf. Perhaps he will tell us what he meant by "so-called". He suggested "It was just because we were physically present in the area that our oil and our reserves were in danger when other peoples were not". This brought out the right hon. Member for Kinross and West Perthshire with a well-merited public rebuke. He told the House only last week:

> Because the Arabs momentarily cut off oil supplies, I cannot follow the argument that there are no political or economic advantages which a British presence can gain anywhere and that, therefore, we should go and go now.—[OFFICIAL REPORT, 20th July 1967; Vol. 750, c. 2487.]

Will the Opposition please tell us to-night—they have repeatedly failed to tell us over the last three years—do they think that we should keep the Aden base, as they promised to do in 1964? Would they stay in the Gulf and, if so, for how long? What is their policy?

On the Far East the split on the Conservative Front Bench is even starker. The high peak of contradiction in the Conservative Party was scaled in this year's defence debates, when the right hon. Member for Wolverhampton, South West sat white and rigid on the Front Bench opposite while at his side the hon. and gallant Member for Winchester argued that Britain should send ships and troops to fight in Vietnam. Is that Conservative Party policy or not? May we have an answer to that question later tonight?

Last week the right hon. Member for Kinross and West Perthshire reminded the House that he was constantly urging the Foreign Secretary to get S.E.A.T.O. reorganised, but what does the right hon. Member for Wolverhampton, South-West say about that? To urge

> that Britain in 1967 can take a leading role in reinvigorating the military alliance in South East Asia . . . seems to me not to be an act of imagination but . . . a symptom of hallucination. Rather like listening to Rip van Winkle talking. One might . . . not be startled to hear that sort of phraseology . . . from Indian Army colonels who retired years ago . . . the reality which is relevant . . . is that we have and can exert virtually no military power in South East Asia.

That is the Opposition spokesman on defence, the self-appointed champion of the Services, the forces' friend, speaking just after the successful end of confrontation. " . . . we have and can exert virtually no military power in South East Asia", he said. Is that the official view of the Opposition on the three years of fighting in Borneo? This was one of the most successful politico-military campaigns in our national history, and I am not surprised that the right hon. Member for Barnet launched a massive attack against his right hon. Friend in the *Sunday Times* the other day, on the theme, "We must not indulge in the fashionable sport of belittling our own role in the world." I agree with the right hon. Member for Barnet. It is about time that the official Opposition spokesman on defence stopped it or that the Opposition got another spokesman.

Holding the views he does, how can the right hon. Member for Barnet speak in support of the right hon. Member for Wolverhampton, South-West today? And how on earth can the right hon. Member for Wolverhampton, South-West continue to sit side by side with all these Rip van Winkles and retired Indian Army colonels on the Opposition Front Bench? I suppose the answer is that adversity makes strange bedfellows.

Other than adversity, there is only one factor which unites the right hon. Member for Wolverhampton, South-West with his colleagues on the Front Bench opposite. That is a terrifying, titanic and total indifference to the cost of defence. The hon. Member for St. Albans, in a recent debate, told us that it was the job of the Defence Secretary to give the Services anything they asked for and to resign if he failed to get it from the Cabinet. Perhaps that is why the party opposite had eight separate Ministers of Defence during the thirteen years they were in power.

Mr. Goodhew: If the right hon. Gentleman will refresh his memory by reading the report of that debate, he will see that I said that his duty was to provide the Services with the weapons they needed to carry out the task given to them, and not to give them all they wanted. He need not misquote me as well as my right hon. Friend the Member for Wolverhampton, South-West.

Hon. Members: Withdraw.

Mr. Healey: At a natural break in a moment, I will quote the hon. Member's words. He made it clear that I should always take the advice of the Services on the equipment they needed. The fact is that even a Conservative Government cannot ignore the cost of defence forever. What the Conservatives did with dogged regularity was to ignore the cost of defence during the planning and development stages of every project and then cancel the project when the expenditure became too high.

That is why in the aerospace field alone they cancelled 30 separate projects on which £200 million had already been spent and left the Royal Air Force worse equipped with supersonic aircraft than Egypt and Indonesia.

Sir Cyril Osborne (Louth): Get on with your own programme.

Mr. Healy: The changes we have made in the programme we inherited from the Conservative Government have already saved the British taxpayer over £750 million during the last three years alone. The further savings announced in this White Paper will raise the rate of saving on Tory plans to £500 million a year in 1971 and something like £800 million a year in the middle 1970s. It is no good the Conservatives arguing that they did not have these plans or that they would not have cost so much.

Sir C. Osborne: Get on with it.

MR. HEALEY: I know that the hon. Member for Louth (Sir C. Osborne) does not enjoy this, but many hon. Members are enjoying it.

The figures I have quoted come straight from the long-term costings I found in the Ministry of Defence when I took office in 1964, just after the right hon. Member for Barnet gave up such languid control of the nation's financial plans as he ever attempted. But, of course, his motto as Chancellor of the Exchequer, as he made clear again the other day, was, "Don't worry, it may never happen."

The right hon. Gentleman may say that the Conservatives would have cut these plans in any case. But they have divided the House against every single cut we have made and have never given a hint of whether they would have made other cuts instead. If they would have made other cuts, let them tell us now what cuts. We have been trying to find out for three years.

But right hon. Members opposite cannot answer, for the right hon. Member for Wolverhampton, South-West, speaking with all the responsibility which he rightly says should invest a Shadow Minister of Defence, has committed his party to a mountain of new expenditure on top even of the plans of the previous Administration. He wants " . . . 'an army in being' . . . equal in armament, training and philosophy to any other in Europe . . ." capable of fighting and winning a conventional war against the whole might of the Red Army. He wants us to be able to achieve command of the sea and command of the air on our own. Has he ever thought what this would cost? He always says that he has not the necessary facilities to do this sort of calculation.

MR. POWELL: The right hon. Gentleman has given us a bit of fiction about our fighting and winning a war against the whole might of the Red Army. I happen to have the passage he refers to with me, and I will supply the House, if I may, with what I actually said, and not what he imagines and attributes to me. I said:

> . . . 'an army in being' . . . equal in armament, training and philosophy to any other in Europe, and of such dimensions and structure, and supported by such reserves, as to be able, and to be seen to be able, to play an important and continuing part in Continental warfare; [OFFICIAL RE-PORT, 6th March, 1967; Vol. 742, c. 1201.]

That is what I said.

MR. HEALEY rose—

HON. MEMBERS: Withdraw.

MR. HEALEY rose—

MR. STEPHEN HASTINGS (Mid-Bedford-shire): On a point of order, Mr. Deputy Speaker. It is now clear, at least to this side of the House, that the Defence Secretary has grossly misquoted my right hon. Friend the Member for Wolverhampton, South-West (Mr. Powell) on three occasions. Would it not be consistent with the ordinary courtesy of the House for the right hon. Gentleman to withdraw?

MR. DEPUTY SPEAKER (MR. SYDNEY IRVING): Order. That is not a point of order. I think that the purpose of the House would be best served if this matter were dealt with in debate.

MR. HEALEY: On that point, I was not quoting the passage the right hon. Member for Wolverhampton, South-West (Mr. Powell) has just quoted. I referred to fighting and winning a conventional war in Europe because the right hon. Gentleman put that view in an earlier speech when he argued with great force that it was obscene and immoral for us to cut the Territorial Army because we must be capable of winning a war in Europe without resort to nuclear weapons. He has recently written a review of a book by General Beaufre in the *Sunday Times*—

HON. MEMBERS: Withdraw.

MR. DEPUTY SPEAKER: Order. This is a very important debate. The Defence Secretary is responsible for the statements he makes. I hope that hon. Members will remember that a large number of hon. Members wish to take part in the debate. I hope that we shall not lose any more time.

MR. HEALEY: I hope that the House will recall that I have given way on at least 17 occasions to interruptions. I hope they will now allow me to conclude without further interruption.

Does the right hon. Gentleman ever think of what all this programme of his would cost? He may say that he has not the facilities to do this sort of work. He often has said it. So I have asked my officials to take his speeches, assume that they are mine, and let me know what would be required on the most restrictive interpretation of his words. The answer, in very rough orders of magnitude, is as follows. The right hon. Gentleman's Army would cost £900 million more than our present Army; his Navy would cost £1,000 million more; his Air Force would cost about £800 million more if it were to provide a defence system against the Soviet manned bombers alone. That is a figure of £2,700 million over the next ten years. But it does not take into account two clear implications of the right hon. Gentleman's statement. If in fact, we were to prepare, as the right hon. Gentleman has repeatedly asked, to fight a long drawn out conventional war, the very much larger war reserves, training facilities and other infrastructure would cost at least another £2,000 million— nearly £5,000 million extra altogether.

The right hon. Gentleman does not seem prepared to accept the fact that the Soviet Union has missiles as well as aircraft. I regret to tell the House that my officials broke down and wept when they were asked to cost an effective anti-ballistic missile system for the United Kingdom. All I can say is that the United States, which has already developed most of the sort of hardware which would be required, has estimated the cost at nearly £15,000 million. The defence policy of the official Conservative spokesman would cost us at least another £2,000 million a year—over twice the cost of the policy of the present government.

The fascinating thing is that this is the defence policy of a party which pledged itself only on Monday to reduce Government expenditure and cut taxation. I hope that the right hon. Member for Barnet (Mr. Maudling), who knows something of economics, will tell us how these objectives are to be reconciled with the defence policy he supports. To use the words of the right hon. Member for Wolverhampton, South-West, either his defence policy or his leader's fiscal policy is a colossal structure of spoof. Perhaps one Leader of the Opposition will tell us which twin is the phoney? The answer, of course, is both. The policy of Conservative Opposition is phoney through and through. It is bogus to the bootstraps.

We are all waiting to hear from the high priest of humbug, the bishop of bogus, the Savanarola of spoof himself. In asking the House to support the Government's Motion, I ask it to reject his Amendment with a majority which is overwhelming, final and complete.

Statement by the Prime Minister, Harold Wilson, in the House of Commons Announcing an Accelerated Withdrawal of Troops from the Far East and the Persian Gulf, 16 January 1968*

With permission, Mr. Speaker, I should like to make a statement.

1. On the 18th December I informed the House that the Government were engaged in a major review of every field of public expenditure as one of the measures necessary to achieve a progressive and massive shift of resources from home consumption, public and private, to the requirements of exports, import replacement and productive investment.

2. This review has now been completed. Our purpose in this review is to make devaluation work, because until we do, until we are earning, year in and year out, a substantial surplus on our overseas payments, we are unable internally or externally to do all the things which, as a nation, we would like to do. But what this means for the immediate future is to ensure that we cut down our demands and our ambitions at home and abroad within the limits of what we can currently earn. At home, it means cutting back on excessive demands, both as individuals and as a community, and abroad it means reassessing our rôle in the world and realistically limiting our commitments and outgoings to our true capacities. On this basis, provided that our recovery is soundly based and lasting, we can go forward. The review we have undertaken, covering as it does our ambitions and expenditure at home, and our commitments and deployment abroad, is an essential step towards making these principles a reality.

3. Our immediate objective, first, is to release resources from home use in order to reinforce the balance of trade, and to do this in a way which realises

Hansard, 5.s., DCCLVI, 1577–84.

every practicable opportunity to reduce Government expenditure overseas. Second, it is to ensure that as the economy moves into expansion, led by the priority areas I have mentioned—exports, import replacement and investment—the total level of demand, public and private, is kept in line with what the productive machine can make available without lurching into inflation and excessive strain on our national resources. Third, and immediately at a time when unemployment, contrary to widespread expectation six months ago, is falling—seasonal factors apart—and demand for labour increasing, it is to ensure that the growing consumer expansion now underway gives way to an export-led expansion.

4. Our aim is not deflation, but expansion based on the growing use of our resources at an ordered pace so that the build-up of exports and the other priority categories does not lead to undue pressure on those resources. A higher proportion of our growing national production must be shifted decisively for the benefit of the balance of payments and investment, and a smaller proportion will be left, therefore, for rising consumer demand and Government expenditure.

5. From every point of view it would be wrong to seek to achieve the necessary reduction in demand solely by restraining the growth of personal consumption, though personal consumption must be sharply restrained. But public expenditure also must make its full contribution. Indeed, if the rate of increase of public expenditure were not severely restrained in the years immediately ahead, unacceptable burdens on the personal consumption of the ordinary family would be required.

6. My statement this afternoon, therefore, relates to public expenditure. The measures will be progressively reinforced as I indicated on 18th December, by all appropriate further measures, budgetary and non-budgetary, to hold back private consumption.

7. These measures which I am announcing today follow the steps announced at the time of devaluation, aimed at restraining both private and public consumption, and are additional to the cuts in defence expenditure, the £70 million cut in the investment programmes of the nationalised industries, the prospective changes in taxation, the hire purchase restrictions, Bank Rate and the tightening of bank lending.

8. These measures accord fully with the policies which we have pursued in the defence of the old parity—the restructuring of industry, the stimulation of investment, technological assistance to industry, an intensified attack on the problems of the development areas, and a policy of severe restraint in prices and incomes. Conceived as they were in the pre-devaluation period, these policies achieved a great deal of what they set out to do: they will be needed in full measure in the new situation we now face. For whatever has to be done by reductions in the growth of public expenditure and in restraining private expenditure, so that we do not spend before we earn, the solution of our problems will basically come from changes in industry and industrial attitudes which are concentrated on increasing what, as a nation we earn, at home and abroad.

9. The measures I shall announce follow a detailed and searching review of policy by the Government in every major field of expenditure, with no exceptions, on the basis that no spending programme could be sacrosanct; and, I repeat, all these are in addition to the measures announced by my right hon. Friend the Home Secretary on 20th November.

10. The House will be aware, from long experience, that the expenditure of any given year is to a very large extent committed by decisions taken two and three years before, particularly where major works such as roads, hospitals and schools and many items of defence production are involved. Because of this time-lag, and the difficulty of making an impact on many continuing projects, we have concentrated on expenditure in the financial year 1969–70, though in some cases, particularly defence, the full saving resulting from our decisions will not be seen until 1970–71 or even later. At the same time, substantial reductions in expenditure in 1968–69 will be achieved. I must, however, tell the House that, so great is the proportion of expenditure governed by programme decisions taken two, three and more years ago, that there will still be a considerable rise in public expenditure in 1968–69 compared with 1967–68, and a further small rise in 1969–70.

11. I begin with defence expenditure, the whole of which has been reviewed against the background of our commitments and alliances. Our decisions have been based on two main principles. First, the House will recognise that it is not only in our own interests but in those of our friends and allies for this country to strengthen its economic base quickly and decisively. There is no military strength whether for Britain or for our alliances except on the basis of economic strength; and it is on this basis that we best ensure the security of this country. We therefore intend to make to the alliances of which we are members a contribution related to our economic capability while recognising that our security lies fundamentally in Europe and must be based on the North Atlantic Alliance. Second, reductions in capability, whether in terms of manpower or equipment, must follow and be based on a review of the commitments the Services are required to undertake. Defence must be related to the requirements of foreign policy, but it must not be asked in the name of foreign policy to undertake commitments beyond its capability. Major foreign policy decisions, therefore, are a prior requirement of economies in defence expenditure; and in taking these decisions we have to come to terms with our rôle in the world. It is not only at home that, these past years, we have been living beyond our means. Given the right decisions, above all given the full assertion of our economic strength, our real influence and power for peace will be strengthened by realistic priorities.

12. We have accordingly decided to accelerate the withdrawal of our forces from their stations in the Far East which was announced in the Supplementary Statement on Defence Policy of July 1967 (Cmnd. 3357) and to withdraw them by the end of 1971. We have also decided to withdraw our forces from the Persian Gulf by the same date. The broad effect is that, apart from our remaining Dependencies and certain other necessary exceptions, we shall by

that date not be maintaining military bases outside Europe and the Mediterranean.

13. Again, by that date, we shall have withdrawn our forces from Malaysia and Singapore. We have told both Governments that we do not thereafter plan to retain a special military capability for use in the area. But we have assured them both, and our other Commonwealth partners and allies concerned, that we shall retain a general capability based in Europe—including the United Kingdom—which can be deployed overseas as, in our judgment, circumstances demand, including support for United Nations operations. During his recent visit to Kuala Lumpur, my right hon. Friend the Commonwealth Secretary told the Government of Malaysia that we wish to reach a new understanding with them about the Anglo-Malaysian Defence Agreement so as to make it fit the changed conditions. As the House knows, the Agreement contains provisions for a review of this nature. He also assured the other Commonwealth Governments concerned of Britain's continued interest in the maintenance of security in South-East Asia, with the forces which will be available here. Meanwhile, if our commonwealth partners so desire and mutually satisfactory arrangements can be made, we would be prepared to assist them in establishing a future joint air defence system for Malaysia and Singapore and in training personnel to operate it. We have informed the Governments of Malaysia and Singapore that we will discuss with them the aid implications of our accelerated withdrawal. We shall amend our force declarations to S.E.A.T.O. as our forces in the area are run down.

14. We shall make an early reduction in the number of aircraft based in Cyprus while maintaining our membership of C.E.N.T.O.

15. On the Gulf, we have indicated to the Governments concerned that our basic interest in the prosperity and security of the area remains; and, as I have said, the capability we shall be maintaining here will be available for deployment wherever, in our judgment, this is right having regard to the forces available.

16. As the House already knows, my right hon. Friend the Foreign Secretary has visited Washington to discuss our intentions with the United States Administration; and my right hon. Friend the Commonwealth Secretary has paid special visits to the four Commonwealth countries concerned with Far East defence so as to discuss with their Prime Ministers the intended changes in our political commitments and consequent military dispositions and the consequences flowing from them. My right hon. Friend the Minister of State, Foreign Office, has paid a special visit to the States of the Gulf for a similar purpose. Other Governments and Organisations concerned have already been made fully aware of our decisions. These decisions were taken in the knowledge, and in the light, of the views of our Commonwealth partners and of our allies directly concerned.

17. We recognise the deep feelings and anxieties of our allies and Commonwealth partners. We recognise, too, that these changes involve risks, but, in the circumstances, we believe they are risks that must be accepted. We are deter-

mined that our commitments, and the capacities of our forces to undertake them, should match and balance each other.

18. These decisions will entail major changes in the rôle, size and shape of the forces, in the nature and scale of the equipment which they will require, and in the supporting facilities which are necessary. Time will be needed to work out the precise implications: these will be embodied in a White Paper to be published and, if the House so wishes, debated later in the year. Nevertheless, I can now give some specific illustrations of the effects of our decisions in advance of the further detailed work.

19. *Manpower.* Cmnd. 3357 envisaged withdrawal from certain east of Suez stations by the mid-1970s, and planned for a reduction by roughly the same date in the establishment of the Services of 75,000 uniformed manpower and 80,000 civilians. As a result of our decisions, and of others that will result from the further planning which is now starting, the active strength of the forces will be reduced by the end of 1971 well below the levels forecast last July in Cmnd. 3357. We would expect that, within about five years or so from now, we shall have reduced the total size of the forces below the long-term strengths we had previously planned. Thus, the eventual saving in Service manpower will be greater than the total reduction of about 75,000 forecast previously for the mid-1970s and we shall achieve it earlier. We shall also be reducing civilian manpower at a faster rate over the same period, and our aim will be to increase the forecast reduction of 80,000 civilians and to achieve this significantly earlier than previously planned.

20. *The Navy.* The aircraft carrier force will be phased out as soon as our withdrawal from Malaysia, Singapore and the Gulf has been completed. There will also be reductions in the rate of new naval construction, for example in the nuclear-powered Hunter/Killer submarines.

21. *The Army.* There will be a considerable increase in the rate of run-down of the Army and in the disbandment or amalgamation of major units. As a result of our accelerated withdrawal from Singapore and Malaysia, the run-down of the Brigade of Gurkhas to 10,000 by the end of 1969 will continue at the same rate until 1971, bringing the total strength of the Brigade to 6,000. The future of the Brigade after 1971 will depend on developments obtaining at that time; there is no question of reducing the strength or effectiveness of the Hong Kong Garrison. There will also be substantial savings on Army equipment and stocks and many of these will be achieved between 1969–70 and 1972–73.

22. *The Royal Air Force.* We have decided to cancel the order for 50 F111 aircraft. Further study is being given to the consequences of this decision on the future equipment of the Royal Air Force. Leaving out of account the results of this study, the cancellation of the F111 is estimated to yield total savings on the Defence budget of about £400 million between now and 1977–78. This figure allows for likely cancellation charges. The saving in dollar expenditure over the period, again allowing for likely cancellation charges, will be well over $700 million. Because of the credit arrangements, these savings will mature over a

period of years. We are discussing with the United States Government future arrangements for offset orders and credit for the Phantom and Hercules aircraft. The reduction in our overseas commitments will make it possible to cut down the transport force.

23. *Support facilities.* The more rapid withdrawal of our forces from outside Europe and the changes we intend to make in their rôle and equipment will impose a massive task on those responsible for providing the most efficient and economical logistic support for the three Services. Very substantial savings in base facilities staff overseas will follow as a consequence of withdrawal. The run-down in the forces will be increasingly reflected in reduced support facilities, such as training establishments in this country, but it is too early yet to indicate the extent of the total reduction of the United Kingdom base as a whole. In spite of the extra planning load placed upon it, we shall energetically continue the process of cutting the size of the Ministry of Defence.

POSTWAR COMMONWEALTH PROBLEMS

Official Declaration of the Commonwealth Prime Ministers' Conference,
12 January 1951 *

The Prime Ministers of the United Kingdom, Canada, Australia, New Zealand, India, Pakistan, Ceylon, and Southern Rhodesia, and the South African Minister for the Interior representing the Prime Minister of South Africa, desire, before concluding the present London meeting, to state in simple terms some of the great principles which have inspired the discussions and strengthened mutual understanding.

Our historic Commonwealth, which comprises one-fourth of the world's population and extends over all the continents and oceans of the world is singularly well constituted to enable it to study and in some measure to comprehend the vexed questions which beset the world. These do not fit neatly into old patterns. In Europe there are grave and urgent problems which must be solved, and in Asia the rise of new nations and new national unities must be recognized, if peace is to be secured on a basis of justice and prosperity.

The Commonwealth has the unique quality of embracing nations and peoples from every continent. Our own meetings have therefore given us special knowledge, and have left us with a special sense of responsibility.

We are, both jointly and severally, pledged to peace. This is not merely a pledge given to other nations; it is solemnly given to our own.

We believe that there are certain courses which must be pursued if real peace is to come.

First, the wounds of the last war must be healed: settlements with Germany and Japan should be made with speed.

Second, we must do what we can to understand those who appear to differ from us. The great antidote to war is hope; its greatest promoter is despair. When we say that war is not inevitable, we do not just mean that we shall prepare and be strong, and that our strength may deter aggression. We also mean that, in a world worn out and distorted by war, there must be an overwhelming majority of the people of all lands who want peace. We must not despair of reaching them. In all our discussions we have made it clear to each other, as we now do to the world, that as Commonwealth Prime Ministers we would welcome any feasible arrangement for a frank exchange of views with Stalin or with Mao Tse-tung. We should, in the name of common humanity, make a supreme effort to see clearly into each other's hearts and minds.

We do not seek to interfere in the affairs of the Soviet Union or China or any

Times, 13 January 1951.

3300

other country; we are simply determined to retain the mastery of our own affairs, without fear of aggression.

It is with these considerations in mind that in the last few days we have directed our efforts to the securing of a cessation of hostilities in Korea, so that around the conference table the great Powers concerned may compose their differences on a basis which will strengthen the United Nations and fulfil the purposes of the Charter.

We all have deep within us a faith in the existence of a purpose of justice in this world, and we believe it to be our duty to forward it by everything we do. Indeed, this sustaining faith derives added strength from the fact that at our meetings it has been simply and sincerely expressed by men of widely different races, traditions, and creeds.

We think it proper to declare once more that the Commonwealth countries, though they have a special and precious association which they value profoundly, do not regard themselves as some sort of exclusive body. They welcome cooperation with other nations. It has been their privilege to be able to work closely with the United States of America, whose efforts in the direction of assisting many war-stricken nations are warmly regarded, and whose practical support of the United Nations has contributed much to the strength of that organization. We will at all times seek, by process of discussion, to promote the utmost harmony among ourselves, and to arrive at common international policies with the United States, and with all other friendly and cooperative nations.

Our support of the United Nations needs no reaffirmation. The Commonwealth and the United Nations are not inconsistent bodies. On the contrary, the existence of the Commonwealth, linked together by ties of friendship, common purpose, and common endeavour, is a source of power behind the Charter.

We of the Commonwealth recognize that the peace and prosperity of the free world cannot be assured while millions live in poverty. We are therefore resolved, while keeping our own economies strong, to promote economic and social development in the under-developed countries, by providing such financial and economic assistance as we can command and by making full use of our resources of scientific and technical experience. The Colombo Plan is practical evidence of this intention. The Commonwealth countries concerned will continue to contribute, to the full extent of their ability, towards the execution of this and similar schemes for developing economic resources and raising social standards.

In brief, the problem of peace is that of removing the causes of war; of easing tension and promoting understanding; of assisting those less-developed nations which need our aid; of being at all times willing to discuss our differences without foolishly assuming that all attempts to secure peace are a form of "appeasement." We will cultivate the friendships we now have, and hope that with wise approaches differences may become less and ultimately disappear.

But, while we say these things with a full heart, we are bound to add that, so long as the fear of aggression exists, we will have to strengthen our defences with all speed and diligence. This may well result in placing heavy burdens upon our peoples. It is our firm belief that the rule of law should govern human conduct; and we are prepared to accept whatever sacrifices may be necessary to uphold, with all other nations, those principles of international law and order which are essential conditions for world peace and progress.

Report of the Monckton Commission Recommending Constitutional Changes for the Federation of Rhodesia and Nyasaland, 2 September 1960*
[*The Federation was established in 1957 and dissolved in 1963.*]

*   *   *

Chapter 19
Summary of Conclusions and
Recommendations

340. After an Introduction (Chapter 1), Chapter 2 describes the historical background to Federation. Chapters 3 and 4 set out the dilemma presented by the present situation in the Federation, the conflict between the numerous, varied and deep-seated criticisms of the present arrangements, and the clear evidence of the economic, material and also political advantages of Federation. Federation cannot, in our view, be maintained in its present form. On the other hand, to break it up at this crucial moment in the history of Africa would be an admission that there is no hope of survival for any multi-racial society on the African continent, and that differences of colour and race are irreconcilable. We cannot agree to such a conclusion. In Chapter 5 we express the view that while the Federation cannot continue unless it commands general acceptance, a dissolution would lead to hardship, poverty and distress. We have considered and rejected three alternative forms of association, and state our view that the three Territories could best go forward if they remained linked in a Federal association, but that it is too much disliked to survive in its present shape. We proceed to outline a number of changes, constitutional and other, to remove the main objections. We endeavour to frame a new design into which all our proposals should be fitted and urge that our recommendations should be considered as a whole.

341. In Chapters 6–18 we have set out these proposals in detail, and we now summarise in the order of those chapters our main conclusions and recommendations.

Chapter 6—The Federal Legislature and Franchise

(1) Two of us make proposals in regard to the composition of the Federal Legislature and the franchise which are in most respects at variance with all other members (*paragraph* 88 *and Reservation* (2)).

**Parliamentary Papers*, 1959–60, XI, Cmd. 1148, 111–20.

(2) If some form of federal association is to continue, Africans must in the immediate future have a much higher proportion of the seats in the Federal Assembly (*paragraph* 88).

(3) The franchise should remain qualitative, and there should be no devalued or weighted votes; it should be broadened to bring a larger number of Africans on to the voters' roll; it should include Africans with experience and judgment, even if without education or income qualifications; and it should be designed to secure the election of a Federal Assembly representative of the broad mass of both African and European opinion (*paragraph* 88).

(4) The Federal Assembly should not be reduced below its present size (*paragraph* 89).

(5) We have not been able to reach agreement on the principles which should govern the proportion of seats as between Africans and Europeans. We therefore set out, with arguments, several possible courses—

(i) Some of us favour the traditional policy of staged development. A possible next stage would be an arrangement whereby some members are elected on communal rolls and others on a common roll. There would be three categories of seats. Taking, for example, an Assembly of sixty members with twenty seats in each category, twenty members would be elected on a communal roll of Europeans, and twenty on a communal roll of Africans, both on a low franchise. The remaining twenty would be elected on a common roll, on a franchise based on the principles stated in (3) above. Alternatively, the balancing element on the common roll might be ten seats, with two sets of twenty-five communal seats (*paragraph* 93 *and Reservation* (3)).

(ii) A smaller number of us believe that the enormous majority of Africans in the population calls for an African majority in Parliament (*paragraph* 94).

(iii) The majority of us consider that the only basis for the division which is fair both to Europeans and Africans, and the one which has the best chance of securing acquiescence by a substantial number of people in both the two principal communities, is parity between them, secured by reserving an equal number of seats for Europeans and Africans (*paragraph* 96).

(iv) Some of us, while supporting parity as an aim, feel that there should be a gradual approach to it, and that at this stage no definite recommendations should be made as to the timing of its introduction, although it should not be delayed longer than necessary. But the largest group of us think that it should be introduced now (*paragraphs* 99 *and* 100).

(6) All members should be elected on a common roll. But measures will have to be taken to ensure that they are sufficiently representative of their own racial community. This might be done through primary elections on communal rolls. If, however, the Governments cannot agree a method of election using a

common roll, it might be preferable for them to declare the common roll as an objective, and to consider whether arrangements should be made, as a last resort and as a purely interim measure, to hold elections on communal rolls (*paragraphs* 101–104).

(7) Electoral divisions would have to be delimited separately for each of the two main racial groups. The choice between two possible methods would have to be examined carefully on the spot (*paragraph* 105).

(8) We think that the Assembly should consist of sixty voting members and a Speaker. As to the distribution of seats between the Territories, there should be ten Africans from each. European seats could be distributed in various ways, but most of us suggest seventeen for Southern Rhodesia, ten for Northern Rhodesia, and three for Nyasaland (*paragraph* 106).

(9) The Speaker should be appointed from outside the Federal Assembly. Alternatively, if it were decided to select him from within the Assembly, he should vacate his seat, which would be filled by a bye-election (*paragraph* 107).

(10) The majority of us consider that a committee should be appointed to make recommendations as to the details of the franchise, and that the Review Conference should consider the composition of such a committee. Most members of this majority consider that this franchise committee should be given additional guidance on broad requirements (*paragraph* 108). Some of us believe that the Review Conference could settle the terms of the franchise without the need for a special franchise committee (*Reservation* (4)).

(11) We also make recommendations on the basic qualifications for the vote. We see no need for a basic literacy test for persons otherwise qualified (*paragraph* 109).

(12) The franchise committee should also consider whether the Federal franchise qualifications should vary from Territory to Territory, bearing in mind that the more voters on the Territorial roll who are disqualified from voting in Federal elections, the more difficult it will be to obtain African support for Federation (*paragraph* 110).

(13) Most of us recommend that the Asian community should be represented in the Assembly by one non-voting member. The franchise committee should consider in what way he should be chosen (*paragraph* 111).

(14) It should be made possible for individual members of the Coloured community to decide for themselves whether they wish to be regarded as Africans or Europeans for the purpose of standing for election and, if communal rolls are adopted, being registered as voters (*paragraph* 112).

Chapter 7—The Territorial Constitutions

(15) Her Majesty's Government should declare as soon as possible that further constitutional advance towards full self-government will be made in the near future in Northern Rhodesia (*paragraph* 114).

(16) A Conference similar to that held recently on the Nyasaland Constitution, and similarly representative of all the main political and racial groups,

should be held without delay to work out the nature and timing of the necessary changes (*paragraph* 114).

(17) Most of us recommend that there should be in Northern Rhodesia an African majority in the Legislature, and an unofficial majority in the Executive Council, so constituted as to reflect the composition of the Legislative Council. Some of us consider that the time has not yet come for an African majority in the Legislative Council (*paragraph* 114). Others think that there should be an African majority in the Executive Council as well as in the Legislative Council (*Reservation* (5)).

(18) If the franchise is not lowered sufficiently to bring a reasonable number on to the voters' roll in any particular area, consideration should be given to reserving special seats for the tribal authorities in those areas, or to electing persons under some system whereby the tribal authorities would form electoral colleges (*paragraph* 117).

(19) It is important that nothing should be done to diminish the traditional respect in which Chiefs are usually held by their communities. All possible steps should be taken to stamp out the intimidation which, apart from its other effects, is undermining the authority and status of the Chiefs (*paragraph* 119).

(20) Barotseland enjoys a special position. Its future status, and its relationship with the Federation and with Northern Rhodesia, require further detailed examination and negotiations between the Paramount Chief and the Governments of the United Kingdom, the Federation and Northern Rhodesia (*paragraphs* 121 *and* 122).

*   *   *

Chapter 11—The Removal of Racial Discrimination and the Development of Partnership

(40) Racial discrimination, though diminishing, remains one of the more important forces working against Federation. In considering reforms it is important to distinguish discriminatory laws which are desirable from those which are unfairly discriminatory (*paragraph* 218).

(41) Racial discrimination exists in all parts of the Federation, but is more rigid and more comprehensively entrenched in Southern Rhodesia. No form of association between the Territories is likely to succeed unless Southern Rhodesia is willing to make further and drastic changes in its racial policies (*paragraphs* 219–221).

(42) The more important discriminatory laws and practices which should be removed or amended include the Pass Laws in Southern Rhodesia, discrimination in Local Government in urban areas, in the public services and in industry, and the Southern Rhodesia Land Apportionment Act (*paragraphs* 222–228).

(43) Governments should take the lead in removing, as quickly as possible, particularly in those enterprises over which they have direct control, all the unfairly discriminatory practices which remain, in order not only to eliminate grievances, but to give a positive impetus to the development of partnership. (*paragraph* 229).

(44) In the field of social, economic and commercial practice, it is both possible and desirable for Governments to legislate to make unfairly discriminatory practices, except in purely private relationships, illegal (*paragraph* 230).

(45) We hope that Governments will legislate so as to ensure that no person who conducts a trade, profession or business by virtue of some sanction of the state, shall be permitted to admit in the conduct of his business any discriminatory practices on grounds of colour, race or creed (*paragraph* 230).

Chapter 12—Safeguards

(46) It is essential to improve the existing safeguards, to devise new ones, and to ensure that their effectiveness continues (*paragraph* 231).

(47) The safeguards should be extended to guarantee individual as well as collective rights (*paragraph* 234).

(48) A Bill of Rights should be included in the Constitution of the Federation (*paragraph* 235).

(49) The Bill of Rights should be drawn up in accordance with the traditions of the English-speaking world, and the current practice of the multi-racial Commonwealth (*paragraphs* 236 *and* 237).

(50) The Bill of Rights would be enforced by the courts, with a right of appeal to the Judicial Committee of the Privy Council (*paragraph* 238).

(51) The Bill of Rights in the Federal Constitution should be incorporated, in identical terms, in each of the Territorial Constitutions (*paragraph* 239).

(52) Federal and Territorial Councils of State should be set up, modelled on the Kenya Council of State (*paragraph* 242).

(53) These Councils of State should not be integral parts of any Legislature. Their main task would be to protect persons against the enactment of legislation unfairly discriminatory on grounds of race, colour or creed (*paragraph* 242).

(54) There should be separate Councils of State for the Federation and for each of the three Territories (*paragraph* 243).

(55) Every member of the Federal Council of State should be a member of a Territorial Council of State, and not a member of any Legislature. Members should be selected on grounds of personal eminence, experience and detachment, to act as wise and impartial men and not as representatives of races or Territories (*paragraph* 244).

(56) The Federal Council of State should consist of twelve persons, with an equal number of members from each Territorial Council of State, appointed by the Governor-General and the four Chief Justices of the Federation, who would also choose an independent chairman having a casting vote only (*paragraph* 244).

(57) While the Northern Territories remain under Her Majesty's Government's protection, each Governor, in consultation with his Chief Justice and with the approval of the Secretary of State, should appoint the members of the Territorial Council of State. which should be composed of not less than six members and an independent Chairman (*paragraph* 244).

(58) Southern Rhodesia should devise its own system of appointing members of its Council of State, but in such a manner as will ensure its independence and freedom from political control; there should be not less than six members and an independent chairman (*paragraph* 245).

(59) We have been unable to agree about the racial composition of the Councils of State (*paragraph* 246). There are three possible solutions:

   (i) An absolute parity between the European and African communities (*paragraph* 247).
  (ii) A less exclusive parity which would not preclude the appointment of Asians and Coloureds (*paragraph* 248).
 (iii) Appointments made without regard to race (*paragraph* 249).

(60) The functions of the Councils of State should be—

   (*a*) to consider proposed substantive legislation and, if it is found to be unfairly discriminatory, to report accordingly to the Legislature;
   (*b*) to consider existing legislation and subsidiary legislation, and, if it is found to be unfairly discriminatory, to report accordingly to the Government and the Legislature.
   (*c*) to acquaint themselves with any unfairly discriminatory trends and report thereon, without dealing directly with individual complaints (*paragraph* 250).

(61) The Councils of State should not have a power of veto, but only of delay (*paragraph* 252).

(62) The application of their powers to ordinary legislation, money Bills and subsidiary legislation are differentiated (*paragraphs* 253–258).

(63) The Councils of State should have no powers in relation to emergency legislation. The duration of such legislation should be limited to two months, unless the Legislature concerned resolves that it should endure for a further stated period (*paragraph* 257).

(64) While a Territory enjoys Protectorate status, a special procedure should apply. If the Council should make a final adverse report, the Bill would be reserved for the signification of Her Majesty's pleasure (*paragraph* 255).

(65) The provisions relating to the Bill of Rights and the Councils of State should be specially entrenched in the Federal and Territorial Constitutions. In the Federal Constitution, amendment of provisions for these safeguards should require (a) the affirmative vote of not less than three-quarters of all the members of the Assembly, and also (b) a special referendum with requirements as stated in paragraph 260.

(66) The Bill of Rights and the Councils of State should be regarded as permanent features in the Federal and Territorial Constitutions, and we trust that Her Majesty's Government will ensure that these safeguards, and the manner of their entrenchment, will be retained at the time when a Territory achieves self-government, and if it wishes to secede, at the time of its secession (*paragraph* 261).

(67) Certain other Articles in the Constitution should be more firmly entrenched than in the manner provided in Article 97 (*paragraph* 262).

* * *

Chapter 16—The Question of Secession

(80) The question has frequently been raised whether Territories have, or should have, legal right of secession. Our view is that the present Constitution does not confer on any of the Territorial Legislatures any right express or implied to secede from the Federation, and that the attainment of responsible Government does not import any such right. This could only be created by an act of the United Kingdom Parliament. We state four possible courses open to Her Majesty's Government in settling a new or amended Constitution. Nothing in constitutional theory makes a right of secession incompatible with the Federal concept (*paragraphs* 287 *to* 290).

(81) It should be made clear before the Review Conference that the question of secession will be discussed there (*paragraph* 294).

(82) Her Majesty's Government should neither leave the question of secession entirely open nor declare the Federation indissoluble (*paragraphs* 296 *and* 297).

(83) A declaration of the intention of Her Majesty's Government to permit secession by any of the Territories, if so requested after a stated time or at a particular stage of constitutional development, would have a very favourable effect and might be decisive in securing a fair trial for the new association. Her Majesty's Government should make such a declaration of intention (*paragraphs* 298 *to* 300).

(84) The timing of a request for secession should be related to a certain stage of constitutional advance in the Territory concerned, or to a period of years from the inception of the new Federal Constitution. If the former is chosen, we consider that the stage should be the attainment of self-government as defined in paragraph 303 (*paragraphs* 301 *to* 303).

(85) A seceding Territory should accept responsibility for its share of the public debt of the Federation, and this could be a condition of any arrangement for secession (*paragraph* 304).

(86) We do not see how it could be made a positive condition of secession that a customs union should be preserved for a number of years, but we think it important that a customs union should be maintained under conditions which the seceding Territory could freely accept without damage to its status (*paragraphs* 305 *and* 306).

(87) A majority of us consider that no special constitutional procedure should be laid down as to the manner in which the wishes of the inhabitants of a Territory with respect to secession should be ascertained. It should be determined by Her Majesty's Government at the time (*paragraph* 309). Some of us recommend that this procedure should be decided at the Review Conference (*Reservations* (12) *and* (13)).

(88) Two alternative formulae as a basis for a declaration of intention by

Her Majesty's Government are put forward for consideration by the Review Conference (*paragraph* 310).

(89) Both give to Her Majesty's Government the right to determine how the wishes of the inhabitants of the Territory at the time should be ascertained. By "the inhabitants" we do not merely mean those qualified for the Territorial franchise at the time (*paragraph* 311).

(90) Under both formulae it is made clear that Her Majesty's Government would continue to afford protection to the Northern Territories until such time as the wishes of their inhabitants with regard to their future are clear. The first formula also makes it clear that Her Majesty's Government would not permit considerations relating to a request of a Territory to secede to affect their views on the pace at which constitutional advances in that Territory should be granted. The second formula would operate independently of a Territory's advance towards self-government (*paragraph* 312).

(91) The declaration of intention should not be embodied in the new Constitution, but the Preamble should be amended so as to include an appropriate reference to it (*paragraph* 314).

(92) Provision for the accession of other territories should be inserted in the Constitution (*paragraph* 316).

* * *

Statement by the Prime Minister, Harold Macmillan, in the House of Commons Announcing the Withdrawal of South Africa from the Commonwealth, 16 March 1961*

The House will know that the Prime Minister of South Africa yesterday decided to withdraw his application for the Union of South Africa to remain a member of the Commonwealth after that country becomes a Republic on 31st May next. Until then, South Africa will remain a member of the Commonwealth. The Prime Minister of South Africa will, therefore, continue to take part in the deliberations of the present Commonwealth Prime Ministers' Conference.

I am sure that I speak for many of us on both sides of the House when I express our deep regret that the Commonwealth ties with South Africa, which have endured for fifty years, are shortly to be severed, and our regret, also, for the circumstances which have made this unavoidable. Remembering that the Commonwealth is an association of peoples of all races, colours and creeds, we must hope that, in the years to come, it will be possible for South Africa once more to play her part in the Commonwealth.

*Hansard, 5.s., DCXXXVI, 1748–53.

The Prime Minister of South Africa has said that he hopes to co-operate in all possible ways with all those members of the Commonwealth who are willing to maintain good relations with South Africa. He has also said that South Africa will remain a member of the sterling area. We, for our part, welcome these statements, and intend to cooperate fully in matters of common interest.

The House will wish to debate the various implications of the situation with which we are now faced. No doubt arrangements can be made through the usual channels for a debate next week.

The House will appreciate that I do not feel free to go into further details until the Conference is over, and the final communiqué has been agreed.

MR. GAITSKELL: We welcome the Prime Minister's suggestion that there should be a debate next week. I think that it is clear to all of us that the Commonwealth, in the last few days, has passed through a great crisis, perhaps the greatest crisis in its history, whose impact was bound to be very great, very decisive, not only in the Commonwealth itself, but far beyond it.

I realise that some take the view that what has happened is a step towards the dissolution and decay of the Commonwealth. For our part, on these benches, we take the contrary view. To us, the outcome, bearing in mind all the circumstances, strengthens our faith that the Commonwealth is an institution of great potential value for humanity.

I hope that I may be permitted to put my remarks in the form of a statement—I think that that is usual on such occasions—and not simply as questions. It can hardly be denied—can it?—that the theory and practice of *apartheid*—the advocacy of a permanent division of men according to the colour of their skin, and involving, in practice, different rights, opportunities and status—is a continuous affront to the vast majority of the inhabitants of the Commonwealth.

SIR K. PICKTHORN: On a point of order, Mr. Speaker. I should be glad to know what rights other hon. Members may have to express their opinions on this occasion.

MR. SPEAKER: At present, I shall have to see. Strictly speaking, what I am allowed to permit on these occasions is some questions, but I do not wish to complicate the situation. I confess, having heard what the Prime Minister has said, that I think that the House might think we should not, perhaps, be as long about this as on another occasion.

MR. GAITSKELL: I fully agree with what you say, Mr. Speaker, but I think that you would agree that it is usual on such occasions to allow a few preliminary observations before one puts the questions to the Prime Minister.

HON. MEMBERS: No.

MR. C. PANNELL: On a point of order, Mr. Speaker. This is the very point that I raised with you yesterday—that is, that there are many precedents for the course which my right hon. Friend the Leader of the Opposition claims to follow. This was particularly so when the right hon. Member for Woodford (Sir W. Churchill) was Leader of the Opposition, in the 1945–50 Parliament, in which the then Speaker ruled in his favour. I am sure that you would not wish my right hon. Friend to be treated with less advantage than his predecessors.

MR. SPEAKER: I have not treated him in any such way. If the hon. Member for Leeds, West (Mr. C. Pannell) agrees with what I am doing about it, I hope that we can now get on.

MR. GAITSKELL: I regret that hon. Members should have misunderstood my intentions in this matter. I will confine myself simply to saying this: we wish profoundly that the dilemma thus created had been resolved by a change in the attitude of the South African Government, but, as this apparently proved to be impossible, it was perhaps best that the Prime Minister of South Africa should recognise the hopeless contradiction of South Africa's staying in the Common-wealth under his Government.

I should like to join with the Prime Minister, if I may, in saying to the people of South Africa, whatever colour they may be, that we hope that, in time, the racial theories and policies adopted by the Union today may be changed and brought into line with those practised in the rest of the Commonwealth, and that they will then return as welcome friends to the Commonwealth.

VISCOUNT HINCHINGBROOKE: On a point of order. Has it not been recognised, from time immemorial, Mr. Speaker, that the Leader of the Opposition has the perfect right to put a question arising out of a Private Notice Question, but not to indulge in moralising on debatable propositions at Question Time? Is he not exceeding the rights usually accorded to him?

MR. SPEAKER: Owing to some noise, I did not myself hear the last sentence the right hon. Gentleman the Leader of the Opposition uttered. My view about this is that it is wisely left to the discretion of the Chair to determine whether the occasion be one on which the right hon. Gentleman should be required strictly to adhere to questions, or whether it is of a more formal character, when some reservations in a non-interrogatory form have been permitted.

MR. GAITSKELL: I will, then, repeat what I said before—that I trust that they will one day return, with different racial policies, as welcome friends to the Commonwealth.

Does the Prime Minister expect that the Prime Minister's Conference will, nevertheless, be issuing a statement on the question of racial policies? Secondly, in view of the decision of the Prime Minister of the Union Government, will the right hon. Gentleman confirm that our attitude to the High Commission Terri-tories remains unchanged, and will he reaffirm our responsibilities to those Territories?

THE PRIME MINISTER: The communiqué will be settled tomorrow. Of course, I am in the hands of my colleagues as a whole as to how they wish the communiqué to be drawn.

It is the case that the withdrawal of the Union of South Africa from the Commonwealth will have no constitutional effects upon the relationship between the High Commission Territories and the United Kingdom, nor will the withdrawal of South Africa affect our responsibilities and obligations towards those Territories, which have repeatedly been made clear.

SIR J. DUNCAN: Without anticipating the debate next week, will my right hon. friend say that the door remains wide open to the Union of South Africa to come back into the Commonwealth if there should be a change of heart?

THE PRIME MINISTER: Yes, Sir. I said that, and the Leader of the Opposition repeated it, and I am glad that my hon. friend has brought it up again.

The tragedy of this event is that we are a comradeship of peoples. There will be very many sad people in South Africa, our friends, our relations, men who have lived there for several generations, others who have only recently gone out. There will be sad people of every kind and every race, and do not let us forget them. We are not a combination of Governments. We are a combination of peoples. Had it been possible to reach agreement, I think that it would have been reached, but it proved not to be so. This seemed the only dignified way out, and I hope that I may be allowed to pay a tribute to the dignity and courtesy of the Prime Minister of South Africa, which was appreciated by all his colleagues, in what was a very good discussion of a very high level. There we are; I agree that we must look to the future.

MR. GRIMOND: Is the Prime Minister aware that there will be widespread agreement in this country with the feeling of sympathy which he has expressed with the people of all races in South Africa who, no doubt, regret this decision as much as anybody and also regret the policies which have made it inevitable?

May I ask two questions which the Prime Minister might consider before the debate? Will he consider giving us information, by a White Paper or in some other way, about his view of the position in the Mandated Territories and British citizenship as it affects South Africa? While I appreciate what he has said about the Protectorates, what will be the position of the High Commissionership of the Protectorates which is now situated in South Africa?

THE PRIME MINISTER: I have already dealt with the question of the High Commission Territories. A number of questions will have to be dealt with and some of them would have had to have been dealt with anyway, probably by legislation, owing to the change from a monarchy to a republic. There will now have to be another set of questions which are being studied by the Departments concerned. The change does not happen until 31st May, and I hope, in the course of the debate, to explain, at any rate in outline, what our major legislative and administrative problems are following from this event.

SIR H. OAKSHOTT: Will my right hon. Friend recognise that there are many of us who fully share his sorrow at the outcome of this issue, and, if I may say so respectfully, who have watched with great admiration his tireless efforts to try to bring about an accommodation satisfactory to everybody? Is he further aware, as he has indicated, that there are many of us who see a distinction between Governments and peoples, and that if the effects of this decision can be mitigated in the way of trade and commerce, to the advantage of all the peoples of the Union, of all colours and races, that will be very much welcomed by many of us?

THE PRIME MINISTER: Yes, Sir.

MR. M. FOOT: In the light of this decision, will Her Majesty's Government review some of the votes which they have cast at the United Nations in recent weeks, in particular their vote this week about South West Africa, since we owe obligations to the people there as well as to those in other parts of Africa?

THE PRIME MINISTER: Certainly, but this is a very complicated question, part of which is a question of the interpretation of the legal position and the advisory opinion of the International Court of Justice, given in 1950. Apart from the substance, there are quite complicated legal questions which we are also studying.

Commonwealth Immigrants Act, an Act Restricting Immigration of Commonwealth Citizens into the United Kingdom (10 & 11 Eliz. II, c. 21), 18 April 1962*
[Further restrictions were placed upon Commonwealth immigration in 1965 and 1968.]

Be it enacted by the Queen's most Excellent Majesty, by and with the advice and consent of the Lords Spiritual and Temporal, and Commons, in this present Parliament assembled, and by the authority of the same, as follows: —

Part I. Control of Immigration

1.— (1) The provisions of this Part of this Act shall have effect for controlling the immigration into the United Kingdom of Commonwealth citizens to whom this section applies.

(2) This section applies to any Commonwealth citizen not being—

(*a*) a person born in the United Kingdom;

(*b*) a person who holds a United Kingdom passport and is a citizen of the United Kingdom and Colonies, or who holds such a passport issued in the United Kingdom or the Republic of Ireland; or

(*c*) a person included in the passport of another person who is excepted under paragraph (*a*) or paragraph (*b*) of this subsection.

*Public General Acts, 1962, 113–17.

(3) In this section "passport" means a current passport; and "United Kingdom passport" means a passport issued to the holder by the Government of the United Kingdom, not being a passport so issued on behalf of the Government of any part of the Commonwealth outside the United Kingdom.

(4) This Part of this Act applies to British protected persons and citizens of the Republic of Ireland as it applies to Commonwealth citizens, and references therein to Commonwealth citizens, and to Commonwealth citizens to whom this section applies, shall be construed accordingly.

2.— (1) Subject to the following provisions of this section, an immigration officer may, on the examination under this Part of this Act of any Commonwealth citizen to whom section one of this Act applies who enters or seeks to enter the United Kingdom,—

(a) refuse him admission into the United Kingdom; or
(b) admit him into the United Kingdom subject to a condition restricting the period for which he may remain there, with or without conditions for restricting his employment or occupation there.

(2) The power to refuse admission or admit subject to conditions under this section shall not be exercised, except as provided by subsection (5), in the case of any person who satisfies an immigration officer that he or she—

(a) is ordinarily resident in the United Kingdom or was so resident at any time within the past two years; or
(b) is the wife, or a child under sixteen years of age, of a Commonwealth citizen who is resident in the United Kingdom or of a Commonwealth citizen (not being a person who is on that occasion refused admission into the United Kingdom) with whom she or he enters or seeks to enter the United Kingdom.

(3) Without prejudice to subsection (2) of this section, the power to refuse admission under this section shall not be exercised, except as provided by subsections (4) and (5), in the case of a Commonwealth citizen who satisfies an immigration officer either—

(a) that he wishes to enter the United Kingdom for the purposes of employment there, and is the person described in a current voucher issued for the purposes of this section by or on behalf of the Minister of Labour or the Ministry of Labour and National Insurance for Northern Ireland; or
(b) that he wishes to enter the United Kingdom for the purpose of attending a course of study at any university, college, school or other institution in the United Kingdom, being a course which will occupy the whole or a substantial part of his time; or
(c) that he is in a position to support himself and his dependants, if any, in the United Kingdom otherwise than by taking employment or engaging for reward in any business, profession or other occupation;

and the power to admit subject to conditions under this section shall not be exercised in the case of any person who satisfies such an officer of the matters described in paragraph (*a*) of this subsection.

(4) Nothing in subsection (3) of this section shall prevent an immigration officer from refusing admission into the United Kingdom in the case of any Commonwealth citizen to whom section one of this Act applies—

> (*a*) if it appears to the immigration officer on the advice of a medical inspector or, if no such inspector is available, of any other duly qualified medical practitioner, that he is a person suffering from mental disorder, or that it is otherwise undesirable for medical reasons that he should be admitted; or
> (*b*) if the immigration officer has reason to believe that he has been convicted in any country of any crime, wherever committed, which is an extradition crime within the meaning of the Extradition Acts, 1870 to 1935; or
> (*c*) if his admission would, in the opinion of the Secretary of State, be contrary to the interests of national security.

(5) Nothing in this section shall prevent an immigration officer from refusing admission into the United Kingdom in the case of any person in respect of whom a deportation order under Part II of this Act is in force.

(6) In this section "child" includes a step-child and an adopted child and, in relation to the mother, an illegitimate child; and for the purposes of this section a person shall be deemed not to be ordinarily resident in the United Kingdom at any time when a condition restricting the period for which he may remain there is in force under this section, whether that period has expired or not.

3.—(1) The provisions of Part I of the First Schedule to this Act shall have effect with respect to—

> (*a*) the examination of persons landing or seeking to land in the United Kingdom from ships and aircraft;
> (*b*) the exercise by immigration officers of their powers of refusal of admission or admission subject to conditions under section two of this Act, and the cancellation, variation and duration of such refusals and conditions;
> (*c*) the removal from the United Kingdom of Commonwealth citizens to whom admission is refused under that section;
> (*d*) the detention of any such persons or citizens as aforesaid pending further examination or pending removal from the United Kingdom.

and for other purposes supplementary to the foregoing provisions of this Act.

(2) The special provisions contained in Part II of the said First Schedule shall have effect for the purposes of the control under this Part of this Act of immigration by Commonwealth citizens who arrive in the United Kingdom as members of the crews of, or as stowaways in, ships and aircraft.

(3) Part III of the said First Schedule shall have effect for the interpretation of Parts I and II of that Schedule.

(4) Her Majesty may by Order in Council direct that the provisions of Part I of the said Schedule relating to persons who land or seek to land in the United Kingdom from ships and aircraft shall extend to persons entering or seeking to enter the United Kingdom by land; and any such Order may make such adaptations or modifications of the said Schedule, and such provisions supplementary thereto, as appear to Her Majesty to be necessary or expedient for the purposes of the Order.

(5) No recommendation shall be made to Her Majesty to make an Order in Council under this section unless a draft of the Order has been laid before Parliament and approved by a resolution of each House of Parliament.

4.— (1) If any person being a Commonwealth citizen to whom section one of this Act applies—

> (a) enters or remains within the United Kingdom, otherwise than in accordance with the directions or under the authority of an immigration officer, while a refusal of admission under section two of this Act is in force in relation to him; or
>
> (b) contravenes or fails to comply with any condition imposed on him under that section or under Part II of the First Schedule to this Act,

he shall be guilty of an offence; and any offence under this subsection, being an offence committed by entering or remaining in the United Kingdom, shall be deemed to continue throughout any period during which the offender is in the United Kingdom thereafter.

(2) If any person knowingly harbours any person whom he knows or has reasonable grounds for believing to have committed an offence under subsection (1) of this section, being an offence committed by entering or remaining within the United Kingdom, he shall be guilty of an offence.

(3) If any person—

> (a) makes or causes to be made to any immigration officer or other person lawfully acting in the execution of this Part of this Act, any return, statement or representation which he knows to be false or does not believe to be true; or
>
> (b) refuses or fails to produce or furnish to any such officer or person any document or information which he is required to produce or furnish to that officer or person under this Part of this Act, or otherwise obstructs any such officer or person in the exercise of his functions thereunder; or
>
> (c) without lawful authority, alters any voucher or other document issued or made under or for the purposes of this Part of this Act, or uses for the purposes of this Part of this Act, or has in his possession for such use, any forged or altered voucher, passport or other document.

he shall be guilty of an offence.

(4) If any person acts in contravention of, or fails to comply with, any provision of the First Schedule to this Act, or of any order made, directions given or requirement imposed thereunder (not being a requirement comprised in conditions so imposed), he shall be guilty of an offence.

5.—(1) This Part of this Act shall continue in force until the thirty-first day of December, nineteen hundred and sixty-three, and shall then expire unless Parliament otherwise determines.

(2) Upon the expiration of this Part of this Act, subsection (2) of section thirty-eight of the Interpretation Act, 1889 (which relates to the effect of repeals) shall apply as if this Part of this Act had been repealed by another Act.

* * *

Statement by the First Secretary of State and Deputy Prime Minister, R. A. Butler, in the House of Commons Accepting the Dissolution of the Federation of Rhodesia and Nyasaland, 1 April 1963*

I will, with permission, make a short statement.

This is my first opportunity of informing the House about the talks on Central Africa which, as the House will be aware, were concluded last Friday afternoon. The object of these talks was to find a basis on which a conference might later be held.

At the outset, I should make it clear that Her Majesty's Government took no decision on these complex matters until all the Governments concerned had had an opportunity to put forward their views. In the light of the views expressed it was necessary for Her Majesty's Government to consider what was the best course to pursue in the interests of all concerned. Her Majesty's Government have accepted that none of the territories can be kept in the Federation against its will, and they have, therefore, accepted the principle that any territory which so wishes must be allowed to secede.

Her Majesty's Government are convinced that this decision was essential before further progress could be made towards their declared objective of policy in Central Africa, that is to say, the evolution of an effective relationship between the territories which is acceptable to each of them.

Because that is their objective, Her Majesty's Government have also clearly stated that they consider it necessary that before any further changes are made there should be renewed discussion in Africa not only on the transitional arrangements required, but also on the broad lines of a new relationship.

*Hansard, 5.s., DCLXXV, 32–37.

I have this morning received a letter from the Prime Minister of Southern Rhodesia asking for certain assurances about the future granting of independence to Southern Rhodesia. This will require close consideration by Her Majesty's Government and I cannot at present take the matter further. I will, however, keep the House informed of any developments that may occur.

MR. STRACHEY: Is the First Secretary of State aware that we on this side of the House welcome his acceptance of the principle that any territory which so wishes must be allowed to secede from the Federation? Does the right hon. Gentleman agree that this question of secession is an entirely different question from the question to which he refers in the latter part of his statement, that of independence for any of the territories? Is he aware that, while we are all anxious to see these territories become independent members of the Commonwealth, we consider that none of them should become independent until it is well on the way, at any rate, to a democratic system with a franchise which gives effective representation to all races?

Would the right hon. Gentleman also agree that no one, by any stretch of imagination, could describe the present Southern Rhodesian Constitution as fulfilling that condition and that neither, for that matter, does the Northern Rhodesian Constitution fulfil that condition? Would he therefore agree that the next step for both territories should be the preparation by this House of a new Constitution containing a broader franchise and better representation? Will the right hon. Gentleman therefore give an assurance to the House that he will not consider independence for these territories until and unless they have new Constitutions based on a substantially broader franchise than at present?

MR. BUTLER: The question of the Northern Rhodesian Constitution is a matter which I also discussed with elected Ministers of the Northern Rhodesia Government and it is agreed that we shall carry these discussions further after the first round of discussions about future relationship—that is, to take one thing at a time.

As for the Southern Rhodesian Government, I cannot go further than my statement that Her Majesty's Government have now under consideration the request of the Southern Rhodesian Prime Minister.

SIR T. MOORE: Is it not a tragedy that this great and noble conception of a multi-racial community should be at an end? Will my right hon. Friend, in his decision on a possible alternative, therefore see that the same ideals that Sir Roy Welensky had in mind are maintained?

MR. BUTLER: Yes, Sir. It is quite clear that the Federation, in its day, achieved a great deal and we are all of us aware of the services rendered by Sir Roy Welensky and the Federal Ministers. What Her Majesty's Government had to come to a conclusion about was whether we could keep people in the Federation against their will, and we came to the conclusion that one can never build up a satisfactory relationship in Central Africa unless and until it is by consent and agreement.

MR. GRIMOND: Does the right hon. Gentleman agree that the end of Federation will require legislation and an Order in Council and that the future of common services will then become the responsibility of Her Majesty's Government in the United Kingdom? Will the right hon. Gentleman ensure that the economic services are continued and the economic links, at any rate, are maintained between the three territories? Will he make clear that Her Majesty's Government do not intend to abdicate their responsibilities for seeing that there is constitutional progress in Southern Rhodesia?

MR. BUTLER: The answer to the first part of that supplementary question is "Yes, Sir." Legislation will be required. The answer about economic links is that they will have to be discussed, I hope, between the Governments principally concerned, namely, the Northern and Southern Rhodesian Governments, in whose two interests the economic links are so important. Naturally, Her Majesty's Government will play their part in helping to work out the economic links and I am obliged to the right hon. Gentleman for bringing up that subject.

On the third point, about abdication in relation to Southern Rhodesia, both under the late Southern Rhodesia Government and the present Southern Rhodesia Government we have never hesitated to put forward our view of the advantage of representative Government.

MR. WALL: Is it my right hon. Friend's intention to negotiate future economic links between three sovereign independent Governments? If so, will he resist pressure from the Opposition, the United Nations and the United States and concede the principle of independence to Southern Rhodesia, which is now practically conceded to Northern Rhodesia?

MR. BUTLER: The principle of independence has not, in fact, been conceded to Northern Rhodesia. All that has been agreed is that there shall be future talks about the future Constitution of Northern Rhodesia which Northern Rhodesians hope will lead towards independence in the end.

The important issue of Southern Rhodesian independence, to which my hon. Friend attaches so much importance, is now under the urgent consideration of Her Majesty's Government.

MR. A. HENDERSON: Can the right hon. Gentleman say what steps Her Majesty's Government propose to take to safeguard the repayment of £114 million worth of Federation of Rhodesia and Nyasaland stock which was subscribed by people in this country with the blessing of Her Majesty's Government?

MR. BUTLER: That is one of the many very difficult matters which will come up for consideration in the future.

*Statement from the Prime Minister, Harold Wilson, to the
Government of Southern Rhodesia, 25 October 1964*

The British Government look forward to the day when Southern Rhodesia can take her place as an independent sovereign State within the Commonwealth. The decision to grant independence rests entirely with the British Government and Parliament and they have a solemn duty to be satisfied that, before granting independence, it would be acceptable to the people of the country as a whole. Indeed the present Government of Southern Rhodesia have already recognised that independence must be based on general consent and that the British Government are entitled to be satisfied about this.

2. The British Government trust therefore that the progress of Southern Rhodesia will proceed on constitutional lines. Nevertheless, in view of reports that there might be a resort to a unilateral declaration of independence. they find it necessary to declare what serious consequences would flow from such an act. The British Government cannot believe that, once the consequences have been made clear, the Government and people of Southern Rhodesia will take an irrevocable step of this kind.

3. A mere declaration of independence would have no constitutional effect. The only way Southern Rhodesia can become a sovereign independent State is by an Act of the British Parliament. A declaration of independence would be an open act of defiance and rebellion and it would be treasonable to take steps to give effect to it.

4. In the final communiqué of the meeting of Commonwealth Prime Ministers in July it was made clear that no Commonwealth Government would be able to recognise a unilateral declaration. There would then be no prospect of Southern Rhodesia becoming a member of the Commonwealth, with all the economic consequences that would then ensue.

5. The British Government would be bound to sever relations with those responsible for such a declaration. It would not be possible for Southern Rhodesia to establish a new and special relationship with the Crown or with Britain. The British Government would not be prepared to advise Her Majesty to accede to any request that she should become a separate Sovereign of a territory which had rebelled. The ultimate result would inevitably be that Southern Rhodesians would cease to be British subjects.

6. The reactions of foreign Governments would likewise be sharp and immediate. With one or two exceptions, they are likely to refuse to recognise Southern Rhodesia's independence or to enter into relations with her. Many of

*Annual Register, 1964, 509.

them might recognise a Government in exile if, as seems probable, one were established.

7. The economic effects would be disastrous to the prosperity and prospects of the people of Southern Rhodesia. All financial and trade relations between Britain and Southern Rhodesia would be jeopardised. Any further aid or any further access to the London market would be out of the question. Indeed most serious consequences would be involved for anyone in the U.K. who afforded aid financial or otherwise to the illegal government, Southern Rhodesia's external trade would be disrupted.

8. In short an illegal declaration of independence in Southern Rhodesia would bring to an end relationships between her and Britain, would cut her off from the rest of the Commonwealth, from most foreign Governments and from international organisations, would inflict disastrous economic damage upon her, and would leave her isolated and virtually friendless in a largely hostile continent.

Television Broadcast by Harold Wilson Warning against the
Consequences of a Unilateral Declaration of
Independence by Rhodesia, 12 October 1965*

Mr. Wilson, the Prime Minister spoke in a television broadcast last night of what he called "the very grave situation" in Rhodesia—"grave because, even as I speak to you tonight, there may be steps taken along a very dangerous road. And the results of these policies may be dangerous not only for Rhodesia but for a far greater area of Africa. They may extend even wider and involve the world." He went on:

After 40 years of limited self-government, the control lay in the hands of 230,000 Europeans, while nearly four million Africans remained effectively without the vote. In effect, under the 1961 Constitution some 90,000 European electors were represented by 50 M.P.s, while perhaps 100,000 Africans qualified for the vote were represented by only 15 M.P.s. It is true that a complicated system provided that as more Africans reached a given educational standard, or got into a higher income bracket, they could have the vote, but this is a very slow process.

The European Government of Mr. Smith has demanded that we now confer independence on the Rhodesian people, on the basis of their existing constitution. And I must make it clear that independence can only be granted by the British Parliament, by an Act of our Parliament. And we have never granted independence except on the basis of democratic majority rule. And this Mr.

*Times, 13 October 1965.

Smith and his colleagues of the Rhodesian National Front resolutely reject. Not in their lifetime, they have said, will they allow it to happen.

For nearly a year we have been in discussion with the Rhodesian Government, with Mr. Smith, to see if we could work out an agreed basis for independence.

What we have been trying to do was to reach an agreed solution on the basis of five principles on which we felt, and on which we feel, we must insist.

First, if we were to break with every previous case and give them independence based on their existing constitution then we must be sure there would be guaranteed and unimpeded progress to majority rule.

Second, we had to be sure that once they had their independence, and no longer subject to the British Parliament, they would not *amend* their constitution so as to make it even less democratic.

Third, we said there must be an immediate improvement in the political status of the four million Africans—we did not say, as in every other case, "one man one vote" immediately—but, an improvement.

Fourth, there must be progress towards ending the racial discrimination, which has developed under the laws and practices of the Rhodesian Government.

Fifth, we insisted, as our predecessors insisted a year ago, that before we could proceed to recommend Rhodesian independence to Parliament, we must be satisfied that the conditions proposed for independence were acceptable to the people of Rhodesia as a whole.

These were the principles—the minimum principles—we laid down. They were endorsed by the Commonwealth Prime Ministers last June. And the Rhodesian Government accepted them as principles. And all our discussions over the past eight or nine months have been about them, and how to turn them into reality.

And I have to tell you tonight that after all these months, and after a week of hard, straight talks, we are no nearer agreement than we were a year ago. On every one of the five principles the disagreement is almost total, absolute. If there is one thing on which Mr. Smith and I agree, it is that on every single issue there is so far no basis for agreement and he has said this inside and outside the Cabinet room.

At the airport last night he seemed to reject any hope of compromise. On a proposal for further talks, he said: "We have talked over several years . . . the gap seems to be so wide that it is impossible to bridge it."

I want you to know this. The talks were very friendly. I can deal with Ian Smith and I recognize his great sincerity even though I disagree with him and even though I feel we are living in different worlds, almost different centuries. Above all I welcome the fact that he stated his case, his beliefs, his principles, absolutely frankly, absolutely straight so there was no room for misunderstanding. And he felt—and said—that we had been equally frank and straightforward.

If we have failed to agree it is because the issues are so deep, so important to both of us, and we would have been guilty of the gravest deception if we had fluffed these issues or pretended the differences were small and capable of being glossed over.

We have tried. And we have failed. And now Mr. Smith has returned home and there are ominous suggestions that the independence he has failed to negotiate will now be seized illegally.

I hope no one—no one in Britain, and still more no one in Rhodesia—will underestimate the gravity of such a step. They have been warned, and warned again of what is involved. They were warned a year ago in the strongest terms by the then Government. We have issued two public statements, in unequivocal terms last October, last April: Mr. Smith is in no doubt that those warnings still stand.

This past week every one of our political parties has urged him to think again. The whole Commonwealth, 21 nations without exception, have reinforced these warnings, this urgent advice not to enter on this dangerous road, and to their warnings have been added the voice—urgent, friendly, compelling—of almost every country with whom Rhodesia has had dealings and would wish in the future to have dealings.

Under our laws, a Rhodesia which took its independence by unilateral action, without the authority of Parliament, would be acting illegally, in a state of rebellion, and we would have to act accordingly. But more than that Rhodesia would, for all practical purposes, be without a friend in the world, unrecognized, illegally governed, alone.

The consequences for Rhodesia and her people would be incalculable. I only wish I could say they would stop there. One of our best-known political journalists wrote last week—before our talks ended—that "Mr. Smith will fly home . . . with a torch in his hand which could set Africa ablaze." This is not the language of panic, or of threats. A U.D.I., a so-called independence illegally taken, could start a chain reaction in Africa of which no one could see the end. Many innocent people, men, women, children, of all races, black and white—could lose their lives. It is a nightmare with which I have to live, that this could be enacted again—on British soil.

We have said, this was the starting point of our talks—and I said to Mr. Smith last week—the Rhodesian people are our own kith and kin. They are our people. But our kith and kin are not confined to Rhodesia.

Once cry havoc, once let slip the ugly passions of race and colour and tribal conflict, it is but a short step to communal rioting—and worse.

I cannot believe that Mr. Smith and his colleagues can go from here and take action which they know to be illegal, and which must destroy the very harmony they seek to establish in their country. At least, after the warnings they have had, they can no longer harbour any illusions about what the British reaction must be, about what the world reaction will be, about what the more incalculable reaction, in terms of human life and human misery, might be.

Before we parted he asked me "What other course is there open for us?" And if I had not had an answer to give I would be even more depressed, even more conscious of our country and the world being caught up in a remorseless wheel of tragedy.

But there is an answer. There is more than one answer, more than one alternative course, and we have urgently held them out to him.

We are prepared to go on talking, to examine even now the possibility of coming at any rate a little closer together on the issues which still so deeply divide us. We have told him we are prepared to work out with him a programme for early independence based on guaranteed progress towards majority rule.

We have made proposals for an interim period working under the existing Constitution, during which Africans would be taken into multi-racial Government, trained as Junior Ministers and Parliamentary Secretaries, while a massive and dynamic programme of education and training is introduced with our help, schools, colleges, as well as training facilities in administration—in Britain, in Rhodesia, in other independent African countries—for the Rhodesian people.

We have proposed, as the Commonwealth Prime Ministers proposed, a constitutional conference representative of the whole Rhodesian people, to hammer out, under the chairmanship of a British Minister, a new and fair and guaranteed basis for independence. Only yesterday I offered to send the Secretary of State to Rhodesia, at any time, for as long as Rhodesian Ministers are prepared to continue the discussions with him.

All these we have proposed. And the Rhodesian Ministers rejected them.

We are not giving up. Too much is at stake. Yesterday I got on the phone to the Prime Minister of Australia, Sir Robert Menzies. Last night I was in direct touch with 19 other heads of Commonwealth Governments.

This evening her Majesty's High Commissioner in Salisbury took to Mr. Smith a personal message from me pressing him, if he continues to reject independence on the terms we have offered, to agree to a new Commonwealth initiative, to a mission of senior Commonwealth Prime Ministers, representing all the Prime Ministers and Presidents and peoples of the Commonwealth, to see if agreement can be reached, without bloodshed, without economic disruption, in harmony and on a basis designed to secure the future stability, security, prosperity, welfare, and independence of a Commonwealth country we all want to help.

I know I speak for everyone in these islands, all parties, all our people, when I say to Mr. Smith: "Prime Minister, think again."

Statement by Harold Wilson in the House of Commons on the
Rhodesian Crisis and the Breakdown of Talks
aboard H.M.S. "Tiger", 5 December 1966

With permission, Mr. Speaker, I should like to make a statement about Rhodesia.

Since my announcement of 27th April that informal talks were to be held the House has been extremely patient and has recognised my inability to give information on the progress of the talks, which it had agreed would be confidential. The time has now come when the House must be put in full possession of the facts as they now stand, more than seven months after Mr. Smith indicated to the Governor his desire to engage in informal talks.

Altogether, three series of talks were held in London and Salisbury at official level before the first visit of my right hon. Friend the Commonwealth Secretary to Salisbury with my right hon. and learned Friend the Attorney-General in September.

These talks were mainly directed to two main issues. First, the method and conditions of a return to legal and constitutional rule in Rhodesia and the determination of the question with whom official negotiations could subsequently take place. Second, an informal exploration in detail of constitutional problems to see what amendments would be needed to the 1961 Constitution to give effect to the six principles which had been the basis of discussions with the legal Rhodesian Government up to 11th November, 1965.

Practically the whole of the discussion during this period was on the problem of an ultimate constitutional settlement, though the representatives of Her Majesty's Government made it plain at the outset and repeatedly warned that a settlement would have to be reached on the problem of return to legality, and warned, too, that before independence could be granted a fair and free test of Rhodesian public opinion would have to be carried out under a constitutional Government.

Mr. Smith, through his officials, insisted on discussing the constitutional proposals first, indicating that he needed to be satisfied about the ultimate constitutional settlement before being ready to discuss what he regarded as a purely procedural matter of the return to constitutional rule. We insisted that before any settlement could be reached both issues would need to be dealt with.

By the time of the visit of my right hon. Friends, in September, no progress had been made in the constitutional talks. Nor, indeed, though my right hon. Friends' visit was extremely useful in informing a wide section of Rhodesian political opinion of our requirements and proposals for a settlement, was there

Hansard, 5.s., DCCXXXVII, 1053–74.

any advance whatsoever on either the constitutional settlement or on the conditions for a return to legality during my right hon. Friends' visit.

Mr. Smith and his colleagues were left by my right hon. Friends in no doubt of our intention to act within the terms of the Commonwealth Prime Ministers' communiqué and no doubt at all about the fact that, while adequate time remained for a settlement if the will were there, the programme envisaged in the communiqué did not admit to unlimited time nor to wasted time. It was not, in fact, until my right hon. Friend again took the initiative in visiting Salisbury on November 25th to 27th, just as we were getting very near the operation of the timetable of which Mr. Smith had been informed, that any signs of movement were detected.

My right hon. Friend returned a week ago with a report indicating for the first time a real possibility that a satisfactory agreement might be reached on the constitutional issues which would give full guaranteed effect to the six principles on which we insisted. The report also indicated, very much for the first time, some sign of movement on the question of return to legality. Mr. Smith had, in fact, indicated that he was prepared to consider returning to the legal 1961 Constitution if a satisfactory constitutional settlement could be agreed. This was said last week for the first time. Mr. Smith said, in fact, to my right hon. Friend that, given a satisfactory solution, he would be prepared to consider surrendering what he called his independence by returning to the legal 1961 Constitution—provided that a satisfactory constitution and settlement could be agreed.

Despite all disappointments—and I can put it no higher—of every round of discussions which we, and indeed our predecessors, have had with Mr. Smith and his colleagues, the Government decided that before we finally had to report to the House, with all the consequences that would ensue, that there was no prospect of an agreement, one last effort should be made.

Accordingly, last Tuesday Mr. Smith was informed that my right hon. Friends and I would be prepared to meet him, on the clear understanding that the purpose of such a meeting would be to reach a final settlement, if it proved possible to reach agreement both on the terms of a constitutional settlement and on satisfactory arrangements for the return to legality. He was informed that I should have full power for this purpose and that it was essential that Mr. Smith should have similar powers and should be authorised to reach a final agreement, if the basis for a settlement were seen to exist.

As the House knows, we met him, and the Governor of Rhodesia, who was accompanied by the Chief Justice, for two days of intensive talks in H.M.S. "Tiger" at the end of last week. I will not weary the House with the successive twists and turns of these discussions—[HON. MEMBERS: "Twists?"] I shall be ready to answer any questions from hon. Gentlemen opposite when I have finished—but their outcome was that we both signed at midnight on Saturday, in the presence of the Governor, a working document setting out in detail all the essentials for a settlement.

On the amendments necessary to the 1961 Constitution which would be required to give effect to the six principles, Mr. Smith and I reached complete agreement, as hon. Members will see when the White Paper is available later this evening. The House will see that the requirements of the six principles have been met in full with effective constitutional and external guarantees.

On the return to constitutional rule, again the document sets out in detail what is required. The programme envisaged that an Order in Council would be made immediately to give the Governor the constitutional powers required for setting up an interim Government. He would then have appointed a broad-based interim Government, to be headed by Mr. Smith, and this Government would have been, in effect, on a legal basis by the middle of this week.

Mr. Smith and I agreed, subject to a condition which he laid down and which I will come to later, possible names for the five non-Rhodesian Front Ministers, European and African, who would be included in this interim administration. The existing Legislature would have been dissolved and the Governor would have exercised full legislative authority. During this period the test of acceptability under the fifth principle would then have been carried out and, provided that it had been completed, fresh elections would have been held not later than four months from the date of restoration of constitutional rule.

Agreement was also reached, without conditions and again in detail, about the procedure, as distinct from the timing, for testing the acceptability of the proposals for an independence constitution to the Rhodesian people as a whole. This was to be done by Royal Commission, to be appointed by Her Majesty's Government, after consultation with the new Rhodesian Government. Censorship was to have been lifted and freedom of political association and activity on democratic lines would have been permitted.

We agreed, also, on a procedure to give effect to the requirement laid down in the Commonwealth Prime Ministers' communiqué for the release of political detainees. To deal with this, a judicial tribunal was to be appointed by the legal Rhodesian Government, but including a British representative nominated by the Lord Chancellor, to consider the detention and restriction of persons on security grounds. Such detention and restriction would have been authorised only if the tribunal was satisfied that the persons concerned had committed, or had incited the committing, of acts of violence or intimidation.

It was agreed that if, as a result of the report of the Royal Commission, Her Majesty's Government were satisfied that the proposed constitutional settlement was acceptable to the people of Rhodesia as a whole, then immediate effect would be given to it by legislation, which we undertook to introduce in this House, the agreement to be further underwritten by a treaty binding both of us to maintain the Constitution. This treaty, as I explained to Mr. Smith, would be registered, as we are required to register it, with the United Nations. And any breach of this treaty, such as a *coup d'état*, either by European or by African extremists, would entitle us—indeed, I feel, would require us—to seek from the United Nations mandatory sanctions under Chapter 7, sanctions not necessarily confined to economic sanctions.

If, as a result of the report of the Royal Commission, Her Majesty's Government decided, however, that the proposed Constitution was not acceptable to the people of Rhodesia as a whole, there would still have been a legal Government under the 1961 Constitution with whom we could have explored alternative new proposals for an independence Constitution.

After all that has happened, the House will understand the anxiety I expressed to Mr. Smith that in these circumstances, if complete agreement had been reached, Mr. Smith, if the Royal Commission reported adversely, might perhaps again illegally declare independence. Nor did Mr. Smith's reply to my expression of anxiety do anything to dispel those suspicions. This would mean that while we had ended sanctions, as we were ready to do this week if Rhodesia returned to constitutional rule, he might once again return to illegality, an easier operation, you might think, than the re-imposition of sanctions. Therefore, I thought it right in these circumstances to leave him in no doubt that if this were to happen we would go immediately and without any preliminaries to the United Nations for effective mandatory sanctions.

Equally, I thought it right to warn him that in conditions of a second U.D.I. he could no longer in all circumstances count on, still less abuse, the assurance I had given before the first declaration, that we would in any circumstances not use force, for example, to reinforce economic sanctions. And in the condition envisaged in a breach of the Treaty to which I have just referred, including a possible *coup d'état,* either by European or African extremists, equally we would not consider ourselves bound by our earlier pledge that force would never be used. Mr. Smith understood this.

By 5 p.m. last Saturday it was open to Mr. Smith to sign an agreement with me covering all the issues providing for an immediate return to constitutional rule, the immediate unwinding of our sanctions provisions, and the urgent initiation of all the procedures leading to independence on terms which I would have no hesitation in recommending to this House as fully implementing all the six principles and that of the guarantees, internal and external, that this House has the right to demand, and as equally implementing the terms of the Commonwealth Prime Ministers' communiqué. This was the position at 5 o'clock last Saturday.

Mr. Smith who had throughout indicated his willingness—within the authority he had been given—to reach agreement on the terms of an appropriate independence Constitution, continued—as he had every right to do—to reserve his position on two points related to the return to constitutional rule.

First, while he was prepared to discuss the procedures for an immediate return to legality—which he had told my right hon. Friend a week earlier he was prepared to consider—he had yet to make up his mind whether he could accept a situation in which he gave up what he called his independence with only the hope and not the certainty that the independence Constitution we had agreed would be shown by the Royal Commission to be acceptable to the Rhodesian people as a whole. While he was confident that it was acceptable to the Rhodesian people as a whole there was, he felt, the possibility that the final verdict might go against him. He continued to insist that the illegal Government should continue, sanctions being lifted, until he knew where he stood as a result of the Royal Commission's report.

I told him that a fair and convincing test of acceptability would be quite impossible in circumstances where an illegal régime was possessed of emergency powers and executive control including broadcasting and television and that we were not prepared to grant even interim recognition which he demanded, particularly since it was clear—as he made clear—that if the verdict went against him he would insist on maintaining his present illegal powers indefinitely. No British Government and few hon. Gentlemen could have agreed to such a proposal. Equally, though we discussed in great detail the composition of the broad-based Government, including the outgoing as well as the incoming personalities, he said that he had not yet accepted the principle that a broad-based Government should be created.

It was understood that having the document as a whole now before him, he would inform me later in the evening whether it was acceptable in its entirety or not. However, after a delay of some hours, Mr. Smith informed me that he had no authority whatsoever from his colleagues to give his agreement on either of these two points, or even to commend our agreed working document to his colleagues. Knowing his difficulties—and I did not underrate them—I agreed that instead of reaching a final settlement which I had authority to do—and I understood that he had come on the same basis—he should return to Salisbury without any commitment on his part either to sign the document as a whole, or even to agree to recommend it to his colleagues. It was, therefore, agreed that both documents should be considered by the British Government, and by Mr. Smith and his colleagues, on the clear understanding that it must be accepted or rejected as a whole, and a straight answer given, "Yes," or "No", by this morning. It was, therefore, understood and agreed that there could be no question of further amendment of the document which expressed clearly a decision on the principles and issues of policy which have been discussed time and time and time again between the British Government and the Rhodesians for many months—indeed, many of them for many years—and which could not, as we both agreed, be fluffed by any form of words which sought to evade that decision.

Before he returned to Salisbury, Mr. Smith, in the presence of the Governor, was left in no doubt about the consequences of any refusal or failure to accept the document. He was told that the consequences set out in paragraphs 10A and 10B of the Commonwealth Prime Ministers' communiqué—on the conditions laid down in those paragraphs—would be set in motion. He was told what this would mean for Rhodesia, and of the immediate dangers for Africa and even more widely, if he and his régime, whose claim to legality has not been recognised by a single country in the world, insisted in continuing on a course which has earned the condemnation of practically the whole of mankind. He was left in no doubt about the action which we would take, and also the action which would be taken internationally. Equally he was left in no doubt about our resolve—however long it might take—to bring to an end a situation which, when he created it, he said would be a nine-days' wonder.

The House knows Her Majesty's Government announced yesterday their acceptance in its entirety of the document Mr. Smith and I worked out together. This evening the House will have heard with sadness that that same document has been rejected by Mr. Smith and his colleagues. They have confirmed that they insist on maintaining their illegality until, in conditions in which no free expression of Rhodesian opinion would be possible, a Royal Commission has reported and independence has been granted.

They have announced that they have accepted the principal changes in the 1961 Constitution which are set out in the document, as a basis for independence. Their refusal to accept the settlement as a whole stems from their insistence on their refusal to return to legality unless they themselves can remain in power while the agreed constitutional settlement is being tested by Rhodesian opinion. The implications of this are obvious, and no one in this House would be ready to accept those implications. Indeed, if reports from Rhodesia which have come this evening are correct, they have also rejected any concept of sharing power with representatives of a wider section of Rhodesian European opinion and they have rejected the proposal that two respected Africans, whose names were agreed between Mr. Smith and myself, should become part of the interim broad-based Government that we have proposed.

At least the House, and the world, have been left in no doubt about the issues which are at stake, after all that has happened since last Thursday. It is clear that power for its own sake and the insistence of retaining that power in the hands of a small unrepresentative minority have dictated the outcome.

I believe that it was right to try to reach a settlement which we could defend consistently with the principles we have proclaimed and consistently, equally, with our honour both in this House and before the bar of world opinion. No one—including many in Rhodesia who have previously put their trust in that group of men—could condone their refusal to accept the settlement which would have provided for them an honourable way out of the situation that not we but the illegal régime created. For us to have accepted what they were demanding would have been a betrayal of the principles on which our own democracy is based and the principles to which the multiracial Commonwealth and the United Nations are dedicated.

When my right hon. Friends and I decided to hold this parley with Mr. Smith, we knew that some might say that we were mistaken to venture on such a task. I believe that we were justified in what we did. The fact that the hand we proffered has been rejected does not alter that conviction. From that rejection certain inevitable consequences must now follow in accordance with the programme that we agreed with our Commonwealth colleagues in September. Mr. Smith was clearly warned of this in terms he clearly understood. He knew that we, the British Government and this House, were not prepared to suffer the destruction of our principles—or of the Commonwealth—for the sake of safeguarding from world opinion the actions of a small and irresponsible minority.

My right hon. Friend the Foreign Secretary will be flying to New York tomorrow to take personal charge, so far as Her Majesty's Government are concerned, of the actions which must follow in the United Nations. My noble Friend, Lord Caradon, has been instructed to ask for an early meeting of the Security Council.

Mr. Speaker, I regret to have had to present this report to the House. [An Hon. Member: "The right hon. Gentleman did not have to."] I am prepared to face hon. Gentlemen opposite in a minute, and to face them with the consequences of their attitude. Until then, I have to say that I regret that I have had to present this report to the House. I believe that we could have done no more.

Mr. Edward Heath (Bexley): The House is grateful to the Prime Minister for coming here tonight and making a statement after the efforts he has been making during the past few days, which, I am sure, the House will believe were fully justified, and I thank the Prime Minister for making that statement.

The House will realise that the statement is one of the utmost gravity, as the right hon. Gentleman himself has emphasised. It will be a bitter blow to millions of people in this country and far beyond that it has not yet been possible to reach a negotiated settlement of this problem.

The situation, as I think the Prime Minister will agree, is a complicated one, judging from his statement, and it is in many ways, as far as Salisbury is concerned, also a confused one. I am sure, therefore, that the House would wish to consider the Prime Minister's statement most carefully, together with the White Paper which, we understand, is to be produced later this evening.

In the meantime, I ask the Prime Minister to clarify the position in what I think is one vital respect. Is it correct to say that the proposals in the working paper fell broadly into two parts, the first being proposals for the Constitution based on the six principles, on which the Prime Minister's words were "The requirements of the six principles have been met in full, with effective constitutional and external guarantees." If that is so, I think that the House would agree that very great progress has been made, and this is a remarkable achievement.

Secondly, the other lot of proposals deal with the method of the return to legality, and it is here that it has not been possible to reach agreement. May I ask the Prime Minister this question on this vital point, which we have always emphasised ever since his statement of 25th January: what was he proposing should be the legal basis for the interim Government to which he proposed Rhodesia should return?

From reports on the tape tonight, it appears that it was being asked that the control of the Armed Forces and the actual appointment of Ministers should be placed under the Governor, and if this were to be under our own Southern

Rhodesia Act, 1965, this would, therefore, be the direct responsibility in both cases of the British Government at Westminster, as I understand the situation. Is this what was being proposed?

While I fully recognise the point made by the Prime Minister about the request of Mr. Smith as far as their own powers in Rhodesia were concerned, could the right hon. Gentleman clarify the point as to what is he proposing for the future interim Government?

Finally, I am sure that the House would feel that where so much agreement has been reached on the constitutional procedures for the future, it would be a matter of the utmost regret if the dire consequences which are to follow, which the Prime Minister has foretold, were to come about as a result of differences about the return to legality on which the whole House was hoping that it would have been possible to reach agreement between the two Governments concerned which would satisfy the principles and requirements of both.

THE PRIME MINISTER: I can reply only by leave of the House.

First, may I say that I agree with the right hon. Gentleman that the statement which I have made is not only one of gravity, but one of some complexity. There is a White Paper available in the Vote Office, or it will be available in a few minutes. I understand that that will have to be studied. I regret that, for reasons which he will understand, I was not able to send the right hon. Gentleman an advance copy of my statement. It was so late that we got final confirmation. I should have liked to have sent it to him.

The right hon. Gentleman said that it is clear that the argument falls into two parts and that progress was made on the constitutional issue—perhaps surprising progress. That progress was not made, not by one inch, during all the months that we have been discussing the matter since April, until my right hon. Friend's visit, on his own initiative, to Salisbury a week ago. [*Interruption.*] We have been talking since April and were willing to talk in January. No progress has been made by one inch on the Rhodesian side to a solution. There was no insistence throughout on a braking mechanism that even the right hon. Gentleman would not have accepted. It was not until my right hon. Friend's visit, during the last few days before the Commonwealth communiqué time-table began to operate, that there was this beginning of movement on the part of Mr. Smith and his colleagues.

It is a fact that after some very hard bargaining—we made a number of concessions, too, although none which I could not defend against the background of the six principles—it was only at the meeting this weekend that we were able to reach agreement here. But I think that it is wrong to suggest that we can separate these two, as the right hon. Gentleman seemed to be trying to do.

In the first place, in my view and that of my right hon. Friends, it is impossible to say that we could operate a free test which is required under the fifth principle which the right hon. Gentleman, my predecessor, insisted on with so much determination against a background of an illegal constitution, armed, as the Leader of the Opposition has said—I quoted this to Mr. Smith—with all the powers of a police State.

But, secondly, it is not only a question of the difficulty, if not impossibility, of making such a test which we argued with Mr. Smith. It is also the fact that if one is to hand over to Mr. Smith and his colleagues, as we were prepared to hand over, the responsibility for a future Rhodesia, this must be based on trust as well as on the test to which I have referred. If he was not willing to agree to return to legality as a condition of that offer—which I know many people have condemned—I do not believe that one would have the conditions of trust which would justify his being given what no Government in this country has given in our generation, and that is the right of independence without majority rule.

We have a very distinguished record in that in successive Governments right hon. Gentlemen opposite as well as ourselves have over many years handed over to their own sovereignty one people after another, and we have always insisted on majority rule first in our lifetime, in the lifetime of most of us. If we have been prepared to hand over to Rhodesia, uniquely, independence without majority rule, I think that it requires some trust and some sense on their part that they are prepared to make some sacrifices. In this case, the only sacrifice that we asked them to make was a sacrifice not of independence, but of an unreal dream world of a Walter Mitty independence which is recognised by no one except them.

There is not a Government in the world which recognises the 1965 Constitution. European Governments of various complexions have been expelling Mr. Van der Byl—known to some hon. Gentlemen opposite—because he did not carry a valid passport.

I hope that no hon. Gentleman opposite will claim that the Rhodesians have a legal independence under the 1965 Constitution. All that we were asking them to accept was that they should return to a legal constitution—under the same Prime Minister. That was all that we were asking. That should not have been difficult. Without that, I submit to the House, there is not the trust which would justify handing over to them responsibility for the conduct of the country and of guaranteeing the progress to majority rule over a period of years which was involved in our constitutional settlement.

The right hon. Gentleman asked what legal basis there would have been if Mr. Smith had accepted return to constitutional rule. The answer is, simply and plainly, the 1961 Constitution. That is all—I will come to the military point in a minute—that we were asking of him, though—it is an arguable point but he and I agree—if he returned under the 1961 Constitution it would be appropriate to dissolve the Rhodesian Parliament, which would first require an Order, which would have been done under the 1961 Constitution in this particular. What would then have been involved would have been that the Governor would dissolve Parliament constitutionally, which would mean that the Governor could govern for four months without Parliament. In these circumstances we proposed that the legislative authority would be vested in the Governor, and in this he would be advised by his own constitutional Rhodesian Government.

We required, also, that it would not be the existing purported Government with all the same members. I do not think that anybody in this House could have agreed to a Rhodesian constitutional Government including Mr. Dupont, who, during this year, has purported to represent the Queen as quasi-regent in Rhodesia. We would have had to insist on his removal. I would add that in my discussions with Mr. Smith there was no controversy about the removal of some of his colleagues.

HON. MEMBERS: Cheap.

THE PRIME MINISTER: This is not cheap. This is a statement of fact.

I would hope that hon. Gentlemen opposite would insist that someone who had purported to be the Governor without the Queen's authority could not be a member of a legal and constitutional Rhodesian Government. If any of those hon. Gentlemen opposite who have enjoyed his hospitality, and have encouraged him in the course that he has followed, believe that he should have been a member of a legal constitutional Government, I hope that they will have the guts to stand up and identify themselves.

I return now to the other point raised by the right hon. Gentleman. It would have been under the 1961 Constitution, as it would have been under the powers of that Constitution, that the Parliament would have been dissolved. But, under the same Constitution, that would have required an election in four months, during which we hoped that the Royal Commission would have completed its task. There would have been no question—and I know that this has worried the right hon. Gentleman for many months, and I have not been free to deal with it because of what I have said—and there has not been any question in any of our discussions with Mr. Smith from May onwards of direct rule, whether direct rule from Whitehall or direct Governor's rule. As I say, I know that that worried the right hon. Gentleman. I only wish that I could have made it clear. He knows why I could not.

As regards control of the Armed Forces, I hope that, now that there has been this break tonight, we shall not start using the facilities which Mr. Smith has for uncorrected means of disseminating information through Government-controlled radio and television and a Government-censored Press, to falsify the facts. We shall publish tonight in a White Paper the document which he and I agreed. I will tell the House now in advance—and hon. Members can study this for themselves—exactly what was involved in the control of Rhodesian troops.

There was no more in the document than that, while the Governor is and always was the titular head and Commander-in-Chief of the Armed Forces, and while he would act as advised by his legal constitutional Government, we would have agreed with Mr. Smith—and he raised no difficulty about this—the appointment of a Defense and Security Council which would consist of the Governor, of the Ministers in the legal Rhodesian Government responsible for defence and for law and order, of the heads of the Armed Forces, who are Rhodesians, of the chief of police, who is a Rhodesian, and of one representative of the British High Commission.

If that is now being presented to Rhodesia so soon as being taking control of the Rhodesian Armed Forces, then I think that I am justified in some of the things which I have said about misrepresentation of the facts.

That would be for four months only—from now until independence. It would only be for this limited period while the Royal Commission was doing its task and while this House, if the Royal Commission so reported, was carrying through the independence legislation. After that, the only reference to defence in the document—and we have agreed this—is that we would enter into discussions for a defence agreement between two sovereign countries.

How that can be represented as control over the Armed Forces, as I understand he is reported to have said to-night, I cannot myself comprehend, though we must always bear in mind, in the overheated atmosphere in Rhodesia, the possibility of being misreported, not least as I gather that he was addressing from outside his offices a crowd of exuberant and perhaps rather extremist supporters.

The right hon. Gentleman came finally to the point where he said that there are dire consequences resulting from this decision. I agree. That is why I so much deplore the fact that, when settlement was within our grasp, we could not get it because they insisted on a constitutional settlement based on "Heads I win, tails you lose". They had to give up their posture of illegality and enter into a legal constitution, and they said that they would not do that until they knew that they were to have legal independence on their own terms. That really is the point. They refused to accept the test of acceptability by the Royal Commission, and said they must hold on to what they have, or what they think they have, so that they could hold on to it for ever if the Royal Commission reported against them.

I am in no doubt where responsibility lies for this break, but I would say to the right hon. Gentleman that it is making too small a thing of this to suggest that we had agreed on all the big things about the Constitution and disagreed over a quibble about the return to legality. The question of the return to legality—[*Interruption.*] I was not suggesting that that is what the right hon. Gentleman said, but I think that it might have been deduced, from some of the noises from behind him when he said it. I know that he is not easily persuaded by those noises, but it is important that he should not be—[*Interruption.*] There is no doubt about the response given by some hon. Members to that statement by the right hon. Gentleman.

I am sure that when the right hon. Gentleman has had time to consider this—and it is only fair that he and the House should have time to consider it—he will feel that this is not a quibble over protocol. It is essentially a matter of principle that this House could not possibly justify handing to those who have voluntarily, for their own purposes, entered into a condition of rebellion, the fact that they should be free to end that rebellion, and end it only on conditions when they got what they wanted.

Mr. J. GRIMOND (Orkney and Shetland): Is the Prime Minister aware that many people will have heard with deep regret of the determination of Mr. Smith to persist in his illegal course of conduct? May we have it quite clear that he has refused all supervision from outside over the return to legality?

Further, may I ask the Prime Minister whether, now that he is taking the serious course of sending this matter to the United Nations, he is in a position to assure the House that if the United Nations agree to mandatory sanctions, they will be effective? I ask that because many of us feel that if we are to have sanctions we should be assured that they will this time be effective.

THE PRIME MINISTER: Yes, Sir. I am not sure to what the right hon. Gentleman is referring when he says that Mr. Smith has rejected all possible terms for outside supervision. The position is as I stated it. We were proposing to act in the most constitutional way in accordance with the Constitution. We did not ask him to go and say to the Governor that he had sinned against the Constitution. We just wanted to authorise the Governor to say that since Rhodesia has no Prime Minister, or no Minister at all, the Governor on noting that vacuum should invite Mr. Smith to fill it on some of the conditions laid down. There was no outside supervision. The only outside supervision would have been, I think I am right in saying, the supervision of the test of acceptability of this proposition to the Rhodesian people as a whole, where Mr. Smith not only agreed, but suggested, that a Royal Commission should be appointed by Her Majesty's Government.

The only other element of supervision would have been the appointment by my noble Friend the Lord Chancellor of one member, and one member only, of a tribunal otherwise appointed by the legal Rhodesian Government to supervise the release from detention of detainees whom it was considered safe to release and who were not there on any criminal charge.

It is our intention that the mandatory sanctions should be effective. I hope to have a chance of saying—I am sorry, Mr. Speaker, but I think that it is important to say this—that we have now, in accordance with our undertaking, proceeded, or shall be proceeding, to move in the Security Council for selective mandatory sanctions against Rhodesia. I am confident that, given their accep tance by the Security Council, all members of the United Nations will fulfil their obligations and will loyally apply the sanctions in question. This does not involve any of the issues which have been the subject of recent public comment.

The first step is to lay down the effective sanctions. If, and it is entirely hypothetical, any country were to decide that it could not conform with the United Nations' decisions, this would create a new situation, which in due course would no doubt be raised. It has not been raised yet. It is not raised this week. But the House must be clear that at the Commonwealth conference I had the fullest support from and understanding of my colleagues, particularly leading African statesmen, that we are committed to selective sanctions against Rhodesia only.

Moreover, they agreed with us that not only must we proceed step by step—and this is a lengthy process—in dealing with this situation, but also, as we said, and they agreed, that this must not be allowed to develop—they understood this—into a confrontation whether economic or military involving the whole of Southern Africa. As the House will join my Commonwealth colleagues in recognising, such a confrontation, economic—and economic might lead to military—could have incalculable consequences for Southern and Central Africa going far beyond the issues raised by the Rhodesian problem. Indeed, as I told my Commonwealth colleagues, it could rapidly dwarf the Rhodesian problem, and nothing would ever be the same in Central Africa again, whether in Rhodesia or some of their own States. Certainly in these circumstances anyone in this House might predict the consequence that my Commonwealth colleagues accepted at this Conference, that in these matters we must continue to be in control of the situation.

Mr. ROBERT MAXWELL (Buckingham): Can my right hon. Friend say what rôle South Africa played in these negotiations? Does he expect South Africa to comply with selective mandatory sanctions? Further, can he tell the House, now that we have regrettably had to hand this matter over to the United Nations, whether the United Kingdom is to bear alone all the economic consequences of these sanctions, and what steps Her Majesty's Government propose to take to alleviate the cost of these sanctions, which are inevitable?

THE PRIME MINISTER: So far as South Africa's actions in the last few days are concerned, I have no direct knowledge of these. We have been in touch with a number of countries—both inside and outside the Commonwealth—which might be affected, but I have no knowledge of what action or line they have taken. As for the future, it is entirely hypothetical to assume that South Africa will or will not take a particular line.

As for the bearing of the burden by this country, the burden that we have been bearing has been exaggerated—perhaps rather damagingly from the point of view of the impact on Southern Rhodesia. I had to point out to Mr. Smith that we had lost about £35 million worth of direct exports over the last year—very serious, and we all regret this—but, on the other hand, our exports have risen by £350 million in total in world markets—so it is possible to exaggerate the effect—although I have left out particular invisibles and certain other things.

As for our bearing the whole burden of economic sanctions, the purpose of making them collective and universal is to ensure that some countries which have been quietly cashing in—or nationals of friendly Governments who have been quietly cashing in—will now have to conform with the general situation. More effective sanctions will be possible, and a much fairer sharing of the burden.

Mr. SANDYS (Streatham): The Prime Minister's statement is a very grave one. I should like him to clarify one point, which he stressed. He said that the proposal was to return to the 1961 Constitution and that there was no question of asking for agreement on direct Governor's rule. I cannot reconcile that with the Prime Minister's statement that during this period the Governor was to have complete legislative power and that the interim Government were to have purely advisory functions. That, surely, is direct Governor's rule. It is the normal kind of rule which comes about in a Colony before it is established with full internal self-government. I should like clarification on that point.

All I would say is that the Prime Minister has told us that there was— [*Interruption.*]

MR. SPEAKER: Order. I hope that the right hon. Gentleman will ask questions at this stage.

MR. SANDYS: I did not hear what you said, Mr. Speaker.

MR. SPEAKER: I asked the right hon. Gentleman if he would ask questions at this stage.

MR. SANDYS: On a point of order. I understood that we were on the Adjournment. I was making a very short speech. I can try to put it in the form of questions, but I did not think that it was necessary. Are we not on the Adjournment?

MR. SPEAKER: Do not let me take away valuable time. We are on the Adjournment, but I think that we get a much wider expression of opinion if we have a number of questions.

MR. SANDYS: Is the Prime Minister aware that he has told us that complete agreement was reached on the basis for a future constitution for Rhodesia which fully satisfied the six points? Does he realise that the British people will need a great deal of convincing that he was right to throw that away on account of disagreement over the procedure during the four months' interim period?

THE PRIME MINISTER: On the right hon. Gentleman's first question, the answer is, yes, it would be a return to the 1961 Constitution. Parts of that are already suspended by Orders approved by this House. We would have to reinstitute, for example, the power of the Governor to appoint the Prime Minister and other Ministers. The fact that there will be no Parliament is permissible under the 1961 Constitution. Parliament is currently in abeyance. Mr. Smith was rather keen on this as we were. The Governor would dissolve Parliament and within four months there must, under the Constitution, be an election. In those difficult circumstances it would be better for the broad-based Government not to have the particular Parliament which has been there up till now. This was no matter of controversy in H.M.S. "Tiger". It might be for the right hon. Gentleman, but if he is to the Right with Mr. Smith, he must get up and tell us.

That is the executive power. Regarding legislative power, it was thought it would not be likely that any legislation would be required during the period we are talking about. In case legislation was required—and I can see circumstances where it might be; for example, to deal with the work of the Royal Commission, the setting up of the Commission on tribunals, and things of that kind—we said we were prepared to clothe the Governor with legislative power by Order in Council approved by Parliament that the Governor, in exercise of that legislative power, would, apart from one or two exceptions, be advised by the legal 1961 Constitutional Government.

I think the right hon. Gentleman, when he studies this, will feel that it is, for all practical purposes, a return to the 1961 Constitution. We did insist that it should be a broad-based Government. I am sure the right hon. Gentleman would have done the same. He knows some of the personalities involved. We have to re-create trust and confidence in that country, including the trust and confidence of the vast proportion of the population who had no vote or voice in choosing the Government that committed U.D.I.

Regarding the second question of the right hon. Gentleman, he was trying to suggest that while we reached agreement, as basically we did, on the Constitution—Mr. Smith has said so, and so it would appear to be so—he said that we threw away the possibility of an agreement by insisting on the conduct that was required in the next four months. If the right hon. Gentleman treats so lightly the issue of the return to legality, which is a matter, however he may disguise it, in constitutional terms of rebellion against established authority—[An HON. MEMBER: "What is the penalty?"] It is not for me to apportion the penalty which he, if I may say so, with great distinction upheld for so many years at the Commonwealth Conference; if he now suggests it is a light matter that anyone taking account of it is throwing away a vital issue, he is sinking a long way from the position which he occupied only two years ago.

With his knowledge, and with my confirmation of that knowledge, he insisted with so much courage on these principles which we have been upholding, that for him to say that they could be carried out on the basis of an irresponsible illegal group of men who rejoice in their irresponsibility and illegality— [*Interruption*]—who have nothing to lose by accepting our invitation to return to legality, then I cannot understand the right hon. Gentleman's argument. The position was that I had the authority, the Governor had the authority, and Mr. Smith had the authority to accept this. Before he left H.M.S. "Tiger" on Saturday night, he could have accepted the Governor's invitation to become the Prime Minister of Rhodesia on the terms I have said. If the right hon. Gentleman says that on those terms I threw away the chance of a settlement, it means that the right hon. Gentleman has lost all sense either of the constitutional argument or of everything he has upheld as a Privy Councillor.

*Speech by a Labour M.P., Frank Allaun, in the House of Commons
on the Nigerian Civil War, 12 June 1968**

I would like to echo the last few words of the hon. Member for Roxburgh, Selkirk and Peebles (Mr. David Steel). In the war in Nigeria atrocities are being suffered by both sides, but even more devastating is the famine which is following in the wake of the war and affecting hundreds of thousands of men, women and children. The *Sun* this morning carried some photographs which most effectively brought home the results of this famine. These children may have black skins, but it hurts their parents as much as it would hurt us to see our children suffering in this way. The fighting in Nigeria may be thousands of miles away, but our Government have great influence in this sphere. And not only great influence. They are deeply involved, because so long as we are sending arms we are partly responsible for the bloodshed.

We are supplying 25 per cent. of the Federal Government's arms. This figure was given to me from an indisputable source. It is 25 per cent. and not 15 per cent., as has been said in some quarters. Even if it were only 1 per cent., it would be 1 per cent. too much for me. British Ferret vehicles are the main instrument of decimation. The whole traffic in arms is, as it has always been, an encouragement to war.

But my main point today is not to press for a unilateral stopping of arms supplies, even though I personally believe that this would be the best way to influence the four other countries who are mainly involved. My main object is to press Her Majesty's Government to get a collective arms ban, to take the initiative in approaching the other Governments to stop exports of arms, whether from Government or private sources.

There are powerful reasons for taking this course. First, it would end the mass slaughter which these modern weapons bring about. Secondly, it would put Britain in a position where she could be respected by both sides as a mediator—which is clearly impossible when she is arming the Federal Government. Thirdly, there are grounds for believing that if we took this lead the Russians, in particular, who are doing just the same as we are, would agree to stop their arms supplies, too, as Czechoslovakia and Holland have already done.

When I put a question on this to the Foreign Secretary at Question Time yesterday he replied that this might be done if it "would be agreeable to both sides".—[OFFICIAL REPORT, 11th June, 1968; Vol. 766, c. 37.] But the right hon. Gentleman knew very well that the Federal side would be unwilling to agree to a suspension of the arms traffic which gives it an overwhelming

*Hansard, 5.s., DCCLXVI, 262-66.

advantage. In other words, it would have to be done by the main suppliers of arms, whether or not it was welcomed with enthusiasm by either of the contending parties.

A fortnight ago I led an all-party deputation of Members of Parliament to the Secretary of State for Commonwealth Affairs, a man for whom I have great respect, a man of compassion and understanding with long experience in African matters. I wish that he could be here today, but we understand that a previous engagement made it impossible. His arguments on that occasion were so weak, so thin and so unconvincing that I left that interview with the view that he did not believe them himself and that he was rationalising to cover up for a policy decided earlier by the Government.

I do not like to say what I am about to allege. I am deeply suspicious that there is a most unworthy motive for our continuing to sell arms to the Federal Government and for our refusal to work for a collective ban. If I am wrong— and I only hope that I am—then I ask the Foreign Secretary immediately and categorically to deny that there is any truth in what I am saying. It is the suspicion that Her Majesty's Government believe that the Federal Government will win and that, as a result, they would be in a position to place big commercial orders in due course.

It is feared that if at any time Her Majesty's Government offended the Federal Government they might lose the chance of these orders—even if it is doing the wrong thing. It is also keeping in with the Federal Government because of British property interests in Nigeria. But humanity must come first, even before orders and property interests.

Oxfam would like it to be known that it is having great difficulty in getting desperately needed food supplies into Nigeria, especially into the area of fighting where starvation is rife. Only a little can be flown in, and at great cost. It urgently needs sea passage preferably through Port Harcourt. On humanitarian grounds alone, could not the British Government press for this free passage?

Lastly, I would make a comment on the British High Commissioner in Lagos. It would be unfair for a Member of Parliament to criticise a civil servant in this House, so I shall not do so. Instead, I shall lay the blame on the Foreign Secretary for allowing things to happen that should not have happened. I remind the House that, during the Crimean War, Lord Cardigan did not travel to the theatre of battle with his troops. He went on an extended cruise with his mistress, calling in at several ports on the Mediterranean on the way.

The British High Commissioner in Lagos has had two months' leave at this time, I understand, enjoying a holiday to which he is entitled. With his wife he spent a fortnight of his leave voyaging back to Nigeria by sea a few days ago. In my view, the Foreign Secretary should have told him in no uncertain manner to jump on the first plane to get back to his scene of duty.

Mr. John Lee: Is it not also true that the High Commissioner is married to a member of the Leventis family and very much tied up with the Federal Government?

MR. ALLAUN: I do not want to enter into that, but I think that the Foreign Secretary has been rather lacking in this matter.

My right hon. Friend the Member for Llanelly (Mr. James Griffiths) has put forward important suggestions for a solution of the problem. A very broad and important committee, of which Lord Brockway is a prominent member, has put forward four points for a solution which I have not time to go into now. The main and first point is that of a cease-fire.

Many hon. Members feel that the present policy of our Government in this matter is wrong and is prolonging and increasing the bloodshed. The purpose of this debate is to press the Government to change their policy. We will listen carefully to the Foreign Secretary's speech to hear whether there has been any effect of the speeches made from both sides of the House, any effect from the movement outside the House—whether there has been an effect in the direction for which we have asked. If not, I should like to back my words with my vote. That will largely depend on the reply by the Foreign Secretary.

Speech by the Foreign Secretary, Michael Stewart, in the House of Commons on the Nigerian Civil War, 12 June 1968

No one could have listened to this debate without being moved and without sharing the deep anxiety which has been expressed by every hon. Member who has spoken, some of whom have a detailed and intimate knowledge of the part of the world we have been discussing and the problems involved.

It would be true to say that, although there have been differences of view, there is very wide general agreement that the objectives of policy should be to stop the slaughter, to avert massacre and famine and to promote, as far as this country can promote, a settlement which would involve both the preservation of the unity of Nigeria and effective and certain assurances for the Ibo people.

This was a view that was expressed particularly by my right hon. Friend the Member for Llanelly (Mr. James Griffiths), the hon. Gentleman the Member for Liverpool, Wavertree (Mr. Tilney) and my hon. Friend the Member for Kingston upon Hull, West (Mr. James Johnson). It is against the background of a common desire for such a policy that we must approach this question.

I realise that hon. Members have said that we are specially concerned about the present, more than about the past and more than about what may lie in the future if the present situation can be led into more hopeful paths. But, so that the House may understand how the Government have approached the problem, it is essential to say something about the past history of it.

The immediate matter which my hon. Friend the Member for Brentford and Chiswick (Mr. Barnes) had in mind in asking for and securing this debate was

*Hansard, 5.s., DCCLXVI, 289–99.

that of the supply of arms. The question will naturally be asked, therefore: how did it come about that we were supplying arms at all to the Federal Government? It is important for a proper judgment of the question to see why that was so.

Before independence, it was natural that we were the traditional suppliers not only of arms, but of military training to Nigeria. She was heavily dependent on us, therefore, in all her defence arrangements. It was we who helped to bring forward Nigeria to independence, so that she took her place in the world as an independent State and was recognised as such by all Governments.

In view of that, I must maintain—though here I am at variance with some, but by no means all, hon. Members—that it would at any rate have been wrong at the outset of the secession for us to have cut off supplies completely from the Federal Government. That would have been to have said to a Government, in effect, "We have put you in a position where you are very heavily dependent on us for the instruments of power. Now, when you are faced by a challenge to your authority, we will put you at a very serious disadvantage." At that time, supplies from this country accounted for 75 per cent. of Nigeria's supplies of arms from all sources. The proportion of current supplies which we provide is, of course, very much less than that.

I do not think that one can avoid the conclusion that if we had taken that action it would have been, and would have been interpreted as being, giving in practice approval, and substantial practical help to the movement for secession.

Apart from my hon. Friend the Member for Kingston upon Hull, West and the hon. Member for Isle of Ely (Sir H. Legge-Bourke), not many hon. Members have stressed the great importance of the issue of secession not only in Nigeria but throughout Africa. It has been a difficulty facing many African States whose boundaries originally were drawn to meet the rivalries of European Powers rather than on any ethnological principle or principle of self-determination.

It has been difficult for such States to weld different tribes into one people. But I believe that African statesmanship expressing itself in the Organisation for African Unity, has been right to maintain the principle that African States should endeavour to weld different tribes into one nation and should regard as a counsel of despair that, whenever it is difficult to bring different tribes together in one nation, the remedy should be secession and disintegration. If that were accepted as a general principle, it would be a very dark outlook for the future of Africa as a whole.

I have laboured that point because, if we do not grasp it fully, we do not understand the attitude of the Federal Government to the question of secession. If we do not understand that, we put ourselves in a position where any actions that we might take are likely to fail in their effect.

I should make one other general point about the question of secession. If it were held right for what was once the Eastern Region of Nigeria to become the independent State of Biafra on the grounds that that is the wish of the Ibo people, is the same thing to be advanced by the very numerous non-Ibos living in the State of Biafra? Once the process of secession is admitted, there may be no end to it without tribal disintegration.

I believe that these considerations are weighty, and that is why I must disagree with some but not all hon. Members and maintain that Her Majesty's Government were right to decide that they could not and ought not to cut off supplies from the Federal Government when the secession began.

Clearly, the British Government would have failed in their duty if they had merely stood there. In view of our past connection, and as a matter of common humanity, we had a duty also to do what we could to help towards a peaceful settlement and, as an essential part of it, to try to remove the understandable fears of the Ibo people.

May I give the House a brief record of what the Government have been doing? In January, 1967, there was the little noticed and inadequately praised work of Mr. Malcolm MacDonald which led to the meeting at Aburi, in Ghana. It has been one of the tragedies of this story that the undertakings entered into at that meeting were given different interpretations by both sides and did not come into effect. But that does not lessen the value and merit of what Mr. MacDonald did, with the Government's support and approval.

Then, throughout the period between March and May, 1967, to which several hon. Members have referred and which has been the subject of some criticism of the Government's attitude, the Government were counselling restraint, a renewal of negotiations between the two parties and, above all, the settlement of the dispute by peaceful means. Indeed, it was during this period that the Federal Government floated the idea that we should guarantee the security of a neutral place in Nigeria at which the leaders could meet. Unhappily, that idea came to nothing, because it was vetoed by Colonel Ojukwu. But, at this point, London was speaking and Lagos was listening. I cannot accept the suggestion that during this period we were failing in our duty or that a deaf ear was turned to us in Lagos. Unhappily, that idea was not acceptable to Colonel Ojukwu.

When the secession occurred in May, 1967, although we could not recognise what claimed to be the independent State of Biafra none the less, in order to make it clear that we were not taking merely a barren legalistic view but wanted to maintain contact despite the fact that we could not recognise Biafra, our Deputy High Commissioner, Mr. Parker, remained at Enugu until the action of the Biafrans in interfering with his communications and molesting his staff made it impossible for him to stay there any longer.

Throughout the autumn and winter of 1967 we gave full support to the work of Mr. Arnold Smith which has been praised by more than one hon. Member during this debate. Despite his efforts, when it appeared that there was not to be any meeting or progress, in April, 1968, my right hon. Friend the Prime Minister took the initiative with Dr. Arikpo, the Federal Commissioner for External Affairs. There was a meeting between Dr. Arikpo, my right hon. Friend the Prime Minister and my right hon. Friend the Commonwealth Secretary, and that helped to make possible the start of talks at Kampala.

The Kampala talks are now—some hon. Members have said broken down—I hope in a state of suspense, but until recently our main hopes for success were in those Kampala talks, and the fact that they were being held at all was due to the efforts which Her Majesty's Government made during the period that I have described. These talks may well be resumed through the talks my right hon. and noble Friend, Lord Shepherd, is now having and will be resuming at the end of this week with the leading figures on both sides.

I thought it right to set out that record so as to make clear that the Government have not been idle during this period. Indeed, it is not an exaggeration to say that in every field in which there has been any approach to, or hope of settlement, it has been our action which has pushed things forward, and any hopes there are of settlement spring in the main from action which we have taken.

I must add to that that if we had taken a decision to cut off the supply of arms to the Federal Government none of those actions could have been taken and we should probably not even have the Kampala talks and the possibility of a resumption of them which we now have. I thought it right to set out those facts from the past.

We must turn now to what is in the minds of so many hon. Members, which was foreshadowed yesterday by a Question put to me by the right hon. Gentleman the Member for Barnet (Mr. Maudling) when he suggested in column 36 of yesterday's HANSARD, that the Government should reconsider their policy on this point—that is the point of the supply of arms—when dangers of massive slaughter appeared to be brooding on the scene, and the same thought was put again emphatically in the speech just made by the right hon. Gentleman the Member for Kinross and West Perthshire (Sir Alec Douglas-Home), when he emphasised what the feeling would be throughout the world if, at this juncture, there were a massacre of the Ibo people, and, in particular, what feeling there would be in this country knowing that we are one of the suppliers of arms to the Federal Government. This one must take into account.

If we make the supposition that it were the intention of the Federal Government not merely to preserve the unity of Nigeria but to proceed without mercy either with the slaughter or the starvation of the Ibo people, or if we were to make the supposition that it were the intention of the Federal Government to take advantage of a military situation in order to throw aside with contempt any terms of reasonable settlement, then the arguments which justified the policy we have so far pursued would fall, and we would have to reconsider, and more than reconsider, the action we have so far taken.

In that sense I do, as the hon. Member for Roxburgh, Selkirk and Peebles (Mr. David Steel) asked me to do, take into account—and I give that phrase the same seriousness and weight as he did—the facts, the evidence and the feelings that have been expressed by so many hon. Members during this debate.

But it is fortunately a supposition that the Federal Government would behave in that manner. It would not be right to treat that supposition as if it were a fact and for me to declare now that it is our policy to stop supplies. I notice that throughout the debate there were many hon. Members who did not want me or urge me to take that rigid and unconditional step.

This is the proposition that I want to put before the House and I shall give certain further reasons why I believe it is the right proposition. As I said, we should reconsider, and more than reconsider, the policy, but I do not believe that it would be right now to treat that supposition as a fact. Indeed, as I shall show there are substantial reasons for not doing so. It is perhaps invidious to single out particular hon. Members in a debate that has been so distinguished by the quality of all the speeches made in it, but I noticed that some hon. Members who spoke most movingly and with great knowledge of the subject refrained from asking me to take what I have called that rigid and unconditional step. I think that they were right, particularly as there are better hopes and possibilities than the grim supposition which I made a little while ago.

MR. FRANK ALLAUN: It is true that nobody asked for unilateral action. Is the objection which my right hon. Friend is now taking to immediate action against collective action by suppliers of arms?

MR. STEWART: I am coming to that point. I wanted to draw the attention of the House to some of what I call the better hopes and possibilities.

What should be the object of our policy—cease-fire, unity of Nigeria, the complete assurance of safety for the Ibo people so that they shall feel delivered from what my right hon. Friend the Member for Llanelly called the terrible choice that they feel sometimes faces them, either to die fighting or to die passively? I do not underestimate the difficulty of reconciling the three objectives of stopping the slaughter, of holding Nigeria together and of giving effective and decisive assurance to the Ibo people, and I think the House will understand that it is not possible for the British Government to set out a blueprint as to how all this should be reconciled or what the terms of settlement can be.

We have offered and continued to offer our good offices, but we are not and should not be accepted as an arbitrator or a mediator. It would be absurd to try and set out a blueprint for a settlement, but there are some matters that bear on the settlement that are worth mentioning and that link with the speech of the right hon. Gentleman who preceded me.

Assurance to the Ibo peoples is bound to involve, in my judgment, some kind of international force to give them some degree of security. Indeed, it is interesting and encouraging to note that at one point General Gowon suggested that part of a settlement could be—I think that he used this term—an international observer force to see that if there were a cease-fire, the Ibos were not impossibly at a disadvantage.

The right hon. Member for Kinross and West Perthshire spoke of a Commonwealth police force. The House will understand that we could not impose such a force except with the consent of the two sides. We have, of course, examined the sheer practicalities of such a thing and I believe, now that discussions are actually going on, that this is one of the matters for which, if consent could be got, we should work as steadily as we can.

The only word of caution I must give is that we cannot impose anything. We are not invited or authorised to act as arbitrators here. We seek with all the resource and imagination we can summon, and with the help, as in this debate, of the collective wisdom of the House, whatever means may bring a settlement, and it is our job to see if we can get the parties concerned to agree to it. It is in that sense necessarily qualified—I hope that the right hon. Gentleman will feel not unnecessarily qualified—that I accept his suggestion.

I now wish to mention a recent statement by Colonel Ojukwu in which he put forward a proposal for an embargo on the supply of arms all round on both sides. It is in this connection that I wish to take up the question of international action to get a cessation of supplies all round. My hon. Friend the Member for Salford, East (Mr. Frank Allaun) intervened about this and the right hon. Member for Kinross and West Perthshire stressed it. I must tell the House that the practical difficulties of getting such an agreement would be very great indeed. In many cases, of course, supplies to both sides are not direct governmental supplies; the action taken by a government is often simply that of permitting, or of not bothering to stop, supplies being sent by private suppliers.

One would, therefore, be dealing with a very wide range of people concerned in this, and to make it effective one would have to require all the Governments concerned, not merely that they should pass some law, or issue some fiats, but that they should be continually active to see that their prohibition on the sending of arms to either side by their subjects was obeyed. I am sorry to have to tell the House that my estimate of the possibilities of reaching agreement on this is not as optimistic as that of my hon. Friend the Member for Salford, East.

When I say that we will look again at this, I would be misleading the House if I said it in a way which gave the impression that it only needs a round of diplomatic activity to get the result. I am afraid that the practical difficulties would be much greater than is sometimes supposed and that there would be the complication that since the sources of supply to the Biafrans are far more—if I may use this word—miscellaneous than those which go to Nigeria, it would perhaps be all too easy to work out an international agreement that would be imperfectly administered and the effect of which would be totally one-sided in operation.

I have, therefore, considered whether one could possibly make this effective by working at the other end; by getting not so much a universal refusal to supply as an effective agreement by both sides not to receive. It is in this connection that Colonel Ojukwu's statement is interesting. It was made very recently and we will have to study it to see if progress can be made on those lines.

MR. J. J. MENDELSON (Penistone): In view of what my right hon. Friend said earlier about the great fear that there might be a massacre of the Ibo people, and of what he said following that, about any action along the lines of an international force depending on the agreement and approval of the two sides, can he not go further and say firmly to the Federal Government that unless they accept a policy of such an international force to ensure that there will not be such a massacre, Her Majesty's Government will not continue with their present policy?

MR. STEWART: In the light of what has been said in the House, it will be entirely right for us to draw the attention of the Federal Government to what feeling is here and to what not only this House but humanity expect of them. However, I do not think that I should tie myself to particular items like that at a time when discussion with the Federal Government is actually going on and I do not think that I could say more than that I note and sympathise with what my hon. Friend has said.

Having mentioned the statement made by Colonel Ojukwu I should also mention certain words and actions by General Gowon which, I think, may put the Federal Government in a more favourable light than some hon. Members were prepared to view them. I believe that we all know that if we start retailing all the fearful happenings in this war, there is much with which both sides and many individuals will feel that they must reproach themselves.

The words and actions of General Gowon to which I draw the attention of the House are these. He has made it clear that he does not desire to invade the Biafran heartlands and that he will try to avoid that step. The Federal Government are not, as it were, poised for an immediate advance upon and destruction of the Ibo people. Next, he has put forward the concept—I referred to this earlier—of an international—I do not think his use of the word would rule out Commonwealth—observer force for the security of the Ibos.

I wish next to mention the action which he has taken on the question of Red Cross supplies and food, in which my right hon. Friend the Member for Llanelly, the right hon. Member for Kinross and West Perthshire and others expressed interest. General Gowon has assured the International Red Cross of the willingness of his Government to accept deliveries of Red Cross supplies to Enugu, Port Harcourt or any other airport under Federal control for onward transport by road to an agreed point in Biafran-controlled territory, to be decided with the Biafran authorities.

The International Committee of the Red Cross has expressed its satisfaction with this proposal as being the best practical means of delivering bulk supplies where they are most needed and it is engaged at present in obtaining the agreement of the Biafran authorities. General Gowon has also offered to supply transport and any assistance the Red Cross might need. This, I think, answers the question which the right hon. Member for Kinross and West Perthshire put. It is important because this is a question not only of medical supplies but of food supplies and of doing what can be done, I wish I could say to avert hunger, but at least to reduce and mitigate it.

MR. DAVID WINNICK (Croydon, South): Arising from my right hon. Friend's statement about the prospect of Red Cross supplies being able to get through, would it be possible for Her Majesty's Government to make additional supplies available, bearing in mind the number of men, women and children who are starving in this war? In other words, will the Government be able to lay on special plans to provide food which is urgently needed by these people?

MR. STEWART: We have already made a gift to the Red Cross for this purpose and I hope—I speak without commitment—that we may be able to do more than that.

I must now return for a few moments to the arguable side of the matter. I would ask the House to believe, in the light of what I have just said about the attitude of General Gowon and of the possibilities—and I would not put it more highly than that—there are of reaching an agreed settlement, that if we were now, particularly in the light of what has been said by General Gowon recently in connection with the Red Cross, to reply by taking the action of stopping arms supplies, that could, I believe, have no other result at present than an estrangement between us and the Federal Government in which the actual power of the Federal Government to do evil if they wished would in no way be lessened; for we are only one among many suppliers, and their will to do good might well be weakened if they received at this stage a rebuff of this kind.

There are not only three possibilities. There are also the contracts to which these possibilities might be turned into facts. The purpose of the talks which my right hon. and noble Friend Lord Shepherd has been having and will shortly be resuming is to make it easier to get back to the real conversations at Kampala. Those lines of contact are still open and my right hon. Friend the Prime Minister and myself will be meeting Chief Enahoro immediately after the conclusion of this debate. I hope that the House will believe that the Government have not dealt with this matter without understanding or compassion. But if we have not on all points been able to satisfy some hon. Members, this has not been due to ignorance of the problem. Certainly, it has not been due to lack of feeling or lack of desire to end the war and to avert the fearful danger which some hon. Members have foreseen and dreaded.

I would hope in the light of this, as the right hon. Gentleman has suggested, that the House might be prepared to leave the matter there, conscious that thanks to the initiative of my hon. Friend the Member for Brentford and Chicwick there has been this opportunity to see that the Government are fully and clearly informed of the wishes of the House.

*Statement by Harold Wilson in the House of Commons on the
Negotiations with the Rhodesian Government Held Aboard
H.M.S. "Fearless", 15 October 1968*

With permission, Mr. Speaker, I should like to make a statement on the talks
about Rhodesia which were held on board H.M.S. "Fearless" in Gibraltar from
9th to 13th October.

First, I should like briefly to mention the events which led the Government to
conclude that it would be right to have such a meeting.

As my right hon. Friend the Commonwealth Secretary and I myself have
repeatedly made clear in the House, we were prepared at any time to engage in
discussions if it seemed that there might be a chance of a settlement and
provided it were understood that such a settlement must fully implement the
requirements of the six principles which have been laid down.

As the House knows, I have more than once before the Recess expressed the
doubt whether, even if Mr. Smith's position changed sufficiently markedly to
make talks worth while, there could be any guarantee that any agreement
initialled by him would be endorsed by his colleagues. During the Recess there
were changes in the membership of his régime, involving the disappearance of
intransigent racialists, and we have also had evidence of the firmness with
which he dealt with his party congress last month. Hon. Members will also have
noted the régime's decision to introduce measures designed to end mandatory
death sentences for certain offences. At the same time, reliable reports reached
us that Mr. Smith would be prepared to enter into meaningful talks.

Accordingly, an Assistant Under-Secretary of State in the Commonwealth
Office was sent to Salisbury on 20th September. He had discussions, first, with
His Excellency the Governor of Rhodesia and the Head of the British Residual
Mission; and, secondly, under the aegis of the Governor, with Mr. Ian Smith. In
addition, he had discussions with other Rhodesians of different races, occupa-
tions and political views who asked to meet him.

On his return to London he reported that he found a widespread feeling in
Salisbury that the recent changes in the political climate there offered some
prospect that a fresh attempt to achieve a settlement might be successful. At
the same time, however, he reported that Mr. Smith had not given him any
indication of a change of position on the fundamental issues which have over
these past five years made agreement impossible. This was particularly the case
in relation to certain non-negotiable requirements on which any British Government must insist as the condition of a settlement. Mr. Smith had expressed his
readiness, however, for an early meeting.

Hansard, 5.s., DCCLXX, 207–23.

Further probings were conducted under the Governor's aegis by the Head of the British Residual Mission. We insisted that Mr. Smith should fully understand that, if talks were to be held, there could be no concessions by us which would undermine or weaken the six principles. We insisted, also, that Mr. Smith should confirm that he understood this. He did, in fact, give this confirmation, at the same time indicating that he, in turn, regarded certain matters as of fundamental importance to himself and to those he represented. Despite this re-affirmation of his own position on the six principles, it nevertheless seemed reasonable to assume that he would be unlikely, before coming to the conference table, to show his negotiating hand, and, in particular, to indicate any concessions he was ready to make.

Accordingly, we met at Gibraltar. On the British side, I was accompanied by my right hon. Friend the Commonwealth Secretary and my right hon. and learned Friend the Attorney-General. On the Rhodesian side, were Mr. Ian Smith, Mr. Howman and Mr. Lardner Burke. The Governor of Rhodesia was present in Gibraltar for the duration of the talks.

It would not be helpful to go over the hard-hitting exchanges in 30 hours of talks except to record that they confirmed that there was and remains a deep difference between the two sides, not only on the requirements for a settlement, but even more on the basic political philosophies which underlie the attitudes expressed. At the same time the talks were conducted in a good atmosphere, having regard to all the circumstances, and within the limitations created by the fundamental differences to which I have referred.

By Saturday night, 12th October, it was clear to both sides that it was unlikely that a settlement would be reached on board H.M.S. "Fearless"—and that this would become no more likely if the discussions lasted several more days. I decided, with Mr. Smith's agreement, to prepare a statement setting out our proposals for a settlement of the Rhodesian dispute.

This statement took account so far as was possible of points made in the discussions. I made clear to Mr. Smith that while there could be no change in the British Government's attitude on the fundamental issues, on other matters there could be further discussion; and that, of course, we should be ready to consider alternative drafts on these non-fundamental matters.

The Government have set out in a White Paper the text of the British statement and the text of the communiqué which was issued in agreement between the two sides. The White Paper also includes yet again the text of the six principles, since we have made it clear before, throughout and since the discussions that there could be no agreement except on the basis of those principles.

The proposals which I gave to Mr. Smith on 13th October incorporate the changes to the 1961 Constitution which were worked out on board H.M.S. "Tiger". In certain cases these changes have been set out with greater precision, particularly as regards the powers of the Senate and the circumstances in which appeals would lie to the Judicial Committee of the Privy Council—the instrument which, in our view, is the best fitted to provide the reinforcement required to guarantee the fulfilment of the second principle. While, no doubt, alternative instruments to this end could be proposed and considered, I am sure hon. Members would agree that the Judicial Committee would provide the most effective guarantee.

The changes suggested in the 1961 Constitution were, and are, designed to meet the first, second, third and sixth principles. The statement makes clear that, provided that there is at all times a "blocking quarter" of directly and popularly elected Africans as a safeguard against retrogressive amendment of the Constitution, the British Government do not insist on any particular composition for the legislature.

The statement further sets out the basis on which the Government would be prepared to accept, as part of an otherwise satisfactory settlement, new procedures to deal with the problem of the return to legality.

Finally, I would draw attention to three further important features of our proposals. First, and this reinforces the "Tiger" proposals relating to the fourth principle, is our insistence on the importance of a vigorous and extended programme for African education, particularly in technical education, including agriculture. We have said that we would be prepared to contribute to this programme a sum of up to £50 million spread over 10 years on a £-for-£ basis. We regard this as imperative in the interests of the African population and of Rhodesia: it would also have an important bearing on the number of Africans able to qualify for the A Roll franchise. Secondly, arising out of our discussions, we have included the proposal that the Royal Commission to be appointed for testing the acceptability of any settlement to the Rhodesian people as a whole, should be instructed also to inquire into the arrangements for the registration of eligible voters under the widely extended franchise which is proposed, with a view to encouraging greater African participation in Rhodesian political life. Thirdly, the House will note what has been said about the need for a broad-based Government, including Africans, to carry Rhodesia through the whole process of introducing the new Constitution, right up to the election of a new Parliament under that Constitution.

The House will recognise the relevance of these three proposals, as well as certain other events, to the creation of the "substantial change of circumstances" which repeatedly I have said in this House must exist to justify our raising with our Commonwealth partners the question of "no independence before majority rule".

And the House will recognise, too, that we will not agree to the implementation of any settlement that has not first been shown to be acceptable to the people of Rhodesia as a whole—the fifth principle, on which all else depends.

As was stated in the communiqué, Mr. Smith said that he would take the British Government's proposals back to Salisbury, without commitment, for consideration with his colleagues there. I said that the Commonwealth Secretary will be available to fly out to Salisbury if Mr. Smith and his colleagues feel that this would assist them in their consideration of the British proposals. Our position at the end of the talks, as throughout these past years, maintains the position repeatedly stated by the Commonwealth Secretary—no sell-out, no slamming the door by us.

We have insisted that our proposals have to be taken as a whole. Any concessions we have been prepared to offer on matters which do not involve the safeguards required for the six principles are available only as part of an agreement which incorporates the clear guarantees on which we have insisted to safeguard those principles. Now, decisions have to be taken in Salisbury. We for our part are keeping the door open. But the key to a settlement is, and must remain, the six principles, which are cardinal to the future of Rhodesia—the future of Rhodesians of all races, for whom the British Parliament stands trustee.

MR. HEATH: The House has heard with regret that it was not possible to reach a settlement during the talks in H.M.S. "Fearless", but we are glad that, as I understand, the talks have not been broken off and that the Commonwealth Secretary stands ready to resume them whenever Mr. Smith and his colleagues wish.

At the same time, I think that the House would feel that there were encouraging features about the talks—the fact that the atmosphere and conduct of the talks generally was so much better than on the previous occasion and that the Prime Minister was able to discuss the question of moving on to a new constitutional legality rather than going back to the old, and to explain the circumstances in which Nibmar would no longer be the policy.

We shall, of course, want to consider the White Paper carefully and perhaps I could suggest to the Prime Minister that we might have a debate on this matter when hon. Members have had a chance of studying the White Paper. We could, perhaps, discuss the timing of the debate through the usual channels to take account of any movements of the Commonwealth Secretary which he may want to make in response to Salisbury.

Secondly, during the debate, if it is not set out in the White Paper, could the Prime Minister explain to us the different means and methods which were discussed of implementing the first and second principles against regression and to ensure movement towards African rule and the part which the Privy Council would play in this matter, and the arguments that were put up against them? To have a debate, we would like to know what were the detailed proposals and the various arguments so that we could weigh the balance.

THE PRIME MINISTER: On the early part of the right hon. Gentleman's question, when he set out his understanding of the position, may I say that the way he expressed it exactly corresponds to the facts as I see them to be today.

Obviously, the House will wish to debate this whole matter. It should, as the right hon. Gentleman suggests, be discussed through the usual channels with a view to finding a convenient time for all hon. Members. It would probably be convenient if this were associated with the debate which is required at this time of the year, in the event of any substantial change in the situation, in relation to the Southern Rhodesia Order, which has to come before both Houses.

In reply to the other point raised by the right hon. Gentleman, I will certainly consider what more explanation can be given. The White Paper which is now available in the Vote Office, or should be at about this time, deals in some detail with our proposals. It sets out in full what were our proposals to Mr. Smith and I think that the right hon. Gentleman will find some information there. He is quite right, if I may say so, in putting his question in a form which links the first and second principles together. They are closely connected, and, right through, all British Governments have insisted that there should be guaranteed, unimpeded progress, and no regressive amendment of the Constitution. We have since that time, when my predecessors were responsible, sought to get guarantees both by internal mechanisms such as the blocking quarter and by external mechanisms.

I think the right hon. Gentleman once suggested a treaty which we discussed on the "Tiger" and, of course, the rôle of the Privy Council as the highest court in construing Rhodesian affairs. I think that one really needs a double-barrelled means of giving the guarantees required for the first two principles. I will not disguise from the House that this has been by far the most difficult of the many difficult problems we had aboard "Fearless". Great progress was certainly made; encouraging progress was made; but I would be misleading the House if I suggested that at the end of the day we had reached an agreement on adequate, copper-bottomed guarantees which would ensure there would be no regressive amendment of the Constitution.

MR. WINNICK: Since the Rhodesian Front believes in maintaining and extending racialism in Rhodesia, is there any possibility at all of an honourable, negotiated settlement between Britain and the illegal régime? Is the Prime Minister aware that many people in the country, and certainly in the Labour movement, would rather see an intensification of sanctions than continuing concessions and talks with the régime which bases itself more on the principles of racial supremacy than on the six principles?

THE PRIME MINISTER: There have been no concessions to the régime. What we have done is to indicate the kind of concession we will be ready to make as part of an overall settlement which could end the five or six years of very unhappy relations between the two countries, the last three of which have been additionally clouded by the illegality of the action taken three years ago.

Of course we deeply deplore—and they understand this—many of the actions taken. At the same time, we should, I think, note that there have been one or two recent moves in the right direction. I have mentioned one piece of legislation they are introducing. In the past year there have been one or two moves of a regressive character. We have to take all these things together before deciding whether to talk.

We have always said that we need sanctions on the basis and to the extent that they carry home a message to the people of Rhodesia that will put them in a position where they will be more willing to talk. We have seen willingness, but have not yet bridged the gap between us.

MR. THORPE: While the whole House and the whole country would welcome an honourable settlement of this issue, may I ask whether the right hon. Gentleman is aware that many of us feel that in the interests of a durable solution we should prefer him to come back without a settlement rather than with an agreement which involved jettisoning any of the six principles involved? Would he confirm that the last 30 hours proved that continuous calls for talks are not in themselves a substitute for a policy still less a solution to the problem?

May I also ask the right hon. Gentleman whether this is an indication that there is likely to be an acceptance in principle by Mr. Smith, but not in detail, to consider the possibility of a joint working party being set up, bearing in mind all the publicity which is attached to the visit of a Cabinet Minister, and the difficulty, thereby, of getting down to close, detailed negotiations?

THE PRIME MINISTER: I thank the right hon. Gentleman for the way in which he began his question. There never was, and, throughout these discussions, equally there has not been, any suggestion of an agreement which was not four-square within the six principles. This was fully understood.

With regard to future progress, I think we must now wait to see what Mr. Smith and his colleagues say. The Commonwealth Secretary stands ready to go out there. This may be necessary and I would very much welcome it if this were agreed. There will be a need for a joint working party. This has been proposed, and following any settlement there would have to be a joint working party to work out details of the constitution. But we have said to Mr. Smith that this statement on these fundamental issues represents our conception of what would be reasonable in the light of our talks last week. We would obviously be prepared to consider alternative drafts.

MR. WHITAKER: As Mr. Smith is reported to have accepted the constitutional part of the "Tiger" proposals, how is it that he objects to the first two of the six principles now? Secondly, as a test of his sincerity is he prepared to accept the offer of help with African education immediately and in any event?

THE PRIME MINISTER: It is not for me, I think, to explain to the House exactly the arguments by which Mr. Smith reaches certain conclusions. It is the fact, of course, that he does not like the six principles. He has never pretended to do so. It is also a fact that he does not like the prospect of majority rule in the foreseeable future. He is, however, sufficiently realistic to recognise that there will be no agreement with any British Government of any party that does not give effect to the six principles.

In these circumstances, it is a question how far he is prepared to stomach the repugnance which is involved in our proposals to get a settlement which will be of great value to Rhodesia and to Rhodesians and which will also help to avert the very great dangers which are lurking in the fairly near future. Some of the dangers, of course, result from the measures of his own régime and are at present in cold storage, awaiting application.

It could well be said that the acceptance of a crash programme of African education would be a good test of sincerity. That was not the only reason we put it forward. I was reasonably encouraged by the attitude on this question.

Another matter to which I drew attention in my statement is the question of a crash programme for registration, because under these proposals there will be up to 1 million Africans enfranchised on the B Roll. Very few of these already registered are enfranchised. We have, therefore, to provide machinery for ensuring what can be done to speed up registration of any African who would like to have the vote, and is entitled to it.

MR. WALL: While congratulating the Prime Minister on the businesslike conduct of the negotiations, may I ask him when he expects a full report from Salisbury on the two questions of the first and second principles.

On the question of educational aid, would he not agree there is also need for economic aid since there is not much good in training people if there are not jobs for them to go to?

THE PRIME MINISTER: On the first question, I cannot say when we expect the reply. I made it clear that we are not pressing Mr. Smith for undue haste. We would rather wait for the right reply, and we would rather have the right reply than speed. There are many difficulties before him and we recognise that. It is not just the reply on the first of the six principles on which some progress, but not enough, was made. It is a reply to the document as a whole. I do not know when that will be. It may be that he will wish to accept my suggestion that my right hon. Friend should go out there before he even forwards a complete reply.

Education is, of course, very important, and it is equally important that there should be jobs for Africans when they are trained and that they should be available on a non-discriminatory basis as between colour and as between races. The biggest impediment, of course, to the expansion of Rhodesian industry and to development of a country of such rich resources—what has been holding it back for three years—has been the existence of the illegal régime and the fact that it is the centre of great international controversy. This was what we were trying to put right last week.

MR. JAMES JOHNSON: While welcoming the Prime Minister's Herculean efforts to get an honourable settlement, may I ask would he not accept the fact that in African history the white community, whether French or English people, have not willingly given up their economic or political privileges? Therefore, what basis has the Prime Minister for thinking that a referendum of Rhodesian white people would not give support to action taken by Mr. Smith now?

THE PRIME MINISTER: I think that that is too gloomy a view of the situation. I have been encouraged. My right hon. Friend the Member for Kettering (Sir G. de Freitas) has already talked to the House about the situation in Kenya following the transfer of power, which we have always said could be an encouragement to Europeans in Rhodesia. I agree that it will not be easy for them. Anyone who saw the television interviews with some allegedly represen-tative Rhodesians last night will not be very encouraged.

The people of Rhodesia will have to recognise the great value to Rhodesia of a settlement and all that follows from it, including the end of sanctions, and they will have to decide whether they are prepared to pay the price. We believe that the price they insist on is totally wrong. We reject the racialist views so often expressed. They will have to decide whether to surrender those racialist views in order to get a settlement.

SIR T. BEAMISH: Since any constitutional settlement must be based on the good faith of both signatories, will the Prime Minister take careful account of the fact that independence qualified by a leading rein for the Privy Council would be unrealistic and a paradox? Will he at any rate give the House an assurance that this is not what he described in his statement as one of the non-negotiable requirements?

THE PRIME MINISTER: I said that the question of the blocking quarter and some guarantee other than the vote in the Rhodesian Parliament are both required to give effect to the first and second principles. I would not call it a leading rein. The hon. and gallant Member will notice, when he reads the White Paper, that in our proposals for an external guarantee we are ready to put a limited term of years upon it. We want to see this question go through the very difficult period of the movement that has to be undertaken by Rhodesia over the next few years if there is to be a settlement.

The hon. and gallant Member will recognise that any discussions such as those last week which could lead to the grant of independence without prior majority rule would be totally unprecedented in the lifetime of any of us in this House. Therefore, in so far as it is unique, to that extent it carries with it great dangers, especially after the controversies inside and about Rhodesia, and I hope that he would agree, on consideration, that with this unique agreement an extra guarantee might well be required.

MR. HECTOR HUGHES: As the constitutional problems involved affect the Commonwealth as a whole, will my right hon. Friend consider summoning or inviting a Commonwealth conference, so as to bring the weight of the whole Commonwealth to a solution of these problems?

THE PRIME MINISTER: Before I announced that we were going to Gibraltar, my right hon. Friend's Department discussed this with the High Commissioners in London and I think that my right hon. Friend has arranged for them to be fully informed about what has happened since our return. In addition, I was in touch with a great number of Commonwealth Prime Ministers during the talks. As the House knows, a number of my right hon. Friends inside the Government and senior officials were entrusted with the job of discussing this with the Commonwealth Prime Ministers and Presidents while actually in Gibraltar. Further, as he knows, there is to be a Commonwealth Prime Ministers' confer-ence in a few weeks' time.

MR. EDWARD M. TAYLOR: If agreement is reached will the Government remove sanctions forthwith? What will be the position with respect to mandatory sanctions if the United Nations does not give any such agreement its blessing?

THE PRIME MINISTER: I am sure that the hon. Gentleman will want to study the White Paper on this point. The linking of the agreement with a settlement, together with the carrying through of the acceptability test by the Royal Commission, is linked with the beginning of the dismantling of sanctions. The question of sanctions arises when these things have been done and there is agreement on the Constitution. We have been carefully into the position of the United Nations. I do not want to make things more difficult, but I do not foresee the difficulties that the hon. Member has referred to.

MR. PAGET: Is my right hon. Friend aware that while I have been critical of the Rhodesia policy in the past, on this occasion, in respect of the manner, the patience, the courtesy, the friendliness, and the sticking point, which is a matter of principle and not legalistic, and also the educational proposals, linked with economic development, my right hon. Friend has my most wholehearted support?

I would like to say to those in Rhodesia that in my view, at any rate, no British Government of any party who wish for continued co-operation between our two countries can offer substantially better terms than these. The South African alternative will be unhappy in the short run and unworkable in the long run.

THE PRIME MINISTER: I should like to thank my hon. and learned Friend both for the tone and the manner of what he said at the opening of his question, and for the wise advice which he is seeking in his last few words to pass on to the people of Rhodesia.

There may have been—there have been—deep differences in the past on this question, but I think that my hon. and learned Friend is right in saying—and I think that the Rhodesians understand—that there is no good now in their trying to play on differences, real or imagined, between the parties in this House or between individuals within any given party. They now have a chance of an honourable settlement. It remains open, and this is giving them plenty of time to consider the position. We all hope that they will accept.

MR. HASTINGS: How does one appeal to the Privy Council after a possible settlement? Can the Prime Minister say whether this proposal was known to Mr. Smith before the talks began? Are there precedents for such an arrangement with any other independent Commonwealth country?

THE PRIME MINISTER: Was it the Privy Council to which the hon. Member was referring?

MR. HASTINGS: Yes.

THE PRIME MINISTER: Yes—because the Privy Council was in the "Tiger" proposals, so was the external treaty between ourselves and Rhodesia. That was with or without other countries guaranteeing it. There was no question of this being new to Mr. Smith. In the visit of the Commonwealth Office official, as well as in the probings which followed his return, this was highlighted as one of the essential matters on which a settlement would have to be reached.

SIR DINGLE FOOT: Did my right hon. Friend and his colleagues represent to Mr. Smith the great importance of immediately releasing those African leaders who represent far more Rhodesians than does Mr. Smith and who have been locked up without trial for the last four years?

THE PRIME MINISTER: As my right hon. and learned Friend will be aware, both in the "Tiger" proposals and in the new document there is provision for the problem of those in detention and those under restriction. We have emphasised throughout, both in our talks on various occasions and in this House, that the test of acceptability could not be a real test unless there were proper machinery for dealing with the problem of detainees and the freedom of expression in Rhodesia during that period. Compared with "Tiger", censorship has been abolished and there will have to be—and I think there would be—a reasonable allocation of broadcasting time and other means for putting different points of view about the acceptability or otherwise of a constitution.

MR. RONALD BELL: Since all the six principles are conditions laid down by the British Government for agreement, and not moral principles, is the Prime Minister satisfied that it is wise to place such emphasis on the two conditions about movement to majority rule when so little use is made by the independent countries of Africa of that system of Government?

THE PRIME MINISTER: A proposal under the first or second principle for a blocking quarter is not a moral principle; it is a technique to give effect to essential principles which themselves derive from the moral attitude of every party in this House. The six principles which have been worked out jointly over the years by successive Governments and endorsed by all parties in this House are an attempt to give practical expression, in constitutional terms, to deeply-held moral principles. I do not disguise the deep differences between Mr. Smith and ourselves on the moral principles which underlie the constitutional techniques. That is why I have said that however repugnant to them it is, it is essential that they should stomach their repugnance and accept these proposals because that is the only way to reach a settlement.

MR. JUDD: Does not my right hon. Friend agree that by definition independence implies that a country is in a position to do what it wishes with its constitution, and that entrenched clauses are worth no more than the paper on which they are written, and that, therefore, Nibmar has always been and remains the key to the substance of the six principles?

THE PRIME MINISTER: My hon. Friend is too gloomy about this matter. When he says that independence must be absolute, without any arrangements for safeguarding the entrenched clauses, that is an argument that I have heard perhaps rather too much of in the past week. I am sorry to see my hon. Friend identifying himself with that point of view, which I do not accept. There have been many cases throughout history, especially during the transitional period—and a very difficult transitional period—where there must be guarantees, external as well as internal. Even some of the most senior and experienced Commonwealth countries that had a long record of local self-government voluntarily accepted some kind of control and guarantee which would fetter their otherwise totally unfettered freedom of action.

SIR D. WALKER-SMITH: The House will want further time to study the proposed functions of the Judicial Committee, as set out on page 9 of the White Paper. But is it not a fact that, whether or not they are good, they are without precedent and constitute a departure from the normal British constitutional principle of the sovereignty of Parliament? Supposing the Privy Council exercised this jurisdiction, how would it enforce it?

THE PRIME MINISTER: The right hon. and learned Gentleman is right. These functions are at any rate almost without precedent. There are near-precedents, but perhaps not absolute ones. They mean restricting the sovereignty of Parliament, and this would no doubt be a unique situation, but we are dealing with a unique situation. The situation in Rhodesia is unique partly because it involves independence before majority rule, and partly because the whole world is deeply suspicious of what has been going on in Rhodesia—the lengths to which they were willing to go in order to maintain their position. Because of this, we are entitled to ask that for a transitional period, and a transitional period only, there should be an external guarantee as well as the guarantee within the proposed Rhodesian Constitution provided by the blocking quarter.

MR. MICHAEL FOOT: Does my right hon. Friend recall that one of the main controversies following the "Tiger" talks was the question of how long it would take under those constitutional proposals for majority rule to be established in Rhodesia? Therefore, could he tell us his calculation of when majority rule would be established in Rhodesia if his proposals were now accepted in their entirety, and confirm that whatever representations he may make to the Commonwealth, the Nibmar pledge which was given to the Commonwealth will stand?

THE PRIME MINISTER: With regard to the time taken under our constitutional proposals for majority rule to be reached, I should find it extremely difficult to give an authoritative answer to my hon. Friend. There are many estimates on this, many of which have been put before the House. Some were as short as one or two elections—seven to 10 years; some were 12 to 15 years. A great deal depends on how many of the Africans who qualify under the 1961 Constitution for the A Roll take up the right to vote by registration. It depends partly on their attitude and partly, we suspect, on the extent to which they are helped to register, which is dealt with in our proposals.

Our educational proposals, which we put forward at great cost to ourselves, great cost to the British taxpayer—this should be understood—will have the secondary effect of increasing the number of qualified Africans and those who would be able to exercise the vote. It would be very difficult to make a clearer estimate than that. We have never proposed immediate majority rule, and I do not think that anyone in the House has. For reasons I prefer not to go into, African nationalist leadership there, and the chances given to Africans for political participation there, compare unfavourably with what has happened in other parts of Africa where there was direct British rule and then local self-government under British rule.

On Nibmar, the position is unchanged. I have said that if there were a change of circumstances we should go to the Commonwealth about it. Some of the things in our proposals relate specifically to what is required in the shape of changed circumstances.

MR. ALEXANDER W. LYON: Did my right hon. Friend ask Mr. Smith when he was on "Fearless" whether he was prepared to explain why, last month, he has twice confirmed that there would never be majority rule in Rhodesia in his lifetime, or in his child's lifetime, if he were genuinely prepared to accept the first principle?

THE PRIME MINISTER: I do not think that it would help if I tried to tell the House everything that was said between us in 30-hour meeting. I assure my hon. Friend that everything relevant was said, more of it looking to the future than to the past on both sides. I have not disguised from the House today, any more than at any other time, that Mr. Smith does not like the first and second principles, or most of the others for that matter. That results from his very different viewpoint on what we have called moral issues on all these questions. What I have raised is the question whether he is prepared to stomach his repugnance in order to accept an agreement that will bring great gain to Rhodesia—to all races in Rhodesia—and help avert some of the very serious dangers threatening Rhodesia from inside and outside.

SEVERAL HON. MEMBERS *rose—*

MR. SPEAKER: Order. We must come to the business of the day.

Statement by Michael Stewart in the House of Commons Announcing
*the Merger of the Foreign and Commonwealth Offices, 16 October 1968**

With your permission, Mr. Speaker, and that of the House, I wish to make a statement on the merger of the Foreign and Commonwealth Offices.

Hansard, 5.s., DCCLXX, 388–89.

On the 15th March my right hon. Friend the Prime Minister announced the intention of Her Majesty's Government to bring about the amalgamation of the Foreign Office and the Commonwealth Office and in a statement on 28th March he explained to the House the reasons for this.

It was announced on 18th September that the new Office would be called the Foreign and Commonwealth Office and that it would come into being on 17th October this year.

This change, therefore, will take effect from tomorrow, and for the first time in modern history the external affairs of this country will be in the charge of one Secretary of State and one Department. For good historical and political reasons we have been the only country in the world to maintain separate Foreign and Commonwealth Offices.

As my right hon. Friend the Prime Minister said in April, the time has now come to amalgamate these two Departments. We shall continue to do everything possible to promote good relations with the world community, whether through the United Nations or with individual countries and groups of countries.

We shall continue to play our full part as a member of the Commonwealth, and to maintain our close association with other Commonwealth Governments. In forming the new Office we have made certain that the interests of the dependent territories will receive the close and sympathetic attention which our responsibility for them requires.

We have not merely put the two existing Departments together: we have examined the tasks of both and constructed a new Office to perform those tasks.

In the planning of the merger, and in the work of both Departments over many years, the country is greatly indebted to the devotion, industry, and skill of its permanent civil servants.

The handling, under Parliament, of the external affairs of this country over the years has called for sensitive judgment, continuous hard work in numerous fields, and the initiation of, and response to, peaceful change—all this in a restless and sometimes violent world. It is in this progressive spirit that the new Department of State will meet the challenge of the future.

PRINCIPAL OFFICIALS

LORD TREASURERS AND
FIRST LORDS OF THE TREASURY

During the seventeenth century the office of Lord High Treasurer was put into commission several times, permanently in 1714 (First Lords of the Treasury). From Sir Robert Walpole's Ministry (1721) the First Lord of the Treasury has usually, although not always, been the leading or Prime Minister; as the functions of that office evolved and increased (see "Prime Ministers") the Chancellor of the Exchequer gradually became the actual head of the financial department.

April	1689	Charles Mordaunt, Viscount Mordaunt, earl of Monmouth (1689); (earl of Peterborough 1697); First Lord
Mar.	1690	Sir John Lowther (Viscount Lonsdale 1696), First Lord
Nov.	1690	Sidney, Lord Godolphin (earl of Godolphin 1706), First Lord
May	1697	Charles Montagu (Lord Halifax 1700, earl of Halifax 1714), First Lord
Nov.	1699	Lord Grey, earl of Tankerville, First Lord
Dec.	1700	Lord Godolphin (*See* 1690), First Lord
Dec.	1701	Charles Howard, earl of Carlisle, First Lord
May	1702	Lord Godolphin (*See* 1690)
Aug.	1710	John Poulett, Earl Poulett, First Lord
Mar.	1711	Robert Harley, earl of Oxford
July	1714	Charles Talbot, duke of Shrewsbury
Oct.	1714	Charles Montagu, earl of Halifax (*See* 1697)
May	1715	Charles Howard, earl of Carlisle
Oct.	1715	Robert Walpole (K.G. 1725, earl of Orford 1742)
April	1717	James Stanhope, Viscount Stanhope (earl Stanhope 1718)
Mar.	1718	Charles Spencer, earl of Sunderland
April	1721	Sir Robert Walpole (*See* 1715)

PRIME MINISTERS

Originally a descriptive designation, the term Prime Minister gradually evolved into the official title of the First Minister of State or leader of the administration. Applied oppro- briously to, and repudiated by, Robert Walpole and later Lord North in the eighteenth century, it fell into disuse during the latter half. The term came into common usage by the mid-nineteenth century and was fully recognized officially in 1905, when King Edward VIII defined the precedence of the Prime Minister.

Between Walpole's Ministry (April 1721) and that of William Pitt (Dec. 1783), a leading minister can usually be identified but it is premature to apply the designation of Prime Minister. Although the Prime Minister usually holds the office of First Lord of the Treasury, prior to Walpole the most important officeholders frequently held such lesser positions as Secretary of State for the Northern Department.

Leading Ministers

April	1721	Sir Robert Walpole, K.G. (1725); (earl of Orford 1742)
Feb.	1742	Spencer Compton, earl of Wilmington
Aug.	1743	Hon. Henry Pelham
Mar.	1754	Thomas Pelham-Holles, duke of Newcastle
Nov.	1756	William Cavendish, duke of Devonshire, First Lord of the Treasury
		William Pitt (earl of Chatham 1766), Secretary of State for the South
July	1757	Duke of Newcastle (*See* 1754), First Lord of the Treasury
		William Pitt (*See* 1756), Secretary of State for the South to 1761
May	1762	John Stuart, earl of Bute [Scot.]
April	1763	George Grenville
July	1765	Charles Watson-Wentworth, Marquess of Rockingham
July	1766	William Pitt, earl of Chatham, First Lord of the Treasury and Lord Privy Seal (to 1768)
Oct.	1768	Augustus Henry Fitz Roy, duke of Grafton
Jan.	1770	Frederick North, called Lord North (earl of Guilford 1790)
Mar.	1782	Marquess of Rockingham (*See* 1765)
July	1782	William Fitz-Maurice Petty, earl of Shelburne [Irish]; (marquess of Lansdowne 1784)
April	1783	Fox-North Coalition Government
		William Henry Cavendish Bentinck, duke of Portland, First Lord of the Treasury
		Lord North (*See* 1770), Secretary of State for Home and Colonial Affairs
		Charles James Fox, Secretary of State for Foreign Affairs

Prime Ministers

Dec.	1783	William Pitt
Mar.	1801	Henry Addington (Viscount Sidmouth 1805)
May	1804	William Pitt

Feb.	1806	William Wyndham Grenville, Lord Grenville ("Ministry of All-the-Talents")
Mar.	1807	William Henry Cavendish Bentinck, duke of Portland
Oct.	1809	Spencer Perceval
June	1812	Robert Banks Jenkinson, called Lord Hawkesbury, earl of Liverpool
April	1827	George Canning
Aug.	1827	Frederick John Robinson, Viscount Goderich (1827); (earl of Ripon 1833)
Jan.	1828	Arthur Wellesley, duke of Wellington
Nov.	1830	Charles Grey, called Viscount Howick, Earl Grey
July	1834	William Lamb, Viscount Melbourne (1828)
Nov.	1834	Duke of Wellington (*See* 1828)
Dec.	1834	Sir Robert Peel, bart.
April	1835	Viscount Melbourne (*See* 1834)
Sept.	1841	Sir Robert Peel, bart.
July	1846	John Russell, called Lord John Russell (Earl Russell 1861)
Feb.	1852	Edward Geoffrey-Smith Stanley, called Lord Stanley, earl of Derby
Dec.	1852	George Hamilton-Gordon, earl of Aberdeen [Scot.]
Feb.	1855	Henry John Temple, Viscount Palmerston [Irish]
Feb.	1858	Earl of Derby (*See* 1852)
June	1859	Viscount Palmerston (*See* 1855)
Oct.	1865	Earl Russell (*See* 1846)
June	1866	Earl of Derby (*See* 1852)
Feb.	1868	Benjamin Disraeli (earl of Beaconsfield 1876)
Dec.	1868	William Ewart Gladstone
Feb.	1874	Benjamin Disraeli, earl of Beaconsfield 1876
April	1880	William Ewart Gladstone
June	1885	Robert A. T. Gascoyne-Cecil, Marquess of Salisbury
Feb.	1886	William Ewart Gladstone
July	1886	Marquess of Salisbury (*See* 1885)
Aug.	1892	William Ewart Gladstone
Mar.	1894	Archibald Philip Primrose, earl of Rosebery [Scot.]
June	1895	Marquess of Salisbury (*See* 1885)
July	1902	Arthur James Balfour (earl of Balfour 1922)
Dec.	1905	Sir Henry Campbell-Bannerman
April	1908	Herbert Henry Asquith (earl of Oxford and Asquith 1925)
Dec.	1916	David Lloyd George (Earl Lloyd George of Dwyfor 1945)
Oct.	1922	Andrew Bonar Law
May	1923	Stanley Baldwin (Earl Baldwin of Bewdley 1937)
Jan.	1924	James Ramsay MacDonald
Nov.	1924	Stanley Baldwin (*See* 1923)
June	1929	James Ramsay MacDonald
June	1935	Stanley Baldwin (*See* 1923)
May	1937	Arthur Neville Chamberlain
May	1940	Winston Leonard Spencer Churchill (K.G. 1953)
July	1945	Clement Richard Attlee (Earl Attlee 1955)
Nov.	1951	Sir Winston Leonard Spencer Churchill, K.G. (1953)
April	1955	Sir Robert Anthony Eden, K.G. (earl of Avon 1961)
Jan.	1957	Maurice Harold Macmillan
Oct.	1963	Sir Alexander Douglas-Home (formerly earl of Home)
Oct.	1964	Harold Wilson
June	1970	Edward Heath

PRINCIPAL SECRETARIES OF STATE

The Secretariat was officially divided into northern and southern departments in 1689. The duties of the two Secretaries evolved during the eighteenth century and the Secretariat was reorganized again in 1782, the northern department becoming the Foreign Office, the southern department the Home Office, and other Secretaryships of State for various departments were later added.

Northern Department		Southern Department	
Mar. 1689	Daniel Finch, earl of Nottingham (earl of Winchilsea 1729)	Feb. 1689	Charles Talbot, earl of Shrewsbury (duke of Shrewsbury 1694)
	June 1690 Earl of Nottingham		
Dec. 1690	Henry Sydney, Viscount Sidney of Sheppey (earl of Romney 1694)	Dec. 1690	Earl of Nottingham
	Mar. 1692 Earl of Nottingham		
Mar. 1693	Sir John Trenchard	Mar. 1693	Earl of Nottingham
	Nov. 1693 Sir John Trenchard		
Mar. 1694	Duke of Shrewsbury (*See* 1689)	Mar. 1694	Sir John Trenchard
May 1695	Sir William Trumbull	April 1695	Duke of Shrewsbury (*See* 1689)
Dec. 1697	James Vernon		
	Dec. 1698 James Vernon		
May 1699	James Vernon	May 1699	Edward Villiers, earl of Jersey
	June 1700 James Vernon		
Nov. 1700	Sir Charles Hedges	Nov. 1700	James Vernon
Jan. 1702	James Vernon	Jan. 1702	Charles Montagu, earl of Manchester (duke of Manchester 1719)
May 1702	Sir Charles Hedges	May 1702	Earl of Nottingham (*See* 1689)
May 1704	Robert Harley (earl of Oxford 1711)	May 1704	Sir Charles Hedges
		Dec. 1706	Charles Spencer, earl of Sunderland
Feb. 1708	Henry Boyle (Lord Carleton 1714)		
Sept. 1710	Henry St. John, Viscount Bolingbroke (1712)	June 1710	William Legge, Lord Dartmouth (earl of Dartmouth 1711)
Aug. 1713	William Bromley	Aug. 1713	Viscount Bolingbroke (*See* 1710)
Sept. 1714	Charles Townshend, Viscount Townshend	Sept. 1714	James Stanhope, Viscount Stanhope (1717); (earl Stanhope 1718)

Dec. 1716	James Stanhope (*See* 1714)	Dec. 1716	Paul Methuen
April 1717	Earl of Sunderland (*See* 1706)	April 1717	Joseph Addison
Mar. 1718	Viscount Stanhope (*See* 1714)	Mar. 1718	James Craggs
Feb. 1721	Viscount Townshend	Mar. 1721	John Carteret, Lord Carteret (earl Granville 1744)
		April 1724	Thomas Pelham-Holles, duke of Newcastle
June 1730	William Stanhope, Lord Harrington (1730); (earl of Harrington 1742)		
Feb. 1742	Lord Carteret (*See* 1721)		
Nov. 1744	Earl of Harrington (*See* 1730)		

10-12 Feb. 1746 Earl Granville (*See* 1721)

Feb. 1746	Earl of Harrington (*See* 1730)	Feb. 1746	Duke of Newcastle (*See* 1724)
Oct. 1746	Philip Dormer Stanhope, earl of Chesterfield		
Feb. 1748	Duke of Newcastle (*See* 1724)	Feb. 1748	John Russell, duke of Bedford
		June 1751	Robert Darcy, earl of Holdernesse
Mar. 1754	Earl of Holdernesse (resigned 9 June 1757, reappointed 27 June 1757)	Mar. 1754	Sir Thomas Robinson (Lord Grantham 1761)
		Nov. 1755	Henry Fox (Lord Holland of Foxley 1763)
		Dec. 1756	William Pitt (earl of Chatham 1766)

April-June 1757 Earl of Holdernesse (*See* 1751)

June 1757	Earl of Holdernesse (*See* 1751)	June 1757	William Pitt (*See* 1756)
Mar. 1761	John Stuart, earl of Bute [Scot.]	Oct. 1761	Charles Wyndham, earl of Egremont
May 1762	George Grenville		
Oct. 1762	George Montagu-Dunk, earl of Halifax		
Sept. 1763	John Montagu, earl of Sandwich	Sept. 1763	Earl of Halifax, (*See* 1762)
July 1765	Augustus Henry Fitz Roy, duke of Grafton	July 1765	Henry Seymour Conway
May 1766	Henry Seymour Conway	May 1766	Charles Lennox, duke of Richmond
		July 1766	William Fitz-Maurice Petty, earl of Shelburne [Irish]; (marquess of Lansdowne 1784)

Jan.	1768	Thomas Thynne, Viscount Weymouth (Marquess of Bath 1789)			
Oct.	1768	William de Zuylestein, earl of Rochford	Oct.	1768	Viscount Weymouth (*See* Jan. 1768)
Dec.	1770	Earl of Sandwich (*See* 1763)	Dec.	1770	Earl of Rochford (*See* 1768)
Jan.	1771	Earl of Halifax (*See* 1762)			
June	1771	Henry Howard, earl of Suffolk and Berkshire			
			Nov.	1775	Viscount Weymouth (*See* 1768)
Mar.	1779	Viscount Weymouth	Nov.	1779	Wills Hill, earl of Hillsborough (marquess of Downshire [Irish] 1789)
Oct.	1779	David Murray, Viscount Stormont [Scot.] (earl Mansfield [G.B.] 1793)			

FOREIGN SECRETARIES

In 1782 the Secretariat underwent a reorganization (see "Secretaries of State"). The northern department was converted into the Foreign Office and Charles James Fox appointed the first Secretary of State for Foreign Affairs.

Mar.	1782	Charles James Fox
July	1782	Thomas Robinson, Lord Grantham
April	1783	Charles James Fox
Dec.	1783	George Nugent-Temple-Grenville, earl Temple (marquess of Buckingham 1784)
Dec.	1783	Francis Godolphin Osborne, called marquess of Carmarthen, duke of Leeds 1789
June	1791	William Wyndham Grenville, Lord Grenville 1790
Feb.	1801	Robert Banks Jenkinson, called Lord Hawkesbury (earl of Liverpool 1808)
May	1804	Dudley Ryder, Lord Harrowby (earl of Harrowby 1809)
Jan.	1805	Henry Phipps, Lord Mulgrave (earl of Mulgrave 1812)
Feb.	1806	Charles James Fox
Sept.	1806	Charles Grey, called Viscount Howick, earl Grey (1807)
Mar.	1807	George Canning
Oct.	1809	Henry Bathurst, earl Bathurst
Dec.	1809	Richard Wellesley, Lord Wellesley [G.B.], marquess Wellesley [Irish]
Mar.	1812	Robert Stewart, called Viscount Castlereagh, marquess of Londonderry [Irish] (1821)
Sept.	1822	George Canning
April	1827	John William Ward, Viscount Dudley and Ward, earl of Dudley (1827)

June	1828	George Hamilton-Gordon, earl of Aberdeen [Scot.]
Nov.	1830	Henry John Temple, Viscount Palmerston [Irish]
Nov.	1834	Arthur Wellesley, duke of Wellington
April	1835	Viscount Palmerston (*See* 1830)
Sept.	1841	Earl of Aberdeen (*See* 1828)
July	1846	Viscount Palmerston (*See* 1830)
Dec.	1851	Granville George Leveson-Gower, earl Granville
Feb.	1852	James Howard Harris, earl of Malmesbury
Dec.	1852	John Russell, called Lord John Russell (earl Russell 1861)
Feb.	1853	George William Frederick Villiers, earl of Clarendon
Feb.	1858	Earl of Malmesbury (*See* 1852)
June	1859	Lord John Russell (*See* 1852)
Nov.	1865	Earl of Clarendon (*See* 1853)
July	1866	Edward Henry Stanley, called Lord Stanley (earl of Derby 1869)
Dec.	1868	Earl of Clarendon (*See* 1853)
July	1870	Earl Granville
Feb.	1874	Earl of Derby
April	1878	Robert A. T. Gascoyne-Cecil, marquess of Salisbury
April	1880	Earl Granville (*See* 1851)
June	1885	Marquess of Salisbury (*See* 1878) (also Prime Minister)
Feb.	1886	Archibald Philip Primrose, earl of Rosebery [Scot.]
Aug.	1886	Stafford Henry Northcote, earl of Iddesleigh
Jan.	1887	Marquess of Salisbury (*See* 1878) (also Prime Minister)
Aug.	1892	Earl of Rosebery (*See* 1886)
Mar.	1894	John Wodehouse, earl of Kimberley
June	1895	Marquess of Salisbury (*See* 1878) (also Prime Minister)
Nov.	1900	Henry Charles Keith Petty-Fitzmaurice, marquess of Lansdowne
Dec.	1905	Sir Edward Grey, Viscount Grey of Fallodon (1916)
Dec.	1916	Arthur James Balfour (earl of Balfour 1922)
Oct.	1919	George Nathaniel Curzon, earl Curzon, marquess Curzon (1921)
Jan.	1924	James Ramsay MacDonald (also Prime Minister)
Nov.	1924	Sir Joseph Austen Chamberlain
June	1929	Arthur Henderson
Aug.	1931	Rufus Isaacs, marquess of Reading
Nov.	1931	Sir John Allsebrook Simon (Viscount Simon 1940)
June	1935	Sir Samuel John Gurney Hoare, bart. (Viscount Templewood 1944)
Dec.	1935	Robert Anthony Eden (K.G. 1954, earl of Avon 1961)
Mar.	1938	Edward Frederick Lindley Wood, Viscount Halifax (earl of Halifax 1944)
Dec.	1940	Anthony Eden (*See* 1935)
July	1945	Ernest Bevin
Mar.	1951	Herbert Stanley Morrison (Lord Morrison of Lambeth 1959)
Oct.	1951	Sir Anthony Eden (*See* 1935)
April	1955	Maurice Harold Macmillan
Dec.	1955	John Selwyn Brooke Lloyd
July	1960	Alexander Douglas-Home, earl of Home
Oct.	1963	R. A. Butler
Oct.	1964	Patrick Gordon Walker
Jan.	1965	Michael Stewart
Aug.	1966	George Brown
Mar.	1968	Michael Stewart
June	1970	Sir Alexander Douglas-Home (formerly the earl of Home)

COLONIAL SECRETARIES

The office of "Secretary of State for the American Colonies," established in 1768, was suppressed by Burke's Sinecure Act in 1782. The Home Office was responsible for colonial affairs between 1782 and 1801, when the Departments of War and the Colonies were united under Lord Hobart. In 1854 a fourth Secretaryship of State was created for War and the Secretary of State for the Colonies administered colonial policy until 1966, when the office was abolished.

From 1870 to 1925 the Colonial Secretary handled relations with both the colonies and the self-governing Dominions, although in 1907 the office was formally divided into three sections: Dominion Affairs, Crown Colonies, and a General Division. In 1925 a separate Dominions Office was created, responsible for business concerning the Irish Free State, Southern Rhodesia, three High Commission territories, and the Imperial Conference in addition to relations with the self-governing Dominions.

Secretaries of State for the American Colonies

Jan.	1768	Wills Hill, earl of Hillsborough [Irish] ; (marquess of Downshire [Irish] 1789)
Aug.	1772	William Legge, earl of Dartmouth
Nov.	1775	Lord George Germain, Viscount Sackville (1782)
Feb.	1782	Welbore Ellis (Lord Mendip 1794)

Secretaries of State for War and the Colonies

Mar.	1801	Robert Hobart, Lord Hobart (earl of Buckinghamshire 1804)
May	1804	John Jeffreys Pratt, earl Camden (marquess Camden 1812)
June	1805	Robert Stewart, called Viscount Castlereagh (marquess of Londonderry [Irish] 1821)
Feb.	1806	William Windham
Mar.	1807	Viscount Castlereagh (*See* 1805)
Oct.	1809	Robert Banks Jenkinson, earl of Liverpool
June	1812	Henry Bathurst, earl Bathurst
April	1827	Frederick John Robinson, Viscount Goderich (1827); (earl of Ripon 1833)
Sept.	1827	William Huskisson
May	1828	Sir George Murray
Nov.	1830	Viscount Goderich (*See* 1827)
April	1833	Edward Geoffrey Smith-Stanley, called Lord Stanley (earl of Derby 1851)
June	1834	Thomas Spring Rice (Lord Monteagle of Brandon 1839)
Nov.	1834	George Hamilton-Gordon, earl of Aberdeen [Scot.]
April	1838	Charles Grant (Lord Glenelg)
Feb.	1839	Constantine Phipps, marquess of Normanby
Aug.	1839	John Russell, called Lord John Russell (earl Russell 1861)
Sept.	1841	Lord Stanley (*See* 1833)
Dec.	1845	William Ewart Gladstone
July	1846	Henry Grey, earl Grey

Feb.	1852	Sir John Somerset Pakington (Lord Hampton 1874)
Dec.	1852	Henry Pelham Pelham-Clinton, duke of Newcastle

Secretaries of State for the Colonies

June	1854	Sir George Grey, bart.
Feb.	1855	Sidney Herbert (Lord Herbert of Lea 1861)
Feb.	1855	John Russell, called Lord John Russell (earl Russell 1861)
July	1855	Sir William Molesworth, bart.
Nov.	1855	Henry Labouchere (Lord Taunton 1859)
Feb.	1858	Edward Henry Stanley, called Lord Stanley (earl of Derby 1869)
May	1858	Sir Edward G. E. L. Bulwer-Lytton, bart. (Lord Lytton 1866)
June	1858	Henry Pelham Pelham-Clinton, duke of Newcastle
April	1864	Edward Cardwell (Viscount Cardwell 1874)
July	1866	Henry Howard Molyneux Herbert, earl of Carnarvon
Mar.	1867	Richard P. C. T. N. B. Chandos-Grenville, duke of Buckingham and Chandos
Dec.	1868	Granville George Leveson-Gower, earl Granville
July	1870	John Wodehouse, earl of Kimberley
Feb.	1874	Earl of Carnarvon (*See* 1866)
Feb.	1878	Sir Michael Hicks Beach (earl St. Aldwyn 1915)
April	1880	Earl of Kimberley (*See* 1870)
Dec.	1882	Earl of Derby (*See* 1858)
June	1885	Frederick Arthur Stanley Lord Stanley (1886); (earl of Derby 1893)
Feb.	1886	Earl Granville (*See* 1868)
Aug.	1886	Edward Stanhope
Jan.	1887	Sir Henry Thurstan Holland, Lord Knutsford (1888); (Viscount Knutsford 1895)
Aug.	1892	George Frederick Samuel Robinson, marquess of Ripon
June	1895	Joseph Chamberlain
Oct.	1903	Alfred Lyttelton
Dec.	1905	Victor Alexander Bruce, earl of Elgin [Scot.] and Lord Elgin [U.K.]
April	1908	Robert Offley Ashburton Crewe-Milnes, earl of Crewe (marquess of Crewe 1911)
Nov.	1910	Lewis Harcourt (Viscount Harcourt 1917)
May	1915	Andrew Bonar Law
Dec.	1916	Walter Hume Long (Viscount Long 1921)
Jan.	1919	Alfred Milner, Viscount Milner
Feb.	1921	Winston Leonard Spencer Churchill (K.G. 1953)
Oct.	1922	Victor Christian William Cavendish, duke of Devonshire
Jan.	1924	James Henry Thomas
Nov.	1924	Leopold C. M. S. Amery (also Dominions Secretary)
June	1929	Sydney James Webb, Lord Passfield (1929), (also Dominions Secretary to June 1930)
Aug.	1931	James Henry Thomas (also Dominions Secretary)
Nov.	1931	Sir Philip Cunliffe-Lister (earl Swinton 1955)
June	1935	Malcolm MacDonald
Nov.	1935	James Henry Thomas
May	1936	William George Arthur Ormsby Gore (Lord Harlech 1938)
May	1937	Malcolm MacDonald
May	1940	George Ambrose Lloyd, Lord Lloyd of Dolobran
Feb.	1941	Walter Edward Guinness, Lord Moyne

Feb.	1942	Robert Arthur James Cecil, Viscount Cranborne (also Dominions Secretary)
Nov.	1942	Oliver Frederick George Stanley
Aug.	1945	George H. Hall
Oct.	1946	A. Creech Jones
Feb.	1950	James Griffiths
Nov.	1951	Oliver Lyttelton
July	1954	Alan Lennox-Boyd
Oct.	1959	Ian Macleod
Sept.	1961	Reginald Maudling
July	1962	Duncan Sandys (also Commonwealth Secretary)
Oct.	1964	Anthony Greenwood
Dec.	1965	Thomas Pakenham, Earl of Longford

BIBLIOGRAPHY

OFFICIAL SOURCES

Parliament

Parliamentary History of England, from the earliest period to the year 1803, The. (Also known as "Cobbett's Parliamentary History of England"). 36 vols. London, 1806-20.

Hansard's parliamentary debates. London, 1804 ff.

Great Britain. Parliament. *Sessional Papers.* (Also known as "Parliamentary Papers"). 1731 ff.

Great Britain. House of Commons. *Journals of the House of Commons, 1547 to date.* London, 1742 ff.

Statutes

The statutes at large, from Magna Charta to the end of the last parliament of Great Britain, held in the 41st year of the reign of King George III, 1800. Edited by Owen Ruffhead. New ed., rev. and continued by Charles Runnington. 14 vols. London, 1786-1800.

The statutes at large of the United Kingdom of Great Britain and Ireland. 29 vols. London, 1804-69.

Public general statutes. London, 1832-67.

Public general acts of the United Kingdom of Great Britain and Ireland. London, 1887 ff.

Foreign Affairs

Great Britain. Foreign Office. *British and foreign state papers.* 1812/14 ff. London, 1841 ff.

Great Britain. Foreign Office. *British documents on the origins of the war, 1898-1914.* 11 vols. Edited by G. P. Gooch and Harold Temperly. London, 1927.

Great Britain. Foreign Office. *Documents on British foreign policy: 1919-1939.* Edited by Medlicott, Dakin, and Lambert. London, 1966.

Legal Proceedings

Howell's state trials. 1163-1820. 34 vols. London, 1809-28.

Annual Register, The: or, a view of the history, politicks & literature of the year 1758, etc.

Antonius, George. *The Arab Awakening: The Story of the Arab National Awakening.* Philadelphia: J. B. Lippincott Co., 1939.

Ashley, Anthony Evelyn Melbourne. *The Life of Henry John Temple, Viscount Palmerston: 1846-1865. With Selections from his Speeches and Correspondence.* 2 vols. London: Richard Bentley & Son, 1876.

Baldwin, Stanley. *Our Inheritance: Speeches and Addresses.* Garden City, N.Y.: Doubleday & Co., 1928.

Battle of Britain, August-October 1940: An Air Ministry Account of the Great Days from 8th August-31st October 1940, The. London: His Majesty's Stationery Office, 1940.

Bright, John. *Speeches on Questions of Public Policy.* Edited by James E. T. Rogers. 2 vols. London: Macmillan and Co., 1868.

Cambridge History of British Foreign Policy, 1783-1919. Edited by Sir Adolphus W. Ward and G. P. Gooch. 3 vols. New York: The Macmillan Co., 1922-23.

Cecil, Lady Gwendolen. *The Life of Robert, Marquis of Salisbury.* 4 vols. London: Hodder & Stoughton, 1932.

Chamberlain, Joseph. *Mr. Chamberlain's Speeches.* Edited by Charles W. Boyd. 2 vols. Boston: Houghton Mifflin Co., 1914.

Chamberlain, Neville. *In Search of Peace.* New York: G. P. Putnam's Sons, 1939.

Chatham, William Pitt, Earl of. *The Speech of the Right Honourable the Earl of Chatham, in the House of Lords, on Friday the 20th of January 1775.* London: Printed for G. Kearsley, 1775.

————; Burke, Edmund; and Erskine, Lord Thomas. *Celebrated Speeches of Chatham, Burke, and Erskine: To which is added, the Argument of Mr. Mackintosh, in the cast of Peltier (Selected by a member of the Philadelphia Bar).* Philadelphia: Key and Biddle, 1835.

Churchill, Winston [Leonard] Spencer. *Blood, Sweat, and Tears.* New York: G. P. Putnam's Sons, 1941.

————. *The Grand Alliance.* Boston: Houghton Mifflin Co., 1950.

————. *The Hinge of Fate.* Boston: Houghton Mifflin Co., 1950.

————. *India: Speeches and an Introduction.* London: T. Butterworth, 1931.

————. *Onwards to Victory: War Speeches of 1943.* Compiled by Charles Eade. London: Cassell and Co., 1944.

————. *The River War: An Historical Account of the Reconquest of the Soudan.* Edited by Col. F. Rhodes. 2 vols. London: Longmans, Green and Co., 1899.

————. *The Sinews of Peace: Post-War Speeches.* Edited by Randolph S. Churchill. Boston: Houghton Mifflin Co., 1948.

————. *The Unrelenting Struggle: War Speeches.* Compiled by Charles Eade. Boston: Little, Brown and Co., 1942.

————. *The World Crisis-1915.* New York: Charles Scribner's Sons, 1923.

Clive, Robert Clive, Baron. *Lord Clive's Speech in the House of Commons, 30th March, 1772, on the motion made for leave to bring in a bill, for the better regulation of the affairs of the East India Company, and of their servants in India, and for the administration of justice in Bengal.* London: J. Walter, 1772.

Codrington, Sir Edward. *Compressed narrative of the proceedings of Vice-Admiral Sir Edward Codrington, during his command of His Majesty's ships and vessels on the Mediterranean station, from the 28th of February 1827, until the 22nd of August 1828.* London: J. Cowell, 1832.

Collection of All the Treaties of Peace, Alliance, and Commerce, between Great Britain and other Powers, from the Revolution in 1688 to the Present Time, A. 2 vols. London: Printed for J. Almon, 1772.

Collingwood, Cuthbert Collingwood, Baron. *A Selection from the Public and Private Correspondence of Vice-Admiral Lord Collingwood: Interspersed with Memoirs of his Life.* Edited by G. L. N. Collingwood. . . . 2 vols. London: J. Ridgeway and Sons, 1837.

Cornwallis, Charles Cornwallis, Marquis. *Correspondence of Charles, First Marquis Cornwallis.* Edited with notes by Charles Ross. 3 vols. London: John Murray, 1859.

Cromer, Evelyn Baring, Earl. "The Capitulations in Egypt." In *The Nineteenth Century and After.* London, LXXIV (1913), 1-10.

Curzon, George Nathaniel Curzon, Marquis of Kedleston. *Lord Curzon's Farewell to India: Being Speeches Delivered as Viceroy and Governor-General of India during Sept.-Nov. 1905, by the Right Honourable Lord Curzon of Kedleston.* Edited by R. P. Karkaria. Bombay: Thacker and Co., 1907.

Dalrymple, Sir John. *Queries Concerning the Conduct which England should follow in Foreign Politics in the Present State of Europe.* London: J. Debrett, 1789.

D'Avenant, Charles. "On Colonies and Plantations. . . ." In *Select Dissertations on Colonies and Plantations.* By those celebrated authors, Sir Josiah Child, Charles Davenant, and Mr. William Wood. Wherein the nature of Plantations, and their Consequences to Great Britain, are seriously Considered. And a Plan proposed, which may settle the Unhappy Differences between Great Britain and America. 8 vols. London: W. Hay, 1775.

Disraeli, Benjamin, Earl of Beaconsfield. *Selected Speeches of the ... Earl of Beaconsfield.* Edited by T. E. Kebbel. 2 vols. London: Longmans, Green and Co., 1882.

Dugdale, Blanche E. C. *Arthur James Balfour, First Earl of Balfour.* 2 vols. New York: G. P. Putnam's Sons, 1937.

Durham, John George Lambton, Earl of. *The Report & Despatches of the Earl of Durham, Her Majesty's High Commissioner and Governor-General of British North America.* 8 vols. London: Ridgway, 1839.

Eden, Anthony. *Full Circle: The Memoirs of Anthony Eden.* Boston: Houghton Mifflin Co., 1960.

"Federation versus Imperialism." *Westminster Review.* London, CVII (June 1902), 636-46.

Fitzmaurice, Edmund. *Life of William, Earl of Shelburne afterwards first Marquess of Lansdowne, with extracts from his papers and correspondence.* 2 vols. London: Macmillan and Co., 1912.

"The German Peril." *Quarterly Review.* London, CCIX (July 1908), 291-98.

Gladstone, William E. *Gladstone's Speeches.* Edited by Arthur T. Basset. London: Methuen & Co., 1916.

————. *A Speech Delivered at Blackheath, on Saturday, September 9th, 1876, together with a letter, on the Question of the East.* London: John Murray, 1876.

————, and Palmerston, Viscount. *Gladstone and Palmerston: Being the Correspondence of Lord Palmerstron with Mr. Gladstone, 1851-1865.* Edited by Phillip Guedalla. New York: Harper & Brothers, 1928.

Goldie, Sir George. Introduction to Vandeleur's *Campaigning on the Upper Nile and Niger*, as reprinted in *Sir George Goldie, Founder of Nigeria: A Memoir*, by Dorothy Wellesley. London: Macmillan and Co., 1934.

Gordon, Major-General Charles George. *The Journals of Major-General C. G. Gordon, C. B., at Kartoum: printed from the original mss.* London: K. Paul, Trench, & Co., 1885.

Government Proceedings Against Fenianism, The. London: Bull, Heaton & Co., 1865.

Grey, Edward Grey, Viscount of Fallodon. *Twenty-five Years, 1892-1916.* 2 vols. New York: Frederick A. Stokes Co., 1926.

Haldane, Richard Burdon Haldane, Viscount. *Before the War.* New York: Funk & Wagnalls Co., 1920.

Hamilton, Sir Ian Standish. *Gallipoli Diary.* 2 vols. New York: G. H. Doran Co., 1920.

Hankey, Maurice Hankey, Baron. *The Supreme Command, 1914-1918.* 2 vols. London: George Allen and Unwin, 1961.

Harleian Miscellany, The; or, A Collection of scarce, curious, and entertaining pamphlets and tracts, as well in manuscript as in print, found in the late (Edward Harley, second) Earl of Oxford's library. 12 vols. London: Printed for R. Dutton, 1808-11.

Hodson, Major William S. R. *Twelve years of a soldier's life in India: being extracts from the letters of the late Major W. S. R. Hodson. Including a personal narrative of the siege of Delhi and capture of the king and princes.* Edited by the Rev. G. H. Hodson. Boston: Ticknor and Fields, 1860.

Holwell, John Zephaniah. *A Genuine Narrative of the Deplorable Deaths of the English Gentlemen, and others, who were suffocated in the Black-Hole in Fort William, at Calcutta, in the Kingdom of Bengal; in the Night Succeeding the 20th Day of June 1756. In a letter to a friend.* London: Printed for A. Millar, 1758.

Imperial Federation League. *The Record of the Past and the Promise of the Future.* London: Cassell and Co., 1886.

Israel, Fred L., ed. *Major Peace Treaties of Modern History, 1648-1967.* 4 vols. New York: Chelsea House Publishers, 1968.

Jellicoe, John Rushworth Jellicoe, Viscount. *The Grand Fleet, 1914-1916: Its Creation, Development and Work.* London: Cassell & Co., 1919.

Jenkinson, Charles, ed. *Collection of All the Treaties of Peace, Alliance, and Commerce, between Great Britain and other Powers, from the Treaty signed at Munster in 1648 to the Treaties signed at Paris in 1783, A.* 3 vols. London: Printed for J. Debrett, 1785.

Jewish Agency for Palestine. *Book of Documents Submitted to the General Assembly of the United Nations Relating to the Establishment of the National Home for the Jewish People.* New York, 1947.

Labour Party. "The British Working Class and the War." In *Labour's Aims in War and Peace.* By C. R. Attlee, Arthur Greenwood, Hugh Dalton and others. With a preface by Lord Snell. London: Lincolns-Prager, 1940.

————. *Report of the Thirty-Fifth Annual Conference of the Labour Party.* London, 1935.

————. *Report of the Fifty-Ninth Annual Conference of the Labour Party held in the Spa Grand Hotel, Scarborough.* London, 1960.

Levy, Benn W. *Britain and the Bomb: The Fallacy of Nuclear Defence.* London: The Campaign for Nuclear Disarmament, 1959.

List of the Society, Instituted in 1787, for the Purpose of effecting the Abolition of the Slave Trade. London, 1788.

Livingstone, Dame Adelaide. *The Peace Ballot: The Official History.* London: Victor Gollancz, 1935.

Lloyd George, David. *British War Aims: Statement by the Right Honourable David Lloyd George.* New York: George H. Doran, 1918.

————. *Memoirs of the Peace Conference.* 2 vols. New Haven: Yale University Press, 1939.

————. *The War Memoirs of David Lloyd George.* 6 vols. London: Nicholson & Watson, 1933-37.

Macaulay, Thomas Babington Macaulay, Baron. *Lord Macaulay's Legislative Minutes.* Selected by C. D. Dharker. Madras: Geoffrey Cumberledge, Oxford University Press, 1946.

Malmesbury, James Howard Harris, Earl of. *Memoirs of an Ex-Minister: An Autobiography.* London: Longmans, Green and Co., 1885.

Marlborough, John Churchill, Duke of. *The Letters and Dispatches of John Churchill, First Duke of Marlborough from 1702 to 1712.* Edited by Sir George Murray. London: John Murray, 1845.

Montgomery, Bernard L. Montgomery, Viscount. *The Memoirs of Field-Marshall the Viscount Montgomery of Alamein, K. G.* Cleveland: The World Publishing Co., 1958.

Monypenny, William F., and Buckle, George E. *The Life of Benjamin Disraeli, Earl of Beaconsfield.* 6 vols. New York: The Macmillan Co., 1920.

Morel, E. D. *The Morrow of the War.* London: Union of Democratic Control, 1914.

Morley, John. *The Life of William Ewart Gladstone.* New York: The Macmillan Co., 1903.

Morse, Hosea B. *The Chronicles of the East India Company Trading to China, 1635-1834.* 5 vols. Oxford: Clarendon Press, 1926.

Narrative of the Recent War in Afghanistan, its Origin, Progress, and Prospects with the official Dispatches of Government, and Authentic Returns of the Killed, Wounded and Missing by Officer in the Honourable East India Company's Service. London: William Strange, 1842.

Nassau Lees, W. *India-Musalmans: Being Three Letters reprinted from the "Times" . . . with an appendix containing Lord Macaulay's Minute.* London: Williams and Norgate, 1871.

Newton, Thomas Wodehouse Newton, Baron. *Lord Lyons: A Record of British Diplomacy.* 2 vols. London: Edward Arnold, 1913.

Notes on the Five Questions in the Ballot Paper. London: National Declaratory Committee, 1934.

O'Brien, Barry. *Thomas Drummond, Undersecretary in Ireland, 1835-40: Life and Letters.* London: Kegan Paul, Trench, 1889.

O'Connell, Daniel. *The Speeches and Public Letters of the Liberator; with Preface and Historical Notes.* Compiled and edited by M. F. Cusack. 2 vols. Dublin: McGlasham and Gill, 1875.

Oliphant, Laurence. *Narrative of the Earl of Elgin's Mission to China and Japan in the Years 1857, 1858, 1859.* New York: Harper and Brothers, 1860.

Pamphleteer, The. London, XXIII (September 1823).

Pinkerton, John. *A General Collection of the Best and Most Interesting Voyages and Travels in all Parts of the World, many of which are now first translated into English, Digested on a New Plan.* 17 vols. London: Longman, Hurst, Rees, and Orme [etc.], 1808-14.

Pitt, William, Earl of Chatham. *Correspondence of William Pitt when Secretary of State with Colonial Governors and Military and Naval Commissioners in America.* Edited by Gertrude S. Kimball. 2 vols. New York: The Macmillan Co., 1906.

Pribram, A. F., ed. *Secret Treaties of Austria-Hungary, 1879-1914, The.* Cambridge: Harvard University Press, 1921.

Proceedings of the Royal Colonial Institute. London, 1869-1909. [Royal Empire Society.] (Annual.)

Raffles, Sir Thomas Stamford. *Statement of the Services of Sir Stamford Raffles.* London: Cox and Baylis, 1824.

Report of the Case of the Queen v. Edward John Eyre on his prosecution in the Court of Queen's Bench, for high crimes and misdemeanors alleged to have been committed by him in his office as Governor of Jamaica.... London: Stevens & Son, 1868.

Schön, Rev. James F., and Crowther, Samuel. *Journals of the Rev. James Frederick Schön and Mr. Samuel Crowther, who with the Sanctuary of her Majesty's Government, accompanied the expedition up the Niger in 1841, in behalf of the Church Missionary Society.* London: Hatchard and Son, 1842.

Seeley, Sir John R. *The Expansion of England: two courses of lectures.* London: Macmillan and Co., 1883.

Sierra Leone Company. *Substance of the Report of the Court of Directors of the Sierra Leone Company to the General Court, held at London on Wednesday the 19th of October 1791.* London: James Phillips, 1791.

Smith, Adam. *An Inquiry into the Nature and Causes of the Wealth of Nations.* 6th ed. 2 vols. London: G. Bell and Sons, 1911.

Smith, Goldwin. *The Empire: A Series of Letters Published in "The Daily News," 1862, 1863.* Oxford: John Henry and James Parker, 1863.

Speeches of the Managers and Counsels in the Trial of Warren Hastings. Edited by E. A. Bond. 4 vols. London: Longmans, Brown, Green, Longman, and Roberts, 1859.

Times. London.

Toynbee, Arnold J., ed. *Survey of International Affairs, 1924.* London: Oxford University Press, Humphrey Milford under the auspices of the British Institute of International Affairs, 1926.

Treaty of Peace, Union, Friendship, and Mutual Defence between the Crowns of Great-Britain, France and Spain Concluded at Seville, on the 9th of November, 1729. London: Reprinted from the *Daily Post-Boy,* 1729.

Trial of Sir Roger Casement. Edited by George H. Knott. Edinburgh: William Hodge, 1917.

United States Department of State. *Peace and War: United States Foreign Policy, 1931-1941.* Washington, D.C.: Government Printing Office, 1942.

Victoria, Queen. *The Letters of Queen Victoria: A Selection from Her Majesty's Correspondence between the years 1837 and 1861.* 3 vols. London: John Murray, 1907.

Wakefield, Edward Gibbon. *A Letter from Sydney, to the Principal Town of Australia.* Edited by Robert Gouger. London: Joseph Cross, 1829.

Walpole, Horace. *Memoirs of the Reign of King George the Second.* Edited by Lord Holland. 3 vols. London: Henry Colburn, 1846.

Walpole, Robert, earl of Oxford. *Observations upon the Treaty between the crowns of Great-Britain, France, and Spain, concluded at Seville on the ninth day of November, 1729.* London: J. Roberts, 1729.

Walpole, Sir Spencer. *The Life of Lord John Russell.* 2 vols. London: Longmans, Green and Co., 1889.

Wellesley, Dorothy. See Goldie, Sir George.

"Why Not an Anglo-German Entente?" *Fortnightly Review.* London, n.s., LXXIV (September 1908).

Young, Arthur. *A Tour in Ireland with General Observations on the Present State of that Kingdom: Made in the Years 1776, 1777, and 1778, and Brought down to the end of 1779.* London: T. Cadell, 1780.

ACKNOWLEDGMENT

The Memoirs of Field-Marshal the Viscount Montgomery of Alamein, K.G., Copyright © 1958, by Bernard L. Montgomery. Reprinted by permission of the World Publishing Company.

INDEX

A

Aberdeen, George Hamilton Gordon, earl of, 147
  speech criticizing policy toward France, 352-53
  speech on Greek independence and the Turkish Empire, 296-301
Abolition Act (slave trade, 1807), 2022-26
Abolition Act (slavery, 1833), 2026-35
Abyssinian crisis, 933-37, 940, 950-58, 958-65, 965-74
Acadia, 38, 119. *see also* Nova Scotia
Accra, British, 2263
Achi Baba, 656, 658
Acre, 2927
Addis-Ababa, 962
Aden, 1342, 1920
  treaty granting control to Britain, 2285
Adkins, Sir Ryland, 665, 668
Adrianople, 601, 603, 649, 2425
Adolphus, Gustavus, 303
Aehrenthal, Baron de, 576
Affray Bill, 2680
Afghan Wars, 2290-2312, 2765-77
Afghanistan, 363, 364, 533-38, 717, 2692, 2693, 2777
Africa. *see also* separate entries
  activity in (1793-1842), 2241-68
  Anglo-French Declaration, 2901-03
  Anglo-German Convention, 2879-84
  expansion into (1861-1913), 2857-2917
  imperial principles concerning, 2885
  independence movements (1953-1968), 3207-29, 3229-42, 3247-58, 3262, 3317-40
  trusteeship in, concept of, 2964-3001
Africa, East. *see* East Africa; German East Africa; Kenya; Uganda; Zanzibar

Africa, North. *see* Egypt; Near East; Sudan
Africa, South. *see* Cape of Good Hope; Orange River Territory; Transvaal; South Africa
Africa, Southeast. *see* Nyasaland; Rhodesia
Africa, West. *see* Gambia; Gold Coast (Ghana); Niger; Nigeria; Sierra Leone; West Africa
Agadir, 580, 584, 588, 591, 612
Agra, 2240, 2618, 2641
agriculture, 1400-01, 1417-19, 1446, 1460, 1646
air defense, 881, 884, 886-92
air-to-air guided missiles, 1341
aircraft carriers, armament of, 761, 765
Airey, General, 2410, 2412, 2414
Alabama claims controversy, 374
  settlement of, Treaty of Washington (1871), 491-97
Albania, 598, 647, 654, 1084
Albert, Charles, 394
Alexander I, Tsar of Russia, 216, 217, 401, 2877
Alexander, General, 1120, 1180, 1182
Alexandria, 287ff, 2283, 2863, 2869, 2913
Alexeieff, General, 695, 696
Algeciras Conference, 611
Algeria, 2904
Algiers, 148, 522, 1173
Allahabad, 2618, 2706
Allaun, Frank, 1316
  speech on the Nigerian Civil War, 3340-42
Allied and Associated Powers, 735, 736
Allied Commission of Control, 813
Alopeus, M., 243
Alphand, Hervé 1267
Als, Robert, 1235, 1267
Alsace-Lorraine, 633, 644, 713ff, 734, 738, 743
Althorp, Viscount, 1552, 1573
Altmark affair, 1102
Ambadkar, Dr., 3099

3383

G

see also nuclear weapons
disarmament treaties, 712, 835-39
Hay-Pauncefote Treaty, 502-03
Jay Treaty, 317-23
Oregon, dispute over boundary, 347-51
Rush-Bagot Convention of 1818, 339-42
Suez crisis, 3164-66
Trent Dispute, 476-80
wars
    War of 1812, 324-39. *see also* separate
      entry
    World War I. *see* separate entry
    World War II, 1125, 1182, 1183. *see also*
      separate entry
    Washington, treaty of (1871), 491-98
    Washington, treaty of (1897), 498-501
    Webster-Ashburton Agreement, 342-47
Universities Act (1908, Ireland), 1625-28
University of Dublin, 1562, 1574-75
Upper Guinea, 1999
Urals, 730, 849
Utrecht, treaties of, 3, 34-39, 40-44, 51, 61, 62,
  66, 71, 92, 117

V

Vaal river, 2524, 2540
Val de Trajans, 2434
Valenciennes, fortress, 235
Van Diemen's Land, 2333-35, 2364, 2365. *see*
  also Tasmania
Vancouver Island, 349, 350, 2817
Vandenberg Resolution, 1250
Varna, 2402, 2453
Vaughan, John Taylor, 1994
Venezuela, treaty with, at Washington (1897),
  498-501
Venice, 171, 377
Vera Cruz, 478
Verdun, siege of, 688
Verona, 255, 256, 257, 258, 259, 260
Versailles, Court of, 347
Versailles Peace Conference (1919), 629-31,
  728-37
Versailles Peace Treaty (1919), 629-31, 737-42,
  743-50, 751-59
Vestry Act, 1575
Vichy government, 1148
Victor Emmanuel I, 394
Victor Emmanuel II, 1183
Victoria, colony of, 2363, 2364
Victoria Nyanza Lake, 2880
Victoria, Queen, 373, 428, 429, 504, 1681,
  1776, 3100
    Jubilee (1887), 2380

letter to the King of the Belgians, 432
letter expressing dissatisfaction with Pal-
  merston, 427
Vienna, Congress of (1814-15), 146ff
Vienna, treaty of (1731), 4, 68-69
Vienna, treaty of (1815), 214-34
Vietnam War, 1085, 1308-18, 1318-25
Villa Viciosa, 276
Villeneuve, Admiral P. C. J. B. S., 197, 198
  197, 198
Vilna, 1188
Virgin Islands, 2033
Vistula river, 735, 849, 1074
Vladivostock, 844
Volksraad, 2535, 2545
Volta, 2882
Volturno, river, 1250
Vyshinski, A. Y., 1205

W

Wade, Sir Thomas, 2475, 2478
Waghorn, R. E., 2968
Waitangi, treaty of, 2353-54
Wakefield, Edward Gibbon
  A Letter from Sydney, 2335-41
Waldeck-Rousseau, Pierre, 2593
Wales, 1846, 1893
Walewski, Count Alexandre, 432, 438
Walker, David, 1425
Wallachia, 2382
Walpole, Horatio, 54, 56, 75
Walpole, Sir Robert, first earl of Orford, 4, 56,
  72-75, 390, 2429
  speech opposing war with Spain, 72-75
  speech defending the Treaty of Seville, 63-
    67
Walsh, Stephen, 665, 759
War Cabinet (World War I), 696, 698
War of 1812, 147, 324-39
War Office, 645
Warbey, William, 3135, 3169
Warren, Sir John, 329
Warsaw, 217, 921, 1039, 1243
Warsaw Pact, 1368
Washington Disarmament Conference (1922),
  760-69
Washington, George, 2585
Washington, treaty of (1871), 491-97
Washington, treaty of, with Venezuela (1897),
  498-501
Waterloo, 146, 234
Watson, Sam, 1374
Wavell, Marshal A. P., first earl, 3199, 3200

تمام